WRITING AFRICAN AMERICAN WOMEN

WRITING AFRICAN AMERICAN WOMEN

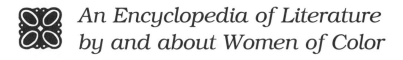 *An Encyclopedia of Literature by and about Women of Color*

Volume 2: K–Z

**Edited by
Elizabeth Ann Beaulieu**

GREENWOOD PRESS
Westport, Connecticut • London

Library of Congress Cataloging-in-Publication Data

Writing African American women : an encyclopedia of literature by and about women of color / edited by Elizabeth Ann Beaulieu.
    p. cm.
   Includes bibliographical references and index.
   ISBN 0–313–33196–0 (set : alk. paper)—ISBN 0–313–33197–9 (v. 1 : alk. paper)—
ISBN 0–313–33198–7 (v. 2 : alk. paper) 1. American literature—African American authors—Encyclopedias. 2. Authors, American—20th century—Biography—Encyclopedias. 3. African American women in literature—Encyclopedias. 4. Women and literature—United States—Encyclopedias.   I. Beaulieu, Elizabeth Ann.
   PS153.N5W756 2006
   810.9'928796073—dc22   2005031487

British Library Cataloguing in Publication Data is available.

This book is included in the *African American
Experience* database from Greenwood Electronic Media.
For more information, visit www.africanamericanexperience.com.

Library of Congress Catalog Card Number: 2005031487
ISBN 0–313–33196–0 (set)
    0–313–33197–9 (vol. 1)
    0–313–33198–7 (vol. 2)

First published in 2006

Greenwood Press, 88 Post Road West, Westport, CT 06881
An imprint of Greenwood Publishing Group, Inc.
www.greenwood.com

Printed in the United States of America

The paper used in this book complies with the
Permanent Paper Standard issued by the National
Information Standards Organization (Z39.48–1984).

10 9 8 7 6 5 4 3 2 1

This work is for Lee Burdette Williams—friend of the second half, sister of my heart's heart, my poem.

❀ Contents

❈ List of Entries

Thematic List of Entries

Autobiography/Narrative Writers

Angelou, Maya
Baker, Josephine
Burton, Annie Louise
Craft, Ellen and William
Delaney, Lucy A.
Delany Sisters
Drumgoold, Kate
Elaw, Zilpha
Holiday, Billie
Jackson, Mattie
Jackson, Rebecca Cox
Jacobs, Harriet
Keckley, Elizabeth
Moody, Anne
Potter, Eliza
Prince, Mary
Taylor, Susie King
Truth, Sojourner

Children's/Young Adult Writers

Boyd, Candy Dawson
Caines, Jeannette
Greenfield, Eloise
Hamilton, Virginia
Hansen, Joyce
Herron, Carolivia
Johnson, Angela
Lattany, Kristin Hunter
McKissack, Patricia
Meriwether, Louise
Nelson, Marilyn
Sanders, Dori
Tate, Eleanora E.
Taylor, Mildred D.
Thomas, Joyce Carol
Walter, Mildred Pitts
Wilkinson, Brenda
Woodson, Jacqueline
Yarbrough, Camille

Sapphire
Spencer, Anne
Terry, Lucy
Tillman, Katherine Davis Chapman
Walker, Margaret
Wheatley, Phillis
Wright, Sarah Elizabeth

Religious Writers

Broughton, Virginia W.
Foote, Julia A. J.
Jackson, Rebecca Cox
Johnson, Amelia E.
Lee, Jarena
Stewart, Maria

Short-story Writers

Anderson, Mignon Holland
Bambara, Toni Cade
Birtha, Becky
Bonner, Marita
Danticat, Edwidge
Ferrell, Carolyn
Lee, Andrea
Millican, Arthenia J. Bates
Moore, Opal
Oliver, Diane
Shockley, Ann Allen
Walker, Alice

Social Activists/Educators

Albert, Octavia V. Rogers
Boyd, Melba
Brown, Hallie Q.
Bush-Banks, Olivia Ward
Cooper, Anna Julia
Coppin, Fanny Jackson
Davis, Angela
Dunbar-Nelson, Alice Moore
Golden, Marita
Graham, Shirley
Grimké, Charlotte Forten
Guy, Rosa

Harper, Frances E. W.
Matthews, Victoria Earle
Mossell, Gertrude
Stewart, Maria
Terrell, Mary Church
Wells-Barnett, Ida B.

Themes

Ancestor, Use of
Beauty
Body
Christianity
Class
Community
Conjuring
Death
Family
Freedom
Healing
History
Home
Identity
Lesbianism
Literacy
Love
Memory
Motherhood
Myth, Use of
Passing
Quilting
Race
Rape
Religion
Sexuality
Slavery
South, Influence of the
Spirituality
Stereotypes
Violence
Whiteness
Womanism
Womanist Conjure
Work

 **K**

KECKLEY, ELIZABETH (1818?–1907)

Most of what we know about Elizabeth Keckley's life as a slave is derived from her postbellum **slave narrative** *Behind the Scenes, or, Thirty Years a Slave, and Four Years in the White House* (1868). She was born in Dinwiddie, Virginia, the only child of Agnes Hobbs, a slave to Colonel A. Burwell, and George Pleasant. Her earliest charge, at age four, was to care for her master's infant daughter, and her first beating came as a result of carelessness in her duty. At fourteen she was sent to live with her master's oldest son, a minister. After the family moved to Hillsborough, North Carolina, Keckley, now eighteen, was whipped by the schoolmaster and later beaten by her master to break her "stubborn pride" until her resistance shamed them into stopping. During four years of persecution by an unnamed white man, she gave birth to her only child, George. Keckley's fortunes began to change, however, after she went to live with the **family** of her old master's daughter. When the Garlands moved to St. Louis, they were so impoverished that Keckley's old mother had to be put out to service. The threat shocked the author into doing what she could to support the family. Before long Keckley had become a dressmaker for some of the best ladies in St. Louis, supporting a family of seventeen persons, black and white.

   Through hard **work** and with loans from some of her women patrons, Keckley purchased **freedom** for herself and her son for $1,200 and was emancipated on November 13, 1855. Her marriage to James Keckley ended when she decided to leave St. Louis in 1860 and head north to improve her fortune. In Washington, D.C., she encountered obstacles to her success as a black businesswoman, but a white customer helped her get established. Women helping women, both black and white, was a hallmark of Keckley's success as a dressmaker.

Soon after her arrival in the nation's capital, Keckley's dressmaking skill led to her working for the wife of Jefferson Davis. Keckley soon achieved her dream: to sew for the inhabitants of the White House. As Mary Lincoln's personal modiste, "Madam Elizabeth," as President Lincoln called her, grew close to the family. Supporting Mary Lincoln through her grief upon the **death** of her son Willie, she became the First Lady's confidante. Keckley's own son, who had joined the Union army, died in 1861 on the battlefield.

In the aftermath of President Lincoln's assassination, Keckley was invaluable to the grieving widow. In Mrs. Lincoln's large debt, however, acquired while she was First Lady, lay the seeds of the "Old Clothes Scandal," and Keckley was asked to help her sell some of her wardrobe in New York City. The disastrous publicity that followed entangled Keckley and led to her increasing poverty and eventual estrangement from the Lincoln family. After teaching at Wilberforce University from 1892 to 1894, Keckley died of a stroke in 1907 in the Home for Destitute Women and Children in Washington, D.C.

Work By

Behind the Scenes, or, Thirty Years a Slave, and Four Years in the White House. 1868. New York: Oxford University Press, 1988.

Work About

Washington, John E. *They Knew Lincoln.* New York: Dutton, 1942.

Beth L. Lueck

KELLEY-HAWKINS, EMMA DUNHAM (?–?)

There is a certain irony that Emma Dunham Kelley-Hawkins published her first novel, *Megda* (1891), under the pseudonym "Forget-Me-Not." While time has preserved her name, her first and second novels (the second is *Four Girls at Cottage City*, published in 1898) and the photo that prefaced *Megda* are all that is known about this author.

While anonymous in her first literary endeavor, its success may have emboldened her to include her name as "Emma Dunham Kelley" in the 1892 reprint of *Megda*. Scholars assume that Kelley married between 1891 and 1898, since in her second volume the appended surname of "Hawkins" appears. However, no records have been located that might tell us more about her life, origins, **family**, or background. Her photo has been read as both racially ambiguous and as unquestionably representing an African American woman of a mixed-race background. Geographically, the choice of a Boston publishing company, James H. Earle, indicates she is probably of New England origin, as do the plots of her novels, Cottage City itself being located on Martha's Vineyard. Her dedication of *Megda* to her "Widowed Mother" who endured "years of hard struggle and self-sacrifice" indicates a childhood touched by trouble, while her dedication of her second novel to "Dear Aunt Lottie, whom I have often and truly called my 'Second Mother'" suggests her reliance on female support for sustenance. The sacrifices and support these women offered may have been in order to enable Kelley's education, evident in her developed writing. However, we must remember that everything where Kelley is concerned is a matter of extrapolation and supposition.

What scholars are left with, besides a tantalizing puzzle, are the novels themselves. Both exemplify the Christian bildungsroman, which preached the sublimation of one's personal desires and ambitions in favor of a higher duty to Christ. This was not presented as effortless: Each novel features a high-spirited heroine who struggles to achieve salvation. The reward for doing so is marriage, with its privileged status of beloved wife and mother.

Ultimately, the plots of both novels are unimportant when compared to their purpose: to educate and form young Christian women who will be impervious to the superficial charms of worldliness, represented as theater, dance, and social elitism. It is here that Kelley's **fiction** differs most substantially from her female African American peers writing at the time: While most were writing what Claudia Tate identifies as "domestic allegories of political desire," which in some way condemned existing racial inequalities, Kelley makes no mention of **race** whatsoever. Indeed, if the photo of Kelley is read as racially ambiguous, her characters are delineated entirely in relation to **whiteness**. Linking whiteness and purity, Kelley's darker-skinned characters are generally presented as less moral than her blond heroines. Critical opinion is divided as to whether Kelley's characters are intended to be white or light-skinned **mulattos**. While some note that Cottage City became Oak Bluffs, an African American vacation spot, the reality is that the composition of Kelley's novel predates such a shift. The fact remains that the text gives us no clues—unless one reads Kelley's photo as racially *un*ambiguous and therefore signifying on the heroines themselves.

Works By

Four Girls at Cottage City. Boston: James H. Earle, 1898.
Megda. Boston: James H. Earle, 1891.

Works About

Hite, Molly. Introduction to *Megda*. New York: Oxford University Press, 1988. xxvii–xxxvii.

McDowell, Deborah. Introduction to *Four Girls at Cottage City*. New York: Oxford University Press, 1988. xxvii–xxxviii.

Shockley, Ann Allen. *Afro-American Women Writers, 1746–1933: An Anthology and Critical Guide*. Boston: G. K. Hall, 1988.

Tarbox, Gwen Athene. *The Clubwomen's Daughters: Collectivist Impulses in Progressive-Era Girls' Fiction*. New York: Garland, 2000.

Tate, Claudia. *Domestic Allegories of Political Desire: The Black Heroine's Text at the Turn of the Century*. New York: Oxford University Press, 1992.

Williams, Julie L. "Emma Dunham Kelley-Hawkins." *African American Authors, 1745–1945: A Bio-Bibliographical Critical Sourcebook*. Ed. Emmanuel S. Nelson. Westport, CT: Greenwood Press, 2000. 311–315.

Jennifer Harris

KENAN, RANDALL (1963–   )

Born on March 12, 1963, in Brooklyn, New York, Randall Garrett Kenan moved to North Carolina when he was six weeks old. Following a temporary stay with his grandfather in Wallace, Kenan settled in Chinquapin, where he was raised by his great-aunt. Early life in the **South**, the landscape for all of Kenan's major **fiction**, was filled with much **death** and many funerals, including the loss of his great-uncle when Kenan was three. Kenan speaks of the event with astonishment when he considers the shock of a three-year-old taking a nap, waking up to find his father-figure dead beside him. Out of that experience, Kenan developed an intense curiosity regarding ghosts and spirits. Buoyed, in part, by his great-aunt's recollections of **family** members dying in her house and their subsequent hauntings, Kenan's awareness of the supernatural grew throughout childhood so that when he turned to authors like Gabriel Garcia Marquez and **Toni Morrison**, he found a vision of the world he identified with and understood.

The small-town South of Kenan's youth allowed him to gain appreciation not only for the supernatural practices of African Americans but for the language of the King James Bible, gospel music, and **spirituals** that accompanied services at First Baptist—one of only two African American churches, both Baptist, in Chinquapin. His inherited faith proved a great influence on him through college, when doubt began; **religion** continues to inform his fiction. The rural setting of Chinquapin also afforded Kenan an agrarian upbringing. On his great-aunt's farm he raised livestock, vegetables, and tobacco. Church and farm life as well as his high school education at the desegregated East Duplin High School in Beaulaville offered invaluable experiences for his work to come, but when he entered college, Kenan had no intention of being a serious writer.

That decision occurred three-quarters of the way through his undergraduate career at the University of North Carolina at Chapel Hill. While there, he majored in physics and intended to be a scientist. His precollege reading had included science fiction writers Isaac Asimov and Arthur C. Clarke, and according to Doris Betts, Kenan expected to fill downtime from his laboratory **work** with the writing of science fiction novels. That plan changed during the summer after Kenan's junior year when he went to Oxford to study literary criticism. His senior year at Chapel Hill included several literary classes as well as a change in major. Among those classes was Betts's senior honors writing seminar. Upon completion of his English degree, Kenan left the South for New York and, with Betts's assistance, contacted Toni Morrison, who secured a job for him at Random House. Kenan repeatedly credits the importance and influence of the English faculty at Chapel Hill in many interviews, and in addition to Betts, he mentions H. Maxwell Steele, Daphne Athas, Louis D. Rubin, Jr., Lee Greene, and Bland Simpson.

Working his way from office assistant to assistant editor in New York, Kenan found time for writing whenever he could. His first novel, *A Visitation of Spirits*, appeared in 1989–four years after his graduation–to favorable reviews. That novel marks Kenan's entrance into the literary world and commences the still-unresolved critical dialogue on his place in the canon. Kenan represents a growing hybridization in both literary criticism and the practice of fiction. As diverse as his own writing, Kenan's literary influences extend beyond African American borders. His affinity for Japanese writers, in particular Yukio Mishima, is well documented, as is the importance he places upon Gabriel Garcia Marquez. He also values the work of southern women writers like Flannery O'Connor, Eudora Welty, and Katherine Anne Porter, as he does Morrison's. Though he aligns himself with **James Baldwin**, Kenan sees important distinctions as well as similarities between them; notably, Kenan is writing as an openly gay author, while Baldwin cloaked his sexual orientation. Like Baldwin's *Go Tell It on the Mountain* (1953), Kenan's *A Visitation of Spirits* has the central protagonist wrestling with his homosexuality against a backdrop of conservative **Christianity**. The growing separation of *Spirit*'s Horace Cross from his **community** and his faith amid issues of self-definition sounds a classic theme in African American **literature**, though his homosexuality confounds tradition. Horace feels distanced from family and friends in Tims Creek, North Carolina, in part because of the desires for other men he works to repress. Cross must confront his religious background in conversations with James (Jimmy) Malachi Greene, his cousin and the pastor of his church. In addition, Cross also must deal with his effeminate schoolmate Gideon and the outward signs of homosexuality he represents as well as encounters with the supernatural and ideas of possession. Written in both narrative and dramatic prose, Cross's story of fragmentation and suicide runs outside of conventional chronological time and shows a young man unable to rectify his sexual orientation with his community's standards of living.

The stories collected in *Let the Dead Bury Their Dead* (1992) represent a further development of Kenan's Tims Creek fiction and move beyond to Washington, D.C., and New Jersey. Nominated for the National Book Critics

Circle Award in Fiction, *Dead*'s stories tell of **history**, incest, death and dying, haunting, **love**, molestation, religion, community, and in several examples, strong women. In "Clarence and the Dead," five-year-old Clarence Pickett is touched with a psychic gift that allows him to communicate with the dead. Balancing the supernatural with the rational world, the community around Clarence looks on in wonder and feels a strange sense of relief when he dies. Clarence's ability to channel the dead proves disturbing to many in the town. His admonition from beyond to the town's also-ran, Ellsworth Batts—unstable since the death of Mildred, his former girlfriend, who offers the advice through the medium of Clarence—causes the controversial pairing of the themes of child molestation and homosexuality to underpin the story.

Homosexuality even affects seventy-year-old Maggie MacGowan Williams in "The Foundations of the Earth." After the death of her gay grandson Edward, Maggie invites his lover Gabriel for a visit. The agnostic Gabriel listens intently to the proselytizing of Maggie's friends gathered on the porch but understands his real reason for being there is to talk openly with Maggie—something that Edward could not do. At once transforming and cathartic, "Foundations" shows that Maggie—a product of her Calvinistic culture—is capable of extending her belief system to accept and embrace both the alternative lifestyle Edward chose and the lover he leaves behind in death. The strength of Maggie's acceptance manifests in her conversations with others, while her courage builds in the long-held family belief of the **healing** properties of sleep. Here, Kenan's use of folk culture underscores his connection to both southern and African American literature. Preserving the customs and manners of his past, Kenan offers Maggie as a woman deeply entrenched in the past yet capable of change. Dynamic in a static landscape, Maggie Williams becomes one of Kenan's finest creations.

"The Origin of Whales" continues Kenan's emphasis on strong women in a story centered on the elderly Essie's babysitting of the overly energetic Thad. In a story that blends **folklore** and the oral tradition against a backdrop of agelessness, Kenan shows that the fun and the serious of life can coexist, and must, because of age. When Essie receives a phone call that one of her contemporaries is hospitalized, the tone of the story changes, but Essie does not give in to the bad news and instead is brought back to the business of living by Thad's request for assistance on his homework. Kenan's most controversial story, "Cornsilk," offers a frank and disturbing look at incest from the perspective of the jilted brother longing for his sister's companionship.

Following the 1992 publication of *Let the Dead Bury Their Dead*, Kenan published a biography of Baldwin in the Chelsea House *Lives of Notable Gay Men* series and began a move from fiction to nonfiction that culminated in his 1999 work *Walking on Water*. Abandoning the fantastic qualities of his fiction for a more factual writing style, Kenan demonstrates his versatility. During this period Kenan also began accepting academic appointments; he has been on faculty at Sarah Lawrence, Vassar, Columbia, University of North Carolina at Chapel Hill, Duke, the University of Mississippi, and the University of Memphis in various creative writing positions.

Kenan's 1999 nonfiction work *Walking on Water: Black American Lives at the Turn of the Twenty-first Century* represents over 600 pages of cross-country conversations and thoughts on the place and advancement of African Americans in America. Reminiscent of Robert Penn Warren's 1965 work *Who Speaks for the Negro?* Kenan's *Walking on Water* offers a unique contribution; it is written by and for African Americans and critically explores the African American influence on popular culture. Melding interviews with children and senior citizens, celebrities and laypeople, with attention to cultural detail, Kenan's meditations show the ongoing prevalence of racism more than a century after the abolition of **slavery**. Beyond that, he writes of the regional differences and influences shaping African America. In this sprawling yet compelling work, Kenan offers no apology for the impossibility of its scope; rather, he successfully provides a penetrating look at disparate cultures comprising African Americans.

Today Kenan continues his work on a novel in his Tims Creek saga that once again shows the intersection of faith and belief with contemporary life. The paucity of scholarship on Kenan's writing creates a noticeable gap in both African American and southern studies. Similarly, his omission from both the first (1997) and second (2004) editions of the *Norton Anthology of African American Literature* hints at an author open to critical consideration and canonical placement. In the ongoing development of African American literary theory, Kenan's **identity** as a southern, African American homosexual may well necessitate a new direction in scholarship, for like the African American women writers preoccupied with place and identity, Kenan, too, remains displaced.

Works By

James Baldwin. New York: Chelsea House, 1994.
Let the Dead Bury Their Dead. New York: Harcourt Brace and Company, 1992.
A Visitation of Spirits. New York: Grove Press, 1989.
Walking on Water: Black American Lives at the Turn of the Twenty-first Century. New York: Alfred A. Knopf, 1999.

Works About

Guinn, Matthew. *After Southern Modernism.* Jackson: University Press of Mississippi, 2000.
Harris, Trudier. *The Power of the Porch: The Storyteller's Craft in Zora Neale Hurston, Gloria Naylor, and Randall Kenan.* Athens: University of Georgia Press, 1996.
Hunt, V. "A Conversation with Randall Kenan." *African American Review* 29.3 (Autumn 1995): 411–420.
Ketchin, Susan. "Randall Kenan." *The Christ-Haunted Landscape: Faith and Doubt in Southern Fiction.* Jackson: University Press of Mississippi, 1994. 277–302.

Rowell, Charles H. "An Interview with Randall Kenan." *Callaloo* 21.1 (1998): 133–148.

Tucker, Lindsey. "Gay Identity, Conjure, and the Uses of Postmodern Ethnography in the Fictions of Randall Kenan." *Modern Fiction Studies* 49.2 (Summer 2003): 306–331.

F. Gregory Stewart

KENNEDY, ADRIENNE (1931–   )

Best known for her play *Funnyhouse of a Negro* (1962) that won her first Obie Award, Adrienne Kennedy has been an influential playwright associated with the **Black Arts Movement**. Her highly acclaimed and often enigmatic works revolve around subjectivity under oppressive structures of **race** and gender, invoked through violent symbolism, radical experimentation, and hauntingly fragmentary lyricism. Her plays significantly pushed the conceptions of African American theater in demonstrating the political potential of abstract theatrical language. Kennedy is also known for her powerful short stories, mystery novels, and a memoir.

Born in Pittsburgh, Pennsylvania, Adrienne Lita Kennedy was the first and only daughter of Cornell Wallace Hawkins, a social worker and an executive secretary for the YMCA, and Etta Hawkins, a schoolteacher. Kennedy credits her mother as an early literary influence but also claims that the direction of her works was affected by the fact that her maternal grandfather was a wealthy white peach farmer. When she was four, her **family** moved to a multiethnic, middle-class neighborhood in Cleveland, Ohio. Soon after receiving a degree in education from Ohio State University, she married Joseph C. Kennedy. He was sent to Korea six months after the marriage, but upon his return the family moved to New York. In New York, Kennedy studied creative writing at Columbia University (1954–1956), American Theatre Wing (1958), and later with Edward Albee at Circle-in-the-Square School (1962). Due to her husband's involvement in developmental efforts in West Africa, the family moved to Ghana in 1961, then to Italy. She had two sons, Joseph, Jr., and Adam, and divorced in 1966. Meanwhile, she was a member of the playwriting unit of Actors Studio from 1962 to 1965 and participated as a founding member of the Women's Theatre Council in 1971.

Kennedy has received three Obie Awards from *Village Voice*, among numerous other awards: two Rockefeller grants, a Guggenheim fellowship, a Third Manhattan Borough President's Award for Excellence, a Lila Wallace Reader's Digest Fund Writer's Award, an Academy Award in Literature from the American Academy of Arts and Letters, and a Pierre LeCompte duNouy Foundation Award. She has been commissioned to write works for the Public Theater, Jerome Robbins, The Royal Court, the Mark Taper Forum, and Juilliard. In addition, Kennedy has been a visiting professor at many universities, including Yale, Princeton, Brown, the University of California at Berkeley, Stanford, and Harvard.

Her first published work, "Because of the King of France" (1960), originally published in *Black Orpheus: A Journal of African and Afro-American Literature*, is a short story about a girl's haunting encounter with her estranged cousin. Kennedy weaves autobiographical detail with expressionism and surrealism to create evocativeness and complexity that continued to surface in her work. In this story, Kennedy places emphasis on cultural specificity of the African diaspora; the work "wears" the mask of conformity to Western cultural values and yet enacts a profoundly different worldview aimed at confronting an oppressive past and reaffirming the humanity and sensibility of black artists.

In *Funnyhouse of a Negro* (1962), coproduced by Edward Albee, Kennedy focuses on the tormented psyche of a young college student, Sarah, who is also in the text simply referred to as "Negro." Kennedy portrays her subjectivity as a site of struggle with crossings of race and gender, as well as family trauma, as painful moments of the past blends into the present. Kennedy dramatizes four aspects of Sarah's self through historical figures: Patrice Lumumba, Christ, Queen Victoria, and the Duchess of Hapsburg. These four figures all embody contradictions and oppressions, such as black and white, male and female, and colonialism and independence. As the play unravels, we learn about the tragic marriage between Sarah's "white mother" and Sarah's father, a dark-skinned aspiring revolutionary. Sarah's mother accompanied her husband to Africa, but she eventually fell out of **love** with him; one night, he raped her in drunken rage. Sarah, the child born of the **rape**, grows up watching her mother lose her mind as her father struggled with guilt. The play leads up to Sarah's final rebuff of her father, his subsequent suicide in a Harlem hotel room, and Sarah's own suicide as she fails to reconcile herself to her roots and the nightmare of her past.

Like her contemporary playwright **Lorraine Hansberry**, the power and distinctiveness of Kennedy's play is fueled by her critique of the social and political condition of black female subjectivity, as well as finding a reference point in personal experience. Yet unlike Hansberry's plays, Kennedy's one-act plays resist easy identification for the audience. Instead of allowing the audience to identify with the characters and follow the plot easily, her plays lead audiences to be shocked with the alienating circumstances in which these characters function. To the audience's bewilderment, setting and characters often keep changing, and the emphasis on repetition and non sequitur breaks down the sense of linear time. Her works are filled with shattering moments of disruption, dislocation, and violation, as she consistently defamiliarizes the audience's assumptions about the enlightened autonomous subjectivity. Her theater consists in producing astonishment rather than empathy and, in that sense, blends the historical avant-garde mode of Bertolt Brecht's epic theater and the modernist modes of surrealism, symbolism, and expressionism.

Kennedy's literary sensibility can be traced in her experimental **autobiography** *People Who Led to My Plays* (1987). Her entry on Lorca, for example, allows us to see her inclination to move away from the "realistic setting" to a "dream setting." Organized loosely in chronological order into six sections, each chapter of her memoir contains short entries that form sequences instead of a long narrative. Her entries are not confined to people like her family and friends but also discuss places, books, music, **film**, and objects from popular culture and everyday life that feed her literary imagination. The eclecticism of the entries allows us access to Kennedy's sensibility that is shaped by the immediate personal life and places that she lived, as well as larger cultural and sociohistorical forces of influence.

Mostly because of her early plays, Kennedy is often characterized as a quintessential postmodern playwright. While we easily recognize postmodern aesthetics in her experimental aspects like fragmentation, decentering, and nonlinearity, Kennedy's early works stand apart from literary postmodernism that fully emerged in the 1970s. Her works do not display fascination with the notions of deconstruction and do not flirt with novelty and marginality as formal strategy of value in itself. For instance, Kennedy's portrayal of fragmented subjectivity is not synonymous with the poststructuralist preoccupation with the breakdown of subjecthood in works of Roland Barthes, in that she never questions the existence of subjectivity itself. Her stylistic experimentation is rather a serious attempt to articulate the previously unimagined consciousness of a racial, gendered, and colonized "other." Her plays anticipate Luce Irigaray's critique of the phallocentric nature of psychoanalytic theory: Is "woman" the unconscious, as Lacan claims, or does woman have one? Kennedy's work presses us to ask similar questions about the impossibility of representing the consciousness of those who are oppressed, not just by the structure of gender but further splintered through race and **class** specificity. Her plays question whether such oppressed subjectivity can be adequately represented through traditional models in Western modernity.

Kennedy's **drama** significantly paved the way for black female writers to articulate marginalized and trivialized realities. Her sensibility is shared in works of later playwrights like **Ntozake Shange** and **Suzan-Lori Parks**, who also challenge the boundaries of realism in their new explorations of **identity** and the human experience. In addition, Kennedy's theater also signals the emergence of **black feminist criticism** in that her works contest for the space of a black female subjectivity against the too often universalized white female subjectivity.

The dramatic retrospective featuring Kennedy during the 1995–1996 season at Signature Theater in New York has prompted renewed critical attention. The Adrienne Kennedy Papers are housed at the Harry Ransom Research Center at the University of Austin, Texas.

Works By

The Adrienne Kennedy Reader. Minneapolis: University of Minnesota Press, 2001.

People Who Led to My Plays. New York: Theatre Communications Group, 1987.

Sleep Deprivation Chamber. New York: Theatre Communications Group, 1996.

Works About

Brockett, Oscar G., and Robert R. Findlay. *Century of Innovation*. Englewood Cliffs, NJ: Prentice-Hall, 1973.

Bryant-Jackson, Paul K., and Lois More Overbeck, eds. *Intersecting Boundaries: The Theatre of Adrienne Kennedy*. Minneapolis: University of Minnesota Press, 1992.

Diamond, Elin. *Unmaking Mimesis*. New York: Routledge, 1997.

Harrison, Paul Carter. *The Drama of Nommo*. New York: Grove Press, 1972.

Kintz, Linda. *The Subject's Tragedy: Political Poetics, Feminist Theory and Drama*. Ann Arbor: University of Michigan Press, 1992.

Robinson, Marc. *The Other American Drama*. Cambridge: Cambridge University Press, 1994.

Rei Magosaki

KINCAID, JAMAICA (1949–)

Well known for her fierce self-assertiveness and frank expressions of her feelings in her writing, Jamaica Kincaid is widely viewed as one of the most important and provocative new voices in the current generation of Caribbean-born women authors. While Kincaid has admitted that she might owe much of her success to the "idea of feminism" and says that she does not mind if people place her in the feminist category, she also refuses to proclaim herself a feminist writer. "[T]hat's just me as an individual," she explains. "I mean, I always see myself as alone. I can't bear to be in a group of any kind, or in the school of anything" (Cudjoe 221). But while refusing the label "feminist writer," she does call herself a feminist and insists, "Every woman is a feminist" (True-heart). Speaking openly about her life and work in her many interviews, Kincaid has frequently commented that everything in her writing is autobiographical. "I've never really written about anyone except myself and my mother. . . . I'm just one of those pathetic people for whom writing is therapy," she has tellingly said of her writing (Listfield 82). A **memory**-haunted woman who continually remembers and tries to make sense of her Caribbean past and her relationship with her mother, Kincaid writes to take control of her obsessive ruminations over the hurts of her past in her ongoing inner conversation with her mother.

Kincaid was born Elaine Potter Richardson in 1949 and grew up in the West Indies on the island of Antigua in the shadow of her mother, Annie Drew, née Richardson. Characterizing her mother as an impressive and powerful woman but also as someone who should never have had children, Kincaid insists that the way she is "is solely owing" to her mother and that, indeed, her mother is the "fertile soil" of her "creative life" (Cudjoe 219, 222). The same mother who gave her daughter words by teaching her how to read when she was three and one half years old and giving her a *Concise Oxford Dictionary* when she was seven later became a source of intense pain, Kincaid recalls, and yet because of her mother, she is able to give voice to the pain. Although admired by her mother for her reading when she was young, later, when Kincaid read obsessively as an adolescent and consequently ignored her household duties at times, her mother became annoyed with her reading habits. When the fifteen-year-old Kincaid, who had been asked to baby-sit her two-year-old brother, Devon, became so absorbed in a book that she failed to notice that his diaper needed to be changed, Annie Drew, in a state of fury, gathered up all of her daughter's treasured books and burned them. As an adolescent, Kincaid came to identify with the bookish—and to her, idealized—world of **literature**, a world, as she would later speculate, she tried to recreate in her writing as she attempted to bring back into her life all the books her mother had burned.

Kincaid was an only child until age nine, and from ages nine to thirteen her life was disrupted by the birth of her three brothers: Joseph, Dalma, and Devon. "I thought I was the only thing my mother truly loved in the world," she states, "and when it dawned on me that it wasn't so, I was devastated" (Listfield). Kincaid also recalls how her mother and stepfather favored their sons over her.

> My brothers were going to be gentlemen of achievement, one was going to be Prime Minister, one a doctor, one a Minister, things like that. I never heard anybody say that I was going to be anything except maybe a nurse. There was no huge future for me, nothing planned. In fact my education was so casually interrupted, my life might very well have been destroyed by that casual act . . . if I hadn't intervened in my own life and pulled myself out of the water. (BBC)

Educated in British colonial schools, Kincaid was a bright student but also was considered difficult by her teachers. "I was always being accused of being rude, because I gave some back chat," as she comments (Garis). Not only did she refuse to stand at the refrain of "God Save Our King," but she also hated "Rule, Britannia" with its refrain, "Rule Britannia, Britannia rule the waves, Britons never ever shall be slaves. I thought that we weren't Britons and that pan so she could help support her family. At first, she sent home her pay checks like a dutiful daughter. "It dawned on me that my mother had made a terrible mistake in her life, that she had had children she could not afford, and I was supposed to help. . . . I remember taking it very badly, that feeling. That was the beginning of feeling outrage and injustice in me, that I should bear that burden" (Jacobs). Coming to realize the great sacrifice that was being asked of her, she stopped sending money to her family, broke off all contact with them, and lived selfishly as she set about reinventing herself. In an act of self-creation that also served as a self-protective disguise, she changed her name to "Jamaica Kincaid" in 1973, choosing the name "Jamaica" to designate her Caribbean origins. In changing her name, Kincaid was also, as she recalls, attempting to disguise herself so that her family would not know that she was writing, for she was afraid that she would fail, and they would laugh at her.

Despite her initial fears of failure, Kincaid became an almost overnight success as a writer. After being befriended by *New Yorker* writer George Trow, who began to quote her in his "Talk of the Town" pieces, she was hired as a staff writer for *The New Yorker* by the editor, William Shawn, who also published her stories in the magazine. And in 1979, she married Shawn's son, Allen—a composer who teaches at Bennington College in Bennington, Vermont—and the couple eventually had two children, Annie and Harold. During the years of her marriage to Allen Shawn—the couple is now divorced—Kincaid rarely spoke about her marriage and her husband and children, determined to protect the privacy of her family life, although she did come to starkly divide her life into her unhappy Antiguan past and her successful writer's—and domestic—life in Vermont. In 1983, with the publication of her first book of stories, *At the Bottom of the River*, Kincaid caught the attention of the critical establishment, and she has since become a widely acclaimed and often studied author, celebrated as an important voice in literature for both her **fiction** and nonfiction works.

In describing the trajectory of Kincaid's literary career and life in the United States, interviewers often invoke the discourse of the American success story and the self-made individual—and her story does indeed follow such a script, as she tells it. But embedded in Kincaid's literary success story is another story that she tells and retells in her writings—in her short-story collection *At the Bottom of the River* (1983), her coming-of-age novel **Annie John** (1985), and her portrait of herself as a young artist in **Lucy** (1990)—as she recounts her abiding struggle to make sense of her painful past and free herself from her obsessive **love**-hate relationship with her mother. "I've come to see that I've worked through the relationship of the mother and the girl to a relationship between

Europe and the place that I'm from, which is to say a relationship between the powerful and the powerless. The girl is powerless, and the mother is powerful," Kincaid has remarked of her writing (Vorda 86). But even as Kincaid came to recognize that she must have "consciously viewed" her relationship with her mother as a "sort of prototype" for the larger social relationship between Antiguans and the British, she also insists that for her writing is "an act of self-rescue, self-rehabilitation, self-curiosity: about my mind, about myself, what I think, what happened to me in the personal way, in thc public way, what things mean" (Birbalsingh 144, 149). "I am someone who had to make sense out of my past," Kincaid insists. "I had to write or I would have died" (Ferguson, "A Lot of Memory" 176).

In an artistic anticipation of *Annie John* and *Lucy*, Kincaid spoke openly and candidly about her Antiguan family in one of her first published stories–the heavily autobiographical "Antigua Crossings," which, like her story "Girl," appeared in June 1978. And yet in her other early stories–most of which originally appeared in *The New Yorker* between 1978 and 1982 and were subsequently published as a collection, *At the Bottom of the River*, in 1983–Kincaid drew on her Antiguan past, but she also worked to halfway conceal what she had revealed as she began to tell the story that drives and gives a kind of emotional urgency to her later work: her troubled relationship with her contemptuous and powerfully destructive mother, Annie Drew. If in *At the Bottom of the River* Kincaid uses a densely allusive and richly poetic style to partially obscure her meaning as she evokes the "bookish" idealized world of literature she came to love while growing up in Antigua, in *Annie John* she recounts, in a simple way, the story of her girlhood in Antigua under the control of her mother as she chronicles the early life of Annie John from ages ten to seventeen, describing Annie John's intense love for the idealized mother of early childhood and her equally intense hatred for the rejecting and shaming mother of adolescence. In *Lucy* Kincaid, through her daughter character, Lucy Josephine Potter, describes her experiences after leaving Antigua and coming to the United States to work as an au pair for a wealthy white family in New York City. A prisoner of her crippling past, Lucy, like Annie John, exists in the shadow of her powerful, and powerfully injuring, mother even though she is physically removed from her. When Lucy, in the final scene in the novel, begins to write, she finds the act of writing a painful process of recovering the past and confronting her abiding feelings of shame and despair.

The angry, contemptuous voice that pervades *Lucy*–a voice that Kincaid identifies as her mother's voice–is also the voice Kincaid adopts to great effect in her openly political writings, such as *A Small Place* (1988), in which she denounces not only the British and American tourists in Antigua and the remembered English colonists of her youth but also the current self-ruling black government in Antigua and the small-minded Antiguans. This voice also pervades Kincaid's portraits of her family–**The Autobiography of My Mother** (1996), *My Brother* (1997), and *Mr. Potter* (2002)–works that are not only self-revealing but are also, in part, self-portraits. In *The Autobiography of My Mother*, which derives from Kincaid's observation that her mother should not have her daughter but also, as we learn in *My Brother*, by her three sons. And in her fictional memoir of her biological father, *Mr. Potter*, Kincaid, as she imagines and writes about the life of her absentee father, Roderick Potter, also deals with the missing and yet ever-present part of her repudiated identity, "Elaine Cynthia Potter," the daughter-narrator in *Mr. Potter*. In telling the shameful story of her illegitimacy—like her biological father, she has a "line drawn through" her—she settles old scores against her biological father. But Kincaid also uses her writing to give narrative—indeed novelistic—dimension to her absent father and to provide a kind of artistic legitimacy to Elaine Potter Richardson, the shamed girl with the line drawn through her.

Kincaid, who traces her beginnings as a writer to William Shawn's acceptance of her writing, recalls how she felt that she had lost her writer's **home** after Shawn was removed as editor of *The New Yorker* in 1987. In 1995 she resigned from her staff job at *The New Yorker* after almost two decades of working for the magazine—from 1976 to 1995—after publicly denouncing *New Yorker* editor Tina Brown, casting the English woman in a familiar role in Kincaid's own personal **drama**: that of the oppressor, both English and maternal, who threatens the inner life of the Antiguan artist/daughter. But if Kincaid once compared the loss of her writer's home at *The New Yorker* to the experience of being orphaned, she has found a new kind of home at Harvard University, where she began to teach as a visiting professor of creative writing in 1992. And she continues to take deep comfort in her domestic and gardener's life in North Bennington, Vermont. For Kincaid, domestic life is part of her writer's life. "I don't consider writing a career or a profession. . . . I think of it as part of my domestic life," she insists (Listfield).

In *My Garden (Book):*—a collection of essays on gardening published in 1999, which began as a gardening column in *The New Yorker*—Kincaid professes her passion for gardening even as she reflects on the relationship of gardening to conquest. Like Kincaid's other works, *My Garden (Book):* draws on Kincaid's life, for as she recounts details of her domestic and gardener's life in Vermont in the present, she continually remembers her Antiguan past. In shaping her garden like a map of the Caribbean and reproducing in her Vermont study the look of the stash of books she once hid as a girl under her one-room house in Antigua—books that gave her comfort and that were burned by her mother— Kincaid remembers the past but also tries to undo some of its pain. Kincaid insists that she does not believe in **healing** and that she cannot and will not forget. "I don't see why I should get along with myself," she remarks in her characteristic way. But in her domestic and gardener's life, which are part of her writer's life, she does find moments of contentment. While she remains haunted by the past, she does find solace in her writing. "I am writing for solace," Kincaid states. "I consider myself the reader I am writing for, and it is to make sense of something, even if to repeat to myself what has happened" (Holmstrom). Even though her creative assets are her memory, anger, and despair, she does find solace in her writing as she becomes the self-authored "Jamaica Kincaid" and, through her ongoing self-narration, fashions for herself a literary life and writer's identity that she finds livable.

Works By

Annie John. New York: Farrar, Straus and Giroux, 1985.
"Antigua Crossings." *Rolling Stone,* June 29, 1978, 48–50.
At the Bottom of the River. 1983. New York: Plume-Penguin, 1992.
The Autobiography of My Mother. 1996. New York: Plume-Penguin, 1997.
Lucy. 1990. New York: Plume-Penguin, 1991.
Mr. Potter. New York: Farrar, Straus and Giroux, 2002.
My Brother. 1997. New York: Noonday-Farrar, Straus and Giroux, 1998.
My Garden (Book):. New York: Farrar, Straus and Giroux, 1999.
"On Seeing England for the First Time." *Transition* 51 (1991): 32–40.
"Ovando." *Conjunctions* 14 (1989): 75–83.
"Putting Myself Together." *The New Yorker,* February 20 and 27, 1995, 93+.
A Small Place. 1988. New York: Plume-Penguin, 1989.
Talk Stories. New York: Farrar, Straus and Giroux, 2001.
"Those Words That Echo . . . Echo . . . Echo Through Life." *New York Times,*
   June 7, 1999, E1.

Works About

BBC World Service. "Her Story: Jamaica Kincaid." November 11, 2001.
   www.bbc.co.uk/worldservice/arts/features/womenwriters/kincaid_life.shtml.
Birbalsingh, Frank. "Jamaica Kincaid: From Antigua to America." *Frontiers of
   Caribbean Literature in English.* Ed. Frank Birbalsingh. New York: St. Mar-
   tin's Press, 1996. 138–151.
Bouson, J. Brooks. *Jamaica Kincaid: Writing Memory, Writing Back to the Mother.*
   Albany: SUNY Press, 2004.
Cudjoe, Selwyn. "Jamaica Kincaid and the Modernist Project: An Interview."
   Caribbean Women Writers: Essays from the First International Conference. Ed. Sel-
   wyn Cudjoe. Wellesley, MA: Calaloux Publications, 1990. 215–232.
Ferguson, Moira. *Jamaica Kincaid: Where the Land Meets the Body.* Charlottes-
   ville: University Press of Virginia, 1994.
——. "A Lot of Memory: An Interview with Jamaica Kincaid." *Kenyon Review*
   16.1 (Winter 1994): 163–188.

Garis, Leslie. "Through West Indian Eyes." *New York Times Magazine*, October 7, 1990, sec. 6, 42–44, 70, 78, 80, 91. www.nytimes.com/books/97/10/19/home/kincaid-eyes.

Holmstrom, David. "Jamaica Kincaid. Writing for Solace, for Herself." *Christian Science Monitor*, January 17, 1996, 14. EBSCO: Academic Search Elite. web0.epnet.com.

Jacobs, Sally. "Don't Mess with Jamaica Kincaid: Author and Gardener, Film Withers as Well as Creates." *Boston Globe*, June 20, 1996, Living Section, 57. Lexis-Nexis Academic Universe. web.lexis-nexis.com.

Listfield, Emily. "Straight from the Heart." *Harper's Bazaar* 123 (October 1990): 82.

MacDonald-Smythe, Antonia. *Making Homes in the West/Indies: Constructions of Subjectivity in the Writings of Michelle Cliff and Jamaica Kincaid*. New York: Garland, 2001.

Paravisini-Gebert, Lizabeth. *Jamaica Kincaid: A Critical Companion*. Westport, CT: Greenwood Press, 1999.

Simmons, Diane. *Jamaica Kincaid*. New York: Twayne-Macmillan, 1994.

Trueheart, Charles. "The Writer's Lessons from Literature and Life: Jamaica Kincaid Meets with Students at Dunbar High." *Washington Post*, November 2, 1991, G1. Dow Jones Interactive–Library Publications. ptg.djnr.com.

Vorda, Allan. "I Come from a Place That's Very Unreal: An Interview with Jamaica Kincaid." *Face to Face: Interviews with Contemporary Novelists*. Ed. Allan Vorda. Houston, TX: Rice University Press, 1993. 77–105.

J. Brooks Bouson

KINDRED

Octavia Butler's stand-alone novel *Kindred* (1979) is the story of a young black woman's journey into America's past and her interactions with her slave and slave-owning **ancestors** who inhabited this past. Dana, an aspiring writer living in California in the mid-1970s, one day feels dizzy; seconds later she finds herself beside a river in which a young, terrified red-headed white boy is drowning. Dana saves the youngster and almost immediately finds herself back in her own **home** and time—wearing wet clothes and with bruises developing on her shoulders where the drowning boy's mother hit her as she tried to administer cardiopulmonary resuscitation (CPR).

Periodically thereafter, Dana is pulled back into the past—to nineteenth-century Maryland, she learns—always seemingly to aid Rufus Weylin, the red-headed boy, who somehow pulls her to him each time he thinks he is dying: She returns home only when she thinks she is about to die in Rufus's world. Dana recognizes Rufus Weylin's name from her **family** Bible but had not realized he was white. According to her Bible's family tree, he fathered a daughter, Hagar, who became Dana's great-grandmother. Dana worries that she must keep Rufus alive so he can sire her family line.

Dana's abrupt travels back in time are full of danger for a young black woman, and her responses and adaptations to life in Maryland during its slave-state days help Butler explore the psychology of **slavery**. Dana must act subservient to survive, and her greatest challenge eventually becomes to keep from internalizing the personality she projects, thus succumbing to a slave mentality. Butler demonstrates how easy it is for even an intelligent, strong-willed, independent woman like Dana to transform from a woman consciously acting the role of a slave to being as psychologically enslaved as any of the Weylin chattel. Butler also shows the process that turns a bright, likable boy like the young Rufus, whose two best friends were black, into a hard-hearted slave master who finds it acceptable to hurt those in his power, even those he loves. As Rufus ages, he becomes adept at the psychology of ownership, using threats, punishments, and deceptions to get what he wants from his slaves, especially Alice, a free black friend in his childhood whom he plots to possess as an adult.

Butler uses a number of women in the story to explore the intersections of **race**, gender, and power issues. Alice, Dana, Sarah, Cassie, and Tess illustrate the peculiar trials female slaves endured, both as sexual objects at the mercy of their masters' whims and as wives and mothers whose attachments to and fears for their children and spouses act as insurance against running away and revolts. Mrs. Weylin, Rufus's mother, illustrates forces helping to shape the slave mistress: the sexual double standard that keeps her from effectively protesting her husband's sexual use of female slaves; her sense that her social status depends on her idleness; and the age's ignorance of psychological problems such as postpartum depression and nervous breakdowns.

Eventually Kevin, Dana's white husband, also becomes trapped in the past, and readers get to see how different this experience is for a white male than for an African American female. Kevin's challenge, readers come to see, is to resist becoming desensitized to the immorality of a slave culture that on its surface often seems rather benign to him. The whites around him accept slavery as a natural social order and fail to notice the cruelties that lurk beneath the calm, quotidian surface of this **class** system. Dana worries that Kevin could learn to do the same.

Dana tries hard to sensitize Rufus to the brutality of slavery, but his inability to control his temper, his deep-seated fear of abandonment, his sense of entitlement, and his growing sexual attraction to her make this a dangerous strategy. As Rufus comes into adulthood, he shows himself more and more a man of his own era, and Dana must compromise more and more of her selfhood to ensure that both Rufus and Alice live long enough to give birth to Hagar. Although Alice catches the brunt of Rufus's power plays and his dangerous possessiveness, Dana too suffers from his angry determination to get his way. Her final, desperate attempt to return to the present (the opening scene of the novel) makes clear that even though she eventually escapes Rufus and the past, she will always be scarred by her experiences on the Weylin plantation, her lost arm an apt metaphor for the lasting damage of slavery on the African American psyche.

Dana is one of a number of strong black female heroes created by Butler. Her firsthand experiences in nineteenth-century Maryland raise a variety of race and gender issues and continue Butler's explorations of the uses and abuses of power. Dana's attempts to "feminize" Rufus—to mold him into a caring nurturer rather than a patriarchal oppressor—meet with only limited success, while Dana's brushes with racism and sexism in her 1970s life make clear that race and gender issues going back to our slavery **history** are so rooted into our social history that they remain unresolved, even many generations following emancipation.

See also Bloodchild and Other Stories; Parable Series; Patternist Series; Xenogenesis Trilogy

Works About

Bedore, Pamela. "Slavery and Symbiosis in Octavia Butler's *Kindred*." *Foundation* 31.84 (2002): 73–81.

Giannotti, Janet. *A Companion Text for Kindred*. Ann Arbor: University of Michigan Press, 1999.

Jesser, Nancy. "Blood, Genes and Gender in Octavia Butler's *Kindred* and *Dawn*." *Extrapolation* 43.1 (2002): 36–61.

Rushdy, Ashraf H. A. "Family of Orphans: Relation and Disrelation in Octavia Butler's *Kindred*." *College English* 55.2 (1993): 135–157.

Grace McEntee

KITCHEN TABLE: WOMEN OF COLOR PRESS

Kitchen Table: Women of Color Press was a progressive publisher in New York established and operated by feminist minority women in the United States with the purpose of publishing writings by women of color. It was founded by Cherríe Moraga, **Audre Lorde**, and Barbara Smith, leading minority feminist writers and scholars. Moraga is a Chicana poet, playwright, and editor. She participated in various feminist movements including organizing women of color groups against **violence**. Barbara Smith is a black feminist critic, writer, and scholar who is one of the pioneers of African American women's studies programs in the United States. She worked as the editor of the Kitchen Table until February 1995. Lorde was a Caribbean black lesbian writer, lecturer, and activist. She dedicated herself to feminism in America and oversees by publishing and organizing activist groups such as Sisters in Support of Sisters in South Africa (SISSA) and the St. Croix Women's Coalition.

With Gloria Anzaldúa, Moraga coedited *This Bridge Called My Back: Writings by Radical Women of Color* (1981), a collection of essays and creative writing by black, Chicana, and Asian feminists, both heterosexual and homosexual. *This Bridge Called My Back* was originally published by Persephone Press, a white feminist publisher in Watertown, Massachusetts. When Persephone Press went out of business in 1983, Moraga and Anzaldúa retrieved the right for *This Bridge Called My Back* from Persephone and developed it into a second edition. However, no publisher in the United States would publish radical writings by lesbian women of color. Realizing the difficulty of publishing feminist writings of minority women in America, Moraga, Smith, and Lorde founded Kitchen Table, with the principle to run it by women of color and to publish works by women of color of all sexualities. One of the first books they published was *This Bridge Called My Back*. It won the Before Columbus Foundation American Book Award in 1986, and it has been widely read, especially in women's studies programs.

Since Kitchen Table's founding in the early 1980s, it has published many remarkable feminist and creative works written by women of color. Their publications present various political, social, and cultural issues in the United States and the world from the perspective of feminist women of color. The topics of their writings include sexism, racism, **lesbianism**, international politics, sisterhood, and **motherhood**, and they present insightful analysis of the social construction of the United States and the world. Recognizing the importance of Kitchen Table's role as one of the few publishers in the United States promoting feminist writings by women of color, The Kitchen Table: Women of Color Press Transition Coalition was formed to support Kitchen Table to develop into "an independent and sustainable nonprofit organization." The members of this coalition are feminist scholars, artists, publishers, and activists such as Joo-Hyun Kang, Cathy Cohen, and Beatrix Gates.

See also Black Feminist Criticism

Works By

Alexander, M. Jacqui, ed. *The Third Wave: Feminists Perspectives on Racism.* New York: Kitchen Table Women of Color Press, 1998.

Beck, Evelyn Torton, ed. *Nice Jewish Girls: A Lesbian Anthology.* New York: Kitchen Table Women of Color Press, 1982.

Brant, Beth, ed. *A Gathering of Spirit: North American Indian Women's Issue.* New York: Kitchen Table Women of Color Press, 1984.

Cichran, Jo. *Bearing Witness.* New York: Kitchen Table Women of Color Press, 1984.

Gomez, Alma, Cherríe L. Moraga, and Mariana Romo-Carmona, eds. *Cuentos: Stories by Latinas.* New York: Kitchen Table Women of Color Press, 1983.

Hylkema, Sarie S., and Mitsuye Yamada, eds. *Sowing TI Leaves: Writings by Multicultural Women.* New York: Kitchen Table Women of Color Press, 1991.

Lorde, Audre. *Need: A Chorale for Black Woman Voices.* Freedom Organizing Series. Vol. 6. New York: Kitchen Table Women of Color Press, 1991.

# #

Moraga, Cherríe, and Gloria E. Anzaldúa, eds. *This Bridge Called My Back.* 2nd ed. New York: Kitchen Table Women of Color Press, 1983.

Morgan, Nancy. *Grenada Notebook.* New York: Kitchen Table Women of Color Press, 1984.

Omolade, Barbara. *It's a Family Affair: The Real Lives of Black Single Mothers.* New York: Kitchen Table Women of Color Press, 1987.

Smith, Barbara, ed. *Home Girls: A Black Feminist Anthology.* New York: Kitchen Table Women of Color Press, 1983.

Toder, Nancy. *Choices.* New York: Kitchen Table Women of Color Press, 1980.

Yamada, Mitsuye. *Camp Notes and Other Poems.* New York: Kitchen Table Women of Color Press, 1992.

——. *Desert Run: Poems and Stories.* New York: Kitchen Table Women of Color Press, 1988.

Yamamoto, Hisaye. *Seventeen Syllables and Other Stories.* New York: Kitchen Table Women of Color Press, 1988.

Youngsook Jeong

KOCHER, RUTH ELLEN (1965–   )

The daughter of a black father and white mother, Kocher was born in Wilkes-Barre, a small city in northeastern Pennsylvania that was once a coal mining center. She grew up in a housing project along the Susquehanna River. Kocher attended the Bucknell University Seminar for Younger Poets and Pennsylvania State University, where she majored in English **literature** and creative writing. She moved to Tempe, Arizona, where she earned her M.F.A. in creative writing in 1994 and her doctorate in 1999 from Arizona State University. Tempe offered a stark contrast to life in Pennsylvania. Kocher's doctoral study emphasized early-twentieth-century women and writers of color. She has taught at Missouri Western State College and Southern Illinois University at Edwardsville and is now a member of the faculty at the University of Missouri, St. Louis, where she teaches creative writing and American literatures. She lives in St. Louis with her husband, Coby Royer, and daughter, Kaylee. She is the winner of the 1999 Naomi Long Madgett Poetry Award and the 2001 Green Rose Prize.

Kocher's scholarly publications offer keys to her poetics. Her articles have explored multiplicity, obstacles to the truth, **passing** and trespassing, and a woman's life as a site of cultural bondage. Kocher's **poetry** is demanding, elusive, multilayered, transgressive, and displacing. Her world is terrifying and beautiful, as she asserts through the Rilke epigraph that opens *Desdemona's Fire* (1999). A feminist reading of Kocher is aided by the goddess Kali. Terrible and beautiful, Kali is represented as a three-eyed, black or blue woman with four arms. She is often depicted with her tongue extended, full breasted, and standing on the chest of her husband, Shiva. Her **home** is cremation grounds. Among her manifold attributes, she is the destroyer of ignorance, the liberator from false notions, the taster of life's offerings, and she who reveals pain and sorrow as a doorway to fullness of being.

Desdemona's Fire takes a mythic approach to the exploration of **identity** and claim. In addition to a retelling of *Othello* (1622), this volume references the Buddha, the Yoruba Orisa Esu Elegba, Eden, and figures from Greek **myth** and *The Odyssey* (800 BCE). Divided into two parts, the collection suggests that identity is the engagement of mother and father through crossroads and crossings, gardens and torn-up places, shadow and light. The poems show identity as origami: a paper-thin construct, folded upon itself. *When the Moon Knows You're Wandering* (2002) examines the awful and frustrating quest for home and self-location. Like Dante's *Inferno* (early fourteenth century), *When the Moon Knows You're Wandering* depicts a poet guided by other poets. James Wright, Osip Mandelshtam, Hilda Doolittle, Martin Luther King, Jr., Norman Dubie, Ruth Stone, Pablo Neruda, Federico García Lorca, and Søren Kierkegaard usher Kocher to evanescence. *One Girl Babylon* (2003) probes captivity and self-alienation. Influenced by the Kabbalah and Western painting, it presents rites of passage for self-reclamation. In the way of Kali, the text is both site of captivity and platform for liberation. Each volume possesses its own secrets of joy, pain, and sorrow. Each presses to reveal new worlds in words.

Works By

"Consequences of Character." *Poets and Writers* (January–February 2002): 44–46, 48.

Desdemona's Fire. Detroit: Lotus Press, 1999.

"O Blessed Verse: Obstructing Truth and the Sanctity of Transgression in Student Poetry." *Creative Writing/Creative Teaching: Pedagogy Forum Handbook.* Fairfax, VA: Associated Writing Programs, 2001.

One Girl Babylon. Kalamazoo: New Issues Press, Western Michigan University, 2003.

"A Question of Survival: An Interview with Allison Deming." *Hayden's Ferry Review* 14 (1994): 74.

"Revisiting a Site of Cultural Bondage: JoAnn Gibson Robinson's Boycott Memoir." *Women as Sites of Culture: Women's Roles in Cultural Formation from the Renaissance to the 20th Century.* Ed. Susan Shifrin. Burlington, VT: Ashgate Press, 2002. 265–274.

When the Moon Knows You're Wandering. Kalamazoo: New Issues Press, Western Michigan University, 2002.

Works About

Bass, Holly. Review of *One Girl Babylon*, by Ruth Ellen Kocher. *Black Issues Book Review* 6.2 (2004): 25–26.

Perrine, Jennifer. Review of *One Girl Babylon*, by Ruth Ellen Kocher. *Indiana Review* (Winter 2004): 111.

Rowell, Charles. "'Within a Field of Knowing': An Interview with Ruth Ellen Kocher." *Callaloo* 27.4 (Fall 2004): 932–944.

Wheeler, Lesley. Review of *Desdemona's Fire*, by Ruth Ellen Kocher. *African American Review* 35.2 (2001): 342–343.

Monifa A. Love Asante

KOMUNYAKAA, YUSEF (1947–   )

In 1994, Yusef Komunyakaa received the Pulitzer Prize for Poetry, the William Faulkner Prize from the Université de Rennes, and the Kingsley Tufts Poetry Award for his book *Neon Vernacular: New and Selected Poems* (1993). These awards catapulted him to international acclaim and established him as one of the finest living poets.

The oldest of six children, Komunyakaa was born in 1947 in Bogalusa, Louisiana, a small town seventy miles northeast of New Orleans. He wrote his first poem for his high school graduation, a 100-lines-long effort that he now terms ridiculous. He would not write again until after he had returned from the Vietnam War, where he served from 1969 to 1970 as an information specialist and won the Bronze Star for gallantry in combat. In 1973 Komunyakaa enrolled in a creative writing workshop at the University of Colorado at Colorado Springs; he reports that he has been writing ever since. He double majored in English and sociology and went on to earn an M.A. in creative writing from Colorado State University and an M.F.A. from the University of California at Irvine.

His earliest and most enduring literary influences include Shakespeare, **Gwendolyn Brooks**, Robert Hayden, **Amiri Baraka**, and the **Harlem Renaissance** poets **Jean Toomer**, **Helene Johnson**, and **Langston Hughes**. The latter three, along with **Zora Neale Hurston**, are in his view the most innovative voices of the Harlem Renaissance.

Critics tend to agree that American **history**, Komunyakaa's war experiences, his childhood in the rural, Jim Crow **South**, and a lifelong **love** of **jazz** and the **blues** inform much of his **poetry**. Receiving far less mention is that many of his best poems focus on women and children and raise feminist concerns. "Stepfather: A Girl's Poem," for instance, is a chilling work that deals with child abuse. Told from a young girl's perspective, she discloses that for years her stepfather's eyes have undressed her. Now, **home** early from **work**, he enters her bedroom and lifts her dress. The particular ending to this tale is left to the reader, for as Komunyakaa explains, he wants his reader to be a "co-creator of meaning." "Re-creating the Scene," from his Vietnam War collection *Dien Cai Dau* ("crazy" in Vietnamese; 1988) paints an equally riveting portrait, this time the gang **rape** (and subsequent cover-up by military officials) of a Vietnamese woman by three Confederate flag–waving soldiers.

With such poems as "*Dui Boi*, Dust of Life" and "Toys in a Field," Komunyakaa explores the particularly horrific effects of the Vietnam War on children, thousands of whom were maimed, physically and psychologically, and orphaned. As "Toys in a Field" ends, the spotlight shifts from a group of Vietnamese children playing among abandoned weapons to–in classic understatement–the little Vietnamese boy with American eyes.

The search for love is another subject that runs through Komunyakaa's writing. His love poems are commonly set in bars or nightclubs, often with the mellow syncopation of a Charlie Parker, Thelonious Monk, or John Coltrane tune reverberating in the background. In "Jasmine," a man and woman make eye contact and flirt from across the room; "Woman, I Got the Blues" features a couple who meet, slow-draw, and bebop, before ending up half-naked on his living room floor; "When in Rome–Apologia" captures a man who, caught up in the music, gives too much attention to another man's wife. Although Komunyakaa's work is at times difficult and not easily decipherable, the love poems have been greeted with great excitement and are among his most commonly anthologized.

Since 1998, Komunyakaa has been a professor of the Council of the Humanities and Creative Writing at Princeton University. In 1999 he was elected a chancellor of the Academy of American Poets. There is wide agreement that his is a vital American voice.

Works By

Blues Notes: Essays, Interviews & Commentaries. Ann Arbor: University of Michigan Press, 2000.

Copacetic. Middletown, CT: Wesleyan University Press, 1984.

Dien Cai Dau. Middletown, CT: Wesleyan University Press, 1988.

I Apologize for the Eyes in My Head. Middletown, CT: Wesleyan University Press, 1986.

Lost in the Bonewheel Factory. Amherst, MA: Lynx House Press, 1979.

Magic City. Hanover, NH: Wesleyan University Press, 1992.

Neon Vernacular: New and Selected Poems. Hanover, NH: Wesleyan University Press, 1993.

Pleasure Dome: New & Collected Poems, 1975–1999. Middletown, CT: Wesleyan University Press, 2001.

Scandalize My Name: Selected Poems. London: Pan Macmillan, 2002.

Taboo. New York: Farrar, Straus and Giroux, 2004.

Talking Dirty to the Gods. New York: Farrar, Straus and Giroux, 2000.

Thieves of Paradise. Hanover, NH: Wesleyan University Press, 1999.

Works About

Aubert, Alvin. "Yusef Komunyakaa: The Unified Vision–Canonization and Humanity." *African American Review* 27.1 (Spring 1993): 119–123.

Conley, Susan. "About Yusef Komunyakaa: A Profile." *Ploughshares* 23.1 (Spring 1997): 202–207.

Mitchell, Verner D. "Remembering Tet: A Conversation with Vietnam War Veteran Poets." *War, Literature & the Arts* 10.2 (Fall–Winter 1998): 1–41.

Salas, Angela M. "Race, Human Empathy, and Negative Capability: The Poetry of Yusef Komunyakaa." *College Literature* 30.4 (Fall 2003): 32–53.

Verner D. Mitchell

KRIK? KRAK!

In the first seven of **Edwidge Danticat**'s nine stories (plus an epilogue) in *Krik? Krak!* (1995), she presents women at various stages living in the aftermath of male destruction. In order to cope following the 1937 massacre of Haitians by Dominican forces, some find comfort through entering the realm of insanity; some resist with silence; some gild their own gutter to forget; some fight in order to die. Danticat's last two pieces occur in New York and deal with more contemporary Haitian American daughters, clearly less aware of what their mothers endured.

In some of the stories it seems as though the more contemporary daughters, both in Haiti and in America, are sentenced to repeat their mothers' folly. But only the casual reader would say that Danticat leaves her female characters to gather themselves up or to fall apart. Instead, the women learn control through ritual. Most successfully, many of the women in these Haiti-centered pieces form a secret society offering protection, a practice later echoed in the States. While Caroline's mother in "Caroline's Mother," the collection's final piece, mourns that the past "fades a person," it is that very past that Danticat's female characters perch on for support, even those who lament **history**'s effects. Danticat purposely leaves many unanswered questions in this work, emphasizing that historical events have no beginning, middle, and end. Instead, Danticat's characters live in a historical moment, without beginning or end, the only sense of history being one's fragmented own.

Further defying the limits of categorization is Danticat's deliberate presentation of nine separate stories. *Kirk? Krak!* is described as a collection, but Danticat's word choice is so precise that the stories read poetically. That Danticat means to imply the ties between the women is clear, but the ties are meted out so rarely that the gulfs between generations can emphasize the difficulty in connecting with history's participants. Yet Danticat's deceptively simple, separate short stories actually depend on one another deeply, as when Marie, who has picked up a discarded corpse from the streets, naming it Rose, transforms the infant into one of the ghost women—her dead mother, aunts, and grandmothers—above her bed. These ties have far less to do with plot than with the emotional understanding of women's lived experience, so much so that when Danticat offers the few direct connections between the women that she does, they profoundly affect the reader's sense of people and place, as when the isolated and imprisoned Défilé is revealed to be surrounded by generations of women.

The presence of absence–absent mothers, aunts, grandmothers–becomes the motive for the construction of a woman's **identity**, echoing the rootless dyasporic existence of Haiti's inhabitants. While the few male characters of Danticat's stories are concerned with the functions of law, Danticat's female characters struggle with the confusion of time. Danticat's female characters turn backward, returning to location, or at least a sense of historical location, confounding time patterns and even physical law. They need to return to points of historical entanglement, repeating their mothers' acts even while resisting them, for Danticat demonstrates it is only through ritualized repetition that a daughter, or a future generation, can hope to escape the cycle and progress. If the repetition were to stop, hope would be lost and the lack of ritualized action becomes a kind of collapse. In the end, it is their mothers' folly that more contemporary daughters must repeat in Danticat's work. That Danticat's daughters repeat their mothers' madness, however, does not mean their destruction but their strength.

Works About

N'Zengou-Tayo, Marie-José. "Rewriting Folklore: Traditional Beliefs and Popular Culture in Edwidge Danticat's *Breath, Eyes, Memory* and *Krik? Krak!*" *MaComère: Journal of the Association of Caribbean Women Writers and Scholars* 3 (2000): 123–140.

Poon, Angelia. "Re-Writing the Male Text: Mapping Cultural Spaces in Edwidge Danticat's *Krik? Krak!* and Jamaica Kincaid's *A Small Place.*" *Jouvert: A Journal of Postcolonial Studies* 4.2 (2000): 30 paragraphs.

Putnam, Amanda. "Mothering the Motherless: Portrayals of Alternate Mothering Practices within the Caribbean Diaspora." *Canadian Woman Studies/Les Cahiers de la Femme* 23.2 (2004): 118–123.

Shea, Renée II. "Edwidge Danticat." *Belles Lettres* 10.3 (1995): 12–15.

Squint, Kirstin. "Exploring the Borderland between Realism and Magical Realism in *Kirk? Krak!*" *Eureka Studies in Teaching Short Fiction* 5.1 (2004): 116–122.

Lisa Muir

 **L**

LANE, PINKIE GORDON (1923–   )

Born in Philadelphia, Pennsylvania, to William and Inez Gordon, Pinkie Gordon Lane has been well acquainted with **death**, change, and survival. Her three siblings did not survive infancy. Her father, a longshoreman, died the year the seventeen-year-old graduated from high school. His death resulted in her postponing college to **work** as a factory seamstress. Five years later, her mother died. Gordon moved to Atlanta to attend Spelman College. During her senior year, she married Ulysses Simpson Lane. After graduating in 1949 she taught in the **South**. In 1955 she entered Atlanta University for graduate study. In 1956 after earning her M.A., the Lanes moved to Louisiana. She taught at Leland College and Southern University, where she served for many years and later directed the English Department. Her only child, Gordon, was born in 1963. She earned her doctorate at Louisiana State University in 1967, the first black woman to do so. In 1970, her husband died. She did not remarry. Lane has traveled extensively and taught at institutions throughout the United States.

Both lauded and critiqued for her intimate, "quiet" occasional **poetry**, Lane has been underappreciated for the measure of her work. Nominated for major awards and belittled for subjective focus and lack of **Black Arts Movement** aggressiveness, Lane's explorations of impermanence, persistence, and cyclical reconfiguration have been largely overlooked. Expert of imagery and metaphor, Lane served as Poet Laureate of Louisiana from 1989 to 1992. Some have ascribed this honor to the dominant role of the Louisiana landscape in Lane's work. If the laureate is an emblem of the Oracle at Delphi and her transfiguring bay leaves, as well as a title for the poet who serves as memorializer and keeper of the flame, Lane's position takes on added appropriateness. Influenced by **Gwendolyn Brooks**, Anne Sexton, **May Miller**, **Margaret Esse Danner**, **Sonia Sanchez**, and Naomi Long Madgett as well as **Clarence Major** and Western male poetics, Lane has developed a body of work devoted to the classical, female trinity of song, **memory**, and meditation and aligned herself with the African tradition of the griot. Like the women poets who have influenced her, Lane reaches through her personal experiences with **love**, death, work, and place to resist containment and claim the patterns, energies, and spaces that are dark and female. Lane dedicated her first collection *Wind Thoughts* (1972) "To All the Beautiful Women of the World." The collection tenders a chain of poems that are linked through verbal play and metaphor. Like her second collection, the Pulitzer Prize–nominated *The Mystic Female* (1978), *Wind Thoughts* professes that the heart and driving force of all things is female. Lane's subsequent collections *I Never Scream* (1985), *Girl at the Window* (1991), and *Elegy for Etheridge* (2000) are in the tradition of **Zora Neale Hurston**. They offer previously visited and new work in new contexts. Like Hurston's great talent, Lane's gift for reorganization and expansion provides for greater understanding of her testimonies of grief, oppression, courage, and connectedness.

Some of Lane's works may be found in the James Weldon Johnson Memorial Collection of Negro Arts and Letters in the Beinecke Rare Book and Manuscript Library at Yale University. The Louisiana State University houses the Pinkie Gordon Lane Papers, compiled by Rose Tarbell.

Works By

Elegy for Etheridge: Poems. Baton Rouge: Louisiana State University Press, 2000.

Girl at the Window: Poems. Baton Rouge: Louisiana State University Press, 1991.

I Never Scream: New and Selected Poems. Detroit, MI: Lotus, 1985.

A Literary Profile to 1977. Baton Rouge, LA: P. G. Lane, 1977.

The Mystic Female: Poems. Introduction by Jerry W. Ward. Fort Smith, AR: South and West, 1978.

A Quiet Poem. Detroit, MI: Broadside, 1980. Broadside Series, No. 80.

"Reflections on Dumas's 'Love Song.'" *Black American Literature Forum* 22.2 (1988): 270–274.

Wind Thoughts: Poems. With photography by S. W. Austin. Fort Smith, AR: South and West, 1972.

Works About

Brown, Dorothy H., and Barbara C. Ewell, eds. *Louisiana Women Writers.* Baton Rouge: Louisiana State University Press, 1992.

Bryan, Violet Harrington. "Evocations of Place and Culture in the Works of Four Contemporary Black Louisiana Writers: Brenda Osbey, Sybil Kein, Elizabeth Brown-Guillory, and Pinkie Gordon Lane." *Louisiana Literature: A Review of Literature and Humanities* 4.2 (1987): 49–60.

Lane, Pinkie Gordon. Sound recording. Interview with Kit Hathaway. Writers' Voices. WRKF, Baton Rouge, LA, February 21, 1980.

Monifa A. Love Asante

LARSEN, NELLA (1891–1964)

Nella Larsen is best known as the author of *Quicksand* (1928) and *Passing* (1929), two short novels of the **Harlem Renaissance** that deal eloquently with the subjects of racial construction and **passing** in the lives of middle-class African American female protagonists. These works of **fiction** are memorable for both their psychological insights into female characters and their taut, lyrical writing style. *Quicksand* received a bronze medal from the Harmon Foundation in 1928. In 1930 Larsen became the first African American woman to win a Guggenheim Fellowship. She used the money to travel to Spain and pursue **work** on a third novel, which was never published. In the same year her short story "Sanctuary" became the center of a plagiarism controversy. Larsen was eventually exonerated, but she published nothing further after this event, although she attempted several other works of fiction during the 1930s. After her return from Spain and an unsuccessful attempt to revive her failing marriage to Fisk University professor Elmer S. Imes, she moved back to New York but gradually withdrew from public literary life during the mid-1930s, cutting off ties with all of her friends in 1937. For the last two decades of her life she worked full-time as a nurse. At the time of her **death** in 1964, she was so removed from her literary fame that no obituary was published and only her nursing colleagues attended her funeral.

An acute observer of social constructions of **race** and **identity**, Larsen also carefully crafted her own public persona. Information about her birthdate, birthplace, **family**, education, and travel has been shrouded in ambiguity and misinformation, some of which was deliberately perpetuated by Larsen herself. Her biographer Thadious M. Davis spent years with primary documents tracing Larsen from her birthplace in Chicago to her eventual **home** in New York City. Davis's biography *Nella Larsen Novelist of the Harlem Renaissance* is deemed the authoritative study of Larsen's life.

Larsen was born on April 13, 1891, as Nellie Walker to Mary Hanson Walker and Peter Walker, a cook, designated "colored" along with his daughter on the birth certificate, although no information was given about his age or nationality. Her elementary school records, however, give her name as "Nellie Larson" and her father's as "Peter Larson." Whether Larson was her stepfather or her birth father with a newly "ex-Negro" name remains unclear, but he was the only parent who signed school records. Her junior high school records list her as "Nellye Larson." In 1907 she left Chicago for Nashville, Tennessee, to complete her high school education at Fisk University, where she enrolled as Nellie Marie Larsen. She stayed at Fisk for only one year, but during the year she adopted "Nella" as the final version of her first name. When Nella entered Fisk, her family moved to a largely Anglo-Saxon neighborhood on Chicago's West Side. Peter Larson changed the spelling of his name to the more Scandinavian "Larsen" at the time of the move; Nella would retain this spelling of her surname for the rest of her life. In the 1910 Illinois census, Peter and Mary Larsen listed their race as "white" and their country of origin as "Denmark." Mary Larsen also reported that she had given birth to only one daughter, Nella's younger sister Anna, who resided with them. Anna's birth year was 1893, the year that Larsen later gave as the year of her own birth. Some records also suggest that before her entrance to elementary school in 1901, Larsen may have lived apart from her family in an institution. These details, and the secrecy surrounding them, give added poignancy to Larsen's fiction, which probes the problems of identity, alienation from family, and the complex psychological dimensions of passing for white.

Although Fisk University in 1907 was the leading black university in the United States, apparently Larsen did not feel at home in this environment for long, as she left after one year. No clear record exists for Larsen's whereabouts between 1908 and 1912. She attended the Lincoln School of Nursing in New York City between 1912 and 1915 as Nella Marian Larsen and then took a position as supervisor of the Nursing Department at Tuskegee Institute. Unlike Fisk, which favored an academic curriculum and had as its vision the creation of race leaders, Tuskegee emphasized vocational training, loyalty, duty, and manual labor. Nella felt even less at home in this African American institution of higher learning than she had at Fisk and left after a year to return to New York.

Larsen's own version of her family background is that she was the daughter of a white Danish mother and a West Indian father who had died when she was two. Her mother's subsequent remarriage to a man of her own race and the birth of another daughter made Nella the only "black" member of this family. While this version of the story certainly explains Nella's estrangement from family, it was also, as Davis points out, a story that also both gave her **freedom** from scrutiny and protected her family's anonymity, especially pertinent as several of her Harlem Renaissance acquaintances had family connections in Chicago. In *Quicksand*, which has autobiographical ties to Larsen's own story, the protagonist Helga Crane has an "Uncle Peter," who has supported her in the past but who also rejects her at the insistence of his new wife when she visits him in Chicago to ask for money. The father of Irene Redfield, in *Passing*, shares the same Chicago house number as the real Peter Larsen. Whether or not Peter Walker and Peter Larsen were the same person, it is clear that Peter Larsen assumed the major responsibility for Nella's upbringing and supported her education at Fisk, which equipped her for a life in the African American **community**. Her mother's name was used only once by Larsen, on her marriage certificate, and was given as Marion

Hansen. Whatever her relation to her mother, it is clear that they were not at all close. Like her protagonist in *Quicksand*, Helga Crane, Larsen spoke of spending time in Denmark with her mother's relatives during her youth and even claimed to have attended the University of Copenhagen as an auditor, but no U.S. passport was issued to Larsen during the relevant time periods. When Helga Crane reacts with panic and suffocation to Robert Anderson's references to family background and pedigree in *Quicksand*, she echoes feelings with which Larsen was all too familiar.

In 1919 Nella Marion Larsen married Elmer S. Imes, then a research physicist and member of a prominent African American family. Their home together was her first real home as an adult, and through her husband she also acquired powerful family connections. The couple lived in the greater New York area, and both continued to pursue their careers—he as a scientist, she as a nurse. Both began to publish as well. While Imes published scientific articles, Larsen began her first literary efforts, a series of pieces based on "pleasant memories of my childish days in Denmark" for **Jessie Redmon Fauset**'s *The Brownies' Book*, which she published in 1920 under the name Nella Larsen Imes. The Imeses moved in a privileged circle of mixed-race acquaintances during the postwar era when new opportunities were opening up for African Americans, and Elmer introduced Nella to several famous persons who later became her close friends, among them the photographer and writer Carl Van Vechten. Although Larsen had no family pedigree to match her husband's, Davis speculates that she played up on the white, Danish part of her heritage to establish a sense of superiority in her relationships with members of the black elite who might have otherwise considered her a "nobody." Nella quit her nursing job at Lincoln Hospital after a change in the administration, then began to work as a volunteer at the New York Public Library, where her recent publications in children's **literature** enabled her to land a job as a librarian in the children's section. She became one of the few persons of color to earn a certificate at the New York Public Library's prestigious school, which later became part of Columbia University. The couple moved to Harlem in 1927. Although the marriage grew troubled and eventually ended in divorce in 1933, it was during her marriage that Larsen produced all of her published writing. In addition to her publications for *The Brownies' Book* and several book reviews, she published a number of stories under the pseudonym "Allen Semi," an anagram for "Nella Imes." By the time her two novels were published in 1928 and 1929, Larsen had decided to use her maiden name professionally.

When Larsen won a Guggenheim Award in 1930, Elmer Imes entered into discussion with Fisk University about a professorship there. During Larsen's travels in southern Europe in 1930–1931, Imes moved to Nashville to begin his job at Fisk. Although she had heard rumors that Imes was involved with another woman during her absence, Larsen moved to Nashville upon her return from Europe, at the urging of the Fisk University president, in an attempt to repair her marriage with Imes. During this time Imes's relationship with a white Fisk employee Ethel Gilbert, who worked as a fund-raiser for the

Fisk Jubilee Singers, continued to be a source of gossip in the community. Attempting a reunion with her husband at Fisk proved disastrous for Larsen in terms of her physical and emotional health. Beyond the pain of his infidelity was her rejection by a man who had once cherished her for a white woman, a pattern perilously close to her own family's rejection of her based on her skin color. Larsen attempted several writing projects during this time, but none came to fruition. In 1933 she finally filed for divorce on the grounds of "cruelty" and was awarded a substantial settlement that enabled her to reestablish herself in New York, this time on the Lower East Side. Harlem had changed dramatically, partly because of the depression, since the Imeses' earlier residence there, and publishers were no longer clamoring for work by black writers. For a few years Larsen continued friendships with several artists and writers—notably the actress Dorothy Peterson and Carl Van Vechten. She "disappeared" from all social life in 1937, leaving mysterious messages with friends, refusing to answer the phone or the doorbell, and then moving to an apartment across the street. She managed to live on alimony payments until Imes's death in 1941, when Larsen took Mrs. Nella L. Imes as her legal name and referred to herself as a widow.

In 1944, Nella Larsen embarked on the last phase of her career, as a full-time nurse working the night shift, first for seventeen years at Governour's Hospital, then at Metropolitan Hospital in New York. Her excellent training and skills enabled her to quickly rise to the level of nursing supervisor. When she died in the early spring of 1964, it was her nursing colleagues who sent flowers and arranged for the funeral. But none of them was close enough to her to find her **body** until a week after her death from acute congestive heart failure in her apartment while reading in bed. During 1963, Nella had traveled to California to see her sister Anna in an attempt to establish connection with her family but returned in a deep depression, her spirits permanently injured. Her sister had refused to allow her to enter her house because of her skin color. Even after Larsen's death in 1964 (her body was discovered on March 30), Anna expressed surprise at being informed by the will's executors that she had a sister and refused direct contact with any representatives of Nella's estate, even though she was the recipient of substantial funds. Larsen's apartment was ransacked during the time of her death, and none of her unpublished manuscripts have come to light. The name on Larsen's death certificate reads "Nella Larsen Imes."

Whatever the reasons for her prolonged silence after a brief period of remarkable literary achievement—psychological trauma, the emotional repercussions of her divorce, the depression and resulting lack of support for black writers, the changing times and contexts—Larsen's cleanly crafted modernist fiction with its evocations of a particular historical moment has earned her a place in the **history** of African American writers. As Thadious Davis eloquently suggests, Larsen, who had long been rejected by her family of origin, could not have anticipated the place her Harlem Renaissance novels would earn for her in the family of African American writers with the flourishing of **black feminist criticism** and the renewed interest in African American writing in the last three decades of the twentieth century.

Works By

Passing. New York: Knopf, 1929.
Quicksand. New York: Knopf, 1928.

Works About

Davis, Thadious M. *Nella Larsen Novelist of the Harlem Renaissance: A Woman's Life Unveiled.* Baton Rouge: Louisiana State University Press, 1994.
Hutchinson, George. *Nella Larsen: A Biography of the Color Line.* Cambridge, MA: Belknap Press, 2006.
Larson, Charles R. *Invisible Darkness: Jean Toomer and Nella Larsen.* Iowa City: University of Iowa Press, 1993.
Wall, Cheryl A. *Women of the Harlem Renaissance.* Bloomington: Indiana University Press, 1995.

Ann Hostetler

LATIMORE, JEWEL C. See Amini, Johari

LATTANY, KRISTIN HUNTER (1931–)

Kristin Hunter Lattany's interest in being a writer was likely kindled by her parents' earliest act on her behalf: choosing her name. Born in Philadelphia, Pennsylvania, to schoolteacher parents George and Mabel Eggleston Hunter, Kristin was named after the main character in *Kristin Lavransdatter*, a novel written by Norwegian novelist Sigrid Undset, winner of the 1928 Nobel Prize for Literature.

From an early age, Lattany wrote. As a child, she wrote **poetry** and articles for school and **community** publications. As a teen and young adult, she was a columnist for the local edition of the *Pittsburgh Courier*, covering social issues including racial disruptions in nearby Camden, New Jersey.

After a brief foray into teaching elementary school at her parents' behest, Lattany returned to writing. Professionally, she wrote ads; independently, she wrote short stories and dramas. In 1955, her hard **work** paid off when she won a national competition sponsored by CBS for her television script *Minority of One*. Her story about a white student being sent to an all-black school was ultimately revised to include a French student at an all-white school due to the broadcaster's concerns about controversy. That was the first—and only—time **race** would be subjugated as an aspect of Lattany's writing.

Lattany's writing typically focuses on themes of poverty, aspirations, pain, **family**, and community in African American life. Her characters are often living in poverty. They contend with primarily economic barriers as they try to escape the slums they live in. Her books are sometimes grim and sometimes optimistic, but they are always realistic.

Her first book, *God Bless the Children* (1964), is the story of Rosalie Fleming, a girl living in a segregated urban neighborhood who wants to make a better life for herself and her family but who ultimately succumbs to despair and **death**. The book won the Philadelphia Athenaeum Award.

In addition to her novels for adults, Lattany has written several works for younger audiences. Her first novel for young adults, *The Soul Brothers and Sister Lou* (1968), is the story of a group of African American teens who see music as their key to leaving the ghetto. After one of the teens is killed by police who mistake an epileptic fit for an assault, they overcome their urge for vengeance and instead record a song of eulogy that becomes an instant hit.

Lattany's writing is both realistic and hopeful. During the course of her career, she has explored a variety of powerful, controversial issues. Recipient of the Moonstone Black Writing Celebration Lifetime Achievement Award, Lattany continues to write today, although she has retired from her university career.

Works By

Boss Cat. New York: Scribner, 1971.
Breaking Away. New York: Ballantine, 2003.
Do Unto Others. New York: Ballantine, 2000.
God Bless the Children. New York: Scribner, 1964.
Guests in the Promised Land. New York: Scribner, 1973.
Kinfolks. New York: Ballantine, 1996.
The Lakestown Rebellion. New York: Scribner, 1978.
The Landlord. New York: Scribner, 1966.
Lou in the Limelight. New York: Scribner, 1981.
The Soul Brothers and Sister Lou. New York: Scribner, 1968.
The Survivors. New York: Scribner, 1975.

Works About

Harris, Trudier. *From Mammies to Militants: Domestics in Black American Literature.* Philadelphia: Temple University Press, 1982.
Polak, Maralyn Lois. "Kristin Hunter: A Writer and a Fighter." *Philadelphia Inquirer*, November 24, 1974.

Heidi Hauser Green

LEE, ANDREA (1953–)

A Harvard graduate and a regular contributor for *The New Yorker*, Lee has been nominated for the National Book Award for her memoir *Russian Journal* (1981), for which she finally won the Jean Stein Award from the American

Academy and the Institution of Arts and Letters. Her work also includes a novel, *Sarah Phillips* (1984), and a collection of short stories, *Interesting Women* (2002). She currently lives and works in Italy, which provided the setting for many of the stories in *Interesting Women.*

The book, which is her best-known work, makes clear that Lee's aesthetics is informed by feminism. The women who populate its pages are "interesting" in that they eschew patriarchal definitions of femininity. For example, Ariel in "The Birthday Present," who invites two prostitutes to spend an evening with her Italian husband as a birthday gift, proves to be no conventional and stereotypical woman. Like Ariel, Lee's women are not afraid to experiment with **love** and openly exhibit sexual desire without being punished for it. Overall, the book creates a mosaic of women who take their chances and are thus active, complex, resourceful, bold, and highly independent. Throughout the pages we are invited to share their point of view, to see gender relations with fresh eyes, and to reconsider traditional definitions of love and womanhood. Similar to other women writers, Lee foregrounds the female voice and perspective, and in doing so she ends up reconstructing female **identity**.

In *Sarah Phillips* the struggle for identity is also on the forefront. Sarah's rejection of the baptismal rite is evident of her need to break free from the limiting black bourgeoisie world. Yet Sarah's attempt at amnesia is often tinted with nostalgia. Throughout her quest, Sarah explores her limits and experiments with relationships **home** and abroad only to realize that she cannot escape her past since her gender identity is inseparable from her racial one. Although the ending of the story may be considered disappointing, as it shows Sarah returning home to all that she had rejected, her desire for a different reality unfulfilled, this disappointment may ultimately give rise to a critique of all those institutions and conventions that hindered Sarah's quest. Furthermore, Sarah's return to her **community** is a common motif in many African American women writers who underline through their work the importance of the cultural past for the individual. In this context, the novel can be said to belong to an African American feminist tradition that privileges both a female perspective and ultimately fights amnesia by underlying that "nothing can be dissolved or thrown away."

In her work, Lee seems to create her own "personal landscape," as she herself confesses in the foreword to her *Russian Journal,* writing only about what pleases and excites her. Thus, the female voice arising from her narratives is strong, highly independent, and feminist in its intent.

See also Black Feminism

Works By

Interesting Women: Stories. New York: Random House, 2002.
Russian Journal. New York: Random House, 1981.
Sarah Phillips. New York: Random House, 1984.

Works About

Enomoto, Don M. "'Creative Destruction' and the Fashioning of a Self in Sarah Phillips." *African American Literature* (Spring 1999): 209–234.

Hogue, Laurence W. "The Limits of Modernity: Andrea Lee's *Sarah Phillips*." *MELUS* (1994): 75–90.

Chrysavgi Papagianni

LEE, JARENA (1783–?)

Known first and foremost for receiving a call to preach, for responding to that call even though a woman, and for writing about it, Jarena Lee, a free black woman from New Jersey, stands out as one of the earliest recognized African American female itinerant preachers. Critics have discussed how the conversion to **Christianity** and the call to preach are important elements of spiritual **autobiography**. Notably, Lee spends a lot of time in her narrative *The Life and Religious Experience of Mrs. Jarena Lee, a Coloured Lady, Giving an Account of her Call to Preach the Gospel* (1836) on her conversion, in part because she may have felt unworthy to receive it, particularly as a woman. Like many early female preachers, Lee was shocked to receive a call from God to preach. After much consideration and testing of God's call, Lee responded by asking permission from Reverend Richard Allen, leader of the African Methodist Episcopal Church in Philadelphia. Not surprisingly, he denied her request on biblical grounds that women should not preach. Lee went on to marry Joseph Lee, a minister, in 1811, and they had two children. Until her husband died in 1818, Lee did not pursue the ministry. Instead, she completed her **domestic** and wifely duties, which she documented with subtle frustration in her narrative. Once a widow, however, Lee petitioned Reverend Allen once again. This time Allen relented, in large part because he heard her spontaneously preaching when substituting at the last minute for another minister. Like her audiences to come, Allen was moved by her fervor as well as her gift for preaching.

Not only did Lee defy gender norms by preaching and writing; as an itinerant preacher she traveled in the public sphere in a way many women did not. Though a free black woman, she continued to visit slave states and mixed-**race** church audiences—a brave task. While in her shorter first autobiography Lee focused more on her conversion and call, in her second autobiography, *Religious Experience and Journal of Mrs. Jarena Lee, Giving the Account of her Call to Preach the Gospel* (1849), she narrates at length the details of her travel to the extent that some critics have seen it more as a travelogue than as a spiritual autobiography. Unfortunately, after 1849, Lee's activities remain unknown. Regardless, it is crucial to understand that Lee helped to inaugurate a tradition, along with **Zilpha Elaw** and **Julia A. J. Foote**, in which feminism and Christianity are interwoven in spiritual autobiography such that one sometimes complements, sometimes contradicts, and sometimes cancels out the other, but they always remain in conversation. While many of the early narratives, like Lee's, were written with the motive of converting followers, it is clear that there is also a covert, and sometimes overt, need to be recognized as a woman with something crucial to say. Part of the outcome of the growth in criticism addressing early African American female itinerant preachers is the understanding that these women linked gender, **spirituality**, and **race** in ways that become important for later writers whose lives or characters also defy gender norms, such as **Zora Neale Hurston** and **Toni Morrison**.

Works By

The Life and Religious Experience of Mrs. Jarena Lee, a Coloured Lady, Giving an Account of her Call to Preach the Gospel. Philadelphia, 1836. Reprinted in *Sisters of the Spirit: Three Black Women's Autobiographies of the Nineteenth Century.* Ed. William L. Andrews. Bloomington: Indiana University Press, 1986. 25–48.

Religious Experience and Journal of Mrs. Jarena Lee, Giving the Account of her Call to Preach the Gospel. Philadelphia, 1849. Reprinted in *Spiritual Narratives.* Ed. Sue E. Houchins. New York: Oxford University Press, 1988. 3–32.

Works About

Andrews, William L., ed. *Sisters of the Spirit: Three Black Women's Autobiographies of the Nineteenth Century.* Bloomington: Indiana University Press, 1986.

Bassard, Katherine Clay. *Spiritual Interrogations: Culture, Gender, and Community in Early African American Women's Writing.* Princeton, NJ: Princeton University Press, 1999.

Brekus, Catherine A. *Strangers and Pilgrims: Female Preaching in America 1740–1845.* Chapel Hill: University of North Carolina Press, 1998.

Grammer, Elizabeth Elkin. *Some Wild Visions: Autobiographies by Female Itinerant Evangelists in 19th-Century America.* New York: Oxford University Press, 2003.

Moody, Joycelyn. *Sentimental Confessions: Spiritual Narratives of Nineteenth-Century African American Women.* Athens: University of Georgia Press, 2003.

Peterson, Carla L. *"Doers of the Word": African-American Women Speakers and Writers in the North (1830–1880).* New Brunswick, NJ: Rutgers University Press, 1998.

Karlyn Crowley

LESBIANISM

It has proven difficult to trace a cohesive social, political, artistic, and cultural **history** of African American women, often exiled from historical annals, relegated to the margins of American culture, and rendered invisible in arts and **literature**. Outlining a unified trajectory of black lesbian feminism, then, is even more problematic. Clearly, African American women engaged in passionate and loving relationships with each other long before the lesbian was identified as a suspect **identity** category. Scholar Karen Hansen recently discovered correspondence between two African American women occurring between 1861 and 1867 that indicated that they shared a deep erotic connection. Addie Brown and Rebecca Primus exchanged **love** letters and likely had an intimate relationship lasting several years. Although only the letters of Addie Brown were recovered, it is clear that both women were deeply committed and loyal to one another.

A great deal of focus has been placed on the white lesbians of the 1920s and 1930s, concentrating on the modernist movement and American ex-patriots Gertrude Stein, Alice B. Toklas, and Djuana Barnes. But analysis dealing with black lesbians of the era has been scant at best, despite that these years were known as the **Harlem Renaissance**, a burgeoning of black cultural and literary activity. Although some discussion has occurred around the bisexuality of **blues** legends Ma Rainey and Bessie Smith, further analysis regarding black lesbians would enrich the study of this period. One scholar who has extended the view on lesbianism in the Harlem Renaissance, Anne Stavney, examined the life of cross-dressing blues performer Gladys Bentley. Gloria A. Hull has also explored lesbian **sexuality** expressed in **Angelina Weld Grimké**'s **poetry** and diary entries. Additionally, Maureen Honey has compiled a collection of poetry by women of the Harlem Renaissance and includes a nuanced and important analysis of women's sexuality and lesbianism.

Another area that demands further excavation is the African American lesbian presence in the early homophile movements. Although the majority of members of the Mattachine Society, formed in 1951, and the Daughters of Bilitis, its lesbian contingent that splintered off in 1955, were mostly white and privileged, there is some evidence that there was at least a small black presence in those organizations. Two scholars who delve into the working-**class** experience of both white and black lesbians, Elizabeth Kennedy and Madeline Davis, have illuminated the existence of a strong black lesbian **community** in 1950s Buffalo, New York. In addition to reconsidering how the working class helped shape the mid-twentieth-century gay and lesbian movements, queer scholars have begun to consider the important black lesbian presence in the Stonewall riots of 1969. By many reports, African American lesbians were at the center of the struggle that occurred when police raided the Stonewall Inn.

Although many believe that the formation of the African American lesbian feminist movement followed the larger, mostly white, lesbian feminist movement in the late 1970s, in fact, black lesbians were concurrently shaping a black lesbian ideology of their own. Though involved in the second wave of the women's movement, the black lesbian feminists knew that their subjugation was not merely predicated on gender and the patriarchy but also on the intricate relationship between **race**, class, and sexuality. The combined issues of racial difference and sexual difference complicated the idea of the universal woman. Just as lesbian feminists questioned their allegiances to the greater women's movement, black lesbians recognized their status as triply marginalized: They were black. They were women. They were lesbian.

Black lesbian feminists experienced and challenged the racism that pervaded the women's movement, and it is important to note that white lesbians were guilty of racism as well. Women of color also dared the white majority in the women's movement to recognize the privilege that their **whiteness** afforded them. Many black lesbian feminists, including **Audre Lorde** and Anita Cornwell, argued that both the women's liberation movement and the lesbian feminist movement mandated that black feminists place their gender or sexual identity above that of their race. While it is true that the impulse to gather and speak out as a black lesbian collective was fueled by racism occurring in the women's movement, it was also fueled by the misogyny and male privilege that pervaded the black **civil rights movement**, the Black Panthers, and the **Black Nationalism** movements. While Barbara Smith, Audre Lorde, Gloria Anzaldúa, and other women of color challenged black male activists and white feminists to investigate and recognize the misogyny, homophobia, and racism running through these movements, they also acknowledged their debt to the earlier movements, where they learned to organize.

One of the first active black lesbian feminist groups, the **Combahee River Collective**, issued a statement in 1977 that outlined the genesis of contemporary **black feminism**. In this essay, the collective does not circumvent the topic of lesbian sexuality, nor sidestep issues of racism and white privilege within the women's movement. It also articulates these women's solidarity with black men without evading a discussion of the sexism that pervaded the early black liberation movements. This seminal piece voices a politics of difference in which no one identity would be privileged over another. In fact, coining the term "identity politics," the Combahee River Collective envisioned a revolutionary society, a world stripped bare of racism, homophobia, classism, and misogyny. Also in 1977, Barbara Smith published her searing and influential "Toward a Black Feminist Criticism" in the second issue of *Conditions*. In this essay, Smith acknowledges that she is one of the first to carve a space for black women writers and a black female presence on the hallowed ground of literature—and that this action is not only unprecedented; it is treacherous.

Since the early work of Barbara Smith, **Alice Walker**, Audre Lorde, and many other artists, theorists, historians, and educators have entered the scene, extending and enriching the archive of black lesbian feminism. In a fascinating study, Siobhan Somerville explores the concurrent cultural impulses at the close of the nineteenth century to pathologize black bodies and queer bodies. Regarding black lesbian **fiction**, the impulse is often revisionist, inserting black lesbians where previously they were absent. For instance, in *The Gilda Stories* **Jewelle Gomez** (1991), creates a world where black lesbian vampires have sexual agency and desire. She swerves from the traditional rendering of the black woman as either a **Mammy** figure or a Hottentot Venus, instead offering a rendering where **myth** is woven with the impulse to acknowledge her foremothers. Although space does not allow for a detailed enumeration of others who have contributed to the canon of African American lesbian literature, it is clear that in the twenty-first century the field is expanding, exciting, and vital.

Works About

Cornwell, Anita. *Black Lesbian in White America*. Minneapolis, MN: Naiad Press, 1983.

D'Emilio, John. *Sexual Politics, Sexual Communities*. Chicago: University of Chicago Press, 1998.

Garber, Eric. "Gladys Bentley: The Bulldagger Who Sang the Blues." *Out/Look* 1:2 (Spring 1988): 52–61.

Gomez, Jewelle. *The Gilda Stories*. Ithaca, NY: Firebrand Books, 1991.

Gross, Larry, and James Woods, eds. *The Columbia Reader on Lesbians and Gay Men in Media, Society and Politics*. New York: Colombia University Press, 1999.

Hansen, Karen. " 'No Kisses Is Like Youres': An Erotic Friendship between Two African American Women during the Mid-Nineteenth Century." *Gender & History* 7:2 (August 1995): 151–182.

Hull, Gloria. *Color, Sex, and Poetry: Three Women Writers of the Harlem Renaissance*. Bloomington: Indiana University Press, 1987.

Kennedy, Elizabeth Lapovsky, and Madeline D. Davis. *Boots of Leather, Slippers of Gold; The History of a Lesbian Community*. New York: Routledge Press, 1993.

Lorde, Audre. "Man Child: A Black Lesbian Feminist's Response." *Conditions* 4 (1979): 124–131.

Moraga, Cherríe, and Gloria Anzaldúa, eds. *This Bridge Called My Back: Writings by Radical Women of Color*. Watertown, MA: Persephone Press, 1981.

Smith, Barbara, et al., eds. *All the Women Are White, All the Blacks Are Men, but Some of Us Are Brave*. Old Westbury, NY: The Feminist Press, 1981.

Somerville, Siobhan. *Queering the Color Line: Race and the Invention of Homosexuality in American Culture*. Durham: NC: Duke University Press, 2000.

Spillers, Hortense J. *Black, White, and In Color: Essays on American Literature and Culture*. Chicago: University of Chicago Press, 2003.

Stavney, Anne. "Cross-Dressing Harlem, Re-Dressing Race." *Women's Studies* 28 (March 1999): 127–156.

Lorna J. Raven Wheeler

LILIANE: RESURRECTION OF THE DAUGHTER

Published in 1994, *Liliane* is as innovative in form as many of **Ntozake Shange**'s other works, including *for colored girls who have considered suicide / when the rainbow is enuf* (1975) and *Sassafrass, Cypress & Indigo* (1983). The character/narrator Liliane comes to us in a collection of narrative fragments and voices. She is an artist who combines creative expression and the making of political **identity** for black women in the United States. Shange's aesthetic here is similar to that in *for colored girls*: It is an embodied **spirituality**, a creative energy based in the erotic as **Audre Lorde** wrote about in her essay on the "Uses of the Erotic" in black women's lives, especially in artistic and political realms.

Liliane struggles through a series of relationship conflicts and attempts to emerge whole: her own self-creation. As in *for colored girls*, there is a dramatic struggle to take control of the language and make it reflect a new, woman-centered reality. The narrative form of *Liliane* is complex. Multiple narrative voices create a pastiche of Liliane's story. Shange appropriates elements of psychoanalytic discourse and distributes them in fragments throughout the narrative. Liliane's analyst inserts her voice into Liliane's narration; suddenly questions to Liliane will appear. But there are more voices than Liliane's and her analyst's. Liliane's childhood friends as well as her lovers also add their voices to the story of her evolving sexual identity.

This novel also orchestrates an international concert, as it were, of voices: Creole, Latino, French, Portuguese, and African. Liliane wishes to make all of them a part of her **community**. She wants to someday learn all of the languages that the slaves ever spoke. This resonates with a choral line repeated in *Sassafrass, Cypress & Indigo* by the three sisters who are also artists of various sorts: They identify with "the slaves who were ourselves." The chapter titles in *Liliane* are dense with imagery, and there is a distinctive vocalized quality to them, as in this call-and-response title: "I Know Where Kansas City Is, But Did Wilbert Harrison Ever Get There?"

Shange's work has contributed to the shape of African American feminist culture for over thirty years.

See also Sexuality; Womanism

Work About

Sayers, Valerie. "A Life in Collage." *New York Times Book Review*, January 1, 1995, 76.

Sharon Jessee

LILITH'S BLOOD. See Xenogenesis Trilogy

LINDEN HILLS

Linden Hills (1985) by **Gloria Naylor** is an offshoot of *The Women of Brewster Place* (1982) that magnifies life in Linden Hills, a black suburb and onetime **home** of Kiswana Browne, a character from Naylor's first novel. In this book, Naylor criticizes the trend of the black upper middle **class** to erase remnants of their heritage as they press forward toward financial progress.

The neighborhood of Linden Hills is designed according to a Dantean model reminiscent of *The Inferno*, in its many spirals and levels of hell. It is a secluded area in which upwardly mobile blacks seek residence, virtually selling their souls to Luther Nedeed in the process. Those who remain closer to their cultural heritage live at the top of the spiral on First Crescent Drive, and those of a heightened moral bankruptcy reflective of Nedeed live closer to Nedeed at the bottom near Tupelo Drive. At the novel's beginning, the Tupelo Realty Company has been owned by the Nedeed **family** for generations.

The figure around which all the other characters revolve is Luther Nedeed. Some critics have noted that his last name translates to "of Eden" or "de-Eden" if viewed backward, for Nedeed is representative of the devil in the text. Residents cannot simply buy a residence in response to a "for sale" sign. Luther Nedeed himself approves leases only on three conditions: (1) the house should stay in the family; (2) if the house must be sold, it must be sold to another African American; and (3) the property can only be gained after signature of a thousand-year-and-day lease. Thus, those who live in Linden Hills have tied both themselves and their families to the Nedeeds for generations to come.

The lives of the characters are revealed as Lester, who is a third-generation resident of First Crescent Drive, and his friend, Willie, from nearby working-class Putney Wayne, travel through the neighborhood doing odd jobs as Christmas approaches. While several stories are revealed, perhaps the major focus of the novel is the matrix of stories involving the Nedeed wives.

For the four generations that the novel spans, the Nedeed wives are called Mrs. Nedeed by their husbands. These wives begin with Luwana Packerville, who the first Luther Nedeed buys from her white master. He keeps the bill of sale as a sign that he still owns her, although she had thought the purchase just a formality. The next Nedeed wife, Evelyn Creton, experiments with culinary methods to kill her husband if not herself. Priscilla McGuire is from a virtual promised land called New Canaan, yet her vibrant spirit fades next to her husband and son. Finally, Willa Prescott marries the last Luther Nedeed well after most of her college mates have married. She finds solace in her **identity** as mother and wife. However, Nedeed banishes Willa and their son to the basement because Sinclair, their son, does not have the signature dark skin of his forefathers. While in the basement, Sinclair dies, and Willa discovers the remnants left behind by the Nedeed wives before her. Ultimately, she ascends the steps, with a dead Sinclair in her arms, to reclaim her role as wife and mother, but in Nedeed's attempt to repress her, they become entangled and mistakenly become engulfed by a fire that sets the entire house ablaze, thus ending the reign of Luther Nedeed and his brand of patriarchy.

Works About

Bouvier, Luke. "Reading in Black and White: Space and Race in *Linden Hills*." *Gloria Naylor: Critical Perspectives Past and Present.* Ed. Henry Louis Gates, Jr., and K. A. Appiah. New York: Amistad, 1993. 140–151.

Collins, Grace E. "Narrative Structure in Linden Hills." *CLA Journal* 34 (1991): 290–300. Reprinted in *The Critical Response to Gloria Naylor*. Ed. Sharon Felton and Michelle C. Loris. Westport, CT: Greenwood Press, 1997. 80–87.

Felton, Sharon, and Michelle C. Loris, eds. *The Critical Response to Gloria Naylor*. Westport, CT: Greenwood Press, 1997.

Gates, Henry Louis, Jr., and K. A. Appiah, eds. *Gloria Naylor: Critical Perspectives Past and Present*. New York: Amistad, 1993.

Sharese Terrell Willis

LITERACY

Learning to read and write occurs within social and ideological contexts. Literacy scholars like Deborah Brandt argue that along with the technical skill of decoding words on a page, becoming literate also demands an understanding of how these skills allow one to participate in cultural and economic life.

In American **history**, slave masters shaped the meaning of literacy for slaves by prohibiting them from learning to read and write as a way to keep them subservient. Slaves commanding language so threatened slave owners that they commonly suppressed communication among slaves and prohibited their use of African languages. So participating in the exchange of written words used by white Americans, for a slave, was typically viewed as a privilege akin to **freedom**—and an act of subversion. The courage and defiance associated with literacy molded the writing skills of the nineteenth-century black female writers studied by Jacqueline Royster, who traces the acquisition of literacy among African Americans to developing a rhetoric of advocacy.

Even though many antebellum free blacks in northern states were taught reading and writing in schools, African Americans as a group faced a culture skeptical of their literacy skills. By the eighteenth century, attitudes throughout Europe brought literacy in association with an elevated status: socially, socioeconomically, intellectually, even morally. Texts produced in Europe during the Enlightenment extolled the progress of the human **race**, moving Western cultures to view rational thinking as the preeminent feature of human existence—literacy being prerequisite to rational engagement. European nations and their colonies found justification for enslaving Africans because they did not qualify for human by white European standards. Proof of African inferiority rested largely on the belief that Africans were not advanced enough to develop a written language, rendering them illiterate. Standards for defining—and redefining—literacy that subordinate African Americans have been used after slavery as well. Up until the Voting Rights Act of 1965, several states used literacy tests to prevent black Americans from voting. Today, labels of illiteracy plague African Americans who confront social and economic limitations because they do not possess the mainstream literacy standards.

The racial judgment associated with "being literate" has put African Americans in the position of proving themselves able to meet the communicative standards set by the white mainstream. Reading and writing standard English has served as a gatekeeper to privileges in publishing, education, and employment. Never were the stakes of these privileges so high as when the first black author emerged. When slave **Phillis Wheatley** published a book of **poetry** in 1773, her master prefaced the edition with his witness to her uncommon abilities "to the great astonishment of all who heard her." Eighteen prominent men of Boston also attested to Wheatley's literacy after interviewing her.

The achievement of literacy by slaves and the works they produced became important tools in the movement to abolish **slavery**. Narrating their accounts of inhumane cruelty under slavery, literate slaves assumed some power in turning public opinion toward abolition. As **Frederick Douglass**'s narrative made most famous, literacy became a symbol of African American potential by asserting arguments from a black perspective and by expressing an **identity** particular to African American experience. Whereas Douglass's narrative establishes literacy as the foundation for a man's identity in a free society, **Harriet Jacobs**'s **slave narrative** offers a woman's view of slavery. In *Incidents in the Life of a Slave Girl* (1861), Jacobs provides insight into the added injuries suffered by women under slavery, describing emotional, physical, and sexual abuse. Jacobs reaches out to her sex, not her race, to resist slavery by "arous[ing] the women of the North to a realizing sense of the condition of two millions of women at the South," as she says in her preface. But viewing literacy as a bulwark against slavery is too simplistic and falls into what Harvey Graff calls the "literacy **myth**." Acquisition of literacy was not enough to reorder the social hierarchy that subordinated blacks.

After Emancipation, concern over the acquisition of literacy for African Americans became subsumed in issues of access to education. In the late nineteenth century, African Americans worked to build an educational system for black students, teaching in boxcars the way Clark Atlanta University started, and in church basements, as was the case at Spelman College. As W.E.B. Du Bois comments in *The Souls of Black Folk* (1903) on the history of African American education, "If the Negro was to learn, he must teach himself." Many great black educators emerged after the Civil War intent on "uplifting" the race, such as **Fanny Jackson Coppin** and Mary McLeod Bethune. African American leaders valorized educated black women who devoted their skills to teaching poor illiterate black children, such as the main characters in **Frances E. W. Harper**'s *Iola Leroy* (1892) and **Victoria Earle Matthews**'s "Eugenie's Mistake." Of the 15,100 African American teachers identified in the U.S. Census of 1890, female teachers (7,864) outnumbered male teachers, introducing a trend that continues today.

For African Americans, literacy education has meant matching up to the standards set by ruling European Americans. Because of the racist origins of the preferred standard, a tradition of challenging it has also persisted among African Americans. **Hallie Q. Brown**, back in the early 1880s, published an elocution textbook, *Bits and Odds*, that put writings by Shakespeare and Mark Twain right beside Negro, Irish, and German dialect pieces, suggesting that any literacy standard is performative and can be learned. **Harlem Renaissance** writers such as **Langston Hughes**, **Zora Neale Hurston**, and **Claude McKay** claimed a unique African American literary expression that used language and rhythms developed in black communities. More recently, linguistics professor Geneva Smitherman has confronted the presumption that being literate means reading and writing in standard English by using black English in her academic articles.

The racist assumptions that separated African Americans from literacy, especially the literacy valued by European Americans, have put in motion two hard-fought efforts to include blacks in the discourses of enfranchised Americans. One drive has been for access to empowered literacy practices; the other toward equal respect for literacy practices in black communities. These two urges lead scholars like Smitherman to recommend that African Americans view literacy acquisition as multiple.

See also Autobiography

Works About

Brandt, Deborah. *Literacy in American Lives*. New York: Cambridge University Press, 2001.
Pattison, Robert. *On Literacy: The Politics of the Word from Homer to the Age of Rock*. New York: Oxford University Press, 1982.
Royster, Jacqueline Jones. *Voices in a Stream*. Pittsburgh: University of Pittsburgh Press, 2000.
Smitherman, Geneva. *Talkin' That Talk: Language, Culture, and Education in African America*. New York: Routledge, 2000.
Winterowd, W. Ross. *The Culture and Politics of Literacy*. New York: Oxford University Press, 1989.

Caleb A. Corkery

LITERATURE

Antebellum Period (1746–1865)

In 1746, when a sixteen-year-old woman penned the poem "Bars Fight," detailing the ambush of two white families by a group of Indians in Deerfield, Massachusetts, her ballad of rhymed tetrameter couplets became the earliest recorded work of literature by an African American of any gender. **Lucy Terry**, a poet, skilled storyteller, and public speaker, argued for three hours before the board of trustees of Williams College, condemning their racist and discriminatory practices when they denied admission to her son. Neither **slavery** nor the fact that she lived during an era when women were expected to be silent prevented Lucy Terry Prince, the mother of six children, from becoming a poet, a teller of tales, and a fighter in the causes of **freedom** and justice. Was she a feminist? Undoubtedly, she would not have referred to herself as such. However, the distinction between feminist and traditionalist is not mutually exclusive. When feminism is defined as those activities by women or men that challenge the status quo (male authority), the label becomes less important than the more instructive analysis of the activities and behaviors of those in question.

While literary historians often refer to 1773 as the beginning of African American literature, citing the publication of **Phillis Wheatley**'s first book of **poetry**, 1746 underscores the fact that whether freeborn or slave, literate or not, African American women, who during the antebellum period suffered under the slave laws and restrictions placed on their **race** as well as their gender, became the creative forerunners of the **black feminist** tradition in literature today. These women rarely had leisure to create literature. Housework, child care, sewing, and food preparation, if one lived in a northern city or was fortunate enough to be a house servant, or, otherwise, hard field labor, prevented the literary expressions of many would-be writers. African American women who managed to write in spite of their conditions are an amazing testimony to the tenacity of human will.

Lucy Terry Prince and Phillis Wheatley mark the beginning only of the African American written tradition. Inasmuch as black women used metaphorical language, poetic rhetoric, and cryptic mother wit, oral literature survived the **Middle Passage**, developed alongside, and informed the burgeoning literate tradition. Black women fully participated in the creation of both the oral vernacular and the literate traditions.

That the first black women writers appear in New England as opposed to the **South** is no accident. As early as 1652, Rhode Island passed the first law against slavery. In 1712, Pennsylvania outlawed the slave trade, and the Great Awakening religious movement that swept the colonies preaching salvation for all included blacks. In contrast, six years before Terry's poem was written, South Carolina made it a crime to teach slaves to write, making life in the southern colonies far less conducive to any literary production than life in the North. Even free blacks in the South could not travel freely nor assemble as blacks could in the North. On the other hand, life in the North was no haven. The hierarchical Puritanical obsession with order made life especially difficult for women deemed "disorderly." Any behavior out of the ordinary could result in one being labeled a witch.

Black women often have been described as headstrong, rebellious, and rarely submissive. While these ideas are part of the **folklore** and stereotyped images of black women, they are not without some veracity. Slavery in North America ignored the gendered division of labor and instead created a system where black men and women were forced to share **work** normally reserved for men only. In fact, black women were forced to work in the cotton, tobacco, and rice fields, whereas white indentured women servants were not. In addition to the hard labor of the fieldwork, black women did the reproductive work but as childbearers were not protected as were other women. Unlike black men, black women also were charged with the **domestic** work in the slave cabins. After working in the fields, it was their duty to cook and clean for black men and children. If they survived, it is not unlikely that strong-willed, self-sufficient women emerged unwilling to genuflect before the throne of male hegemony.

The antebellum women's movement by 1820 was well established. Black and white women agitated for education, temperance, abolition, and women's suffrage. The ideology of "Separate Spheres" and the "Cult of True Womanhood" emerged to reinforce the notion that woman's proper sphere, a trope for place, was the **home**. A true woman was pious, pure, and submissive, interested only in and circumscribed by domestic duties. These ideas influenced black feminists in interesting ways as they wrote to subvert the restrictive definition yet appropriate to themselves the privileges of womanhood.

In 1826, Isabella Van Wagener walked away from slavery in New York a year before it was outlawed, changed her name to **Sojourner Truth**, and left a legacy of oral texts that inform the black feminist literary tradition. In 1831, **Maria Stewart** became the first woman of any race to participate in public political debate. At the age of twenty-eight, she addressed an audience of the New England Anti-Slavery Society at Boston's Franklin Hall and published *Meditations from the Pen of Mrs. Maria W. Stewart* (1832). In 1836, Sarah Forten adopted the pseudonym Ada and began her contribution as a poet and essayist in the *Liberator*. Forten advocated for antislavery and women's rights and helped to organize the Female Anti-Slavery Society. In 1819, against all social and religious custom, **Jarena Lee** began to preach. She published *Life and Religious Experience of Jarena Lee, a Coloured Lady, Giving an Account of Her Call to Preach* in 1836. **Ann Plato** printed *Essays; Including Biographical and Miscellaneous Pieces, in Prose and Poetry* (1841) in Hartford, Connecticut, making her the first black person to publish in this genre. Mrs. Juliann Jane Tillman, ignoring the restrictions placed on women by the African Methodist Episcopal (AME) Church, began to preach in 1844. While her sermons are not preserved in any literary format, Mrs. Tillman overcame the objections of both her husband and brother to take a feminist stance in the masculine domain of the clergy. **Zilpha Elaw**'s *Memoirs of the Life, Religious Experiences, Ministerial Travels and Labours, of Mrs. Zilpha Elaw, an American Female of Colour; Together with Some Account of the Great Religious Revivals in America* (1846) was published in London by the author.

Publication, always difficult, was especially so for women who for the most part were not highly educated and who belonged to a race of people whose very humanity was called into question by the prevailing science of the day. Undaunted, they published their own works or had them published abroad or as pamphlets like Mary Ann Shadd Cary, a prolific writer of essays and letters who printed the pamphlets *Conditions of the Colored People* (1849) and *A*

Plea for Emigration, or Notes of Canada West (1852). In 1854 **Frances E. W. Harper**'s *Poems on Miscellaneous Subjects* was published in Boston and Philadelphia, making her one of the most popular black poets of this era. Her famous "Bury Me in a Free Land" and "The Slave Mother" appeared in this volume.

The first black woman novelist, **Hannah Crafts**, wrote *The Bondwoman's Narrative* in the early 1850s. **Harriet E. Wilson** published *Our Nig* in 1859. Her fictionalized biography is a political indictment of the system of servitude in the North. **Charlotte Forten Grimké** published *The Slave Girl's Poems* in the *Liberator* in 1856 and 1860. *The Deeper Wrong; or,* ***Incidents in the Life of a Slave Girl***, was published in 1861 by **Harriet Jacobs**, pseudonym Linda Brent, and picked up by a London publisher in 1862. This work introduced into literature the sexual coercion of black women by white slaveholding men. Jacobs establishes the sexual vulnerability of black women with her autobiographical novel, and it becomes an underlying motif in the literature during the period of Reconstruction.

Reconstruction (1865–1910)

During the Civil War (1861–1865) black women literally fought for freedom. Harriet Tubman led as many as 800 soldiers in military raids, while other women disguised as men and fought alongside the soldiers. Still others worked as army nurses, cooks, and laundresses. Reconstruction was the federal government's effort to reunite the country and to secure economic and civil rights for the newly freed blacks when the war ended. The Civil Rights Act of 1866 enfranchised black men who voted themselves into political offices. This exercise in democracy enraged southern whites, many of whom could not conceive of racial equality. White southerners enacted black codes to limit the rights of the newly freed. Black freedom was met with white **violence** in the form of race riots and individual attacks on black people. Black optimism that followed the 1863 emancipation was squelched, and freedom for many blacks remained elusive. The circumstances for black women workers in freedom were not significantly different from what they had been during slavery. As wage earners, they faced seven-day workweeks and double duty in their homes. In 1881, 3,000 laundry workers in Atlanta organized the grassroots Washerwoman Strike. Reconstruction ended in 1877, and the federal government and Freedman's Bureau withdrew from the South, leaving black people without protection or resources to defeat the rising tide of white racism. The Ku Klux Klan made lynching as much a part of its organization as the hoods and burning crosses. Women and children were not excluded from Klan violence, as they too were lynched.

As hard-won freedoms disappeared, black women organized clubs and associations, which included benevolent associations, mutual aid societies, local literary societies, and numerous church organizations, to benefit the race and offered themselves as ambassadors of the black **community** to white America. They identified education and **literacy** as the keys to success and for maintaining their freedom. Racism in the national women's movement, the suffragettes, and the temperance movement, undermined black women's effort to voice their concerns, thus forcing black feminists to form separate organizations.

Black women writers protested injustice for black people in general and for black women in particular. During the antebellum period they were writers, editors, and publishers even though restricted to the "women's pages" of newspapers and journals. In the "woman's era," they became editors of ladies' magazines. These magazines influenced what black women bought, wore, read, and cooked and how they thought about certain issues. In 1894, *Woman's Era* was created for black women. *Our Women and Children* (1888), *Ringwood's Afro-American Journal of Fashion* (1891), and *Half-Century Magazine for the Colored Homemaker* (1916–1925) are other examples. **Pauline Hopkins** became editor in chief of the *Colored American Magazine* in 1900. The black press, *Colored Citizen* (1866), and *Afro-American* (1885) also offered opportunities for black women writers and editors.

Black women writers adapted the **slave narrative** as a literary genre to suit their own political and artistic needs. Prior to the Civil War whites seemed to possess a voyeuristic impulse to read slave narratives, but following the war the narratives were not in vogue and stories of ex-slaves had no audience. Black women writers adapted their narratives to attract a readership. Some writers drew on the Christian biblical tradition and others on explicitly political and secular forms. The postbellum narrative reinterpreted slavery and declared that it was damaging to everyone, master and slave alike. To what extent being published depended on this reinterpretation is not known. **Elizabeth Keckley**'s narrative is the prototype. Keckley's narrative, like Jacobs's, deals with the sexual vulnerabilities of black women. Another literary model to emerge during Reconstruction centers on the American dream of individual success through hard work and perseverance.

In 1872, Frances Harper's *Sketches of Southern Life* set the standard for black political poetry that combines formal structure with experimental form (dramatic narrative) and black vernacular rhythms. **Julia A. J. Foote** wrote *A Brand Plucked from the Fire* (1886); Clarissa Thompson, *Treading the Winepress; or, A Mountain of Misfortunes* (1885–1886), a serialized novel; and Garrison serialized *A Ray of Light* (1889–1890). These works ushered in a new era for black women writers. In 1890 **Amelia E. Johnson**'s novel *Clarence and Corinne; Or, God's Way*, Josephine Henderson's collection of poems, *Morning Glories*, and **Octavia V. Rogers Albert**'s *The House of Bondage or, Charlotte Brooks and Her Friends* appeared within months of each other. The landmark publication in 1892 of **Anna Julia Cooper**'s *A Voice from the South* and **Ida B. Wells-Barnett**'s *The Reason Why: The Colored American Is Not in the World's Columbian Exposition* and *Southern Horrors: Lynch Law in All Its Phases* equal in importance the works of Booker T. Washington and W.E.B. Du Bois, but until recent feminist scholarship rediscovered them, they were little known. Black women's writing, as Cooper pointed out, had been witnessed but not proclaimed. Cooper proclaimed the black woman's need for sexual autonomy, and Wells-Barnett led the fight against lynching by making the world aware of the number of people lynched, the crimes of which they were accused, and pointing out the innocence of the majority of those accused.

By the 1890s women had established the genre labeled *domestic literature.* Amelia Johnson, Sarah Allen, **Emma Dunham Kelley-Hawkins**, Ruth Todd, Marie Burgess Ware, J. McHenry Jones, Pauline Hopkins, and Frances Harper adapted popular white women's domestic **fiction** to dramatize and protest the plight of black people. The basic theme of this kind of fiction included a lone heroine forced to make her way in the world without parental guidance or support. After many trials, she triumphs, marries, and lives happily ever after. In black women's fiction, the heroine's marriage becomes a means for enhancing and continuing her efforts to uplift the race.

Black women writers used their pens to advance political agendas. Frances Harper's speech to the World's Congress of Representative Women at the Columbian Exposition in Chicago on May 20, 1893, heightened black women's desire for political power. They also made concerted efforts to counter the distortions and **stereotypes** of the Plantation School of southern writers who romanticized slavery and southern life. Defending the virtue of black womanhood became a major motif in the works of black women writers. Some women tried to write across the color line by using racially ambiguous characters, others focused on **religion** and morality like Emma Dunham Kelly-Hawkins in *Megda* (1891), refusing to be limited by race issues, continuing a tradition begun by Terry and Wheatley. **Lucy A. Delaney**'s *From Darkness Cometh Light; Or, Struggles for Freedom* (1892) synthesized religious issues with those of race. Cooper's book was a feminist manifesto that demanded racial, sexual, and social equality. Just as there were race men, so too were there race women. These black women writers considered themselves spokespersons for both their race and their gender.

Gertrude Mossell called the twentieth century the "Woman's Century." In many ways she was correct, for during the twentieth century women fought for and won the vote, greater access to higher education, affirmative action and equal protection for women (resulting from the **civil rights movement**), an approach toward parity between men and women's salaries, and reproductive rights.

Some women of the Reconstruction era became transitional figures, living and working well into the middle of the twentieth century. **Mary Church Terrell**, founder and first president of the National Association of Colored Women's Clubs (1896), was the apotheosis of the New Woman, breaking from the Victorian idea of the Cult of True Womanhood, the standard by which women measured themselves and were measured by others. A true woman's virtues were piety, purity, submissiveness, and domesticity. The growing consumer culture and materialistic society fueled by the Industrial Revolution threw the known world into chaos. The stereotyped ideal woman confined to her proper sphere—the home—was the only stabilizing force in the world gone money mad. Only female virtue could be counted on to save men from themselves, so they claimed.

Clearly a contradiction existed between the ideal and the real lives of women, especially so for wage-earning black social critics and political organizers. In the Age of Reform, these women followed their own mandate to uplift their race through education, service, and community building, which took them far beyond the so-called feminine sphere.

Harlem Renaissance (1910–1940)

The dates of the Harlem Renaissance have fluctuated over the years. Generally confined to the 1920s, recent literary historians have argued that the flowering of literary talent and other cultural expressions began at a much earlier date. All of the activity was not confined to Harlem; Washington, D.C., Chicago, and Philadelphia were also centers of black artistic expression, and for that reason the term is a bit of a misnomer. The term "New Negro movement," by which the era is also known, to some scholars seems more accurate.

The Harlem Renaissance was far more than a literary movement. It consisted of visual artists, musicians, actors, playwrights, and dancers as well as poets and novelists, essayists, short-story writers, and white philanthropists who provided financial support to the aspiring artists. Garland Anderson's full-length play *Appearances* becomes the first written by a black person to open on Broadway, in 1925. Duke Ellington's move to New York in 1922 becomes a driving force on the **jazz** scene, and Madame C. J. Walker's, the first female millionaire black or white, move to the city and her **beauty** salon helped create the elements that produced the New Negro.

The flowering of literary talent in black women began earlier than the 1920s. Five books by black women were published in 1910: Cordelia Ray's *Poems*, Gertrude A. Fisher's *Original Poems*, Maggie Pogue Johnson's *Virginia Dreams*, Christiana Moody's *A Tiny Spark*, and **Katherine Davis Chapman Tillman**'s *Fifty Years of Freedom, a Play in Five Acts*. The next years would see the publication of Carrie Clifford's *Race Rhymes* (1911), *A Narrative of the Negro* by Lelila Amos Pendleton (1912), and *A Biography of Norris Wright Cuney* (1913), written by **Maud Cuney-Hare**. They continued to publish in a steady stream, and while the themes of these works were not necessarily feminist, the mere fact that they possessed the chutzpah to claim a public voice was itself a feminist act.

Black periodicals and newspapers continued to provide significant outlets for black women writers. *Half-Century Magazine for the Colored Homemaker* (1916–1925) and black newspapers—the *Pittsburgh Courier* (1911), *Chicago Defender* (1912), and *Philadelphia Tribune* (1912) among the most popular—were important for employing black women as editors and developing a black readership. The founding in 1910 of *Crisis* magazine, the official publication of the National Association for the Advancement of Colored People (NAACP), edited by W.E.B. Du Bois, created still another outlet. From number 20 Vesey Street in New York City, Du Bois made encouraging and developing black literary and artistic talent one of the magazine's goals. In October 1919, **Jessie Redmon Fauset** became literary editor for the *Crisis*, taking it to new heights. Another magazine to contribute significantly to the publication of young black renaissance writers was the official publication of the National Urban League, *Opportunity*, launched in October 1911, when the Committee for Improving the Industrial Conditions of Negroes in New York, the Committee on Urban Conditions, and the National League for the Protection of Colored Women merged to address the problems of urban blacks. Pauline Hopkins, for the second time in her career, became editor in chief of a magazine, the Boston publication *New Era*, in 1916. In 1918, *Negro World*, published by Marcus Garvey, brought another political perspective to Harlem and the world. *Woman's Voice*, a periodical established by black women in 1919, addressed black women and highlighted their own achievements.

The black feminist agenda begun during the era of Reconstruction continued under the leadership of transitional women from that decade. In 1914, Mary Church Terrell wrote the Delta Creed of the Delta Sigma Theta Sorority. The feminist aspect of this creed demands continued protest against double standards of morals. The National Association of Colored Women's Club (NACWC) formed in 1896, the merger of the National Federation of Afro-American Women, the Women's Era Club of Boston, and Colored Women's League of Washington, D.C., to promote the education and protect the rights of women and children, raise the standards of the home, improve conditions for **family** living, work for moral, economic, social, and religious welfare of women and children, secure and enforce civil rights for the race, and promote interracial understanding. Terrell's agenda called for job training, wage equity, and child care. The clubwomen raised funds for kindergartens and vocational schools, and in 1912 they launched a national scholarship fund for college-bound black women. NACWC endorsed the suffrage movement in 1912, two years before its white counterpart, the General Federation of Women's Clubs. Community service, child care and equal pay still remain principal black feminist issues.

In 1916, the first birth-control clinic in the United States opened in Brooklyn, New York. Also in 1916, **Georgia Douglas Johnson** published three poems in the *Crisis*, and **Angelina Weld Grimké**'s controversial play *Rachel* appeared, challenging the notions of **motherhood**. Black women contributed to the *Birth Control Review*, introducing new themes of liberation that challenged Victorian mores. Mamie Mary Burrill, an educator, actor, and playwright, published her one-act feminist play in 1919, *They That Sit in Darkness* in the *Review* in the same issue as Angelina Grimké's short story "The Closing Door." Burrill's play encouraged the use of birth control. Birth control and voluntary motherhood were becoming a black feminist philosophy that they thought would benefit the race.

Grimké, a closeted lesbian, and Burrill at one time were lovers. Their relationship, uncovered in letters researched by black feminist scholar Gloria Hull, introduces another dimension to female **sexuality** and reveals the painful frustration of unclaimed identities by women writers of the Harlem Renaissance. In the speech "The Social Emancipation of Woman," Grimké sees woman as man's equal and calls for the right to vote and the freedom to reject traditional marriage and motherhood, as she had chosen to do. In 1918, the Cornhill Company published Georgia Douglas Johnson's *The Heart of a Woman and Other Poems*. The poems, highly autobiographical and explicitly feminist, deal with motherhood and the frustration of gender roles, although these elements of her poetry were not discussed during the Harlem Renaissance. Not until the rediscovery of Johnson by feminist scholars does the rereading of her poems enable their feminist perspective. Johnson's second volume of poetry, *Bronze: A Book of Verse* (1922), was published by B. J. Brimmer Co. in Boston. In the poem "Aliens," Johnson introduces the "neo-treatment" of the tragic **mulatto**. The poem entitled "Black Woman" clearly rejects motherhood, and her one-act play, *Safe*, carries the theme further by having a young mother commit infanticide at the same time that a young black boy is being lynched. Thus she combined feminism with racism, creating a perspective unique to black women.

Alice Moore Dunbar-Nelson's diary (1921–1931) provides valuable insight about her life during this era, revealing her lesbian longings and her critique of black men's attitudes regarding black women, which she characterizes as stultifying and imitative of white men. Jessie Redmon Fauset's novels, for so long dismissed as middle-class novels of manners, have been recovered by black feminist scholars. Deborah McDowell has designated Fauset as a pioneer black feminist. Her novels show women controlling their own lives, and her themes of incest, promiscuity, and sexual exploitation are unconventional. Angela Murray and Martha, characters in **Plum Bun** (1928), clearly articulate a feminist perspective regarding women's roles as homemakers and mothers. **Nella Larsen**'s **Passing** (1928) also portrays sexism in her delineation of the Reverend Mr. Pleasant Green, a black preacher who exploits the women in his congregation. Larsen's is perhaps the first to expose in fiction the negative behavior of black men, choosing a clergyman, the most respected position in the black community. Decades later, **Alice Walker** and other feminist black writers would be harshly criticized for exposing the foibles of black men in their literary creations.

Black women writers of the 1920s embraced more literary genres including **drama**, the short story, and biographies. Playwrights of the era included Ruth Gaines-Shelton who wrote the prize-winning comedy and satire of black church politics; *The Church Fight* (1925); **May Miller**, the most widely published woman playwright of the Renaissance; Eulalie Spence; and **Marita Bonner**, who wrote *The Purple Flower* (1928), a revolutionary play using the term "white devils" long before the Black Muslim rhetoric of the 1960s. Bonner's play was published in *Crisis* as well as her avant-guarde essay "On Being Young, a Woman and Colored" (1925), which critiqued racism and sexism.

At the height of what Alain Locke termed the New Negro movement, he guest edited the March 1925 issue of *Survey Graphic* that announced "Harlem: Mecca of the New Negro." Locke articulated the New Negro's social, political, and artistic position with a compilation of works by the writers later published in his anthology, also titled *The New Negro*. Elsie Johnson McDougald's essay in *Survey Graphic*, "The Double Task: The Struggle of Negro Women for Sex and Race Emancipation," defined the New Negro woman. McDougald challenged the representation of black women in American society. Focusing on advertising and the arts, she critiqued the stereotypical treatment of black women's sexuality and discussed the **class** differences that existed among black as well as white women, criticizing the monolithic way in which black women were perceived. **Hallie Q. Brown**'s 1926 publication of *Homespun Heroines and Other Women of Distinction* documents for posterity the contributions of black women, one of the few works to do so before the contemporary efforts of feminist scholars.

One of the greatest changes to occur during the "Jazz Age" was the financial support available to writers. From the William E. Harmon Foundation, Nella Larsen won a prize for her novel ***Quicksand*** (1928), and *Crisis* received money from Amy Spingarn to support literary prizes. *Opportunity Magazine*, edited by Charles S. Johnson, awarded prizes for poetry, short stories, essays, and plays. But it would all come crashing down with the collapse of the New York Stock Exchange. Financial support dried up, not all at once, but gradually support decreased as the interest of wealthy whites waned.

For black Americans the 1930s was an extension of the vitriolic hatred that emerged during the southern Reconstruction, except that it now extended, as **Malcolm X** once observed, to the Canadian border. The 1895 publication of Ida B. Wells-Barnett's *Red Record: Tabulated Statistics and alleged Causes of Lynchings in the United States 1892–1894* and *Southern Horrors: Lynch Law in all its Phases* (1893), as well as the formation and work of the NAACP, combined to make America and the rest of the world aware of dysfunctional southern democracy. For several decades, Klan activity decreased, although it did not cease, but in 1915 the Klan reemerged and by the middle of the 1920s claimed as many as 4 million white women and men members. In an effort to explain this resurgence of hatred, some historians have suggested that the declining agricultural prices, economic hardship on the white farmers, and the migration of large numbers of black people to the North could have provoked the scapegoating of blacks, Jews, and "foreigners." However, economic depression cannot fully explain the phenomenon because the Klan also flourished in communities that were prosperous. The economic depression then simply heightened feelings of animosity toward black people. This very aspect of American life and culture is what has made black women writers and intellectuals into a different kind of feminist. During slavery, the black woman could not be free until her family was free. During the postbellum years of Reconstruction, she privileged family and community by focusing on racial uplift. Even during the "progressive" period known to whites as the "Roaring Twenties," the "Red Summer of Hate" that occurred in 1919, the Rosewood Massacre of 1923, and the failure of antilynching legislation were clear reminders that nowhere in America could black women be just women–feminist, focusing on issues pertaining to themselves. They were black women, and that fact alone altered their agenda.

During the depression, black wage-earning women found their jobs taken by white housewives who had not been employed outside of their homes. With almost one-third of the people in the United States unemployed, those at the bottom of the economic rung were hardest hit—black women. When relief came in the form of government assistance (1933), the New Deal disproportionately benefited white men. Sex segregation of the labor force enabled the public works projects to discriminate against all women. In 1935 Eleanor Roosevelt, Mary McLeod Bethune, and black clubwomen formed what was referred to as Mrs. Roosevelt's black cabinet. They advocated for equal treatment of women and black people and addressed the discriminatory practices of the New Deal like lower pay for minorities and women and the majority of relief jobs going to white men.

The climate that black women writers faced continued to be overwhelmingly political. Between 1930 and 1939, there were twenty-one lynchings. A new generation of writers would need to assume the mantle as the elder feminists passed away. In August 1930, Pauline Hopkins died from injuries she sustained in a fire. Ida B. Wells-Barnett died in 1931. A young Ella Baker would continue in their footsteps. In 1935 she published an essay with Marvel Cooke, "The Bronx Slave Market," in *Crisis*, protesting the exploitation of black women domestic workers. Jessie Fauset published two more novels in the 1930s, *The Chinaberry Tree* (1931) and *Comedy: American Style* (1933), making her the most prolific novelist of the Harlem Renaissance.

An interesting aspect of the New Deal was the Federal Writers' Project of the Works Progress Administration (WPA). Some black writers were able to take advantage of this program devised to employ artists and bring art to the public as well as record the story of Americans in photographs, paintings, and narratives. **Zora Neale Hurston**, **Margaret Walker**, and **Dorothy West** were fortunate enough to participate in the project. The salary was deplorable but the experience invaluable for developing their fiction. The WPA supported a Federal Theater Project as well. During the depression, **Shirley Graham** directed the Negro Theater of the WPA in Chicago. Graham, a graduate of Oberlin College and emerging playwright, produced *Elijah's Ravens* in 1930 and in 1932 *Tom-Tom*. Black artists, more than other black folk, were able to continue to be productive through the federally funded programs in spite of the economic depression.

Throughout the 1930s and 1940s newspapers continued to enable black women to publish and through their written word influence others. The black press was the major medium of mass communication. Black people who might not afford books could and did purchase the newspaper. Marian Campfield, city editor of the *Chicago Bee* in the 1930s and 1940s, was directly responsible for the newspaper's general reporting and focused remarkable attention on the coverage of women. She also used the newspaper to sell black **history** and literature books and raise the consciousness of black readers. **Gwendolyn Brooks**'s first published poems appeared in the newspaper. In 1947 when the *Bee* folded, Campfield became women's editor of the *Chicago Defender*.

Zora Neale Hurston's 1935 publication of *Mules and Men* and 1937 novel, *Their Eyes Were Watching God*, laid the groundwork for contemporary black feminism. Hurston divorced herself from politics, something that her predecessors had been unable to do. She did not protest against racism or discrimination, and her attitude toward it was not anger but amazement. It astonished her that anyone could deny themselves the pleasure of her company. Her attitude angered many class-conscious black people who felt that she exposed the worst aspects of black folk culture in her work and did not protest in ways that they deemed acceptable. For her uniquely feminist stance she earned black male scorn, and not until decades later would her works be appreciated.

As the spotlight slowly faded from Harlem, a renaissance of sorts began to emerge in Chicago. Margaret Walker, Gwendolyn Brooks, **Margaret Taylor Goss Burroughs**, **Richard Wright**, and others were Chicago Renaissance artists supported by the Federal Art Project (a division of the WPA) and the locally sponsored South Side Community Art Center. The American Negro Exposition in Chicago from July 4 to September 2, 1940, brought attention to the South Side as a center for culture and art. When Margaret Walker won the Yale University Younger Poet's Award in 1942, for her first volume of poetry, *For My People*, it marked the new era for black women poets who had not published a volume of poetry since 1918. The young Margaret Walker's call for "a second generation full of courage" did not fall on deaf ears, and although her famous poem ends with the masculine imperative for a race of men to rise and take control, she inspired her sisters to rise as well.

Protest Movement (1940–1959)

The end of the Great Depression and the beginning of World War II mark a period of unprecedented political protest for black Americans. As the Great Migration brought the so-called Negro problem to the North where de facto segregation limited black freedom just as de jure had in the South, African Americans demanded their rights. The war against fascism abroad would intensify the battle against racism at home. Chicago and other major cities had restrictive neighborhood covenants that even though illegal still effectively kept black people limited to ghettoes. Violence continued to mark white response to black progress. In 1943 race riots erupted in Detroit and Harlem. Ironically, Detroit was nicknamed the "Arsenal of Democracy" because of the defense plants that manufactured war weapons. The Congress of Racial Equality (CORE), the NAACP, and the Brotherhood of Sleeping Car Porters protested the treatment of black people and the segregation of blacks in the military. Mary McLeod Bethune organized the National Council of Negro Women (NCNW) in 1935 to express black women's concerns regarding national and international affairs. The national headquarters, established in Washington, D.C., in 1942, published the *Aframerican Women's Journal*. Collectively these groups protested everything from the lack of human and civil rights, unequal pay, fair housing, equal educational opportunities as well as the right to fight in the U.S. armed forces as full-fledged citizens of democracy during World War II. Black women were excluded from the WAVES (Women Accepted for Volunteer Emergency Service) until near the end of the war, although they served as WACS (Women's Army Corps) and nurses and in the U.S. Civilian Air Patrol.

In 1945 with the publication of *A Street in Bronzeville*, Gwendolyn Brooks answered Margaret Walker's charge in *For My People* and began what later characterizes the works of black women writers: their literary talking to each other through their speakerly texts. *Bronzeville*, the alternate name given to Chicago's Southside ghetto by its black residents, focuses on the ordinary lives of the people confined to kitchenette apartments, captures the cadence of black speech patterns, and masters formal poetic devices in ways that make Brooks's poetry more politically astute and feminist than many were willing to grant. Even she claimed to have been more political after her encounter with young students of the **Black Arts Movement** who criticized her formal poetry. However, "The Mother," with its arresting first line, speaks volumes about gender, race, and class, as does "Kitchenette building," particularly with regard to artistic production. The Pulitzer Prize–winning *Annie Allen* (1949) and Brooks's only novel *Maud Martha* (1953) contain feminist subtexts that indict sexist and racist oppression of black women.

The atomic age ushered in by the end of World War II, the postwar economy that produced a rise in blue-collar jobs, and the possibility of achieving the American dream of a house in the suburbs, two-car garage, television set, two and a half kids and a dog for many black people remained unattainable. The success of Richard Wright's *Native Son* (1940) cast literary protest into the mode of natural realism. While his influence is undeniably great in terms of social protest fiction, many other writers regarded Wright's mode passé. They focused instead on integration and the challenges of modern life. One of the challenges continued to be the marginalization of black people and the refusal of America to live up to its promise of democracy. **Ann Petry**'s novel *The Street* (1946) moved beyond the naturalistic tradition of Richard Wright by demonstrating the interconnections of race, gender, and class. In *The Living Is Easy* (1948) by Dorothy West satirizes Boston's black petit bourgeoisie and critiques patriarchy with her feminist portrayal of Cleo, a headstrong woman who refuses gender typing.

The 1950s' popular culture of Sputnik, Donna Reed, June Cleaver, and *Father Knows Best* was unprepared for the Civil Rights Movement that forced massive changes in the fabric of American culture. The 1954 Supreme Court decision of *Brown v. Board of Education*, the Montgomery Bus Boycott, and all of the federal legislation that followed appeared to enact what Reconstruction had left undone. A fitting close to this era of protest was **Lorraine Hansberry**'s hit *A Raisin in the Sun* (1959). The play articulated the integrationist impetus of many black people who hoped for inclusion in American society. Ironically, for other black people, integration would prove to be too little, too late. Beneatha, the Afrocentric feminist who challenges traditional gender roles, articulates the most forward-looking aspect in Hansberry's play because by the end of the decade integration was becoming suspect, especially for urban blacks in ghettoes of the North and West.

Black Arts Movement (1960–1969)

From the end of the 1950s throughout the revolutionary 1960s, America was forced to awaken from its dream of peace and prosperity. A sexual revolution occurred that destroyed any remaining Victorian mores. A new psychology espoused by Wilhelm Reich postulated that sexual repression was destructive, distorted psychological development, and led to authoritarian behavior including fascism and racism. The youthful cry "Make love not war" spoke for the antiwar peace movement against the Vietnam War as well as for sexual freedom. However, the decade of the 1960s was anything but peaceful and loving. In 1963 President John F. Kennedy's assassination unleashed a wave of violence that would bring white America face to face with what African Americans had suffered for centuries. Thus, Malcolm X's statement about the chickens coming home to roost was not insensitive to the pain Kennedy's assassination caused; rather it was seizing a teachable moment in order to show America that the violence they had allowed to go unchecked as long as it was confined to the black communities had now come for them. The decade ended with the murders of Malcolm X, Martin Luther King, Jr., and Robert Kennedy.

The Black Arts Movement was the literary counterpart to the political Black Power movement that split from the nonviolent civil rights movement of the 1950s. The Black Arts Movement was as different from **protest** literature as Black Power was from passive resistance. Whereas the latter stressed integration and racial harmony, the former expressed **Black Nationalism** and revolution. Poetry became the dominant genre of the movement. For Black Americans, particularly the young, the lyrics of popular music summarized the movement's sentiments. James Brown's 1969 "I'm Black and I'm Proud" epitomized the era, and Aretha Franklin's rendition of "Respect" articulated what black women were demanding. In the 1960s the New Negro turned black. In poetry **Amiri Baraka** called for words that could kill, and **Nikki Giovanni** posed the question, "Nigger can you kill?" No longer could critics refer to black women's poetry as prim and proper.

The Black Arts Movement differed from previous literary eras in several significant ways. The first and most obvious was in the appropriation and use of language heretofore deemed derogatory. Both the words *nigger* and *black* were used to undermine white definitions. Alternate spelling of words to reflect urban black speech and the lack of capitalization and/or punctuation characterizes the movement's poetics. The second major shift was that of audience. Black Arts Movement writers addressed their works to the black masses. As a result of this shift in focus, they expected the critiques to come from black people and ignored white criticism as irrelevant.

Black women poets, militant and feminist, articulated feminism differently from their antebellum and postbellum sisters. They differed from women of the protest period as well, and not just in terms of degree and technique. While it is true that Black Arts Movement poets were not subtle, they screamed and cursed, and moreover, they were the first generation of black women writers to openly reject and criticize their mothers. Clearly, not all militant feminists took this approach, but enough did to call attention to the shifts taking place. They were daughters of revolution and poets of rebellion. Nothing was sacrosanct, and mother-daughter relationships were scrutinized.

Carolyn Rodgers's "Jesus Was Crucified" is an early poem in which she critiques **Christianity** and her mother's seeming willingness to be nailed to the cross of white America. Rodgers later recognizes her mother as the bridge she "crossed over on." Nikki Giovanni's "Woman Poem" clearly is a feminist comment on gender roles as well as a critique of how black women treat each other. Many of the black women writers of the Black Arts Movement (BAM) begin with militant reactions to racism and evolve into militant feminism, something not counted on by black male critics, theoreticians, and definers of the black aesthetic. Theories of black art and black aesthetic did not include or acknowledge a feminist premise.

It would take time for black women novelists to catch up in print with the publications of the women poets. Many of the poets assumed responsibility for publishing their own works. Performance poets had the advantage of creating a following from their public readings as well as marketing their poetry on record albums and tape recordings. Margaret Walker's *Jubilee* (1966), a historical novel about her great-grandmother's life from slavery to Reconstruction, although published during the BAM, adhered to an earlier tradition. Certainly it celebrated female wisdom and strength by portraying Vyry as a self-sustaining woman, but it could not, in light of historical facts, condemn the gender roles.

On the other hand, **Sarah Elizabeth Wright**'s novel *This Child's Gonna Live* (1969) and **Kristin Hunter Lattany**'s novels present settings that enable the interrogation of gender, race, and power, especially in *The Soul Brothers and Sister Lou* (1968). *Coming of Age in Mississippi* (1968) by **Anne Moody** introduces a woman-centered **autobiography** instead of a race-centered one. The end of the decade saw the publication of books for young people by black women writers not only interested in instilling pride of history but joy and power for the female gender. **Virginia Hamilton**'s *Zeely* (1967) is one of the first black publications to examine race and gender in **children's and young adult literature**. The 1970s would witness a flowering of feminist fiction and other writing, undoubtedly begun during the Black Arts Movement but not published until the decade of the movement had ended.

Contemporary (1970–Present)

The women's liberation movement characterized the 1970s. Shirley Chisholm's political autobiography *Unbought and Unbossed* (1970) and **Toni Cade Bambara**'s anthology *The Black Woman* (1970) ushered in the new wave feminism for black women. The 1971 publication of *MS.* magazine, the widespread availability of the birth-control pill and other forms of contraception, the Supreme Court's decision in *Roe v. Wade* granting women the constitutional right to abortion, Chisholm's election to Congress in 1968, making her the first black congresswoman, her run for the presidency in 1972, the creation of Black Women Organized for Political Action (BWOPA 1973), and Congress' passing of the Equal Rights Amendment and sending it to the states to ratify made this a decade of victories for women.

By the end of the 1960s, the civil rights movement collided with feminism. Black women marginalized within the civil rights and Black Power movements faced what Frances Beale called their double jeopardy: race and gender. Black female strength and sacrifice for family and community had become suspect and, according to some social scientists, threatened **black masculinity**. *The Negro Family: The Case for National Action* (1965), known as the infamous Moynihan Report, critiqued the black family as pathological because of its failure to imitate the white patriarchal model. The study introduced into currency the term *black matriarch* as a negative signifier for usurping male authority and for symbolically castrating black men. If the public arena defined the black man's domain, black feminists would turn to the home as the site for their resistance. It was home that women chose to write about; as sisters, mothers, daughters, lovers, and wives, they constructed the stories that they knew best.

The year 1970 proved to be a watershed for black women writers. Race no longer took precedence over gender issues, nor did the needs of family and community. Rather, these feminists insisted that race and gender could not be separated—that both must be reckoned with simultaneously. They challenged the oppressive nature of male privilege, and the politics of self became an overarching concern. **Mari Evans**'s collection of poetry *I Am a Black Woman* proudly proclaimed her female strength, and **Maya Angelou** celebrated matriarchal strength in *I Know Why the Caged Bird Sings*. **Toni Morrison** and Alice Walker published feminist novels that critiqued black men as husbands and fathers. Cholly Breedlove as incestuous rapist in *The Bluest Eye* and Brownfield Copeland, child abuser, wife beater, and murderer in *The Third Life of Grange Copeland* represented what many black men perceived as attacks aimed for literary castration of their body politic.

In 1974, the publication of **Ann Allen Shockley**'s lesbian novel *Loving Her* broadened and deepened the politics of black female literary representation as well as examined the nature of black and white women's relationships to each other. **Pat Parker**'s bold declaration in *Pit Stop* (1974) that her lover was a woman urged many black lesbians to claim their identity and linked, in the minds of many black women and men, **lesbianism** with feminism. However, even among radical white feminists, racism alienated many lesbians of color. The **Combahee River Collective** *Black Feminist Statement* revealed the intersectionality of race, sexual orientation, class, and gender and challenged white feminists to recognize and to not deny difference.

By the middle of the decade, **Ntozake Shange**'s feminist choreopoem *for colored girls who have considered suicide/when the rainbow is enuf* (1975) opened on Broadway. Both **Sherley Anne Williams** and **Gayl Jones** published books in 1975. Jones's *Eva's Man* contains the literal castration (with teeth) of a man by the central character, Eva Medina Canada. In 1977, **Wanda Coleman**'s *Art in the Court of the Blue Fag* extended the challenge, begun in the 1960s, to eradicate the "nice lady poetry" of previous decades. Her use of black English and ghettoez continued the audacity of the women poets from the Black Arts Movement, **Jayne Cortez**, **Sonia Sanchez**, and others.

The decade closed with **Audre Lorde** claiming all of her identities: black woman, mother, daughter, feminist, lesbian, and poet with the publication of *The Black Unicorn* (1978). *Kindred*, the critically acclaimed science fiction novel by **Octavia Butler**, was published in 1979, making her the first black woman recognized in the genre. The decade was one that honored black women in all of their shapes, forms, and fashions and challenged black men to reject the ideas of male privilege and oppressive hierarchical structures including within the family. Not only were black feminist voices heard; their efforts were rewarded. In 1978 Sonia Sanchez received the American Book Award for her collection of poems *I've Been a Woman*. Morrison's **Song of Solomon** (1977) won the National Book Critics Circle Award, and **Lucille Clifton** was named Poet Laureate of Maryland.

Politically, the decade spelled disaster for the law and order Republican Nixon administration that apparently believed that it was above the law. Vice President Spiro Agnew was forced to resign in 1973 and pleaded no contest to tax fraud. The Watergate scandal forced Richard Nixon to resign in August 1974. The Nixon White House represented the so-called silent majority who were tired of civil rights, human rights, and women's rights. Despite the scandals and setbacks, they would not be silent for long and would erect stiff opposition against gains in civil and women's rights.

The political reaction of the silent majority resulted in the activism of the Moral Majority in the 1980s. Fundamentalist Baptist preacher and leader of the Moral Majority, Reverend Jerry Falwell led the most organized backlash against abortion, gay rights, and affirmative action. The organization was influential in helping to elect conservative candidates to political office. Despite efforts to the contrary, in 1983 the Supreme Court reaffirmed the *Roe v. Wade* decision. However, in 1982 the states failed to ratify the Equal Rights Amendment.

Works by black women writers continued to flourish in spite of Reaganomics and the trickle-down economic theory. The 1982 publication of Alice Walker's clearly feminist novel *The Color Purple* politicized many black women who were uncomfortable identifying themselves with the F word. Thus in 1983, Walker coined the term **womanism** as more appropriate for black feminists. Womanism, defined in her collection of essays *In Search of Our Mothers' Gardens* (1983), was an all-inclusive as opposed to exclusive term. Many people thought of feminists as man-hating separatists at best and lesbians at worst. Walker's term embraced women who preferred women's culture, loved each other sexually or nonsexually, loved men, sexually or nonsexually, and who were in charge of their own lives and responsible for their own happiness. Feminism paled in comparison to womanism, like lavender in the presence of purple.

Not all black women writers shunned the feminist label. Michelle Wallace in *Black Macho and the Myth of the Superwoman* (1979) embraced feminism in her critique of sexism within the black community. She reaped the wrath of many blacks both men and women. Sociologist Robert Staples wrote a heated reply titled "The Myth of Black Macho: A Response to Angry Black Feminists" in the *Black Scholar* (March–April 1979).

Black lesbians found it necessary to establish their own press. In 1980, Lorde and other politically active women founded the **Kitchen Table: Women of Color Press**. The press was responsible for bringing to print seminal works including *This Bridge Called My Back* (1983) and *Home Girls: A Black Feminist Anthology* (1983). The 1980s also witnessed the emergence of black women feminist theorists. In 1981 bell hooks's *Ain't I a Woman* examined issues of racism and feminism. Her 1984 publication *Feminist Theory from Margin to Center* was among the first to bring the study of black feminist politics into the academy. Prior to hooks, Gloria Hull, Patricia Bell Scott, and Barbara Smith edited the groundbreaking book *All the Women Are White, All the Blacks Are Men, but Some of Us Are Brave: Black Women's Studies* (1982), an indictment of the academy's black and women's studies programs for their failures to acknowledge black women in terms of both race and gender.

Black feminist theorists not only examined the politics of black feminism and exclusion but also undertook the serious critical study of black feminist artistic works. Barbara Christian's *Black Women Novelists: The Development of a Tradition* (1980) and *Black Feminist Criticism: Perspectives on Black Women Writers* (1985), Hazel Carby's *Reconstructing Womanhood: The Emergence of the Afro-American Novelist* (1987), Joanne Braxton's *Black Women Writing Autobiography* (1989), and Marcia Ann Gillespie's "The Myth of the Strong Black Woman" in *Feminist Frameworks* (1988) shaped the study of black feminist literature.

The 1980 publication of *The Black Woman*, edited by La Frances Rodgers-Rose, extended the issues raised in Bambara's 1970 volume of the same title, particularly by discussing the black woman's role in the family. As in the past, magazines and journals edited by black women offered publication opportunities unavailable elsewhere. *SAGE: A Scholarly Journal on Black Women* began publication in 1981 and addressed issues ignored in other publications such as black mother-daughter relationships and black female-male relationships.

Popular culture during the decade of the 1980s shifted from the highly political, socially engaged activity of the previous two decades to an obsession with MTV music videos, cable television, and personal computers. The beginning of Internet culture, the outbreak of AIDS (acquired immunodeficiency syndrome), twenty-four-hour television news (CNN), hip-hop, and break dancing as well as the widespread use of the banal phrase "shop until you drop," aimed to remind women of their gender-based role as consumers, acted like anesthesia on the politically conscious.

The 1990s brought a change in political atmosphere and an end to Republican politics. President Bill Clinton's sex scandal, his impeachment trial, and O. J. Simpson's murder trial foreshadowed issues that still plague feminists today: sexual harassment, pornography, abuse, violence, and death. Other major issues facing contemporary feminists include equal treatment in military academies and in the armed services, leadership in religious organizations and worship, surrogate motherhood, balancing family and career, and after so many years, once again the issue of women's reproductive rights.

American women have made steady progress in spite of political backlash to impede their progress for total equality. Black women, feminist or not, have worked to advance the cause. The final decades of the twentieth century began with the unprecedented appointment of a woman as bishop in the Episcopal Church. That woman, the Rt. Reverend Barbara C. Harris, was black. The Episcopal Women's Caucus and other feminist groups worked to raise the consciousness of both men and women to achieve this advancement in the private and sacrosanct area of organized religion. As executive director of the Episcopal Publishing Company and publisher of the *Witness* magazine, Harris used the written word to work for women's rights.

The 1990s saw the rise of black women novelists like **Terry McMillan**, whose work became increasingly popular. Other writers to continue or extend the trend of writing feminist novels in the sense that they contain strong women characters and address women's issues of sexual and political liberation include **Marita Golden**, **Tina McElroy Ansa**, **Gloria Naylor**, **Bebe Moore Campbell**, Lorene Cary, Shay Youngblood, and poets Natasha Trethewey and **Sapphire**. The black feminist intellectual tradition continues to be uncovered and documented. Patricia Hill Collins's 1990 publication *Black Feminist Thought* and her 2004 book *Black Sexual Politics: African Americans, Gender, and the New Racism* are excellent examples of the ongoing work of black feminists.

The twentieth-first century offers another kind of publication opportunity for writers through the electronic media, and many black women writers will take advantage of E-publications. As long as issues of equity and racial and gender discrimination constitute a part of the black woman's experience in America, undoubtedly there will continue to be black feminist writers.

Nagueyalti Warren

LITTLE, MALCOLM. See Malcolm X

LIVING IS EASY, THE

The Living Is Easy (1948) was the first novel of **Harlem Renaissance** author **Dorothy West**. Originally, the book was to have been serialized by the *Ladies' Home Journal*. West recalls her elation at the unprecedented fee she was to have received; she also recalls the decision of the editorial board of Blackwell's, who published the magazine, to retract the offer, as they feared losing both advertising dollars and southern subscribers. Instead, *The Living Is Easy* was published by Houghton and Mifflin in 1948.

West's novel is drawn from her upbringing by an extended southern **family** in a northern household that strove to achieve the respectability of Boston's black Brahmin caste. Nevertheless, she rejects many of their prejudices and satirizes others. At the center of the novel is Cleo Judson, the southern wife of a Boston businessman. Cleo ruthlessly maneuvers to destroy her sisters' marriages and prospects for independence as a means of gathering them and their children around her in her northern home. Abusing her husband's generosity, terrorizing her shy and adoring daughter into corroborating her lies, and demanding that her family recognize her authority, Cleo is a less-than-sympathetic character and one uncommon in African American **literature** at the time. Yet she is always believable in her desire to better her family—whatever her methods—and to be loved. West's portrait of Cleo's daughter provides a perfect counterpoint; Judy's childish perspective on, and conflicted **love** for, her mother allows a more sympathetic portrayal than an adult perspective would.

The Living Is Easy includes many thinly veiled portraits of individuals West knew or with whom she was familiar. Booker T. Washington is treated with dignity, despite West's initial impulse to represent him comically, stemming from her family's disdain for his politics. Editor Monroe Trotter appears as Simeon Binney, though he was offended by West's representation of his family as "genteel poor." Businessman J. H. Lewis is represented as Mr. Harnett. But most notable is the resemblance of the Judson family to West's own, from the occupation of the father and aunts to the number of siblings, and the characters of all. West admits that her mother was the model for Cleo. According to her niece, this and the revelation of other family secrets in *The Living Is Easy* was not without controversy; the book "caused such a catastrophic uproar in the family that most members stopped speaking to Dorothy. To this day many family members still don't speak to each other as a direct result of that book" (McGrath 124). But West defends the character of Cleo, saying that her meanness had a positive effect on future generations. The portrait of West's mother recorded by her niece concurs: "The fact that she was mean and gave those girls a life a high intellect and misery is key" (McGrath 125). This is also key to *The Living Is Easy*—how one woman can inspire both creativity and repression and can be a subject of both adoration and hatred.

Works About

Cromwell, Adelaide M. Afterword to *The Living Is Easy*. New York: Feminist Press, 1982. 349–364.

Dalsgard, Katrine. "Alive and Well and Living on the Island of Martha's Vineyard: An Interview with Dorothy West, October 29, 1988." *Langston Hughes Review* (Fall 1993): 28–44.

McDowell, Deborah E. "Conversations with Dorothy West." *Harlem Renaissance Re-examined*. Ed. Victor A. Kramer. New York: AMS, 1987. 265–282.

McGrath, Abigail. "Afterward: A Daughter Reminisces." *This Waiting for Love: Helene Johnson, Poet of the Harlem Renaissance*. Ed. Verner D. Mitchell. Amherst: University of Massachusetts Press, 2000. 123–130.

Rodgers, Lawrence R. "Dorothy West's *The Living Is Easy* and the Ideal of Southern Folk Community." *African American Review* 26.1 (1992): 161–172.

Sanders, Pamela Peden. "The Feminism of Dorothy West's *The Living Is Easy*: A Critique of the Limitations of the Female Sphere through Performative Gender Roles." *African American Review* 36.3 (2002): 435–446.

Steinberg, Sybil. "Dorothy West: Her Own Renaissance." *Publishers Weekly*, July 3, 1995, 34–35.

Jennifer Harris

LOFTON, RAMONA. See Sapphire (author)

LORDE, AUDRE (1934–1992)

Audre Lorde called herself a "black lesbian feminist poet warrior mother" (Hall 146). She was born in depression-era New York to Linda Belmar Lorde and Frederic Byron Lorde, immigrants who never quit thinking of the West Indies as **home**. For Audrey Geraldine, their youngest child, the Caribbean island of Grenada became "my truly private paradise," if only in her imagination (*Zami* 14). In the experimental **autobiography *Zami: A New Spelling of My Name*** (1982), Lorde emphasizes that American racism was a "new and crushing reality" for her parents, who had emigrated as young adults in hopes of better employment (69). The positions they found were low paying and exhausting. In 1928, the year before the first of her three daughters was born, Linda Lorde lost her twelve-hour daily job as a scullery maid when a New York teashop owner realized that she was black instead of Spanish.

Yet Lorde also describes her mother as a powerful woman, strong in ways that distinguished her from most other women, regardless of **race**. At home, she mixed oils to heal bruises; on the streets, she projected an image of "in-charge competence" (*Zami* 16). Years later, Lorde understood that Linda Lorde must have worked hard to hide her actual powerlessness as a black female foreigner from her children. The biographer **Alexis De Veaux** says Audre Lorde was "both intimidated and erotically fascinated" by her mother, while she regarded her father as a "hardworking, silent, and shadowy figure" (14). Lorde told an interviewer for *Christopher Street* magazine that neither parent "thought of our upbringing in feminist terms," yet they raised their daughters outside the "feminine **stereotype**" (Hall 23).

Byron Lorde was determined to have a "dynasty," with a doctor, a teacher, and a lawyer in the next generation; the sex of his children was irrelevant to his dream (Hall 18). Ambitious to improve his own status, he attended night school and managed buildings for white owners before saving enough money to invest in boarding houses and other rental property. During World War II he also worked at a manufacturing plant to avoid the draft, and his wife assisted him at his Harlem real estate office, often leaving the older daughters to babysit for Audre. In *Zami*, Lorde relates that she slept in her parents' bedroom as a young child and envied her sisters, Phyllis and Helen, for their "magical and charmed existence" in a tiny bedroom where she was not welcome (43). Although her siblings considered her the spoiled baby of the **family**, De Veaux suggests that Lorde's own early **memories** "became almost mythic constructions of an ugly duckling" (14): overweight, stuttering, darker skinned than her sisters or mother, clumsy, and alone. She was further isolated by extreme nearsightedness and by her limited efforts at verbal communication.

Lorde credits Augusta Baker, a children's librarian, with introducing her to a life-saving resource after Linda Lorde brought Audre to the 135th Street branch library at the age of four. Enthralled by Mrs. Baker's storytelling, she let her mother teach her the alphabet so that she could read books in large type. Audre's new language skills extended to oral expression; she often spoke to her family in lines of **poetry**. Before she began school, she dropped the "y" from "Audrey" and printed her whole name as one smooth word, AUDRELORDE. Thus, "Audre" became the first of many transformations alluded to in the subtitle of *Zami: A New Spelling of My Name*. "Zami," she explains, is the Carriacou island word for "women who work together as friends and lovers," and Lorde's "biomythographical" memoir depicts many of the supportive women in the first three decades of her own life (255).

In *Zami*, she describes her mother as a devout Catholic who prayed to the Virgin Mary at every crisis yet followed such West Indian traditions as lighting candles before All Souls Day. Aside from Audre's brief enrollment in a public school's sight conservation kindergarten, the three children attended parochial grade schools, but Audre's objections to traditional Christian **religion** began early. She challenged the nuns' instruction at the all-black St. Mark's Academy, where her sisters were known for their obedience to authority. After the Lordes moved to a white ethnic area of Upper Harlem in 1945, Audre was teased by her new classmates as the first black student at St. Catherine's School.

Her sensitivity toward racism was heightened on a trip to Washington, D.C., when her family was refused counter service in an ice cream parlor across from the Supreme Court. At thirteen, Audre was "outraged"; she told interviewer Nina Winter that when she returned home, she typed "an impassioned plea for justice filled with every cliché you can imagine" (Hall 15). That same year, she began to attend the academically distinguished, all-female Hunter High School, where she was the only black member of The Branded. She portrays this outsider group in *Zami* as a "sisterhood of rebels" that conducted séances, read the British Romantics, and exchanged their own poems (81). Diane di Prima, in particular, became a lifelong friend and supporter of Lorde's work. During high school, Lorde's favorite writers included Edna St. Vincent Millay and Helene Magaret; she published her first poem in *Seventeen* after it was rejected by the Hunter literary magazine.

In Harlem, she had a separate group of black female friends and was especially close to Genevieve Johnson, an adventurous ballet dancer and one of the few African Americans at Hunter High. Gennie's suicide at fifteen was painfully difficult for Lorde, who called her "the first person in my life that I was ever conscious of loving"; she later regretted that their relationship had not been sexual (*Zami* 87). With Gennie, she roamed New York in a series of disguises. "Bandits, Gypsies, Foreigners of all degree, Witches, Whores, and Mexican Princesses—there were appropriate costumes for every role," she says (88). De Veaux comments on Lorde's "ambivalent" **sexuality** (33), observing that her intense friendships, like her strong attraction to some of her women teachers, "were unquestionably homoerotic" (28). At the same time, she dated white males, despite her parents' disapproval; during her first year at Hunter College, she had an abortion. In spring of 1952, Lorde attended weekly meetings of the Harlem Writers Guild, where she met **Rosa Guy** and **Langston Hughes**; one of her poems appeared in the group's quarterly journal.

Lorde made sporadic progress on a college degree in **literature** and philosophy, supporting herself with pink-collar and blue-collar jobs in hospitals and factories. Retreating from the political climate of the McCarthy era, she spent several months of 1954 in Mexico. The **beauty** of Cuernavaca sharpened her insight into the possibilities of poetry, and she was so intrigued by Mexican legends that she wrote the short story "La Llorona" about a Medea-like mother figure. Lorde's encounter with the journalist Eudora Garrett clarified her sense of lesbian **identity**. In *Zami*, she describes their relationship in erotic, almost mythic terms; after her return to New York, she became increasingly involved in "gay-girl" culture.

Lorde compared young lesbians to their "sister Amazons," riding Dahomey's "loneliest outposts" (*Zami* 176). She read Gertrude Stein and felt "crushed" when the *Ladder*, a lesbian magazine, rejected her poetry submissions (210). Few black lesbians were out of the closet, but Lorde said gay girls were "the only Black and white women who were even talking to each other" in 1950s America, "outside of the empty rhetoric of patriotism and political movements" (225). Whether butch or femme, she adds, lesbians saw their "connection in the name of woman" as their source of power. At the end of *Zami*, Lorde remarks that, during her twenties, her life became "increasingly a bridge and field of women" (255). She pays tribute to several friends and relatives but also to the African goddess MawuLisa and her trickster daughter Afrekete, who are subjects of several of her poems. Even though she mentions completing her coursework at Hunter and earning a graduate degree in library science from Columbia University, Lorde's most important female teachers in *Zami* were not in the classroom.

For several years, Lorde thought of herself not as a writer but as a librarian who wrote. In studying library science, she hoped to gain access to the sort of information that could improve society. Setting up libraries for children in Manhattan and Mt. Vernon was also a creative outlet. In 1962, she married Edwin Ashley Rollins, a legal aid attorney whose sexuality was as complicated as hers; Lorde continued her lesbian liaisons. The same year, her poetry was anthologized in two collections; however, she did not publish her first book until 1968, when Poets Press, run by her high school friend Diane di Prima, printed *The First Cities*. With several poems about **love**, **motherhood**, and children, the volume was considered less confrontational than much contemporary African American poetry. Lorde told *Callaloo* editor Charles Rowell that she felt women were excluded, to a large degree, from the **Black Arts Movement**.

Although they had a young daughter and son, Elizabeth and Jonathan, Rollins encouraged Lorde to accept a National Endowment for the Arts residency grant in the spring of 1968 at Tougaloo, the historically black college from which **Anne Moody** had graduated. During this period of great racial tension, members of Mississippi's White Citizens' Council practiced target shooting near the campus at night to frighten black residents. Lorde said her experience as a creative writing instructor at Tougaloo was "pivotal" in her decision to begin a new career as a writer and teacher (Hall 94). Over the next two decades, she taught at New York universities, including Hunter College, where she was named Thomas Hunter Professor in 1987. **Jewelle Gomez** was a student in her poetry workshop at Hunter.

At Tougaloo, Lorde met Frances Clayton, a visiting psychology professor from Brown University, who became her longtime partner after she divorced Rollins in 1970. De Veaux observes that Lorde chose to "reinvent herself" in "a life wholly grounded in lesbian identity"; the feminist movement and "an African, female-centered **spirituality**" became crucial elements of this identity (De Veaux 111). Her 1970 collection *Cables to Rage* includes the long poem "Martha," which some literary critics see as her first published expression of **lesbianism**. Establishing a household with Lorde on Staten Island, Clayton shared in raising the children to adulthood. In an interview with **James Baldwin** for *Essence* magazine, Lorde revealed her worries about the dangers faced by black adolescents, including destructive images of **black masculinity**.

When a major company, W. W. Norton, published *Coal*, her fifth collection, in 1976, Lorde reached a larger reading audience. Her seventh book, *The Black Unicorn* (1978), with its inventive use of **myth**, was especially well received. But Lorde was as well known for her social activism as she was for her eleven volumes of poetry. Several of the speeches and essays gathered in her books *Sister Outsider* (1984) and *A Burst of Light* (1988) reflect her involvement in major movements of the 1960s through the 1980s: women's liberation, gay/lesbian rights, and the **civil rights movement**. These pieces include "Sexism: An American Disease in Blackface," "Eye to Eye: Black Women, Hatred, and Anger," "I Am Your Sister: Black Women Organizing Across Sexualities," "Turning the Beat Around: Lesbian Parenting 1986," and "Age, Race, Class, and Sex: Women Redefining Difference."

"Difference" was a key word for Lorde, who saw herself as both an outsider and a bridge. In 1981, with Barbara Smith, she cofounded **Kitchen Table: Women of Color Press** as a resource for those women who were often overlooked by mainstream publishers because of their ethnicity. Lorde was alert to divisions within communities to which she belonged. Discussing African American gender battles, she told **Mari Evans** that black men must admit that obstacles to their own liberation come from the "same constellation of intolerance for difference" that produces "sexism and woman-hating" (Hall 78). Critical of some white feminists for undermining the goals of **black feminism**, Lorde nevertheless forged alliances across races, including her long friendship with poet Adrienne Rich. When Lorde, Rich, and **Alice Walker** were nominated for the 1974 National Book Award in poetry, they refused to act as if they were in competition. Rich, as the winner, read a statement prepared by all three poets, accepting the prize for all "unheard" women (Hall xxi).

After Lorde dissolved her partnership with Frances Clayton and moved to the Virgin Islands to live with social scientist Gloria Joseph in the late 1980s, she spoke out increasingly against American intervention in world affairs. In 1982, she had criticized the U.S. military invasion of Grenada; later in the decade, she described the negative impact of American companies and American tourism on St. Croix. Lorde's international perspective on land-rights struggles and other global issues was broadened by travel to Africa, Europe, and Australia. Beginning in 1984, she made several teaching trips to Berlin, where she compared prejudice against Afro-Germans to prejudice against Jews. Lorde told interviewers for *Listen* magazine that the white women's movements in America and Germany would "fall apart" if they failed to acknowledge that "racism is a feminist issue" (Hall 167). In collaboration with Orlanda Women's Press editor Dagmar Schultz, Lorde helped to organize the first Afro-German anthology, published in 1986 as *Farbe bekennen* and translated in 1991 as *Showing Our Colors: Afro-German Women Speak Out.*

In Germany, Lorde sought homeopathic alternative therapies for liver cancer, metastasized from the breast cancer that had necessitated a mastectomy in 1978. She spoke with Schultz about the importance of acquainting women's organizations with available treatments because cancer is "a woman's concern" and "a feminist concern of the twenty-one-year-old feminist who doesn't know it is" (Hall 135). Lorde told interviewers that struggles with cancer helped her to formulate a theory of the erotic, celebrating the pleasures of the **body**, including her love of laughter and dance. In 1981, the American Library Association named Lorde's ***The Cancer Journals*** Gay Caucus Book of the Year; her 1988 essay collection *A Burst of Light* includes "A Burst of Light: Living with Cancer." In this long essay, she describes cancer as "another face of that continuing battle for self-determination and survival that Black women fight daily, often in triumph" (49). Lorde emphasizes that women should engage the "core problems" confronting their nations because "Feminism must be on the cutting edge of real social change if it is to survive as a movement in any particular country" (64).

In October 1990, more than 2,000 people from twenty-three countries gathered in Boston to honor Audre Lorde at the conference "I Am Your Sister: Forging Global Connections across Difference." The same year, she was awarded the Publishing Triangle's Bill Whitehead Memorial Award for

Lifetime Achievement in Gay and Lesbian Literature. New York State appointed her to a two-year term as Poet Laureate in 1991, a term she was unable to complete. On November 17, 1992, Lorde died in Christiansted, St. Croix, supported by Gloria Joseph and three close friends from Germany: Dagmar Schultz, Ika Hügel, and May Ayim. Thousands of mourners attended a memorial service on January 17, 1993, at New York's Cathedral of Saint John the Divine, where tributes were paid by Lorde's children, **Sonia Sanchez**, **Angela Davis**, and many others. Her biographer Alexis De Veaux sums up her complex relation to the feminist movement, which initially offered Lorde a "longed-for home" (122). Involvement with white feminists, however, led her to "challenge their perspectives on sexuality, the meaning of feminist sisterhood, and race" (De Veaux 122). As Lorde famously said, "Your silence will not protect you" (*Sister Outsider* 41). In speaking her challenges, she changed the shape of the movement.

Works By

Between Our Selves. Point Reyes, CA: Eidolon Editions, 1976.
The Black Unicorn. New York: W. W. Norton, 1978.
A Burst of Light: Essays. Ithaca, NY: Firebrand Books, 1988.
Cables to Rage. London: Paul Breman, 1970.
The Cancer Journals. San Francisco: Spinsters Ink, 1980.
Chosen Poems Old and New. New York: W. W. Norton, 1982.
Coal. New York: W. W. Norton, 1976.
The Collected Poems of Audre Lorde. New York: W. W. Norton, 1997.
The First Cities. New York: Poets Press, 1968.
From a Land Where Other People Live. Detroit: Broadside Press, 1973.
The Marvelous Arithmetics of Distance: Poems 1987–1992. New York: W. W. Norton, 1993.
The New York Head Shop and Museum. Detroit: Broadside Press, 1974.
Our Dead behind Us. New York: W. W. Norton, 1986.
Sister Outsider: Essays and Speeches. Trumansburg, NY: Crossing Press, 1984.
Undersong: Chosen Poems Old and New. Rev. ed. New York: W. W. Norton, 1992.
Zami: A New Spelling of My Name. Watertown, MA: Persephone Press, 1982.

Works About

Brogan, Jacqueline Vaught, and Cordelia Candelaria Chavez, eds. *Women Poets of the Americas: Toward a Pan-American Gathering.* Notre Dame: University of Notre Dame Press, 1999.
Chawla, Louise. *In the First Country of Places: Nature, Poetry, and Childhood Memory.* Albany: State University of New York Press, 1994.
De Veaux, Alexis. *Warrior Poet: A Biography of Audre Lorde.* New York: W. W. Norton, 2004.

Hall, Joan Wylie, ed. *Conversations with Audre Lorde.* Jackson: University Press of Mississippi, 2004.

Jones, Suzanne W., ed. *Writing the Woman Artist: Essays on Poetics, Politics, and Portraiture.* Philadelphia, PA: Temple University Press, 1991.

Keating, Ana Louise. *Women Reading/Women Writing: Self Invention in Paula Gunn Allen, Gloria Anzaldúa, and Audre Lorde.* Philadelphia, PA: Temple University Press, 1996.

Nelson, Emmanuel S., ed. *Critical Essays: Gay and Lesbian Writers of Color.* New York: Haworth, 1993.

Snyder, Sharon L., Brenda Jo Brueggemann, and Rosemarie Garland-Thomson, eds. *Disability Studies: Enabling the Humanities.* New York: Modern Language Association of America, 2002.

Steele, Cassie Premo. *We Heal from Memory: Sexton, Lorde, Anzaldúa, and the Poetry of Witness.* New York: Palgrave, 2000.

Wiley, Catherine, and Fiona R. Barnes, eds. *Homemaking: Women Writers and the Politics and Poetics of Home.* New York: Garland, 1996.

Wilson, Anna. *Persuasive Fictions: Feminist Narrative and Critical Myth.* Lewisburg, PA: Bucknell University Press, 2001.

Joan Wylie Hall

LOVE

Love is a universal and essential human emotion and, as such, is a dominant theme in the creative works of African American writers from **slavery** to **freedom**. In the **literature** love manifests itself from ideal and spiritual love to erotic and sexual love.

The earliest African American literature of the eighteenth century primarily consists of narratives by slaves about their predicament. The topic of love rarely comes up. For example, **poetry** by **Phillis Wheatley** (1753–1784) focuses on themes of freedom and **religion**. The love that she refers to is the love of God. This is typical of many of the works of this period.

Early works from the nineteenth century also include many of the **slave narratives**. Writers such as **Sojourner Truth**, Nathan Beauchamp, Elizabeth Johnson Harris, Emma Crockett, **William Wells Brown**, and others created autobiographical works. The themes of survival and the quest for freedom dominate this period. **Harriet Jacobs** (1813–1897) went against traditional nineteenth-century values by choosing to have a sexual relationship with a white man to protect her children and **family** from the persistent sexual harassment by her master. In doing so she preserved her right to choose, her integrity, and her self-esteem—a form of love. The complications caused by this action make her narrative ***Incidents in the Life of a Slave Girl*** (1861) an interesting and important slave narrative of the nineteenth century. **Paul Laurence Dunbar** (1872–1906) was among the first black writers not born in slavery. He addressed the difficulties encountered by members of his **race** and the efforts of African Americans to achieve equality in America. He sometimes wrote poetry in the style of classic English poets, for example, "Invitation to Love." Other times he wrote in an evocative black American dialect of his times. "A Negro Love Song" is written in this style.

From 1917 until about 1935, an outburst of creative activity among African Americans occurred in all fields of art. The **Harlem Renaissance** was more than a literary movement and more than just a social revolt. The theme of love in African American literature is more prominent from this point forward. **Gwendolyn B. Bennett** (1902–1981) was known for raising her voice against social injustice and hatred, in the hope that the past would never be repeated. Her poetry shows a great range of emotions from hatred to a healthy self-love as seen in her poems "Hatred," "Secret," "Sonnets," and "To a Dark Girl." **Alice Moore Dunbar-Nelson** (1875–1935) wrote about race and gender conflicts. She also published occasional stories in magazines and newspapers. Her diaries written during the 1920s and 1930s deal with topics such as **sexuality**, **family**, and **work**. Her compilation of stories *Laughing to Stop Myself from Crying* (2003) deals with the subject of adultery, which men disguise as love. **Zora Neale Hurston**'s (1891–1960) landmark novel *Their Eyes Were Watching God* (1937) portrays a woman's search for self-fulfillment. Her idea of true love in marriage slowly erodes as her husband becomes abusive and disinterested in her. Janie reinvents herself into a lively woman after his **death** and finally finds love with another man. Many of **Ann Spencer**'s (1882–1976) poems deal with the human search for **beauty** and meaning in life and are not devoid of love. "Black Man O' Mine," for instance, uses erotic imagery to celebrate black love. The major theme in **Angelina Weld Grimké**'s (1880–1958) poetry is lost love. Her poetry is a record of her attempt to love and be loved by another woman–"The Garden Seat," for example. Strangely, some of her poetry is written in the nineteenth-century classic male poet's voice. Her poem "My Shrine" is a good example of this style. **Nella Larsen**'s (1891–1964) novels primarily deal with issues of **identity**, not love. **Langston Hughes** (1902–1967) is the most influential poet and essayist of this period. He melded the beats of **jazz**, sweetness, and the simplicity of folk songs in his poetry. His works, even when not explicitly dealing with the topic of love, are filled with love for people. **Ralph Ellison**'s (1914–1994) *Invisible Man* touches on the subject of love only peripherally. The unnamed hero is searching for the ultimate truth. His search gets him expelled from his southern college and brings him to New York, where he finds brotherhood in a communist group. After being disenchanted, the hero quits the Communist Party, wondering: "Could politics ever be an expression of love?"

The 1970s saw an upsurge in feminist African American literature. **Maya Angelou** (1928–) is one of the earliest modern feminist voices in African American literature. Her themes are love and the universality of all lives. Her autobiographical novel *I Know Why the Caged Bird Sings* was published in 1970. The protagonist, Marguerite Johnson, is a victim of her color and her gender. She has internalized the belief that black is ugly. The **autobiography** tells us about her childhood life torn between the loving grandmother and the glamorous mother as well as her sufferings from color prejudice and sexual abuse. All of this was enough to keep a little girl spellbound for a long time, until she comes out of her shell, confronts the world, and becomes a champion of the black woman's cause. Patrice Gaines's (1949–   ) *Laughing in the Dark* (1995) has a similar theme. It is a story of one woman's journey from the dark world of racial prejudice, sexual abuse, assaults, and broken relationships to a brighter world where her daughter would be proud of her, where she would become a woman capable of independence and love and would live with dignity. It is a journey toward the land of self-esteem.

E. Lynn Harris has written about love, friendships, and family. His first novel, *Invisible Life* (1991), is a coming-of-age story of a young black man who is confused about his sexuality. His search for answers and for lasting love brings him to New York where following a serious illness and death of a friend he is finally able to face the truth about himself. *Wild Women Don't Wear No Blues* (1993) is a nonfiction collection of writings by **Marita Golden** and fourteen other African American women authors. The pieces are very personal and provocative. The women talk about their experiences of love, lust, and a strong quest for freedom. They show us ways to become better men or women and how to create better loves.

Sonia Sanchez (1934–   ) is a prominent playwright and poet of this era. Her plays deal with the themes of love, beauty, time, change, **history**, and music. She examines black women's characterizations in her works to show the evolution of the black female through time. In her poetry collection *Like the Singing Coming off the Drums: Love Poems* (1998), Sanchez writes of the many forms love can take, such as burning, dreamy, disappointed, and vulnerable. **Ann Petry**'s (1908–1997) novel *The Narrows* (1953) deals with the forbidden love affair between a twenty-six-year-old black man and a wealthy married white woman. This classic novel deftly evokes a racially divided era in America's not-so-distant past. **Elizabeth Nunez**'s novel *Grace* (2003) is a moving love story. It shows us how a deferred dream can take its toll on a marriage and how life can sometimes put us to the test. Another one of her novels, *Discretion* (2002), is written in oral storytelling style. Here she explores monogamy versus the African culture of polygamy. The main character faces the dilemma of loving two women at once. In fiery language, bell hooks (1952–   ) writes about racism and sexism. Yet her book *All About Love: New Visions* (2000) explores the ultimately elusive question, "What is love?" *All About Love* shatters the **myths** of the sentimental and often fleeting aspects of love such as lust. She explores the problems that frequently arise from the confusion between the two; hooks reveals that the true force of love lies in its spiritual, redemptive power.

Nikki Giovanni's (1943–   ) poetry is well known for its call for black people to realize their identities and understand their surroundings as a part of a white-controlled culture. She is considered a leader in the black poetry movement. Her poetry collection *Love Poems* (1997) contains bold, romantic, and some erotic poems such as "Seduction," "I Wrote a Good Omelet," and "My House." **Rita Dove** explores the mother-daughter **drama** of love in her book of poetry *Mother Love* (1995).

Two important collections of short stories and novel excerpts by black women writers edited by Mary Helen Washington were published in 1975 and 1980. *Black-Eyed Susans* contains the voices of groundbreaking female authors such as **Toni Morrison**, Jean Smith, **Gwendolyn Brooks**, **Toni Cade Bambara**, **Alice Walker**, and **Paule Marshall**. For the first time in literature black women were defining themselves and breaking the **stereotype** of the black woman as strong but shrill. The stories all deal with the experience of being black and female. Two topics that specifically deal with the theme of love are black mother/daughter relationships and the disappointment of romantic love. In the second collection, *Midnight Birds*, the voices are more brave and free. Women's friendships and solidarity form the basis for new love for these women now. They demonstrate the strength found in each other's help and support.

As is evident so far, narratives written during slavery had little room for romantic or familial love. As more of the freed slaves began writing, the early works began showing an awareness of sexuality. These works primarily deal with love in terms of sexual relationships. The real liberation of the soul took a long time to happen. We see more and more narratives dealing with the emotional complexities of love in contemporary African American literature written by both men and women. Gwendolyn Brooks's ***Maud Martha*** (1953), for example, is about an ordinary woman living her ordinary life who faces racism, sexism and classism every day. This simple act of being able to experience love in its natural form was missing in literature written during slavery. Toni Morrison explores ambiguous areas of love in her novels such as *Jazz* (1992), ***Beloved*** (1987), and ***Sula*** (1973), where **violence** is paradoxically an act of love. Eva Peace in *Sula* kills her son Plum to save him from lifelong suffering caused by his emasculated existence. In *Beloved* the mother kills her baby daughter to spare her from a life of slavery. Both of these mothers choose physical death over the death of the spirit for their children. Equally ambiguous in moral terms is Joe Trace's murder of his lover Dorcas in *Jazz*. The novel shows how racial tensions and oppression can lead to distorted love. Alice Walker in her 1983 Pulitzer Prize–winning novel ***The Color Purple*** equates abusive behavior with an expression of self-hatred and shows that healthy self-definition stems from self-knowledge and self-love. She portrays lesbian love as natural and freeing. Her novel *The Way Forward Is with a Broken Heart* (2000) is an exploration of love, sex, and friendship. The autobiographical story "To My Young Husband" contains a series of letters written by a black woman to her white ex-husband.

No feminist study of black literature would be complete without mentioning **Gloria Naylor**'s (1950–   ) novel ***The Women of Brewster Place*** (1983). The stories of seven women whose lives touch each other at Brewster Place make up the novel. The novel deals with many complex issues, but in the end there is hope. Love and hope serve as a backdrop for social ills such as homophobia, racism, sexism, violence, and alcoholism. **Audre Lorde** (1934–1992) often described herself as "a black lesbian feminist mother lover poet." She wrote poetry about racism in the feminist movement, sexism among African Americans, and about **lesbianism** and love. She said that there is no such thing as universal love in literature. There are only specifics. As such, almost every work of literature can be said to be about love, since it is a basic human instinct.

Works About

hooks, bell. *Salvation: Black People and Love.* New York: William Morrow, 2001.
Robotham, Rosemarie. *The Bluelight Corner: Black Women Writing on Passion, Sex, and Romantic Love.* New York: Three Rivers Press, 1998.
Smiley, Tavis, ed. *Keeping the Faith: Stories of Love, Courage, Healing, and Hope from Black America.* New York: Doubleday, 2002.

Pratibha Kelapure

LOVE

Toni Morrison's eighth novel, *Love* (2003), is set on the East Coast in the 1990s in a town called Silk. The book recounts the traumatic lives of the women who orbit Bill Cosey, the owner of Cosey's Hotel and Resort, once a prestigious vacation spot for African Americans. *Love* is a culmination of the themes in Morrison's earlier novels: the sexual abuse of a child, the spiritual bond of girlfriends, intra and interracial tensions within the black **community**, the intricate emotional ties of **family**, the complexity of mother love, the nuances of madness, and the power of the black patriarch.

As in Morrison's second novel *Sula* (1973), a friendship between two girls from different socioeconomic classes drives the story. Too young to recognize culturally designated difference that might otherwise separate them, Christine (granddaughter of Bill Cosey) and Heed the Night (illiterate daughter of poor parents) form a bond of friendship that ultimately transcends the restrictive, selfish, and sexualized relationships of the adult world. However, the girls, both scarred in early adolescence by Bill Cosey's sexual impulses yet trapped by their desire for his approval, attention, and affection, allow their **love** for each other to manifest itself as hate for over fifty years.

The rift begins when fifty-two-year-old Cosey commits the novel's unspeakable act: He marries the eleven-year-old Heed. Cosey refrains from intercourse with his child bride for a year, until she begins to menstruate. When they return from their delayed three-day honeymoon, the bewildered Heed finds an enemy where she had left a friend. Encouraged by her mother's prompting, Christine feels displaced in her grandfather's affections, but Heed does not understand her friend's anger. Each girl's sense of betrayal develops into a literal and figurative battle of wills that drives the story.

The novel opens with Christine and Heed in their sixties, both living in the Cosey mansion but separated by two floors, an obscurely worded will, and a shared resentment. Never fully conquering her illiteracy and unable to erase the community's **memory** of her lower-**class** origins, Heed has spent her life in the shadow of her long-deceased husband, "Papa," whose portrait hangs above her bed. She is also emotionally scarred by the miscarriage of her only pregnancy, the result of a single adulterous affair. Christine, sent to boarding school by a mother battling madness, has lived a distinctly different life. After a failed marriage to a cheating Private, a long stint in the **civil rights movement** with a man named Fruit, three arrests, seven abortions, a brief respite in a house of prostitution, and a three-year affair with a married doctor that ends with her displacement and arrest, Christine returns to Silk in 1976 with a few pair of underwear and the twelve diamond engagement rings her grandfather had won at cards. Although she nominally returns to tend her dying and insane mother, she stays even after her mother's **death**, intent on reclaiming her inheritance.

Cosey's will, scratched in the margins of a hotel menu, bequeathed the bulk of the estate to his "sweet Cosey child," an appellation both Christine and Heed claim. Their two-decade-long battle intensifies with the arrival of Junior Viviane, a young woman with wild hair, a short skirt, merged toes, and long leather boots. Junior, a character who would have felt at **home** at the Convent in Morrison's seventh novel *Paradise* (1998), has emerged from a life of poverty, illiteracy, and juvenile detention in answer to Heed's ad for a personal assistant. Willing to physically resist unwanted sexual advances (the Corrections Administrator attempts and fails to force oral sex from her), Junior also prefers rough sex. Her sexual relationship with fourteen-year-old Romen Sandler encapsulates in graphic form the relationships between Bill Cosey and his women. He abuses for his own gratification; however, the women, shaped by a patriarchal system that stunts their self-esteem, are complicit in their own subjugation. It is fitting that Junior and Romen's sexual relationship turns physically violent only in the attic of Cosey's long-abandoned hotel.

The hotel is also the site of Christine and Heed's ultimate reconciliation. Junior has taken Heed to the hotel to find a box of old menus, from which Heed plans to forge a will that leaves the estate more clearly to her. Christine follows, finding them in the hotel's attic just before the rotting floor gives way and Heed falls into the bedroom below. The scene allows a metaphoric regrounding: The world that Bill Cosey built, the very ground beneath their feet, collapses. Left together, alone, Heed's frail body broken, the two friends reconcile, reviving their secret childhood language and understanding that in different ways they had both been commodities, sold on a patriarchal market.

Regardless of whether Cosey "bought" Heed from her poverty-stricken parents as some suspect, Cosey's money did allow him certain freedoms. No one openly condemns his marriage to Heed because he is the wealthy, powerful, well-connected patriarch. Although individual characters privately condemn his act, the novel itself refrains from condemning Bill Cosey the man. As Morrison readers expect, a morally questionable (and arguably reprehensible) act is contextualized within a cultural and psychological domain. Cosey is not the saint Vida Sandler remembers him as, nor is he the "Good Man" of Junior's dreams. He is a man warped by his father's racial betrayal, prevented by cultural convention from marrying the one woman he truly loves, and abandoned to his own sense of power. Although this contextualization mediates his act, it does not excuse it. The women in his life pay the cost of his pain, loneliness, and unrestrained masculine impulse to create, control, and coerce.

The text offers Romen Gibbons as an alternative to Bill Cosey and his destructive abuse of patriarchal power. Early in the novel, Romen releases a girl tied and gang-raped at a party rather than take "his turn." Rejected by his friends who construct his act as one of weakness and betrayal, Romen finds temporary solace and self-respect in his rough sexual relationship with Junior. By novel's end, however, Romen rejects a violent articulation of **black masculinity** for a compassionate one. Romen speeds to the hotel to help the Cosey women. Although he brings only one back alive, the friends remain united in spirit.

The italicized voice that closes the novel—the same voice that opens it—is that of L., the title character and a voice from beyond the grave. Christine and Heed remember L., Cosey's longtime cook, as the only stable adult in their lives. However, by novel's end, L. is also revealed as the controlling force in the text, ultimately thwarting even Bill Cosey's desires. After Cosey makes a will bequeathing everything to the "sporting woman" Celestial, who figures throughout the novel as his one true love, L. poisons him, substituting her own version of his will, the one scrawled on a hotel menu. L.'s act redirects Cosey's fortune and the lives of the Cosey women, bringing them together in hate so that they could find love.

L. tells the reader that every story has a monster. In *Love*, it may be the Police-heads, mysterious creatures who rise from the sea to punish wayward women and children; it may be men who turn women's love for them into hate for each other; or it may be the power of love itself. Ultimately, Bill Cosey destroyed the lives of the women who loved him because they let him, the novel's warning to women. Its promise: If love for men can destroy them, love for each other can save them.

See also Literacy; Sexuality; Violence

Works About

Davis, Thulani. "Book & the Arts—Morrison: *Love*." *The Nation*, December 2003, 30–31.

Green, Charlie. Review of *Love*, by Toni Morrison. *Missouri Review* 27.1 (2004): 182–183.

"Nobelist Morrison Writes of Love." *Library Journal* 128.10 (2003): 92–95.

Julie Cary Nerad

LUCY: A NOVEL

"My mother...was a betrayer of her sex," **Jamaica Kincaid** remarks as she draws a connection between the mother character in her 1990 novel *Lucy* and her own mother, Annie Drew (Listfield). In *Lucy*, a novel Kincaid says is filled with "thick female stuff," she wants to be "very frank," "unlikable," and "even unpopular" (Listfield; Perry 506). *Lucy*, she insists, is not about "**race** and **class**" but instead is about "a person figuring out how to be an artist, an artist of herself and of things" (Kennedy). In *Lucy*, Kincaid, who was born Elaine Potter Richardson, continues her ongoing fictional recreation of her early life begun in her coming-of-age novel *Annie John* (1983) as she describes her experiences after leaving Antigua and coming to the United States to **work** as a nanny. Because of the similarities in the experiences and memories of Annie John and Lucy Josephine Potter, who shares Kincaid's birthday and the surname of her biological father, Roderick Potter, and because of the close connection between Kincaid's life and that of her characters, informed readers are likely to read *Lucy* as a sequel to *Annie John*. *Lucy* is connected to but also represents an important departure from *Annie John* as it records Kincaid's experiences after she left Antigua and as it describes Kincaid's attempt to forge a new invented writer's **identity** and to become the self-possessed "Jamaica Kincaid" rather than the mother-dominated "Elaine Potter Richardson."

The linear, but fragmented, sections of the novel describing Lucy's first year in the United States are so constantly interrupted by Lucy's intrusive memories of her past on a small unnamed island in the Caribbean that she seems to live as much in the past as in the present in an unnamed city, unspecified places that readers knowledgeable about Kincaid's life readily identify as Antigua and New York City. Plagued by the same depressive feelings that overwhelmed Annie John, Lucy, as she settles into the **home** of the wealthy white couple—Lewis and Mariah—who have hired her to serve as an au pair, recognizes the grip that the past has on her as she obsessively recalls her Antiguan **family**. Ambivalent in her response to Mariah, Lucy is in part drawn to and even idealizes Mariah, but she also repeatedly expresses scorn for Mariah's joyful embrace of life, which becomes symptomatic to Lucy of Mariah's political naïveté and unthinkingly privileged way of life.

Once told by her mother that she was named for Lucifer, Lucy turns this maternal insult into a badge of honor. Even though Lucy/Lucifer represents an oppositional "bad" identity—an identity forged in defiance of the repressive societal rules and regulations enforced by the shaming mother—Kincaid's character, despite her physical separation from her mother, still exists, as she comes to see, in the shadow of her powerful, and powerfully injuring, mother. When Mariah learns that Lucy was deeply hurt when growing up because her mother preferred her sons over her daughter, she explains the universality of Lucy's experience of gender shaming and gives Lucy a copy of Simone de Beauvoir's *The Second Sex* to read, but Lucy eschews the universalizing assumptions of de Beauvoir's feminist theory, focusing instead on her own subjective experiences as a daughter. Continuing the story of Annie John by recalling the scene in which Annie's mother denounced her daughter for behaving like a slut, Lucy writes a cold and condemning letter to her mother in which she declares that she finds her life in the United States as a slut very enjoyable. But behind Lucy's defiant anger and bitterness lies a deep sense of woundedness, for she has spent ten of the twenty years of her life, as she comes to recognize, mourning the end of her great **love** affair with her rejecting mother. Aware that she is reinventing herself, Lucy, as she begins to write in the journal given to her by Mariah at the end of the novel, remains a prisoner of her unhappy past as she becomes an artist not only of **memory** but also of anger and despair.

See also The Autobiography of My Mother

Works About

Bouson, J. Brooks. *Jamaica Kincaid: Writing Memory, Writing Back to the Mother.* Albany: SUNY Press, 2004.

Ferguson, Moira. *Jamaica Kincaid: Where the Land Meets the Body.* Charlottesville: University Press of Virginia, 1994.

Kennedy, Louise. "A Writer Retraces Her Steps: Jamaica Kincaid Finds Herself in Her Words." *Boston Globe*, November 7, 1990, Living Section, 85. Lexis-Nexis Academic Universe. web.lexis-nexis.com.

Ledent, Bénédicte. "Voyages into Otherness: *Cambridge* and *Lucy*." *Kunapipi* 14.2 (1992): 53–63.

Listfield, Emily. "Straight from the Heart." *Harper's Bazaar* 123 (October 1990): 82.

Mahlis, Kristen. "Gender and Exile: Jamaica Kincaid's *Lucy*." *Modern Fiction Studies* 44.1 (1998): 164–183.

Paravisini-Gebert, Lizabeth. *Jamaica Kincaid: A Critical Companion.* Westport, CT: Greenwood Press, 1999.

Perry, Donna. "An Interview with Jamaica Kincaid." *Reading Black, Reading Feminist: A Critical Anthology.* Ed. Henry Louis Gates. New York: Meridian-Penguin, 1990. 492–509.

Simmons, Diane. *Jamaica Kincaid.* New York: Twayne-Macmillan, 1994.

J. Brooks Bouson

 **M**

MAJOR, CLARENCE (1936–)

With more than two dozen books to his credit, Clarence Major's prolixity is matched only by his artistic versatility. Born in Atlanta, Georgia, in 1936 to Clarence and Inez (Huff) Major, Major's artistic ability was evident at a very young age. In *Come By Here: My Mother's Life* (2002), Major's memoir of his mother, Inez Major proudly recounts the story of when Clarence's schoolteacher, Mrs. Bellamy, shows her his drawing of a car, pointing out that Clarence's car, unlike the other children's cars, had four wheels rather than only two and how this was a sign of exceptional artistic ability. Mrs. Bellamy advised Mrs. Major to encourage her son, suggesting that one day he would make her proud.

By 1948 Major would be taking art lessons from Gus Nall in Chicago and, between 1951 and 1953, was attending the prestigious Art Institute of Chicago on a fellowship. If Major demonstrated a **love** of drawing and painting rather early in life, he also showed a passion for reading and writing (and Major's novels make it clear that painting has greatly influenced his writing and his interest in formal experimentation). According to Inez Major, while attending Wendell Phillips Elementary School in Chicago, the same school **Nella Larsen** attended between 1901 and 1907, young Clarence would come home from the Oakwood Public Library with a stack of books; Clarence spent so much time reading that she, though encouraged, worried about him not getting enough exercise. But his mother's fears would be replaced with pride when in 1954 *The Fires That Burn in Heaven*, Major's first book of **poetry**, was printed. Major's writing life had begun.

With the publication of *Come By Here*, readers of Major's work are better able to appreciate the important role his mother played and continues to play in his life. Though authored by Major, *Come By Here* is Inez Major's story as recounted in first person by Inez herself. One of Major's strengths is his ability to create strong female voices, and in *Come By Here*, Inez's voice, as she tells of her life in the segregated **South** and then in Chicago, comes through poignantly, often passionately, with little or no sentimentality. And while, from a feminist standpoint, it could be argued that in *Come By Here* Inez's voice is subordinated (because mediated) by her son's—as critics have argued is the case in the court scene in **Zora Neale Hurston**'s ***Their Eyes Were Watching God*** (1937), in which Janie's voice is subordinated to Hurston's— Major has made it clear in a number of interviews that he believes it is possible for a man to write from a woman's perspective, and vice versa. Major's pen has given birth to a number of memorable women, including Annie Eliza, the black matriarch of *Such Was the Season* (1987).

In *Such Was the Season, Come By Here*, and *Painted Turtle: Woman with Guitar* (1988), Major deftly creates powerful women with distinct voices and personalities, and each of these works has been well received by feminist critics who have found in Annie Eliza, Inez Major, and Painted Turtle unique, independent spirits, making their way in singular fashion, often unaided (Inez) or in defiance of her people (Painted Turtle). And while Major has been praised for his ability to write from a female point of view, his first and most controversial novel, *All-Night Visitors* (1969), an amalgamation of four or five failed novels, has drawn a lightning storm of criticism for the way in which the male protagonist objectifies women.

All-Night Visitors, set in Chicago, is the story of a young black man, Eli Bolton, and his attempt to piece together not only the "jigsaw puzzle of [his] heritage" but of his fragmented life. Abandoned by his mother as an infant, Eli was raised in an orphanage, where he was beaten severely by the violent female warden, watched a young boy gut a puppy with a switchblade, and felt an undefined sexual attraction for the cook who, with her "coal-black skin" and "giant tits," was not only the object of his desire but the source of a deep longing for his absent mother. In one of the more graphic scenes in the novel, Eli, now in Vietnam, recounts a "sadistic inhuman monstrous incident" in which Moke and Dokus Mangy, two fellow soldiers, violently **rape** and kill a child, an incident that would haunt Eli throughout his life.

But while violent scenes such as this are rare in *All-Night Visitors*, Eli's protracted sexual encounters with a host of women, from dropouts and runaways to Harvard-bound college students, are not. From Tammy, the twenty-year-old homeless woman, whose name, the narrator tells us, is not really important, to Anita, with her natural fellatio skill, the women who come in and out of Eli's life are simply objects, "things" meant to satisfy his sexual desire. In the opening scene of the novel, Eli comes home to find Tammy, who he has taken in, sleeping, and he begins to think of a way to get her to wake up and perform oral sex on him. He does not want to have sex with her because the dried sperm on her pubic hair turns him off; the clean receptacle of her mouth, he explains, is more appealing. And when Tammy would not wake up, Eli feels an evil streak come over him. He wants to *force* her. He wants to force her mouth open like a doll and choke her with his penis.

In Anita Eli finds a woman whose sexual knowledge, her ability to please men, is "in the very pores of her skin." This sexual knowledge, according to Eli, is like "deep wisdom," a knowledge that is in her genes, and Major puts Anita's knowledge on display in an oral sex scene that goes on for roughly ten pages. Both Tammy and Anita, to Eli, are sex objects, "the idea of a body, a commodity," nothing more, nothing less. And Eli's attitude suggests that women, or at least these women, are genetically wired to perform sexually. Neither Tammy nor Anita is granted a sense of individuality or autonomy. They are only seen through the eyes of Eli, whose misogynistic attitude toward women is the most blatant and unsettling aspect of this formally experimental novel.

While Tammy and Anita (and Eunice) function only to satisfy Eli's enormous sexual appetite, Cathy, a young white woman and a "volunteer in service to America" (VISTA), has a more positive affect on Eli. As he does with all of the other women he encounters, Eli longs to possess Cathy sexually. Yet Cathy is different from the other women in Eli's life. When Cathy leaves to go to California, Eli becomes depressed, and he realizes Cathy had become a kind of mental crutch for him. But in stark contrast to his past relationships, Eli regains the ability to love through his relationship with Cathy. Cathy functions as a catalyst for Eli's regeneration. And while Cathy's role, in this sense, is admirable, the emphasis, as it has been throughout the novel, is on Eli Bolton (*El* in Hebrew, Eli tells us, means god), and women only serve to bolster his existence. The only altruistic act we see Eli perform in *All-Night Visitors* comes when he invites a Puerto Rican woman and her children into his apartment, evidence of his newly regenerated capacity to love.

If in *All-Night Visitors* women are simply objects of the male protagonist's sexual desire, and therefore play a subordinate role, in *Such Was the Season*, with Annie Eliza at center stage, Major shows his ability to create a character whose sense of individuality and autonomy, despite being in her late sixties, is still intact. *Such Was the Season* is Annie Eliza's first-person account of her nephew Juneboy's weeklong visit to her **home** in Atlanta, Georgia. In contrast to Major's early novels, *Such Was the Season* is told in a straightforward narrative and has a wonderfully intimate feel to it. Because Annie Eliza is personally telling us—whom she often addresses directly as "child" or "girl"—her story, we are able to get inside Annie Eliza's head and to appreciate her self-described old-fashioned ways. She admits to being just a "plain down-to-earth common sense person." It is also clear, however, that Annie Eliza is quite serious. Her **religion** is very important to her, as is her **family** (Annie Eliza has two sons, Jeremiah, a preacher, and DeSoto, a police officer), but when Jeremiah gets caught up in the Greenhouse Tomato conspiracy, she is unwilling to shield him from the wheels of justice (social or divine).

While Annie Eliza feels an abiding fealty toward her family and friends, she does not hesitate to criticize those with whom she disagrees. She endlessly criticizes Renee, Jeremiah's wife, for her materialism and her modern ways, and while she eventually supports Renee's decision to run for elected office (and changes her party affiliation from Republican to Democrat, to the dismay of some of her friends), her initial reaction betrays a latent conservatism, a conservativism evidenced by her (admittedly paradoxical) reaction to Jeremiah's **sermon** on women's rights. She believes that women have all the rights they deserve and that they tend to mess up the ones they already have. And that, she says, is "the truth!" Yet Annie Eliza goes on to criticize Jeremiah for not preaching about strong, liberated women, like Mary in the Bible. She begins to think about her own mother and how she is the perfect example of a strong woman, one who "took her own rights and made everybody respect them." Major will say the same thing about his own mother in *Come By Here*.

In Annie Eliza we get a portrait of a woman in all her complexity. Her voice, like her independent spirit, is strong and her attitude, feisty. One moment she is telling Juneboy (a pathologist) that he is welcome to stay with her for a year if he wants to, yet in the next she admits to being tired of having him around. His presence has not only exiled her to the couch but has made her life feel scattered. Major's achievement here is his ability to bring Annie Eliza to life, to give her the same kind of vitality that would mark the life not only of his mother, Inez, but also that of the legendary Zuni, Painted Turtle.

Painted Turtle: Woman with Guitar is the story of Mary Etawa, a Zuni folksinger and poet who, Old Gchachu prophesied, would become legendary among the Zuni. While Major's first five novels are formally experimental, *Painted Turtle* is equally unique in form and style, combining both poetry and prose, and captures beautifully the story of a young woman struggling to find her voice in song. Raped and subsequently impregnated at a very young age, eventually giving birth to twins (a sign of bad luck), Mary Etawa, known as Painted Turtle, becomes a prostitute and leaves her people for the cantina circuit, playing her songs of sorrow and redemption to sleepy drunks in sleepy towns throughout the Southwest. Painted Turtle's story is narrated by Baldwin "Baldy" Saiyataca, a Navajo-Hopi mixed-blood musician and Painted Turtle's lover, the man to whom Painted Turtle would tell her story. Major began this novel with Painted Turtle recounting her own story firsthand, as Annie Eliza would in *Such Was the Season* and Inez would in *Come By Here*. Unable to find Painted Turtle's voice, he turned to a male narrator, yet Painted Turtle's voice comes through in her songs and in Major's prose if we listen closely as her life unfolds.

The **beauty** of Major's poetry and prose comes from its highly visual nature. As a skilled painter, Major has translated his visual **literacy** into the kind of prose that leaps off the page, giving us portraits of multifaceted women like Annie Eliza, Painted Turtle, and, of course, Inez Major, for whom Major's artistic accomplishments are not only a cause for celebration but a source of great pride.

Works By

All-Night Visitors. 1969. Unexpurgated ed., Boston: Northeastern University Press, 1998.
Come By Here: My Mother's Life. New York: John Wiley, 2002.
Configurations: New and Selected Poems, 1958–1998. Port Townsend, WA: Copper Canyon, 1998.
The Dark and Feeling: Black American Writers and Their Work. New York: Third Press, 1974.
Dirty Bird Blues. San Francisco: Mercury House, 1996.
Emergency Exit. New York: Fiction Collective, 1979.
Fun and Games: Short Fictions. Duluth, MN: Holy Cow!, 1990.
The Garden Thrives: Twentieth Century African-American Poetry. New York: HarperCollins, 1996.
Juba to Jive: A Dictionary of African-American Slang. New York: Viking, 1994.
My Amputations. New York: Fiction Collective, 1986.
Necessary Distance: Essays and Criticism. Minneapolis, MN: Coffee House Press, 2001.
NO. New York: Emerson Hall, 1973.
One Flesh. New York: Dafina, 2003.
Painted Turtle: Woman with Guitar. Los Angeles: Sun and Moon Press, 1988.
Reflex and Bone Structure. New York: Fiction Collective, 1975.
Some Observations of a Stranger at Zuni in the Latter Part of the Century. Los Angeles: Sun and Moon Press, 1989.
Such Was the Season. San Francisco: Mercury House, 1987.
Swallow the Lake. Middletown, CT: Wesleyan, 1970.
Symptoms and Madness. New York: Corinth, 1971.
Waiting for Sweet Betty. Port Townsend, WA: Copper Canyon Press, 2002.

Works About

Bell, Bernard W. *The Afro-American Novel and Its Tradition.* Amherst: University of Massachusetts Press, 1987.
——, ed. *Clarence Major and His Art: Portraits of an African American Postmodernist.* Chapel Hill: University of North Carolina Press, 2001.
Bradfield, Larry D. "Beyond Mimetic Exhaustion: The *Reflex and Bone Structure* Experiment." *Black American Literary Forum* 17 (1983): 120–123.
Bunge, Nancy, ed. *Conversations with Clarence Major.* Jackson: University Press of Mississippi, 2002.
Klinkowitz, Jerome. *The Life of Fiction.* Urbana: University of Illinois Press, 1977.

Benjamin D. Carson

MALCOLM X (1925–1965)

Malcolm X was a Black Nationalist leader whose birth name was Malcolm Little. He made famous speeches on racism and the **civil rights movement** and was critical of other African American civil rights leaders' strategies of integration and nonviolence; he called for active protest against white racism and proclaimed Pan-African internationalism. He wrote *The Autobiography of Malcolm X* (1966) with the help of African American writer **Alex Haley** in 1963–1964; it was published posthumously. His speeches are also published in several books such as *Malcolm X Speaks* (1990).

Malcolm X was born in 1925 to a Baptist preacher, Reverend Earl Little, and his wife Louise. Earl Little was a loyal follower of Marcus Garvey, a Black Nationalist from Jamaica, and a member of the Universal Negro Improvement Association. Louise was an educated **mulatto** born as the result of **rape** by a white man. Their **family** lived in constant threat from the Ku Klux Klan (KKK) while Earl Little preached Garvey's **Black Nationalism**, called "Back to Africa," to the black **community**. Their house was burned by the KKK, and in 1931, when Malcolm was six, Earl Little was run over by a trolley car. People in the community believed that he was killed by the local KKK. After Earl's **death**, Louise took care of the family by herself for several years, but later she had a nervous breakdown and was institutionalized in Kalamazoo. Her children were separated and sent to foster homes.

In spite of his family difficulties, Malcolm X was a successful and popular student. He was elected class president by white classmates in the seventh grade. However, when he expressed his wish to be a lawyer, his favorite teacher told him that it is "no realistic goal for a nigger." This experience disappointed him so deeply that he shut down his feelings from white people and the American system. When he was fourteen, he left school and went to Boston to live with his sister Ella. Although his sister was well established in the black community, he quickly became involved in criminal life. He became a hustler, a pimp, and a thief, gaining his nickname "Detroit Red." He was arrested for burglary and sentenced to ten years in prison, which is an unusually long period for such a crime. In prison, he was introduced to the Nation of Islam (NOI), whose adherents are commonly known as Black Muslims. NOI was first established in 1930, following W. D. Fard's teaching, and Fard's mentee Elijah Muhammad was the leader of the NOI. Besides learning about Islam, Malcolm read various books about **religion** and philosophy and developed a deeper understanding of Islamic teaching and politics surrounding black people.

After he was released from prison, he joined the Nation of Islam and changed his last name to X. He married Betty Sanders, whose name was Betty X after she joined NOI, in Lansing in 1958. They had six daughters, including the twins Betty was pregnant with when he was assassinated. He became a Muslim minister in New York and a famous spokesperson for Black Muslims. His speeches were eloquent and powerful, so he drew attention from blacks and the media. As Malcolm become more famous and popular, other Black Muslim leaders, including Muhammad, felt threatened and jealous. Malcolm also started to criticize Muhammad for his lavish lifestyle and affairs with women. Upon John Kennedy's assassination, he commented that Kennedy "never foresaw that the chickens would come home to roost so soon," although Muhammad ordered him not to comment on the assassination. Malcolm X was suspended, and he finally broke with Muhammad and the NOI the next year, 1964. He organized "Muslim Mosque, Incorporated (MMI)," a Black Nationalist political organization.

After Malcolm X left NOI, he traveled to Africa, the Middle East, and Europe, where he made speeches in parliaments and met the heads of states in many countries. In Mecca, where he earned his religious name El-Hajji Malik El-Shavazz, he started to think that people of other races, including white, could be allies against racism. He organized the Organization of African American Unity (OAAU), through which he tried to develop Pan-African internationalism. At the African Summit Conference he attended to represent the OAAU, he called attention to the issue of blacks in the United States. His trip abroad also changed his attitude toward women. He was impressed and influenced by the active role of women in African organizations. Black Muslims emphasize women's **domestic** role and patriarchal order, and Malcolm X's speeches reveal a patriarchal view of women. However, his organization gave a more active and equal role to women than did the Nation of Islam. Women in the NOI were not allowed to be part of the decision-making process. In the OAAU, Lynn Shrifflet had the leading role from its establishment in 1964, and one of the active leaders was Sara Mitchell. During his trips, he was welcomed by political and social leaders in many African and Middle Eastern countries; the French government, however, did not permit his entrance to the country.

On February 21, 1965, when Malcolm X started to speak at an OAAU rally, he was fatally shot. Talmadge Hayer, Norman 3X Butler, and Thomas 15X Johnson were arrested for his murder and sentenced to life in prison. Since he had become famous, he often felt his life was threatened, and his house was fire-bombed in 1965. He often said publicly that Black Muslim leaders wanted to kill him, but the day before his assassination, he told Alex Haley that he had started to think that the people who were trying to kill him were not Black Muslims.

His outspoken, eloquent, direct speeches about **race** and Black Power inspired and appealed to blacks and also scared many white people. He was called a "black supremacist," a "hatemonger," and a "dangerous fanatic." The moderate civil rights movement activists also considered him an extremist. He was cynical about the moderate civil rights movement of Martin Luther King, Jr. He believed that integrating into American society would not liberate blacks but that uniting and offering strong resistance would.

See also Autobiography

Works By

The Autobiography of Malcolm X. 1966. New York: Ballantine Books, 1999.
Malcolm X Speaks: Selected Speeches and Statements. Ed. George Breitman. New York: Grove Weidenfeld, 1990.

Works About

Baldwin, James. *One Day When I Was Lost: A Screenplay Based on the Autobiography of Malcolm X.* New York: Dial, 1973.
Bloom, Harold. *Alex Haley & Malcolm X's The Autobiography of Malcolm X.* Philadelphia, PA: Chelsea, 1996.
Breitman, George, ed. *Assassination of Malcolm X.* New York: Pathfinder, 1976.
——. *The Last Year of Malcolm X: The Evolution of a Revolutionary.* New York: Merit, 1967.
Clarke, John Henrik. *Malcolm X: The Man and His Times.* New York: Macmillan, 1969.
Davies, Mark. *Malcolm X: Another Side of the Movement.* Englewood Cliffs, NJ: Silver New York University Press, 1996.
Gallen, David. *Malcolm X: As They Knew Him.* New York: Carroll and Graf, 1992.
Goldman, Peter. *Death and Life of Malcolm X.* Urbana: University of Illinois Press, 1973.
Sales, William W., Jr. *From Civil Rights to Black Liberation.* Boston: South End, 1994.
Stickland, William. *Malcolm X: Make It Plain.* New York: Penguin, 1994.
Wolfenstein, Eugene. *The Victims of Democracy: Malcolm X and the Black Revolution.* Berkeley: University of California Press, 1981.

Youngsook Jeong

MAMA

Set in the 1960s, **Terry McMillan**'s first novel *Mama* (1987) is a narrative of a poverty-stricken black **family** that resides in the fictional Point Haven, Michigan. A departure from many contemporary African American novels that feature portrayals of child rearing, *Mama* is a revisionary text that deconstructs the **myth** of **motherhood** to include discussions about the tensions between ideal motherhood and realistic versions of this role. Mildred Peacock, the wife of Crook Peacock and mother of five children, Freda, Money, Doll, Angel, and Bootsy, struggles to keep her family together throughout bouts with an abusive, drunken husband and poverty.

The title of the novel suggests that readers will witness the ins and outs of a mother of a typical black northern family. Ironically, however, the setting of the novel and the images used to describe the text imply that the Peacock family is indeed a typical black family, but one similar to that of a southern plantation family. The streets of Point Haven are mostly packed dirt. The houses are rundown and resemble shacks, and many of the homes lack a father figure. In homes such as the Peacocks', a father figure is present, but readers are alerted to the fact that this is only temporary, as the marriage between Crook and Mildred is volatile. Moreover, the 1960s setting suggests that readers should pay attention to the oppression that the women in the novel suffer at the hands of the black male characters. Ironically, the 1960s is a moment in black **history** where racial uplift was the mantra; however, the residents of Point Haven were not beneficiaries of such movement.

Throughout the novel, readers witness Mildred's transformation from a woman who places significant value on pregnancy and childbirth to a divorced mother of five on welfare, to a factory worker, then a prostitute, and finally, an entrepreneur in the sense that she opens her own day-care center by the end of the novel. In the early stages of her transformation Mildred hangs on to dominant Eurocentric ideologies regarding femininity and motherhood. Although her first marriage is dissolved, she holds out hope for marital bliss; however, her focus has changed. Her subsequent marriages are defined by necessity and practicality. Mildred learns early on that marriage for **love** does not fit her historical subjectivity as a black woman. Instead, she marries for food for her children and money for rent.

Similar in many ways to McMillan's life, the narrative of *Mama* reminds us of the problematic relationship between dominant ideologies and black women's realties. Set during a time of racial uplift, McMillan presents a female character who learns to redefine womanhood on her own terms.

Works About

Dandridge, Rita. "Debunking the Motherhood Myth in Terry McMillan's *Mama*." *CLA Journal* 41.4 (1998): 405.
Eisenbach, Helen. "Profile of a First Novelist: Terry McMillan and Mama." *Writer's Digest* 67 (1987): 58.

Catherine Ross-Stroud

MAMA DAY

Mama Day (1988) by **Gloria Naylor** captures a black **community** separate from the mainland United States in geography and ideology. The people of Willow Springs develop and maintain their own customs, their own sense of **spirituality**, and their own life's tempo. The progenitor of Willow Springs is Sapphira, a woman who somehow obtained the deed to the land and her bill of sale from the slave master Bascombe Wade. These two acts firmly set her in charge of her own fate and the future of Willow Springs. In this authority, she names her seven sons for Old Testament prophets. The next generation produces seven sons with New Testament names. Miranda Day, who comes to be called Mama Day, is one of three daughters of the next generation.

Then there are Peace, Grace, and Hope before the final generation in first cousins Ophelia (Cocoa) Day and Willa Prescott Nedeed (of ***Linden Hills***, 1985).

Day is the name that Sapphira gives to her descendants, and by **family** order it sticks regardless of marriage. The genealogy in the front of the book indicates that Willa disregarded this family rule. Whether in the Day line or not, all the residents of Willow Springs look to Sapphira as a kind of great mother with divine or magical powers. For them she is the beginning of life in Willow Springs, not Bascombe Wade, and they look to Mama Day for guidance in the present. Mama Day is herself a spiritual force whom residents seek out for **healing**, going beyond the natural if necessary. She is seemingly interminable, close to 100 years old and showing no signs of decline.

Mama Day is as much about the **love** story of George and Cocoa as it is about community, healing, and faith. It is the relationship between Cocoa and her new husband George that drives the reader and the plot to Willow Springs. The island's customs are baffling to George because he has no sense of community or family, as he was raised in a **home** for boys. In this alienation from his roots, George represents the growing body of African Americans who have no sense of their **history** and their relationship to their communities. George was intimidated by Cocoa's sense of her family legacy and confused by the community's dependence on what he considered to be illogical, inefficient customs such as building a bridge to the mainland only sturdy enough to last until the next storm.

For all its emphasis on women's strength, the novel is troubled by the mother/daughter relationship. The relationship between Mama Day and Cocoa is perhaps the closest mother/daughter relationship in the novel; they are actually great-aunt and great-niece, not mother and daughter. However, the relationships of biological mothers and daughters in the novel are corrupted by insanity and finally **death**. Mama Day's own mother and Cocoa's mother succumbed to their insanity.

Although a jealous Willow Springs woman put a hex on Cocoa, Cocoa will not yield to the insanity that plagues her because George ultimately sheds his own blood as a messiah figure to save her life. At the novel's end, George's spirit is still in Willow Springs, and Cocoa goes to visit and talk to him once a year as they rehash their story, trying to get it right.

Works About

Cowart, D. "Matriarchal Mythopoesis: Naylor's *Mama Day*." *Philological Quarterly* 77.4 (1998): 439–459.

Korenman, Joan S. "African-American Women Writers, Black Nationalism, and the Matrilineal Heritage." *CLA Journal* 38.2 (1994): 143–161.

Pearlman, Michel. "An Interview with Gloria Naylor." *High Plains Literary Review* 5 (Spring 1990): 98–107.

Perry, Donna. "Gloria Naylor." *Backtalk: Women Writers Speak Out.* Ed. Donna Perry. New Brunswick, NJ: Rutgers University Press, 1993. 217–244.

Prahlad, Sw. Anand. " 'All Chickens Come Home to Roost': The Function of Proverbs in Gloria Naylor's *Mama Day*." *Proverbium: Yearbook of International Proverb Scholarship* 15 (1998): 265–281.

Puhr, Kathleen M. "Healers in Gloria Naylor's Fiction." *Twentieth Century Literature: A Scholarly and Critical Journal* 40.4 (1994): 518–527.

Sharese Terrell Willis

MAMMY

The Mammy **stereotype** originated during the late antebellum period, as one of a number of caricatures developed to refute the growing body of eyewitness testimonies—in **slave narratives**, abolitionist newspapers, and memoirs—of the harsh brutality of **slavery**. The Mammy figure—middle-aged or elderly, obese and dark-skinned, hardworking and loyal, her satisfaction with her subordinate position evident in her broad smile and hearty laugh—was developed as a rejoinder to northern white readers' growing awareness of the sexual subjugation of black female slaves. While first-person accounts like **Harriet Jacobs**'s *Incidents in the Life of a Slave Girl* (1861) and *Narrative of the Life of Frederick Douglass* (1845), depict black women servants terrorized by the sexual desires of their masters and, in the case of Harriet Jacobs, willing to take extreme measures to escape his predatory desires, representations of the Mammy depict her as proud to serve the white **family** that owns her and even willing to risk her life in defense of her white employer-owners. At the same time, her age, obesity, and skin color were interpreted through the aesthetic lens of white supremacy and, as such, were presented as irrefutable evidence of Mammy's inherent unattractiveness to white men.

"Aunt" or "Auntie," the titles by which Mammy was most often known (hence the **Aunt Jemima** of pancake-flour fame and Aunt Chloe, the loyal matron in Harriet Beecher Stowe's *Uncle Tom's Cabin* [1852]) overtly suggest her acceptance as "one of the family" by the household that she served. At the same time, however, the "Auntie" label suggests the degree to which any identities or attachments (as wife or mother) to her black family were subordinated to the interests of the white landowners she served. Indeed, a key component of the Mammy **myth** is her prioritization of the welfare of her master's children over the nurturance and upbringing of her own. In addition, the "Auntie" title, with its allusion to family, implies a connection between Mammy and her white mistress and master that, while intimate, is unambiguously nonsexual.

Historical evidence indicates that the Mammy was primarily a figure of myth, with little basis in the reality of plantation life. The popular image of antebellum slave life, characterized by gracious mansions, surrounded by acres of fields, tended by dozens of African American workers who performed every duty from agricultural labor to household maintenance to child care, is largely the product of late-nineteenth-century nostalgia and fantasy, reinforced and further disseminated in the first half of the twentieth century through **films** like *Birth of a Nation* (1915) and *Gone With the Wind* (1939). In reality, however, the overwhelming majority of white slaveholders could afford no more than a few slaves, most of whom were needed for fieldwork and other agricultural duties.

If the fiscal realities of slavery fail to support the economic viability of the Mammy phenomenon, so too do the social realities of slavery undermine the physical stereotypes associated with that figure. Many historians have pointed out that the realities of household servitude under slavery point to a woman servant whose physical attributes are very much in contradiction to those associated with the Mammy stereotype. In those households that did employ slaves as domestics laborers, house servants tended to be young (fewer than 10 percent of black women lived past fifty years of age), thin (black slaves were poorly fed), and of mixed-**race** descent, quite the opposite of the fat, jolly, matron of plantation myth.

As a mythic figure, however, the Mammy has permeated almost every aspect of U.S. culture, influencing the popular perception of slavery, subservience, and black womanhood even into the present day. Many scholars have suggested that the prototype for this figure was first introduced in Harriet Beecher Stowe's *Uncle Tom's Cabin*, in the figure of Aunt Chloe, introduced in the following passage: "A round, black, shiny face is hers, so glossy as to suggest the idea that she might have been washed over with the whites of eggs.... Her whole plum countenance beams with satisfaction and contentment from under a well-starched checkered turban." The link between Stowe's vision of a plantation Mammy and the many representations of that figure to follow is clear. As influential as Stowe's physical description of Mammy would turn out to be, however, it was her reference to Aunt Chloe's **domestic** skill—"Aunt Chloe was universally held and acknowledged" as "the first cook of the neighborhood"—that foreshadowed the most common incarnation of this image, in the form of what author Phil Patton refers to as a "commercial icon."

Indeed, Mammy has achieved her widest recognition, her greatest longevity, and her deepest incursion into the heart of the American **home** and into the collective imagination of the United States as a commercial image. Much attention has been paid in recent years to depictions of Mammy in film—Hattie McDaniel's iconic portrayal of Mammy (for which she received African America's first Academy Award) in *Gone With the Wind*, Louise Beavers's 1934 portrayal (and Juanita Moore's 1959 reprisal) of a Mammy-like servant in the "tragic **mulatto**" melodrama *Imitation of Life*, and others. Indeed, these productions created lasting and heartfelt images that continue to both attract and disturb viewers today. Any qualities or associations reflected in these roles only reinforced the messages that were being transmitted in U.S. households every day, through white and black Americans' daily contact with a veritable army of household products that used images of the Mammy as a trademark.

In addition to Aunt Jemima pancake products, there was Luzianne coffee, Aunty brand citrus fruits, and a variety of household laundry detergents, cleansers, produce brands, and baking supplies. Add to these the variety of functional decorative items depicting the Mammy, primarily intended for use in the kitchen and dining rooms. Such objects included cookie jars, salt and pepper shakers, syrup dispensers, toothpick holders, and peg boards. The overall effect of these items was to associate household maintenance—especially cleaning and food preparation—with the cheerful subservience of the black domestic. At the same time, Mammy's bright gaze and contented smile—staring out at white homemakers from their kitchen walls and cabinets, refrigerator shelves, and countertops—conferred a form of approval on their efforts, an approval that was noteworthy. As Phil Patton explains, the ubiquitous presence in white women's households of images of these " 'idealized servant types,' especially during the first half of the 20th century, suggested heartiness, quality, [and] the approval of those who really ran the kitchen, who knew food."

While modified, updated Mammy images still appear on a handful of products, this figure primarily lives on in film and on television. Contemporary depictions of the Mammy serve a far more troubling purpose than the simple approval for white women's domestic efforts their commercial and decorative counterparts confer. In their happy and dedicated service to white families—by both their literal presence within their white television homes and their implied presence within the homes of their white viewers—the Mammy-like protagonists in films like Queen Latifah's *Bringing Down the House* and television programs like Nell Carter's *Gimme a Break* offer absolution to white descendants of Euro-American slave owners and to those whose connection to slavery is indirect but whose white skin privilege is rooted in the unequal hierarchy of the slave system. Their adoption of the white employers' personal interests and challenges as their own communicates that most conciliatory and comforting of all messages, for which Mammy is most beloved—above and beyond her smiling countenance, her witty rejoinders, and her expert cooking skills. In her happy service and unshakable loyalty Mammy comforts all those who see her with the simple message that simple, hardworking black people like herself desire nothing more than that status that is conveyed by the **love** of one's white employers.

See also Douglass, Frederick; Neely, Barbara; Plantation Tradition

Works About

Bogle, Donald. *Toms, Coons, Mulattoes, Mammies, and Bucks: An Interpretive History of Blacks in American Films*. New York: Continuum, 1994.

Goings, Kenneth. *Mammy and Uncle Mose: Black Collectibles and American Stereotyping*. Bloomington: Indiana University Press, 1994.

Patton, Phil. "Mammy: Her Life and Times." *American Heritage* (1993): 78–87.

Ajuan Maria Mance

MARSHALL, PAULE (1929–)

Paule Marshall has emerged as a major writer of feminist, African American, and Caribbean American **fiction** in the latter half of the twentieth century. Born of Barbadian parents, Marshall writes narratives of self-discovery often embodied in black female characters but encompassing larger social critiques of gender, **race**, and economics in Western capitalist culture. Marshall's body of **work** includes five novels and two collections of short stories. For her works, the most well known of which are ***Brown Girl, Brownstones*** (1959), ***The Chosen Place, the Timeless People*** (1969), and ***Praisesong for the Widow*** (1983), Marshall has garnered prestigious awards such as a Guggenheim Fellowship, the Columbus Foundation American Book Award, and a MacArthur Foundation Fellowship. Her stories chronicle the pitfalls of sexism, racism, and materialism in Western culture but reveal the hope of renewal through the embracing of cultural heritage and communal relationships.

Born in 1929 in Brooklyn, New York, Marshall spent her childhood within a close Caribbean and immigrant **community**. Her parents came from Barbados and returned with nine-year-old Marshall for an influential visit after which the budding writer was inspired to compose her first lines of **poetry**. Since those early verses, Marshall's writing has explored the female and Caribbean voices of her youth with affection and honesty. In her famous essay "The Making of a Writer: From the Poets in the Kitchen" in *Reena and Other Stories* (1962), Marshall credits the gathering of her mother's friends around the kitchen table for teaching and inspiring the art within her. From the hours of conversation she overheard, Marshall says, she learned to weave a story with grace, truth, and humor.

Marshall's grappling with the obstacles of black life in Western culture have been appreciated by many scholars including biographer Joyce Pettis and critics Dorothy H. Dennison, Hortense J. Spillers, and Barbara Christian. Marshall's writing follows many different characters as they struggle to define themselves within a materialist culture that devalues African and West Indian heritage. Some of her characters, like Marshall herself, travel back to their Caribbean homeland and rediscover a wholeness missing from their lives. The journey of self-discovery becomes symbolic and thematically connects much of Marshall's oeuvre.

In her exploration of dominated peoples in a patriarchal and capitalist culture, Marshall's writing can also be considered globally feminist. Not only does she examine issues specifically feminine such as familial and marriage relationships, **motherhood** and childbirth, and female friendship and community, but Marshall's work also illustrates alternate forms of self-identification in a dominant culture. Finding strength in the tension of community rather than in strict self-reliance, and epiphany within cultural tradition rather than in typical Western self-enlightenment, marks Marshall's writing as largely feminist in scope.

Many of Marshall's young female protagonists spend their childhood attempting to balance the demands of **family** versus the outside culture. As children of immigrant parents, Marshall's characters must learn to balance their own growing dreams with the expectations of a demanding community. Selina, in *Brown Girl, Brownstones*, constantly negotiates the conflicting demands of her mother and father, as well as those of her new American **home** and her West Indian heritage. Likewise, Merle and Avey, in *The Chosen Place, the Timeless People* and *Praisesong for the Widow*, respectively, must figure out how to first define themselves as wives and then redefine themselves as women after their marriages end. In both marriage and family responsibilities, Marshall's characters often encounter some aspect of African or West Indian heritage that helps them unearth new paths toward self-discovery.

Motherhood and childbirth recur in Marshall's texts as constant issues in the lives of her female characters, representing both mothers and daughters. Not only do the characters face these questions of **identity** common to most women, but they also must look past their roles as someone's mother or daughter to find fulfillment. Marshall does not allow her protagonists to become dominated by their role as wife, mother, or daughter but instead portrays their struggles as individuals in tension with those roles. ***Daughters*** (1991) especially confronts the role of motherhood and childbirth in the personal lives of the characters Estelle and Ursa as well as the political life of the country of Triunion; abortion becomes a central metaphor for loss, pain, and ultimately the regeneration of the personal and the communal.

Female friendship and community are constant backdrops in Marshall's stories. From her own **love** of her mother's friends to the many descriptions of women's communities in her writing, Marshall clearly locates both problems and solutions in the gathering of women. Often groups of black and immigrant women provide both tension and support for the development of Marshall's protagonists. Selina must struggle against her mother's group of friends in order to find her own individuality, for example, but where the community does not exist for Avey in *Praisesong for the Widow*, the character must seek it out in order to find **healing** within herself.

Marshall's stories should be considered feminist for the many themes she develops around women's emotional, physical, and spiritual lives. But her constant interest in her male and female characters' ability to heal and regenerate can be understood as more broadly feminist. Whereas the traditional Western masculine narrative locates an individual's enlightenment in internal and intellectual exploration, Marshall's texts demand her characters' interaction with the self and the community. Incorporating individualism and communal identity, present cultural norms as well as ethnic heritage, Marshall's characters do not focus on the self to the exclusion of all else. On the contrary, Marshall illustrates that the only possibility for healing an oppressive **history** and encouraging an egalitarian future comes through interaction with self and community. The tensions created by her characters' honest confrontations of these many pressures place her within feminist discourse.

While many of Marshall's themes focus primarily on female characters and community, men also figure prominently in her stories. Not all of Marshall's characters are female, nor are they all of African or West Indian descent. But the lives of African Americans and women come to represent the inequalities present in an often disjointed and materialistic mainstream American culture. The journeys toward wholeness that Marshall's characters experience offer a path to healing and self-integration available to the culture as a whole. Marshall shows that rejuvenation is possible for those willing to confront often painful histories to reconcile generations of oppression.

Marshall has lectured in creative writing and black **literature** at many prestigious institutions such as Yale, Columbia, and Oxford. She currently holds the Helen Gould Sheppard Professor in Literature and Culture at New York University.

See also Fisher King, The

Works By

Brown Girl, Brownstones. 1959. Afterword by Mary Helen Washington. Old Westbury, NY: Feminist Press, 1981.
The Chosen Place, the Timeless People. 1969. New York: Vintage, Random House, 1984.
Daughters. 1991. New York: Plume, Penguin Books, 1992.
The Fisher King. 2000. New York: Scribner, 2001.
Praisesong for the Widow. 1983. New York: Plume, Penguin Books, 1992.
Reena and Other Stories. 1962. Old Westbury, NY: Feminist Press, 1983.
Soul Clap Hands and Sing. 1961. Introduction by Darwin T. Turner. Washington, DC: Howard University Press, 1988.

Works About

Billingslea-Brown, Alma J. *Crossing Borders through Folklore: African-American Women's Fiction and Art.* Columbia: University of Missouri Press, 1999.
Brock, Sabine. "Transcending the 'Loophole of Retreat': Paule Marshall's Placing of Female Generations." *Callaloo* 10.1 (Winter 1987): 79–90.
Collier, Eugenia. "The Closing of the Circle: Movement from Division to Wholeness in Paule Marshall's Fiction." *Black Women Writers (1950–1980): A Critical Evaluation.* Ed. Mari Evans. Garden City, NY: Anchor Press/Doubleday, 1984. 295–315.
Coser, Stelamaris. *Bridging the Americas: The Literature of Paule Marshall, Toni Morrison, and Gayl Jones.* Philadelphia: Temple University Press, 1995.
DeLamotte, Eugenia C. *Places of Silence, Journeys of Freedom: The Fiction of Paule Marshall.* Philadelphia: University of Pennsylvania Press, 1998.
Denniston, Dorothy H. *The Fiction of Paule Marshall: Reconstructions of History, Culture, and Gender.* Knoxville: University of Tennessee Press, 1995.
Pettis, Joyce. *Toward Wholeness in Paule Marshall's Fiction.* Charlottesville: University Press of Virginia, 1995.

Spillers, Hortense J. "Chosen Place, Timeless People: Some Figurations on the New World." *Conjuring: Black Women, Fiction, and Literary Tradition.* Ed. Marjorie Pryse and Hortense J. Spillers. Bloomington: Indiana University Press, 1985. 151–175.

Laura Baker Shearer

MATTHEWS, VICTORIA EARLE (1861–1907)

Victoria Earle Matthews was among the literary elite of her day, a national leader in the struggle for the rights of black women, and an instrumental figure in the social reform to "uplift" African Americans. When she was thirty-three, a column in *Woman's Era* predicted her name would become a household word. Given her contributions, American **history** has made little notice of her, perhaps because of her early **death** to tuberculosis at age forty-five or because many of her writings have been lost.

Matthews succeeded through much adversity in her life, a path she worked to recreate for other women of her **race**. Born a slave in Fort Valley, Georgia, Victoria Earle endured a cruel master who her mother escaped from after several attempts. Victoria's mother earned enough money after eight years to return for her **family** to bring them to New York. Once in school, Victoria showed great promise as a student but was forced to leave school to help provide for her family. She found employment in a **home** with an extensive library, which her employer allowed her to use when time permitted.

At eighteen, she married William Matthews and began a successful journalistic career. Initially she substituted for reporters at several prominent daily papers, such as the *New York Times* and *New York Herald*. Eventually she became a highly sought-after reporter, by both black and white newspapers.

Matthews's extant writings portray her as an advocate for and educator of her race. Through her columns she defended the morality of black women and the progress of African Americans; she also wrote tributes to heroes of abolition. "We owe it to our children to uncover from partial oblivion and unconscious indifference the great characters within our ranks," she says in a piece on Harriet Tubman. Of the nine short stories she published in the *A.M.E. Church Review*, three have survived. Perhaps Matthews's best-known work, "Aunt Lindy: A Story Founded on Real Life," represents one of the first uses of a dialect-speaking Negro as a central character. She also edited a collection of works by Booker T. Washington in *Black-Belt Diamonds* (1898).

Complementing Matthews's **work** as a writer was her leadership among organizations advocating for her race and sex. She helped sponsor a fund-raising rally for anti-lynching crusader **Ida B. Wells-Barnett** in 1892. The same year she also established the Women's Loyal Union of New York and Brooklyn. In

1895, Matthews joined the effort to organize a national black women's club by speaking at the first National Conference of Colored Women on "The Value of Race Literature," highlighting the accomplishments and distinctiveness of African American literary works. She later became chair of the executive committee of the Federation of Afro-American Women.

With the death of her only child in 1897, Matthews followed a calling to help other people's children. She established the White Rose Industrial Association after witnessing how southern black women became exploited as prostitutes when migrating to northern cities. Inside the Association's home, new arrivals to New York City found shelter and training in **domestic** skills, as well as access to a library rich in African American history and **literature**. It is believed she contracted tuberculosis doing her mission work at the wharves in New York Harbor.

Works By

"Aunt Lindy: A Story Founded on Real Life." By Victoria Earle. New York: J. J. Little and Co., 1893.

Black-Belt Diamonds: Gems from the Speeches, Addresses and Talks to Students of Booker T. Washington. Ed. Victoria Earle Matthews. New York: Fortune and Scott, 1898.

"The Value of Race Literature: An Address Delivered at the First Congress of Colored Women, Boston, Massachusetts, 1895" and "The Awakening of the Afro-American Woman." *With Pen and Voice: A Critical Anthology of Nineteenth-Century African-American Women.* Ed. Shirley Wilson Logan. Carbondale: Southern Illinois University Press, 1995. 126–148, 149–155.

Works About

Brown, Hallie Quinn. *Homespun Heroines and Other Women of Distinction.* Xenia, OH: Aldine, 1926. Reprint, New York: Oxford University Press, 1988. 208–216.

Davis, Elizabeth Lindsay. *Lifting as They Climb.* Washington, DC: National Association of Colored Women, 1933. 232–234.

Dickson, D. Bruce, Jr. *Black American Writing from the Nadir: The Evolution of a Literary Tradition, 1877–1915.* Baton Rouge: Louisiana State University Press, 1989. 51–55.

Lawson, Scruggs. *Women of Distinction: Remarkable in Works and Invincible in Character.* Raleigh, NC: Scruggs, 1893. 30–32.

Logan, Rayford W. *The Negro in American Life and Thought: The Nadir, 1877–1901.* New York: Dial, 1954. 322.

Mossell, N. F. *The Work of the Afro-American Woman.* New York: Oxford University Press, 1988. 61–63.

Osofsky, Gilbert. *Harlem, the Making of a Ghetto: Negro New York, 1890–1930.* New York: Harper and Row, 1963. 56–57.

Penn, I. Garland. *The Afro-American Press and Its Editors.* 1891. New York: Arno Press, 1969. 375–377.

Shockley, Ann Allen. *Afro-American Women Writers, 1746–1933: An Anthology and Critical Guide*. Boston: G. K. Hall, 1988. 181–184.

Caleb A. Corkery

MAUD MARTHA

Gwendolyn Brooks's only novel, published in 1953, relates the autobiographical coming-of-age story of a poor, dark-skinned African American woman living on the South Side of Chicago during the 1930s and 1940s. The novel comprises thirty-four brief chapters, or vignettes, that offer not a narrative about its heroine but rather glimpses of her intellectual and emotional struggles on various occasions during her childhood and young adulthood. Some of these occasions are traditional landmarks in a girl's maturation into womanhood: her grandmother's **death**, her first boyfriend, her marriage, the establishment of her married **home**, and the birth of her first child. Others emphasize the heroine's day-to-day existence: children on their way to elementary school, the young couple reading in bed, and Maud Martha's struggle to dress a chicken, for example. Overall, the novel immerses us in the ordinariness of Maud Martha's life, which is uniquely her experience but, simultaneously, representative of the vast majority of lives. By giving us a complex, imaginative heroine who identifies more with the dandelions in her backyard than with the rarer **beauty** of lilies, Brooks teaches her reader to value the commonplace.

Critics tend to concentrate on the novel's aesthetics and thematic coherence. Brooks brings the tightly compressed but vividly precise language of her **poetry** to her prose work. Each chapter conveys a mood, delicately evoked through telling images. She effectively employs juxtaposition, alliteration, fragmentation, and repetition—stock tools of the poet's trade—in delineating moments in Maud Martha's development. By representing Maud Martha as sensitive, creative, and acutely observant, Brooks gives us a portrait of the artist as a young woman. Brooks's aesthetic choices enable her to suggest succinctly such broadly resonant themes as the relationship between life and death, the damaging effects of white racist and black color-conscious definitions of beauty, and the chafing constraints that gender norms place on potentially extraordinary women.

The novel has been instructively compared with **James Baldwin**'s *Go Tell It on the Mountain* (1953) and **Ralph Ellison**'s *Invisible Man* (1952), which were published contemporaneously with it. While Ellison's and Baldwin's debut novels garnered serious critical attention and appreciation, only quiet and cursory notice was given to *Maud Martha*, despite Brooks's status as a Pulitzer Prize–winning poet. **Black feminist** critics subsequently attributed this difference in reception not only to the shorter length and stylistic innovations of Brooks's work but also to the extent that it frustrated expectations that African American novels would portray a protagonist's heroic response to epic and tragic racial conflict. *Maud Martha* instead relentlessly filters issues of **class**, **race**, and gender oppression through the interior world of its heroine, who in turn remains confined within the claustrophobic **domestic** realm. It is ironic that this novelistic critique of the silencing of women was marginalized precisely because it speaks, though in a third-person narrative voice, almost entirely through Maud Martha's thoughts and impressions. Only recently has the novel been recognized as significant in the African American literary tradition, especially as a forerunner of the particular concerns of late-twentieth-century black women novelists.

Works About

Christian, Barbara. "Nuance and the Novella: A Study of Gwendolyn Brooks's *Maud Martha*." *Black Feminist Criticism*. New York: Pergamon Press, 1985. Reprinted in *A Life Distilled: Gwendolyn Brooks, Her Poetry and Fiction*. Ed. Maria K. Mootry and Gary Smith. Urbana: University of Illinois Press, 1987. 239–253.

Lattin, Patricia H., and Vernon E. Lattin. "Dual Vision in Gwendolyn Brooks's *Maud Martha*." *Critique* 25 (Summer 1984): 180–188. Reprinted in *On Gwendolyn Brooks: Reliant Contemplation*. Ed. Stephen Caldwell Wright. Ann Arbor: University of Michigan Press, 1996. 136–145.

Shaw, Harry. "*Maud Martha*: The War with Beauty." *A Life Distilled: Gwendolyn Brooks, Her Poetry and Fiction*. Ed. Maria K. Mootry and Gary Smith. Urbana: University of Illinois Press, 1987. 254–270.

Washington, Mary Helen. "Plain, Black, and Decently Wild: The Heroic Possibilities of *Maud Martha*." *The Voyage In: Fictions of Female Development*. Ed. Elizabeth Abel, Marianne Hirsch, and Elizabeth Langland. Hanover: University Press of New England, 1983. 270–286.

Evie Shockley

McELROY, COLLEEN (1935–   )

An award-winning writer of poems, stories, dramas, and memoirs, Colleen Johnson McElroy has spent much of her life in motion. Born in 1935 in St. Louis to Ruth Celeste and Purcia Purcell Rawls, McElroy's parents divorced when she was three, leading to her first move, into her grandmother's **home**. It was there, while playing with her grandmother's Victrola, that McElroy developed a "romance with language." When Ruth married army sergeant Jesse Johnson in 1943, the **family** resettled in various locations, including Germany and Wyoming. After earning an associate's degree at Harris-Stowe College in 1956, she attended the University of Maryland and the University of Pittsburgh before earning her bachelor's and master's of science degrees in language patterns at Kansas State University. McElroy worked as a speech clinician and a television talk show moderator before completing her doctorate at the University of Washington in 1973, when she joined the faculty. In 1983, she became the first black woman at the University of Washington to be promoted to full professor.

McElroy's passion for language has assumed both scholarly and creative dimensions. In 1972, she published a study of language development in preschoolers, followed the next year by her first collection of **poetry**, *The Mules Done Long Since Gone*. This chapbook grew out her frustration with 1960s-era poems that mythologized African American women's experiences. Inspired by her Washington surroundings—as much by fellow poets Richard Hugo and Denise Levertov as the rainy, mountainous landscape—McElroy's early poetry draws upon her discovery of black poets like **Anne Spencer**, **Gwendolyn Brooks**, **Margaret Walker**, **Langston Hughes**, and Robert Hayden. She has since published nine collections of poetry, including *Queen of the Ebony Isles* (1984), which won the Before Columbus Foundation's American Book Award in 1985. In *Queen*, McElroy explores territories both familial and exotic, moving from mother-daughter relationships through Latin American travels to comic book heroines.

The recipient of numerous National Endowment for the Arts (NEA) fellowships and Fulbright residencies, McElroy has traveled widely, listening to storytellers and learning new ways to render human experience. Not surprisingly, her writing often draws from **memory**, whether the experience originates in her past or is sparked by someone else's words. Her story collections *Jesus and Fat Tuesday* (1987) and *Driving Under the Cardboard Pines* (1990) explore acts of complicity and resistance, from the controversial seduction/**rape** of a nineteenth-century backwoods girl ("A Brief Spell by the River") to the joyride of a black war widow through postriot Watts ("Sister Detroit"). In 1999, her passion for storytelling and travel converged in *Over the Lip of the World: Among the Storytellers of Madagascar*, a collection of translations and travel memoirs. Attuned to ways language transcends time, place, and **race**, McElroy is a writer constantly returning "home/a stranger in love with words/with tart sweet clusters of poems."

Works By

Bone Flames. Middletown, CT: Wesleyan University Press, 1987.

Driving Under the Cardboard Pines and Other Stories. Berkeley, CA: Creative Arts Books, 1990.

Jesus and Fat Tuesday and Other Short Stories. Berkeley, CA: Creative Arts Books, 1987.

Lie and Say You Love Me: Poems. Tacoma, WA: Circinatum Press, 1981.

A Long Way from St. Louie: Travel Memoirs. Minneapolis, MN: Coffee House Press, 1997.

Looking for a Country under Its Original Name. Yakima, WA: Blue Begonia Press, 1984.

The Mules Done Long Since Gone. Seattle, WA: Harrison-Madrona Press, 1972.

Music from Home: Selected Poems. Carbondale: Southern Illinois University Press, 1976.

Over the Lip of the World: Among the Storytellers of Madagascar. Seattle: University of Washington Press, 1999.

Queen of the Ebony Isles. Middletown, CT: Wesleyan University Press, 1984.

Travelling Music: Poems. Ashland, OR: Story Line Press, 1998.

What Madness Brought Me Here: Collected Poems—1968–88. Wesleyan Poetry Series. Hanover, NH: University Press of New England, 1990.

Winters without Snow. San Francisco: I. Reed Books, 1979.

Works About

"Colleen J. McElroy." faculty.washington.edu/dragnldy/poet.

Koolish, Linda. *African American Writers: Portraits and Visions*. Jackson: University Press of Mississippi, 2001.

Ontles, Linden. "An Interview with Colleen J. McElroy." *Writer's Chronicle* (October–November 2000): n.p.

Strickland, Daryl. "Seattle's Black Voices—For Authors of Color, the Local Literary Scene Is Filled with Promise." *Seattle Times*, February 16, 1997, M1.

Rebecca Meacham

McKAY, CLAUDE (1889–1948)

Claude McKay, poet, novelist, and journalist, was born Festus Claudius McKay on September 15, 1889, in Jamaica, West Indies. Both of McKay's parents were farmers, and McKay's early **poetry** exhibited an interest in the life of "folk" people, like his parents, who were struggling to gain economic stability in an often-unstable economic environment. The youngest of eleven children, McKay was sent at an early age to live with an older brother and his **family** in order that he could gain access to a better education. McKay's brother was a schoolteacher who had a large collection of English novels, poetry, and scientific texts. McKay was encouraged to pursue his interest in reading and writing, and he began writing poetry at age ten. In 1907 while apprenticing to a wheelwright, McKay met Walter Jekyll, who would be influential in his development as a writer. It was due to Jekyll's influence that McKay constructed his early poetry using Jamaican Creole (a.k.a. Patois), in effect capturing the true essence of the "folk" culture from which he was raised. Jekyll would later set some of McKay's dialect verse to music.

In 1911 McKay became a constable in Spanish Town, Jamaica, an experience that would be reflected in his early poetry, *Songs of Jamaica* and *Constab Ballads* (both 1912). McKay's decision to write his poetry in Jamaican Creole spoke of his criticism of colonial and postcolonial British influence in the Caribbean. The collections *Songs of Jamaica* and *Constab Ballads* reflect McKay's social awareness as well as his understanding of the different economic locales he occupied; *Songs of Jamaica* deals with McKay's life in the country, while *Constab Ballads* reflects his time in urban Kingston and Spanish Town. McKay's concern for the working-**class** members of the **community** is maintained in his second collection of poetry. It is during his time as a constable that McKay gathered the material for his collection *Constab Ballads*. This collection not only reflects his experience in urban Jamaica; it provides insight into McKay's struggle to reconcile his societal position as a constable with his view of himself as product of a peasant community. This is perhaps most heartfelt in his poem "The Heart of a Constab." McKay's Jamaican Creole poetry helps to affirm his connection to his Caribbean **home** and demonstrate his awareness of the political climate in the Caribbean, an awareness that continued to appear in McKay's work even after his migration to the United States. McKay's determination, in Creole poetry, to link himself with the peasant populations is critical as it reflects the position McKay would take during the **Harlem Renaissance**, maintaining concern for and interest in the lifestyle of working-class blacks in Harlem.

Written under the pseudonym Hugh Hope, McKay's poem "Song of the New Soldier and Worker," though written in 1920 during McKay's "pre-communist period" and while he was living in England, clearly could have been applied to Jamaican country folk or to the low-class blacks of Harlem.

In 1912 McKay migrated to the United States to attend Tuskegee Institute in Alabama, hoping to pursue a career in agronomy. While at Tuskegee, McKay felt firsthand the reality of black and white relations in America, experiencing the overt racism that was still a way of life in the United States. From 1913 to 1914 he attended Kansas State University, studying agriculture, before moving to New York City in 1914. It was through the financial support of Walter Jekyll that McKay was able to make this move to the American North.

In 1917 McKay began publishing ("Invocation" and "The Harlem Dancer") under the pseudonym of Eli Edwards. McKay's notoriety came in 1919 when he published "If We Must Die" in Max Eastman's the *Liberator*; "If We Must Die" is often identified as one of the critical starting points of the Harlem Renaissance (a.k.a. New Negro movement). The poem was written during the Red Summer of 1919, a period of racial **violence** against blacks. The poem's ardent influence came not only from its insistence on maintaining the struggle for equality but also because of its open recognition of the humanity of African Americans and the black experience in America. McKay was identified by other writers of the Harlem Renaissance, such as **Langston Hughes** and **Countee Cullen**, as an inspirational leader. McKay's Harlem Renaissance **literature** focused on contemporary **race** issues. He chose to focus on the working-class community rather than the middle-class population that W.E.B. Du Bois and Alain Locke wanted to see exhibited in art during this time period. Du Bois's attempt to make the Harlem Renaissance a movement of art as a form of propaganda and his insistence that artists present positive images of a middle-class, educated, upwardly mobile community caused conflict for writers such as McKay who desired to represent a "true" image of the black experience in America. McKay and the members of the Harlem School of Writers resisted Du Bois's and Locke's political agenda and produced art that reflected the experience of the working-class people.

McKay's Harlem Renaissance poetry breaks from the literary tradition he developed in his writing in the West Indies. His use of the traditional sonnet form and standard English to discuss racial issues pertinent to early 1900 America was a noticeable change from his previous use of "folk" language. Despite McKay's shift in language, his interest in the working-class community is maintained and reflected throughout his literary pieces written in America and during his time in Europe.

Although the Harlem Renaissance is often presented as a Harlem-centered phenomenon, like many artists of the time McKay spent little time in Harlem. He lived in England from 1919 to 1921 where his interest in Karl Marx and Marxism began. McKay spent a year working for the Marxist periodical *Workers' Dreadnought*. Upon returning to New York in 1921 McKay began working for the *Liberator* as an associate editor. He continued to write, publishing the essay "How Black See Green and Red." *Harlem Shadows*, McKay's collection of poetry, was published the following year.

In 1922–1923 McKay journeyed to Russia and addressed the Third Communist International in Moscow. These years mark his expatriate years in Europe and North Africa. In 1925 McKay wrote and destroyed his first novel *Color Scheme*. In 1927 Alain Locke, often identified as the "father" of the Renaissance movement, published *Four Negro Poets*, which contained work by McKay.

McKay's novel *Home to Harlem* was published in 1928 with much acclaim, though not without some controversy. The novel's candid portrayal of the working-class Harlem community directly subverted the focus on middle-class ideals that was the hallmark of the Renaissance. *Home to Harlem* focused on the life of a young black soldier living in Harlem after his return from World War I. McKay has often been criticized for writing *Home to Harlem* in response to and modeled after Carl Van Vechten's *Nigger Heaven* (1926) in order to gain prominence from the coverage that *Nigger Heaven* had received. Although a relationship between the two texts cannot be denied, McKay's distinct and particular use of dialogue and his focus on the lower class of Harlem clearly distinguish his work from Van Vechten's.

In 1929, McKay published *Banjo* while living in France. Both McKay and the novel *Banjo* influenced Léopald Sédar Seghor, Aimé Césaire, and other participants of the Negritude movement.

Banana Bottom was published in 1933. This novel is McKay's literary return to the Caribbean, focusing on the homecoming of a young woman who had been sent to England to be educated. The book emphasizes the importance of a return to home and culture in determining **identity**.

McKay had moved to Morocco in 1930, but due to financial concerns, he returned to the United States in 1934. The following year he published the essay "Harlem Runs Wild." He participated in the Federal Writers' Project in 1936. McKay published his autobiographical text *A Long Way from Home* in 1937. In 1940 *Harlem: Negro Metropolis* was published.

McKay never returned to Jamaica, becoming a U.S. citizen in 1940. During the later years of his life, McKay suffered from high blood pressure and heart disease. Having previously given up his association with communism, McKay developed a strong Catholic faith, moving to Chicago in 1944 to work for the Catholic Youth Organization. McKay died of congestive heart failure in 1948 in Chicago; he was buried in New York following a service in Harlem. *My Green Hills of Jamaica*, McKay's second **autobiography**, was published post-humously in 1979.

From a feminist perspective, *Home to Harlem* is perhaps McKay's most crucial text. In a first reading of *Home to Harlem*, Jake, McKay's African American protagonist, appears to be a character of simple means, driven by his sexual desires and without any sense of morality. His movement throughout the novel is made possible by his encounters with women; these encounters are primarily sexual and exploitative. The women in the novel lack motivation and are political and socially unaware. They are portrayed as primitive beings driven by their **sexuality** and base emotion. The women reflect the racial and cultural biases of the Harlem community at that time. For most of the novel, the majority of women are limited to purely physical tasks–having sex, drinking alcohol, or fighting each other over the men.

On one level, *Home to Harlem* can be read as a romance novel, paralleling Jake's relationship and search for Felice. Jake's relationship with Felice serves to pull the novel together. Felice is the first woman, and appropriately the last woman, that Jake encounters when he is in Harlem. *Banjo*, where we find the couple still together and still "in **love**," clearly establishes the viability of Jake and Felice's relationship. The movement of the novel parallels Jake's search for Felice after they lose contact. However, Jake must assert his manhood before he and Felice can meet again. It is ironic that Jake's journey to manhood, signified by his search for Felice, is made possible through his demoralizing and limited relationships with women. Jake's movement in the novel is hinged on his relationships with women. *Home to Harlem* uses women as social markers, and this is particularly noticeable in the emphasis on color that pervades the novel. The narration uses color and erotic female images to characterize the local hangout, the Congo, as "African." Rose, the singer at the Congo, is compared to a leopard, a description that complicates any reading of the text. Rose is objectified throughout the novel; to Jake, she is a sexual object. Rose is, however, significant to Jake's "rite of passage," because she is symbolic of the type of woman that Jake can never commit to. Rose is the antithesis of the proper woman; the text renders Rose's character in a negative light, positing her as an unacceptable female figure. When Rose, in an attempt to pacify Jake, demands that Jake beat her, Jake's denial helps to solidify Rose's inadequacy. Rose acts as a springboard for Jake's psychological advancement; she provides Jake with a lesson that allows him to continue on his journey. McKay's representation of women as "steps" for male acquisition of status and power places women in a marginal position, leaving them without a viable voice and without a legitimate role within society.

Collections of McKay's works are held as follows: James Weldon Johnson Collection at Yale University; Schomburg and H. L. Mencken collections at the New York City Public Library; the William Stanley Brathwaite Papers at Harvard University; the Alain Locke Papers at Howard University; the NAACP Papers in the Library of Congress; the Eastman Papers at the University of Indiana, Bloomington; the Rosenwald Fund Papers at Fisk University; the Countee Cullen Papers at Dillard University.

Works By

Banana Bottom. 1933. Chatham, NJ: Chatham Bookseller, 1970.
Banjo. New York: Harper and Brothers, 1929.
Constab Ballads. Jamaica, 1912.
Gingertown. c. 1931. Freeport, NY: Books for Libraries Press, 1972.
Harlem: Negro Metropolis. New York: E. P. Dutton, 1940.
Harlem Shadows. New York: Harcourt, Brace and Company, 1922.
Home to Harlem. 1928. Chatham, NJ: Chatham Bookseller, 1973.
A Long Way from Home. 1937. New York: Harcourt, Brace and World, 1970.
Songs of Jamaica. Jamaica, 1912.

Works About

Cooper, Wayne F. *Claude McKay: Rebel Sojourner in the Harlem Renaissance: A Biography*. Baton Rouge: Louisiana State University Press, 1987.
Lee, Robert A. *Harlem on My Mind: Fictions of Black Metropolis*. New York: St. Martin's Press, 1988.
LeSeur, Geta. *Claude McKay's Marxism*. New York: Garland, 1989.
McLeod, A. L. *Claude McKay as Historical Witness*. New Delhi: Sterling, 1989.
Nelson, Emmanuel S. *Community and Individual Identity in the Novels of Claude McKay*. New Delhi: Sterling, 1992.
Tillery, Tyrone. *Claude McKay: A Black Poet's Struggle for Identity*. Amherst: University of Massachusetts Press, 1992.

Josie Brown-Rose

McKISSACK, PATRICIA (1944–   )

Patricia L'Ann Carwell McKissack grew up in the segregationist **South** experiencing many of the horrors and inequities of Jim Crow. These experiences left her with a deep understanding of the necessity to have representative voices that tell the countless stories of the people of the United States. After graduating from Tennessee State University in Nashville in 1964, McKissack married her college sweetheart Fredrick and became a junior high school teacher in Missouri. As the mother of three boys, Fredrick Jr. and twins Robert and John, and years spent as a teacher, McKissack witnessed firsthand the lack of writings for children that underscored African American heritage and culture. In the face of this drought, McKissack picked up her pen and began to write of the African American way of life.

The depth of McKissack's narrative can be attributed, in part, to her experiences growing up in a **family** that practiced and appreciated oral storytelling. Her maternal grandmother and fraternal grandfather often regaled the family with stories of what it was like growing up African American during the early decades of the twentieth century. These stories fueled her mind and planted a seed that prepared her for a storytelling future. McKissack's **historical fiction** and nonfiction narratives celebrate wide-ranging African American experiences and contributions that bring alive the facts and figures of African American **history** in an accessible way for children. Although McKissack writes of both male and female leading characters, many of her books present prominent female characterizations that position young African or African American girls as role models for young readers today. McKissack designs her work to be suitable for the youngest reader, with stories that include *Ma Dear's Aprons* (1997), *Goin' Someplace Special* (2000), and *Flossie and the Fox* (1986), and for older readers including *A Picture of Freedom: The Diary of Clotee, a Slave Girl* (1997), *Color Me Dark: The Diary of Nellie Lee Love, the Great Migration North* (2000), and *Nzingha: Warrior Queen of Matamba* (2000), all showcasing outstanding young female heroines.

McKissack and her husband have worked together on many publications. These collaborations include the *Great African Americans* biography series that relates the lives of **Ida B. Wells-Barnett**, **Mary Church Terrell**, **Zora Neale Hurston**, and Madam C. J. Walker, to name only a few. McKissack's writings, which number over 100, have received numerous awards including the Newbery Honor Award, Coretta Scott King Award, *Boston Globe/Horn* Award, and Image Award for Outstanding Literary Work for Children. In 2004 McKissack won the King Author Honor Book award for her 2003 publication *Days of Jubilee: The End of Slavery in the United States*.

Works By

African-American Inventors. Brookfield, CT: Millbrook Press, 1994.

African-American Scientists. Brookfield, CT: Millbrook Press, 1994.

Aztec Indians. Chicago: Children's Press, 1985.

Black Hands, White Sails: The Story of African-American Whalers. New York: Scholastic, 1999.

Cinderella. Illustrated by Tom Dunnington. Chicago: Children's Press, 1985.

The Civil Rights Movement in America from 1865 to the Present. Chicago: Children's Press, 1987. 2nd ed., 1991.

Color Me Dark: The Diary of Nellie Lee Love, the Great Migration North. New York: Scholastic, 2000.

Madam C. J. Walker: Self-made Millionaire. Illustrated by Michael Bryant. Berkeley Heights: Enslow, 1992.

Work About

Roethler, Jacque. "Three Phases of the Black Aesthetic—Ann Petry's *Tituba of Salem Village*, Eloise Greenfield and Lessie Jones Little's *Childtimes*, and Patricia McKissack's *Sojourner Truth: Ain't I a Woman*." *Journal of African Children's and Youth Literature* 6 (1994–1995): 56–73.

Wanda G. Addison

McMILLAN, TERRY (1951–   )

Born in Port Huron, Michigan, on October 18, 1951, Terry McMillan is the daughter of Madeline Washington Tillman and Edward McMillan. After her parents' divorce when McMillan was thirteen, her mother supported the **family** by working in a factory. One of six children, McMillan attended Michigan public schools, where as a library worker she discovered works by black authors such as **James Baldwin** and **Zora Neale Hurston**; however, at this point, McMillan admits to not reading these authors out of embarrassment and fear. Moreover, McMillan was not sure if these black writers would have anything different to say than Thomas Mann, Henry David Thoreau, and Ralph Waldo Emerson.

It was not until junior college at the City College of Los Angeles that McMillan became reacquainted with black writers. Her enrollment in an African American **literature** course is where she finally read Baldwin and Hurston. While inspired by these writers, she was also influenced by the work of **Langston Hughes** and **Frederick Douglass**. McMillan asserts that she did not consider emulating these authors. McMillan goes on to explain that she was just reading them at the time, not thinking of herself in any way as a writer. She was just in awe that there were black people who wrote books.

After her completion of studies at Los Angeles City College, McMillan spent six years as a student at the University of California in Berkeley, where she initially considered majoring in sociology. Still not defining herself as a writer, McMillan began writing political essays and editorials for a magazine called *Black Thoughts*. Soon she was recruited as a writer for the university magazine.

In her junior year at Berkeley, McMillan was required to declare a major. Still not defining herself as a writer, McMillan was perplexed as to what major she should choose. After initially choosing sociology as her major, she soon discovered that it was not intellectually and spiritually sustaining. It was not until her adviser suggested journalism that McMillan was able to envision herself in a profession that would be fulfilling, though she still ignored her gift as a writer. She did not consider something (writing) that came so easily to her as warranting serious consideration as a career choice. McMillan was reminded by her adviser that difficulty choosing a career is not a requirement for being taken seriously as an adult. Instead, one should choose a career path that one has a passion for instead of one that is expected. Armed with her adviser's advice, McMillan officially declared journalism as her major.

Although McMillan declared journalism as her major, she soon discovered that this, too, was not fulfilling. It was not until McMillan's senior year at Berkeley, when enrolled in a **fiction** course taught by **Ishmael Reed**, that she recognized her connection with words. There she acknowledged her passion for creative writing. It was also in Reed's course where her short story "The End" was published. On the advice of Reed, McMillan moved to New York upon her graduation from the University of California, Berkeley, in 1979, with a journalism degree in hand.

In New York, at the advice of Reed, McMillan joined the Harlem Writers Guild. With the encouragement of her fellow writers in the guild, McMillan began to take herself seriously as an author. In 1983, while a single parent to her son Solomon, a graduate student in the M.F.A. program in **film** at Columbia University, and a typist, McMillan enrolled for a two-week stint at an artists' colony in upstate New York, where she completed a draft of what would be her first novel, *Mama*.

After the completion of her formal education, McMillan began her teaching career. She has held positions at Stanford University, the University of Wyoming, and the University of Arizona in Tucson where she gained tenure. Following her teaching career, McMillan began to focus all of her attention on writing full-time. Her first novel, *Mama* (1987), gained McMillan wide recognition; however, it is her second novel *Disappearing Acts* (1989) that brought McMillan to fame. Her third novel, *Waiting to Exhale* (1992), became an instant *New York Times* bestseller and remained on the bestsellers list for thirty-eight weeks. The novel then became an award-winning motion picture. As a result, African American women across the United States gathered in theaters where applause and cheering was heard as the protagonists of the film claimed their right to self-actualization. Following *Exhale*, McMillan's fourth novel, *How Stella Got Her Groove Back* (1996), was an instant success. Described by McMillan as the novel closest to autobiographical, *Stella* remained on the *New York Times* bestsellers list for twenty-one weeks and sold more copies than the wildly popular *Waiting to Exhale*. That novel was also transformed into a major motion picture.

Largely based on McMillan's own life, *Stella* tells the story of a May/December relationship, but with a twist: The older partner is female. While all of her novels can be labeled as departures from the conventional forms of the female quest for romance narrative, *Stella* is at the forefront of such challenges in that McMillan creates a female protagonist who demands her right to be in touch with her passions—something women are traditionally socialized to repress.

Similar to her novel, McMillan traveled to the Caribbean for a respite after suffering the losses of her mother and her best friend. It was in Negril, Jamaica, that McMillan met and fell in **love** with twenty-year-old Jonathan Plummer, a hotel worker, who helped McMillan rediscover her passion for her art and for love. With Jonathan, McMillan was able to experience unconditional acceptance—something she did not always experience while dating men her own age. In interviews, McMillan has described the early stages of the relationship as something that is happening for the time being. However, the couple was married in 1999 after a five-year courtship.

With the publication of her fifth novel, *A Day Late and a Dollar Short* (2001), McMillan comes full circle in her discussion of the importance of gender and racial pride. *A Day Late* can be described as McMillan's "adult" novel because it is the work that is the greatest departure from the romance novel form. The characters operate as reminders to the reader of the dangers of not looking backward and acknowledging "truths," in order to learn how to move forward. The novel closes with what the narrator (and indirectly McMillan) sees as important rules to live by: have hope and faith; remember family is all one has; self-forgiveness is the first step toward peace; if one does not love herself, then she will not attract and keep love in her own life.

Writing novels that are loosely structured like popular romance fiction is racially and politically risky for black women writers. Such a form carries sentimental connotations that are in direct opposition with the unspoken demands that black literature should be artistic, but artistic in a way that exemplifies the work's political significance. At first glance, one may view McMillan's work as apolitical. However, a closer look reveals that McMillan came of age during the 1960s **Black Arts Movement** where black authors were supposed to reflect racial uplift. All of her novels include representations of characters with redeeming qualities. Through these characters, readers are left with a sense of hope as they witness McMillan's commentary on the complexities and the **beauty** of black life.

Similarly, McMillan's novels serve to revise the narrative of what it means to be a woman in today's society. The female characters in her novels come to the realization that their oppression is borne out of the refusal to let go of dominant ideologies of womanhood. McMillan constructs plot lines that show her female characters on both sides of the master narrative. First, McMillan's women are constructed in plot lines where the female characters ascribe to the rules of the Cult of True Womanhood. By novel's end, these characters discover that self-empowerment and liberation come when one defines herself on her own terms.

See also Interpretation of Everything, The

Works By

Breaking Ice: An Anthology of Contemporary African-American Fiction. Ed. New York: Viking, 1990.

A Day Late and a Dollar Short. New York: Viking, 2001.

Disappearing Acts. New York: Viking, 1989.

How Stella Got Her Groove Back. New York: Viking, 1996.

The Interruption of Everything. New York: Viking, 2005.

Mama. New York: Washington Square Press, 1987.

Waiting to Exhale. New York: Viking, 1992.

Works About

Dandridge, Rita. "Debunking the Beauty Myth with Black Pop Culture in Terry McMillan's *Waiting to Exhale*." *Language, Rhythm, and Sound: Black Popular Cultures into the Twenty-first Century*. Ed. Joseph K. Adjaye and Adrianne R. Andrews. Pittsburgh: University of Pittsburgh Press, 1997. 121–133.

——. "Debunking the Motherhood Myth in Terry McMillan's *Mama*." *College Language Association* 41.4 (1998): 405–416.

Ellerby, Janet Mason. "Deposing the Man of the House: Terry McMillan Rewrites the Family." *MELUS* 22 (1997): 105–113.

Harris, Tina M. "Waiting to Exhale or Breath(ing) Again: A Search for Identity, Empowerment, and Love in the 1990's." *Women and Language* 21.2 (1998): 9–20.

Patrick, Diane. *Terry McMillan: The Unauthorized Biography*. New York: St. Martin's Press, 1999.

Reid, E. "Beyond Morrison and Walker: Looking Good and Looking Forward in Contemporary Black Women's Stories." *African American Review* 34.2 (2000): 313.

Richards, Paulette. *Terry McMillan: A Critical Companion*. Westport, CT: Greenwood Press, 1999.

Catherine Ross-Stroud

MEMORY

Preserved and contested, cohesive and divisive, infallible and faulty, memory remains one of the central themes in African American women's writing. In the hands of female African American writers, memory often becomes paramount to logic or knowledge. As a vessel of the past, memory is sacred; as an organizing textual device, it raises issues of questions of reliability. For example, one finds the painful memories of **slavery** recorded in various **slave narratives** and sees them transform into a shared, cultural memory present in **historical fictions**. In other forms, the embodiment of memory is in the **ancestor** figure whose stories reveal one's inheritance. Regardless of its shape, the tangible intangibility of memory informs African American **fiction**, prose, and **poetry**.

As a literary device, memory looms large, becoming, at times, a character unto itself. There are educable moments where one character imparts wisdom through memories, but memory often proves unreliable. Imbued with psychological qualities, as in **Gwendolyn Brooks**'s "When You Have Forgotten Sunday: The Love Story," memory takes on yet another form. There, associations dictate the outcome of memory. Unquestionably multifaceted, memory is at best a duality that prevents a single, fixed definition. Similarly, memory, though discriminatory in what one chooses to remember, is not hierarchical insofar as characters both ordinary and extraordinary rely upon it. From something as trivial as a birthday meal to something as meaningful as the rivers **Langston Hughes**'s speaker recalls in "The Negro Speaks of Rivers," memory's confluence with and contribution to knowledge remain unmistakable.

Harriet Jacobs uses the recollections of her time both in slavery and her flight from it to compose her *Incidents in the Life of a Slave Girl* (1861). In that book, Jacobs offers a look at the devastating effects physical and sexual violation cause. More so, Jacobs positions slavery as the primary memory of African American women and establishes an ultimate legacy to which all memories may return. In contemporary African American women's writing, however, the triumph over slavery replaces the cruel inhumanity of the institution. Unlike historical knowledge, the memories preserved in slave narratives offer an alternative entrance into understanding. Time's role in memory certainly changes recollections by softening some incidents or adding strength to others so that long-forgotten sources feel a new bruise. For example, a flood of **family** memories triggered by the **death** of her father sustains **Lucille Clifton**. In *Generations: A Memoir* (1976), Clifton comes to see the power of memory to transform the present. Her father's reliance on memories of his life and the knowledge that he was descended from Dahomey women offer Clifton a lineage and a legacy. By holding on to his preslavery Dahomey heritage, Clifton's father sees memory as empowering rather than crippling. Likewise, Clifton takes from her father's memory the realization of its corrective quality that illuminates the past as something more far-reaching than slavery.

Perhaps the most well known of characters serving this theme, Sethe in **Toni Morrison**'s *Beloved* (1987) confronts both memory and rememory. More immediate and visual, rememory is often involuntary and lacks the depth and detail of memory. Akin to a photograph rather than an entire experience, Sethe's rememory of Sweet Home, for example, is deceptive and limited, while her actual memory of the place retains omitted details. In *Beloved*, memory is repressed and the consequences reveal memory's more dangerous capacities. Meanwhile, the men of Ruby, Oklahoma, in Morrison's *Paradise* (1998) change the nature of memory from selective and personal to ironclad and indisputable. In the hands of Steward and Deacon Morgan, memory becomes a propagandist tool used to keep order among the **community**. The Morgans' transformation of memory into **myth** offers not only self-proclaimed justification for the Convent massacre but also an additional caveat to the power of memory. Here, masculine memories dictate what is appropriate to feminine memory; communal memory transforms into knowledge, while individual memories become discredited.

Similarly, **Gloria Naylor**'s *Bailey's Café* (1992) echoes and expands the dangers of memories that become sentimental and static. While Eve uses her memory of each grain of delta dust as a reminder of how bad the past can be, she carries that knowledge into her present and moves forward in order not to repeat it. Others who stay at her house have to learn that the past is not a prison and memory can be misleading. Still, for Sadie, who never enters Eve's house, memories delude her alcohol-induced reality and prevent her from moving beyond the passive life of memory into activity and decision.

Amy Hill Hearth's editorial decisions in *Having Our Say: The Delany Sisters' First 100 Years* (1993) expose the problem one faces in creating an order for the recounting of memory. While Sarah L. and A. Elizabeth Delany told their century's worth of memories to that *New York Times* reporter, she chose to structure the book primarily around their memories of racial tensions. Thus, she crafted memory to a specific end and in the process changed its dynamic, stream-of-consciousness quality into something artificial and contrived—in other words, from healthy narrative into propaganda.

Additionally, withheld memory can privilege conjecture over knowledge, as **Nella Larsen** illustrates in ***Passing*** (1929) by never revealing Irene Redfield's true, initial disdain for Clare Kendry. Brooding over memories can destroy life, as the case of Joe Starks in **Zora Neale Hurston**'s ***Their Eyes Were Watching God*** (1937) demonstrates. Starks holds on to the memory of Janie's insult and allows it literally and metaphorically to kill him. Like Jacobs and Morrison, **Alice Walker**, **Paule Marshall**, **Ntozake Shange**, **Rita Dove**, and **Gayl Jones** provide additional examples of the multitude of African American women who use memory in their writing to show its perversions and clarifications. In the individual memories of *Beloved*'s Sixo or the communal memory behind ***Song of Solomon***'s (1977) Not Doctor Street we see the power of memory to isolate and recall importance otherwise lost in the same manner **Nikki Giovanni** does in "Knoxville, Tennessee." In all these diverse manifestations, memory consistently offers a window to the past that connects individual and communal African American **history**.

See also Delany Sisters

Works About

Carby, Hazel V. *Reconstructing Womanhood: The Emergence of the Afro-American Woman Novelist.* New York: Oxford University Press, 1987.

Griffin, Farah Jasmine. *"Who Set You Flowin'?" The African-American Migration Narrative.* New York: Oxford University Press, 1995.

Morrison, Toni. "Memory, Creation, and Writing." *Thought* 59 (1984): 385–390.

F. Gregory Stewart

MEN OF BREWSTER PLACE, THE

The Men of Brewster Place (1998), the sequel to **Gloria Naylor**'s award-winning first novel, ***The Women of Brewster Place*** (1980), focuses on the lives of seven men who live in the Brewster Place project. Naylor establishes an intertextual relationship between the two works by repeating the narrative structure, seven related stories, that she used in her first novel and by resurrecting Ben, a character who dies in the first book, to serve as narrative voice in *The Men of Brewster Place*. Although the sequel examines the lives of seven black men struggling to discover what it means to be black and male, women also play a prominent role in the book.

Ben describes his relationship with three women. His Grandma Jones, a hardworking woman who washed clothes to earn money, reared Ben. She taught him the value of self-reliance and the dignity of hard **work**. His wife, Elvira, lacks the compassion and tolerance that ennobled his grandmother. Convinced of her ugliness and unworthiness like Pauline Breedlove in **Toni Morrison**'s *The Bluest Eye* (1970), Elvira worships everything associated with white culture and hates all things black. Elvira humiliates Ben and tramples on his manhood, making him feel worthless and inadequate. Moreover, she is openly hostile and abusive toward their crippled daughter. Consequently, the daughter suffers from a severe case of low self-esteem. Ben tries to shield his daughter from Elvira's attacks, but he cannot protect her from the sexual exploitation that she experiences from her white employer.

Naylor calls attention to other mothers in the book. Mildred, mother of Brother Jerome, the mentally retarded **blues** musician, remains emotionally detached from her son. He spends his days and nights alone playing the blues on the piano, and he entertains his mother's guests on demand. Significantly, Jerome's father abandons Mildred and their son, leaving her without the emotional and financial support that she needs to cope with their disabled son. Keisha, also a single mother with two little boys, is verbally abusive toward her sons and seems to view them as an unwanted burden. Like Mildred, Keisha feels used and abandoned by her sons' father. Basil, whose mother in *The Women of Brewster Place* had to rear him without a husband, marries Keisha to offer her sons a loving, nurturing environment like his mother provided for him. Ceil, the long-suffering wife of Eugene, the bisexual dockworker, is also a mother whose husband refuses to behave responsibly. Despite Eugene's repeated infidelity, she clings to him, allowing him to leave her alone to care for their child and to return when his guilty conscience overwhelms him. Like Ben, Eugene despairs over a painful sense of unfulfilled manhood. Because he has failed to achieve his dream of owning his own **home**, Eugene sees himself as less than a man. Like many women, Ceil blames herself for their dysfunctional marriage. She is a classic example of a woman whose **love** for her husband covers his faults and enables him to wallow in self-pity.

For the Rev. Moreland T. Woods, women are merely objects of pleasure. Although he respected and admired his strong, Jamaican grandmother, he shows little or no regard for other women, including his wife. Like Rev. John Pearson in **Zora Neale Hurston**'s *Jonah's Gourd Vine* (1934), Reverend Woods routinely violates his marriage vows. His wife accepts his infidelity as inevitable. Ironically, Reverend Woods's reputation for infidelity works against him when a disgruntled **community** activist hires several pregnant women to picket city hall, claiming that Reverend Woods is their babies' father. Reverend Woods is forced to resign his seat on the City Council. Through her portrayal of Ben's daughter, Mildred, Keisha, Ceil, and the nameless women in Reverend Woods's narrative, Naylor highlights ways in which black women are exploited and devalued.

Works About

Fowler, Virginia C. *Gloria Naylor: In Search of Sanctuary.* New York: Twayne, 1996.

Gates, Henry Louis, and K. A. Appiah, eds. *Gloria Naylor: Critical Perspectives Past and Present.* New York: Amistad, 1993.

Hall, Chekita T. *Gloria Naylor's Feminist Blues Aesthetic.* New York: Garland, 1998.

Harris, Trudier. *The Power of the Porch: The Storyteller's Craft in Zora Neale Hurston, Gloria Naylor, and Randall Keenan.* Athens: University of Georgia Press, 1996.

Montgomery, Maxine. Review of *The Men of Brewster Place*, by Gloria Naylor. *African American Review* 34.1 (Spring 2000): 176.

Elvin Holt

MERIDIAN

The central question of *Meridian*—whether or not the title character would kill for the revolution—illustrates **Alice Walker**'s own ambivalence about the **civil rights movement** and the **Black Arts Movement**. Published in 1976 after Walker left the **South**, the novel chronicles Meridian's shifting self through adolescence, college, and adulthood, though not in chronological order: Walker said that she wanted the novel's structure to mimic that of a "crazy quilt," in which time sense and story focus may seem disjointed but in fact are intricately planned. Augmented with tangential anecdotes, like the stories of Feather Mae and Louvinie, Meridian's story depicts the unique struggle of a black woman in 1950s–1970s America.

Meridian Hill is raised by a judgmental and indifferent mother and a kind and distant father, neither of whom explains their constant rejoinder to "be good." Consequently, Meridian gets pregnant by and marries Eddie, after which she understands her own mother's disaffection for **motherhood**. Having a child, for both Meridian and her mother, signals an end to independence, excitement, possibility, and joy. Rather than perpetuate her mother's resentment, Meridian gives up her son, leaves Eddie, and attends the all-black Saxon College. At Saxon, once Saxon Plantation, she meets Anne-Marion, whose energy and militancy contrast with Meridian's own sense of quiet suffering and reserve. They become involved in civil rights protests and with a group of civil rights workers. Meridian falls in **love** with one of the workers, Truman, but only consummates their affair after he begins dating Lynne, a white New Yorker also working in the movement. Their unsatisfying encounter results in pregnancy; Meridian aborts the fetus, undergoes tubal ligation, and experiences a profound depression, of which Truman is unaware.

Truman and Lynne marry, have a daughter, and live in the South, working for the movement. Just as Anne-Marion contrasts with Meridian, so too does Lynne. Lynne's **whiteness** endangers the black men in their group, providing white racists with fodder for their acts of **violence** against black men. After Tommy Odds is shot, he becomes bitter and blames Lynne, not just because her presence may have incited violence but because all white people are guilty of all racial injustice. Tommy's subsequent **rape** of Lynne acts as a wedge between her and Truman; Lynne becomes disillusioned with the movement, and Truman begins seeing other women. After their daughter is killed and they move to New York, Lynne and Truman separate.

Meridian stays in the South, working for civil rights. She lives like a monk, or a mystic, without possessions or the support of a civil rights group. Living in a series of small communities, she stands up to incidences of racism, after which she experiences both physical deterioration and spiritual transcendence. She also acts as a referee and a comforter to both Lynne and Truman, who begin to see by her example the true mission of the civil rights movement. After several years, Meridian decides that she is done with self-sacrifice and leaves her mystic's life, replaced by Truman.

Walker's novel shows that while the civil rights movement may have been internally divisive because of sexual politics, racial ambivalence, and lofty but abandoned ideals, individuals can achieve real change. Meridian's decision not to kill for the revolution later manifests as her later determination that no one—Martin Luther King, Jr., Medgar Evers, and others—should die for it, either. This tension between sacrifice and confrontation illuminates Meridian's **work** for civil rights as well as the other characters' development, plot trajectory, and Walker's presentation of the **history** of the civil rights movement.

Works About

Ahokas, Pirjo. "Hybridized Black Female Identity in Alice Walker's *Meridian*." *America Today: Highways and Labyrinths*. Ed. Gigliola Nocera. Siracusa, Italy: Grafià, 2003. 481–488.

Barker, Deborah E. "Visual Markers: Art and Mass Media in Alice Walker's *Meridian*." *African American Review* 31.3 (1997): 463–479.

Barnett, Pamela E. "'Miscegenation,' Rape, and 'Race' in Alice Walker's *Meridian*." *Southern Quarterly: A Journal of the Arts in the South* 39.3 (2001): 65–81.

Brown, Joseph A., S.J. "'All Saints Should Walk Away': The Mystical Pilgrimage of *Meridian*." *Callaloo* 12.2 (1989): 310–320.

Byerman, Keith. "Gender and Justice: Alice Walker and the Sexual Politics of Civil Rights." *The World Is Our Culture: Society and Culture in Contemporary Southern Writing*. Ed. Jeffrey J. Folks and Nancy Summers. Lexington: University Press of Kentucky, 2000. 93–106.

Collins, Janelle. " 'Like a Collage': Personal and Political Subjectivity in Alice Walker's *Meridian*." *CLA Journal* 44.2 (2000): 161–188.

Danielson, Susan. "Alice Walker's *Meridian*, Feminism, and the 'Movement.' " *Women's Studies: An Interdisciplinary Journal* 16.3–4 (1989): 317–330.

De Lancey, Frenzella E. "Squaring the Afrocentric Circle: Womanism and Humanism in Alice Walker's *Meridian*." *Literary Griot: International Journal of Black Expressive Cultural Studies* 5.1 (1993): 1–16.

Hall, Christine. "Art, Action and the Ancestors: Alice Walker's *Meridian* in Its Context." *Black Women's Writing*. Ed. Gina Wisker. New York: St. Martin's Press, 1993. 96–110.

Hendrickson, Robert M. "Remembering the Dream: Alice Walker, *Meridian* and the Civil Rights Movement." *MELUS* 24.3 (1999): 111–128.

Nadel, Alan. "Reading the Body: Alice Walker's *Meridian* and the Archeology of Self." *MFS: Modern Fiction Studies* 34.1 (1988): 55–68.

Pifer, Lynn. "Coming to Voice in Alice Walker's *Meridian*: Speaking Out for the Revolution." *African American Review* 26.1 (1992): 77–88.

Sengupta, Ashis. "Search for Black Womanhood in Alice Walker's *Meridian*." *Quest* 106 (1994): 221–224.

Weston, Ruth D. "Inversion of Patriarchal Mantle Images in Alice Walker's *Meridian*." *Southern Quarterly: A Journal of the Arts in the South* 25.2 (1987): 102–107.

Kate Cochran

MERIWETHER, LOUISE (1923–   )

Though her literary light shines less brightly than her contemporaries', Louise Meriwether has written in a variety of genres, producing works that highlight African American **history**, culture, and achievements. Her first novel *Daddy Was a Number Runner* (1970), praised by **James Baldwin** for its candor and insight, is still her best-known work.

The only daughter of Marion Lloyd Jenkins and Julia Jenkins, Meriwether was the third of their five children. Born in Haverstraw, New Jersey, she relocated with her **family** to Harlem while still a child. Meriwether later completed a B.A. in English at New York City College and earned an M.A. in journalism from the University of California in Los Angeles (1965).

The degrees in English and journalism indicate Meriwether's early **love** of writing. As a journalist, Meriwether worked for the *Los Angeles Sentinel*, contributing biographical articles on accomplished but little-known African Americans. Upon joining the Watts Writers' Workshop in the mid-1960s, Meriwether turned her full attention to **fiction** writing. Meriwether spent five years writing *Daddy Was a Number Runner*, and excerpts were published in *Antioch Review* and *Negro Digest*. The completed novel was published by Prentice-Hall in 1970.

Daddy Was a Number Runner is a coming-of-age novel told from the perspective of a thirteen-year-old black girl living in depression-era Harlem.

Francie Coffin adores her number-running father James, who tells his children stories about their African heritage. As the depression continues, it becomes increasingly difficult for the Coffin family to survive economically. Unable to provide for his family, James leaves rather than bear witness to its disintegration. Francie's maturation process includes a shift from loyalty to her father to identification with and appreciation of her mother, Henrietta. Meriwether brilliantly illuminates the consequences of James's abandonment while fostering empathy for both parents. The harshest judgment of James comes from Francie when she learns he has moved in with another woman; evoking his stories about the **ancestors**, Francie tells her father that he forgot that he was one of Yoruba's children.

Despite the critical acclaim for her first novel, Meriwether turned her attention from adult to **children's and young adult literature**. Motivated by the omissions and distortions in American history books, Meriwether published juvenile biographies of three important African Americans: Civil War hero Robert Smalls, heart surgeon Daniel Hale Williams, and civil rights activist **Rosa Parks**. Her insistence on inclusive and truthful history inspired both her literary pursuits and her political activism. Meriwether played a key role in the protest by black **community** members that blocked the proposed **film** adaptation of William Styron's historically inaccurate *The Confessions of Nat Turner* (1967).

Meriwether returned to fiction writing in the 1990s and published two more novels. *Fragments of the Ark* (1994) revisits the story of Robert Smalls, this time as **historical fiction** that imagines and explores the personal relationships of the historical characters. Painstakingly researched, the novel fills in gaps in American history while telling a compelling story of the impact of **slavery** on individuals, families, and communities. Meriwether's third and most recent novel, *Shadow Dancing* (2000), takes place in 1980s New York. Set in the black professional **class**, the novel has some autobiographical traces in terms of the main character, a writer for *BlackSpeak* magazine who moves from journalism to fiction writing, echoing Meriwether's own career path.

Whether fiction or fact, Meriwether's writing engenders respect for African American ancestors and achievers. Her literary contributions deeply enrich our understanding of history and humanity.

Works By

Daddy Was a Number Runner. Englewood Cliffs, NJ: Prentice-Hall, 1970. New York: Feminist Press, 1986.

Don't Ride the Bus on Monday: The Rosa Parks Story. Englewood Cliffs, NJ: Prentice-Hall, 1973.

Fragments of the Ark. New York: Simon and Schuster, 1994.

The Freedom Ship of Robert Smalls. Englewood Cliffs, NJ: Prentice-Hall, 1971.

The Heart Man: Dr. Daniel Hale Williams. Englewood Cliffs, NJ: Prentice-Hall, 1972.

Shadow Dancing. New York: One World/Ballantine, 2002.

Works About

Collins, Janelle. " 'Poor and Black and Apt to Stay That Way': Gambling on a Sure Thing in Louise Meriwether's *Daddy Was a Number Runner.*" *Midwest Quarterly* 45.1 (2003): 49–58.

Dandridge, Rita. "From Economic Insecurity to Disintegration: A Study of Character in Louise Meriwether's *Daddy Was a Number Runner.*" *Negro American Literature Forum* 9.3 (1975): 82–85.

——. "Meriwether, Louise." *Black Women in America.* Ed. Darlene Clark Hine. New York: Oxford University Press, 1993. 2:783–784.

Duboin, Corinne. "Race, Gender, and Space: Louise Meriwether's Harlem in *Daddy Was a Number Runner.*" *College Language Association Journal* (2001): 26–40.

McKay, Nellie. Afterword to *Daddy Was a Number Runner*, by Louise Meriwether. New York: Feminist Press, 1986. 209–234.

Walker, Melissa. *Down from the Mountaintop: Black Women's Novels in the Wake of the Civil Rights Movement, 1966–1989.* New Haven, CT: Yale University Press, 1991.

Janelle Collins

MIDDLE PASSAGE

Scholars, historians, and scientists have not been able to settle on the exact number of enslaved Africans who were transported across the Atlantic on the crossing called the Middle Passage because of the sheer numbers who died en route and the lack of historical documentation providing specific numbers. The number has been estimated to be anywhere from 10 to 60 million. The route from the coast of Africa that cargo ships took to transport slaves to the French and British Caribbean Islands, South America, North America, and Central America consisted of one of the most brutal forms of human rights abuses historically.

Slave narratives such as ***Incidents in the Life of a Slave Girl*** (1861) by **Harriet Jacobs** and *The Interesting Narrative of the Life of Olaudah Equiano, or Gustavus Vassa, the African* (1791) by Olaudah Equiano captured the country's imagination when they were published. Jacobs's account provides insight into the plight of female slaves, and much like her life of sexual abuse at the hands of her master, it has been documented that African women on slave ships endured **rape** and other forms of abuse.

Along with the autobiographical accounts of the enslaved were testimonies by unlikely eyewitnesses. The English surgeon Alexander Falconbridge took many voyages on slave ships as a paid surgeon, saw horrifying atrocities, and recounted his experiences. His nonfictional description *An Account of the Slave Trade on the Coast of Africa* (1788) provides vivid detail of the horrors the enslaved endured, making specific references to the imminent **death** and extreme suffering the female slaves faced. His experiences led him to fight for the abolition of **slavery**. His account became popular among abolitionists, and he eventually governed a colony of freed slaves in Sierra Leone.

Compelling fictional accounts of the horrors of the Middle Passage include **Toni Morrison**'s *Beloved* (1987) and **Charles Johnson**'s *Middle Passage* (1990). With astounding detail, Morrison carefully crafts and fictionalizes the horrors of slavery that the Middle Passage resulted in. Sethe's infanticide is another atrocity that the enslaved were forced to engage in as a way to avoid the brutality of slavery. To escape the unknown anguish that lay ahead, slaves committed suicide by throwing themselves overboard and perhaps even committed infanticide.

In 1807 the British Parliament prohibited the slave trade, and America followed suit, banning the slave trade in 1808. However, the legacy of the Middle Passage and the slave trade continue to reverberate worldwide. African women were valued solely for their reproductive capabilities and strength to withstand the harsh life on plantations in the new world. Their children became property, and their offspring with white slave masters created a perplexing caste and color system that privileged light skin and kept African Americans' inferiority intact. The psychological, physical, and economic repercussions have not yet been fully comprehended and, because of the complicated nature of the events, have remained unmeasured.

Works About

Burnside, Madeleine, and Rosemarie Robotham, eds. *Spirits of the Passage: The Transatlantic Slave Trade in the Seventeenth Century.* New York: Simon and Schuster, 1997.
Diedrich, Maria, Henry Louis Gates, Jr., and Carl Pedersen. *Black Imagination and the Middle Passage.* New York: Oxford University Press, 1999.
McMillan, Beverly. *Captive Passage: The Transatlantic Slave Trade and the Making of the Americas.* Washington, DC: Smithsonian Institution Press, in association with the Mariners' Museum of Virginia, 2002.
Pettinger, Alasdair, ed. *Always Elsewhere: Travels of the Black Atlantic.* London: Cassell, 1998.

Zisca Isabel Burton

MILLER, MAY (1899–1995)

May Miller, the daughter of writer and professor Kelly Miller, contributed to the New Negro literary movement of the mid-1920s, establishing her place as an important female voice in an era of burgeoning civil rights and social consciousness. Miller's plays, **poetry**, and prose convey the African American woman's experience with female characters of various ages and backgrounds who are deliciously compelling and densely textured. Miller's characters, both male and female, frequently grapple with the division between knowledge and emotion, and the human condition and a higher power. She often uses children and images of childhood to explore the assimilation of innocence with knowledge and the transformation of girl to woman, boy to man. Miller's works also engage in the juxtaposition of **slavery** and the fight for **freedom** with the modern African American struggle for equality. Her works underscore her conviction that education is the way to elevate the African American condition and empower black women. The influence of South Carolina **folklore** lends a wistful air to her poetry and a cultural richness to her plays that bespeaks Miller's **love** of language and learning.

Miller grew up in Washington, D.C., and graduated from Howard University in 1920, earning her degree in **drama**. During her college years she acted, directed, and produced numerous plays, winning an award for her one-act play *Within the Shadows*. But it was with a third-place award for her play *Bog Guide* (1925), a tale of a daughter's revenge for the **death** of her father, that established Miller as a member of the early **Harlem Renaissance**. In 1929, Miller's one-act drama *Scratches*, a commentary on black poverty, **class** differences, and **stereotypes**, was published in *Carolina Magazine* of the University of Carolina at Chapel Hill. In 1930, William Richardson identified Miller as one of the most promising black playwrights and anthologized Miller's *Riding the Goat* (1928) and *Graven Images* (1930) in his *Plays and Pageants from the Life of the Negro* (1930). In 1935, Richardson and Miller collaborated on *Negro History in Thirteen Plays*, in which three of Miller's plays appeared: *Christophe's Daughters*, *Soujourner Truth*, and *Harriet Tubman*.

For twenty years Miller taught English and speech at the **Frederick Douglass** High School in Baltimore, Maryland. In 1943, Miller retired from teaching and returned to Washington, D.C., where she began to concentrate exclusively on writing poetry. Miller's first collection of poetry, *Into the Clearing*, was published in 1959; followed by *Poems* (1962); *Lyrics of Three Women*, with Katie Lyle and Maude Rubin (1964); *Not That Far* (1973); *The Clearing and Beyond* (1974); *Dust of Uncertain Journey* (1975); *Halfway to the Sun* (1981), a volume of children's poetry; and *The Ransomed Wait* (1983). Miller served as poet-in-residence at Monmouth College in 1963, University of Wisconsin in 1972, Bluefield State College in 1974, Exeter Academy in 1973 and 1976, and Southern University in 1975. Miller was the poetry coordinator (1964, 1965) and chairperson of the **literature** panel (1970–1978) for the Friends of Art Commission of the Arts and Humanities in the District of Columbia. She has been widely published in journals and anthologies.

Works By

The Clearing and Beyond. Washington, DC: Charioteer Press, 1974.

Collected Poems. Detroit: Lotus Press, 1989.

Dust of Uncertain Journey. Detroit: Lotus Press, 1975.

Halfway to the Sun. Washington, DC: Washington Writers Publishing House, 1981.

Into the Clearing. Washington, DC: Charioteer Press, 1959.

Lyrics of Three Women: Katie Lyle, Maude Rubin, and May Miller. Baltimore, MD: Linden Press, 1964.

Negro History in Thirteen Plays. Ed. Willis Richardson and May Miller. New York: Associated Publishers, 1935.

Not That Far. San Luis Obispo, CA: Solo Press, 1973.

Poems. Thetford, VT: Cricket Press, 1962.

The Ransomed Wait. Detroit: Lotus Press, 1983.

Works About

Miller, Jeanne Marie A. "Georgia Douglas Johnson and May Miller: Forgotten Playwrights of the New Negro Renaissance." *College Language Association Journal* 33.4 (1990): 349–366.

Molette, Barbara. "Black Women Playwrights." *Black World* 25 (1976): 28–34.

Young-Minor, Ethyl A. "Staging Black Women's History: May Miller's *Harriet Tubman* as Cultural Artifact." *CLA Journal* 46.1 (2002): 30–47.

Debbie Clare Olson

MILLICAN, ARTHENIA J. BATES (1920–   )

Arthenia J. Bates Millican was born on June 1, 1920, in Sumter, South Carolina, to Susan Emma David Jackson and Calvin Shepherd Jackson. Bates was always inspired by the written word and published her first poem at the age of sixteen. She received a B.A. degree in 1941 from Sumter College in South Carolina and pursued an M.A. degree at Atlanta University in Atlanta, Georgia, where she was able to participate in a creative writing workshop led by **Langston Hughes**. Hughes took Bates under his wing as a protégée. This relationship nurtured her craft and would lead to a prolific career in several genres. She graduated in 1948 and would continue her lifelong **love** of learning. She eventually received a doctorate degree in 1972 from Louisiana State University, writing her dissertation on **James Weldon Johnson** and his influence on the African American literary tradition.

In addition to being a lifelong student, Millican is also an educator, her teaching career spanning four decades. At Morris College, Millican served as chair of the English Department. She also taught English at Norfolk State University, Mississippi Valley State University, and Southern University, from which she retired in 1980.

In 1976, Millican received a fellowship from the National Endowment for the Arts for her short story "Where You Belong." She has been named a distinguished alumnus of Morris College, and collections of her works are maintained at the Sumter County Historical Society, South Carolina Library at the University of South Carolina, and Beinecke Library at Yale University.

Throughout the years, Millican has published **poetry**, **fiction**, and non-fiction in a myriad publications ranging from *Essence Magazine, Negro Digest,* and *College Language Association Journal.* She was a contributing editor for the literary journal *Callaloo* from 1976 to 1984 and *Obsidian: Black Literature in*

Review from 1974 to 1976. She also served as contributing editor to the compilations *James Baldwin, a Critical Evaluation* (1977) and *Sturdy Black Bridges: A Vision of Black Women in Literature* (1979).

In 1969, Millican published the critically acclaimed collection of short stories *Seeds beneath the Snow: Vignettes from the South.* Each of the twelve stories focuses on life in the black rural **South** and examines many of the influential forces of the South—relationships between parents and children, husbands and wives, people and God. In 1973, Millican published her first and only novel, *The Deity Nodded.* She currently resides in her hometown of Sumter, South Carolina.

Works By

"The Autobiography of an Idea." *African American Review* 27 (1993): 25–28.
"A Ceremony of Innocence." *Full Measure: Modern Short Stories on Aging.* Ed. Dorothy Sennett. Saint Paul, MN: Graywolf Press, 1988.
The Deity Nodded. Detroit: Harlo Press, 1973.
Hand on Full Throttle. Baton Rouge, LA: Franklin Press, 1993.
Seeds beneath the Snow: Vignettes from the South. Washington, DC: Howard University Press, 1969.

Roxane Gay

MODERNISM

Literary **history** has long placed African American "modernism" as separate from the "**Harlem Renaissance**," although friendships and influences between black and white writers of this era were many. American modernism thus defined refers to works by a group of primarily white European American writers inspired by European experimental writing, especially that of the French symbolists. The Harlem Renaissance, on the other hand, is a term equally racialized in its application to black writing produced between World Wars I and II. The Harlem Renaissance has most frequently been characterized in terms of its contribution to a "Negro aesthetic," informed by debates between advocates of racial uplift through the arts (W.E.B. Du Bois) and advocates of expressive black culture through the idiomatic and vernacular (**Langston Hughes** and **Zora Neale Hurston**). While modernism tends to be distinguished by its experimental character, Harlem Renaissance writing is most often characterized by its central concern with the subject matter of **race** and embodiment, emphasizing experience over experiment in its obsession with African American culture and struggle. These distinctions between the mind (literary experiment) and the **body** (experience), associating white modernist writing with the mind and black modern writing with the body, articulate a racist dichotomy that has played out since the Enlightenment and that has found its latest incarnation in the critical dialogues between "essentialism" and "constructivism" in the **identity** politics of the late twentieth century.

With recent reevaluations of modernism in the wake of postmodernism, critics are articulating an array of "modernisms" in American **literature**, including writing by black American authors. A closer investigation of the relationship between black and white writers during the world wars of the first half of the twentieth century reveals a relationship between them that was far more nuanced and complex than previous accounts suggest. Recent studies of **Jean Toomer** and **Nella Larsen**, for instance, investigate the relationship of these writers to modernist writers and artists as well as their influence on the development of modernist aesthetics. Other writers who used literary experimentation while exploring African American subjects include **Ann Petry**, **Gwendolyn Brooks**, Melvin Tolson, Robert Hayden, and **Ralph Ellison**.

A number of recent studies have gone beyond the examination of individual African American writers in relation to modernism and have focused on the ways in which the development of African American art during this period created a foil for developing white artists who wished to "alienate" themselves from the status quo. The ways in which both black and white cultural production shaped each other is the subject of several pioneering studies by Houston Baker, Michel Berube, Aldon Nielsen, Michael North, and Eric Sundquist. As the list of authors here suggests, this has been an area in which the work of male scholars predominates. Their work is valuable but should also suggest, in the context of a feminist encyclopedia of African American writers, the need for more studies of women writers and more theorizing by women critics in this area.

In *The Dialect of Modernism*, North argues that African American culture was essential to the development of mainstream modernism because the impersonation of black voices by such writers as Gertrude Stein ("Melanctha") and T. S. Eliot (dubbed "Possum" by Ezra Pound in the spirit of the "Uncle Remus" tales) was essential to the development of literary personas "alienated" from the status quo. This impersonation of blacks by white writers complicated the use of dialect and experimentation with literary style among African Americans, as the literary "dialect" available was often invented by whites, rather than speech reflecting black cultural authenticity. North interprets the **film** *The Jazz Singer* (1927) as an archetypal tale about this sort of appropriation. And as Nielsen points out in *Reading Race*, the persistence of modernism's debt to African American culture and cultural impersonation is illustrated in the dedication of John Berryman's second "Dream Song" to Daddy Rice, credited with inventing the Jim Crow dance in 1828. On the other hand, African American writers during the Harlem Renaissance often felt constrained by white patrons from writing about social issues, lest they violate the stylistic conventions of modernism.

From the beginning, Harlem Renaissance literature was infused with the spirit of literary experiment and a consciousness of style and invention, although critics have often deliberately overlooked style in order to focus on content in black writing. Jean Toomer, often credited as the author whose experimental work *Cane* initiated the Harlem Renaissance with its publication in 1923, was well read in the French symbolists and incorporated what he learned from them into his portraits of southern black women in *Cane* as well as in the suggestive, elusive structure of this three-part book of short, lyrical prose passages interspersed with poems. Toomer's literary colleagues during this period included modernist writers and artists such as Waldo Frank, Alfred Stieglitz, and Sherwood Anderson. When he traveled with Toomer in the **South**, modernist Waldo Frank often passed for black. Although William Faulkner never acknowledged a debt to Jean Toomer, the opening passages of *Light in August* (1932), written a few years after the publication of *Cane*, reflect a stylistic treatment of the rural South akin to that of Toomer's in *Cane*'s first section, set in rural Georgia, especially in the portrait of Lena Grove.

Among African American women modernists, the work of Nella Larsen stands out, particularly her short novels **Quicksand** (1928) and **Passing** (1929), that bear comparison to F. Scott Fitzgerald's *The Great Gatsby*, published a few years before, in their concise, elegant, symbol-laden prose, particularly with regard to its use of color. While Fitzgerald's celebrated use of color symbolism associates characters and their dreams in *The Great Gatsby*, the use of color in Larsen's work draws the reader's attention to the crudeness of the stark black and white terms used to describe the color spectrum of race in America and to foster nuances and complexity in the reader's understanding of race and culture. Larsen's innovative use of modernist literary techniques to reveal the complex surface tension inherent in interracial relationships and racial mixing shows how modernism and social issues, textual experiment and lived experience, can be effectively interwoven. Furthermore, *Quicksand* not only incorporates modernist literary techniques; its plot brings together the European and the American, two worlds in which the protagonist finds herself constructed differently, but in both places as a body rather than as a stylish text. In fact, *Quicksand* can be read as a parable of the African American modernist author in the racialized literary context of the 1920s—no matter how hard she works at attending to "surfaces"—literary experiment—and no matter how hard she works at escaping the limits of physical experience—the racial body—she is still construed as a "body" by others, whether in the context of a black college in the American South as the body who will breed the "talented tenth" or in Denmark as the "exotic primitive" on which the white European artist (Axel Olson) projects his own desire for warmth and sexual fulfillment. Larsen's novel *Quicksand*, like Toomer's *Cane*, uses the bodies of black women as a metaphor to dramatize the mind/body dichotomy underlying racially charged distinctions between "modernist" work and work that is socially conscious.

Gwendolyn Brooks's **Maud Martha** (1953) can be viewed as a response to Stein's Melanctha, a reappropriation of the body and voice of the dark-hued black woman. Thus from the beginning, modernist texts by African American writers displayed not only a double consciousness but a triple consciousness—inflected by both race and gender awareness in the construction of the "black body" in racial discourse. A mind/body dualism that insists on dichotomizing aesthetic creation and experiential authenticity haunts not only conversations about modernism and race but also the broader disciplines of African American and feminist criticism. African American critics (especially during the 1960s and 1970s) have chastised African American writers who drew on European or modernist forms as not being true to the charge of African American literature—to articulate art from the black experience. **Black feminist criticism**, during its rise in the 1980s, was rife with dispute over the authenticity of representations of African American women's experience by African American women writers, and whether criticism should be based on essentialist notions of culture or theorized by what was often viewed as "European American" ideological paradigms.

Contemporary African American poets have integrated experimental poetics and the exploration of subjectivity, defying the binaries of identity politics while exploring the ways in which social and political realities are constructed through language. They have drawn on an experimental heritage of modern American poetics including the contributions of African American vernacular and **jazz** as well as the innovations of language **poetry**. Some of the women in the forefront of contemporary experimental writing include **Elizabeth Alexander**, **Harryette Mullen**, Claudia Rankine, **Sapphire**, and Natasha Trethewey.

Works About

Baker, Houston A., Jr. *Modernism and the Harlem Renaissance*. Chicago: University of Chicago Press, 1989.

Berube, Michael. "Masks, Margins, and African-American Modernism: Melvin Tolson's *Harlem Gallery*." *PMLA* 105.1 (1990): 57–69.

Hostetler, Ann. "The Aesthetics of Race and Gender in Nella Larsen's *Quicksand*." *PMLA* 105.1 (1990): 35–46.

Hutchinson, George. *The Harlem Renaissance in Black and White*. Cambridge, MA: Harvard University Press, 1997.

Morrison, Toni. *Playing in the Dark: Whiteness and the Literary Imagination*. Cambridge, MA: Harvard University Press, 1992.

Nielsen, Aldon L. *Reading Race: White American Poets and the Racial Discourse in the Twentieth Century*. Athens: University of Georgia Press, 1988.

North, Michael. *The Dialect of Modernism: Race, Language, and Twentieth-Century Literature*. New York: Oxford University Press, 1994.

Sundquist, Eric. *To Wake the Nations: Race in the Making of American Culture*. Cambridge, MA: Harvard University Press, 1993.

Wall, Cheryl A. *Women of the Harlem Renaissance*. Bloomington: Indiana University Press, 1995.

Ann Hostetler

MOODY, ANNE (1940–   )

By most accounts, today Anne Moody lives an almost reclusive life, although her formative and young adult years are well documented in her powerful **autobiography** *Coming of Age in Mississippi* (1968). The eldest daughter of sharecroppers in Wilkinson County, Mississippi, her younger years were shaped by a somewhat nomadic existence as her **family** moved quite frequently. To help out financially, Moody began working at the age of nine as a **domestic** for various white families in the area. It was then that she was exposed to the racial inequality and injustice to which blacks were subjected; however, this new awareness sparked a spirit of defiance in Moody that would drive her passion for social activism at the dawn of the **civil rights movement**.

By the time Moody was in her early teens, she had heard of several lynchings in the **South**. But one lynching in particular instilled in her a hatred and intense, almost palpable fear of whites–the 1955 lynching of Emmett Till. In *Coming of Age in Mississippi* she says, "Before Emmett Till's murder, I had known the fear of hunger, hell, and the Devil. But now there was a new fear known to me–the fear of being killed just because I was black" (107). Moody did not, however, allow her fear to incapacitate her.

She earned excellent grades in school and was a standout basketball player. She attended Natchez Junior College in 1961 on a basketball scholarship and continued her education at Tougaloo College, where she earned a Bachelor of Science degree in 1964.

During college, Moody became active in the civil rights movement. She joined the Congress of Racial Equality (CORE), the Student Nonviolent Coordinating Committee (SNCC), and the National Association for the Advancement of Colored People (NAACP). Her activities exposed her and her family to retaliation from racist factions in the South, but she was a determined woman who was committed to the fundamental goals of the civil rights movement.

Moody participated in numerous voter registration drives in Mississippi. She also traveled to various counties speaking out against racism and black apathy for the movement. She helped set up boycotts and was a demonstrator during the "sit-in" movement at a Woolworth lunch counter in Jackson in 1963. She helped organize protest marches, including one in response to Medgar Evers's murder. Moody experienced threats and intimidation by white officials and the Ku Klux Klan and was jailed several times. It was the assassination of John F. Kennedy, however, that filled her with a sense of hopelessness.

Her autobiography ends by foreshadowing her disillusionment about the movement effecting positive social changes in Mississippi. She eventually broke away from the organized movement and relocated to New York. Moody published one other novel, but her autobiography detailing her years of social activism is what earned her the most acclaim.

Works By

Coming of Age in Mississippi. New York: Dell, 1968.
Mr. Death: Four Stories. New York: Harper, 1975.

Works About

Cullen-Dupont, Kathryn, ed. *American Women Activists' Writings: An Anthology, 1637–2002.* New York: Cooper Square Press, 2002.

David, Jay, ed. *Growing up Black: From the Slave Days to the Present—25 African Americans Reveal the Trials and Triumphs of Their Childhoods.* New York: Avon Books, 1992.

McKay, Nellie Y. "The Girls Who Became the Women: Childhood Memories in the Autobiographies of Harriet Jacobs, Mary Church Terrell, and Anne Moody." *Tradition and the Talents of Women.* Ed. Florence Howe. Urbana: University of Illinois Press, 1991. 105–124.

Toni E. Smith

MOORE, OPAL (1953–   )

Opal J. Moore—poet, short-story writer, educator, scholar, and literary critic—is a Chicago native who graduated with a B.F.A. from Illinois Wesleyan University's School of Art in 1974. It was at Wesleyan that feelings of powerlessness in the face of racism led Moore to begin writing journals and **poetry**. Moore continued writing at the University of Iowa, where she earned an M.A. from the School of Art in 1981 and an M.F.A. from the Iowa Writers' Workshop in 1982. In 1985 she took a position with Virginia State University teaching creative writing and African American **literature**. In addition to faculty appointments at Virginia Commonwealth University, Kassel University, and Radford University, Moore has also taught as a Fulbright Lecturer at Johannes Gutenberg-Universität in Mainz, Germany, and was Jessie Ball DuPont Visiting Scholar at Hollins College. In 1997 she joined the faculty of Spelman College, where she is currently serving as chair of the Department of English.

Moore, once coeditor of the "Cultural Pluralism" column in *Children's Literature Association Quarterly*, has focused much of her scholarship on visual and textual representations of African Americans in **children's literature**. In her essay on the censorship of **Maya Angelou**'s *I Know Why the Caged Bird Sings* (1970), Moore asserts that children do not need to be protected from the novel's difficult themes but rather should be allowed to grapple with the harsh truths it portrays. Similarly, Moore's **fiction** and poetry cast a clear, unflinching gaze on reality and frequently address the painful struggles of women attempting to live "sane lives." Her 1995 short story "The Fence" tells of a young black girl's beginning lessons of survival in the face of, among other things, her uncle's sexual abuse. Moore's 1999 poem "A Woman's

Virtue: Sister I Need to Hear You Sing That Song" remembers the suffering of uncelebrated women, silent and silenced.

Moore's work often deals with making sense of the everyday: with the small incidents that go on to shape life's larger purposes. One such shaping incident for Moore was her mother's attempt to teach her children table manners by insisting that they "excuse" themselves before leaving the dinner table. Moore, who only understood "excuse me" as a request for forgiveness, refused to utter what she perceived as a false admission of guilt, and so sat silently. Moore credits her mother for recognizing her refusal as meaningful and not punishing her apparent disobedience. Questions of obedience are taken up in her most recent work, a collection of poetry titled *Lot's Daughters* (2004), which focuses on the choices women make to obey or defy cultural directives. The collection also reflects on what it means for women to "look back" and considers the stories and practices that people keep secret within a culture. Currently, Moore is collaborating with artist Arturo Lindsay on a collection of images and poems that excavate the story of the *Delfina*, a Portuguese slaver ship on which fifty-one people died en route to Rio de Janeiro in 1832.

Works By

"The Day Nelson Mandela Is Voted President." *From Whence Cometh My Help: The African American Community at Hollins College.* Ed. Ethel Morgan Smith. Columbia: University of Missouri Press, 2000. 31–32.

"Enter, the Tribe of Woman." *Callaloo* 19.2 (1996): 340–347.

"Eulogy for Sister." *Callaloo* 19.3 (1996): 622–623.

"False Flattery and Thin History: A Study of Three Novels for Children." *The Black American in Books for Children: Readings in Racism.* Ed. Donnarae MacCann and Gloria Woodard. 2nd ed. Metuchen, NJ: Scarecrow, 1985. 129–143.

"The Fence." *African American Review* 29.1 (Spring 1995): 47–55.

"Freeing Ourselves of History: The Slave Closet." *Obsidian II* 3 (Spring 1988): 68–75.

"Git That Gal a Red Dress." *Honey Hush! An Anthology of African American Women's Humor.* Ed. Daryl Cumber Dance. New York: Norton, 1998. 531.

"A Happy Story." *Callaloo* 39 (1989): 274–281.

"I Fly Away: John's Song." *Callaloo* 19.3 (1996): 624–627.

"Landscapes: Shakin'." *Black American Literature Forum* 19.3 (1985): 113.

"Learning to Live: When the Bird Breaks from the Cage." *Censored Books: Critical Viewpoints.* Ed. Nicholas J. Karolides, Kee Burress, and John M. Kean. Metuchen, NJ: Scarecrow, 1993. 306–316.

Lot's Daughters. Chicago: Third World Press, 2004.

"The Mother's Board." *Callaloo* 19.1 (1996): 101–106.

"A Pilgrim Notebook, Part I: The Odyssey." *Homeplaces: Stories of the South by Women Writers.* Ed. Mary Ellis Gibson. Columbia: University of South Carolina Press, 1991. 231–242.

"A Small Insolence." *Callaloo* 24 (1985): 304–309.
"The Taste of Life Going On." *Furious Flower: African American Poetry from the Black Arts Movement to the Present*. Ed. Joanne V. Gabbin. Charlottesville: University of Virginia Press, 2004. 199.
"Walking Liberty." *Connecticut Review* 20.2 (1998): 60.
"A Woman's Virtue: Sister I Need to Hear You Sing That Song." *Callaloo* 22.4 (1999): 979–980.

Work About

MacCann, Donnarae, and Olga Richard. "Picture Books about Blacks: An Interview with Opal Moore." *Wilson Library Bulletin* 65 (June 1991): 24–28.

Stacy Grooters

MORRISON, TONI (1931–)

Chloe Anthony Wofford was born in Lorain, Ohio, in 1931, the second of four children born to George Wofford and Ramah Willis Wofford. They had moved north to escape a life of sharecropping and vigorous southern racism. They succeeded on both counts. George became a shipyard welder, and in the ethnically diverse steel town, Chloe grew up without encountering the worst of American racism. Although she was the only black child in her first-grade class, she was also the only one who already knew how to read. From early childhood, Morrison was an avid reader, a pastime fostered by her parents. The Woffords told their children stories and **folklore** from the black **community** and thus instilled in them a deep appreciation for and interest in heritage.

After graduating with honors from Lorain High School, in 1949 Chloe Wofford moved to Washington, D.C., and matriculated at Howard University, one of America's most distinguished traditionally black universities. While at Howard, Chloe changed her name to "Toni," an abbreviated version of her middle name, reportedly because people had difficulty pronouncing "Chloe." In a 1990s interview, Morrison admits regret at having made the change; however, even earlier, the theme of claiming one's name surfaces in her **fiction**. In her third novel, *Song of Solomon* (1977), Milkman Dead cannot connect past to present nor understand his own heritage until he discovers his grandfather's true name. By obscuring **identity**, the name Macon Dead—assigned by an intoxicated and indifferent white official at the Freedman's Bureau—encapsulates white culpability in the cultural breach between Africans and diasporic people. Similarly, the protagonist of her fourth novel *Tar Baby* (1981) has two names: Jadine (the name used by blacks in the novel) and Jade (the name used by whites). The dual names signify the pressure the character feels to define and claim an identity in a culture that defines and delimits individuals by **race**, gender, and **class**. But in 1953, when Toni Wofford graduated from Howard with a Bachelor of Arts degree, majoring in English and minoring in classics, her novels were still almost two decades in the future. Her immediate goal was a master's degree from Cornell University in Ithaca, New York. Having completed a thesis on suicide in the work of William Faulkner and Virginia Woolf, she graduated in 1955.

After two years of teaching at Texas Southern University in Houston, Toni Wofford returned to Howard University as a member of the faculty. There she met Harold Morrison, a Jamaican architect. The couple married in 1958 and had two sons, Harold Ford and Slade Kevin. In 1964 they divorced, and Morrison left her teaching position at Howard. With her sons, Morrison moved to Syracuse, New York, and took a job as a textbook editor for Random House. During this period, Morrison began writing at night after her children were in bed. She found writing therapeutic, a balm for the loneliness she felt. In 1967, she transferred to Random House's headquarters in New York City and became a senior editor. In that capacity, she edited many acclaimed African American women writers, including **Toni Cade Bambara** and **Gayl Jones**.

Morrison also continued to teach during these years, holding appointments at State University of New York–Purchase (1971–1972) and Yale University (1976–1977). In 1983, having already published four acclaimed novels, she left Random House and, in 1984, was appointed Albert Schweitzer chair at the State University of New York (SUNY) at Albany. She stayed at SUNY–Albany until 1989 when she was named Robert F. Goheen Professor of the Council of the Humanities at Princeton University. The appointment made Morrison the first black woman to hold a chair at an ivy league university.

Throughout Morrison's distinguished career, she has taught at a number of prestigious colleges and universities, including Bard College, Rutgers University, and Princeton University. She delivered the Clark Lectures at Trinity College, Cambridge, and the Massey Lectures at Harvard University. She has also received numerous honorary degrees, including those from Brown, Columbia, Dartmouth, Georgetown, Harvard, Sarah Lawrence College, University of Pennsylvania, and Yale. Although Morrison is perhaps best known for her fiction, she has written successfully in several other genres as well, including **drama**, **children's and young adult literature**, short story, and criticism. Morrison has published *Playing in the Dark: Whiteness in the Literary Imagination* (1992) and two collections of critical essays: *Race-ing Justice, Engendering Power: Essays on Anita Hill, Clarence Thomas, and the Construction of Social Reality* (1992) and *Birth of a Nation'hood: Gaze, Script, and Spectacle in the O. J. Simpson Case* (1997). Her awards include the highest writers can receive. Morrison is a member of the National Council on the Arts and the American Academy and Institute of Arts and Letters. She won a National Book Critics Circle Award and the Distinguished Writer Award from the American Academy of Arts and Letters in 1977; the Pulitzer Prize in 1988; the Pearl Buck Award and the title of Commander of the Order of Arts and Letters in

1994; and the National Book Foundation Medal for Distinguished Contribution to American Letters in 1996. In 1993, Morrison was awarded the
Nobel Prize for Literature, making her the first African American and only
the eighth woman to receive the prize. The body of work for which she was
awarded the Nobel Prize began with a simple story.

In the late 1960s, Morrison had joined a writing group for which she
penned a short story. That story became the basis of her first novel, *The
Bluest Eye* (1970). In *The Bluest Eye*, Morrison established her recurrent concern with the meaning and place of black female identity; the novel explores
the psychological damage the white standard of **beauty** does to black girls in
America. Pecola Breedlove wants the blue eyes that will validate her identity
and make her worthy of **love**. Although Morrison's fiction often focuses on
the place of African American women in a racist, patriarchal culture, it also
explores the ways black men are psychologically shaped by those same cultural influences. Many writers of Morrison's generation explore such themes;
however, Morrison's work allows for a nuanced complexity that many other
writers miss. Morrison's novels often turn on a specific act that is morally
reprehensible. In *The Bluest Eye*, this act is Cholly Breedlove's **rape** and im-
pregnation of his daughter. Although these acts—which include child rape,
incest, child abuse, infanticide, and murder—are condemned, the perpetrators themselves are not. Morrison places her characters within contexts that
explain, if they do not excuse, each character's complex actions. Cholly
Breedlove, warped as a young teen by white racism, is certainly not a hero;
however, many readers ultimately feel some compassion for him despite his
heinous act.

Morrison shifts her focus away from the **family** dynamic that fuels *The
Bluest Eye* to focus on black female friendship in her second novel, *Sula* (1973).
The story of Nel Wright and Sula Peace, *Sula* explores not only the psychological connection between two young girls, disparate in class and desperate for friendship, but also the ways black women are subject to and
defined by community. The black community of The Bottom, like so many
of Morrison's fictional communities, is necessary for growth, happiness, and
self-knowledge, but it can also be crippling, especially for black women. The
novel thus explores the communal forces that shape and limit Nel and Sula's
identities and the psychological consequences of the rift in their friendship.
Nel is a respectable married woman with two children whose husband leaves
her after an adulterous affair with Sula; Sula is a demonized single, childless
woman who (like her mother) openly expresses her **sexuality** by sleeping
with any man she chooses. After their break, Nel lives in an emotional abyss,
and Sula dies alone, one suffering the consequences of living within the
confines of patriarchal community and the other, those of living outside of it.
More popularly received than her first novel, *Sula* earned the nomination for
the National Book Award and thus helped solidify Morrison's place as a
premier writer of her time.

Her bestselling third novel, *Song of Solomon* (1977), offers for the first time a
male protagonist, Milkman Dead. However, the story is as much about the

women in Milkman's life as it is a record of his journey to trace his family's heritage, another theme that Morrison develops in later novels. In *Song of Solomon*, Morrison offers, as she did in *Sula*, a three-generational matriarchal family. *Sula*'s Eva, Hannah, and Sula are revised in Pilate, Reba, and Hagar. Lacking a navel, Pilate functions as a maternal force that exceeds the confines of embodiment, just as she exceeds the restrictions of the patriarchal community. Her daughter also rejects traditional, patriarchal morality by celebrating her sexuality with an abandon that seems as joyous as it is innocent. Hagar, however, is one of Morrison's many characters who loves too much. She dies after being rejected by her cousin Milkman with whom she has had a fourteen-year affair. Like her great-grandmother Ryna, Hagar cannot live without the man she loves. The novel garnered international attention for Morrison as the main selection of the Book-of-the-Month Club, the first novel by a black author to be selected since **Richard Wright**'s *Native Son* in 1949. The novel also won the National Book Critics Circle Award and the American Academy and Institute of Arts and Letters Award.

Tar Baby (1981), Morrison's fourth novel, turns the focus away from the black community to explore more directly the complex connections between blacks and whites. Even within her most interracial setting, however, the novel continues to focus on familiar themes: black heritage, black female subjectivity, and the mysteries of mother love. Jadine Childs is an internationally successful model who struggles to understand her identity in a world that defines people by race, class, and gender. Margaret Street, one of Morrison's few white female characters, also struggles to understand her self and her role in a world that classifies people by educational level and economic status. In a complex reaction to her early **motherhood** and her much-older husband, Margaret abuses her only child, a son whom she also idolizes. As in *The Bluest Eye*, *Tar Baby* explores the causes and consequences of victimization on both victims and victimizers.

Morrison's fifth novel, **Beloved** (1987), is the first book of a loosely defined trilogy that chronicles three important historical moments in African American and American **history**: **slavery**, the Great Migration, and the civil rights era. *Beloved*, which met with significant critical and popular acclaim, focuses on the psychological damage of slavery and the consequences of a mother's love so thick it transcends reason. The protagonist, Sethe, is a newly escaped slave who murders her daughter to keep her safe from the slave-catchers who have come to reclaim them under authority of the Fugitive Slave Act of 1850. The baby returns, first in spirit, then in flesh, to haunt Sethe's life until she can come to terms with her own brutal act of love. After the book failed to win the National Book Award in 1987, forty-eight prominent black writers published an open letter in the *New York Times Book Review*, lauding the work. In 1988, Morrison won the Pulitzer Prize in Literature.

Jazz (1992), Morrison's sixth novel and second in her trilogy, explores the effects of the Great Migration of rural, southern blacks to northern, urban centers in the first two decades of the twentieth century. The novel focuses on the psychological damage caused by dislocation at the individual, familial, communal, and cultural levels. As in *Song of Solomon*, the male protagonist, Joe Trace, must return to the **South** to come to terms with a familial past that includes abandonment and uncertainty. His wife, Violet, must reconcile an identity fractured by time and place and accept her feelings of loss and lack, because she has no children. Although the story, which is told in discourse that is both communal and female, begins with Joe's murder of his young lover, it ends with reconciliation and a new surrogate family for Joe and Violet.

With the publication of **Paradise** in 1998, Morrison completed her trilogy. Like *Jazz*, *Paradise* focuses on the effects of dislocation. The novel also explores the gendered and generational gap that opened in the civil rights era for an all-black community in rural Oklahoma. As in many of Morrison's novels, the characters must reconcile past with present and self with community before they can achieve any sense of identity. The characters (mainly women) must also heal the psychological damage done to them by a violent racist and patriarchal world. *Paradise* is arguably Morrison's strongest statement on the damaging effects of patriarchy on both men and women, as nine of the leading townsmen murder five women in the novel's opening scene. The tensions in this novel are not just between men and women, however; they are also about internal psychological tensions created by racial, sexual, and moral trauma. The ending, both ambiguous and hopeful in typical Morrison style, allows an image of strong, independent, united, and healed women.

Morrison's eighth novel **Love** (2003) explores many of the themes of her earlier novels: female friendship, community, patriarchy, class, sexual abuse, sexuality, dislocation, heritage, marriage, and love. The novel details the relationships between one man, Bill Cosey, and the women whose lives he shapes. What drives the story, however, is the relationship between two women whose hate is both born from and dissolved in love. *Love* is an apt title not only for her eighth book but also for Morrison's oeuvre, as in many ways the manifestions and manipulations of love are what each of her novels explores.

Works By

Beloved. New York: Knopf, 1987.
The Bluest Eye. New York: Holt, Rinehart and Winston, 1970.
Jazz. New York: Knopf, 1992.
Love. New York: Knopf, 2003.
Paradise. New York: Knopf, 1998.
Playing in the Dark: Whiteness in the Literary Imagination. Cambridge, MA: Harvard University Press, 1992.
Race-ing Justice, En-gendering Power: Essays on Anita Hill, Clarence Thomas, and the Construction of Social Reality. Ed. and intro. Toni Morrison. New York: Chatto and Windus, 1992.

Song of Solomon. New York: Knopf, 1977.
Sula. New York: Knopf, 1973.
Tar Baby. New York: Knopf, 1981.

Works About

Beaulieu, Elizabeth Ann, ed. *The Toni Morrison Encyclopedia.* Westport, CT: Greenwood Press, 2003.

Bloom, Harold. *Toni Morrison.* Philadelphia: Chelsea House Press, 2002.

Deans, Gary, dir. *Toni Morrison Uncensored.* Princeton, NJ: Films for the Humanities and Sciences, 2003.

Fultz, Lucille P. *Toni Morrison: Playing with Difference.* Urbana: University of Illinois Press, 2003.

Mbalia, Doreatha D. *Toni Morrison's Developing Class Consciousness.* Selinsgrove, PA: Susquehanna University Press, 2004.

"Nobel Laureates: Toni Morrison and William Faulkner." Introduction by William Harris. Special issue, *Proteus: A Journal of Ideas* 21.2 (2004): 1–51.

Taylor-Guthrie, Danielle, ed. *Conversations with Toni Morrison.* Jackson: University Press of Mississippi, 1994.

Julie Cary Nerad

MOSES, MAN OF THE MOUNTAIN

Zora Neale Hurston published *Moses, Man of the Mountain,* her third novel, in 1939. As is obvious from its title, the novel is a re-creation of the biblical story of Moses, but this story has a black cast of characters. While the focus for the most part is on the presentation of Moses as a "born leader," gender concerns are a constant in the development of the story line. The gender issue is established early in the novel as we witness the oppression under which Hebrew women must deliver their babies. These women are forced to deliver in silence for fear that their cries would draw the attention of the Egyptian soldiers who are on alert because of the rumors that a Hebrew leader is to be born. Other indications of the oppression or devaluation of women are found in the following incidents: the Egyptian Pharaoh's daughter is told that all she was born for was to serve as a "passageway for boy children"; Jethro is called "weak" because he has all daughters, no sons; it is suggested that women are faithless in that they are always ready to go with the conqueror; vanity and pettiness are often presented as female traits; and when the spoils of war are catalogued, women are listed along with cows, mules, wine, and household vessels.

The most obvious and dramatic examples of sexual bias, however, are connected with the presentation and development of Miriam, sister to Moses and Aaron. Although Hurston shows her to be clever, creative, and intelligent, Miriam is only reluctantly recognized as a person of voice by Moses;

more often than not, Hurston shows that Moses resents Miriam's intrusions and her attempts to be a part of the leadership. For instance, when Moses summons the Elders to discuss the plight of the Israelites, he is surprised (and not pleased) when he sees Miriam among them.

Miriam, like the other women in the novel, is accused of being vain and self-centered, focused on her own success and wealth. Moses's wife, Zipporah, is presented as short-sighted, looking back at what men had been, while Moses, the born leader, is able to look forward to what men can become. While women are criticized for their ambition, Hurston demonstrates that men who focus on achieving success and wealth are not criticized. When Aaron brags to Moses about what a great and powerful man he (Aaron) will be once they arrive in Canaan, he is not denigrated for his self-serving aspirations. At one point, Moses becomes frustrated with the outspokenness of both Aaron and Miriam and calls them to the Tabernacle to be judged by God. God punishes Miriam by making her a leper, and she remains very silent for the rest of her life, speaking only in whispers. Aaron, who has been just as outspoken, is not punished. Miriam has been subdued to the point that when she wants to die, she seeks consent from Moses.

Perhaps in the end, Moses realizes that the actions of Miriam have been pivotal in his assuming the position of "born leader" and in the Hebrews' ultimate achievement of **freedom**, because after her **death**, Moses makes sure that the young Israelites remember her efforts. While this action may appear to preserve the positive characterization of Moses, Miriam still suffers in the end.

Hurston presents Miriam as an exceptional female character, one who does not conform to the traditional female roles of wife and mother. Moses even tells Miriam at one point that the trouble with her is that nobody ever married her. Perhaps Hurston uses *Moses, Man of the Mountain* and Miriam to demonstrate that the woman who would defy gender limitations determined by the society in which she lives is destined to struggle.

Works About

Caron, Timothy P. " 'Tell Ole Pharaoh to Let My People Go': Communal Deliverance in Zora Neale Hurston's *Moses, Man of the Mountain.*" *Southern Quarterly* 36.3 (Spring 1998): 47–60.

Wallerstein, Nicholas. "Feminist/Womanist Liberation Hermeneutics and the Kyriologic of Zora Neale Hurston." *Literary Griot: International Journal of Black Expressive Cultural Studies* 11.2 (Fall 1999): 97–115.

Johnnie M. Stover

MOSS, THYLIAS (1954–)

Thylias Rebecca Brasier Moss was born on February 27, 1954, in Cleveland, Ohio. Her **family** was working **class**, with her mother, Florida Missouri Gaiter Brasier, working as a maid and her father, Calvin Theodore Bruiser, working for the Cardinal Tire Company. Moss was an only child and met her husband when she was sixteen years old and married him at age nineteen. They have two sons together, Dennis and Anisted. Having written her first short story at age six and her first poem at age seven, Moss intended from an early age to become a professional writer. She graduated with honors from John Adams High School and attended Syracuse University for two years. She later returned to college and received her B.A. in creative writing from Oberlin College in 1981. In 1983, she finished her M.A. in English at the University of New Hampshire.

The author of six collections of **poetry**, two plays, and a memoir, Moss has been publishing steadily since her first collection of poetry, *Hosiery Seams on a Bowlegged Woman*, was published in 1983. She won the Academy of American Poets College Prize for the poem "Coming of Age in Sandusky" and was named first-runner-up for the Best of Great Lakes Prize for a First Book for *Hosiery Seams on a Bowlegged Woman*. Books to follow were *Pyramid of Bone* (1989), *At Redbones* (1990), *Rainbow Remnants in Rock Bottom Ghetto Sky* (1991), *Small Congregations: New and Selected Poems* (1993), *I Want to Be* (1993), *Last Chance for the Tarzan Holler* (1998), and *Tale of a Sky-Blue Dress* (1998).

Moss's poetry has been described as having an angry, hostile, and sometimes resentful tone. Her themes range from personal **identity**, **freedom**, racism, human brutality, womanhood, **motherhood**, and **spirituality**. Although not all her poems are specifically for and about women, there is a decidedly feminist perspective present in her work. The poems in *Hosiery Seams* are reflective, emotional, and individual, whereas in *Pyramid of Bone* she begins to pose questions about larger issues regarding womanhood, spirituality, and ethnicity. She does this using thought-provoking imagery and sometimes tormented wording. *At Redbones* is a bit less negative in tone and seems to be influenced by her own childhood experiences in church and with her father's whiskey-induced Saturday night philosophical musings. The collection focuses on racism and brutality, problems she faced as a young black woman growing up. Her fourth book, *Rainbow Remnants in Rock Bottom Ghetto Sky*, departs from the rage of her first collection and focuses on joyous women's issues like pregnancy, identity, friendship, and womanhood itself. Moss uses unique metaphors in this collection, which were generally not well received by critics. Moss's feminist themes are continued in *Last Chance for the Tarzan Holler*, which includes topics such as motherhood, **sexuality**, and spirituality.

Perhaps Moss's most powerfully feminist book is her memoir *Tale of a Sky-Blue Dress*, in which Moss describes the abuse she suffered as a child. A teenage babysitter who lived in the same apartment building as the Mosses subjected Moss to physical, emotional, and sexual abuse, shattering the safe, comfortable world her parents had created for her. At the babysitter's encouragement, Moss was raped by the babysitter's brother. As a result of this abuse, Moss had several adolescent relationships with men that were abusive.

Works By

At Redbones. Cleveland, OH: Cleveland State University Press, 1990.
The Dolls in the Basement. Produced by New England Theatre Conference, 1984. (Play.)
Hosiery Seams on a Bowlegged Woman. Cleveland, OH: Cleveland State University Press, 1983.
I Want to Be. Illustrated by Jerry Pinkney. New York: Dial, 1993. (For children.)
Last Chance for the Tarzan Holler: Poems. New York: Persea, 1998.
Pyramid of Bone. Charlottesville: University of Virginia Press, 1989.
Rainbow Remnants in Rock Bottom Ghetto Sky. New York: Persea, 1991.
Slave Moth: A Narrative in Verse. New York: Persea Books, 2003.
Small Congregations: New and Selected Poems. Hopewell, NJ: Ecco Press, 1993.
Tale of a Sky-Blue Dress. New York: Avon Books, 1998. (Memoir.)
Talking to Myself. Produced in Durham, NH, 1984. (Play.)

Work About

Bloom, Harold. *The American Religion.* New York: Simon and Schuster, 1992.

Kyla Heflin

MOSSELL, GERTRUDE (1855–1948)

Gertrude Bustill was born to a prosperous Philadelphia **family** who could trace their ancestry in the United States back to the time of the Revolutionary War. She began her career in Philadelphia as a schoolteacher, and although she would ultimately make her greatest mark in the field of print journalism, she viewed herself throughout life as an educator and civic reformer.

By the early 1870s, Bustill had become a regular contributor to several of the city's leading black periodicals such as the *AME Church Review*, *Philadelphia Echo*, and the *Independent*. Her work also appeared in Philadelphia publications directed primarily at a white readership, including the *Philadelphia Times*, the *Philadelphia Inquirer*, and the *Philadelphia Press*. Outside of the city, she printed editorials and reports in several national periodicals like *Indianapolis World*, *Ladies' Home Journal*, and *New York Freeman*.

The *New York Freeman*, which grew to be one of the largest and most influential African American newspapers in the country during the Reconstruction era, proved fertile ground for Bustill's social and political interests. In December 1885, she began her own column, "Woman's Department," the first women's column in an African American newspaper. A firm supporter of women's suffrage and educational reform, Bustill used her column to advise African American women about uplift through vocational opportunities and independent thinking. She offered practical advice on such matters as dealing with recreant husbands, rearing children, and managing money.

In 1893, Gertrude Bustill married Nathan F. Mossell, a Philadelphia physician and the founder of **Frederick Douglass** Memorial Hospital. The marriage produced two daughters and resulted in the new appellation, Mrs. N. F. Mossell. Under this name, Mossell published a collection of eight essays and seventeen poems called *The Work of the Afro-American Woman* (1894). In 1902, she authored the children's book *Little Dansie's One Day at Sabbath School* (1902).

Her 1894 essay collection chronicles the achievements of black women, listing inventors, land prospectors, and musicians, among others. In "A Sketch of Afro-American Literature" and "The Afro-American Women in Verse" she pays tribute to the literary innovations of women of color and takes a particular interest in the bourgeoning work of **race** historians. She points out the attractiveness of a career in the field of journalism and proffers useful advice to beginning women journalists in areas ranging from newspaper layout to interviewing techniques. Her essay "The Opposite Point of View" goes on to challenge conventional gender proscriptions, which maintained that a woman's only true vocation was **motherhood** and **domestic** service for her husband. A happy woman, Mossell argues, must possess a mind of her own.

Throughout her life, Mossell remained active in the black **community** of Philadelphia. She worked tirelessly as a fund-raiser for African American health services and as a sponsor for black media, helping originate the idea for the founding of the Associated Negro Press. In 1899 she organized the Philadelphia branch of the Afro-American Council, the forerunner of the National Association for the Advancement of Colored People.

Works By

Little Dansie's One Day at Sabbath School. Philadelphia: Geo S. Ferguson Company, 1902.
The Work of the Afro-American Woman. 2nd ed. Philadelphia: Geo S. Ferguson Company, 1908.

Works About

Streitmatter, Rodger. *Raising Her Voice: African American Women Journalists Who Changed History.* Lexington: University Press of Kentucky, 1994.
Tate, Claudia. *Domestic Allegories of Political Desire: The Black Heroine's Text at the Turn of the Century.* New York: Oxford University Press, 1992.

Judith Mulcahy

MOTHERHOOD

Mother Africa—the birthplace of humanity. Images of motherhood in African American feminist **literature** are rooted in the foundations of African culture.

The transcending resonance of the experiences of all African mothers lingers in the heart of each African American mother. **May Miller**'s "One Blue Star" describes a black mother's connection to Africa's maternity:

> And I, who had but once conceived, who had for one brief period only felt life within my womb, knew the stirring of generations within me, suffered the agony of multitudinous birth. Life of dim eras, of far-flung continents swept through and over me. . . . I was one with timelessness—I became the black mother.

The image of the mother is deeply rooted in every aspect of African society, **folklore**, and culture, and the image of the African mother filters through in all aspects of life.

In African **family** units the relationship between mother and child is of primary importance and is the foundation for a healthy kinship group. African mothers forge deep and lifelong bonds with their children. For women, their mothers teach them all of the **domestic** arts as well as the feminine ones. Men honor their mothers and provide for their comfort and security. Grandmothers also hold a special place in African society as the holders of family **history**, folklore, and other traditions. Grandmothers command very high status in African society and are perceived as occupying a special place between the earth-bound family and the **ancestors**. Grandmothers are an integral part of the familial relationship and are deeply respected and valued in African kinship groups. The **rape** of Africa by white societies' slave traders threatened to destroy the African family and, most particularly, the maternal relationship.

Grandmothers were particularly important within the fractured remnants of slave families and were the bearers of surviving tradition and wisdom. Older female slaves took on the role of grandmother and/or mother to those young black children who were ripped from their mothers' loving arms. For those fortunate slaves who were not sold from their nuclear kin, their blood grandmothers became the bedrock upon which small family groups were allowed to exist. In **Harriet Jacobs**'s *Incidents in the Life of a Slave Girl* (1861), the horrors of **slavery** rival the greater horror of losing the **love** and respect of her grandmother. For Jacobs, an estrangement from her grandmother is unthinkable. In **Zora Neale Hurston**'s *Their Eyes Were Watching God* (1937), Janie spends considerable time being taught by her grandmother, Nanny. In one poignant scene, Nanny passes on the experience of her slavery and explains to Janie her mixed heritage. When the master's mistress finds out that Nanny's child was half white, the mistress threatens her with a hundred lashes. Nanny took her baby, Janie's mother, and fled in the night to eventual **freedom**. Janie learns from her grandmother that she has the freedom to dream. Marilyn Fullen-Collins's "Mama" describes the speaker's grandmother who "grins big and safe." In **Alice Moore Dunbar-Nelson**'s "The Stones of the Village" (1905) a young boy's grandmother is the only parent he has ever known. In **Paule Marshall**'s affecting tale "To Da-Duh, in Memoriam" (1967) a young modern black girl meets her grandmother in Barbados for the first time. Marshall's story is a charming, yet bittersweet, meeting of old ways and new, of a grandmother who tries to impart to her citified granddaughter the wonders of her age-old wisdom and of her beloved Barbados. In Nora Brooks Blakely's poem "To Grandmother's House We Go" her grandmother represents the venerable forces of love. **Black feminist** literature is resplendent with images of African American grandmothers, whose acumen and perseverance gave birth to, and prepared, generations of black mothers.

African American feminist writers own, define, and celebrate their maternity, a vitalizing expression of freedom from white racist beliefs about black women. Whites defined black motherhood within the context of slavery, thereby devaluing black maternity, creating then reaffirming white **stereotypes** of black motherhood as occupying only certain roles: **Mammy**, breeder, or cook. Harriet Jacobs in *Incidents in the Life of a Slave Girl* describes her grandmother's reputation as a great cook. In **Frances E. W. Harper**'s novel *Iola Leroy* (1892), Iola loves her Mammy, "just as much as I do my own mother." In her defense of slavery, Iola argues that her Mammy "loves us just as if we were her own children" despite the fact that Mammy could be sold at a whim. **Dorothy West**'s "Mammy" is a clever satire uniting the role of Mammy, the modern welfare system, and slavery. A Negro Welfare Investigator is charged with reviewing an application for Old Age Assistance from Mrs. Mason, former Mammy to the Colemans. Mrs. Coleman desperately wants Mammy back. The young Black Investigator must return Mammy to the Colemans, despite Mammy's protest and desire for freedom. Her application for benefits is denied. In **Rita Dove**'s play *The Darker Face of the Earth* (1994), Phoebe tells of the fate of her mother, a faithful Mammy and servant to the Big House, who catches the fever by sneaking food to infected field hands.

Slavery fractured and dissipated the very condition of motherhood for African American women, reducing and then defining black motherhood as merely breeding for profit, a commodification of their bodies as well as a commodification of their ability to reproduce. African American motherhood itself was also a victim of white defeminization of black women. Black female slaves were regarded as nothing more than breeders, effectively separating white ideals of motherhood from black motherhood, thereby justifying the removal of a black woman's children by slaverholders. **Sojourner Truth** describes her pain as a slave mother in her 1851 speech at the Women's Convention in Akron, Ohio: "I have borne thirteen chilern and seen 'em mos' all sold off into slavery, and when I cried out with a mother's grief, none but Jesus heard—and ar'n't I a woman?" Black female slaves had to defend against both white denial of their femininity as well as denial of their right to feel the human condition of motherhood. **Mary Prince**, in *The History of Mary Prince, a West Indian Slave* (1831), gives a chilling account of her mother, who was given the task of preparing her own children for the auction block; her mother then had to transport her children to the marketplace and stand by and watch while each one was sold. Maya Angelou's "Grandmothers" begins with a mother's flight to freedom and the terrified children she struggles to save.

African American feminist literature is suffused with heart-wrenching images of children torn from their mothers. Tragic images like these are common throughout **slave narratives** as black writers, both women and men, attempt to articulate the numbing horror of children ripped from their mothers' arms and sold to an unknown fate. Frances E. W. Harper's "The Slave Mother" describes a mother's torment as her son is taken from her. Much of Harper's **poetry** contains images of children severed from their mother's arms. In "Bury Me in a Free Land" the speaker witnesses "her babes torn from her breast/like trembling doves from their parent nest." In Harper's "Eliza Harris" (1853) a desperate mother runs to freedom to save her child. In **Toni Morrison**'s *Beloved* (1987), Sethe attempts to kill her children to save them from the slave catcher; to Sethe, the only way to save her children from suffering the hell of slavery is to "put [her] babies where they'd be safe." Paul D tells Sethe her love is "too thick." Morrison's *Beloved* exposes how slavery disfigures and corrupts that thick love bond between mother and child, laying bare slavery's assault upon African American mothers.

Motherhood and mothering images take on a wide variety of forms in African American feminist literature. As black women writers validate their femininity in their works, they also recapture and reframe their experience as mothers, free of white constructs. In **Jessie Redmon Fauset**'s *Plum Bun: A Novel without a Moral* (1929), Angela learns from her mother that there is a dazzling world of joy and freedom that is wholly black. The motherhood bond was discombobulated by the commodification of the black **body**, both male and female. African American feminist writers reconfigure the white dehumanization of black motherhood by revealing, within their essays, poetry, and **fiction**, a profoundly authentic motherhood experience that survived all efforts to destroy it. Gladys Casely Hayford's "The Nativity" celebrates the wonder and unity of black motherhood. In Frances E. W. Harper's "My Mother's Kiss," a young man expresses the gentle **memory** of his mother's comfort. The simple kiss pressed "on my brow" that represents when "all my life was fair." **Marita Bonner**'s "One Boy's Story" presents a charming and loving portrait of a mother from a child's point of view. **Alice Walker**, in "In Search of Our Mothers' Gardens" (1983), explores the artistic repression of the African woman who "dreamed dreams no one knew. . . . Our mothers and grandmothers, some of them; moving to music not yet written. And they waited. They waited for a day when the unknown thing that was in them would be made known; but guessed, somehow in their darkness, that on the day of their revelation they would be long dead." And in Frances E. W. Harper's "The Two Offers" (1859), the rich gift of motherhood becomes the greatest artistic endeavor of all: "Every mother should be a true artist, who knows how to weave into her child's life images of grace and beauty, the true poetry capable of writing on the soul of childhood the harmony of love and truth, and teaching it how to produce the grandest of all poems—the poetry of a true and noble life."

African American feminist writers' rich literary voices continue the boundless connection between all African American mothers, who captivate their daughters with age-old wisdom and a compelling sense of belonging. Their voices continue the tradition of the souls of many mothers lifting and supporting each other, timeless and eternal.

Works About

Beaulieu, Elizabeth Ann. *Black Women Writers and the American Neo-Slave Narrative: Femininity Unfettered*. Westport, CT: Greenwood Press, 1999.

Berry, Cecelie S., ed. *Rise Up Singing: Black Women Writers on Motherhood*. New York: Doubleday, 2004.

O'Reilly, Andrea. *Toni Morrison and Motherhood: A Politics of the Heart*. Albany: State University of New York Press, 2004.

Patton, Venetria K. *Women in Chains: The Legacy of Slavery in Black Women's Fiction*. Albany: State University of New York Press, 2000.

Wilkie, Laurie A. *The Archaeology of Mothering: An African-American Midwife's Tale*. New York: Routledge, 2003.

Debbie Clare Olson

MULATTO/A

The word *mulatto*, derived from the word *mule*, embodies within it the idea that people with one parent of African descent and one parent of European descent fit uneasily, if at all, into the existing natural and social orders. The question of whether Africans and Europeans were separate species, and mulattoes hybrids between the two, was debated by American and European scientists throughout much of the nineteenth and early twentieth centuries. In **literature**, the idea that mulattoes are inevitably divided beings, beset by a crippling internal conflict between opposing racial tendencies, was most common during the early twentieth century, especially in **fiction** that constructed **race** through the conventions of naturalism. This literary movement, influenced by Social Darwinism, treated human character as the product of interactions between genetic inheritance and environment. In 1933, African American poet and critic Sterling Brown coined the phrase "tragic mulatto" to refer to the internally conflicted biracial characters in fictions of his own day, including Geoffrey Barnes's *Dark Lustre* (1932) and, better known now thanks to two movie adaptations, Fannie Hurst's *Imitation of Life* (1934). **Nella Larsen**'s *Quicksand*, published in 1928, portrays a heroine similarly torn between conflicting racial heritages, though with considerably more nuance than the fictions Brown criticized, through his use of the term "tragic mulatto," for their simplistic portrayal of supposedly inherent racial traits.

Sterling Brown also used the term "tragic mulatto" to refer to characters in earlier fictions, particularly those of the abolitionist era. However, as he recognized, these mid-nineteenth-century characters shared little with their early-twentieth-century counterparts except their authors' apparent belief that certain traits are both heritable and racially linked. In antebellum fictions, mulattoes, rather than being crippled by their mixed racial heritage, are often the most admirable of the slave characters, possessing intelligence, bravery, and **beauty** beyond that of their darker-skinned counterparts (and, sometimes, their white masters). When they die—as they often but not always do—it is because of external conflict with a racist society that has not made a place for them (though, their creators imply, it could and should), not because of an internal conflict between supposedly incompatible racial heritages.

Despite their ability to expose the illogic and injustice of social systems based on race, the mulatto characters in abolitionist fiction were open to the criticism, often raised by proslavery reviewers, that they exemplified the best traits of their European **ancestors** rather than their African ones, and so presented a poor argument for either abolition or racial equality. Perhaps the most famous characters in this category are Eliza and George Harris of Harriet Beecher Stowe's 1852 *Uncle Tom's Cabin* and the title character of **William Wells Brown**'s 1853 *Clotel, or the President's Daughter*. Brown's novel follows a slave daughter of Thomas Jefferson on her journey through households representing various manifestations of the slave system, ending in Clotel's eventual escape, through suicide, from the slave catchers, and the survival of her daughter in exile in Europe. Brown, perhaps as a result of observing audience reactions to abolitionist lectures by the light-skinned escaped slave **Ellen Craft** and her dark-skinned husband **William Craft**, seems to have been especially aware of the potential pitfalls of focusing on mulatto characters. Although he kept his heroine light-skinned through several revisions of the novel, he transformed his original mulatto hero into an equally heroic character of unmixed African descent in later versions of the book. Stowe, too, created a heroic black character in her second antislavery novel, *Dred* (1856), but also included a sensitive and intelligent mulatto hero, Harry Gordon.

Abolitionist writers' tendency to focus on light-skinned protagonists, and especially light-skinned heroines, carried over into postbellum African American fiction. Authors including **Frances E. W. Harper**, **Charles Chesnutt**, **Pauline Hopkins**, and **Jessie Redmon Fauset** centered novels around mulatto protagonists. The dark-skinned heroine of **Gwendolyn Brooks**'s 1953 *Maud Martha* is usually cited as the first major exception to this pattern. In some turn-of-the-century novels, such as Harper's 1892 *Iola Leroy* and Hopkins's 1900 *Contending Forces*, the focus on light-skinned characters played some of the same roles it had in abolitionist fiction, reminding readers of the socially constructed nature of racial dividing lines and exposing—though often somewhat obliquely—the sexual victimization of black women by white men. For Hopkins as well as Chesnutt, and later Larsen, mulatto characters also provided an opportunity to examine the social and psychological significance of **passing**.

While mulatto characters often allowed African American authors to explore in useful ways the intersecting constructions of race and **class**, the prevalence of light-skinned protagonists in the early African American fictions had other, less positive, effects on the developing African American literary tradition. As **Alice Walker** points out in her 1982 essay "If the Present Looks Like the Past, What Does the Future Look Like?" (republished in 1983 in *In Search of Our Mothers' Gardens*), one of the most troubling legacies of the literary focus on mulatta heroines is its ability not only to reflect but also to help perpetuate Eurocentric standards of beauty, and the associated phenomena of colorism and light-skin privilege, both in American society at large and within African American communities.

The recovery of nineteenth-century African American women's literature in the last quarter of the twentieth century provided new insight into the systems of sexual and racial domination, ranging from **rape** to more complex forms of sexual exploitation, that led to the birth of mulattoes. The 1987 republication of **Harriet Jacobs**'s 1861 **slave narrative** *Incidents in the Life of a Slave Girl*, long thought to be a novel but revealed by Jean Fagan Yellin's research to be based on real people, places, and events, opened a window on the complicated choices made by a slave woman who, threatened with rape by her master, evaded him by choosing another white man to father her children and later negotiated the task of telling her story to an audience of white northern women whose concepts of sexual morality were shaped by their own relatively sheltered experience. **Harriet E. Wilson**'s 1859 *Our Nig*, republished by Henry Louis Gates in 1983, centers around a mulatta heroine whose more unusual origins reveal intersections between class and race; her white mother, abandoned by a white seducer, accepts an offer of marriage from an African American man, only to abandon their daughter, Frado, to a form of indentured servitude that is little different from **slavery** after her black husband dies and she returns, with a new lover, to a white world that would not accept her mixed-race daughter.

Fiction of the late twentieth century also explores African American women's exploitation during and after slavery and the continuing legacy of those experiences in contemporary black women's lives. **Gayl Jones**'s 1975 *Corregidora* tells the story of a 1930s **blues** singer charged by her great-grandmother with remembering the story of her own and her daughter's exploitation by the same white master and still seeing the effects of this white heritage—jealousy from darker-skinned black women, desirability to black men—in her own life. **Octavia Butler**'s 1979 *Kindred* traces the legacy of slavery further into the twentieth century, telling the story of an African American woman in 1976 who finds herself repeatedly transported to the nineteenth century to rescue a young white boy who will grow up to coerce her great-great-grandmother into a sexual relationship and so become her ancestor. **Barbara Chase-Riboud**'s *Sally Hemings*, also published in 1979, explores in detail the same relationship that had inspired William Wells Brown's *Clotel*: the then-rumored, now almost certainly confirmed, long-term liaison—in Chase-Riboud's interpretation, a genuine **love** affair—between Thomas Jefferson and his late wife's slave and half sister, Sally Hemings.

In more recent years, authors have begun to explore the experiences of biracial children conceived in the very different, but still complicated, racial atmosphere that prevailed during the civil rights struggle of the 1960s and its aftermath in the 1970s. **Danzy Senna**'s 1999 novel ***Caucasia*** tells the story of two sisters, one light-skinned like their white mother and one dark-skinned like their black father, separated by their parents' divorce but eventually reunited as each seeks to define her own **identity**. James McBride, in his 1997 memoir *The Color of Water*, reflects on the experience of growing up with a Jewish mother who passed as black, while Rebecca Walker, daughter of Alice Walker, tells her own story in *Black, White, and Jewish: Autobiography of a Shifting Self* (2002).

Though American understandings of race have changed considerably over the course of the last two centuries, much can still be learned about the construction of racial identity in the United States by examining the lives—real or fictional—of Americans who embody two or more different "racial" heritages. At the same time, if an accurate picture of the workings of race in America is to be formed, such accounts cannot be the only or even the dominant voice but instead must continue to be balanced by others exemplifying the full variety of African American experiences.

Works About

Brown, Sterling. "Negro Character as Seen by White Authors." *Journal of Negro Education* 2.2 (April 1933): 179–203.

Carby, Hazel. *Reconstructing Womanhood: The Emergence of the Afro-American Woman Novelist.* New York: Oxford University Press, 1987.

Christian, Barbara. *Black Women Novelists: The Development of a Tradition, 1892–1976.* Westport, CT: Greenwood Press, 1980.

Fredrickson, George M. *The Black Image in the White Mind: The Debate on Afro-American Character and Destiny, 1817–1914.* New York: Harper and Row, 1971.

Gossett, Thomas F. *Race: The History of an Idea in America.* 1963. Reprinted with new preface and bibliography. New York: Oxford University Press, 1997.

Sollors, Werner. *Neither Black Nor White Yet Both: Thematic Explorations of Interracial Literature.* New York: Oxford University Press, 1997.

Catherine E. Saunders

MULES AND MEN

One of the strengths of Part I of **Zora Neale Hurston**'s ethnography *Mules and Men* (1935) is its evaluation of gender roles within specific southern black folkloric communities, represented here primarily by the people of Eatonville, Florida. Part II takes Hurston into the world of Hoodoo where she becomes a student of several Hoodoo priests, eventually becoming a priest herself. While Part II is an interesting account of the secretive world of Hoodoo ceremonies, this entry focuses on the gender issues more clearly raised in Part I of this text.

Hurston used her own literary voice to develop an ethnography that did justice to the authenticity of black folktales by placing the predominantly black male text within a black female frame. What emerges is a richer and more realistic picture of the black storytelling **community** than a strict, unadorned anthropological listing of the tales could have provided. In constructing this study, Hurston also gives the reader insight into how the struggle over the control of language affects the public and private places of the men and women of the community, pitting black males against black females in linguistic battles for power. In Part I of *Mules and Men*, twenty-eight of the storytellers are men, while only four are women; of the seventy stories related, sixty-five are told by men, five are told by women, and only one (Mathilda Mosley's "Why Women Always Take Advantage of Men") is told from a woman's perspective. The more Hurston experienced these storytelling sessions (which were called "lying" sessions), the more she recognized how gender specific the tales were. While the storytellers in traditional West African villages were usually women, Hurston shows how that tradition reverses itself in these African American communities, mirroring the European American tradition of privileging the male. Hurston confronts and tackles this cultural reversal in the structuring of *Mules and Men* by putting her female voice in the privileged position as overall narrator.

The residents of Eatonville located their primary site for lying on the porch of Joe Clarke's store. But, as Hurston demonstrates, the actual physical site was not crucial when it came to the act of storytelling; the community could function anywhere as long as there was a storyteller, a story, and an audience that shared the same sense of community, thus creating a common setting. The storytelling in *Mules and Men* shifts to a number of locations as the participants move around to various open spaces: the sawmill, the swamp, the fishing lake, and so on. What is notable, however, is that the lying sessions recorded by Hurston all take place outside—that is, in what was traditionally seen as the public male space. The indoor spaces—the "jook" joints and houses—seem to resist the act of storytelling. Even when the men visited Hurston at her **home** to share their lies with her, they take her outside to do it. That indoor, private, female, **domestic** space is not conducive to the male appropriation of storytelling, so they remove the telling to their venue as a reassertion of their power and control.

After recounting her Hoodoo adventures in Part II of *Mules and Men*, Hurston ties the two parts of the ethnography together and asserts her own power as storyteller by relating the tale of "Sis Cat." "Sis Cat" is an apt conclusion to *Mules and Men* because, as a folktale that Hurston herself tells, it brings full circle the anthropological, literary, cultural, and gender factors that Hurston encounters and tries to re-present in her ethnography. Just like the clever and subversive Sis Cat, she has successfully devoured the mouse and can now calmly sit back, "washing [her] face and usin' [her] manners."

See also Folklore

Works About

Andrews, Adrianne R. "Of *Mules and Men* and Men and Women: The Ritual of Talking B(l)ack." *Language, Rhythm, and Sound: Black Popular Cultures into the Twenty-first Century.* Ed. Joseph K. Adjaye and Adrianne R. Andrews. Pittsburgh: University of Pittsburgh Press, 1997. 109–120.

Wall, Cheryl A. "*Mules and Men* and Women: Zora Neale Hurston's Strategies of Narration and Visions of Female Empowerment." *Black American Literature Forum* 23.4 (Winter 1989): 661–700.

Johnnie M. Stover

MULLEN, HARRYETTE (?–)

Harryette Mullen is a poet and critic who was born in Florence, Alabama, and raised in Texas. Known for her experimental poetics and her critical attention to often overlooked black writers, Mullen is the author of six books of **poetry**, including *Tree Tall Woman* (1981), *Trimmings* (1991), *S*PeRM**K*T* (1992), *Muse & Drudge* (1995), *Sleeping with the Dictionary* (2002), *Blues Baby: Early Poems* (2002), and a book-length critical study titled *Freeing the Soul: Race, Subjectivity, and Difference in Slave Narratives* (1999). Among other honors, she has received the Gertrude Stein Award in Innovative Poetry, the Rockefeller Fellowship from the Susan B. Anthony Institute for Women's Studies, and nominations for the National Book Award and the National Book Critics Circle Awards. Mullen is associate professor of English and African American studies at the University of California at Los Angeles.

The poems in Mullen's first book, *Tree Tall Woman*, are written in a voice intended to represent black **community**, but it is a voice she now describes as not entirely her own. In response to this realization, Mullen began to write poems in which the subjectivity of the speaker would shift. The books that followed demonstrate a break with forms of poetry in which the range of possibilities in speaker's **identity** is assumed to be static and knowable. In *Trimmings*, Mullen explores the way the category "woman" is constructed through language about women's clothing. Her short prose poems allow the many meanings of words associated with feminine clothing or objects for women (including articles of clothing, colors, and clothing metaphors) to direct the narrative. In the next book, *S*PeRM**K*T*, Mullen explores consumption and capitalism through prose poems about the supermarket. Each poem takes a different area of the supermarket as a field of language through which meta-narratives about **race**, **class**, and gender are inscribed. The personas of both books trouble the idea of an authentic, stationary self.

After publishing *Trimmings* and *S*PeRM**K*T*, Mullen noticed that her audiences had become increasingly white, a stark difference from her audience for *Tree Tall Woman*. In response, she set out to write *Muse & Drudge*, a book of poems that would unite her audiences by continuing to use innovative forms and by bringing a varied, inclusive perspective on African and diasporic traditions. Mullen's next book, *Freeing the Soul*, is a critical study of the ways in which narrative silences and other conventions of the **slave narrative** genre are gendered. She followed with *Sleeping with the Dictionary*, a highly acclaimed book in which narratives about gender, race, nationality, and class are threaded through poems with a playful take on the dictionary and thesaurus. *Blues Baby* includes the poems of *Tree Tall Woman* as well as other early poems that were previously uncollected.

Mullen's feminist concerns can be read in the content of her works, but they are also present in her attention to form. Her explorations of women's language, women's dress, and the ways in which the spaces women inhabit shape their narratives give form to her poems and critical essays. In Mullen's work, representations of gender are complicated by other forms of difference, such as race, nation, and class.

Works By

Blues Baby: Early Poems. Lewisburg, PA: Bucknell University Press, 2002.
Muse and Drudge. Philadelphia, PA: Singing Horse Press, 1995.
Sleeping with the Dictionary. Berkeley: University of California Press, 2002.
S*PerM**K*T. Philadelphia, PA: Singing Horse Press, 1992.
Tree Tall Woman. N.p: Energy Earth Communications Inc., 1981.
Trimmings. New York: Tender Buttons, 1991.

Works About

Bedient, Calvin. "The Solo Misterioso Blues: An Interview with Harryette Mullen." *Callaloo* 19.3 (1996): 651–669.
Frost, Elizabeth. "Signifyin(g) on Stein: The Revisionist Poetics of Harryette Mullen and Leslie Scalapino." *Postmodern Culture* 5.3 (May 1995).
Griffith, Farah Jasmine, Michael Magee, and Kristen Gallagher. "A Conversation with Harryette Mullen." 1997. epc.buffalo.edu/authors/mullen/interview-new.htm.
Pearcy, Kate. "A Politics of Opposition? Race and the Avant-Garde." *Poetry and the Public Sphere.* The Conference on Contemporary Poetry, April 24–27, 1997. english.rutgers.edu/pierce.htm.

Mendi Lewis Obadike

MURPHY, BEATRICE M. (1908–1992)

Beatrice M. Murphy was born in Monessen, Pennsylvania, in 1908. Though a lesser figure of the **Harlem Renaissance** and the ensuing years, Murphy did play a significant role in encouraging the artistic and literary endeavors of young black writers. She spent the majority of her life in Washington, D.C., where she graduated from Dunbar High School in 1928. Her literary career began as a poet and writer with the African American newspaper the *Washington Tribune*, and she eventually became the publication's reviews editor. Murphy converted to Catholicism in the 1930s and began to extend her efforts toward her **community** as part owner of a circulating library that would eventually become part of a special library collection.

During the 1940s, Murphy worked for the Office of Price Administration (OPA), a federal agency established during World War II to prevent wartime inflation. The OPA could control prices and ration consumer products and was successful in keeping the consumer market stable during the war years. The agency was disbanded in 1947.

Like many artists and writers during the 1950s, Murphy was persecuted during the McCarthy era, a time when the U.S. government, following the lead of Senator Joseph McCarthy, actively sought out members of the Communist Party. Murphy was accused of membership in a subversive community organization, but she successfully disproved the charges and, unlike many of her peers, was able to clear her name. During the 1960s, Murphy gained prominence in the black literary community through her **work** with the Negro Bibliographic and Research Center (NBRC), which eventually became known as the Minority Research Center. The Negro Bibliographic and Research Center aimed to chronicle the works of African American writers and published a journal titled the *Negro in Print*, a bibliographic survey. Murphy served as editor of this journal between 1965 and 1972. After Murphy moved on to other endeavors, the NBRC continued to chronicle the black community through a variety of bibliographic tomes covering subjects including black English and the black church.

Throughout her lifetime, Murphy was a tireless advocate for black writers—promoting their work whenever possible and offering support, emotional and otherwise, to writers in need. Murphy's special collections form the bulk of material at the Black Studies Division of the Martin Luther King, Jr. Memorial Library in Washington, D.C. The noncirculating reference collection includes rare books, textiles, pamphlets, bibliographies, **slave narratives**, and other historical artifacts. She died in 1992.

Works By

Ebony Rhythm: An Anthology of Contemporary Negro Verse. Ed. Beatrice M. Murphy. Freeport, NY: Books for Libraries Press, 1968.
Get With It Lord. Washington, DC: Wineberry Press, 1990.
Love Is a Terrible Thing. New York: Hobson Book Press, 1945.
The Rocks Cry Out. Detroit: Broadside Press, 1969.
Today's Negro Voices: An Anthology by Young Negro Poets. Ed. Beatrice M. Murphy. New York: Julian Messner, 1970.

Roxane Gay

MURRAY, PAULI (1910–1985)

Pauli Murray was a remarkable woman whose life and career mark her as a true Renaissance woman. A lifelong warrior for civil rights, she challenged both racial and gender discrimination policies at the University of North Carolina at Chapel Hill and Harvard, respectively, and though both challenges were unsuccessful, they were crucial steps to eliminating the exclusive policies at both schools. She received her undergraduate degree from Hunter College in New York City and went on to attend law school at Howard University, where she engaged in several nonviolent protests in the 1940s, long before their popularity in the 1950s and 1960s. Murray received graduate degrees in law from the University of California at Berkeley and Yale University; later she would practice law as well as teach at the Ghana School of Law and at Brandeis, where she not only taught law but also was responsible for helping to design their first African American Studies program. Murray was also an ardent advocate for women's rights, coining the phrase "Jane Crow" to refer to women's second-class status in the United States and serving as one of the founding members of the National Organization for Women (NOW) in 1966. In 1973, at the age of sixty-two, Murray entered divinity school and in 1977 became one of the first women, and *the* first African American woman, ordained a priest in the Episcopal church in the United States. Murray died on July 1, 1985.

Murray was also a gifted writer and is most well known for her autobiographical works. *Proud Shoes* (1956) chronicles the story of her maternal grandparents, Robert and Cornelia Fitzgerald, who raised her, the former a free black man from Chester County, Pennsylvania, who came to North Carolina during Reconstruction as a teacher devoted to educating the newly freed slaves, and the latter the offspring of a slave woman named Harriet and her owner Sidney Smith, a member of a prominent Orange County family, who raped her repeatedly. Later Sidney's brother Frank would claim Harriet for himself and produce three more daughters. Mary Ruffin Smith, the Smith brothers' unmarried sister, raised eyebrows when she took the girls into her household, brought them up much differently than other Smith slaves, including instilling in them a sense of their aristocratic blood, and bequeathing each of them substantial parcels of land upon her **death**. The book is a milestone, not only for its recounting of the success of an African American **family** during Reconstruction and the early twentieth century but also for the way it tells the national story of America's tangled **race** relations and racial identities; it makes a worthy companion to **Harriet Jacobs**'s *Incidents in the Life of a Slave Girl* (1861).

In 1987, two years after her death, *Song in a Weary Throat: An American Pilgrimage*, the **autobiography** she was working on with editors up to the time of her death, was published. The autobiography recounts Murray's awakening to both racial and gender inequities and eloquently explains how she shaped herself into the civil rights' activist and feminist she became. The autobiography won the Lillian Smith Award in 1987, was widely and positively reviewed, and was later reprinted by the University of Tennessee Press as *Pauli Murray: The Autobiography of a Black Activist, Feminist, Lawyer, Priest, and Poet.*

Murray also published one volume of **poetry**, *Dark Testament and Other Poems* (1970), which has largely been neglected but deserves greater attention. The collection can be characterized as containing a significant number of poems that speak to racial and economic injustices as well as a section of beautiful, striking, and conflicted **love** poems that are particularly intriguing, especially in light of the struggles Murray underwent in the 1930s and 1940s with her gender **identity** and **sexuality**, when most of the love poems were written. Murray found herself emotionally and sexually drawn to women but was unable to accept **lesbianism** as a respectable identity. Her distress over her attractions to women and her deep belief that she was really biologically a man resulted in several psychiatric hospital stays and finally abdominal surgery to assure her that she did not have "hidden" male sex organs. Following this surgery, Murray seems to have relinquished her struggle over her gender and sexuality and turned her energies toward her **work**; nonetheless, the love poems are significant for they can be read as helping to establish an African American lesbian tradition in poetry brought to fruition in the work of such writers as **Audre Lorde**, **June Jordan**, and **Pat Parker**.

Works By

The Constitution and Government of Ghana. With Leslie Maxwell. London: Sweet and Maxwell, 1961.
Dark Testament and Other Poems. Norwalk, CT: Silvermine, 1970.
Pauli Murray: The Autobiography of a Black Activist, Feminist, Lawyer, Priest, and Poet. 1987. Knoxville: University of Tennessee Press, 1989.
Proud Shoes: The Story of an American Family. 1956. Boston: Beacon Press, 1999.
Song in a Weary Throat: An American Pilgrimage. New York: Harper and Row, 1987.
States' Laws on Race and Color. 1955. Athens: University of Georgia Press, 1997.

Works About

Bucher, Christina. "Pauli Murray: A Case for the Poetry." *North Carolina Literary Review*, no. 10 (2004): 59–73.
"Dialogue: Pauli Murray's Notable Connections." *Journal of Women's History* 14.2 (2002): 54–86.
Drury, Doreen Marie. " 'Experimentation on the Male Side': Race, Class, Gender, and Sexuality in Pauli Murray's Quest for Love and Identity, 1910–1960." Ph.D. diss., Boston University, 2000.
O'Dell, Darlene. *Sites of Southern Memory: The Autobiographies of Katherine Du Pre Lumpkin, Lillian Smith, and Pauli Murray.* Charlottesville: University of Virginia Press, 2001.

Christina G. Bucher

MYTH, USE OF

Readers typically associate the word *myth* with classical figures such as Odysseus or Hercules, but many African American female writers allude to biblical myths more frequently than classical ones to develop images and metaphors that reflect the struggle for **freedom** and dignity in a sexist and racist world. Christian mythology is an integral part of African American **literature** and dates back to the singing of **spirituals**, which are biblical songs sung by the earliest slaves. Black female writers are especially fond of using biblical examples of hope to engage their readers' imagination. The Jews' captivity described in Exodus is mentioned so frequently by female authors that scholars now consider the Jews' enslavement as a common trope that captures the African Americans' experience with **slavery**. **Frances E. W. Harper** in *Moses: A Story of the Nile* (1869) discusses her personal sacrifices in relation to the Jews' bondage; likewise, **Phillis Wheatley** in her letter to Samson Occom likens slave owners to the Egyptians and slaves to the chosen people of God. The **history** of African American feminist literature spans approximately only 250 years, yet a majority of black female writers express a common thematic concern: the struggle of black women to seek dignity and freedom in a racist and sexist environment. Central to the literary expression of this struggle are the biblical myths used as thematic declarations by black feminist writers who searched for a voice, respect, and the freedom to explore their **identity** through literary writings.

Biblical myths play an important part in eighteenth- and nineteenth-century black women's literature. Phillis Wheatley's *Poems on Various Subjects, Religious and Moral* (1773) represents one of the few literary works that mingle biblical and classical myths to underscore thematic concerns. "To the University of Cambridge, in New-England" invokes the aid of the Muses of epic **poetry**, then alludes to the Jews' captivity and, later the shedding of Jesus' blood. Wheatley's book created a stir among readers who believed that artistic expressions such as poetry were beyond the capabilities of slave girls like Wheatley, yet her skillful poetics and grasp of current events, which exposed the horrors of slavery, earned laudatory reviews from her contemporaries, including **Sojourner Truth**.

Wheatley's biblical metaphors and their relation to slavery encouraged other feminists such as Sojourner Truth (born Isabella) to use the Bible's teachings to critique social concerns such as slavery and women's rights. Truth was illiterate, but she convinced Olive Gilbert to write and publish the *Narrative of Sojourner Truth* (1850), a **slave narrative** that in part silences a minister's accusations by pointing out that Christ came into the world through the efforts of God and a woman and that no man had any part in the birth of Christ. Truth uses biblical myths to support her struggles for freedom, but her views infuriated the leaders of numerous religious sects, including Methodist, Baptist, Episcopal, Presbyterian, and Universalist ministers, who often used the Bible as an authoritative document to support racial and patriarchal oppression.

The question of biblical interpretation dates back to the practice of singing spirituals, which were songs that depicted the slaves' interpretations of biblical myths. The spirituals were an oral expression of hope and redemption that encouraged the slaves to struggle against oppression, and while scholars are uncertain whether or not women composed spirituals, black women's literature certainly echoed the spiritual songs' thematic use of biblical myths to encourage their struggles against oppression.

For feminists such as Sojourner Truth and **Maria Stewart**, the Bible clearly describes exemplary human behavior. Truth's most famous speech "Ar'nt I a Woman?" (1851) challenged racial and sexual **stereotypes** by reminding the audience that Jesus was befriended numerous times by women, such as Mary and Martha. Stewart also utilized biblical metaphors and myths to raise awareness of feminist struggles. Her *Productions of Mrs. Maria W. Stewart* (1835) is a social critique that scholars credit for encouraging subsequent writers to use literature to effect political and cultural changes, but by the time Stewart begins writing, black feminists are already beginning to address gender as well as slavery concerns.

Writers such as Frances E. W. Harper and Ada (Sarah L. Forten) contributed to antislavery journals such as the *Liberator* and the *Abolitionist* but were also well known for emphasizing a lifestyle that followed biblical teachings. Harper's *Poems on Miscellaneous Subjects* (1854) addresses the anguish of slave mothers who lost their children, and the conclusion of "Woman's Political Future" reminds audiences that Rome once protected the apostle Paul because he was a natural citizen. Harper ultimately suggests that, like Rome, America too should care for its own citizens, male and female, black and white.

Harper's works encouraged other black women to find their literary voice, though by the time the Civil War ends, the literary structure of the **protest tradition** begins to change. Writers still refer to biblical teachings and metaphors, but within an evolving literary style. In the landmark novel *Our Nig; or, Sketches from the Life of a Free Black, in a Two-Story White House, North* (1859) by **Harriet E. Wilson**, she examines the typical African American by incorporating literary realism into a text that features, in part, a questioning of heaven's existence for the African **race**. Nineteenth-century feminists do not doubt the existence of God or the validity of the Scriptures, but changing literary styles suggest that subtle transformations in cultural attitudes toward race and gender are taking place before and after the Civil War.

The Civil War brought an end to slavery but not to the struggle for the rights of African Americans. Many black women aided the Civil War effort with their writings, and they continued to fight against patriarchal social structures after gaining their freedom. Feminists such as Frances E. W. Harper encouraged other writers such as **Anna Julia Cooper** to aid the cause of black women everywhere. Cooper was one of the first black women to receive a Ph.D., and she is remembered by scholars for her lifelong **work** educating black women by using a philosophical approach firmly rooted in biblical morals and beliefs.

Promoting biblical myths and teachings became easier with the emergence of an African American press, which featured publications such as *Freedom's Journal* and the *Mystery*. The African American press allowed writers such as **Pauline Hopkins** and **Ida B. Wells-Barnett** to reach an audience sympathetic to their political and social exhortations for equality. Hopkins's ***Contending Forces***: *A Romance of Negro Life North and South* (1900) addresses social concerns of African American women, and later activists such as W.E.B. Du Bois credit Hopkins for bringing to America's attention the tension that precedes social changes. The African American press also enabled a generation of black writers to promote social upheaval through their writings, and by the time World War I began, black men and women were publishing works in every genre and style. The African American press greatly aided the efforts of social reformers, and subsequent writers were encouraged to use literature to effect cultural changes. Many feminist writers of the **Harlem Renaissance** produced literature concerned with patriarchal oppression and, like their predecessors, relied upon biblical myths to address racism and sexism.

The quest for freedom and respect continues for writers of the Harlem Renaissance, but the women authors most commonly associated with this era—**Zora Neale Hurston**, **Gwendolyn B. Bennett**, and **Anne Spencer**—are well known for their reliance on biblical and classical myths to discuss feminists concerns. Hurston's ***Their Eyes Were Watching God*** (1937) celebrates the individual woman's triumphs over sexism and poverty, but in terms that recall biblical teachings. Hurston's novel begins with Pheoby and Pearl discussing other townspeople, but Pheoby soon rebukes Pearl for implying that couples should use their marital beds only to praise God. Spencer uses classical and biblical myths to celebrate gender and race; in "Before the Feast of Shushan," she creates a monologue that extols the independence of women by parodying the first twelve verses of the Book of Ester, which tells of King Ahasuerus's anger at Queen Vashti's refusal to come when he calls. And Spencer concludes "At the Carnival" (a poem celebrating the poetry of **Paul Laurence Dunbar**) by alluding to Neptune to praise Dunbar's poetry. Like Hurston, Spencer and others such as Bennett underscore their works with parodies of biblical myths, though the range and scope of their imagery expand considerably over that of the previous generation's writers.

The women writing after the Harlem Renaissance often celebrated the mundane to emphasize their struggles, though many authors still drew from biblical myths to enhance their poetic expressions. **Gwendolyn Brooks**'s *A Street in Bronzeville* (1945) captures the everyday life of Chicago's ghettos, but through metaphors that recall the struggles of black women and their reliance on the Bible. The speaker in "the preacher: ruminates behind the sermon" begins by speculating about God's probable loneliness, then immediately suggests that His stern master persona promotes isolation. **Margaret Walker**'s poetry has been noted by scholars for its rich biblical imagery, due undoubtedly to the influence of her father, a minister; indeed, critics often liken the title poem of Walker's *For My People* (1942) to a sermon. Black writers, however, still center their writings on the struggles (especially racism and sexism) of women everywhere.

Ann Petry and **Lorraine Hansberry**, for example, reproach the naive efforts of black women trying to survive in a patriarchal society. Petry's ***The***

Street (1946) concentrates on the efforts of a black woman's failure to secure a respectable living for herself and her son. And in Hansberry's ***A Raisin in the Sun*** (1959) the implication that Beneatha will probably never attend medical school undercuts Mama Younger's marginal success at the play's end; Beneatha's dream is deferred by Walter's mismanagement of most of the family's money.

The focus on the struggles of young women and their relation to biblical myths shifted during the **Black Arts Movement** of the 1960s. Writers such as **Sonia Sanchez** abandoned the use of biblical myths to emphasize the struggles for individuality. Sanchez's "Summer Words of a Sistuh Addict" features a rebellious narrator who uses drugs to alter her feelings immediately after attending church services; **Carolyn Rogers**'s poem "Jesus Was Crucified" features a speaker who discredits the Bible's teachings and celebrates individual expression. The writers of the Black Arts Movement are known more for their celebration of liberty and black culture than for their use of biblical myths as literary expressions, though later writers such as **Maya Angelou** return to biblical myths to underscore feminist motifs.

Angelou's *And Still I Rise* (1978) encourages women to confront destructive forces in their lives; likewise, **Toni Morrison**'s *Song of Solomon* (1977) address the history of racial struggles in America, and **Adrienne Kennedy**'s *Funnyhouse of the Negro* (1969) centers on the harmful effects of cultural clashes between Africans and Europeans. Literary works by black women today often maintain subtle references to biblical myths; Celie in **Alice Walker**'s *The Color Purple* (1982) grieves about abusive treatment in letters addressed to God; **Rita Dove**'s poem "Receiving the Stigmata" alludes to the five wounds of Christ; and the speaker in **Michelle Cliff**'s "Within the Veil" states plainly that God's love alone will not overcome racism. Beginning with **Lucy Terry**, black women writers have expressed their frustrations with racism and sexism, and although the structure of literary expressions has evolved from folk and gospel songs to highly polished prose, poetry, and **drama**, the cry for freedom—and its relationship to biblical myths—is still heard today.

See also Christianity; Religion

Works About

Bassard, Katherine Clay. *Spiritual Interrogations: Culture, Gender, and Community in Early African American Women's Writing.* Princeton, NJ: Princeton University Press, 1999.

Harris, Trudier. *Saints, Sinners, Saviors: Strong Black Women in African American Literature.* New York: Palgrave, 2001.

Hubbard, Dolan. *The Sermon and the African American Literary Imagination.* Columbia: Missouri University Press, 1994.

James N. Ortego II

 **N**

NARROWS, THE

Through its main characters, Link Williams and Camilla Treadway, **Ann Petry**'s *The Narrows* (1953) studies the psychology of **race** and its pernicious impact on both black and white communities. Set in New England, Petry's third novel builds upon naturalistic elements introduced in *The Street* (1946), yet extends themes introduced in this award-winning novel by exposing the impact of racism not just on individuals but on communities as a whole. Unlike other black writers who, at the time, used predominantly black settings to study the impact of racism on African Americans, Petry's choice to situate the novel within a disconnected New England city mirrors her feminist critique of the isolation and psychic fragmentation that occurs when black Americans are separated from their past, their people, and their **history**.

The Narrows tells the story of Dartmouth-educated Link, a black man who, through a chance, heroic encounter, meets and falls in **love** with Camilla, the married, well-to-do daughter of the town's most affluent and powerful white **family**. Hiding her marriage and status behind a false name, Camilla begins a relationship that ends abruptly when Link learns that she is married and that their engagement is a sham. Camilla cries **rape**, Link is arrested, and in the midst of a very public media scandal, he is kidnapped and murdered. In the same way that 116th Street in Harlem served as the setting for Petry's literary excavation of the impact of place upon the human psyche in *The Street*, the relationship between Link and Camilla offers a similarly poignant commentary on the pervasiveness of racism in both black and white communities. Each character has inherited a set of behavioral codes formed from a racist history; in the end, neither can escape the stereotypical roles that history has created.

Even though black women play primarily supporting roles in *The Narrows*, the novel's focus on **community** connects it to a tradition of black women's **fiction** where, even without a female protagonist, the **literature** nevertheless maintains feminist elements. Protagonist Milkman Dead's reclamation of his collective history in **Toni Morrison**'s *Song of Solomon* (1977) is facilitated, in part, by female relatives Pilate and Hagar; Link's downfall, in contrast, is that he lacks female family members to connect him to his history. Petry's fictional Monmouth, Connecticut, is completely dislocated from black culture and history. In the end, Link's tragedy is not that he is naive and weak; his tragedy is that he lives without a familial connection to black women and, by extension, his cultural heritage.

Works About

Barry, Michael. " 'Same Train Be Back Tomorrer': Ann Petry's *The Narrows* and the Repetition of History." *MELUS* 24.1 (Spring 1999): 141–159.

McDowell, Margaret B. "*The Narrows*: A Fuller View of Ann Petry." *Black American Literature Forum* 14.4 (Winter 1980): 135–141.

Shanna Greene Benjamin

NAYLOR, GLORIA (1950–   )

The oldest child of migrants from Robinsville, Mississippi, Gloria Naylor grew up in the burroughs of New York City. She was born on January 25, 1950, just one month after Roosevelt and Alberta McAlpin Naylor left the **South** in search of better **work** opportunities for themselves and better education for their future children. Roosevelt worked as a transit worker, while Alberta worked as a telephone operator.

Although it would not be until she enrolled at Brooklyn College that Naylor would realize the existence of **black feminist** writers, her own familial legacy gave Naylor her first gleanings of black feminists. Her maternal great-aunt Sadie worked in vaudeville, while another great-aunt, Aunt Mae, was "a successful bootlegger" who also owned two apartment buildings in Harlem that served as way stations for **family** members making their transition to a better life for themselves. Of the family stories that Naylor inherited was one of her paternal grandmother, Callie Canada Naylor, who was reported to have held a shotgun to Gloria Naylor's grandfather and a young woman. Her maternal grandmother, Luecelia Johnson McAlpin, was rumored to have had an affair with the local blacksmith, who visited quite frequently, despite the fact that the McAlpins did not own a horse.

Naylor's mother, Alberta, was the conduit to this feminist legacy as she emphasized the acquisition of knowledge as the key to advancement. Restricted from checking out books from her local library in Mississippi, Alberta saved money from a weekend job to join a book club that would send her books. In fact, it was Alberta who insisted that her children not be born in Mississippi because of the state's paltry record of restricting education to blacks. It was also Naylor's mother who fought and won the battle with her husband to ultimately settle in Queens, where she believed their children would receive better educations than in the upper Bronx, where Roosevelt felt most comfortable.

As a child, Naylor had a shy temperament that her mother recognized, giving her a diary to express herself. The young Naylor was a voracious reader and would dream stories that would continue from night to night. She also fantasized about the idea of being a writer, but she did not believe that to be even a remote possibility until her introduction to **Toni Morrison**, **Ntozake Shange**, and **Alice Walker** while Naylor was a student at Brooklyn College.

In 1963, Alberta Naylor joined the Jehovah's Witnesses religious group, and two of her three daughters accompanied her, including the oldest, Gloria. Still, Gloria was not baptized into the faith until 1968 when she was eighteen years old. (The group only allowed adults to be baptized.) Instead of going to Hunter College at this point, as she had planned, Gloria Naylor began full-time ministry, a trek that would last seven years. During that time, she lived in Dunn, North Carolina, and Jacksonville, Florida, as part of her ministry duties. However, in 1975, when Armageddon had not arrived as the Jehovah's Witnesses had prophesied, Naylor left the sect and enrolled in Brooklyn College.

Before graduating from Brooklyn College in 1981, Naylor had worked full-time as a switchboard operator, published a short story in *Essence* magazine, and sealed a deal to publish ***The Women of Brewster Place*** (1982). In this six-year span, Naylor was introduced to black women novelists, and by the end of it, she was among their ranks. For the first time, she read **Gwendolyn Brooks**, **Nikki Giovanni**, and other black women writers and began to identify with these women. In the works of these writers, she discovered feminism and African American **literature** and expanded her self-definition as more than her parents' child, a Christian, and a switchboard operator. Before her discovery of Toni Morrison in a creative writing class, Naylor wrote **poetry** but did not have confidence in her ability to write prose **fiction**. Naylor's first short story was published in *Essence* in 1979. A contract with Viking followed shortly thereafter. The *Essence* story in addition to several others became *The Women of Brewster Place*, essentially a collection of seven short stories made a cohesive unit by the common residence that the characters share at a dead-end street punctuated by a brick wall that separates the characters from the rest of the city.

Naylor subsequently enrolled in Yale University to pursue a Master of Arts in Afro-American studies with plans to pursue a Ph.D. in American studies. Her plans were thwarted by her realization that academic inquiry and creative writing required different levels of energy and that her allegiance was to her creative work. After one year in the master's program, Naylor negotiated an arrangement that would allow her to use ***Linden Hills*** (1985) as the thesis required for graduation. *Linden Hills* was a follow-up to *The Women of Brewster*

Place in which Naylor explored issues inherent in the increase of the black middle and upper **class**. In 1983, Naylor was also writer-in-residence at Cummington Community of the Arts. From 1983 to 1984, she was visiting lecturer at George Washington University, and in 1984 she became a contributing editor to *Callaloo*, a leading African and African American literary journal.

Her other accomplishments include service as a cultural exchange lecturer with the United States Information Agency in India in 1985, a stint as scholar-in-residence at the University of Pennsylvania, and a visiting professorship at New York University in 1986, a visiting lectureship at Princeton University (1986–1987), and a visiting professorship at Boston University (1987). She also served as a Book-of-the-Month Club judge in addition to serving as the Fannie Hurst visiting professor at Brandeis University in 1988. She has adapted **Bailey's Café** (1992) into a play and founded One Way Productions, an independent **film** production company. In addition, she has written for *Southern Review*, *Ms.*, *Life*, *Ontario Review*, and *People*.

One of the common threads to be found in at least Naylor's first four novels is the strength inherent in communities of women. Whether the strength is embraced or not, the reservoir is there for sustenance if it is desired. In *The Women of Brewster Place*, women are there to nurture in times of disappointment and heartache. In *Linden Hills*, it is not the living women who reach out to each other for support but the dead Nedeed wives who speak to Willa through the relics in the basement, telling her of past horrors and that her own despair is nothing new. Perhaps they, as the reader and author herself do, want her to choose a path other than that they lived. **Mama Day** (1988) is steeped in the mysteries of womanhood, of ushering forth life and even creating it or withdrawing it. Still, it is a woman who is sought out to wield power over life and **death** and a woman who leads the characters in their reverence for their **ancestors**.

Although Naylor's body of work bears tremendous emphasis on the trials and triumphs of the African American woman, her work ultimately becomes the story or stories of the black couple—male/female, female/female, and male/male. Naylor and other black women writers have often been criticized for the negative portrayal of black men in their novels. However, Naylor has commented that she went to great lengths to do the converse in *The Women of Brewster Place*. A kind of justification and airing of the men's perspective is given in her fifth book, **The Men of Brewster Place** (1998). Largely, though, her work is about how women have negotiated, survived, or succumbed to their often tumultuous relationships with men or the structures or barriers to progress that they impose.

The concept of space is a strong one in Naylor's novels. In each, the characters are set apart from some other person or group of people. For instance, the residents of Brewster Place are separated from the rest of the city by a brick wall. They come to embrace this city-mandated seclusion, forming their own sense of **community**. Nonetheless, they finally reject the wall for the restriction that it represents and the despair that festers as a result of its presence. Space operates on at least two levels in *Linden Hills* in which Willa has been relegated to a dungeonlike space as punishment for having a light-skinned child. While a space of confinement, the basement also privies Willa to women's stories that she would not have known otherwise. Alternately, the entire novel is concerned with what the most desirable space is to be in and what price the characters are willing to pay to be in that space of residence—the space also of certain relationships and a particular professional existence. For Linden Hills residents, the price of living in their suburban space causes havoc in the other segments of their lives to the point of divorce, alcoholism, specious marriages, and even suicide. In the first two novels, residential space appears to be defined by a construct of **whiteness** either directly or through some reaction to white oppression. In *The Women of Brewster Place*, the residents are outcasts from the mainstream of the city. In *Linden Hills*, blacks create their own enclave, realizing an unspoken exclusion from other places. However, the characters in *Mama Day* claim their own space. Although once owned by a slave master, Willow Springs is owned by the black residents of Willow Springs never to be relinquished to whites again. It is an unspoken agreement that Willow Springs belongs to the people of Willow Springs only. They claim that in its geographical separation from the United States it does not even belong to or in the United States. Naylor demonstrates the very tenuous connection between the two worlds in the bridge that goes out intermittently. No permanent bridge is desired. The people of Willow Springs own their space in a way that other Naylor characters do not. Finally, the world in *Bailey's Café* is a place of escape, actually the last hope for survival. At first, it is the only place the characters can go, but it becomes a place where the characters choose to stay, a place where characters find they belong. Because of the ethereality of the café, those exiles or runaways can be at **home** and coexist with one another.

Willa's story is threaded throughout *Linden Hills*. On the surface, she has all the advantages of a modern woman (education and a strong familial legacy of women) that would lead one to believe that she would choose for herself the benefits now available to women, a broader definition of womanhood other than mother and wife, at any cost. To the readers' and the author's dismay, she chooses to be a wife and mother even to the death. Even in marrying Luther Nedeed, she chooses the ideal of marriage over the value of herself. When her husband restricts her to the basement, she learns that her marriage has never been about her and would never be. She serves only a biological function for her husband, as all of the Nedeed wives before her had done. Willa never usurps her feminine power, as she has the opportunity to do.

Mattie Michael's story is more complete than any other in *The Women of Brewster Place*. The reader sees her sexual initiation, the rejection she receives from her father when she refuses to tell him the name of her baby's father, her migration, and her struggle as a single mother. Although Mattie is an elderly woman for much of the novel, she perhaps never loses her innocence, and that is to her undoing. Her wide-eyed, youthful innocence leads to her first sexual encounter with Butch Fuller, which leads to her pregnancy. It is also her same trusting nature that leads her to post bail for her son who was charged with murder. When her son skips bail, she moves to Brewster Place. There, she is the mother to all, finding a place where the others are even more lost than she is. On Brewster Place, Mattie seems to find direction. Brewster Place needs a mother and finds one in Mattie Michael.

Works By

Bailey's Café. New York: Harcourt, Brace, Jovanich, 1992. Paperback reprint, New York: Vintage/Random House, 1993.

Children of the Night: The Best Short Stories by Black Writers, 1967 to Present. Ed. Gloria Naylor. Boston: Little, Brown, 1995.

Linden Hills. New York: Ticknor and Fields, 1985. Paperback reprint, New York: Penguin, 1986.

Mama Day. New York: Ticknor and Fields, 1988. Paperback reprint, New York: Penguin, 1989.

The Men of Brewster Place. New York: Hyperion, 1998.

The Women of Brewster Place: A Novel in Seven Stories. New York: Viking, 1982. Paperback reprint, New York: Penguin, 1983.

Works About

Andrews, Larry. "Black Sisterhood in Gloria Naylor's Novels." *CLA Journal* 33.1 (1989): 1–25.

Donlon, Joycelyn. "Hearing Is Believing: Southern Racial Communities and Strategies of Story-Listening in Gloria Naylor and Lee Smith." *Twentieth Century Literature* 41.1 (1995): 16–35.

Felton, Sharon, and Michelle C. Loris, eds. *The Critical Response to Gloria Naylor.* Westport, CT: Greenwood Press, 1997.

Fowler, Virginia C. *Gloria Naylor: In Search of Sanctuary.* Twayne United States Authors Series, #660. New York: Simon and Schuster Macmillan, 1996.

Gates, Henry Louis, Jr., and K. A. Appiah, eds. *Gloria Naylor: Critical Perspectives Past and Present.* New York: Amistad, 1993.

Kelley, Margot Anne, ed. *Gloria Naylor's Early Novels.* Gainesville: University Press of Florida, 1999.

Lattin, Patricia Hopkins. "Naylor's Engaged and Empowered Narrative." *College Language Association Journal* 41.4 (1998): 452–469.

Whitt, Margaret E. *Understanding Gloria Naylor.* University of South Carolina Press, 1999.

Sharese Terrell Willis

NEELY, BARBARA (1941–)

Barbara Neely began her writing career in 1981 with the publication of her short story "Passing the Word" in *Essence*; since then her stories have appeared in a variety of magazines and anthologies. In 1992 she published her first novel, a mystery titled *Blanche on the Lam*; the immediate popularity of her sleuth character ensured the success of the Blanche books that followed. Neely is now best known as the author of the Blanche White mystery novels.

Blanche on the Lam introduced Neely's protagonist, a middle-aged, heavyset, dark-skinned African American **domestic** worker saddled with the incongruous and redundant name Blanche White and blessed with a personality marked by its feisty humor. Blanche's no-nonsense behavior and her savvy tell-it-like-it-is observations immediately endeared her to readers. Although Blanche solves some mystery in each novel, her assertive personality and outspoken commentary on social issues often take front seat to the plot. Neely has Blanche respond to social ills both through her behavior and her pointed observations about life. The Blanche mysteries illustrate how racism, classism, and sexism permeate everyday life, especially for the poor and for women of color.

Neely's use of **detective fiction** as a vehicle for speaking out about social injustices is just one more dimension of a life that has centered on social activism. Born in Lebanon, Pennsylvania, in 1941, Neely went through school being, more often than not, the only African American in her classes. In 1971 she moved to Philadelphia, where she worked for the Philadelphia Tutorial Project and became involved with various inner-city issues, especially housing. This interest led to her earning a master's degree in urban studies from the University of Pittsburgh. Upon graduation she took a job with the Pennsylvania Department of Corrections, where she helped to establish and then run the state's first **community**-based women's correctional facility.

Concern for social inequities is a constant in Neely's life, expressed through a wide range of jobs—including administering a YWCA and a Head Start program—and despite several relocations. During a stint in Raleigh, North Carolina, she produced radio shows for the African News Service and was a writer for *Southern Exposure*. She has been a director for Women for Economic Justice and was a founding member of Women of Color for Reproductive Freedom. Neely has received several awards for her commitment to social action, including the Women of Courage and Conviction Award for Literature. In addition to her current writing career, Neely hosts *Commonwealth Journal*, a radio public affairs program. She lives in Jamaica Plain, Massachusetts.

Not surprisingly, Neely's fiction is an extension of her social activism. But it is also good entertainment. When the first Blanche White mystery, *Blanche on the Lam*, hit the market, it garnered enthusiastic reviews and won several accolades, including the prestigious Agatha, Macavity, and Anthony awards. Neely followed this success with three other Blanche White books, *Blanche among the Talented Tenth* (1994), *Blanche Cleans Up* (1998), and *Blanche Passes Go* (2000). Each story highlights some social ill, and Blanche offers plenty of opinions about the problem as she does her sleuthing.

Blanche on the Lam examines the effects of **race** and **class** stereotyping, with special focus on how the **Mammy (Aunt Jemima) stereotype** affects African American women. Blanche spells out the power these social constructions of race have to do psychic damage and the strength it takes to resist internalizing their demeaning images. Blanche fits the Mammy physical type, and she is a longtime domestic worker, but her very un-Mammy-like thoughts and behavior leave no doubt that she has not bought into this stereotype, although she sometimes manipulates this image to become invisible or to stay safe. Her need to do so is just one of the indignities that comes with being "the help."

Blanche among the Talented Tenth criticizes the African American color hierarchy, in which lighter skin brokers into greater social status. Blanche sadly notes how this attitude has produced a large market for skin lighteners, hair straighteners, and other products that tempt African Americans to accept a white world's standard of **beauty**. In *Blanche Cleans Up* Neely address issues that are not as specifically race related as those in her first two books. Here a cluster of social ills weaves through the story, including homophobia, lead poisoning, and teen pregnancy. In *Blanche Passes Go* Neely uses her protagonist to illustrate the life-changing effects of physical **violence** on women. In this story Blanche tries to come to terms with her long-ago **rape**. Her search for peace and **healing** is difficult, partly because she keeps noticing other brutalized women, including victims of sexual assaults, domestic violence, and murder.

In addition to her social commentary, Neely contributes to the mystery genre a memorable cast of African American characters, helping to fill a need in this mass-market category. Casting her sleuth as a heavyset, middle-aged domestic worker with dark skin and an attitude is a particularly strong contribution, filling a near void in a genre with plenty of strong, sassy women sleuths but few of color, few not trim and fit, few near poverty, and few who use their stories as vehicles for social commentary.

See also Detective Fiction

Works By

Blanche among the Talented Tenth. New York: St. Martin's, 1994.
Blanche Cleans Up. New York: Viking, 1998.
Blanche on the Lam. New York: St. Martin's, 1992.
Blanche Passes Go. New York: Viking, 2000.

Works About

Bailey, Frankie Y. "*Blanche on the Lam*, or The Invisible Woman Speaks." *Diversity and Detective Fiction.* Ed. Kathleen Gregory Klein. Bowling Green, OH: Bowling Green State University Popular Press, 1999. 186–204.
Carroll, Rebecca. *I Know What the Red Clay Looks Like.* New York: Crown Trade, 1994. 174–184.
Geiger, Shirley Tolliver, and Natalie Hevener Kaufman. "Barbara Neely's Blanche White Series." *Clues: A Journal of Detection* 22.2 (2001): 95–108.
Herbert, Rosemary. *The Fatal Art of Entertainment: Interviews with Mystery Writers.* New York: G. K. Hall, 1994.

Jablon, Madelyn. " 'Making the Faces Black': The African-American Detective Novel." *Changing Representations of Minorities East and West*. Ed. Larry E. Smith and John Rieder. Honolulu: College of Languages, Linguistics and Literature, University of Hawaii, 1996.

Mueller, Monika. *Sleuthing Ethnicity: The Detective in Multiethnic Crime Fiction*. Madison, NJ: Fairleigh Dickinson University Press, 2003.

Plummer, Bonnie. "Subverting the Voice: Barbara Neely's African American Detective." *Clues: A Journal of Detection* 20.1 (1999): 77–88.

Tolson, Nancy D. "The Butler Didn't Do It So Now They're Blaming the Maid: Defining a Black Feminist Trickster through the Novels of Barbara Neely." *South Central Review: The Journal of the South Central Modern Language Association* 18.3–4 (2001): 72–85.

Witt, Doris. "Detecting Bodies: Barbara Neely's Domestic Sleuth and the Trope of the (In)visible Woman." *Recovering the Black Female Body: Self-Representations by African American Women*. Ed. Carla L. Peterson. New Brunswick, NJ: Rutgers University Press, 2001. 165–194.

Grace McEntee

NELSON, MARILYN (1946–)

Poet Marilyn Nelson is also an award-winning writer for children, a skilled translator, and critic. She was born in Cleveland, Ohio, the daughter of Melvin M. Nelson, a career serviceman in the U.S. Air Force who wrote **poetry** and **drama**, and Johnnie Mitchell Nelson, a teacher who was herself the descendant of teachers. Growing up largely on military bases, Nelson had started composing poetry by age eleven and was writing seriously by the time she was in college. She holds a B.A. from the University of California, Davis; an M.A. from the University of Pennsylvania; and a Ph.D. from the University of Minnesota.

Nelson's books of poetry include *For the Body* (1978), the title of which suggests the collection's central metaphor; *Mama's Promises* (1985), which further considers the **body** as grounds of female **spirituality**; and the multigenerational **family** collage *The Homeplace* (1990), which won the 1992 Annisfield-Wolf Award and was a finalist for the 1991 National Book Award. Later collections are *Magnificat* (1994) and *The Fields of Praise: New and Selected Poems* (1997), which won the 1998 Poets' Prize and other awards and was a finalist for the 1997 National Book Award. Another collection that treats a remarkable historical subject, *Carver: A Life in Poems* (2001), won several awards, was named a Newbery Honor Book and a Coretta Scott King Honor Book, and became a finalist for the 2001 National Book Award.

Nelson has translated poems by Halfdan Rasmussen, Inge Pedersen, Thornkild Bjornvig, and others; has written a young adult book, *Fortune's Bones* (2004), to be performed with music by Ysaye Barnwell of Sweet Honey in the Rock; a book of sonnets for young adults, *A Wreath for Emmett Till*

(2005); and other publications. Nelson's version of Euripides's play *Hecuba* appeared in the Penn Greek Drama Series in 1998. She has also published articles on **Paule Marshall**, on poetic form, on N. Scott Momaday, and on the tradition of African American writing.

Nelson's many awards include a John Simon Guggenheim Fellowship that supported her work on "The Cachoiera Tales," (2005) a long poem depicting a group of Aframerican tourists in Brazil on a pilgrimage that evokes Chaucer's *Canterbury Tales* (1380). In addition, Nelson has received two Pushcart Prizes; two creative writing fellowships from the National Endowment for the Arts; a Fulbright Teaching Fellowship; the 1990 Connecticut Arts Award; and a Contemplative Practices Fellowship from the American Council of Learned Societies. In June 2001, Nelson was named the poet laureate of the state of Connecticut for a five-year term.

Nelson has taught in Denmark and Germany; at St. Olaf College; at the University of Connecticut, where the Thomas J. Dodd Research Center houses a selection of her papers; at the University of Delaware; and as a visiting writer at many other schools in the United States and abroad. With Martín Espada, she directs the Third World Villanelle Society.

Works By

Cachoiera Tales and Other Poems. Baton Rouge: Louisiana State University Press, 2005.
Carver: A Life in Poems. Asheville, NC: Front Street Books, 2001.
The Fields of Praise: New and Selected Poems. Baton Rouge: Louisiana State University Press, 1997.
For the Body. Baton Rouge: Louisiana State University Press, 1978.
Fortune's Bones. Asheville, NC: Front Street Books, 2004.
The Homeplace. Baton Rouge: Louisiana State University Press, 1990.
Magnificat. Baton Rouge: Louisiana State University Press, 1994.
Mama's Promises. Baton Rouge: Louisiana State University Press, 1985.
A Wreath for Emmett Till. New York: Houghton Mifflin, 2005.

Works About

Adcock, Betty. Review of *Carver: A Life in Poems. Southern Review* 39.3 (Summer 2003): 650–670.
Dick, Rodney Franklin. "Creative and Constructive Tensions: A Discussion of the Poetry of Marilyn Nelson (Waniek)." M.A. thesis, University of Louisville, 2000.
Gardiner, Susan. "Bootleg, Jackleg Medicine: Curing as Only Generations Can." Review of *The Homeplace. Parnassus* 17.1 (1992): 65–78.
Hacker, Marilyn. "Double Vision." Review of *The Fields of Praise: New and Selected Poems. Women's Review of Books* 15.8 (May 1998): 17–18.
Kitchen, Judith. "I Gotta Use Words." Review of *The Fields of Praise: New and Selected Poems. Georgia Review* 51.4 (Winter 1997): 756–776.

Pettis, Joyce. "Marilyn Nelson." *African American Poets: Lives, Works, and Sources*. Westport, CT: Greenwood Press, 2002. 262–269.

Rosengarten, Theodore. "America in Black and White." Review of *A Wreath for Emmett Till*. *New York Times Book Review*, November 11, 2004, 43.

Williams, Miller. Review of *The Fields of Praise: New and Selected Poems*. *African American Review* 33.1 (Spring 1999): 179–187.

Katharine Rodier

NEO-SLAVE NARRATIVE

Generally speaking, neo-slave narratives can be defined as fictional texts whose primary unifying feature is their central thematic focus on new world **slavery**. Many of these narratives were written to fill in the gaps and recover the silences often left in the original **slave narratives** and as such engage with themes of **history**, **memory**, and **identity**. Like the slave narratives and abolitionist **fiction**, which appeared in a variety of forms and for a variety of reasons, neo-slave narratives are also heterogeneous. Yet despite this formal variety, neo-slave narratives can be loosely organized into two general types: narratives that mimic the autobiographical form of the original slave narratives and narratives that engage with the larger cultural and historical effects of plantation slavery.

Although there are quite a few slave narratives by and about women, the most famous being **Harriet Jacobs**'s *Incidents in the Life of a Slave Girl* (1861), an overwhelming majority of the original slave narratives focused on the lives of male slaves. This was despite the fact that the average new world slave was female. As a result, issues of gender and **sexuality** became paramount to many writers of neo-slave narratives.

Early narratives such as **Harriet E. Wilson**'s *Our Nig* (1859) and **Hannah Craft**'s *The Bondswoman's Narrative* (2002) take the form of first-person narratives. Like the female slave narratives by Jacobs and **Mary Prince**, these narratives tend to focus on the specific details of female enslavement. They recount the unique distinctions of slavery as experienced by women. More specifically, the writers of this type of neo-slave narrative frequently engaged with the manner in which **sexuality** became another way for slave owners, both male and female, to abuse their slaves. They also attend to the particularities and difficulties of slave families. They spend a great deal of time discussing the difficulties of being a female slave and in particular a light-skinned female slave. Although these narratives also attend to the various ways in which slave women were victimized, they also provide evidence of female agency.

A significant number of African American female writers began to turn to the neo-slave narrative in the 1960s and 1970s during the burgeoning women's movement. Writers such as **Toni Morrison** and **Sherley Anne Williams** frequently sought to foreground the political ramifications of the neo-slave narrative form. These writers very often focused on the specifically female aspects of questions of history, memory, and identity, which were fore-grounded in the slave narrative form. In these narratives, women are often represented as the repositories and carriers of the African American communities' histories and memories. While many of the male slave narratives engaged with the question of identity from a frequently singular perspective, the female authors often complicated these questions of identity by focusing on the fluid, fragmentary, or communitarian aspects of identity and history.

Many of the female writers of neo-slave narratives not only sought to recover the voices of the marginalized and previously silenced but also questioned the appropriateness of the singular form of the progressive narrative often modeled on the novel form. These writers frequently incorporated alternative methods of storytelling thought to better accommodate the specifics of new world slavery and the cultural heritage of the African diaspora such as employing narrative methods that emphasized orality, fragmentation, and provisionality thought to be connected to a shared and universal African heritage.

The neo-slave narratives that mimic the original first-person slave narratives frequently focus on issues of individual identity. The writers of neo-slave narratives often emphasize the interiority or psychology of the slaves and new world slavery, a topic frequently overlooked in the original narratives, which took as their mandate to describe the institution of slavery itself.

The second group of narratives include texts such as **Gayl Jones**'s *Corregidora* (1975), Edward P. Jones's *The Known World* (2003), and **Octavia Butler**'s *Kindred* (1979) and engage with the peculiarities and paradoxes inherent in new world slavery as an institution as well as questions of communal history. For example, *Corregidora* depicts the very different manner in which memories of slavery are recalled and interpreted by different generations of the African diaspora.

Texts such as ***Dessa Rose*** (1986) by Sherley Ann Williams, *Middle Passage* (1990) by **Charles Johnson**, and *Cambridge* (1992) by Caryl Phillips draw upon the connections between history and how stories of slavery are written and by whom. For example, in the case of *Dessa Rose*, although the character of Mr. Nehemiah is supposed to be writing an "objective" history of slavery, his perspective is shown to be compromised by his inability to see slaves and Dessa herself as anything other than animals. Williams contrasts this with Dessa's ability to "read" Nehemiah despite the fact that she is illiterate. Unlike Nehemiah, who is enthralled by Enlightenment positivism, Dessa's alternative knowledge enables her to narrate the truth of her story to her descendants.

Another theme prevalent in this second group of narratives concerns notions of history, including our knowledge and understanding of the institution of new world slavery as history. For example, in the novel *Cambridge*, Phillips foregrounds the impossibility of comprehending the full story of slavery without paying attention to those frequently marginalized by history, such as women and blacks.

One of the most famous neo-slave narratives is Toni Morrison's novel *Beloved* (1987). Although the narrative primarily focuses on the story of Sethe, its use of postmodern and poststructural ideas and narrative form, as well as its exploration of the psychology of slavery, it is also concerned with detailing and elaborating the role of the **community** during slavery.

One of the unifying themes common to both types of neo-slave narratives is that of the persistence of history and its entanglement with personal and communal memories of slavery. Just as African American feminist historians acknowledge that the past is never just the past, these revisions of new world slavery highlight the manner in which the institution and effects of new world slavery continue to haunt us both as individuals and as members of a global community.

See also Family; Historical Fiction; *Jubilee*

Works About

Andrews, William. *To Tell a Free Story: The First Century of Afro-American Autobiography (1760–1865)*. Chicago: University of Illinois Press, 1989.

Beaulieu, Elizabeth Ann. *Black Women Writers and the American Neo-Slave Narrative: Femininity Unfettered*. Westport, CT: Greenwood Press, 1999.

Rushdy, Ashraf. *Neo-Slave Narratives: Studies in the Social Logic of a Literary Form*. New York: Oxford University Press, 1999.

Nicole N. Aljoe

NUNEZ, ELIZABETH (1944–)

Elizabeth Nunez was born in Trinidad on February 18, 1944, and immigrated to the United States after receiving her secondary school education. She earned a B.A. degree in English from Marian College Fond du Lac in Wisconsin in 1967 and a master's (1971) and Ph.D. (1976) in English from New York University. She is presently a CUNY Distinguished Professor of English at Medgar Evers College, the City University of New York. In 1986 Nunez, along with John O. Killens, founded the National Black Writers Conference sponsored by the National Endowment for the Humanities.

Nunez has written six novels: *When Rocks Dance* (1986), *Beyond the Limbo Silence* (1998; IPPY Award-Independent Publishers Book Award Multicultural Fiction, 1999), *Bruised Hibiscus* (2000; American Book Award, 2001), *Discretion* (2002), *Grace* (2003), *Prospero's Daughter* (2006). She has edited *Defining Ourselves: Black Writers in the 90s* (1999, with Brenda M. Greene) and *Stories from Blue Latitudes: Caribbean Women Writers at Home and Abroad* (2005, with Jennifer Sparrow).

Nunez investigates the ways in which women and men in the African diaspora negotiate **love**, hate, resentment, desire, and greed in patriarchal societies that have in place prescriptions for the way they are to think and behave. Her settings on the continent of Africa, the Caribbean Islands, and the United States introduce the reader to an international cornucopia of characters, ideas, rituals, and beliefs. She demonstrates how an abundance of elements unfolds in a myriad of environments. At every narrative curve, her plush and vivid descriptions of land make obvious her love for Africa and New York and her intense adoration for Trinidad, its culture and **history**.

Each of Nunez's stories explores the myriad of ways Afro-Caribbean/American women negotiate emotions, desires, and identities that inevitably compel them to summon the courage to consider and initiate agonizing decisions. A Nunez protagonist is a woman who will disturb the stability of her marriage or any other union either via infidelity, the sheer need to protect her children, or to answer the call for self-protection from a union threatening to strangle the very spirit from her **body**. Her novels *When Rocks Dance* and *Bruised Hibiscus* best illustrate the women Nunez creates who fight for individuality and expression inside relationships and cultures that demand unabbreviated adherence to sociocultural norms.

When Rocks Dance, her debut novel, is set at the turn of the twentieth century on Trinidad, the Caribbean island under British colonial rule. The quest for Trinidadian soil by Afro-Caribbean women is the main focus of the novel. Emilia Heathrow consorts with Hrothgar Heathrow, a British plantation landowner, because he promises her land if she bears him male heirs. All of her children are strangled in childbirth because Emilia has yet to pay homage to the African tradition and ritual of obeah. After she consults with and obeys the edicts of Taro, the obeahman, Emilia has a daughter she names Marina. Emilia and Marina, however, are displaced from Hrothgar's house due to a misunderstanding of his last will and testament; Emilia then invests her hope for the acquisition of land in Marina—without disseminating Taro's knowledge to her. Emilia's neglect places the spiritual life of Marina, who is married and pregnant, in danger. Nunez's panoply of characters, settings, imagery, and symbolism illustrate her belief that if Afro-Caribbean women give over their souls and spirits to British colonial dictates for land acquisition, they will only experience unhealthy dispirited relationships—even the threat of **death**. Once Emilia and Marina reconcile themselves to obeah, their lives are rightly aligned. Marina can regenerate life and finally own Trinidadian soil.

Bruised Hibiscus is set in British colonial Trinidad in 1954. Nunez interlaces a story around a real-life horrific crime whereby a decapitated white woman's body wrapped in a coconut bag is found by a fisherman on Freeman's Bay. A **rape** witnessed between a hibiscus bush by two native Trinidadians—Zuela and Rosa, the daughter of a white English landowner—happened prior to the murder. Even though these young girls share this scene in girlhood, they go their separate ways. The murder and decapitation of the white woman reunite Zuela and Rosa in their adulthood.

Nunez explores wider social issues: colonialism, racism, sexual and emotional abuse, and power relations between men and women of different races. But her study of the negotiations made by Zuela and Rosa as they manage their abusive marriages makes for a more textured narrative. Zuela, "adopted" by Ho Sang, a sadistic Chinese immigrant battling his own demons, has borne ten children by him. Not only does she endure his insistence on having intercourse while she is pregnant; she also lives under the constant threat of being made homeless. One of the things he demands of her is to "smoke" opium for him and blow the smoke into his nostrils and mouth to satisfy his addiction. She agrees so that Ho Sang will never cast his eyes on her children. But Ho Sang rapes her daughter Agnes while she is away. Once Zuela sees Agnes curled up in a fetal state, counting her fingers, she unleashes her rage and blows enough opium on Ho Sang that he overdoses.

Zuela's love for her children and the "blessing" of shelter provided by Ho Sang undergird her life. Through Zuela, Nunez makes known the harrowing circumstances of young girls made powerless due to circumstances beyond their control. Ho Sang takes full advantage of Zuela's vulnerable state (her youth and lack of **family**) made manifest by her own father's inability to protect her as well as the installed notions of patriarchy in Trinidad. What is intriguing, however, is once Zuela decides to escape Ho Sang, she is aided by Tong Lee, an admirer of Zuela from afar, with whom she and her children live a healthy, fulfilled life.

Rosa, on the other hand, fails to survive. The daughter of white English landowners, Rosa bears up under the constant psychological and verbal abuse of her husband, Cedric, son of a black fisherwoman and East Indian man—all without the support of her mother, Clara Applegate. Nunez creates a character who must come to terms with her reason for marriage: Rosa marries Cedric only to satisfy her own sexual desires. After her appetite for Cedric diminishes, Cedric becomes irrational and cruelly aggressive in his treatment of Rosa. Fueled by the murders in Trinidad, Rosa travels to the Shrine of Our Lady of Fatima in the economically depressed village of Laventille. Here, Zuela's and Rosa's paths converge, only to be marred by memories of the rape that bruised the hibiscus bush during their adolescence.

The 1960s is the setting for *Beyond the Limbo Silence*. The novel is a painstaking journey into a young Trinidadian woman's coming of age in the United States during the turbulent civil rights era. A small Catholic college in Oshkosh, Wisconsin, awards college-bound Sara Edgehill a full scholarship. A black Catholic priest acts as messenger, and tells her family the college is determined to unearth fresh raw talent from Trinidad, a place considered by the college administrators as a "primitive" environment. A myriad of experiences causes Sara to examine her Trinidadian sensibilities as well as her upbringing. Sara, quite knowledgeable of **race** relations in Trinidad, has to negotiate her **identity** in the United States, a nation whose racial politics cut deeper. Attendant to her coming of age is the demystification of the America she has learned about through **film**. All the while Sara has to come to terms with the troubled past of her elders: It is legend that Bertha "Mad Bertha," Sara's White Creole great-grandmother, goes insane after abandoning Sara's grandmother and being cast out by her family for the shame she has brought upon them by becoming impregnated by a native West Indian. The possibility that the "sins" of her great-grandmother could be visited upon her causes her anxiety. Although Sara thrives in her new Midwestern **home**, she is all too aware that students from other countries use strategies to assimilate and erase difference in the all-white setting. The childish ignorance of her native land, Trinidad, its history, and its customs expressed by the privileged young white women in the college alienates Sara from them. That they attempt to taunt her into carrying a bucket on her head without dropping it, for example, humiliates Sara. Not that she is ashamed of her people, but the incident brings Sara to the realization of the **stereotypes** held for West Indians by the young women in the college. She carries a greater weight of awareness of her skin color since her parents make subtle references to their disappointment that her skin is too dark. All of these perceptions, beliefs, and feelings get challenged as Sara is pulled into the vortex of the civil rights movement. The intimate relationship she forms with Sam Maxwell, an attractive black law student, alleviates much of her alienation, but even that union casts a burden on her. Sara's and Sam's interactions with each other bring up the problem of native- and foreign-born African Americans. Even though Sam and Sara have the same skin color and hold dear affection for each other, Sam's fervent involvement with the **civil rights movement** and his strong comradeship with black and white activists weigh heavily on the union; the relationship eventually crumbles under Sam's commitment to his beliefs.

Nunez takes another turn in her writing whereby her male protagonists have to wrestle with the reality that lovers and/or wives no longer share common ground with or interest in them or the partnerships they have formed. As a result, they desperately fight for their marriages, all the while searching themselves for the culprit that made the tear in the seam; some of them rescue their women from depression and others from memories that haunt them. Some remain in partnerships out of sheer commitment only.

Discretion begins with the ruminations of Oufola Sindede, an African-born male who has moved through the political ranks to become foreign ambassador to the United States for his unnamed country. He is married yet feels a passionate love for his lover, Marguerite, a New York artist living in Harlem. Nunez takes a nonjudgmental stance as she explores the "what if" of a desire and affection held by a man who loves two women—a love that is compromised by his commitment to his wife and marriage. Important to the novel is Nunez's survey of the complexities of marriage and how its elements of stability and constancy hold their own merit. What is more, Nunez's characterization of Marguerite illustrates the angst and/or the interior discomfort of the "other woman" who enters into an extramarital relationship. In the end, Oufola chooses to remain with his wife, as both he and Marguerite bear up under the knowledge of their love for one another.

Grace opens with the contemplative voice of Justin Peters, a Harvard-educated professor of British and classic **literature** who has come to realize that his wife, Sally Peters, has lost interest in him and the marriage. Their only stabilizing force is their daughter Giselle. Justin refuses to allow Sally's disinterest to deter him from finding out why. Through a course of actions,

Justin anchors Sally as he encourages her to face a vortex of haunting memories and horrific events that have assaulted her ability to create **poetry**. In the process, Justin faces his own frailties only to summon the courage to be gentle and patient until Sally finally sees herself again first as a poet, then as a mother, and finally, as a wife. Justin's belief in Sally's abilities summons in her the strength to be.

Works By

Beyond the Limbo Silence. Seattle: Seal Press, 1998.
Bruised Hibiscus. Seattle: Seal Press, 2000.
Defining Ourselves: Black Writers in the 90s. Ed. Elizabeth Nunez and Brenda M. Greene. New York: Peter Lang Press, 1999.
Discretion. New York: Ballantine, 2003.
Grace. New York: One World/Ballantine, 2003.
Prospero's Daughter. New York: One World/Ballantine, 2006.
Stories from Blue Latitudes: Caribbean Women Writers at Home and Abroad. Elizabeth Nunez and Jennifer Sparrow. Emeryville, CA: Seal Press, 2005.
When Rocks Dance. New York: Putnam, 1986.

Works About

Creque-Harris, Leah. "*When Rocks Dance*: An Evaluation." *Caribbean Women Writers: Essays from the First International Conference*. Ed. Selwyn R. Cudjoe. Wellesley, MA: Calaloux Publications, 1990. 159–163.
"Elizabeth Nunez." PanMedia Features. www.panmedia.com.jm/features/nunez.htm
Rahming, Melvin B. "Theorizing Spirit: The Critical Challenge of Elizabeth Nunez's *When Rocks Dance* and *Beyond the Limbo Silence*." *Studies in the Literary Imagination*, Fall 2004.

Kwakiutl L. Dreher

O

OLIVER, DIANE (1943–1966)

Diane Oliver was born on July 28, 1943, in Charlotte, North Carolina, the daughter of William Robert and Blanche Rann Oliver. She grew up in Charlotte during the time of the 1954 Supreme Court decision on *Brown v. Board of Education*, which desegregated schools. Not letting racism or sexism stop her, Oliver graduated from West Charlotte High School and enrolled at the University of North Carolina at Greensboro in 1960.

During her college years, she started her brief but flourishing writing career by being the managing editor of the school newspaper the *Carolinian*, studying under the poet Randall Jarrell, and writing short stories. In 1964, Oliver won a college writing contest sponsored by *Mademoiselle*. Her award was being its guest editor for June. Her first short story "Key to the City" was published in the 1965 fall edition of *Red Clay Reader*. Because of this story, she obtained a scholarship to the University of Iowa and used it to enroll in its Writers' Workshop in 1965.

More published stories followed. In the spring issue of *Sewanee Review*, her first and third stories "Key to the City" and "Neighbors" were published (1966). Oliver's second and fourth stories "Health Service" and "Traffic Jam" were published in the November 1965 and July 1966 issues of *Negro Digest*. Eventually, she was awarded the O'Henry Award for Short Fiction and received an Honorable Mention in *Mademoiselle*'s **fiction** competition.

Oliver's promising career was cut short at the age of twenty-two. A few days before receiving her Master's in Fine Arts degree, she died in an automobile accident on May 21, 1966. The University of Iowa bestowed her degree posthumously.

Oliver's work infuses the natural southern tradition with issues of feminism and **race**. Influenced by such authors as William Faulkner, **Richard Wright**, and **Lorraine Hansberry**, she still has her own unique style. All of her stories focus on strong but struggling black women of the 1960s who are trying to survive in a society that is unsympathetic to their plight. Usually abandoned by a father or a significant other, they try to keep what remains of their **family** intact. Unfortunately, they eventually are abandoned or ignored by the society that they reach out to for assistance. Despite these problems, they demonstrate determination against the forces that threaten to destroy them; however, they usually end up being resigned to their unfortunate circumstances, creating a downward spiral that seems impossible to escape. By writing these stories set in rural and city settings, Oliver shows how not only racism and sexism but indifference as well are major problems.

Oliver's amazing achievements at such a young age clearly indicate that she was destined to be one of the most important writers of her generation regardless of her sex and race. Oliver was ahead of her time; her short stories serve as a precursor to the budding feminist movement of the 1970s. Furthermore, her influence is also reflected in the more positive and sympathetic social changes of that same era. Although her career was tragically brief, her stories are relevant today.

Works By

"Key to the City." *Red Clay Reader* 2 (Fall 1965). Folder 168.
"Health Service." *Negro Digest* 15 (November 1965).
"Neighbors." *Sewanee Review* 74 (Spring 1966).
"Traffic Jam." *Negro Digest* 15 (July 1966).

Works About

Adoff, Arnold, ed. *Black on Black*. New York: Macmillan, 1968.
Chambers, Bradford, and Rebecca Moon, eds. *Right On! Anthology of Black Literature*. New York: New American Library, 1970.
Hamer, Judith A., and Martin J. Hamer, eds. *Centers of the Self: Stories by Black American Women from the Nineteenth Century to the Present*. New York: Hill and Wang, 1994.
Kratt, Mary. *The Imaginative Spirit: Literary Heritage of Charlotte and Mecklenburg County, North Carolina*. Charlotte, NC: Public Library of Charlotte and Mecklenburg County, 1988.
Llorens, David. "Remembering a Young Talent." *Negro Digest* 15 (September 1966).

Major, Clarence, ed. *Calling the Wind: Twentieth Century African-American Short Stories.* New York: HarperPerennial, 1993.

Margolies, Edward, ed. *A Native Sons Reader.* Philadelphia: Lippincott, 1970.

Mizener, Arthur, ed. *Modern Short Stories: The Uses of Imagination.* 1971. New York: Norton, 1979.

Mullen, Bill, ed. *Revolutionary Tales: African American Women's Short Stories, from the First Story to the Present.* New York: Laurel, 1995.

Prize Stories of 1967: The O'Henry Awards. Garden City, NY: Doubleday, 1967.

Watson, R., and G. Ruark, eds. *The Greensboro Reader.* Chapel Hill: University of North Carolina Press, 1968.

Devona Mallory

OSBEY, BRENDA MARIE (1957–)

What is most remarkable about the **poetry** of Brenda Marie Osbey is the vivid sense of New Orleans mystique, beautiful, yet haunting, that carries the reader into the mesmerizing allure of Louisiana's African American Creole culture. Osbey creates portraits of black womanhood resplendent with dimensions of **beauty** and madness, melancholy and innocence, **love** and hate. Her poetry weaves a spicy symbiosis between woman and place, exploring the charm and complexities within each.

Osbey's first published volume, *Ceremony for Minneconjoux* (1983), combines love, murder, and insanity in a series of small visceral portraits—murky windows through which Osbey carefully guides the reader. *In These Houses* (1988) continues her theme of madness as she explores the traditional realm of women—the house. Akin to Charlotte Perkins Gilman's *Yellow Wallpaper* (1892), Osbey probes the dark side of the female world behind closed doors, as her "houses" exemplify the inscrutable balance between sanity and madness. *In These Houses* also includes a glossary of cultural terms and place names that work to further draw the reader into the African American Creole world. *Desperate Circumstances, Dangerous Women* (1991) is a book-length narrative poem replete with hoodoo **spirituality**, where past and present are inextricably entwined into daily Marigny life. Osbey's most recent publication, *All Saints: New and Selected Poems* (1997), continues her tendency to merge the past and present by exploring **death** and the important role **memory** plays in keeping lost loved ones alive. Osbey has also been published in numerous journals, collections, and anthologies.

While Osbey's poems are an affirmation of the strength and charisma of black womanhood, frequently through images of hands and feet, they also offer a unique ambience of African American Creole culture, and each poem is a fetching reminder of the unity of black women's experiences that transcend time and place. Osbey's use of local idioms, coupled with the bewitching sounds and images of memorable characters, create a poetic dance of mesmerizing black womanhood.

Osbey received her B.A. from Dillard University and an M.A. from the University of Kentucky, and she attended the Universitè Paul Valèry at Montpèllièr, France. She was awarded the Academy of American Poets Loring-Williams Award and a 1984 Associated Writing Programs Poetry Award and has been a fellow of the MacDowell Colony, the Fine Arts Work Center in Provincetown, the Kentucky Foundation for Women, the Millay Colony, and the Bunting Institute of Radcliffe College, Harvard University. She was the recipient of a 1990 National Endowment of the Arts Creative Writing Fellowship. She was awarded the 1993 Louisiana Division of the Arts Creative Writing Fellowship. Osbey's collection of poetry *All Saints* received the American Book Award in 1998. Osbey was awarded the Camargo Foundation Fellowship for 2004 and was in residence at Cassis, France, completing her newest manuscript. She has taught French and English at Dillard and African American and third world literatures at the University of California at Los Angeles. She has been twice appointed scholar-in-residence at Southern University and visiting writer-in-residence at Tulane University. Osbey currently teaches at Loyola University in New Orleans.

Works By

All Saints: New and Selected Poems. Baton Rouge: Louisiana State University Press, 1997.
Ceremony for Minneconjoux. 1983. Charlottesville: University Press of Virginia, 1985.
Desperate Circumstances, Dangerous Women. Brownsville, OR: Story Line Press, 1991.
In These Houses. Middletown, CT: Wesleyan University Press, 1988.

Works About

Bryan, Violet Harrington. "Evocations of Place and Culture in the Works of Four Contemporary Black Louisiana Writers: Brenda Marie Osbey, Sybil Kein, Elizabeth Brown Guillory, and Pinkie Gordon Lane." *Louisiana Literature Review* 4.2 (1987): 49–80
Lowe, John. "An Interview with Brenda Marie Osbey." *Southern Review* 30.4 (1994): 812.

Debbie Clare Olson

OUR NIG

Harriet E. Wilson's 1859 text *Our Nig; or, Sketches from the Life of a Free Black, In a Two-Story White House, North, Showing That Slavery's Shadows Fall Even There* existed in near obscurity until a scholarly second edition was published in 1983. In this groundbreaking edition, Henry Louis Gates, Jr., provides evidence to confirm Wilson's **race** and gender, thus proving *Our Nig* was the first novel published in the United States by an African American writer and the first published by an African American woman. Additional recovery **work** within the field of nineteenth-century African American **literature** may at some point disprove the "first novel" status of *Our Nig*, but it will nevertheless remain a significant and remarkable work.

Published for the author in 1859 in Boston, *Our Nig* emerged in a time and place of fervent abolitionism. Unlike the numerous first-person **slave narratives** published, read, and distributed for abolitionist ends, *Our Nig*'s third-person narrator conveys Frado's life in the North as an indentured black servant. Anticipating the final chapters of **Harriet Jacobs**'s *Incidents in the Life of a Slave Girl* (1861), Wilson exposes that racism and racial oppression exist in the North as well as the **South**.

Frado's story illustrates the extreme physical and emotional hardships a young African American girl encounters in a racist society. At age six, Frado is left with the white Bellmont **family** when her father dies and her mother cannot support her. Thus abandoned, Frado becomes an indentured servant to the Bellmont family and victim to the abuses of the tyrannical "she-devil" Mrs. Bellmont. Although Mr. Bellmont and several Bellmont children are sympathetic toward Frado, they cannot fully protect her from Mrs. Bellmont's cruelties. At age eighteen, Frado is able to leave the Bellmont **home**. Her troubles, however, do not end; economic survival is difficult due to society's racist attitudes, and she suffers ill-health caused by a lifetime of abuse. Frado's troubles are compounded when she is abandoned by her husband and must support herself and their young son on her own. Frado attempts to make a living sewing straw bonnets and selling hair tonic, but at several points she becomes dependent on public aid and the kindness of the few sympathetic Bellmonts. In the concluding paragraphs of the novel, the narrator notes that Frado is still an invalid and asks for the readers' sympathy and aid.

Critics are divided as to whether this text is **fiction** or **autobiography** since it embodies elements of both. Strong parallels exist between Frado and Wilson; *Our Nig* has provided strong leads for finding biographical information about Wilson. For reasons that are not entirely known, Wilson's self-published text received little, if any, critical notice or public attention. Thus *Our Nig* spawns two stories: a nineteenth-century story about an African American woman who hopes her story will support her and her son in a racist world, and a twentieth-century story about the challenges of reconstructing the life of the African American woman who wrote a literary landmark.

Works About

Carby, Hazel. *Reconstructing Womanhood: The Emergence of the Afro-American Woman Novelist*. New York: Oxford University Press, 1987.

Gates, Henry Louis, Jr. Introduction to *Our Nig; or, Sketches from the Life of a Free Black*, by Harriet E. Wilson. 2nd ed. New York: Vintage, 1983.

Stern, Julia. "Excavating Genre in *Our Nig*." *American Literature* 67.3 (September 1995): 439–466.

Tate, Claudia. *Domestic Allegories of Political Desire: The Black Heroine's Text at the Turn of the Century.* New York: Oxford University Press, 1992.

Heidi L. M. Jacobs

P

PARABLE OF THE SOWER. See Parable Series

PARABLE OF THE TALENTS. See Parable Series

PARABLE SERIES

The most recent novels of science **fiction** writer **Octavia Butler** are install-ments in her Parable series, which so far include *Parable of the Sower* (1993) and *Parable of the Talents* (1998). *Parable of the Sower* is a postapocalyptic tale that opens in 2024 with national, state, and local governments no longer able to provide reliable communication, electrical, health, or safety services. Years of drought, epidemics, and economic depression have left water as expensive as food, and gasoline and electricity affordable only to the rich. Hoards of homeless people depend on looting, prostitution, or assault to get the neces-sities of life. Desperate women sell themselves or their children for food. Violent drug gangs roam the streets; a new popular designer drug provides, with its high, an intense attraction to fire, so arson and even self-immolation abound. What is left of middle-class urban populations have walled in their communities; they keep armed patrols and leave their neighborhoods only in groups.

Protagonist Lauren Olamina lives in one such **community**, where families struggle to maintain a life that approximates better times. Lauren sees that a yearning for the past has blinded her neighbors to their need to prepare for the worst. She places some of the blame on traditional religions, which valorize faith, hope, and suffering, not action. Lauren does not believe in her father's Baptist God or in any **religion** she has heard of; she does, however, feel that people need some kind of faith system to help them survive. So she formulates a new religion, Earthseed, that asks individuals to take responsibility for shaping the future. This religion recognizes Change as the deepest, most fundamental principle of life; hence, it preaches that God is Change. But this God is not to be worshiped; rather, Earthseed followers are urged to anticipate and prepare for Change, adapt to Change, and to foster the responsible shaping of Change, thereby shaping God. One of Earthseed's goals is for humankind to branch out from Earth, a move necessary for species survival. The destiny of Earthseed, Lauren preaches, is to take root among the stars. She means this literally.

Lauren's ability to adapt to and shape change is tested when her neighborhood is razed by a band of violent looters. One of the few survivors, she heads north in search of **work** and safety. The novel follows a quest pattern as Lauren begins to collect other travelers around her; they eventually become her first Earthseed converts. The group is ethnically diverse, underscoring Butler's insistence that solutions to social problems should reflect contributions from many groups and be for everyone. Lauren lives in a world reverting to racism, sexism, segregation, and even **slavery**, but her group welcomes members from a variety of ethnic origins, from both genders, and from a wide range of generations and economic classes. Lauren does not offer fellowship to the violent, the mentally deranged, or those who have become desensitized to their own humanity, but she takes in the weak and vulnerable as well as the strong.

Parable of the Talents picks up in 2032. The early part of the novel gives Lauren's memories of the final days of her commune, which grew and prospered until a fast-growing fundamentalist group, Christian America, branded Earthseed a dangerous cult and sent their Ku Klux Klan–like militia to wipe it out. Imprisoned and brutalized in an internment compound reminiscent of a Nazi concentration camp, Lauren almost lost her will to shape Change but finally found the courage to strike back against her oppressors.

The story's present occurs years later, with the country on the road to economic recovery, with most mob **violence** in the past, and with a right-wing Christian America president. Lauren by now has rejected the idea of concentrating Earthseed into a single commune; her religion must spread quickly if it is to be an effective agent of change. So she turns to public media and locally run community seedgroups to spread her faith.

A second plotline follows Lauren's eighteen-year-old daughter Larkin. Kidnapped as a baby during the raid on the commune, she has been raised in a Christian American **home** in which she feels unloved. Larkin (renamed Asha Vere) is an unhappy young woman who comes to blame her mother for her misery. A third major character is Lauren's brother Marcus, whose response to the horrors he has lived through is to become a preacher for Christian America. Marcus and Lauren, unable to reconcile their differences, part after a brief reunion, and when Marcus eventually locates Larkin, he does not tell his sister. Instead, he forms a secret relationship with his niece, the only relative he feels close to.

Contrasting religious visions form the backdrop of this story. The fundamentalist Christian America with its ultraconservative political agenda is used to explore how a repressive religious climate targets women. Lauren's Earthseed is used to propose an alternative approach to social change; it also explores the heartbreaking choices a leader of a movement must sometimes make. At the novel's end Lauren is a respected religious leader—some call her a saint—but she has been unable to heal her damaged relationships with Marcus and Larkin, her only living **family**.

Lauren Olamina follows in the footsteps of Butler's other strong African American female protagonists who courageously seek new perspectives and solutions. These women reject patriarchal worldviews in favor of more inclusive, compassionate, egalitarian models of life. In *Parable of the Sower*, Lauren acts out an archetypal hero's quest, demonstrating how that story changes when it addresses women's concerns, everything from including tampons in one's survival pack and valorizing nurturing to an emphasis on sexist social practices and violence against women. Lauren founds her commune on feminist principles: inclusion, egalitarianism, nurturing, and family. *Parable of the Talents* tracks the results of her quest—its triumphs and joys as well as its hardships and costs. *Parable of the Sower* is a Nebula Award finalist; *Parable of the Talents* is a Nebula winner.

See also Bloodchild and Other Stories; Kindred; Patternist Series; Xenogenesis Trilogy

Works About

Gant-Britton, Lisbeth. "Octavia Butler's *Parable of the Sower*: One Alternative to a Futureless Future." *Women of Other Worlds: Excursions through Science Fiction and Feminism*. Ed. Helen Merrick and Tess Williams. Nedlands: University of Western Australia Press, 1999. 277–294.

Phillips, Jerry. "The Intuition of the Future: Utopia and Catastrophe in Octavia Butler's *Parable of the Sower*." *Novel* 35 (2002): 299–311.

Stillman, Peter G. "Dystopian Critiques, Utopian Possibilities, and Human Purposes in Octavia Butler's *Parables*." *Utopian Studies* 14 (2003): 15–35.

Grace McEntee

PARADISE

Toni Morrison's eighth novel *Paradise* (1998) is a historical odyssey chronicling the gendered and generational effects of the Civil Rights era and the Black Power movement in Ruby, Oklahoma, a rural, patriarchal, all-black town where, by covenant with God, no one dies. The novel is divided into nine sections, each titled for a female character, and begins with a graphic description of patriarchal **violence**: Nine of Ruby's leading townsmen murder five women living at the Convent. Throughout the novel, what happens in the predawn hours of that July day in 1976 is slowly and intricately woven into an unfolding of Ruby's complex **history**.

In 1890, nine dark-skinned black families, fleeing both the racism of the Redemption **South** and the prejudice of light-skinned blacks, established Haven, Oklahoma. Returning from World War II to find Haven failing financially and morally, the fifteen men (descendants of the original nine) take their families and the Oven, the symbolic center of the town despite its associations with the womb, and move 240 miles west to begin again. Their new haven remained nameless until 1954 when Ruby Morgan died because no white hospital would admit her. A constant reminder of American racism, the town's name reinforces its protective, exclusionary impulse. However, Ruby's efforts to isolate itself ultimately prove futile; the town cannot escape the sociopolitical changes sweeping the United States in the 1960s and 1970s. Indeed, one of the primary struggles in the novel results from the efforts of Ruby's youth to challenge their parents' generation. Unable to accept any challenge to their patriarchal authority and unwilling to acknowledge their own culpability in the town's unrest, Ruby's men need a scapegoat. They find one in the women of the Convent.

A sprawling mansion erected by an embezzler, the Convent was originally replete with sexually explicit décor: paintings, faucets, doorknobs, ashtrays all shaped as men's and women's genitals or depicting graphic sexual encounters. After one orgy in the nearly completed mansion, the embezzler was arrested. Years later, his house, located seventeen miles outside of Ruby, was redeemed by Catholic nuns as Christ the King School for Native Girls. The nuns promptly destroyed, hid, or painted over any sexual material, just as they "cleansed" the native Arapaho girls of their native language and customs. Thus, the Convent evolved from a place of sexual exploitation of women to one of repression, oppression, and enforced conformity to a particular set of moral and cultural codes. After losing funding, however, the school—known by then as the Convent—underwent one final transformation, one that finally resisted women's sexual and cultural oppression. At novel's opening, it is a haven for the dispossessed, abused, confused, weary, or abandoned and the **home** of Consolata (Connie), Mavis, Grace (Gigi), Seneca, and Pallas (Divine).

Consolata Sosa is brought by Mother Mary Magna to the Convent in 1925 at the age of nine, having been sexually abused and abandoned in the streets of Brazil. At thirty-nine, she has an intense affair with Deacon Morgan, ten years her junior, already married, and one of Ruby's most prominent men. Deek ends the affair after Connie bites his lip and licks his blood during sex. Echoing Paul D's critique of Sethe in Morrison's fifth novel ***Beloved*** (1987), Deek argues to himself that her behavior is that of an animal. However, the text suggests that he ends the affair because he cannot reconcile his patriarchal mores or his **black masculinity** with Connie's deep, unrestrained female

sexuality. After the affair, Connie saves Deek's son's life by "stepping into" him and thus becomes friends with Soane, Deek's wife. Their relationship encapsulates the connections between Ruby and the Convent: These two women **love** the same man and give life to the same son; however, their similarities are obscured for Ruby's citizens by differences of convention. One is redeemed in marriage, the other considered a whore.

By 1971, when Mother Mary dies, wayward women—all scarred by the men in their lives—have already begun to join Connie in the Convent. The first, who comes in 1968, is twenty-seven-year-old Mavis, a woman running from the accidental murder of her newborn twins and convinced that her husband and three remaining children are trying to kill her. Reminiscent of the haunting power of a mother's guilt in *Beloved*, Mavis begins to hear the laughter of her dead twins and stays without ever deciding to. Grace (Gigi), who loves to be naked, joins them in 1971, running from bloody memories of the Oakland riot and searching for the preplanned rendezvous spot with a lover who never shows. After an affair with Coffee Smith (the Morgans' nephew) that ends abusively, she focuses her sexual energy on the newcomer, Seneca. In 1973, Seneca is twenty-three and on a failed mission to get bail money for her boyfriend. Abandoned by the mother she thought was her sister, abused by a foster brother, and used as a sex toy by a rich woman for three weeks, Seneca repeatedly cuts herself to see the blood pool in surgically precise wounds. The sixteen-year-old Pallas, most likely the white girl shot in the novel's opening line, arrives pregnant in 1975. She is running from the **memory** of her boyfriend having sex with her mother and of two white men chasing her in the night. In 1976, Pallas delivers a baby boy.

After Connie begins to receive visits from a strange, floating man with cascading brown hair, she starts to tell the Convent women of Piedade, a beautiful, maternal woman who sings like paradise. Connie inspires the women to a new sense of purpose: They clean themselves, shave their heads, begin to **work** together, and participate in sessions of "loud-dreaming" that allow them to excise the ghosts that haunt them. They paint images of themselves, their pasts, and their fears on the basement floor and walls and tell each other their stories. When Soane sees them again, just before the attack, she believes they are no longer haunted. As they dance in the predawn rain, they have become holy women. Meanwhile, Ruby's men participate in their own ritual. They prepare for battle, eating rare steak and gathering their weapons. The Convent's menless women—signs of their failure, disintegration, loss of control, and their own human weaknesses—must be eradicated to ensure the patriarchal stasis of Ruby.

Ruby's citizens, marshaled by Lone DuPres, the town's aging and no-longer-needed midwife, arrive too late. Although the women put up a fight, they are all presumably shot. After Deek unsuccessfully attempts to stop his twin brother Steward from shooting Connie, a rift opens between the twins. Deek begins to understand that the isolated, unchanging, patriarchal new "haven" they had attempted to create was impossible, that they had become what their grandfathers hated: those who attack and destroy others because they are seen as different. When the coroner arrives, the bodies, along with Mavis's Cadillac, are gone. In their place is an inexplicable opening, a door or a window, into another plane. Billie Delia Cato, who once found refuge in the Convent, believes that the women have left to prepare for battle against Ruby, men, and all who have subjugated them. The readers do see each of the women again, as they confront people from their pasts, armed, determined, and united. Regardless of whether the women have survived the attack or occupy some liminal, spiritual space, the novel ends with hope for reconciliation between genders and generations. The strong, militant image of women armed for battle is juxtaposed with the final image of Connie sitting at the ocean's edge with her head in Piedade's lap, in peace and in Paradise.

See also Community; Identity; Motherhood

Works About

Aguiar, Sarah Appleton. " 'Passing On' Death: Stealing Life in Toni Morrison's *Paradise*." *African American Review* 38.3 (2004): 513–519.

Kearly, Peter R. "Toni Morrison's *Paradise* and the Politics of Community." *Journal of American & Comparative Cultures* 23.2 (Summer 2000): 9–16.

LeSeur, Geta. "Moving beyond the Boundaries of Self, Community, and the Other in Toni Morrison's *Sula* and *Paradise*." *CLA Journal* 46.1 (September 2002): 1–20.

Michael, Magali Cornier. "Re-imagining Agency: Toni Morrison's *Paradise*." *African American Review* 36.4 (Winter 2002): 643–661.

Sweeney, Megan. "Racial House, Big House, Home: Contemporary Abolitionism in Toni Morrison's *Paradise*." *Meridians: Feminism, Race, Transnationalism* 4.2 (2004): 40–67.

Widdowson, Peter. "The American Dream Refashioned: History, Politics and Gender in Toni Morrison's *Paradise*." *Journal of American Studies* 35.2 (August 2001): 313–335.

Julie Cary Nerad

PARKER, PAT (1944–   )

Pat Parker was born on January 20, 1944, in Houston, Texas, the youngest of four daughters in a working-**class** African American **family**. In the early 1970s she moved to Oakland, California, where she became involved in a range of political activism including participation in the Black Panther Party and the Black Women's Revolutionary Council. She also played a part in the formation of the Women's Press Collective. Between 1978 and 1987 Parker was medical coordinator of the Oakland Feminist Women's Health Center, where her tireless **work** made her a national leader on issues of women's health, particularly regarding **domestic** and sexual **violence**. Parker has also been actively involved in diverse gay and lesbian organizations.

Parker's narrative **poetry** draws strongly from working-class oral traditions employing vernacular speech, wry humor, and strong language to attack social injustice while avoiding the pitfalls of didacticism in political poetry. As such, her words, which incorporate chants, curses, and jokes, require hearing as well as reading. Indeed Parker's poetry was honed not only in bookstore readings but in bars and coffeehouses. Often her work incorporated musical performances. In Parker's powerful performances the activist and artist found their sharpest articulation.

Her poetry was part of a much larger personal and political engagement. Both as a political activist and as a poet Parker was at the forefront of efforts to link struggles for racial, gender, and sexual equality and against class exploitation. Parker's work expanded the visions of her contemporary political allies to bring racial equality together with gay liberation while bringing a black working-class feminist perspective to recurring themes of **love**, political alliances, family legacies, and ultimately liberation and justice.

In all of this, Parker's work resists containment by notions of **identity**, whether queer or feminist, which suggest a singular or unified subjectivity. Instead her work emphasizes unity within diversity. Her work continues to speak to the silences around matters of **race** and class within lesbian feminism and the women's movements in the United States.

Parker's writings speak against the ongoing marginalization of working-class lesbians and lesbians of color within much of contemporary queer theory. At the same time they situate queer theory within the particular histories of working-class lesbians and lesbians of color.

Central to Parker's poetry are the tensions around notions of identity. These tensions express a creative political force through the author's consciousness of producing poetry from experiences of multiple oppression.

Parker's poems are elements of struggle that refuse marginalization in the face of racism in women's communities and homophobia in African American communities. In addition, and crucially, her words also tear away middle-class presumptions of mainstream movements against racial, gender, and sexual oppression. Underlying all of this is a constant commitment to the possibilities of social transformation, even as she offers critiques of specific strategies for change that have limited the movements in which she has participated.

Through her poems and her activism Parker asserts a radical identity, beyond capture by essentialist categories. In an essay titled "Revolution: It's Not Neat or Pretty or Quick," which appeared in *This Bridge Called My Back*, she states, "I am a feminist. I am neither white nor middle class. And the women that I've worked with were like me. Yet I'm told that we don't exist and that we didn't exist."

Although some critics dismiss Parker's straightforward style, the directness of her poems articulates a transgressive and contestatory identity spoken from the sites where complex power relations intersect. Parker's poems affirm the identities of the silenced while always remaining conscious of the disapproval and contradictions that serve to keep those identities silent in a society marked by homophobia, racism, and class exploitation.

For Parker these identities are collectively experienced and articulated, and her words speak of, from, and to collective resistance. Poetry is but one tool in the construction of those "liberation fronts" in which the ongoing struggles for collective transformation, or revolution, are engaged.

Works By

Child of Herself. Oakland, CA: Diana Press, 1972.
Lesbian Concentrate. Los Angeles: Olivia Records, 1977.
Movement in Black: The Collected Poetry of Pat Parker 1961–1978. Trumansburg, NY: Crossing Press, 1983.
Pit Stop. Oakland, CA: Diana Press, 1973.
Where Would I Be Without You? The Poetry of Pat Parker and Judy Grahn. Los Angeles: Olivia Records, 1976.
Womanslaughter. Oakland, CA: Diana Press, 1978.

Works About

Annas, Pamela. "A Poetry of Survival: Unnaming and Renaming in the Poetry of Audre Lorde, Pat Parker, Sylvia Plath and Adrienne Rich." *Colby Library Quarterly* 18 (1982): 9–25.
Callaghan, Dympna. "Pat Parker: Feminism in Postmodernity." *Contemporary Poetry Meets Modern Theory.* Ed. Antony Easthope and John O. Thompson. Toronto: University of Toronto Press, 1981. 128–138.
Culpepper, Emily E. "A Genius for Putting the Emphasis Where It Belongs." *Gay Community News*, September 3–9, 1989, 12.
Folayan, Ayofemi, and Stephanie Byrd. "Pat Parker." *Contemporary Lesbian Writers of the United States: A Bio-Bibliographical Critical Sourcebook.* Ed. Sandra Pollack and Denise D. Knight. Westport, CT: Greenwood Press, 1993. 415–419.
Garber, Linda. "Lesbian Identity Poetics: Judy Grahn, Pat Parker, and the Rise of Queer Theory." Ph.D. diss., Stanford University, 1995.

J. Shantz

PARKS, ROSA (1913–2005)

Rosa Parks, a seamstress, boarded a bus in Montgomery, Alabama, on December 1, 1955. When told to give up her seat, in accordance with Jim Crow laws that mandated blacks were to give up their seats to whites, Parks refused. As a result of her refusal, she was forcibly removed from the bus, arrested, jailed, and fined. News of Parks's courageous stance and subsequent treatment ignited the passion that fueled the Montgomery bus boycott and earned her the title "mother of the **civil rights movement**."

Parks was born in Tuskegee, Alabama, in 1913. Her mother, Leona Edwards, was a schoolteacher, and her father, James McCauley, was a carpenter. She spent her early years in Pine Level, Alabama, in the **home** of her maternal grandparents. In 1924, Parks, her mother, and brother relocated to segregated Montgomery, Alabama. She attended the Montgomery Industrial School for Girls, which she commonly referred to as "Ms. White's school." Despite the curriculum's focus on **domestic** science, Parks gained vital knowledge beyond home economics. It was at Ms. White's school that Parks experienced being treated with dignity, regardless of **race** or gender.

After graduating from Ms. White's school, Parks continued her education at Booker T. Washington High School, where she graduated in 1928. She attended the Alabama State Normal School (Alabama State University) but was unable to complete her degree, due to the illnesses of her mother and grandmother. In 1932, she married Raymond Parks, a barber whom she credits with further awakening her activism. Parks's civic responsibility was reflected in her membership in the Montgomery Voters League, the National Association for the Advancement of Colored People (NAACP), and the Youth Council.

The day after she was arrested for refusing to give up her seat, Parks and the Women's Political Council produced and distributed 52,000 leaflets concerning a one-day bus boycott. The boycott was so successful that the Montgomery Improvement Association, led by the Reverend Martin Luther King, Jr., decided to continue its strike until white lawmakers met black demands and ended the practice of segregation on city buses. On December 20, 1956, the U.S. Supreme Court declared that segregated seating on the buses in Montgomery, Alabama, was unconstitutional. Parks is cited as having said she had no idea that the small action of refusing to give up her seat would facilitate the dismantling of segregation laws throughout the **South**. Parks and her husband subsequently moved to Detroit, Michigan, in 1957, due to numerous **death** threats. However, Parks continued her activism.

Parks was awarded the Congressional Gold Medal, the highest civilian honor, by President William Clinton in 1999. Parks received many additional accolades and honors as a result of her strong civic commitment to human rights and efforts to incorporate the disenfranchised. In hopes of encouraging youth and promoting high scholastic achievement, she founded the Rosa and Raymond Parks Institute for Self-Development. In *Rosa Parks: My Story* (1992), *I Am Rosa Parks* (1999), and *Quiet Strength* (2000), she humbly articulates her pioneering efforts to bring about equality and change. Pioneer Rosa Parks died on October 24, 2005.

Works By

I Am Rosa Parks. With Jim Haskins. New York: Puffin, 1999.
Quiet Strength. With Gregory J. Reed. New York: Zondervan Press, 2000.
Rosa Parks: My Story. With Jim Haskins. New York: Scholastica, 1992.

Works About

Brinkley, Doug. *Rosa Parks: A Penguin Life*. New York: Viking Adult, 2000.

Meriwether, Louise. *Don't Ride the Bus on Monday: The Rosa Parks Story*. Upper Saddle River, NJ: Prentice Hall, 1973.

Wilson, Camilla. *Rosa Parks: From the Back of the Bus to the Front of the Movement*. New York: Scholastic, 2000.

Karen Arnett Chachere

PARKS, SUZAN-LORI (1964–   )

Suzan-Lori Parks was born in Fort Knox, Kentucky, but grew up in several different places due to her father's career as an army colonel. As a result of her parents' interest in truly experiencing the places they lived, she had opportunities to be fully immersed in other cultures. For example, while living in Germany she attended a German high school instead of the American schools for the children of military personnel. At this point as a teenager, she had already begun writing short stories, and she credits working so closely with another language as pivotal in her ability to capture language and dialogue.

Parks attended Mount Holyoke College, a women's liberal arts college, and studied **fiction** writing with renowned author and essayist **James Baldwin**, who after hearing her read her works aloud, suggested she consider **drama**. The exploration of works by African American playwrights **Adrienne Kennedy** and **Ntozake Shange** were key in the development of her art form. Both Kennedy and Shange provided a more freeing and individualistic context for Parks, who was looking to tell her stories in ways that were not structured by the confines of traditional drama. Her own first plays were similarly experimental, and although she won honors from the theater department for her first work *The Sinner's Place*, it was declined production because of its innovative form.

This was not a setback for Parks, who continues to write and shape her art in a way that allows her to manipulate the confines of traditional drama. In fact, her approach to language has become a signature quality to her work. And as a result of her commitment to representing her talents on stage in her own way, language, time, and sense of **history**, she has reaped tremendous success. Her interviews and writings reveal that she is interested in examining the known history in order to discover things that have been missing or hanging on the sides of the cracks; she is committed to telling the unchronicled events.

Her writing is imbued with posing and answering questions regarding the individual and collective **identity** of African Americans and people in general. She not only tells these stories through words but with sound, using repetition that often has the ability to create a hypnotic effect. Although the theatrical and phonetic way in which she writes may look daunting to the reader, Parks has been successful at carrying on a tradition of African American culture and writing where the English written word is deliberately taken apart and reshaped to make new meaning. This not only allows the audience to experience the story through several senses and through their imagination, but for Parks, who is interested in challenging the actors, she gives them an opportunity to experience it in their diction and diaphragm. Parks is invested not only in providing **work** for black actors but also in challenging more than their emotional instrument.

The playwright, screenwriter, and novelist has received numerous accolades for her work. Most recently, in 2002 she won the Pulitzer Prize for her play *Topdog/Underdog* only days after the play opened on Broadway, making her the first African American woman to win for drama. She was the Pulitzer Prize finalist in 2000 for the play *In the Blood* that tells the story of a homeless black woman who is a single mother of several children by different fathers. In 2001 she received a $500,000 MacArthur Foundation "genius grant." In addition, she garnered the 1990 Obie Award for Best off-Broadway Play for *Imperceptible Mutabilities in the Third Kingdom* and the Whiting Foundation Writers Award. She won the MacArthur Award in 1986. She has received two National Endowment for the Arts Fellowships for Playwrights, the Lila-Wallace Reader's Digest Award, and the CalArts/Alpert Award in the Arts and has been awarded grants by the Rockefeller Foundation, Ford Foundation, New York State Council on the Arts, and New York Foundation for the Arts.

In addition to writing for the stage, she has also written three plays for radio: *Pickling* (1990), *Third Kingdom* (1990), and *Locomotive* (1991). She has written two screenplays, *Anemone Me* (1990) and *Girl 6* (1996), which was directed by Spike Lee, and a novel, **Getting Mother's Body** (2003). She is currently working on an adaptation of **Toni Morrison**'s novel **Paradise** (1998) and a stage musical, *Hoopz*, about the Harlem Globetrotters.

Parks holds degrees from Mount Holyoke College and the Yale School of Drama. She has taught or worked as writer-in-residence at several institutions including the Yale School of Drama, the University of Michigan, New School for Social Research, and the Pratt Institute for the Arts. She is currently the director of the California Institute for the Arts and lives in Venice Beach, California.

See also Venus

Works By

The America Play and Other Works. New York: Theatre Communications Group, 1995.
Betting on the Dust Commander. New York: Dramatist Play Service, 1990.
The Death of the Last Black Man in the Whole World. Theatre, Summer/Fall 1990.
Fucking A. In *Red Letter Plays.* New York: Theatre Communications Group, 2002.
In the Blood. American Theatre (March 2000): 31.
Topdog/Underdog. New York: Dramatist Play Service, 2001.
Venus. New York: Theatre Communications Group, 2001.

Works About

Basting, Anne Davis. "Performance Review: *Venus* by Suzan-Lori Parks." *Theatre Journal* 49.2 (May 1997): 223–225.

Bernard, Louise. "The Musicality of Language: Redefining History in Suzan-Lori Parks's 'The Death of the Last Black Man in the World.'" *African American Review* 31.4 (Winter 1997): 687.

Dixon, Kimberly D. "An I am Sheba me am (She be doo wah waaaah doo wah) O(au)rality, Textuality and Performativity: African American Literature' Vernacular Theory and the Work of Suzan-Lori Parks." *Journal of American Drama and Theatre* 11.1 (Winter 1999): 49–66.

Drukman, Steven. "Suzan-Lori Parks and Liz Diamond: Doo-a-Diddly-Dit-Dit." *Re-direction: A Theoretical and Practical Guide*. Ed. Rebecca Schneider and Gabrielle Cody. London: Routledge, 2002. 352–365.

Jiggetts, Shelby. "Interview with Suzan-Lori Parks." *Callaloo* 19.2 (1996): 309–317.

Solomon, Alisa. "Signifying on the Signifyin': The Plays of Suzan-Lori Parks." *Theater* 21.3 (1990): 73–80.

Wilmer, S. E. "Restaging the Nation: The Work of Suzan-Lori Parks." *Modern Drama* 43.3 (Fall 2000): 442–452.

Young, Jean. "The Re-objectification and ReCommodification of Saartjie Baartman in Suzan-Lori Parks' *Venus*." *African American Review* 31.4 (Winter 1997): 699–708.

Brandon L. A. Hutchinson

PASSING

In the context of African American culture, *passing* refers to the act of denying an African American ancestry and assuming a white **identity**. Perhaps because the concept of racial passing calls into question the relation between physical appearance and identity and thus challenges the very definition of **race**, it has been one of the most explored and controversial themes in African American **literature**.

The passing character is often portrayed in late-nineteenth- and early-twentieth-century American literature as a tragic victim—one who enjoys a certain amount of power in assuming a white identity but must, in the end, return to his or her cultural roots. Some African American authors would depict doomed interracial couples and **mulattoes** to emphasize the danger of miscegenation and the folly in denying African heritage. For example, in *The Garies and Their Friends* (1857), Frank J. Webb presents the story of an interracial couple who attempt to escape racial prejudice by moving to Philadelphia but ultimately cannot and are eventually murdered. Their light-skinned son, who is discovered passing for white and attempting to marry a white woman, is socially rejected. **Charles Waddell Chesnutt** uses passing characters in *The Wife of His Youth* (1889) and *The House behind the Cedars* (1900) to expose the dangers of being seduced by white cultural values. Rather than portraying **whiteness** as an identity to be envied, Chesnutt shows that the consequence of adopting white values is the loss of the self.

If these narratives encourage African Americans to unite in a defined **community**, some African American writers would deploy the narratives of passing to illustrate the precarious nature of the color line. In what is recognized as the first African American novel, *Clotel, or The President's Daughter* (1853), for example, **William Wells Brown** draws a sympathetic portrait of the quadroon daughter of Thomas Jefferson and his slave Sally Hemings, even as he reminds his audience that with the rise of such interracial coupling, racial heritage will become increasingly difficult to define. In what is recognized as the first extensive exploration of racial passing, **James Weldon Johnson**'s *Autobiography of an Ex-coloured Man* (1912) complicates the very idea that one who has a mixed racial heritage can claim an identity as either an African American or a white man. Its depiction of a fair-skinned man who denies his African American heritage to enjoy the privileges of being white ends in complete ambivalence with a short description of the protagonist's psychological turmoil over his success at passing.

In more complex and subtle ways, some African American women writers have used the theme of passing to critique both racism and misogyny. **Frances E. W. Harper**'s heroine in *Iola Leroy; or, Shadows Uplifted* (1892), for example, is a light-skinned heroine who embraces her African American identity and actively engages in her fate by refusing to marry a white doctor and vowing to **work** for the progress of African American people. Because the protagonist marries another light-skinned African American character who also refuses to pass, however, to some extent the novel suggests the impossibility of social progress without marriage. Similar to Harper's protagonist in her refusal of a white man for an African American as a husband is **Jessie Redmon Fauset**'s all but white character Angela Murray in *Plum Bun* (1928). For Angela, who refashions herself as Angèle Mory when passing for white, passing yields a state of empowerment and social prestige, but only for a short time. To some extent, then, *Plum Bun* represents passing as a clash between feminist empowerment and racial denial. Mixed-race African American women have no recourse but to rely on their racial brothers or fathers to attain social visibility. Not only does Fauset portray the impossibility of African American women's independence, thereby subtly criticizing the patriarchal ideology of African American culture, but also she shows how the phenomenon of passing brings out new, more complex forms of prejudice. In the ironically titled *Comedy: American Style* (1933), for example, a dark-skinned character commits suicide because he is rejected by his light-skinned mother and sister.

Nella Larsen, one of the most intriguing writers on the concept of passing, would further complicate and greatly expand the concept of racial passing. Her work in *Quicksand* (1928) and *Passing* (1929) not only reacts against conventional ways of representing the narrative of passing but also widens the term to encompass other aspects of identity, especially **class**, gender, and

sexuality. For this reason, several critics from Martha J. Cutter to Judith Butler suggest that Larsen's representations of passing are empowering in that they emphasize the fluidity of identity and destabilize traditional oppressive boundaries. In *Quicksand*, Helga Crane "passes" by continually adopting new identities, and the striking deterioration of her roles as the narrative moves forward—from independent teacher to entrapped wife and mother—illustrates the extent to which cultural prejudice about the expected role of a black woman, even within the black community, actually damages African American culture. After experiencing empowerment through her ability to change her identity as one would a wardrobe, the heroine's fate as a minister's wife imprisoned in her own **body** strongly suggests that without feminist revision, African American beliefs about gender would ensure political regression for the entire race.

If *Quicksand* satirizes the conventional narratives of passing, which at times radically reinforce racist and sexist boundaries, *Passing* introduces two light-skinned heroines who approach their mixed racial identity very differently. Like Helga Crane, Irene Redfield occasionally enjoys the privileges of being an exotic "other" but ultimately perceives passing as a deception and denial of identity. Unlike both Helga and Irene, trapped as they are by their choices to assume conventional roles as decidedly African American women, Clare Kendry not only refuses to confine or direct her desire but also escapes the text altogether through an enigmatic **death** in the end. To some extent, then, *Passing* fragments the meaning of the term *passing* so that it indicates the performances of various identities, the deaths or "passings" of others, and the obliteration of the idea of a single definable self.

Larsen's transformative representations of passing foreshadow its treatment in contemporary literature, where it is no longer simply about crossing a color line as an empowering strategy used to transcend boundaries of race, gender, class, and sexual, ethnic, and national identity. Though the concept of racial passing remains controversial as it threatens the idea of a purely African American identity, the broader idea of passing has come to play a crucial role for contemporary scholars who see identity as a performance or an act, rather than a simple biological claim.

Works About

Berzon, Judith R. *Neither White nor Black: The Mulatto Character in American Fiction*. New York: New York University Press, 1978.

Fabi, M. Giulia. *Passing and the Rise of the African American Novel*. Chicago: University of Illinois Press, 2001.

Ginsberg, Elaine K., ed. *Passing and the Fictions of Identity*. Durham: Duke University Press, 1996.

Pfeiffer, Kathleen. *Race Passing and American Individualism*. Amherst: University of Massachusetts Press, 2003.

Smith, Valerie. "Reading the Intersection of Race and Gender in Narratives of Passing." *Diacritics* 24.2–3 (1994): 43–57.

Sollors, Werner. *Neither Black nor White Yet Both: Thematic Explorations of Inter-racial Literature.* New York: Oxford University Press, 1997.

Kathleen M. Helal

PASSING

Nella Larsen's second novel, *Passing*, published in 1929, explores a relationship between two African American women who are able to pass for white, a social practice common among light-skinned urban African Americans at the time of Jim Crow laws, black migration, and the one-drop rule. While some "passed" for occasional convenience (for instance, to eat at a restaurant or to sit in a preferred section of a train), a few others entered white society, completely shedding their African American **identity**, as in the case of **James Weldon Johnson**'s *Autobiography of an Ex-coloured Man* (1912). Irene Redfield, the protagonist of *Passing*, belongs to the former category. Married to an African American doctor in New York, she is comfortably well off and securely established within the black bourgeoisie. But her accidental meeting of a childhood acquaintance, Clare Kendry, at a Chicago hotel, where both are **passing** for white, shakes her to the core. The stunning and unforgettable Clare, with her mixed-race **family** background, has embraced passing as a way of life as the glamorous wife of a white businessman who is unaware of her mixed racial heritage. She expresses a desire, through Irene, to reconnect with her African American roots, although doing so is perilous to her current lifestyle.

Much of the novel focuses on Irene's intense fear of and fascination with Clare and, in return, Clare's pursuit of the reluctant Irene. The psychological tension invokes the doppelganger theme: The two women become shadows of what the other both fears and desires. For Clare, Irene represents acceptance and connections within middle-**class** black society, which has treated Clare as an outsider. For Irene, Clare represents the outrageous—living a bald-faced lie on her own terms, without regard for rules, morals, or responsibility to the **race**. Irene's life, on the other hand, is centered around playing by the rules. One of her triumphs is keeping her restless husband, Brain, in practice in New York, distracting him from a desire to explore the riskier dream of living and working in South America. Managing the desires of others in order to serve her needs for a certain social status and standard of living is at the center of Irene's adult existence. Clare's presence in her life threatens to reveal to Irene the self-centered nature of her own life and the lies she is also living.

The tension builds as Clare engages Irene's complicity in her charade—forcing her to pass as white, along with another acquaintance, Gertrude, at a meeting with Clare's husband in which he reveals his distaste for Negroes and divulges his nickname for Clare, "Nig." Irene's paranoia mounts as she suspects Clare of seducing her husband, Brian, conflating Clare's daring and

Brian's restlessness into a double threat. The melodramatic ending, in which Irene and Clare exchange places as perceived victim and perpetrator, makes it clear that only one of them can survive, introducing another meaning of "passing." The "peace" (Irene) and "clarity" (Clare) symbolized by the names of the protagonists cannot coexist; one is achieved at the repression of the other.

Larsen's keen insights into the psychology of passing and her skillful, spare narrative have intrigued critics since its revival in the 1970s by **black feminist criticism**. The strange tension between Clare and Irene has led some critics to posit a latent homoerotic tension between the women. A recent Lacanian reading of this text by Brain Carr posits that, in fact, *Passing* is about "nothing." While the object of desire may, in fact, be nothing, the desire to pass was caused by material circumstances in a highly race stratified time and place. Although Larsen herself did not pass for white, her mixed parentage gave her grounds for understanding the complexities of racial construction. That her own family may have rejected her in order to pass for white is a possibility suggested by Larsen's biographer, Thadious Davis.

See also Harlem Renaissance; Lesbianism; Mulatto; *Quicksand*; Sexuality

Works About

Carby, Hazel. *Reconstructing Womanhood: The Emergence of the Afro-American Woman Novelist.* New York: Oxford University Press, 1987.

Carr, Brian. "Paranoid Interpretation, Desire's Nonobject, and Nella Larsen's *Passing.*" *PMLA* 119.2 (March 2004): 282–295.

Davis, Thadious. *Nella Larsen, Novelist of the Harlem Renaissance: A Woman's Life Unveiled.* Baton Rouge: Louisiana State University Press, 1994.

McDowell, Deborah. Introduction to *Quicksand* and *Passing.* New Brunswick, NJ: Rutgers University Press, 1996.

Wall, Cheryl A. *Women of the Harlem Renaissance.* Bloomington: Indiana University Press, 1995.

Ann Hostetler

PATTERNIST SERIES

Octavia Butler's Patternist series consists of (in the saga's chronological order) *Wild Seed* (1980), *Mind of My Mind* (1977), *Patternmaster* (1976), *Clay's Ark* (1984), and *Survivor* (1978). These novels follow the rise of a **race** of telepaths and describe the culture these beings create, sometimes with centuries separating the stories. Of these works, *Wild Seed* has received the most critical attention.

The first in the series, *Wild Seed* relates the beginnings of the telepathic culture. Doro, the founding father, is a being like none other. The origin of his power is unknown, but Doro is apparently immortal, for he is able to project his consciousness into a new **body** at will, an act that both feeds him and provides a surge of pleasure. Consuming the "selves" of persons with mental talents such as telepathy or telekinesis is especially satisfying, so over time Doro collects and breeds telepaths as an ongoing source of food and pleasurable kills. Eventually whole settlements of his special people exist, with residents who both **love** and fear him.

The story opens when Doro meets an African named Anyanwu, herself a near immortal. But Anyanwu's longevity comes from her power to heal, not from stealing others' bodies. She can repair any organism whose genetic structure she is familiar with, and she can shape shift into any creature whose anatomy she understands. Unlike Doro, who takes over others' bodies, Anyanwu stays alive by altering her own genetic makeup, living most often as an elderly woman but sometimes changing into a young woman, a man, a porpoise, leopard, bird, or dog.

Doro forces Anyanwu to go with him to America and join his colony there; allusions to the cross-Atlantic slave trade are obvious. For many years she lives quietly, happily married to one of Doro's sons, a man devoted to her, and breeding with whomever Doro brings to her—the usual pattern for Doro's people. Anyanwu needs to feel connected to **family**; her greatest sorrow is that she outlives all those she loves. Her family members have been granted immunity from Doro's feedings, but Doro still uses them to coerce Anyanwu to his will. After many decades, Anyanwu's beloved husband dies, and she finally flees Doro, whose casual killings she abhors. She knows he must kill to live, but her attempts to curb his unnecessary kills have been futile; she hopes now to find a sanctuary where she can live peacefully, surrounded by loved ones.

The story follows Doro's search for her and their final showdown. Neither comes out a winner; their strengths, although opposites in nature, are equal in force. The story ends with their recognition that although their natures are irreconcilable—Doro a killer, Anyanwu a healer—they (and only they) can provide one another companionship lasting perhaps for eternity. To effect this, though, they must learn to accept one another. Anyanwu must let Doro kill; Doro must accept Anyanwu's rules about what kills are off limits. This is a story of the feminine principle versus masculine principle: Anyanwu, a life force, advocates familial ties, equality, **community**, **domesticity**, and **healing**, while Doro, a **death** force, refuses social obligation, preferring solitary individuality, patriarchal authority, rootlessness, and **violence**. The book ends with an uneasy alliance between the two.

Mind of My Mind picks up some generations later and follows the life of Mary, the most powerful telepath Doro has yet sired. After "transition," the risky period when one's powers become active, Mary finds she has the ability to mentally link other telepaths to herself—and once linked, they are unable to regain autonomy. She uses her power to create The Pattern—an ever-growing community of linked telepaths. Together they construct a social system that provides a haven for tormented telepaths unable to function elsewhere, a place where one's powers can be explored, augmented, and made productive.

As Mary seeks out telepaths from around the world and compels them to join her–her own kind of feeding–Doro begins to fear what his daughter is creating. The story ends with the showdown between the two. Like Anyanwu, Mary represents an alternative to Doro's tyranny, but she also enslaves, albeit much more benevolently. And both Mary and Doro oppress the easily enslaved nontelepathic "mutes." Collectively, these two books explore the uses and abuses of power.

Patternmaster occurs eons after the telepaths' complete conquest of the mutes. With telepaths in charge, society has evolved into a feudal, nontechnological age. The story follows two brothers' rivalry for the position of Patternmaster, controller of The Pattern. The protagonist is the younger son, Teray. As he makes a daring move to claim The Pattern, Teray comes to understand the consequences of continuing the telepaths' feudal social structure, a structure bereft of compassion that pits telepaths against clayarks, a race of monstrous mutants. The previous book in the series, *Clay's Ark*, relates the evolution of these mutants, whose origins began when an astronaut brought a dreadful genetic plague back to Earth. The last book in the series to be written, *Clay's Ark* is only loosely connected to the rest of the Patternist series. *Survivor*, the final story, tracks the life of Alana, a girl who escapes the plague by migrating to another planet. There, she becomes a victim of war between two rival factions, which she undertakes to reconcile. Alana is one of Butler's early female protagonists who strives to bring people and races together.

This series collectively explores the effect of enormous power on individuals and societies, and it suggests that a feminist model of government that values compassion and equality, uses power to help others, and brings people together as family, not master/servant, is the only model where happiness and contentment are likely. Only those characters who think in terms of family, personal connections, and healing find even a modicum of peace in these books.

See also Bloodchild and Other Stories; *Kindred*; Parable Series; Xenogenesis Trilogy

Works About

Alaimo, Stacy. "'Skin Dreaming': The Bodily Transgressions of Fielding Burke, Octavia Butler, and Linda Hogan." *Ecofeminist Literary Criticism: Theory, Interpretation, Pedagogy*. Ed. Greta Gaard and Patrick D. Murphy. Urbana: University of Illinois Press, 1998. 123–138.

Govan, Sandra Y. "Homage to Tradition: Octavia Butler Renovates the Historical Novel." *MELUS* 13 (1986): 79–96.

Ramírez, Catherine S. "Cyborg Feminism: The Science Fiction of Octavia Butler and Gloria Anzaldúa." *Reload: Rethinking Women + Cyberculture*. Ed. Mary Flanagan and Austin Booth. Cambridge: MIT Press, 2002. 374–402.

Grace McEntee

PERRY, PHYLLIS ALESIA (1962–   )

The 1998 publication of Phyllis Alesia Perry's debut novel *Stigmata* granted the young author membership into the ranks of the highly acclaimed African American female writers from the **South**. These writers are women who have lived almost exclusively in the South or who living elsewhere have chosen not to sever ties with their historical and **family** southern roots. In many instances, these women authors have used **historical fiction** to chronicle the sojourn of their people, tracing their journey back to the land of those **ancestors** who still exercise a firm grip on the lives of the authors' twenty- and twenty-first-century fictional characters. By doing so, as does Perry in *Stigmata* and her other writing, these historically conscious writers establish a sense of unity between the past and present, evidenced by a reaffirmation of sisterhood.

Perry, a native southern, was born in Atlanta, Georgia, and grew up in Tuskegee, Alabama. She graduated from the University of Alabama in 1982 with a degree in communications and worked for several southern newspapers after college. While writing for the *Alabama Journal*, she was a member of a team of reporters who won the Pulitzer Prize and a Distinguished Service Award of the Society of Professional Journalists, Sigma Delta Chi, for the investigation of Alabama's high infant mortality rate.

The publication of her first novel in 1998 brought Perry worldwide attention as a young but serious novelist. The carefully crafted book tells the story of a young woman whose existence is unexpectedly altered by the inheritance of a trunk and handmade quilt from her deceased grandmother. Sensing a cloud of mystery surrounding the quilt, the main character, Lizzie, goes on a journey to confront her family's past.

Following the publication of *Stigmata* in Germany and the United States, the book quickly found its way to bookstores in Great Britain, the Netherlands, Spain, and other countries. The novel became the Book of the Month Club Quality Paperback Selection and was nominated for the Quality Paperback Book Club New Voices Award. Perry also received the Georgia Author of the Year award in the first novel category in a ceremony held on the campus of Mercer University in 1999.

Her latest book is *A Sunday in June* (2003), a prequel to the earlier written *Stigmata*. *A Sunday in June* relates the story of three Alabama sisters living in the early years of the twentieth century. These young women are far from normal. They carry their grandmother's gift of second sight: They can see into the future and experience the pain of the past. Unexpectedly, the sisters experience paranormal connections to the days of **slavery** in America's past.

The novelist grew up in a **home** where writing was encouraged. Her father, Harmon Perry, preceded his daughter's association with the southern white press. He was the first African American reporter hired by the *Atlanta Journal*. During his reporting at the *Journal*, the elder Perry was part of a group of writers that received an award for investigation of racial tensions between Atlanta's African American and white citizenry. Additionally, he won four awards from the Georgia Press Association in recognition of the quality of his individual **work**.

As a female novelist, Perry has been compared to other writers in the rich tradition of African American literary artists such as **Toni Morrison** and **Alice Walker**. Perry currently lives in Atlanta, Georgia.

See also Quilting

Works By

Stigmata. New York: Hyperion, 1998.
A Sunday in June. New York: Hyperion, 2003.

Shirley Walker Moore

PETRY, ANN (1908–1997)

Born Ann Lane to Peter C. and Bertha James Lane on October 12, 1911, Ann Petry spent the first thirty years of her life in and around Old Saybrook, Connecticut, a small New England town that informed her literary aesthetic and **work** ethic. The consummate New Englander, hardworking and self-reliant, Petry graduated from high school in 1925 and earned her Ph.G. from then Connecticut College of Pharmacy in New Haven in 1931. Petry returned to Old Saybrook to work in the **family** drugstore business until 1938, when she married Louisiana native George D. Petry and moved to New York. Committed to becoming a writer, Petry worked as a journalist for the Harlem-based *Amsterdam News* and as a reporter for the Harlem weekly the *People's Voice*. While employed at the *People's Voice*, Petry edited the woman's page and soon thereafter helped to found Negro Women, Inc., an advocacy group for Harlem consumers. After honing her craft at Mabel Louise Robinson's creative writing workshops, Petry published "On Saturday the Siren Sounds at Noon" in the *Crisis*, the official publication of the National Association for the Advancement of Colored People (NAACP), in 1943. This short story marked the beginning of Petry's notoriety in popular literary circles.

To be sure, Petry's life and work testify to her commitment to women's issues in the public and literary spheres. Specifically, Petry's **literature** offers a **black feminist** critique of **violence**, poverty, **motherhood**, **race**, **class**, gender, and **sexuality**. Her work shifts the gaze of naturalistic **fiction** established by **Richard Wright**'s *Native Son* (1940) from the black man to the black woman; her work expands African Americanist notions of **home** through her depictions of black life in New England; her work recasts literary conventions and tropes within the context of **black feminism** and a black feminist experience; her work offers a fearless look at the needs and desires of black women in a world overrun by racism and sexism; her work sings a **blues** song for a black female experience that places survival—the singing of one's song even in the face of tragedy—above all else.

Petry inherited this survivalist ethic as well as her self-assuredness from the strong-willed women in her family. Even though Petry's first profession, pharmacy, suggested that she might follow in the footsteps of her father, it was the tenacity and entrepreneurial spirit of her mother and maternal aunts that encouraged her to view the world through eyes unencumbered by fallacious gender limitations. Bertha Lane, mother, wife, and sister, was also a hairdresser, barber, chiropodist, creator of cleaning products for the home, and maker of tonics for the hair. One aunt was, like Petry's father, a licensed pharmacist; the other was an educator. All three helped Petry to see that powerful women existed and that this strength was her birthright.

Author of a wide variety of texts—short fiction, three novels, **children's and young adult literature**, a screenplay, and several essays—most of Petry's blues narratives explore black experience in America. The tale that started Petry's literary career, "On Saturday the Siren Sounds at Noon," (1943) tells the story of a troubled black man who is reminded of the day he found his children burned to **death** at home, left alone by his philandering wife, whenever he hears the air raid test siren on Saturday afternoon. Rendered through flashbacks, readers learn that, overwhelmed by anger at his wife who placed her own selfish needs over the protection of their children, the protagonist murders her and commits suicide by throwing himself into the path of an oncoming train. Even though the story offers little in the way of explicitly feminist themes, Petry's manipulation of **history** (the tale was based on true events) and desire to speak on behalf of otherwise silenced voices (in this case, African American men) demonstrate the feminist foundation upon which her work stands.

Intent on expanding the settings and spaces typically associated with African American experience, Petry's literary oeuvre also reflects a complex rendering of the psychology of black and white experiences, both communal and individual, in America. Petry's award-winning first novel, *The Street* (1946), tells the story of Lutie Johnson: an industrious black woman who moves from Long Island to Connecticut, then to Harlem in search of a better life for herself and her son. While living on 116th Street in Harlem, Lutie must learn to deal with the "street"—a metaphor for the race, gender, and class conflicts that accompany her new life. As an attractive black woman, Lutie's **beauty** becomes a liability as she must constantly ward off advances from a cadre of men in her **community**: a neighbor who wants her to become a prostitute; the building superintendent who, infuriated by Lutie's rebuff to his sexual advances, introduces her son Bub to a life of crime; and a rich white Harlemite who also wants Lutie for himself. As a poor inner-city woman without much success in securing gainful employment, the street becomes emblematic of the oppression that faces Lutie at every turn. While many scholars and readers consider *The Street*, like other texts by Petry, to be overwhelmingly depressing, her style reflects her early training in journalism. In *The Street*, Petry reports with an unflinching journalistic eye the story of a woman on the periphery of American life—a story that would otherwise be left untold. This novel, therefore, reflects her feminist impulse to give voice to marginalized women's experiences.

In her second and third novels, *Country Place* (1947) and ***The Narrows***
(1953), Petry returns to New England settings and fixes her black feminist
gaze upon white and black communities to explore the destructive nature of
intolerance and prejudice within each. *Country Place* centers around two sets of
characters—most of whom are white—and their inability to reconcile gender
and class tensions in the small town of Lennox, Connecticut. Without major
black characters or a story line driven by racial conflict, *Country Place* was a
hard sell among critics and readers accustomed to Petry's biting commentary
on race and gender. Petry's willingness to step beyond the arbitrary constraints of what constitutes "black" literature, however, expanded the subject
matter and settings available to black writers. In this profound feminist act,
she rewrote the rules and expanded the territory for all African American
writers by turning her New England experiential knowledge into transformative literature. *The Narrows*, also set in New England, builds upon naturalistic elements introduced in *The Street* by exposing the impact of racism on
individuals as well as the communities they represent. In this tragic tale of
interracial **love** between a well-educated black man and a well-bred white
woman, Petry explores the impact of American history, and the **stereotypes**
and racist values formed out of that history, upon black and white relations.
A raw exploration of the politics of gender, race, violence, community, and
class, *The Narrows* continues Petry's feminist analysis of the intellectual and
spiritual costs of black psychic fragmentation established in earlier works.

As a black feminist interested in telling stories with communal value, Petry
turned to children's fiction and nonfiction in 1955 to extend the choices for
African American youth interested in culturally relevant texts. As in Petry's
fiction, her nonfiction for black youth also offers deep psychological portrayals of complex figures. *Harriet Tubman, Conductor on the Underground Railroad*
(1955) and *Tituba of Salem Village* (1964) relate the stories of their protagonists—
the first, a former slave who helped to free hundreds of slaves, the second, a
female slave from Barbados who was accused of being a witch during the
Salem witch trials—with elegance and depth. By challenging established tropes
and accepted norms, Petry's work anticipates the literature of later black
women writers who relate African American experience through a distinctly
black feminist lens.

Works By

Country Place. Boston: Houghton Mifflin, 1947.
Miss Muriel and Other Stories. Boston: Houghton Mifflin, 1971.
The Narrows. Boston: Houghton Mifflin, 1953.
"The Novel as Social Criticism." *The Writer's Book*. Ed. Helen Hull. New
    York: Harper, 1950. 32–39.
"On Saturday the Siren Sounds at Noon." *Crisis* 50 (December 1943):
    368–369.
The Street. Boston: Houghton Mifflin, 1946.
Tituba of Salem Village. New York: Crowell, 1964.

Works About

Drake, Kimberly. "Women on the Go: Blues, Conjure, and Other Alterna-
    tives to Domesticity in Ann Petry's *The Street* and *The Narrows*." *Arizona
    Quarterly* 54.1 (1998): 65–90.
Holladay, Hilary. *Ann Petry*. New York: Twayne, 1996.
McKay, Nellie. "Ann Petry's *The Street* and *The Narrows*: A Study of the
    Influences of Class, Race, and Gender on Afro-American Women's Lives."
    Women and War. Ed. Maria Diedrich. New York: Berg, 1990. 127–140.
Puschmann-Nalenz, Barbara. "Ann Petry: Mother Africa." *The African
    American Short Story 1970–1990*. Ed. Wolfgang Karrer and Barbara Pusch-
    mann-Nalenz. Trier: Wissenschaftlicher, 1993. 29–40.
Wilson, Mark K. "A MELUS Interview: Ann Petry–The New England
    Connection." *MELUS* 15.2 (1988): 71–84.

Shanna Greene Benjamin

PLANTATION TRADITION

The plantation tradition refers to a body of **literature** that offers a nostalgic representation of "the Old **South**" as well as a highly romanticized portrait of the institution of **slavery**. Revolving around life on agricultural southern estates primarily in the 1830s, 1840s, and 1850s and composed primarily by white southern authors, literature of the plantation tradition insists on the nobility of the white southern aristocrat and the virtuous passivity of the white southern belle and contests the image of slavery as a violent and dehumanizing institution that was presented in antebellum **slave narratives** such as **Frederick Douglass**'s *Narrative of the Life of Frederick Douglass* (1845) and **Harriet Jacobs**'s ***Incidents in the Life of a Slave Girl*** (1861) and abolitionist novels such as Harriet Beecher Stowe's *Uncle Tom's Cabin* (1852). In addition to avoiding any mention of the physical, psychological, or sexual abuse of slaves and obscuring their desire for liberation, plantation literature typically portrays the plantation **community** as a stable and harmonious **family** unit and likens the relationship between masters and slaves to that of caring parents and their loving, obedient children.

The representation of the plantation community as a cohesive and content family largely depends on its depictions of African American slaves as devoted and docile servants, which helped generate a number of racist **stereotypes** that were later propagated in other cultural forms, including **film** and advertisement. One of the most prominent of these stereotypes is the **Mammy** figure. Immortalized in Margaret Mitchell's bestselling novel *Gone With the Wind* (1936), "Mammy" presents an image of a completely desexualized and simple-minded black woman who consistently demonstrates an unwavering loyalty to and affection for her white mistress, even, in some cases, to the extreme of preferring to care for the white children in her charge over nurturing her own children. The male counterpart to the Mammy stereotype in plantation literature and an identifiable progenitor of the popular minstrelsy shows of the early twentieth century is the Sambo figure, a content, childlike character who wants nothing more than to continue his tranquil existence as a slave and to please and entertain his white masters.

Plantation literature first emerged in the decades prior to the Civil War with the publication of works such as John Pendleton Kennedy's *The Swallow Barn, or a Sojourn in the Old Dominion* (1832), a work that consists of several sketches that relay the "seeings and thinkings" of northerner Mark Littleton during his first visit to the South and his stopover at the southern estate of Frank Merriwether. Addressed to a northern audience, Littleton, though initially morally opposed to slavery, becomes convinced during this journey that while slaves might become more "respectable" in another social system that afforded them self-governance, they could not possibly obtain any greater state of happiness than they already had on the southern plantation. The success of *The Swallow Barn*, which was republished in 1851, paved the way for the appearance of numerous other plantation novels, including Caroline Gilman's *Recollections of a Southern Matron* (1836), William Gilmore Simms's *Woodcraft* (1852), and Caroline Hentz's *The Plantation's Northern Bride* (1857).

While effecting the emancipation of African Americans and, accordingly, the deconstruction of the socioeconomic structure of the "Old South," the Civil War did not terminate the plantation tradition. Rather, plantation literature gained new prominence during the post–Reconstruction era with the publication of Thomas Page Nelson's *In Ole Virginia* (1887), a collection of stories narrated mainly by loyal ex-slaves who fondly recall life in the Old South. In addition to epitomizing the racist conventions of the antebellum plantation tradition, Nelson's collection also marks what Lucinda H. MacKethan has identified as a major development in plantation literature of the late nineteenth century–the creation of dialect plantation stories told through the perspective of African American narrators. While in the hands of writers such as Page, this form of narration functioned to further emphasize African Americans' "simplicity" and desire to please, it also complicated the political implications of the tradition, as Joel Chandler Harris's famous collection of dialect tales, *Uncle Remus: His Songs and His Sayings* (1880), illustrates. Although the debate over Harris's relationship to the racist ideology of the plantation tradition continues, critics such as Amy Kaplan have complicated the prevailing assumption that the text uncritically participates in the tradition. Like Page's *In Ole Virginia*, *Uncle Remus*, Kaplan claims, "participate[s] in the nostalgic recuperation by framing slave stores in the voice of an elderly black 'uncle' entertaining a white boy, but the stories themselves often speak in the subversive voice of a popular oral tradition that provided a cultural source of resistance to slavery and racism in the past and the present" (244).

The majority of plantation literature of the post–Reconstruction era, however, was generally written to support the maintenance and expansion of systematic forms of racial oppression. Whereas prior to the Civil War, it aimed to counteract the influence of abolitionists, after Reconstruction, it typically served to promote segregation. In addition to offering an idealized depiction of the antebellum South that posited a connection between social order and prosperity and forms of racial "control," plantation literature's stereotypical portrayal of African Americans led to the construction of other racist character types such as the **Jezebel** figure, an overly sexualized and morally deviant black temptress, and what has been termed "the Black beast," an image of an animalistic and violent black male that was propagated in Thomas Dixon's radically conservative, white-supremacist novels, particularly *The Clansman: A Historical Romance of the Ku Klux Klan* (1905). These images fueled the idea that African Americans posed a moral and physical threat to white southerners and, therefore, that interaction between the races should be severely restricted. Moreover, the stereotypes rooted in plantation literature also helped support the systematic disenfranchisement of African Americans in the South that was instituted primarily through poll taxes, property requirements, and **literacy** tests. In essence, the portrayal of African Americans as both simple-minded children and moral deviants insinuated that they lacked the mental capabilities and moral requirements necessary to make decisions for themselves, let alone for others.

African American artists' efforts to dismantle the racist **myths** of the plantation literature have constituted a major tenet of African American literary history. Such efforts are perhaps most overt in **Charles Waddell Chesnutt**'s *The Conjure Woman* (1899), which consciously evokes the conventions of the plantation tradition only to subvert them. Reminiscent of Page's *In Ole Virginia*, the work is a collection of stories about plantation life prior to emancipation told by ex-slave Uncle Julius in black dialect and framed by the narrative of a white northerner. When he is initially introduced in the first story of the collection, "The Goophered Grapevine," Julius immediately recalls the Sambo figure of conventional plantation literature. Sitting leisurely on a bench, eating grapes in an exaggerated way, he reveals a fearful superstition of "goopher" and displays a strong eagerness to both aid and entertain two white northerners, John and Annie. Julius's tale about the haunted McAdoo plantation, however, suggests that this initial appearance is nothing more than a veneer, as it centers on the systematic economic exploitation of African Americans that calls attention to the reality that, after years of having labored on the abandoned vineyard, Julius does not have the financial resources to purchase it; moreover, it can be interpreted as an effort to scare off the white northern couple who does. Although the strategy ultimately fails, and John and Annie eventually purchase the vineyard, the tale underscores the superficiality of the stereotypical image of African Americans as devoted and docile servants, the image on which plantation literature's nostalgic depiction of the Old South largely relies.

While a notable trend in African American literature in general, revisions of the representations of slavery and African Americans in literature of the plantation tradition have played a particularly prominent role in African American women's writing throughout the past two centuries. Jacobs's antebellum slave narrative, for instance, challenges the tradition by countering the romanticized image of slavery as a paternal institution with revelations of her own experiences of physical, psychological, and sexual abuse during her enslavement on a southern plantation, and **Frances E. W. Harper**'s *Iola Leroy* (1892), which depicts a formerly enslaved heroine as she attempts to locate her lost relatives after Emancipation, emphasizes how slavery destroyed rather than constituted a form of family.

Literature by African American women of the twentieth century has continued to debunk the "plantation myth" in diverse and complex ways. While novels written during the "Jim Crow" era such as **Nella Larsen**'s *Passing* (1929) and **Zora Neale Hurston**'s *Their Eyes Were Watching God* (1937) examine the multifaceted destructive legacies of slavery for the African American community, more recent works such as **Alice Walker**'s *The Color Purple* (1982), **Gloria Naylor**'s *The Women of Brewster Place* (1982), and **Toni Morrison**'s *Beloved* (1987) have, for instance, highlighted the strengths, complexities, and diversity of African American women that the stereotypes of the plantation tradition vehemently deny.

Works About

Kaplan, Amy. "Nation, Region, and Empire." *The Columbia History of the American Novel.* Ed. Emory Elliott. New York: Columbia University Press, 1991. 240–266.

MacKethan, Lucinda H. "Plantation Fiction, 1865–1900." *The History of Southern Literature.* Ed. Louis D. Rubin et al. Baton Rouge: Louisiana State University Press, 1985. 209–218.

——. "Plantation Tradition." *The Oxford Companion to African American Literature.* Ed. William L. Andrews et. al. New York: Oxford University Press, 1997. 579–582.

Nowatzki, Robert C. " 'Passing' in a White Genre: Charles W. Chesnutt's Negotiations of the Plantation Tradition in *The Conjure Woman.*" *American Literary Realism* 27.2 (1995): 20–36.

Taylor, William R. *Cavalier and Yankee: The Old South and American National Character.* Cambridge, MA: Harvard University Press, 1979.

Kara L. Mollis

PLATO, ANN (1820–?)

Not much is known about the life of Ann Plato. What little is known comes mainly from the only book she published, *Essays: Including Biographies and Miscellaneous Pieces of Prose and Poetry* (1841), and from various printed sources. Plato's volume is the second published by an African American woman. She also has the distinction of being the first African American woman to publish a collection of essays and one of the first to publish **poetry**. From the information provided, she may have been a free African American who lived in

Hartford, Connecticut, and was certainly a member of Hartford's Talcott Street (Colored) Congregational Church.

Her book contains four biographical compositions, sixteen short essays, and twenty poems. The book itself was produced inexpensively and suggests that limited copies were published for the local area. Reverend James W. C. Pennington, the pastor of her church, wrote the introduction, which is known more for the information he leaves out about Plato. In this introduction, he states that Plato is a member of his church but does not record the amount of time that she has been a member. He says she is young but never gives her age. The only **family** information he provides claims she comes from modest means.

Unfortunately, Plato is even less forthcoming about her background. At the time of publication, she was either studying to be a teacher or already one. Lending credence to this theory, other sources state that she taught at one of the all-African American schools in Hartford, the Elm Street School, otherwise known as the South African School, from 1844 to 1847. Even though Plato is African American, she makes few references specifically to **race**. However, one of her poems, "To the First of August," positively refers to the end of **slavery** in the British West Indies, which occurred on August 1, 1838.

Plato's essays and poetry correspond to the typical standards of the time. The main topics of her essays are **religion** and education, while her poetry follows the elegiac technique of the eighteenth century. Plato's essays have a didactic and uplifting tone that enhances her attempts to convert readers to Protestantism at the same time it seems that she tries to convince them that the African American students of Hartford need a better educational system. She does not need to mention race; it is implicit in her message. The various types of work correspond to the typical style of the time because she has to prove that African Americans have the capacity and capability to be educated according to the standards of the day. Plato's purposeful citations of historical figures such as Aristotle, Benjamin Franklin, and John Milton enhance this action.

Information about Plato stops after 1847. Because of the lack of information and her adherence to the writing techniques of her time period, her value to African American **literature** has been overlooked until recently. Hopefully, more extant information will become available that demonstrates Plato's bravery in defending the rights of all African Americans to be educated.

Work By

Essays: Including Biographies and Miscellaneous Pieces of Prose and Poetry. Intro. Kenny J. Williams. New York: Oxford University Press, 1988. xxvii–liii.

Works About

Loggins, Vernon. *The Negro Author, His Development in America.* Port Washington, NY: Kennikat Press, 1964.

Robinson, William H., ed. *Early Black American Poets*. Dubuque, IA: William C. Brown, 1969.

White, David O. "Hartford's African Schools, 1830–1868." *Connecticut Historical Society Bulletin* 39 (April 1974): 47–53.

Devona Mallory

PLUM BUN

Jessie Redmon Fauset's second novel *Plum Bun: A Novel without a Moral*, first published by Frederick A. Stokes in 1928, focuses clearly and intensely on one particular character, Angela Murray. Philadelphia born, Angela is a white-skinned daughter of a dark-colored father and a light-colored mother; she is, to cite a bitter conjunction used several times in the novel, a "white nigger." She thanks God that she has inherited her mother's paleness, unlike her dark sister, Virginia. *Plum Bun* is, in part, a bitter meditation on segregation between blacks and whites—even within families. Angela's father cannot be acknowledged in the streets by Angela and her mother.

On reaching adulthood, the individualistic, ambitious Angela moves to New York. She eschews black **community**, settling in the Village, where she can learn to draw and paint in white colleges. All the time she passes for white, hiding her ethnic **identity**. She is courted by a number of white men and is accepted into the company of white, middle-**class** groups. Frequently she hears friends and suitors, particularly the rich Roger Fielding, make extremely violent remarks against blacks. Her response is not to flee the company of these racists but to be convinced further that her mixed-**race** origins are a curse that must be suppressed at all costs, because only whites can have a fulsome life. On one highly symbolic occasion, Angela pretends not to know her sister Virginia, "cutting" her, lest the black-hating Roger discover her ethnic identity.

The appalling attitudes and conduct of Roger work effectively to bring Angela to her senses. His attacks on both blacks and on her chastity encapsulate the novel's twin anxieties: the subjugation of African Americans by whites and the subjugation of women by men. When eating in a restaurant, Roger acts swiftly to ensure that a black **family** does not receive service, even offering to pay any legal costs that the establishment might incur. He worries, with sincerity, about any possible illness that seeing the blacks may have caused Angela, but he does not ask her opinion about the situation. He arrogantly deigns to speak for them both. Angela and Roger sleep together, before marriage has been even discussed. It is unclear about how much force he uses to achieve the "surrender" of Angela, but it is clear that he is the sole instigator of the sexual union.

Gradually, Angela quashes her naive notion that **passing** will earn her **freedom** from racial prejudice. Infuriated when a talented black classmate is refused a scholarship on grounds of color, Angela declares her true racial affiliations, earning the respect of her sister and of her favored suitor, Anthony, a young **mulatto** of Brazilian origin. She learns that pretending to be white will not impede racism; the only possible advantage would be to achieve material comfort at a cost of personal integrity. She also learns, however, that not all whites despise blacks and that not all men are reckless and violent toward women. *Plum Bun* is, supposedly, "a novel without a moral," but the moral is loud and clear: All systems of generalized prejudice are fundamentally flawed and inappropriate.

See also Chinaberry Tree, The; Comedy: American Style; Passing, There Is Confusion

Works About

Feeney, Joseph J. "Black Childhood as Ironic: A Nursery Rhyme Transformed in Jessie Fauset's Novel *Plum Bun.*" *Minority Voices* 4.2 (1980): 65–69.

Kroell, Sonja. "A Bitter Journey: 'The Passing' Mulatta as 'Expatriate' in Jessie Redmon Fauset's *Plum Bun.*" *Prospero* 2 (1995): 35–45.

McDowell, Deborah. "Introduction: Regulating Midwives." *Plum Bun: A Novel without a Moral*, by Jessie Redmon Fauset. Boston: Beacon Press, 1990. ix–xxxiii.

Pfeiffer, Kathleen. "The Limits of Identity in Jessie Fauset's *Plum Bun.*" *Legacy* 18.1 (2001): 79–93.

Rueschmann, Eva. "Sister Bonds: Intersections of Family and Race in Jessie Redmon Fauset's *Plum Bun* and Dorothy West's *The Living Is Easy.*" *The Significance of Sibling Relationships in Literature.* Ed. J. S. Mink and J. D. Ward. Bowling Green, OH: Bowling Green State University Popular Press, 1992. 120–131.

Tomlinson, Susan. "Vision to Visionary: The New Negro Woman as Cultural Worker in Jessie Redmon Fauset's *Plum Bun.*" *Legacy* 19.1 (2002): 90–97.

Zachodnik, Teresa. "Passing Transgressions and Authentic Identity in Jessie Fauset's *Plum Bun* and Nella Larsen's *Passing.*" *Literature and Racial Ambiguity.* Ed. Teresa Hubel and Neil Brooks. Amsterdam: Rodopi, 2002. 45–69.

Kevin De Ornellas

POETRY

Stylistically, African American feminist poetry negotiates two traditions. On the one hand, it strives to equal the formal principles of traditional, European forms such as the Shakespearean sonnet. On the other hand, African American feminist poetry–like other forms of black **literature** such as the poetry of the **Harlem Renaissance**–seeks to achieve new forms adequate to the struggle against patriarchal formality itself. Thematically, this poetry represents the African American woman as heroic in her own right. Unlike *The Odyssey* (800 BCE), *Paradise Lost* (1667), or *The Canterbury Tales* (1380), the heroes of such lyrics do not embark on grandiose trips, focusing instead on life as it is lived in the **community** or at **home** and illustrating a more understated form of heroism that includes such roles as witness to racial discrimination, mother, and celebrant of African American **history** and culture.

While the majority of African American feminist poets write from their experiences as women, such male poets as **Claude McKay**, **Jean Toomer**, and **Langston Hughes** have also written feminist verse celebrating the African American woman and defending her against racial **violence**. McKay's "The Harlem Dancer" (1917), for example, represents the double life of a lovely African American performer reminiscent of **Josephine Baker**, a representation that takes the form of a traditional Shakespearean sonnet. Illustrating that the African American poetic tradition can indeed master the stylistic qualities of canonical writers, McKay's fourteen-line sequence follows precisely the Shakespearean rhyme scheme, with the last couplet offering the final twist; this African American **beauty** is not simply prostituting herself for the gaze of others but, rather, has managed to transcend her earthy reality, ultimately becoming more worthy than her position on the streets acknowledges. Likewise, Toomer's "Portrait in Georgia" (1923), while written in a wholly unique form that relies on flashes of images separated by em-dashes, also pays homage to Shakespeare as a master but goes one step beyond in order to signify on the idea of objectified beauty that Shakespeare portrays in his famous sonnets. Shakespeare's Sonnet 130, for example, enumerates the physical features of a woman; similarly, Toomer's "Portrait" depicts the portrait of a lady, but it also depicts the portrait of a lynching in Georgia, comparing a woman's hair to "a lyncher's rope" and describing her **body** as "white as the ash / of black flesh after flame."

Like Toomer, Hughes juxtaposes lynching–unlikely material for a poem dedicated to a woman–with the lyric. "Song for a Dark Girl" (1927) appears, in the first line, as a simple song with an uncomplicated and catchy rhythm similar to a child's song. However, Hughes undercuts the assumption established by his rhythm with the violent representation of a young black woman's lynching. Here, he repeats two phrases within parentheses: "(Break the heart of me)" and "(Bruised body high in air)"–the most powerful lines in the poem, despite, or because of, the parentheses themselves. In "Song for a Dark Girl," Hughes necessarily connects **race** with this young lover's lynching, putting into tension such key phrases as "black young lover" and "white Lord Jesus." This reference to a "white Lord Jesus" seeks to undercut racist language and practices by calling attention to the uninformed assumption that Jesus was, in fact, white.

While these three Harlem Renaissance poets have achieved a feminist poetics in their own right, perhaps the most powerful feminist statements regarding historical atrocity come from African American women themselves. **Rita Dove**'s "Parsley" (1983) refers to the moment on October 2, 1957, when the dictator of the Dominican Republic, Rafael Trujillo (1891–1961), ordered 20,000 blacks killed because they could not pronounce the letter *r* in *parejil*, the Spanish word for parsley. The poem develops that narrative in two sections, refusing consolation even in the end by suggesting that the general "will/ order many, this time, to be killed/for a single, beautiful word" (lines 70–72). In linking the beauty of language, in this case, the poetical sounding *parejil* with the brutality of humankind, Dove actually reinforces the strangely productive relationship between poetry and historical calamity. For Dove, the only possible way to communicate traumatic events is through the language of poetry, a language that, while beautiful, has the power to carry with it the most brutal acts of **violence**.

African American feminist verse not only focuses on violence against women, however. It also celebrates the physical attributes of African American woman traditionally devalued by the mainstream Anglo-Saxon aesthetic. Like her poem "My Race," **Helene Johnson**'s "What Do I Care for Morning" (1927) establishes binary oppositions between morning and evening, as well as the sun and the moon. Typically, morning is associated with the sun, which is also associated with **whiteness**, while evening is associated with the moon and with darkness. Yet Johnson complicates the sun versus moon, day versus night, and white versus black oppositions by proclaiming the "whiteness" of the moon for her celebration of night. Johnson undoes simplistic race rhetoric, for instance, by asking for "the beauty of the evening/ [with] the moon like a love-sick lady,/Listless and wan and white." The formal properties of this poem **work** simultaneously as an acceptance of—and rejection of—Anglo-American conventions for canonical poetry. In the opening and closing four lines, Johnson seems to reject the expectations for end rhymes in her lines, but in the middle she has a formal, iambic meter and rhyme scheme, pairing "night" with "white," "hill" with "still," and "hair" with "fair." **Nikki Giovanni**'s 1968 "On Hearing the Girl with the Flaxen Hair" takes this project one step further by associating hard work on the cotton plantation with African American beauty. It is work and experience that make one beautiful, she suggests in this poem, not innocence and protection from the grit of everyday life.

Audre Lorde's "Coal" (1976) draws on associations between the hard work performed in coal mines and the beauty of blackness. Further, "Coal" is self-consciously experimental, using words to function as parts of speech that are different from their traditional uses. For example the "I" of the first line is not a pronoun but a noun: "I is the total black, being spoken." In lines 3 and 7, "open" seems to work neither as a verb nor exactly as an adjective but as an idea: "there are many kinds of open," and "Some words are open like a diamond." By placing the image of coal beside the image of diamonds—both substances created from carbon—Lorde alludes to the process of evolving (as a woman, as a carbon) under tremendous pressure while also theorizing the radical potential of language.

Contemporary poetry about African American beauty is more forthcoming, by contrast. **Lucille Clifton**'s "Homage to My Hips" (1991) celebrates the attributes of "big," "mighty," and "magic" hips. Written without the formal use of capitalization, this poem rejects the Anglo Saxon ideal of narrow hips on a woman and, ultimately, illustrates the sexual power of such girth. Patricia Smith's "Blonde White Woman" (1992) similarly rejects the cultural imposition of white beauty. In keeping with **Toni Morrison**'s *The Bluest Eye* (1970), Smith tracks her maturation as a woman from her blonde fantasies as a young girl to her commitment to reading *Ebony* on the morning train.

Often, such poems idealizing African American beauty emphasize the relationship between beauty and desire, in keeping with Mae V. Cowdery's "Insatiate" (1936). This poem establishes a tension between constancy (line 20) and uncertainty (line 27), appearing to offer up sexual desire as a synecdoche for African American women's experience as a whole. In the first three stanzas of the poem, for example, it appears impossible fully to satisfy the persona; however, this fact changes significantly when she imagines what it would be like if her **love** took another lover. Paradoxically, this dynamic "cures" the persona of her insatiability, demonstrating the vexed sexual politics in the African American women's literary tradition that continues today with such writers as **Terry McMillan**.

By contrast, African American feminist poetry appears to celebrate stability rather than uncertainty when it addresses the theme of **motherhood**. For example, the exemplary poetry of **Gwendolyn Brooks** uses issues of motherhood to bridge concerns of race and representation with **class** and gender tensions. The granddaughter of an escaped slave, Brooks was the first African American to receive the Pulitzer Prize. Brooks published her first poem at the age of thirteen in the popular magazine *American Childhood* and received encouragement early in her career from the African American modernist poet Langston Hughes. From the beginning, Brooks followed Hughes in focusing on the lives of ordinary African Americans in her work. Her poetry examines the contradictory impulses, choices, and lifestyles of contemporary African American women, depicting women's encounters with racial and class oppressions, sexual betrayal, and the racial violence during the pre–civil rights era of the late 1940s.

Brooks's "The Mother" (1945) is a poem that at first appears to be inappropriately titled, as the perspective it takes is of a woman who chose not to be a mother. And yet, with the first line, "abortions will not let you forget," the poem seems to say that memories of "the children you got that you did not/get" always make one a mother. As such, this poem introduces a paradox from the beginning and continues to oscillate between examples of mothering, on the one hand, and an illustration of what it means to forgo motherhood, on the other hand.

"The Mother" is also significant to Brooks's oeuvre–indeed, to the history of African American feminist poetics–because it dismantles rhyme schemes out of suspicion of traditional forms that celebrate consistencies in rhyme and meter. For example, there are three lines in this poem that do not fit the rhyme pattern at all. In a poem about decisions that do not let a mother forget, these very "failures" appear to succeed in "not letting" the reader forget.

Ai's "The Mother's Tale" (1986) also celebrates motherhood while simultaneously refusing to romanticize it. Although it begins as an apparently comfortable dialogue between mother and child, "The Mother's Tale" eventually turns into a confusing tangle of love, jealousy, possession, and abuse, often shifting not only representations of affect but perspective as well. Finally, **Toi Derricotte**'s 1983 *Natural Birth*—a volume that has gone out of print and has since resurfaced in a new volume with a compelling new author's note (2000)—uses lyric to describe what it is like to become pregnant accidentally at nineteen while being expected to overturn all negative **stereotypes** of African American women. Derricotte, in her introduction, suggests that the form her poem took in dealing with the pregnancy, labor, birth, and eventual life with her newborn son was unrecognizable to her—and to her editors—early on but was later celebrated because of this very experimentalism.

While the formal properties of African American feminist poetry about motherhood tend to be as messy as childbirth and motherhood itself, the verse written by African American feminists about life in the United States and the double consciousness that accompanies it appears to be more measured even when raging against injustice. **Phillis Wheatley**'s "On Being Brought from Africa to America" (1773) reveals her formal training with the prominent Boston **family** who owned her. When she was eight years old, Wheatley was taken from West Africa and brought to Boston in July 1761. Wheatley worked in the house for this family rather than the fields and expresses satisfaction with her life. Still, it is hard not to read her poem as deeply ironic in our present day. Wheatley writes in the opening line, "Twas mercy brought me from my pagan land"—which leads us to wonder how bad life was at home that a little girl of eight would be grateful for being taken from her family and put to work in a foreign country. Many critics read this poem not as sarcastic but rather as evidence of the success of Christian missionaries, who told people from Africa that they were "saving" them into eternal life after they had lived previously as "pagans" in Africa. Wheatley, perhaps, was the ideal student, as evidenced by her flawlessly constructed iambic pentameter so valued by the Anglo poets of her day. She was not entirely complacent, however. Wheatley lent a strong voice for improved race relations. In this poem, she undoes the strong sentiment that pits white people against black people, by suggesting in her last couplet that true Christians would organize society through the contrast of "Christians versus non-Christians" rather than "slaves versus their owners."

Written over 150 years after Wheatley's tribute to America, **Georgia Douglas Johnson**'s "The True American" (1927) not only defines the African American son as a true American but, in the process of doing so, also redefines what it means to be American generally. For example, most readers, when seeing a title like "The True American," may consider a person's citizenship only within the nation's borders; however, Johnson extends the meaning of the "true" American to include a site of coalescing nations and of cosmopolitanism—a particularly powerful move significant for its ability to redefine African Americans within U.S. society. A potentially controversial poem for its time period, Johnson embeds her message in a more traditional form, conveying formal, if not thematic, complacency.

In addition to providing political and philosophical insights about life in the United States, African American feminist poetry also addresses the day-to-day reality of living in American communities. **Margaret Walker**'s "Childhood" (1942) is often read as a biographical portrait of the poet, who lived in Ishkooda, a town south of Birmingham, Alabama, until she was five, and later near New Orleans, Louisiana. Embracing more traditional verse forms, the poem is a sonnet; the first octet describes life in Ishkooda, and the sestet describes New Orleans. Strikingly, this poem seems to have less to do with childhood–as its name suggests it might–than about the recognition of unhappy miners and famine, terror, flood, and plague, which are hardly things associated with childhood. Yet perhaps this is the point. Walker buries within a perfect sonnet with a perfect lulling rhythm–itself associated with children's songs–the experiences of oppressed others that children often recognize before adults, who typically bury them under the details of their daily lives. The poetry of Gwendolyn Brooks similarly juxtaposes child's play with adult concerns. Her poem "a song in the front yard" (1945), for example, is a revision of William Blake's *Songs of Innocence* (1789) and *Songs of Experience* (1794), using the "front yard" as a symbol for innocence and the "back yard" as a symbol for experience. "I've stayed in the front yard all my life," reports the persona: "I want a peek at the back / Where it's rough and untended and hungry weed grows."

If Brooks's persona has played too often in the front yard, then Tracie Morris's persona in "Project Princess" (1998) has played too often in the back. However, the poem's title alone establishes a potential oxymoron from the beginning, begging the questions: Can a young woman both be a princess and from the projects? Is the difference in worlds between the projects and the princess something that can be negotiated? Further, Morris's "project" might be less about housing projects than about the narrative of the poem's "urban goddess" seeking self-improvement (a personal project) via her own style.

Upon an initial reading, it is unclear whether Morris's persona embraces or dismisses the "princess" in the U.S. projects. At first, the speaker's tone seems catty, even judgmental, as the short staccato sounds of the *t*'s and *d*'s and *p*'s hint at a kind of impatience and mocking disapproval. However, we learn later that this is probably not the case, as the poem's last lines embrace this attitude of survival–much like Claude McKay's "Harlem Dancer": "It's all about you girl. You go on. Don't you dare stop."

As Morris's performance poetry suggests, African American feminist poetry has changed dramatically since the eighteenth century when Phillis Wheatley began writing in verse. While Wheatley's formal training and poetic talents suggested to her readership that African American poets were indeed able to master traditional verse forms, contemporary performance poetry focuses not only on how a poem *sounds*–a quality that all poetry shares–but also on the staged theatrics of poetry. When poets such as Morris *perform* their poetry, they enliven poetry by taking it off of the page and presenting it bodily through sound and motion. The result is an actual embodiment of the feminist project of African American poetry—an invocation of the movement of Josephine Baker as well as the lyrical insights of all who have contributed to this rich and remarkable tradition.

See also Alexander, Elizabeth; Amini, Johari; Angelou, Maya; *Annie Allen*; Baraka, Amiri; Bennett, Gwendolyn B.; Birtha, Becky; Black Feminism; Black Feminist Criticism; Boyd, Melba; Carter, Xam Wilson; Coleman, Wanda; Cullen, Countee; Danner, Margaret Esse; Dunbar, Paul Laurence; Evans, Mari; *for colored girls who have considered suicide/when the rainbow is enuf*; Jordan, June; Kocher, Ruth Ellen; Komunyakaa, Yusef; Lane, Pinkie Gordon; Major, Clarence; *Maud Martha*; Moss, Thylias; Mullen, Harryette; Nelson, Marilyn; Osbey, Brenda Marie; Parker, Pat; Rodgers, Carolyn; Sanchez, Sonia; Shange, Ntozake; Spencer, Anne; Thomas, Joyce Carol; *Thomas and Beulah*; White, Paulette Childress; Williams, Sherley Anne; Womanism

Works About

Harper, Michael S., and Anthony Walton, eds. *Every Shut Eye Ain't Asleep: An Anthology of Poetry by African Americans since 1945.* Boston: Little, Brown, 1994.

Honey, Maureen, ed. *Shadowed Dreams: Women's Poetry of the Harlem Renaissance.* New Brunswick, NJ: Rutgers University Press, 1989.

Reed, Ishmael, ed. *From Totems to Hip-Hop: A Multicultural Anthology of Poetry across the Americas 1900–2002.* New York: Thunder's Mouth Press, 2002.

Smith, Barbara, ed. *Home Girls: A Black Feminist Anthology.* New Brunswick, NJ: Rutgers University Press, 2000.

Stetson, Erlene, ed. *Black Sister: Poetry by Black American Women, 1746–1980.* Indianapolis: Indiana University Press, 1982.

Aimee L. Pozorski

POLITE, CARLENE HATCHER (1932–   )

Carlene Hatcher Polite was born on August 28, 1932, in Detroit, Michigan, to John and Lillian Cook Hatcher, who were international representatives of the UAW–CIO (United Auto Workers–Congress of Industrial Organizations). Growing up in a secure middle-**class** atmosphere, she possessed the financial and creative **freedom** to accomplish whatever she wanted. She studied at Sarah Lawrence College but later quit to attend the Martha Graham School of Contemporary Dance. She was an accomplished professional dancer and later instructor of dance at various theaters from 1955 to 1963.

Demonstrating her parental influence, Polite's career shifted from dancing to practicing politics and fighting for civil rights for African American artists and intellectuals. As a Democrat, Polite was elected to the Michigan State Central Committee in 1962. To protest the Birmingham church bombings, in June 1963, she coordinated and participated in the Walk for Freedom and the

November 1963 Freedom Now Rally. Also in 1963, she was an active member of the National Association for the Advancement of Colored People (NAACP) and organized the Northern Negro Leadership Conference.

Polite's career interests again shifted, this time to writing. Although she had started writing prose poems at twelve, she wanted to develop this gift undistracted. So she moved to Paris, France, in 1964, where she lived until 1971. Under the influence of her mentor, French editor Dominique de Roux, who encouraged her to move after they met in Detroit, she published the novel *The Flagellants* in French in 1966. It was translated into English a year later. Because of this novel, Polite received a National Foundation on the Arts and Humanities Fellowship in 1967 as well as a Rockefeller Foundation Fellowship in 1968. Back in America, her second and last novel, *Sister X and the Victims of Foul Play*, was published in 1975. In 1971, Polite became an associate professor of English at the State University of New York at Buffalo. Currently, she is an associate professor emeritus of that university.

Her published novels have been largely overlooked because of their experimental and unique nature. Influenced by existentialism and satire, Polite's unique prose style and form and her use of various African American dialects that honor the oral tradition reflect the emotional highs and lows in dancing choreography. Besides the influence of dancing, her novels are infused with symbols and ideas of African American culture and art and deal with issues of **race**, **identity**, and freedom from oppression. Polite's unique combination of dance elements and activism in her novels place her among her contemporaries such as **Ishmael Reed**, Charles Wright, William Melvin Kelley, and Ronald Fair. She paves the way for African American postmodern **fiction** writers such as **Gayl Jones**.

Polite's career changes—from dancer and instructor to civil rights and political activist, author, and academic scholar—demonstrate her ability to be fully creative, insightful, and totally adaptable to the changing times. Polite's success in a variety of fields is a prime example to all African Americans that much can be accomplished through hard **work**, creativity, and determination.

Works By

The Flagellants. New York: Farrar, 1967.
Sister X and the Victims of Foul Play. New York: Farrar, 1975.
"Speak, Brother." *Mademoiselle* (January 1968): 95, 138–141.

Works About

Fabre, Michel. *From Harlem to Paris.* Urbana: University of Illinois Press, 1991.
Fabre, Michel, and John A. Williams. *Way B(l)ack Then and Now: A Street Guide to African Americans in Paris.* Paris: Center for American Culture Studies at the Sorbonne, 1992.
Lottman, H. R. "Authors and Editors." *Publishers Weekly,* June 12, 1967, 20–21.

Robinson, William H., ed. *Nommo: An Anthology of Modern African and Black American Literature.* New York: Macmillan, 1972.

Watkins, Mel, and Jay David, eds. *To Be a Black Woman: Portraits in Fact and Fiction.* New York: Morrow, 1970.

Devona Mallory

POSSESSING THE SECRET OF JOY

Possessing the Secret of Joy (1992) brings back many characters from **Alice Walker**'s earlier novel *The Color Purple* (1982). Tashi is the young African woman that Celie's son Adam marries in *The Color Purple*. Like *By the Light of My Father's Smile* (1998), the story is told from the perspective of a variety of characters including members of Tashi's **family**, Tashi, the anthropologist Pierre, and two psychotherapists. Tashi's sister dies as a young girl due to a complication with the tribe's traditional initiation rite of female genital mutilation. Female genital mutilation is performed on girls around the age of eleven and involves, with some variation, the removal of the clitoris and inner and outer lips of the vulva, scraping away the inside of the vagina, and is finalized with a tight sewing up of the wound. As the mythical tribe the Olinka become increasingly influenced by other cultures, including Christian missionaries, the practice of female genital mutilation begins to dwindle among those converted. To preserve the tradition before her move to the United States and as rebellion against others who warn her, Tashi goes to M'Lissa, the Olinka tribe's administrator of this particular practice. It is only after this ritual is performed that Tashi realizes the magnitude of her actions, blocks the **memory** from her mind, and suffers for most of her life. Tashi seeks therapy in America as she descends further into madness to distance herself from the loss of her **sexuality**. Tashi feels her only recourse for what was done to her is to pay retribution to M'Lissa. The novel ends with Tashi's execution for murdering M'Lissa, a venerable icon of the Olinka.

Walker describes in painful detail the procedure of female genital mutilation, a description that is further explicated in her **film** *Warrior Marks* (1993) and the nonfiction account of the film's making by the same name. In some ways this novel is her political stance on female genital mutilation and her call to arms for women to join together and eliminate this practice that continues globally today and denies women pleasure from all sexual activities. This particular custom passed on by oral tradition eradicates the ability for women in such places to question the ideology behind such practices. In the case of Tashi, all her adulthood searching for why her sexuality was stripped does not provide her with a clear understanding of this initiation rite, why it started, and why it has not perished. Scholars have focused on many aspects of this novel including **myth**, characters as archetypes, and didactic use of **literature**.

See also In Search of Our Mothers' Gardens; Womanism

Works About

Gates, Henry Louis, Jr., and K. A. Appiah, eds. *Alice Walker: Critical Perspectives Past and Present.* New York: Amistad, 1993. 27–36.
Lauret, Maria. *Alice Walker.* New York: St. Martin's Press, 2000. 159–192.

Laura Madeline Wiseman

POTTER, ELIZA (1820–?)

Though behind-the-scenes, tell-all books rarely get honorable mention in the genre of women's **literature**, Eliza Potter's **autobiography** *A Hairdresser's Experience in High Life*, published anonymously "for the author" in 1859, gives a rare glimpse into nineteenth-century manners and customs and an unusual critique of white standards of **beauty** and fashion. As a literary achievement, her autobiography was the first in the genre of behind-the-scenes books by African Americans, setting the stage for African American women writers such as Lillian Rogers Parks (seamstress/maid to the White House, 1929–1961) and **Elizabeth Keckley**, who also wrote biographies about their experiences in service to white employers. Many African American women held a historical position as marginal observers to the intimate secrets of white society, and Potter's *A Hairdresser* provides unique historical and social context for the study of posh Cincinnati society and the white woman's world.

While there is very little archival information about Potter, it is known that she was **mulatto**, grew up in New York, moved to Philadelphia when she married, gave birth to two mulatto children, a girl and a boy, and then promptly gave in to her desire for "roving." Potter's autobiography provides a unique and compelling view into the world of white fashion and beauty. Potter recounts with humor, wit, and sophistication her experiences as a prominent hairdresser to Cincinnati's upper-**class** white society. She was witness to the intimate details of polite white society and recreates genteel Cincinnati society through her distinctive rhetorical style. Though her profession required her to create images of white style for her clients, she was a harsh critic of the white standard of beauty and fashion, an interesting juxtaposition. Her candid portrayal presents her experiences, not as a subservient young black woman but as an autonomous woman full of enthusiasm, resourcefulness, and quiet dignity.

Potter's autobiography also serves as a window through which to view the manners and customs of the various societies where she lived and worked. Potter traveled extensively, never content to be in one place for too long, and from her unique perspective observed the nuances of social customs and behaviors in such places as New York, Saratoga, Canada, Paris, and London. Potter's observations provide a wealth of information about social nuances and interpersonal relations between various classes and genders of nineteenth-century American society. Not surprisingly, within the various social customs, Potter exhibited a high degree of personal reverence and never failed to enlighten those who were negligent in exhibiting proper courtesy or respect for her person and/or her position. Potter's demeanor elicited equal treatment from both men and women, regardless of color or class.

Potter enjoyed an unusual autonomy, relying on her skills as a hairdresser to achieve an economic **freedom** unusual for a woman, especially a black woman of that time. Though she enlightens the reader with the intimate secrets of white society, she remains an invisible observer throughout her own tale, revealing only scant information about herself. Potter was married briefly, which she explains as a very natural expectation for young black women. But she considered her stint at matrimony a weakness and instead went "roving," a prelude to the modern woman's quest for independence. Potter was an advocate for abolition and took in many young black women to train them in the art of hairdressing. She used her skills to help other black women achieve an independent, self-directed existence.

Work By

A Hairdresser's Experience in the High Life. 1859. *The Schomburg Library of Nineteenth-Century Black Women Writers.* Introduction by Sharon G. Dean. London: Oxford University Press, 2005.

Debbie Clare Olson

PRAISESONG FOR THE WIDOW

Paule Marshall most fully develops her concerns with cultural heritage, individual and collective **memory**, and self-integration in her third novel, *Praisesong for the Widow* (1983). Continuing the themes of fragmented **identity** introduced in her earlier novels **Brown Girl, Brownstones** (1959) and **The Chosen Place, the Timeless People** (1969), Marshall enacts one character's journey toward personal enlightenment and self-discovery through reconnection with African ritual and heritage. This novel received the Columbus Foundation American Book Award and cemented Marshall's literary reputation as a major African American woman writer in the twentieth century.

The novel's protagonist, Avey Johnson, begins the story as a woman embedded in the materialist American life. When her husband dies, Avey finds herself completely disconnected from herself, her physical well-being, and her heritage and thus unable to approach her new life as a widow. Her journey toward self-discovery begins, unbeknownst to her, on a Caribbean cruise and with a vigorous physical illness. As she sails, Avey begins to recollect early memories of **family** and **religion**; these memories continue to regress into the collective memory of her **ancestors** and their capture into **slavery**. Amid these memories, Avey's physical illness and her location on a sailing vessel reenact the **Middle Passage**.

Initiated with her **body**'s negative reaction to her ancestors' enslavement, Avey continues to physically experience and reconnect with her personal and cultural past. When she becomes delayed in her return to New York, she encounters an island **community**, the Carriacou people. It is in these relationships that Avey's physicality turns from a negative purging to a positive and regenerative experience. Through the Carriacou, Avey comes in contact with African rituals and traditions she previously disparaged. As the novel progresses and Avey learns to grieve both her personal loss and eventually her ancestral enslavement, she finds wholeness through physical expression. The story climaxes with Avey's joining in a ceremonial African dance, where she at first tentatively and then robustly dances for her **ancestors**.

Praisesong for the Widow explores many of the themes Marshall introduces in her earlier works. Here she presents an American woman of Caribbean and African heritage who must find reconciliation with her personal past as well as her ancestral **history** in order to find peace and self-integration. Avey experiences a more full and hopeful rejuvenation than Marshall's early characters, however, as she reintegrates her ancestral heritage through physical ritual. This connection of the mind and body through collective memory offers the most complete opportunity for personal and social **healing** that Marshall presents in any of her writings to this point. Marshall embodies in Avey's reclamation of her heritage the potential for individual and cultural healing and progress. Notably, *Praisesong for the Widow* is dedicated to Marshall's own ancestor, her grandmother "Da-duh."

Works About

Christian, Barbara. "Ritualistic Process and the Structure of Paule Marshall's *Praisesong for the Widow*." *Black Feminist Criticism: Perspectives on Black Women Writers*. New York: Pergamon Press, 1985. 149–158.

Cobham, Rhonda. "Revisioning Our Kumblas: Transforming Feminist and Nationalist Agendas in Three Caribbean Women's Texts." *Postcolonial Theory and the United States: Race, Ethnicity, and Literature*. Ed. Amritjit Singh and Peter Schmidt. Jackson: University Press of Mississippi, 2000. 300–319.

Hoefel, Roseanne. "Praisesong for Paule Marshall: Music and Dance as Redemptive Metaphor in *Brown Girl, Brownstones* and *Praisesong for the Widow*." *MaComère: Journal of the Association of Caribbean Women Writers and Scholars* 1 (1998): 134–144.

Kitch, Sally L. "Motherlands and Foremothers: African American Women's Texts and the Concept of Relationship." *Analyzing the Different Voice: Feminist Psychological Theory and Literary Texts*. Ed. Jerilyn Fisher and Ellen S. Silber. Lanham, MD: Rowman and Littlefield, 1998. xvii, 141–165.

McKoy, Sheila Smith. "The Limbo Contest: Diaspora Temporality and Its Reflection in *Praisesong for the Widow* and *Daughters of the Dust*." *Callaloo* 22.1 (1999): 208–222.

Olmstead, Jane. "The Pull to Memory and the Language of Place in Paule Marshall's *The Chosen Place, the Timeless People* and *Praisesong for the Widow*." *African American Review* 31.2 (1997): 249–267.

Rogers, Susan. "Embodying Cultural Memory in Paule Marshall's *Praisesong for the Widow*." *African American Review* 34.1 (2000): 77–93.

Sandiford, Keith. "Paule Marshall's *Praisesong for the Widow*. The Reluctant Heiress, or Whose Life Is It Anyway?" *Black American Literature Forum* 20 (1986): 371–392.

Scarboro, Ann Armstrong. "The Healing Process: A Paradigm for Self-Renewal in Paule Marshall's *Praisesong for the Widow* and Camara Laye's *Regard du Roi*." *Modern Language Studies* 19.1 (1989): 28–36.

Waxman, Barbara Frey. "Dancing Out of Form, Dancing into Self: Genre and Metaphor in Marshall, Shange and Walker." *MELUS* 19.3 (1994): 91–106.

Laura Baker Shearer

PRINCE, MARY (1788–?)

Born a slave in Brackish Pond, Bermuda, Mary Prince published what is considered the first full-length narrative by a female slave, *The History of Mary Prince, a West Indian Slave, Related by Herself*, in England in 1831. In this often harrowing narrative, Prince documents her experiences under **slavery**, detailing the physical and often psychological abuse she was forced to suffer as a female slave.

In excructiating detail Prince describes the trauma of learning what it means to be a slave as a young girl, including being sold at a slave market, flogged while naked, raking salt for ten years in the harsh marshes of the Turks islands, and being subjected to sexual abuse. In 1828 Prince's owners, the Woods, agreed to take her with them to England. While in London, the Woodses' continued and increased abuse of Prince culminated in her decision to walk away from slavery. In 1772, abolitionist and lawyer Granville Sharpe had successfully argued in the case of James Somerset, the black versus Charles Stewart, that since British common law made no explicit reference or provisions for slavery, that at least while physically in the metropole of Great Britain, slaves were free.

Because her husband was still in Antigua, Prince desired to return to him there but wanted to do so as a free woman. With the aid of the Anti-Slavery Society, she sued the Woods, claiming that since they had violated the Amelioration Act of 1823, which prohibited excessive cruelty by slave owners, she should be completely manumitted. As a means to document evidence of their cruelty, Prince dictated the details of her life, which were transcribed by Susanna Strickland, an aspiring poet, and edited by Thomas Pringle, a writer and the secretary of the Anti-Slavery Society. Because the narrative provided a female slave's perspective, it became immensely popular and went through three editions in quick succession. Hoping to hinder public acceptance of the narrative, writer James MacQueen in an article for *Blackwood's Magazine*, accused Pringle and Prince of fabricating the narrative to spread abolitionist propaganda. Pringle sued MacQueen for libel, and although judgment was found in his and Prince's favor, the damages paid by MacQueen were a paltry £3. This ideological triumph would be short-lived, however, because the court decided against Prince in her suit for **freedom**, claiming she had exaggerated her abuse by the Woods out of revenge. Other than the trial summaries in *The Times*, and attendance at Susanna Strickland's wedding to Captain Moody, further written documentation of Prince is limited to a brief mention in Strickland's 1851 short story "Rachel Wilde, or, Trifles from the Burthen of Life," in which the main character, loosely based on Strickland, admits that she knows the narrative is not false, because she took it down herself.

Prince's narrative highlights not only the various spectacular punishments she and other female slaves were forced to endure but also the complexity of power relationships under slavery. Although a female slave, the narrative details Prince's entrepenerurial endeavors and participation in both the formal and informal aspects of the **plantation** economy. She describes how she would make money by hiring herself out and selling produce and goods at local markets. Also, Prince documents her efforts to assert what critic Jenny Sharpe has described as "a certain kind of freedom" by choosing to develop sexual relationships with white men who could help her attain freedom. Although other critics have focused on Prince's inability to fully and completely document her sexual **history** due to the strictures of readership, what is most remarkable about Prince and her narrative is the manner in which she asserts her voice. In particular, she relates a story in which she saves one of her master's daughters from being beaten by him. Also, at several points in the narrative she speaks directly to her readers, claiming voice and authority though her experiences as a slave. She even details the many ways in which her masters engaged in hypocritical Christian behavior.

Prince's narrative is often treated as problematic because it was dictated to and edited by white amanuenses. However, the prohibition on teaching slaves to read and write complicates this privileging of single-author narratives. As she says in her narrative, Prince's goal was to "tell the truth to the English people." If her narrative were not taken down, it would probably not exist. Her narrative leaves us with a compelling portrait of the fortitude and resilience of slave women under a system that sought to destroy them emotionally and physically.

Work By

The History of Mary Prince, a West Indian Slave, Related by Herself. Ed. Thomas Pringle. London, 1831.

Works About

Haynes, Roberta R. "Voice, Body and Collaboration: Constructions of Authority in *The History of Mary Prince*." *Literary Griot* 11.1 (1999): 18–32.

Paquet, Sandra Pouchet. "The Heartbeat of a West Indian Slave: *The History of Mary Prince*." *African American Review* 26.1 (1992): 131–146.

Rauwerda, A. M. "Naming Agency and 'A Tissue of Falsehoods' in *The History of Mary Prince*." *Victorian Literature and Culture* (2001): 397–411.

Salih, Sarah. Introduction to *The History of Mary Prince*, by Mary Prince. London: Penguin Books, 2000.

Sharpe, Jenny. " 'Something Akin to Freedom': The Case of Mary Prince." *Differences* 8.1 (1996): 31–55.

Whitlock, Gillian. "The Silent Scribe: Susanna and 'Black Mary.'" *International Journal of Canadian Studies* 11 (1995): 249–260.

Nicole N. Aljoe

PROTEST TRADITION

The written record of black women's protest efforts spans two centuries, extending from the early-nineteenth-century writer-activist **Maria Stewart** to contemporary figures comprising the **womanist** cultural formation. This tradition, including its social message, rhetorical strategies, and literary devices, has evolved historically according to the social and political conditions in which black women lived and worked. They have protested black women's multilayered burden of interlocking (**race**, gender, and **class**) oppressions to white America, black men, and the bourgeois rulers—what **black feminist** critic bell hooks calls the white supremacist capitalist patriarchy. Whether enslaved or bonded, black women have written for and to one another throughout the tradition, inspiring and nurturing each other's creativity, **spirituality**, and vision of human possibility.

Maria Stewart was the first woman, black or white, to deliver a political speech to a gender-mixed audience; she did so in 1832 in Boston. She was a staunch advocate of black **freedom** and women's independence and saw no contradictions inherent in black women's freedom. She wrote for the *Liberator* and *Freedom's Journal* on behalf of abolitionist and nationalist agendas. In 1835 she published selected essays and selected speeches in *Productions of Mrs. Maria W. Stewart*. Inspired by militant political analyst David Walker, and defying the cult of domesticity, Stewart felt compelled by spiritual calling to fight for abolition and expose colonizationist programs. Ahead of her time, she is well known for her daunting speeches and writings on blacks' right to self-defense, women's equal worth and value in the struggle, and the unflinching way in which she delivered her ideas publicly. She was a forerunner and inspiration to other black women of similar tenacity and vision in her century like **Sojourner Truth**, **Rebecca Cox Jackson**, Harriet Tubman, and **Anna Julia Cooper**.

Stewart's audience was both black and white; each was exhorted with different agendas. In her speeches and writings she uses varying rhetorical strategies and literary techniques, as well as varying intellectual sources, to express her social critique and vision of human possibility. She was an early crafter of the black Jeremiad, mastering the black idioms of thundering exhortation, parataxis, anaphora, and the rhythmic patterns of call and response. She drew on the Constitution, classical **literature**, and the Bible to fashion her prose and speeches. To whites Stewart spoke and wrote of the impending doom of black rebellion if they continued enslaving blacks, who had no choice in her eyes but to defend themselves by any means necessary. God would be on the side of the vanquished, and a mighty thunder would smite the slaveholders, she exhorted. This was a particularly bold stance for any black person of this period, and especially for a black *woman*, because whites, particularly Irish and German Americans, rioted black neighborhoods with impunity to contain black social mobility and autonomy. She charged blacks with the responsibility of defending their homes and suing for citizenship rights, for they had built up America.

Black women were integral to the struggle, she argued, citing historical and biblical instances where women played key roles in their others' survival. Stewart is known as one of the earliest proponents of women's rights in America and the first black woman to speak out publicly. For her outspoken opinion, often contrasting that of her black male contemporaries, she was retired from the public lecture circuit fairly early in her career by her male contemporaries. Stewart continued her crusade, writing for abolitionist periodicals, and later wrote her **autobiography**.

Runaway slave women protested the contradiction between **slavery** and the country's professed ideals of self-evident freedom and Christian brotherhood. **Harriet Jacobs**'s *Incidents in the Life of a Slave Girl* (1861), **Harriet E. Wilson**'s *Our Nig* (1859), and *Celia: A Slave* (1991) by Melton McLaurin are well known. Telling their stories and educating the nation on the horrors of bonded women's lives was challenging, for they had to express themselves in generic codes (of **domestic fiction** and True Womanhood ideology) that contradicted their experiences of racialized gendered powerlessness. Gender made slave women sexually exploitable by white slaveholders to reproduce human capital for the system and forced them into moral dilemmas that diverged from black men's experiences and that white women could have never even imagined. Slave women's vulnerability to **rape** raised quandaries of whether to birth or spare their child a life of misery (abortion and infanticide)—particularly if it were a female; of whether to endure forced sex by slaveholders to protect their families from abuse. Their autobiographies were conscious (yet subtle) protests against racist mythologies of slave women "**Jezebels**" who raped white slaveholders. They aimed to set the record straight on the increasing population of **mulattos** in the **South**. Ex-slave women's memoirs also revealed how their experiences of slavery were gendered differently from men's. The escape prospects of slave mothers were burdened by having children. They also exposed the hypocrisy of white womanhood as anything but pious and honorable—as cruel, conniving, and spiteful when dealing with blacks. Written with literary genius and narrative strategy, many slave women's autobiographies are some of the earliest analyses of intersectionality in black feminine subjectivity.

In *A Voice from the South* in 1892 Anna Julia Cooper eloquently described black women's dilemmas in relation to the suffragist movement and racial uplift in the late nineteenth century, including the omission of black women's concerns in both struggles. She criticized the institutionalization of patriarchy via racial uplift, pointing out the hypocrisy of black men creating roadblocks to black women's education and social equality. Echoing Stewart decades later, Cooper was one of the first to argue that blacks could never be free until emancipation was extended to black women: that the Negro race's entrance into "**history**" as a subject is not complete until black women are empowered as subjects. From the late nineteenth century to the 1940s, covering both Reconstruction and the **Harlem Renaissance**, black women launched an antilynching crusade through journalism, theater, novels, and short stories. Among these were **Ida B. Wells-Barnett**, **Angelina Weld Grimké**, **Alice Moore Dunbar-Nelson**, Mary Burrill, **Georgia Douglas Johnson**, **May Miller**, Regina Andrews, and Myrtle Smith Livingston. They were a part of the anti-lynch movement and used journalism and theater to stake a claim to public discourse of protest. Wells-Barnett launched a scathing exposé of lynching in her newspaper articles and pamphlets. In the *Red Record* and other journal publications, she tackled the politically charged subject at the heart of lynching, white women's duplicity, which scandalously hinted that white women were anything but chaste. Not only was their purity suspect, her critique implied; they willingly transgressed the patriarchal law with the most hated target of white men's rage—black men. Lynching was a tactic that white men used to terrorize blacks into political and economic submission, which simultaneously functioned to clear white women of suspicion that they had coveted the unspeakable. Disseminating such deconstructions of lynching and dissecting its underlying political economy in national periodicals and pamphlets got Wells-Barnett run out of Memphis with a healthy reward for her capture.

At the height of the Harlem Renaissance, the **poetry** and plays of Grimké, Nelson, and Burrill also demystified the predominant rationale for lynching black men and argued for blacks' right to self-defense. They often exposed the role of white women in maintaining the system of white dominance and attacked the real reasons behind lynching, white hatred of black suffrage and social mobility. They dramatized connections between **motherhood** and lynching in efforts to stir white women's maternal sensibility, which contributed to the eventual formation of the Association of Southern Women for the Prevention of Lynching in 1930. Writers often drew on Christian imagery as a way of shoring up the contradiction between America's professed religious values and the system of second-class citizenship set up for blacks. The politics and aesthetics of the Harlem Renaissance literati underwent a significant change in black women's protest productions in the black arts and social protest movements of the 1960s and 1970s.

The voices of revolutionary protest in the 1960s and 1970s became more demanding and militant in poet-writer-activists such as **Sonia Sanchez**, **Nikki Giovanni**, **Toni Cade Bambara**, **Margaret Walker**, **Pat Parker**, **Mari Evans**, **Alice Walker**, and **Gwendolyn Brooks**. As in the productions of antilynching crusaders before them, the undercurrent of urgency to end state-sanctioned terrorism against blacks runs throughout their works. Experimentation with innovative verse structures and language by these poets reflected their affirmation of black life and culture and their rejection of dominant literary and poetic standards. They drew on a black urban wisdom and reached back to a diasporic cultural past for poetic inspiration and looked less to biblical or classical **literature** for substance. They drew on the hip slang of the black urban idiom, incorporating so-called ungrammatical constructions like multiple negation, the invariant "be," the zero copula and possessive, and clipped verb endings. They used other gestures like call and response and signifying from the **blues** (and black church), as well as other features like tonal semantics and narrative sequencing, which are rooted in certain African oral traditions.

Unrelenting critics of America's democratic hypocrisy, many black women activist-writers refused to allow readers the comfort of distance from the harsh realities of black struggle that language as a system of signifying often affords. Their protest repertoire included the intransigence of white supremacy, police brutality and state repression, urban poverty and environmental racism, as well as specific incidents in the struggle like the assassinations of Martin Luther King, Jr., and **Malcolm X** and the murder of James Chaney, Andy Goodman, and Michael Schwerner in Mississippi in 1964.

Many writers connected the oppression of the African diaspora to the historical persecution and annihilation of indigenous Americans and European Jewry. Pat Parker's "Where Will You Be, When They Come" (1978) cleverly uses the language, imagery, and symbolism of Nazi fascism to frame the historical oppression of blacks and queers and to raise black consciousness of the necessity of solidarity in revolutionary struggle. Often these poets also related blacks' experience to other anticolonial struggles in Africa and Asia/Pacific Islands and demystified the military's function—including the state's recruitment of black male revolutionaries—in maintaining Western dominance and black oppression both in America and abroad. This is a thematic of Sonia Sanchez's "final solution/the leaders speak" (1979) in which the poet outlines the available choices of blacks: either assimilate to the American democracy agenda—that is, fight the white man's wars to colonize other colored peoples—or die in the prisons, projects, and poverty. Black women poets drew on a wide range of rhetorical techniques and poetic structures from the black vernacular and African orature and idiom, as well as the classical tradition. Some included circumlocution, ellipsis, satire, onomatopoeia, diasporic folktales, hyperbole, irony, alliteration and assonance, dys/tactical constructions, and grammatical disruptions.

Black women also dared to take up questions that many black male revolutionaries shied away from, like the rule of pigmentocracy (or colorism) in black communities as a legacy of slavery engendering black self-loathing and shame and undermining black unity. **Toni Morrison**'s *The Bluest Eye* (1970), Alice Walker's *Meridian* (1976), and **Kristin Hunter Lattany**'s *God Bless the Child* (1964) explore this subject, as well as others like black male sexism and oppression of black women. Black women and the writers who expressed their concerns found themselves in a peculiar position in the women's and black movements: invisible in the movements' agendas but usable as an resource of endless energy, labor, and emotions for these movements. This is the void of silence and omission out of and against which many black women writers protested to their own comrades. Many writers responded to direct pronouncements by Stokely Carmichael that the only place for women in the revolution is prone as baby-making machines. Writers like **Audre Lorde** and Alice Walker explored the ways that this view of black women was not only sexist and counterrevolutionary but also racist—no different from how white slaveholders viewed bonded women a century earlier. Much of black women's literary protests today fall under the rubric of "**womanism**," which Alice Walker defined in her 1983 collection of short stories, poems, and essays *In Search of Our Mothers' Gardens*. Walker formulated the concept as a testimonial to black women's struggle, creativity, and spiritual resilience in surviving and making a life in racist-sexist America. She resignified its original pejorative sting of "acting womanish," a term that is often hurled at young black girls to remind them of their place in the **family/community** hierarchy, to a more positive meaning of precocious and curious. Her works explore how black women's lives are underwritten by a matrix of race, gender, and class oppression in which they must navigate through ideologically charged paths and contradictory social positionings in pursuit of fulfilling paths. *Meridian, The Color Purple* (1982), *You Can't Keep a Good Woman Down* (1981), and *In Love & Trouble* (1973) especially examine subjects of taboo in black communities like incest, rape, **lesbianism**, interracial relationships, colorism, black bourgeois assimilationism, and domestic abuse. Perhaps nothing was more perplexing and insulting to Walker, as for others before her such as Cooper, than black men's disinterest in disarming patriarchal institutions and relations of servitude. Some of Walker's more insightful critiques involve showing how racism inheres in certain forms of black male chauvinism such as the idea that black women's primary contribution to the struggle lies in birthing future warriors, which echoes white slaveholders' degradation of slave women as breeders (raw material) of (future) human capital (wealth). Many contemporary writers, some from the 1960s and 1970s, are part of this womanist cultural formation that has continued protesting black people's economic, patriarchal, and racial plight and the suffering of black women from within.

Works About

Davies, Carol Boyce. *Black Women, Writing and Identity: Migrations of the Subject.* New York: Routledge, 1994.

Foster, Frances Smith. *Written by Herself: Literary Productions by African American Women, 1746–1892.* Bloomington: Indiana University Press, 1993.

Grasso, Linda. *The Artistry of Anger: Black and White Women's Literature in America, 1820–1860.* Chapel Hill: University of North Carolina Press, 2002.

Hartmann, Susan. "Pauli Murray and the 'Juncture of Women's Liberation and Black Liberation.'" *Journal of Women's History* 14.2 (Summer 2002): 74–77.

Migliorino, Ellen Ginzburg. "Maria Stewart and Mary Ann Shadd: Pioneers in the Fight for Black Women's Rights." *America Today: Highways and Labyrinths.* Ed. Gigliola Nocera. Siracusa, Italy: Grafià, 2003. 431–437.

Moore, Opal. "The Productions of Maria W. Stewart: Rebellious Domesticity and Black Women's Liberation." In *Early America Re-explored: New Readings in Colonial, Early National, and Antebellum Culture.* Ed. Klaus H. Schmidt and Fritz Fleischman. New York: Peter Lang, 2000. 441–465.

Reid, Margaret. "A Rhetorical Anlysis of Black Protest Poetry of the Revolutionary Sixties." *MAWA Review* 1.2–3 (Summer–Fall 1982): 50–55.

Stover, Johnnie. M. *Rhetoric and Resistance in Black Women's Autobiography.* Gainesville: University Press of Florida, 2003.

Angela Cotten

QUICKSAND

Nella Larsen's first and best-known novel *Quicksand*, published in 1928 by Knopf, was greeted with acclaim, winning a Bronze Medal from the Harmon Foundation and words of praise from W.E.B. Du Bois as the best piece of **fiction** written by an African American since **Charles Waddell Chesnutt**. The novel tells the story of Helga Crane, a young woman of mixed parentage—a Danish American mother and a West Indian father—who becomes an outsider in her own **family** when her mother remarries a white man and has a child with him. Larsen's penetrating psychological character study moves beyond earlier representations of the tragic **mulatto** to reveal the ways in which **race** and gender inevitably construct **identity** and consciousness. Helga attempts to transcend racial categories by defining herself in terms of "taste"—surrounding herself with material possessions and aesthetic surfaces. But when she is confronted with the economic, social, or genetic basis of such material surfaces, as well as her own sexual desires, Helga responds with flight. Beginning with her artfully arranged teacher's apartment at Naxos, a fictitious Negro College where Helga is employed, she moves through a series of spaces that provide diminishing possibilities for self-realization as she struggles to define herself.

The meaning of the title becomes evident as her story progresses; the harder she struggles, the deeper she sinks. Each of Helga's moves—from Naxos to Chicago to New York to Copenhagen to New York to Alabama—is precipitated

by a crisis involving a confrontation with race or **sexuality**. She flees from
Naxos when its handsome young president, Robert Anderson, suggests that
she is a woman of good breeding. She leaves Chicago when her last family
connection, her Uncle Peter, withdraws his support at the insistence of his new
white wife. Helga finds a job as companion to a wealthy widow and "race
woman" who takes her to New York, but she is put off by the attitudes of black
Harlemites toward whites and those who associate with them. Overwhelmed
by a **jazz** party scene at a Harlem nightclub, she decides to leave for relatives in
Copenhagen, where she is taken in and pampered by relatives who are en-
chanted with what they perceive as her exotic nature. In Denmark Helga is
courted by a famous painter but refuses to marry him when she realizes that he
values her as an "exotic other," a sexual object rather than for herself. Returning to New York, Helga runs from a potential sexual encounter with
Robert Anderson, now the husband of her closest friend, and takes refuge in
a church revival meeting where she meets a southern preacher whom she
ends up marrying. Her move with him to rural Alabama is a reversal of the
migration narrative of upward mobility and economic opportunity; her
four pregnancies within two years mock her earlier attempts to establish a
destiny independent of race and gender as biologically constructed. Because
Helga does not feel at **home** in either black or white society, her character
highlights the "constructed" nature of race and the ways in which it is internalized.

    Black feminist criticism has restored *Quicksand* to the canon of African
American women's writing. Some critics have viewed the ending as flawed
and hasty; others, notably Deborah McDowell, have viewed *Quicksand* as a
pioneering exploration of black female sexuality. Hazel Carby has noted that
Larsen's fiction provides the urban counterpart to **Zora Neale Hurston**'s
evocation of the heroine's journey to selfhood in ***Their Eyes Were Watching
God*** (1937). The story of Helga Crane bears some resemblances to Nella
Larsen's life, as revealed in Thadious Davis's biography.

See also Harlem Renaissance; Passing; *Passing*

Works About

Carby, Hazel. *Reconstructing Womanhood: The Emergence of the Afro-American
Woman Novelist.* New York: Oxford University Press, 1987.
David, Thadious. *Nella Larsen, Novelist of the Harlem Renaissance: A Woman's Life
Unveiled.* Baton Rouge: Louisiana State University Press, 1994.
Hostetler, Ann. "The Aesthetics of Race and Gender in Nella Larsen's
Quicksand." *PMLA* 105.1 (January 1990): 35–46.
McDowell, Deborah A. Introduction to *Quicksand* and *Passing.* 1929. New
Brunswick, NJ: Rutgers University Press, 1996. ix–xxxvii.
Wall, Cheryl A. *Women of the Harlem Renaissance.* Bloomington: Indiana Uni-
versity Press, 1995.

Ann Hostetler

QUILTING

Quilting is a process that has been a part of the African American culture for over 200 years. The process seems simple but requires time and artistic flair. Quilting involves "piecing" together strips or squares of fabric into larger blocks that are then connected by hand sewing, machine sewing, or even knotting the fabric together. These connected blocks of fabric are formed into larger blocks to produce a bed-size covering. A second layer of batting or soft material is next, with a final piece of fabric attached to the back, forming three layers. This is a process that is time-consuming, particularly if all of the steps are done by hand, as would have been the case during **slavery**.

In the past, typically, women were the primary quilters in the **family**, although then and now, a few men quilted as well. When one considers the contributions of women to the support and care of their families, it is easy to overlook quilting; however, this process reaps many benefits in the black culture, among them helping to form a shared **community** of quilters who through their talent express a sense of pride, creativity, and **love**. In addition, quilting is a way to pass along African Americans' cultural heritage, and the quilts themselves serve as historical artifacts in the African American community.

In a practical sense, quilting was a necessity in most slave families. They had only minimal provisions for their comfort, and warm blankets were a luxury, so the women would make quilts to keep everyone warm. These women had to be resourceful, so they might use flour or corn meal sacks as fabric for the quilts. They also used clothing and various pieces of material. Of course the women were expected to **work** the fields each day, but after their daily labor, they would gather with other women on the plantation to work on their quilts. These slave women might work on one quilt until it was completed and then begin another. No doubt, this was a time to commiserate with others about the sadness and fears of slave life, but it was also a time to experience some comfort by sewing into the quilt the love they had for their families.

Black women quilting to express their love for their families is still an African American tradition today. In many families, mothers and grandmothers give their children and grandchildren quilts to mark milestones in their lives, such as a high school or college graduation or an engagement or marriage. Sometimes, particularly valuable hand-stitched quilts may be passed down from one generation to the next. Many times the quilts are used for their intended purpose, but in some cases, the idea of using these priceless heirlooms is seen as shortsighted and unappreciative of their value. In a story by **Alice Walker** titled "Everyday Use" (1973), the author explores this ongoing dilemma.

Whatever one feels about this question, there is no question that quilting is a way of expressing creativity. Quilts are "pieced" together in various patterns and geometric shapes. The colors are many times vivid and bold, and when hung outside on a fence or line, the quilts can be seen from great distances. Numerous techniques and styles exist for putting the fabric together, thus altering the appearance of the quilts and their aesthetic qualities. For example, quilts can be constructed in blocks, strips, or even strings of fabric. Various genres of quilts also exist, such as Bible quilts, story quilts, or appliquéd quilts. One well-known quilter was former slave Harriet Powers, who is famous for her quilts that depict stories from the Bible; one of these can be seen at the Smithsonian Museum of American History.

For African Americans, quilting provides a connection to heritage and **ancestors**. Many times, young girls watch their mothers quilting and, in doing so, learn the tradition themselves, which they then pass down to their children. Because clothing is often used for the fabric, the mothers sometimes tell stories about the person who wore the clothing, or events that person experienced when they wore the clothing.

These stories are ways of remembering family **history**. During slavery, important records, such as births and deaths, were not formally documented, and family members were sold so frequently that keeping track of family histories became tenuous at best. Quilting very easily fit in with the oral tradition and became a way of maintaining a connection to the slaves' ancestors and "documenting," in some sense, family lore.

In recent years, quilt lovers and scholars have begun tracing the history of quilting in the African American culture. This has proven to be a formidable task because many of the slave quilts were not preserved. However, quilt experts like Maude Southwell Wahlman, Gladys-Marie Fry, and others have conducted countless hours of research and have interviewed hundreds of African American quilters all across the country in search of a more in-depth understanding and appreciation of African American quilting, particularly from a historical and cultural perspective. Their research continues today.

One topic hotly debated among scholars recently is the idea that slave quilts were used to provide information to runaway slaves traveling the **Underground Railroad**. This possibility is the topic of quilt researchers Jacqueline L. Tobin and Raymond G. Dobard in their book *Hidden in Plain View: A Secret Story of Quilts and the Underground Railroad.* Researchers will no doubt continue to debate this topic.

Some may think of quilting as insignificant "women's work" and the quilts as simple bed covering, but to do so is to diminish one source of the history and legacy of a culture and a people. African American quilts are artifacts that tell a story about blacks in this country and provide a link to their roots in Africa.

Works About

Eli, Leon. *Who'd a Thought It: Improvisation in African American Quiltmaking.* San Francisco: San Francisco Craft and Folk Art Museum, 1987.

Fry, Gladys-Marie. *Stitched from the Soul: Slave Quilts from the Antebellum South.* Chapel Hill: University of North Carolina Press, 1990.

Southwell Wahlman, Maude. *Signs and Symbols: African Images in African American Quilts.* Atlanta, GA: Tinwood Books, 2001.

Tobin, Jacqueline L., and Raymond G. Dobard. *Hidden in Plain View: A Secret Story of Quilts and the Underground Railroad.* New York: Doubleday, 1999.

Toni E. Smith

 # R

RACE

Race plays a crucial role in the treatment of women and in American attitudes about women, and feminist **literature**, especially that written by African American women, reflects this reality. Using their literature as a response to institutionalized racism, black women writers have continually challenged **stereotypes** of black women and men that have permeated society. While black men like **Ralph Ellison**, Frantz Fanon, W.E.B. Du Bois, **Langston Hughes**, **Richard Wright**, and **James Baldwin** are typically viewed as writers who brought the discourse of race to the forefront of America's consciousness, their female counterparts were also addressing the issue of race in their writings, though these did not instantly receive the same amount of recognition. Black women writers' concern with race and the ways it has intersected with gender and **class** produces literature that illustrates the unique and multifaceted experiences of black women.

African American women writers have long argued that black women's experiences are informed by a combination of their race, gender, and class and that one cannot be separated from the other, or privileged over the other forms of discrimination. The desire to integrate inseparable **identities** has been a fundamental issue for many African American women. Contemporary books such as the groundbreaking *All the Women Are White, All the Blacks Are Men, but Some of Us Are Brave* (1982), edited by Gloria T. Hall, Patricia Bell Scott, and Barbara Smith, and *Inessential Woman: Problems of Exclusion in Feminist Thought*

(1989), by Elizabeth V. Spelman, started conversations about this faulty categorization. **Sojourner Truth**'s "Ain't I a Woman" Women's Convention speech in Akron, Ohio, in 1851 testified to the importance of gender in a world that refused even to recognize black women as women. Because of race, black women were delegated to positions of inferiority and were denied membership to the "Cult of True Womanhood" that focused on the attributes of piety, purity, submission, and domesticity that afforded middle-class white women respect and deference from society. Black women were immediately excluded from this classification of womanhood because of their race. It was *because* of race that black women were subjected to the philosophy that they were automatically inferior and not "real" women to be respected.

In America, black women's experiences began with the brutal institution of **slavery** that denigrated men and women based on race. The literature frequently examines the societal view of black women's inferiority that began with slavery and still continues today to some degree. The literature enlisted the support of white Americans and reached out to other blacks with libratory messages of hope and empowerment. Born into slavery, both Sojourner Truth and Harriet Tubman provided black female writers with powerful examples of bravery and eloquence in the face of the utter disregard of slave women's rights. Olaudah Equiano and **Frederick Douglass**'s **slave narratives** struck a nerve with white America, and around the same time, black female writers started to raise the issue of gross inequality and the lot of the enslaved. *The Bondswoman's Narrative* by **Hannah Crafts** (1850), *Incidents in the Life of a Slave Girl* by **Harriet Jacobs** (1861), and *Our Nig; or, Sketches from the Life of a Free Black, In a Two-Story White House, North. Showing that Slavery's Shadows Fall Even There* by **Harriet E. Wilson** (1859) were some of the first texts by black women designed to appeal to the outside world to consider the brutality and injustice of slavery. These works focus on the inequalities that had become normalized in American society and the ways these young women's lives were dominated by **violence** and prejudice. Contemporary depictions of slavery, such as **Sherley Anne Williams**'s *Dessa Rose* (1986) and **Octavia Butler**'s *Kindred* (1979) illustrate the ways race irrevocably impacted the main characters' lives in their poignant narratives.

The Emancipation Proclamation of 1865 freed the enslaved and led the country into Reconstruction from 1865 to 1870, which proved to be the beginning of an erosion of the rights to **freedom** that emancipation had afforded. Many black female activists who fought for racial equality in America helped bring institutionalized racism to the forefront of society's consciousness and provided the impetus for many activists and women writers to protest the system of inequality in America. Activists like **Ida B. Wells-Barnett**, **Mary Church Terrell**, Mary McLeod Bethune, **Anna Julia Cooper**, and Fannie Lou Hamer dedicated their lives to eradicating discrimination and struggled gallantly against the complicated nature of a racist system. Many black women's literary works at the time exposed the complex issues within the black **community** such as miscegenation, light-skin privilege, and internalized racism that were some of slavery's legacies. Slavery established a complicated demarcation of race that classified blacks as **mu-lattos**, quadroons, and octoroons, based on the amount of "black blood" they had. Through the story of a young woman who is raised in a wealthy white **family** without knowledge that her mother is half black, **Frances E. W. Harper**'s *Iola Leroy, or Shadows Uplifted* (1892) addresses the realities of black life in America after slavery. Iola refuses to pass for white once she knows the truth of her heritage; instead, she goes on to uplift the African American community by embracing her sense of social responsibility, becoming involved in suffrage for African Americans. The writers often illustrate the **work** of activists and in many cases were activists themselves. Harper's response to the injustice of slave laws was to contribute her time and energy as a lecturer as part of the antislavery movement. The roles of the black woman writer often included being an activist, artist, and truth-teller in a society that undervalued the creative contributions of African Americans, especially the women.

When regular American universities remained closed to African Americans on the basis of race, historically black colleges provided places of intellectual growth. In the years following emancipation, historically black colleges received federal aid, and African Americans could receive a higher education, which was a welcome relief from the prohibition against teaching slaves to read in the antebellum period. African Americans perceived education as a way to escape the limiting constraints of racism, since through education came power and a chance to receive qualifications that would offer life improvements. In 1881, the ten women, including former slaves, with whom Spelman College was started helped the founders Sophia B. Packard and Harriet E. Giles embark on their mission to provide black women and girls with excellent instruction. This mission, and others like it, played a vital role in the perception and acceptance of black female intellect. Many pieces of **fiction** refer to the role of education in the perceived improvement of black people's lives. **Lorraine Hansberry**'s *A Raisin in the Sun* (1959), the first play by a black woman to be produced on Broadway, examines Beneatha Younger's dream to become a doctor and the brighter future that she has because of her college education and her desire to learn more about her connection to Africa. *Meridian* (1976) by **Alice Walker** describes the title character's journey, including college life, ending with her work that encourages traditionally disenfranchised African Americans to register to vote. In this novel the focus of many women's colleges at the time to produce ladies is subtly critiqued. *Daddy Was a Number Runner* (1970) by **Louise Meriwether** ends with Francie Coffin's mother pleading with her to get an education so that she can avoid her mother's fate of becoming a **domestic**–a fate many black women lived during the Great Depression of the 1930s. **Nikki Giovanni**'s 1969 essay "I Fell Off the Roof One Day (A View of the Black University)" outlines the necessity of all-black institutions that were under attack at the time for being racist. The promise of historically black colleges and all the opportunities that they represented in the 1800s provided a sense of hope that would not last long.

The Supreme Court's *Plessy vs. Ferguson* decision in 1896 heralded the legalization of segregation in America and made the discrimination, hatred, and fear of blacks legal. The brutal Jim Crow laws, named after a black minstrel, regulated every aspect of black life and kept blacks and whites separated physically (for example, banning intermarriage), politically (making it illegal for blacks to vote), and philosophically (prohibiting political organizing in favor of equality). The Jim Crow era eliminated any notion of equality that emancipation had promised. These laws continued to mandate separate facilities for blacks and whites until the 1954 *Brown v. Board of Education* decision, which legally dismantled segregation. Sarah and Elizabeth **Delany** share their reality during these repressive years in their **autobiography** *Having Our Say: The Delany Sisters' First 100 Years* (1997), vividly conjuring up a world in which they could not drink from the same water source in a public park as white people. The two sisters additionally mention the influence of the Ku Klux Klan on society and its horrifying effect on the psyche of blacks.

During the Jim Crow years, the **Harlem Renaissance**, spanning from 1920 to the 1930s and coinciding with the Great Migration of blacks from the rural **South** to the North, provided blacks an opportunity to escape the rigid negative connotations of their race and celebrate their creativity. African American artists experimented with artistic forms, creating **jazz** and new forms of **poetry**, prose, dance, and art. Alain Locke, the African American Rhodes Scholar and Harvard graduate, named the purveyors of this cultural explosion the "New Negro," a black person with a sense of social responsibility to uplift the black community with art, education, and self-respect. Locke edited an anthology of the same name in 1925, showcasing young African American authors such as Langston Hughes and **Claude McKay** and forcing the literary world to take these black writers seriously. At the same time, writers like **Zora Neale Hurston**, **Jessie Redmon Fauset**, and **Nella Larsen** addressed issues of race in their fiction, as did singers **Billie Holiday** and **Josephine Baker**, ushering in a new outlook on African Americans' contributions to art and literature. Fauset became the literary editor at *Crisis* magazine, the journal of the National Association for the Advancement of Colored People (NAACP), while W.E.B. Du Bois was the editor, helping to publish authors such as **Jean Toomer** and **Countee Cullen**, who were making tremendous contributions to the conversation on race in America. Fauset explored the roles of race and internalized racism in her prose. In her 1928 novel ***Plum Bun***: *A Novel without a Moral*, Fauset's protagonist Angela Murray realizes she looks white and eventually ends up living as a white woman in New York, facing not racism but sexism. During this time many African American writers needed to have white patrons to provide much-needed financial support in the publishing world. Both Zora Neale Hurston and Langston Hughes received financial support from their patron Charlotte Osgood Mason, with whom they eventually parted ways because of the restrictive relationship. Hurston's 1935 anthropological ***Mules and Men*** provides an insight into black culture that many literary figures denounced as being too focused on **folklore**. Alice Walker revived Hurston's works after she fell into obscurity after her **death**.

The Harlem Renaissance segued into the **protest** movement and opened the door for authors like **Gwendolyn Brooks**, who became the first black woman to win a Pulitzer Prize in 1950, for *Annie Allen*, which explores injustice in America.

The beginning of the civil rights era found an American society that historically separated women's inexplicably intertwined identities of race and gender. Civil rights groups often delegated women to the margins, and black women also found themselves excluded from the struggle for women's rights. As Black Nationalists, women like Assata Shakur and **Angela Davis** protested police surveillance of blacks and were incriminated and jailed for their outspoken activism. Shakur's autobiography *Assata* (1987) exposes the reality of political prisoners in America who were discriminated against based on their race. The **Black Arts Movement**, which was embraced as the artistic articulation of the Black Power movement, provided a means for authors to articulate their outrage over the political and social discrimination that African Americans continued to experience. **Maya Angelou**, **Rosa Guy**, Nikki Giovanni, **Sarah Elizabeth Wright**, and **Sonia Sanchez** were prominent African American women writers in this period; their writing generated literary responses from black feminist literary critics such as bell hooks, Barbara Christian, and Barbara Smith, who began the conversation of the role of black women's literature as libratory discourse. Other black feminists critics such as Nellie Y. McKay, Hazel Carby, Deborah McDowell, Mary Helen Washington, and Cheryl Wall continued the conversation. **Toni Cade Bambara**'s 1970 anthology *The Black Woman* gave a voice to women such as **Audre Lorde**, the black lesbian feminist poet whose poem in the text is about natural **beauty**, and Abbey Lincoln, the great jazz singer who is concerned with the many burdens that black women experienced. **Toni Morrison**'s *The Bluest Eye*, published in the same year, examined the effects of racism on the psyche of the main character Pecola Breadlove and provided the world with further insight into racial politics in America.

Contemporary writers such as Alice Walker, **Gloria Naylor**, Toni Morrison, **Bebe Moore Campbell**, **Paule Marshall**, and **Suzan-Lori Parks** all make social and political statements about the role of race in America. The Pulitzer Prize–winning and Nobel Laureate Toni Morrison challenges readers with the deliberate omission of race in her description of the protagonists in the novel *Paradise* (1998). This omission was viewed as a bold move, revealing the significance of race in black women's fiction, by withholding the racial identities of the characters. Alice Walker's *Anything We Love Can Be Saved: A Writer's Activism* (1997) explores the struggle many black female activists engage in and reminds her readers of the social activism of many black female authors. In 1987, **Rita Dove** won a Pulitzer Prize for *Thomas and Beulah* (1986), the story of her grandparents' lives. Bebe Moore Campbell's novel *Your Blues Ain't Like Mine* (1982) offers a profoundly complex story revolving around the most notorious lynching in America. The story of the murder of the teenaged Emmett Till is brought to life in the brilliantly crafted narrative of revenge, redemption, and denial.

Many African American women authors have been expected to portray black women in a positive light to counteract the fundamentally racist images presented historically in **film**, literature, and the news media. Some writers have risen to this challenge, others have rejected it, but most have addressed race or racism in a variety of ways in their writing. The literature has countered the stereotypes of black women as the contemptuous "**Sapphire**," the asexual, self-sacrificing "**Mammy**," and the overly sexual "**Jezebel**." The literature has also provided black women with the voice to dispute the discrimination and subjugation of African Americans, and women of all races have used the literature as a forum for social activism, presenting protagonists as activists or engaging in activism themselves. Using literature as the tool for liberation, black women have come from the most debasing period of **history** and have managed to recover their self-respect through their creativity and their social and political activism.

See also Black Feminist Criticism; Black Nationalism; Civil Rights Movement; Whiteness

Works About

Giddings, Paula. *When and Where I Enter: The Impact of Black Women on Race and Sex in America.* New York: William Morrow, 1984.

Holloway, Karla. *Codes of Conduct: Race, Ethics, and the Color of Our Character.* New Brunswick, NJ: Rutgers University Press, 1995.

hooks, bell. *Black Looks: Race and Representation.* Boston: South End Press, 1992.

Morrison, Toni. *Playing in the Dark: Whiteness and the Literary Imagination.* Cambridge, MA: Harvard University Press, 1992.

Smith, Barbara. *The Truth That Never Hurts: Writings on Race, Gender, and Freedom.* New Brunswick, NJ: Rutgers University Press, 1998.

Zisca Isabel Burton

RAHMAN, AISHAH (1936–)

Aishah Rahman (born Virginia Hughes) is a playwright and author whose avant-garde and surrealist works are considered "underground classics." Although her plays tend not to be performed in major, mainstream theaters, they have been hailed and widely appreciated by smaller audiences at university campuses, in regional theater, and in off-Broadway productions. In many of her works, she produces a surreal ambience by utilizing strong symbolism, the unexpected, and the irrational. She is particularly skilled at revealing the quirks and obsessions found in her various characters. She also incorporates what she calls a "**jazz** aesthetic," which unveils a particular character's multiple "levels of reality." Many of her plays are centered on the life of a famous artist or person, whom she portrays in a fictionalized setting.

Rahman was born in New York City and grew up in Harlem. She received a B.S. in political science from Howard University in 1968 and a master's degree in playwriting and dramatic **literature** from Goddard College in 1985. She taught at Nassau Community College and was director of the Henry Street Settlements Playwrights Workshop at New Federal Theatre. Rahman became a faculty member at Brown University in 1992, where she continues her teaching career. She is also the founder and editor of *NuMuse*, a journal that includes plays and essays by student and professional writers from Brown University. A recipient of fellowships from the Rockefeller Foundation and the Foundation of the Arts, she has also been honored with the Doris Abramson Playwriting Award, a Theater Communications Group Collaborative Grant for Artists, and several Audelco Awards.

Rahman's creative work started to receive attention in the early 1970s, when she wrote a play about the jazz phenomenon **Billie Holiday**, titled *Lady Day: A Musical Tragedy* (1972). One of her more celebrated works, *Unfinished Women Cry in No Man's Land While a Bird Dies in a Gilded Cage*, was premiered at the New York Shakespeare Festival in 1977. This play juxtaposes the suffering and challenges of five unwed mothers who must make difficult choices regarding the future of their babies with the **death** of jazz legend Charlie Parker, who passed away on March 12, 1955, in the apartment of his former lover who is a rich baroness. Rahman also wrote the **blues** musical *The Tale of Madame Zora* (1986), which is centered on the life of **Zora Neale Hurston**. Then in collaboration with composer Akua Dixon Turre, she wrote the libretto for *The Opera of Marie Laveau* (1989), which was renamed *Anybody Seen Marie Laveau?*, and is based on the New Orleans voodoo queen. Some of her other plays include *The Mojo and the Sayso* (1987), *Only in America* (1993), *Chiaroscuro: A Light and Dark Comedy* (2000), and *Mingus Takes (3): Three One Acts* (2003). In addition, she has published a memoir titled *Chewed Water* (2001), which was originally titled *Illegitimate Life*. This memoir tells of her coming of age in Harlem during the 1940s and 1950s and details the first eighteen years of her life as the foster child of a woman who abused her both emotionally and physically. It also recounts how she worked to overcome obstacles in her life and developed the desire to become a playwright.

See also Drama; Harlem Renaissance; Historical Fiction; Memory

Works By

Chewed Water: A Memoir. Hanover, NH: University Press of New England, 2001.
The Mojo and the Sayso. New York: Theatre Communications Group, 1988.
Plays by Aishah Rahman. New York: Broadway Play, 1997.
"To Be Black, Female and a Playwright." *Freedomways* 19 (1979): 256–260.
"Tradition and a New Aesthetic." *MELUS* 16.3 (1989–1990): 23–26.
Unfinished Women Cry in No Man's Land While a Bird Dies in a Gilded Cage. New York: Drama Jazz House, 1984.

Works About

Hatch, James V., and Ted Shine, eds. *Black Theatre USA: Plays by African Americans, 1847 to Today*. Rev. ed. New York: Free Press, 1996.

Koger, Alicia Kae. "Jazz Form and Jazz Function: An Analysis of *Unfinished Women Cry in No Man's Land While a Bird Dies in a Gilded Cage*." *MELUS* 16.3 (1989–1990): 99–111.

Mahone, Sydné, ed. *Moon Marked and Touched by Sun: Plays by African-American Women*. New York: Theatre Communications Group, 1994.

Maynard, Suzanne. "1997 Interview with Aishah Rahman." www.brown .edu/Departments/English/Writing/rahmanmaynard.

Nouryeh, Andrea J. "*Mojo and the Sayso*: A Drama of Nommo That Asks, 'Is Your Mojo Working?'" *Black Theatre: Ritual Performance in the African Diaspora*. Ed. Paul Carter Harrison, Victor Leo Walker II, and Gus Edwards. Philadelphia: Temple University Press, 2002. 285–295.

Peterson, Bernard L., Jr., ed. *Contemporary Black American Playwrights and Their Plays: A Biographical Directory and Dramatic Index*. New York: Greenwood Press, 1988.

Deborah Weagel

RAINBOW ROUN MAH SHOULDER

Linda Beatrice Brown's first novel, *Rainbow Roun Mah Shoulder* (1984), tells the story of Rebecca Florice Letenielle from 1915 to 1954 as she struggles with her gift/curse of **healing**, with her relationships with **religion**, men, other women, and with Jim Crow discrimination. The story opens in New Orleans in 1915 and closes in North Carolina in 1954 and traces Rebecca's journey to becoming Florice and finally her full self.

In 1915 New Orleans Rebecca is conflicted about her relationship with her husband Mac and over loyalty to the church and her attraction to priest Father Theodore Canty. Finally she flees to North Carolina, where Mac leaves her. With Mac gone, she drops the name Rebecca and begins going by Florice. Living with her sister Marie, Florice is befriended by Alice Wine and settles in Jacksonville, North Carolina, to **work** as a cook and babysitter. When Marie and her husband move to Chicago, Florice and Alice decide to move to Greensboro, where they find work as cooks at a Negro college. The foreground story of their lives is shadowed by a background that includes a chilling lynching and lack of opportunities for blacks in the **South**.

In Greensboro, Florice once more falls in **love** with a clergyman, Robert Brown, a married preacher. When he leaves town, she tries to take her own life in a horrifying voodoo ritual. Saved by her friend Alice, Florice gradually comes to terms with herself and with the gift for healing that she has long denied. Because some see her as a witch, Florice insists that those she heals keep her role in their cure a secret. Part of her personal growth is in her relationship with her goddaughter, Ronnie Johnstone. Ronnie also has gifts that Florice helps her learn to appreciate. Florice finally leaves Greensboro to visit Robert on his deathbed and to seek the peace of the beach for her own final hours. All of these events are illuminated by the deeply spiritual values that Florice holds and develops.

To underscore the evolving nature of Florice's and her other characters' lives, Brown interweaves italicized sections in the narrative that describe the life cycles of butterflies and moths, stressing the necessary stages of molting or changing form, of assuming protective coloring, and of being toxic to some predators. The novel ends with a passage describing the diversity of size and shape of butterflies and moths and the widespread nature of their habitats, reinforcing for us the metaphor that butterflies and moths, like people, are vastly different from one another but serve vital functions in the continuation of all life.

Brown's style in this first novel resounds with poetic diction, creating scenes of vivid intensity and/or lasting **beauty** in the readers' minds as the story takes the readers through terrible experiences to arrive at Rebecca Florice's final rainbow vision. The enduring support of friends and **family** in the individual's struggle for self-knowledge and spiritual certainty emerge as the chief thematic values in a work that combines beauty and power.

See also Historical Fiction; Violence

Works About

Greenwall, Bill. Review of *Rainbow Roun Mah Shoulder. New Statesman* 111.2859 (January 10, 1986): 27.
Review of *Rainbow Roun Mah Shoulder. Library Journal* 110 (March 1, 1985): 92.

Harriette C. Buchanan

RAISIN IN THE SUN, A

A Raisin in the Sun (1959) was the first play by a black female playwright to be produced on Broadway. The author, **Lorraine Hansberry**, led the way for recognition of both female and male black artists on the Great White Way by becoming the first black recipient of the New York Drama Critics Circle Award for Best Play. She was only the fifth woman and the youngest person to receive the award. Its premier production brought together the talents of Lloyd Richards, the first black director on Broadway in over fifty years, who would go on to become dean of the Yale School of Drama and artistic director of the Yale Repertory Theater, and future Oscar-winning actor Sidney Poitier, as Walter Lee Younger, Jr. The cast also included three powerful female actors in the roles of the other Younger adults: Claudia McNeil as Mama Lena; Ruby Dee as Ruth, and Diana Sands as Beneatha. All these actors would reprise their roles for the 1961 Columbia Pictures **film**, directed by Daniel Petrie, which garnered Hansberry a nomination for Best Screenplay of the Year by the Screenwriters' Guild of America and the Gary Cooper Award for "outstanding human values" at the 1961 Cannes Film Festival. Adapted as the musical *Raisin*, the play won Broadway's Tony Award for Best Musical of 1974. Black female playwrights like **Adrienne Kennedy** and **Ntozake Shange**, while diverging from Hansberry's realistic mode, have found inspiration in her example and success in bringing their own black characters to the stage.

A Raisin in the Sun confronts the disadvantaged situation of poor, working-class black families in Chicago's Southside. The play's setting, a small two-bedroom apartment with a shared bathroom down the hall, is **home** to three generations of the Younger **family**: Mama Lena Younger; her adult children, Walter Lee, a chauffeur, and Beneatha, a student with ambitions to be a doctor; Walter's wife, Ruth, like Mama, a **domestic** worker; and Walter and Ruth's son Travis. Their circumstances offer little hope for bettering their social conditions. The dramatic tensions arise from Mama's receipt of a $10,000 life insurance payment on her deceased husband. The play's epigraph, which also provides the title, is a **Langston Hughes** poem, "Harlem," from his collection *Montage of a Dream Deferred* (1951). The Younger family and the demoralizing effects of dreams too long deferred become Hansberry's montage. The money offers the Youngers the hope of a better life, but the means of realizing their dreams differ, especially for Walter Lee and Mama. Walter Lee wants the money to invest in a liquor store. Instead, Mama uses part of it as a downpayment on an affordable house in Clybourne Park, an all-white neighborhood. Recognizing her son's desperation, Mama relents and hands over to him the remainder of the money, part of which is meant for Beneatha's medical school education. Walter Lee foolishly entrusts it to one of his potential business partners, who disappears with it. Tempted to recoup part of his losses, he achieves personal triumph when he rejects the bribe from the Clybourne Park Improvement Association to stay out of its white neighborhood and asserts his pride in himself and his family and their right to live peacefully wherever they choose. At the play's end, the Youngers' determination to move carries hope, but not without the sense of their continuing struggles as black Americans for basic human rights against the white majority's bigotry, represented by the Clybourne opposition.

Walter Lee's discovery of his moral center forms a significant part of the **drama**, but *Raisin*'s female characters draw much of the play's attention, celebrating in diverse ways the potential of womanhood. Despite the **memory** of Walter Sr., the Younger apartment is an intensely female space with its three adult women; Mama considers it her house. Hansberry's presentation invokes the **stereotype** of the emasculating black matriarch who considers the black male incompetent and unreliable. But Mama's transcendence comes in recognizing before it is too late her son's destructive hopelessness, and she acts decisively to rectify the damage. Despite her overbearing ways, Mama is a figure of **love**, nurturance, and growth, symbolized by her plant and her association with gardens. Her daughter-in-law, the play's other mother, is less strident but equally strong. Ruth's insights often reconcile the family's tensions.

Her pregnancy emphasizes her vitality, but her plans for an abortion, because of their impoverished circumstances, provide one of the play's strongest social commentaries, for Ruth's livelihood, looking after the children of other mothers, presumably white, falls short of allowing her to mother her own black children.

Beneatha suggests endless possibilities for black womanhood. Intelligent and ambitious, she places her studies before marriage. Her motivation to become a doctor, to cure people, suggests her social conscience. Intent on exploring her black **identity**, she pursues an interest in Africa. She is also the female character against whom misogynistic attitudes are most often directed. Walter openly questions her intent, as a female, to become a doctor. Her two suitors, George Murchison of the black monied **class** and the African Asagai, are both preoccupied with her attractiveness and are intent on molding her into their conception of the desired female. Partly through the influence of the play's other women, Beneatha learns compassion without any loss of self-assertion.

The dramatic power of *A Raisin in the Sun* has not diminished since its opening on Broadway almost half a century ago. Subsequent productions, such as the twenty-fifth Anniversary Revival at the Roundabout Theater in New York (1986), and the American Playhouse Television version, based on this production (1989), restored some of Hansberry's original material, sharpening its enduring appeal. The play's themes of racial and sexual discrimination, social injustice, the conflict between material needs and moral values, and independence for black peoples worldwide remain relevant, and Hansberry's dramatic ability to lay bare the rich inner life of her characters, balancing despair and hope, anguish and humor, makes the play timeless. Its revival on Broadway in the spring of 2004, with Sean Combs (rap artist Puff Daddy/P. Diddy) in the role of Walter Lee and Phylicia Rashad as Mama, ensures its exposure to a new and diverse audience.

See also Beauty; Black Masculinity; Motherhood

Works About

Anderson, Mary Louise. "Black Matriarchy: Portrayals of Women in Three Plays." *Negro American Literature Forum* 10.3 (Autumn 1976): 93–95.

Bernstein, Robin. "Inventing a Fishbowl: White Supremacy and the Critical Reception of Lorraine Hansberry's *A Raisin in the Sun*." *Modern Drama* 42 (1999): 16–27.

Brown, Lloyd W. "Lorraine Hansberry as Ironist: A Reappraisal of *A Raisin in the Sun*." *Journal of Black Studies* 4.3 (March 1974): 237–247.

Clark, Keith. "Black Male Subjectivity Deferred?: The Quest for Voice and Authority in Lorraine Hansberry's *A Raisin in the Sun*." *Black Women Playwrights: Visions on the American Stage*. Ed. Carol P. Marsh-Lockett. New York: Garland, 1999. 87–111.

Domina, Lynn. *Understanding A Raisin in the Sun: A Student Casebook to Issues, Sources, and Historical Documents*. Westport, CT: Greenwood Press, 1998.

Gourdine, Angeletta K. M. "The Drama of Lynching in Two Blackwomen's Drama, or Relating Grimké's *Rachel* to Hansberry's *A Raisin in the Sun.*" *Modern Drama* 41.4 (1998): 533–545.

Hays, Peter L. "*Raisin in the Sun* and *Juno and the Paycock.*" *Phylon* 33.2 (1972): 175–176.

Miller, Jeanne-Marie A. "'Measure Him Right': An Analysis of Lorraine Hansberry's *Raisin in the Sun.*" *Teaching American Ethnic Literatures: Nineteen Essays.* Ed. John R. Maitino and David R. Peck. Albuquerque: University of New Mexico Press, 1996. 133–145.

Washington, J. Charles. "*A Raisin in the Sun* Revisited." *Black American Literature Forum* 22.1 (1988): 109–124.

Wilkerson, Margaret B. "*A Raisin in the Sun*: Anniversary of an American Classic." *Performing Feminisms: Feminist Critical Theory and Theatre.* Ed. Sue-Ellen Case. Baltimore, MD: Johns Hopkins University Press, 1990. 119–130.

Rita Bode

RAPE

Rape has been a major motif in African American **literature**, reflecting the predominance of rape as both a fact and a trope in American culture. Rape was a regular practice within the institution of **slavery**, particularly the rape of black female slaves by white men with power over them. It is not surprising, then, that the **slave narrative** and other early African American literature deal with this reality. Sometimes such interracial rapes are named explicitly as such. More often, in an era when depictions of **sexuality** of all kinds, including sexual **violence**, were unspeakable, such rapes were implied by a narrative "blackout" and the woman's subsequent pregnancy. The term *rape* itself may not have been used in slave narratives and other early accounts of interracial relations; our contemporary understanding of the term as nonconsensual sex, often involving sexual violence, is a recent one. In early U.S. culture, "rape" was one man's theft of a woman's **body** from another man (specifically her father or her husband); rape was a power struggle between men. The man who "owned" the woman—father, husband, or slave master—was seen to have rights over her sexuality, whether or not the woman was an enslaved or a free person. The woman's consent, then, was not seen as a primary issue but was superceded by the will of the man who had property rights over her.

While many early African American writers may condemn what we would today call rape, they are more likely to condemn it as part of a larger system of slavery and white privilege, in which an enslaved woman's ownership of her proper body and her ability (or inability) to consent are always already denied, than to single it out as a specific social ill to be protested. Even so, many explicit and even more implicit rapes appear in the pages of U.S.

literature about slavery, including **William Wells Brown**'s *Clotel, or The President's Daughter* (1853) and Harriet Beecher Stowe's *Uncle Tom's Cabin* (1852), among many other works. Later African American writers, too, return to this earlier **history** of white enslavers raping enslaved black women. Often the reality of the rape of enslaved women by white men serves as a metaphor for what was done to African Americans in the United States; in such literature African Americans may be figured as both victims and children of rape.

Angela Davis has argued that rape has not only been a reality in the lives of African Americans; it has also served as a cultural trope, or encapsulating image, for black-white relations in America. Even as white male power was embodied and solidified by the ability to control/dominate black female bodies, there was also emerging "the **myth** of the black rapist," a myth that had helped to justify slavery but that gained its greatest life after Emancipation. In this American cultural mythology (ironically a reversal of the more prevalent reality of white male rapes of black females), black men innately lusted after white women, whom they would readily rape if they were not kept in check (by white men). Rumors of black men attempting to rape white women abounded. (For example, the famous 1953 lynching of fourteen-year-old Emmett Till was instigated by rumors that he had ogled and whistled at a white woman.) Although the actual occurrences of such rapes were almost surely minimal relative to the myth, the myth had tremendous power in inciting fear and in creating the "need" to police black male bodies. Such policing was sometimes legal—for example, many of the Jim Crow laws developed for this reason—and sometimes illegal or extralegal—for example, many lynchings were instigated by the accusation that the black man had raped or sexually abused a white woman. An exemplary novel illustrating the myth of the black rapist is **Richard Wright**'s *Native Son* (1940). Bigger Thomas is hailed into this myth and is so afraid of being accused of raping a white woman, Mary Dalton, that he ends up accidentally killing her. In the end, his **death** sentence assuages the outrage aroused by the fantasy of a black man committing sexual violence on a white woman—whereas Bigger's *actual* rape and murder of his black girlfriend Bessie arouses little outrage from the white populace or even from Bigger himself.

Because the myth of the black rapist was used to justify lynchings of black men, antilynching activist women were put in a difficult position on the issue of rape. For example, **Ida B. Wells-Barnett**, one of the most famous antilynching activists, had to at times undermine white women's charges of rape in order to defend black male victims of lynching. Such tensions between black and white women in the women's movement around this issue have persisted. The "Second Wave" feminist movement of the 1960s and 1970s partially replicated the racialized trope of rape. While it was very important in bringing about legislation to protect rape victims and prosecute rapists, feminist antirape activism was not always careful enough in disentangling ideological mythologies of **race** from the facts and realities of rape. Susan Brownmiller, for example, in her groundbreaking book *Against Our Will*, inadvertently perpetuates the myth of the black rapist by claiming that black and underprivileged men may be more likely to rape because more acceptable forms of masculine power are unavailable to them. Such arguments end up unreflectively incorporating racist myths into antirape activism. Furthermore, such Second Wave feminist antirape activism, in singling out rape as a distinct issue, sometimes overlooked interconnections among violence, racism, and economic inequities. So the analysis and protest of conditions that give rise to rape may have been minimized in relation to the call to prosecute rapists and aid rape survivors. Since rape charges have been disproportionately leveled against black men, African American feminists could once again find themselves caught between both sides of the rape issue. Furthermore, enduring U.S. cultural myths of black women (and other women of color) as more promiscuous and/or "tougher" and "harder" than white women have led black women's charges of rape to be taken less seriously and treated with less legitimacy than white women's complaints of rape.

Meanwhile, rapes of African American women remain both far too prevalent and at the same time far too invisible in the mainstream U.S. cultural consciousness, and many feel that the rapes of black women (by both black and nonblack men) remain the least prosecuted and the most neglected instances of rape in the United States (and elsewhere). Much of African American literature, particularly in the last half-century, and particularly by women, attempts to rectify this neglect. **Maya Angelou**'s *I Know Why the Caged Bird Sings* (1970), **Alice Walker**'s *The Color Purple* (1982), **Toni Morrison**'s *The Bluest Eye* (1970), **Ntozake Shange**'s *for colored girls who have considered suicide/when the rainbow is enuf* (1976), and **Sapphire**'s *Push* (1996) all powerfully address the effects of rape on black girls and women.

While this entry has focused on the rape of women by men (the most commonly understood notion of the term), "rape" could be understood more generally as any kind of nonconsensual sexualized violence. In this understanding, lynchings, especially those involving castration and/or sodomy (both of which are documented practices in vigilante violence as well as in military and police brutality), could be seen as a kind of rape. Such acts of sexual violence against men of color by authority figures (legitimate or illegitimate) gain particular power metaphorically from their sexist signification as emasculation and castration. Nonconsensual sexual violence, in a variety of forms, including interracial and intraracial, remains rampant. Likewise, both literal and metaphoric rapes remain active tropes in U.S. literature and culture.

See also Black Masculinity

Works About

Brownmiller, Susan. *Against Our Will.* New York: Simon and Schuster, 1975.
Davis, Angela. "Rape, Racism and the Myth of the Black Rapist." *Women, Race and Class.* New York: Random House, 1981. 172–201.

Smith, Valerie. "Split Affinities: The Case of Interracial Rape." *Conflicts in Feminism.* Ed. Marianne Hirsch and Evelyn Fox Keller. New York: Routledge, 1990. 271–287.

Deborah Thompson

REED, ISHMAEL (1938–   )

Ishmael Reed's reputation as a major player in Africa American literature has been built on writing that spans more than thirty-five years. He has produced a diverse body of work that includes **fiction**, **poetry**, and essays that celebrate all facets of life for black Americans while at the same time satirizing American political, religious, and literary expression.

In satirizing various elements of American life, Reed's own work has received mixed reviews from an eclectic assortment of critics. These critics include authors such as **James Baldwin** and Harold Bloom. In addition, his work has been reviewed in publications such as the *Boston Globe* and the *Saturday Review.*

Reed's work, racy and provocative, attempts to deconstruct Western civilization. Reed is also known for his political activism. Of the many books he has written, the most useful to look at here is *Mumbo Jumbo* (1972). Not only is *Mumbo Jumbo* controversial, but it is also filled with a mixture of artistic forms that render the text complex. In *Mumbo Jumbo* Ishmael Reed exposes and interrogates the conflict between traditional cultures and modern/Western civilization employing such techniques as voodoo, witchcraft, and **jazz**.

Voodoo (sometimes spelled voudou, vodou, or voudun) means God Creator or Great Spirit. However, it has been greatly distorted and misused as a justification for human sacrifices, vampires, dripping blood, and devil worship. Reed uses the characterization of Jes Grew as a **healing** agent for the Negro communities of the 1920s. Hence, Reed emphasizes that voodoo plays a major role in the life of Africans in the diaspora in the portrayal of events, characters, and forms of symbolism throughout the text. Numerous characters in *Mumbo Jumbo* are associated with voodoo rituals. Papa Labas, for example, can be viewed as a "witch doctor" who prepares medicine for ailing African Americans. Departing from Western medicine, Reed construes voodoo with its many spirits as something that is outside of chronological time and has infinite spirits that can be used to heal.

Papa Labas, functioning as a witch doctor, practices hoodoo, a blend of African, Indian, Haitian, and European folkloric mythical systems. He is a voodoo doctor like many others before him who resided in New Orleans, where the Jes Grew antiplague began. Reed presents voodoo as not necessarily religious but as an eclectic mixture of practices that are less rigid and less structured than traditional Western **religion**. According to Lawrence Hogue, voodoo symbolizes flexibility, adaptability, mysteriousness, heterogeneity, and individual creativity. As a result, voodoo has the potential to infiltrate all other major religions and nationalist movements.

Hogue, in his analysis of *Mumbo Jumbo*, posits that Reed "uses jazz aesthetics to undermine instrumental reason and to show how the novel and Western metaphysics are constructs." As such, difference and absolute truth, among other concepts, do not exclusively belong to European-centered postmodernism. By extension, Reed in *Mumbo Jumbo* demonstrates the universality of jazz, which is a creation of African Americans and the first original American music form. *Mumbo Jumbo*, like jazz, is improvisational and fluid. This fluidity allows Reed to create a text that goes beyond a typical Western novel.

Reed, in *Mumbo Jumbo*, attempts to show the significance of reconciling African traditions with the beliefs in the future and power of Jes Grew while incorporating other unorthodox characters. Whereas Western thought characterizes voodoo as foolishness, Reed suggests that voodoo's traditions are important to reconciling Africans in the diaspora with their historical roots. Jes Grew is also a symbol of African culture and traditions dispersed throughout the diaspora attempting to drive out European ghosts that haunt the minds of Africa's children. Although the music that carries the healing of Jes Grew sounds different in different parts of the world, it carries the same cure and has the same effect on its people, dancing the dance of liberation.

Works By

Airing Dirty Laundry. Reading, MA: Addison-Wesley, 1993.
Blues City: A Walk in Oakland. New York: Crown, 2003.
Flight to Canada. New York: Random House, 1976.
Japanese by Spring. New York: Atheneum, 1993.
The Last Days of Louisiana Red. New York: Random House, 1974.
Mumbo Jumbo. Garden City, NY: Doubleday, 1972.

Works About

Dick, Bruce Allen, ed. *The Critical Response to Ishmael Reed*. Westport, CT: Greenwood Press, 1999.
Hogue, W. Lawrence. "Postmodernism, Traditional Cultural Forms, and the African American Narrative: Major's *Reflex*, Morrison's *Jazz*, and Reed's *Mumbo Jumbo*." *Novel: A Forum on Fiction* 35.2–3 (Spring–Summer 2002): 169–193.
Ludwig, Sami. "Ishmael Reed's Inductive Narratology of Detection." *African American Review* 32 (1998): 435–444.
McGee, Patrick. *Ishmael Reed and the Ends of Race*. New York: St. Martin's Press, 1999.
Swope, Richard. "Crossing Western Space, or the Hoodoo Detective on the Boundary in Ishmael Reed's *Mumbo Jumbo*." *African American Review* 36.4 (Winter 2002): 611–629.

Juluette Bartlett Pack

RELIGION

Religion has always been part of the African American experience and hence part of the literary heritage as well. However, demonstrations of both religious expression and allegiance have been contentious. The forcible transport of slaves to America began a process of deculturalization in which the adoption of **Christianity** played its part in the deemphasizing of the slaves' human rights, cultural background, and right of return to Africa.

Slavery and its consequences created a Christian **community** of African Americans who sought to detach Christian spirit and **identity** with the racist and ethnophobic attitudes of slave owners and white Christian communities. Ballads and folksongs identify strongly with the exiled tribes of Judah and with the "desert wanderings" of Old Testament heritage. At the same time, other traditions of religious observance survived: the practice of non-Western rituals and the maintenance of a spirit-led "voodoo" heritage among some Haitians and African Americans is one cultural expression of the survival of African religious traditions. The Christian community among African Americans played a key part in the development of the **civil rights movement**, especially under Martin Luther King. Following **Rosa Parks**'s memorable act of civil disobedience, women were a key part of this movement and have always had a strong role in African American religious life. However, Christianity has never been the sole monotheistic religion among African Americans; Sylviane A. Diouf's book *Servants of Allah: African Muslims Enslaved in the Americas* estimates that from 10 percent to 25 percent of all enslaved Africans shipped to the Americas from the seventeenth to the nineteenth century were Muslims. In 1887 Edmond Blydon published *Christianity, Islam and the Negro Race*, which argued that Islam was a more appropriate religion for African Americans, an idea taken up by many in the twentieth century. This was followed by the Ahmadiyya movement, an Islamic order with roots in nineteenth-century India that began proselytizing in the United States during the 1920s. The Nation of Islam followed, in 1930. Made famous by the **work** of **Malcolm X**, this movement preaches a racially segregationist creed and is highly repressive to women. Malcolm X himself disowned this movement, embracing orthodox Islamic belief. Feminist scholars of African American culture have been careful to distinguish between the free and liberated identities of Islamic black and African American women in general and the very oppressive conditions prevailing for female members of the Nation of Islam.

In recent years, theology from Africa has begun to play a role in the African American religious experience, with writers such as Ernest Ezeogu and Emmanuel Katongale publishing in the West. Theologians such as Mercy Amba Oduyoye have engaged with African religious identity from a feminist perspective. Feminist scholars working in this field have had to engage not merely with the aftereffects of white colonization but with the highly discriminatory legacy of African phallocentrism and the reality that many African women are highly oppressed today.

Women writing of the African American experience in religious terms have used different labels with which to do so. **Womanism** has sought to draw parallels between feminist questions of identity and experience and the African American experience. **Alice Walker**'s theory and writing have acted as a significant founding influence.

Religion remains a site of struggle and of conflict, as well as a vibrant part of African American life. It is a contested site of feminist identity but also a potentially joyous and celebratory aspect of African American identity and culture and may be seen as a creative and affirming force.

See also Spirituality

Kerry Kidd

RODGERS, CAROLYN (1945–)

Born in Chicago, Illinois, on December 14, 1945, Carolyn Marie Rodgers attended the University of Illinois and Chicago's Roosevelt University and holds postsecondary degrees from Chicago State University (B.A.) and the University of Chicago (M.A.). Rodgers published her first volume of **poetry**, *Paper Soul*, in 1968. Since that time she has produced an impressive range of broadsides, collections, and works in other genres (short stories and a play); but Rodgers is primarily recognized for her audacious and insightful poetry on **race**, gender, and the revolutionary politics of the **Black Arts Movement**. Her stinging condemnations of white supremacy, her witty and irreverent critiques of masculinist bias in the Black Nationalist art and politics, and alternately, her unabashed celebration of black male **beauty** alongside her thoughtful explorations of mother-daughter relationships have found a warm reception in the pages of African American and women's **literature** anthologies. The outrageousness, anger, and the liberal use of vulgarity that defined Rodgers's earliest poems were well received by many in the broader literary establishment, even as these elements of her work were criticized within her own black arts **community**. One of Rodgers's most highly acclaimed poems, "The Last MF," is a direct response to those male writers within the Black Arts Movement who condemned her use of expletives as unwomanly and inappropriate, even as they continued to use many of the same words and phrases in their own work.

Rodgers was deeply influenced in her development as a poet by her participation in the Organization of Black American Culture (OBAC) Writer's Workshop, where she encountered such influential black arts poets as Haki Madhubuti (formerly Don Lee) and **Johari Amini** (formerly Jewel Latimore). Eventually OBAC would change its name to the **Gwendolyn Brooks** Writers' Workshop to reflect that poet's instrumental involvement in Chicago's growing African American poetry community. Another early influence on Rodgers's development was the mentorship of Hoyt W. Fuller. Described by the poet as her "literary father figure," Fuller encouraged Rodgers's growth as a poet and was a key force, along with Brooks, behind the publication of her first book.

Composed of poems written by Rodgers and selected by Brooks, and with an introduction by Fuller, *Paper Soul* was a critical success that brought increased attention and accolade to the poet and her work. In the months following the publication of this volume, Rodgers was honored with the first Conrad Kent Rivers Memorial Fund Award. Shortly after the appearance of her second book, *Songs of a Blackbird* (1969), the poet was presented with the Poet Laureate Award of the Society of Midland Authors, as well as a grant from the National Endowment for the Arts.

Rodgers's 1975 volume *How I Got Ovah: New and Selected Poems* represents a change in her focus and her perspective. Having experienced her own and other young poets' embrace of and eventual departure from the strident excesses of the black arts aesthetic, Rodgers sets forth in this, the first of two volumes that she published with the mainstream Doubleday Press, to reexamine her relationship to the rigid politics of the Black Arts Movement. In the poems of *How I Got Ovah* Rodgers places special emphasis on the intersections between blackness and womanhood and the way those links open up for her a new understanding of the personal **history** of struggle, survival, and victory embodied in the figure of her mother. The culmination of Rodgers's journey through revolutionary nationalism and into a new understanding of black womanhood is summed up in the closing line from "It Is Deep (don't never forget the bridge that you crossed over on)," in which her mother is the "sturdy Black bridge" that supports her. While Rodgers's black liberation–based consciousness remains firmly in place, some of the less tolerant aspects of the black arts aesthetic (the dismissal of "negroes" as counterrevolutionary adversaries, the rejection of **Christianity** as a tool of white supremacy) have given way, in this poem, to a broader capacity to recognize and honor the diversity of black struggle.

Since *How I Got Ovah*, Rodgers has further expanded her vision for black liberation and consciousness, exploring feminism, Christianity, and **love** as tools for group empowerment, self-awareness, and transcendence. In *The Heart as Ever Green* (1978), Rodgers ponders the nature of truth, transformation, and renewal, using images and impressions from nature to offer a message of hope. *The Heart as Ever Green* was the last volume that Rodgers published with Doubleday. Between 1978 and 1980 she created her own imprint, Eden Press, through which she continues to release collections that record her ever-expanding vision of empowerment and spiritual growth.

In addition to producing her own work, Rodgers remains active in fostering the development of younger writers. She has taught at a number of postsecondary institutions, including Columbia College, University of Washington, Malcolm X Community College, Albany State College, and Indiana University. She has served as a book critic for the *Chicago Daily News* and as a columnist for the *Milwaukee Courier*, and she is a member of the Organization of Black American Culture.

See also Black Feminism

Works By

Eden and Other Poems. Chicago: Eden Press, 1983.
Finite Forms. Chicago: Eden Press, 1985.
The Heart as Ever Green. New York: Doubleday, 1978.
How I Got Ovah: New and Selected Poems. New York: Doubleday, 1975.
Morning Glory: Poems. Chicago: Eden Press, 1989.
Paper Soul: Poems. Chicago: Third World Press, 1968.
Songs of a Blackbird. Chicago: Third World Press, 1969.

Works About

Ford, Karen. *Gender and the Poetics of Excess: Moments of Brocade.* Jackson: University Press of Mississippi, 1997.

Parker-Smith, Bettye J. "Running Wild in Her Soul: The Poetry of Carolyn Rodgers." *Black Women Writers (1950–1980): A Critical Evaluation.* Ed. Mari Evans. Garden City, NY: Anchor Press/Doubleday, 1984. 395–397.

Sales, Estella M. "Contradictions in Black Life: Recognized and Reconciled in *How I Got Ovah.*" *CLA Journal* 25.1 (1981): 74–81.

Ajuan Maria Mance

SALLY HEMINGS

The United States' national consciousness is embedded with a historical ro-
manticism that spurs most citizens to embrace a messianic optimism. In short,
many Americans believe that God blesses, guides, and preserves the American Experiment despite some missteps along the divinely appointed path.
Most important, they expect that most past wrongs will eventually be made
right. Many Americans turn hostile when parts of that three-part formula are
exposed as a lie, which accounts for the critical ice storm that swamped
Barbara Chase-Riboud's 1979 novel *Sally Hemings*.

The author, who lives in France, raised a largely undesired question: Could
a white master hold romantic **love** for a black slave?

The novel, inspired by Fawn Brodie's *Thomas Jefferson: An Intimate History*
(1974), blends imagined dialogue with the heady social scene of eighteenth-
century Paris. Most reviews cast the work as bad writing and worse **history**.
In interviews, Chase-Riboud acknowledged the scarcity of firsthand reports
on Jefferson's and Hemings's love lives. Hemings's papers were burned after
her **death**. Jefferson did not write about Sally or the children other than as
property, although during his life Richmond journalist Thomson Callendar
charged that Jefferson fathered several children by her. In the end, she said
the real aim of the work is for Americans to consider the country's "**mulatto**"
character. That was a lot to expect for the time.

Two years prior, the **film** version of **Alex Haley**'s novel *Roots* (1976), a **slavery**-to-**freedom** saga of a black **family**, spurred most Americans to acknowledge a horrible slave legacy. Chase-Riboud pushed the public consciousness to move past the widely touted images of raped black slave girls and grapple with consensual, romantic relations between white masters and African slave women. She punched a perennial "hot button"—interracial relationships.

Despite *Sally Hemings*'s bestseller status, many in literary circles remain cool toward its merit. The consensus is that the author broke too many rules and leaves the reader confused. Criticisms range from unauthentic dialogue to a convoluted plot to a misrepresentation of Jefferson's racial attitudes.

Sally Hemings provokes thought about the real nature of women, **race**, and family, considerations for which most Americans are unprepared. Even in 2004, after genetic evidence has shown what a Thomas Jefferson Memorial Foundation (TJMF) report dubbed "a strong likelihood" that the third president fathered at least one of Hemings's children, most white Jefferson descendants and scholars do not accept Hemings's descendants as family. "Honorable people can disagree," TJMF president Daniel Jordan wrote on the organization's Web site.

Still, the notion of romance between a black person and a white person in the midst of the degenerate American slave industry touches a spot in most American hearts. Many people want to believe some small good exists in even the most horrendous circumstances.

Works About

Andrews, Tina. *Sally Hemings: An American Scandal: The Struggle to Tell the Controversial True Story*. Collingdale, PA: Diane Publishing Company, 2002.

Gordon-Reed, Annette. *Thomas Jefferson and Sally Hemings: An American Controversy*. Charlottesville: University Press of Virginia, 1998.

Lanier, Shannon. *Jefferson's Children: The Story of One American Family*. New York: Random House, 2000.

Lewis, Jon, and Peter S. Onuf, eds. *Sally Hemings and Thomas Jefferson: History, Memory and Civil Culture*. Charlottesville: University Press of Virginia, 1999.

Woodson, Byron W., Sr. *A President in the Family: Thomas Jefferson, Sally Hemings and Thomas Woodson*. Westport, CT: Praeger Trade, 2001.

Vincent F. A. Golphin

SALT EATERS, THE

Published in 1980, **Toni Cade Bambara**'s first novel concerns the legendary healer Minnie Ransom's attempt to return Velma Henry to some form of health and stability following her attempted suicide. Velma sits with Minnie

Ransom in the center of the Master's Mind, a group of twelve supporters and aides to Ransom, at the Southwest Community Infirmary. The novel's **healing** story, occupying just over two hours of chronological time, fragments into a past and future journey recalling and foretelling Velma's life, Minnie's training, and their connections to other characters inside and out of the peripheral setting of Claybourne, Georgia. At once spiritual, apocalyptic, mysterious, cacophonic, and destabilizing, *The Salt Eaters* offers a unifying epiphany of creation and **community**.

Velma Henry's life is one of devotion to activism within her community. Through time shifts and the dialogue of other characters, one sees Velma's dedication to causes pushing her forward into still other responsibilities that ultimately alienate her from her **family**. Her growing dissatisfaction with her marriage to Obie and the disintegration of their collective **work** at the Academy of the 7 Arts (a community education facility) as well as her recent alleged sabotage of records and files at the nearby nuclear power plant become the latest events in a long litany of tensions taking their toll on Velma. Her growing dissatisfaction with life proves the catalyst for other characters to reflect upon their own lives. Meanwhile, her healing becomes one of Ransom's most difficult because Velma cannot quickly answer the pivotal opening question of the novel, "Are you sure, sweetheart, that you want to be well?"

Juxtaposed with Velma's suicidal temperament, other characters populating the novel also speak to the varying degrees of wellness. With their blending of traditional songs, stories, and customs, the Seven Sisters, a multicultural performance troupe including Velma's sister Palma, offer a healthy alternative to racial strife and division. Conversely, a man with a questionable past, Doc Serge, the eccentric administrator of the Infirmary, revels in self-**love** as the source of his strength. Dr. Julius Meadows, however, as the newest doctor at the Infirmary, lacks such strength and stability. Haunted by recurring thoughts of the Welfare Man, the African American male who takes advantage of the women in his life while eschewing responsibility, Meadows must move beyond generalizations of masculinity and blackness in order to find harmony in his **identity**. The wholeness that Campbell, the manager of the Avocado Pit Café, demonstrates affirms the novel's push toward wellness. He sees in the great, thunderous noise that coincides with Velma's healing a sign of Damballah, the god of order and creation. Campbell possesses the clarity that Meadows lacks and toward which Velma aspires.

Through Minnie Ransom's work, Velma comes to see a future filled with challenges greater than the ones already faced. Yet, she accepts the healing and becomes certain of her desire to be well. Though critical commentary notes the difficulty of the novel, that Bambara's work offers important consideration of one of the central questions of **black feminism/womanism**— cannot be denied. *The Salt Eaters* does not resolve the tensions that shape it; rather, it offers readers a meditation on social activism and the necessity of community as the strength of the individual and order as the remedy for chaos.

Works About

Bambara, Toni Cade. "What It Is I Think I'm Doing Anyhow." *The Writer on Her Work*. Ed. Janet Sternburg. New York: W. W. Norton, 1993. 155–168.

Hull, Gloria. " 'What It Is I Think She's Doing Anyhow': A Reading of Toni Cade Bambara's *The Salt Eaters*." *Home Girls: A Black Feminist Anthology*. Ed. Barbara Smith. New York: Kitchen Table: Women of Color Press, 1983. 124–142.

Kelley, Margot Anne. " 'Damballah Is the First Law of Thermodynamics': Modes of Access to Toni Cade Bambara's *The Salt Eaters*." *African American Review* 27.3 (1993): 479–493.

Page, Philip. " 'Across the Borders': Imagining the Future in Toni Cade Bambara's *The Salt Eaters*." *Reclaiming Community in Contemporary African American Fiction*. Jackson: University Press of Mississippi, 1999. 78–115.

F. Gregory Stewart

SANCHEZ, SONIA (1934–   )

Sonia Sanchez is one of the most recognized individuals associated with the **Black Arts Movement**. During that time, Sanchez emerged as a fresh and fierce voice that embraced black speech and sought to tell the truth about the black condition. Both qualities have remained part of Sanchez's work, now spanning more than three decades. She has authored a dozen books of **poetry**, three children's books, and several plays and contributed to or edited more than twenty anthologies. In addition to her literary production, she has traveled the world reciting her poetry and has taught at various universities. In 2000, Sanchez retired from Temple University after teaching there for more than twenty years. Sanchez has three children from two marriages: her daughter, Anita, and her twin sons, Morani Meusi and Mungu Meusi.

Sanchez was born Wilsonia Benita Driver in Birmingham, Alabama, on September 9, 1934, to Lena and Wilson Driver. She had an older sister, Patricia, and later a half brother, Wilson. As a child, she faced tremendous loss. Her mother died when she was a year old. Having lost her mother, Sanchez was raised in Alabama by her grandmother until her **death** five years later.

The death of her grandmother proved to be a significant turn in her life. While her grandmother was alive, Sanchez grew fond of the southern black language she heard her speak and often tried to imitate it. Following her death, Sanchez began to stutter, and verbal communication became difficult and embarrassing. She turned to writing things down as a means of expressing herself. Over the next three years Sanchez continued writing as she and her sister moved between different **family** members and friends.

At the age of nine, Sanchez and her sister moved to Harlem with their father. Although she finally overcame her stutter as a teenager, Sanchez continued writing, and her work was greatly influenced by the vibrant environment of New York City. On the streets she heard an urban black language that was different from what she had heard in Alabama. Sanchez describes the language she heard as having its own cadence and rhythm, as being hip, smart, and straightforward. As in Alabama, she liked what she heard and would imitate it. Her father, a musician, took her to hear **jazz** and **blues** artists. The impact of the language and music would resonate in her poetry.

Sanchez also encountered a new world of **literature**. She regularly visited the public library and voraciously read book after book, discovering writers such as **Countee Cullen** and **Margaret Walker**. She was shocked and inspired by how many black writers existed. Later, Sanchez stumbled upon the Schomburg Library (now the Schomburg Center for Research in Black Culture), which specialized in books by and about black people. She could hardly believe that such a library existed. Here she read W.E.B. Du Bois and **Zora Neale Hurston** for the first time. Although happy to discover the books, Sanchez was upset that such a discovery seemed to be in spite of rather than a result of her education. She had recently graduated from Hunter College, yet she had never heard of these writers. Resentful and angry that her education had not included this **history** and literature, she cried right there in the library.

Experiences such as this were motivation for Sanchez. She has said that poetry was for her a means of protest against the mistreatment and denigration of black women and men. Since her childhood she recognized something was wrong with the way black people were treated, but she did not know how to articulate it. Her involvement with the Congress of Racial Equality during the **civil rights movement** and her participation in the subsequent struggles for Black Power and **Black Nationalism** helped her articulate what she felt was wrong and unjust. On several occasions Sanchez has named **Malcolm X** as an influential figure in her life and work. His forthright and critical views of white America and his counsel to black America were highlighted by the black language that Sanchez had already come to regard as powerful.

In 1955, Sanchez graduated with a degree in political science from Hunter College. She then studied with the poet Louise Bogan at New York University. During the 1960s her poems were published in several leading black journals including *Nommo* and *Negro Digest*. It was in 1969 that her first book of poetry, *Home Coming*, was published. Around the same time she also wrote two plays, *The Bronx Is Next* (1968) and *Sister Son/ji* (1969).

In these works Sanchez brashly criticizes the institutional racism that exploits the contributions and hinders the development of black people in the United States. At the same time she promotes ideals of self-esteem, respect, unity, and **love** in the black **community**. Sanchez addresses the relationship between black women and men, taking issue with sexist characterizations of the struggle for racial justice that were so often offered by male leaders. Her stance was that black women should not settle for secondary status. *The Bronx Is Next* is especially explicit in this regard.

Her subsequent poetry, *We a BaddDDD People* (1970), and plays, *Uh Huh, But How Do It Free Us?* (1973) and *Malcolm/Man Don't Live Here No More* (1972), similarly criticize the oppressive conditions that stifle the intellectual, spiritual, and economic development of black men and women. In *Love Poems* (1973) Sanchez turned her focus to intimate relationships and episodes in her life. This was a departure from the militant themes but still rooted in promoting the ideals of respect and love in the black community.

In response to much of this work, Sanchez faced criticism for being too confrontational with whites as well as for dragging feminist issues into the black struggle. Some also claimed she was repeating herself without saying anything new. Her supporters embraced her provocative voice and critical content. Many felt that confrontation was a necessary part of the Black Arts Movement.

In addition to the content of her work, Sanchez became known for her use of black language and her live readings. The rhythm and cadence that she heard on the street took center stage in her poetry. For Sanchez, this was the most appropriate language to communicate honestly with her black audience and get to the truth of their history and the oppressive environment they were in. The call and response, singing, and chanting that marked her readings were also integral to the forthright communication that the language afforded her. In her writing, the language was represented through the formal use of abbreviated spellings, dashes, and other devices.

Sanchez's writing, teaching, and activism attracted the attention of the Federal Bureau of Investigation (FBI). In 1969 she helped to establish the black studies program at San Francisco State College (now University), and she recalls FBI attempts to have her evicted from her apartment because of the curriculum she was teaching. She then joined the newly formed black studies program at the University of Pittsburgh (1969–1970), where she developed a course on black women, believed to be the first of its kind. Subsequent appointments included Rutgers University (1970–1971), Manhattan Community College of the City University of New York (1971–1973), Amherst College (1972–1975), the University of Pennsylvania (1976–1977), and finally, Temple University (1977–2000).

FBI interest in Sanchez was partially due to the perception that she was a Black Nationalist. This perception was heightened after she joined the Nation of Islam in 1972. One of Sanchez's most acclaimed books, *A Blues Book for Blue Black Magical Women* (1974), was published while she was a member of the Nation. Described as a spiritual **autobiography**, the collection reflects her involvement with the organization and is a celebration of the evolution of black women. Despite the fact that the Nation expected women to play a background role in the organization, Sanchez maintained her stance of equal involvement for black women and men. Knowing that her beliefs were in constant conflict, and that some in the organization did not support her as a writer, she left the Nation in 1975.

The timing of Sanchez's departure from the Nation coincided with the decline of the Black Arts Movement. Despite these apparent disruptions, Sanchez remained active and continued to write and teach. *Homegirls and Handgrenades* (1984) was awarded the American Book Award from the Before

Columbus Foundation in 1985 and was followed by *Under a Soprano Sky* (1987). Her recent work includes *Does Your House Have Lions?* (1997), which was nominated for NAACP (National Association for the Advancement of Colored People) Image and National Book Critics Circle Awards; *Like the Singing Coming Off the Drums: Love Poems* (1998), which was dedicated to slain rapper Tupac Shakur; and *Shake Loose My Skin: New and Collected Poems* (1999).

Sanchez has acknowledged that her earlier writing was aggressive but that it reflected her anger and growing consciousness at the time. Over the years, as her views changed, so did her work. Perhaps not as confrontational as before, her work remains a means of protest against what she believes is unjust and has grown to connect the problem of racism and sexism with environmental concerns, war, and other global issues. Sanchez is still driven by the love of language and humanity that helped forge her voice decades ago.

See also Baraka, Amiri; Giovanni, Nikki

Works By

A Blues Book for Blue Black Magical Women. Detroit: Broadside Press, 1974.
Home Coming. Detroit: Broadside Press, 1969.
Homegirls and Handgrenades. New York: Thunder's Mouth Press, 1984.
It's a New Day: Poems for Young Brothas and Sistuhs. Detroit: Broadside Press, 1971.
I've Been a Woman: New and Selected Poems. Sausalito, CA: Black Scholar Press, 1978.
Shake Loose My Skin: New and Collected Poems. Boston: Beacon Press, 1999.
Under a Soprano Sky. Trenton, NJ: African World Press, 1987.
Wounded in the House of a Friend. Boston: Beacon Press, 1995.

Works About

Blackshire-Belay, Carol Aisha, ed. *Language and Literature in the African American Imagination.* Westport, CT: Greenwood Press, 1992.
Curb, Rosemary K. "Pre-feminism in the Black Revolutionary Drama of Sonia Sanchez." *The Many Forms of Drama.* Ed. Karelisa V. Hartigan. Lanham, MD: University Press of America, 1985. 19–29.
Joyce, Joyce A. *Ijala: Sonia Sanchez and the African Poetic Tradition.* Chicago: Third World Press, 1996.
Kelly, Susan. "Discipline and Craft: An Interview with Sonia Sanchez." *African American Review* 34.4 (2000): 679–687.
Leibowitz, Herbert. "Exploding Myths: An Interview with Sonia Sanchez." *Parnassus* 12.2–13.1 (1985): 357–368.
Melham, D. H. "Sonia Sanchez: Will and Spirit." *MELUS* 12.3 (1985): 73–98.
Pettis, Joyce. *African American Poets: Lives, Works, and Sources.* Westport, CT: Greenwood Press, 2002.

Tate, Claudia, ed. *Black Women Writers at Work*. New York: Continuum, 1983.

Raquel Rodriguez

SANDERS, DORI (1935?–   )

Dori Sanders was born where she still lives, on one of York County, South Carolina's largest black-owned farms, established by her father in 1915. The daughter of a school principal and farmer and a housewife, she was the eighth of ten children. Her father always made sure the children had reading matter for the times between chores, and they also enjoyed making up and telling one another stories. As they grew up, most of the children went off to be educated and did not return, but she and one brother remained to **work** on the farm. She felt she was an underachiever but truly loved the farm work she continues to do during the season. During the off season she was living in Maryland with a sister when an employer saw her jottings and encouraged her to write. Motivated by this and other friends, she wrote a novel, which was not accepted, but the publisher encouraged her to submit further writings, and they accepted and published *Clover* in 1990. Published for adults, this accessible novel won excellent reviews, attained bestseller status, and was widely read by young adults as well.

Clover Hill is a gifted, strong-willed, ten-year-old rural African American child whose widowed father abruptly remarries a college friend, an educated white woman. On their wedding day, the newlyweds are in an automobile accident, and her beloved father dies. Her stepmother, Sara Kate, declares her intention to remain and raise her new stepdaughter, even though Clover's relatives distrust Sara Kate. Told by Clover in a convincing vernacular voice, the novel has periods of humor and poignancy as the two wrangle over different foodways and have other misunderstandings as they try to forge a **family**. **Race** is one issue here, but other obstacles include city versus country and the odd situation of strangers sharing a common grief and learning to respect each other.

Sanders's second novel is *Her Own Place* (1993), about the life of Mae Lee Barnes, a hardworking, determined mother of five who is eventually abandoned by her husband. She buys her own farm with money she earns working at a munitions plant during World War II, plus a loan from her parents, and raises her children to be successful, as the **South** she knows changes around her. After her retirement, Mae Lee becomes the first black volunteer hospital auxiliary member, and there are humorous moments as the old volunteers adjust to the new. Throughout, Mae Lee Barnes shows strength and shrewdness as she pursues her dreams for her family. Because the heroine is a mature woman, this is generally considered an adult rather than a young adult novel. Sanders has also written a popular cookbook, *Dori*

Sanders' Country Cooking: Recipes and Stories from the Family Farm Stand (1995), which combines family recipes and anecdotes with great charm.

Works By

Clover: A Novel. Chapel Hill, NC: Algonquin Books, 1990.
Dori Sanders' Country Cooking: Recipes and Stories from the Family Farm Stand. Chapel Hill, NC: Algonquin Books, 1995.
Her Own Place: A Novel. Chapel Hill, NC: Algonquin Books, 1993.

Works About

Contemporary Authors. Vol. 206. Detroit: Thomson Gale. 306–308.
Hine, Darlene Clark, ed. *Facts on File Encyclopedia of Black Women in America: Literature.* Vol. 2. New York: Facts on File, 1997. 152.
Mabunda, L. Mpho, ed. *Contemporary Black Biography.* Vol. 8. Detroit: Gale Research. 219–221.
Mautz, Roger, ed. *Contemporary Southern Writers.* Detroit: St. James Press, 1999. 323–324.

Susan L. Golden

SAPPHIRE (Author) (1950–)

Born Ramona Lofton at Ft. Ord in 1950, Sapphire spent her early years moving with her military **family** to other bases in California, Texas, and Germany. After her parents divorced, she lived in Philadelphia and Los Angeles. She spent the early 1970s studying dance and identifying with the counterculture. After moving to New York in 1977, she graduated from City College and began teaching in various **literacy** programs for children and adults. For years, she indefatigably gave legendary (and controversial) readings at lesbian and black performance spaces, including Gap Tooth Girls and the Nuyorican Poets Café. In 1994 she received the MacArthur Foundation Scholarship in **poetry** and won first place in *DownTown Magazine*'s Year of the Poet III Award. She received an M.F.A. from the writing program at Brooklyn College, where she studied with Susan Fromberg Shaeffer and Allen Ginsberg, in 1995. She lives in New York City and is working on a second novel.

Important strands of American ideology—especially an abiding faith in the individual-in-**community**'s power to construct a self—thread through Sapphire's life and work. Hitchhiking to San Francisco at twenty-one, she began writing and dancing and changed her name. Traces of this "hippie" phase linger in her work, as does the exhilaration of resisting America's war culture. The **Black Arts Movement** and nascent feminist theater facilitated her escape from the denials of 1950s America. Her now rare *Meditations on the*

Rainbow (1987) deliberately evokes the title, colors, and experimental mono-logues of **Ntozake Shange**'s *for colored girls*, which Sapphire saw in progress. The "rainbow" on Sapphire's cover, however, is made of barbed wire, and many of the colors refer not to skin but to sexual practices. (The book is dedicated to "…the homosexuals, lesbians, queers, faggots, dykes, fairies, zami queens, jaspers, wimmen lovers and bulldaggers of the rainbow.") While Shange's characters find god in themselves "and love her fiercely," Sapphire politicizes and sexualizes that vision in "black," chanting desire for a volcanic earth goddess, in whose womb "god / is / the / clit / a / burning / red / projectile / amidst / the / damp / earth, / secretions / of /creation."

Haunted, driven by sexual betrayals, the early voice cannot forget or for-give. Without abating the angry energy of *Meditations on the Rainbow*, *American Dreams* (1994) places Sapphire's conflicted self within a particular family and social **history**, where ambition twists the dreamers. The abusive past of black/white and even black/black relationships entangles them. She sees that the split incestuous father—community leader by day/child rapist at night may himself have been abused or abandoned, that America has been built on "**rape** cul-ture." Split between the hallucinatory comforts of the *Donna Reed/ Father Knows Best* mind-set and the abuse in her own family, the poet's voice inhabits other victims in order to articulate their /her horror. "Mickey Was a Scorpio" sets a Disney fantasy against the sensations of a young girl being raped by her father. "Wild Thing" imagines the world of the young men convicted of raping the Central Park jogger in 1989, when few defended their humanity. (In light of the dismissal of their convictions in 1996, her poem now looks more prescient than sensational.) At the time, however, Jessie Helms made Sapphire a ce-lebrity when he denounced her poem in the battle over National Endowment for the Humanities (NEH) funding of artists' works; John Frohnmayer de-fended her work and lost his job.

Sapphire's first novel, *Push* (1996), shows her progress on several fronts. Her $500,000 advance from Knopf and selection by the Book of the Month Club occasioned both admiring and critical comments. Her story of a child almost erased by abuse also provoked praise and blame. Most critics were captivated by the voice—ignorant, terrified, rebellious, dissociated, witty, evolving—of Precious Jones, a fourteen-year-old, illiterate, poor, black mother of two children by her own father, who manages to dream and laugh in a wasteland of contempt. Sapphire has emphasized that *Push* is Precious's story; its success is the uneven but powerful rendition of that voice. Patterned on a composite of her students, Precious *lives* for Sapphire; she is a more con-vincing character than her abusive parents, or even the good teacher, Blue Rain, whom **Cheryl Clarke** has called "the Shug Avery" of *Push* (1996). Indeed, Sapphire both celebrates and rewrites **Alice Walker**'s *The Color Purple*. Rain reads the book to her struggling students and points out its "fairy tale ending." The students' journals echo Celie's desperate letters to God, but Precious's world is meaner than Celie's, and she gets no inheritance from her "real" father, except a positive HIV (human immunodeficiency virus) test. She is still homeless, and her children still spring from incest, though in her son's **beauty**, she says, "I see my own." Her acquisition of literacy has enlarged her world, but the ending hardly guarantees triumph, or even survival, though, crucially, *she* writes it.

In *Black Wings and Blind Angels* (1999), Sapphire takes up earlier poetic themes differently. Her "Breaking Karma" series continues to articulate ceremonies of change; the "Gorilla in the Mist" poems and "Neverland" expand the contradictions of **black masculinity** in the grotesquely funny voices of, for instance, the penile implant nurse, the white racist cop, and Michael Jackson. In "False Memory Syndrome," she reverses her history, trying on agency. In poems like "My Father Meets God," she imagines the **freedom** of forgiveness. In "A Window Opens" and "Leave the Lights On," she is not erasing her life as sexworker, lesbian, or celibate woman but announcing another controversial change: loving men. Likewise, she experiments with form, resisting in "Villanelle" and "Sestina," producing in "Dark Sores" and "Today," tumbling into a new voice in "Broken." In some ways she has finished—she has made it; in others, her journey has just begun.

See also Lesbianism

Works By

American Dreams. New York and London: High Risk Books/Serpent's Tale, 1994.
Black Wings and Blind Angels. New York: Knopf, 1999.
Meditations on the Rainbow. New York: Crystal Bananas Press, 1987.
Push. New York: Knopf, 1996.

Works About

Baxt, Helen. "Sapphire Pushes Ahead" (Interview). *Hues* 2.1 (January 1997): 34. *ProQuest: Gender Watch.* Keyword: Sapphire. Capital University Library, Columbus, OH.
Bishop, Jacquie. "Finger in the Chest." Review of *American Dreams. Lambda Book Report* 4.4. (May 1994): 30. *ProQuest: Gender Watch.* Keyword: Sapphire. Capital University Library, Columbus, OH.
Doane, Janice, and Devon Hodges. *Telling Incest: Narratives of Dangerous Remembering from Stein to Sapphire.* Ann Arbor: University of Michigan Press, 2001.
Gordon, Fran. "Breaking Karma: A Conversation with Sapphire." *Poets and Writers* (January–February 2000): 24–31.
Juno, Andrea. "Sapphire" (interview). *Angry Women.* San Francisco: Re/Search Publications 6, 1991. 163–176.
Miller, Lisa. "Sapphire—Interviewed." *Urban Desires* 2.5 (September 1996). desires2.desires.com/2.4/Word/Reviews/Docas/sapphire.
Pela, R. L. "Big Books, Big Bucks: Major Publishers Are Paying Whopping Advances for Books by Gay and Lesbian Writers but Are Readers Getting

Their Money's Worth?" *Advocate*, January 21, 1997, 91. *ProQuest: Gender Watch.* Keyword: Sapphire. Capital University Library, Columbus, OH.

Roiphe, Katie. "Making the Incest Scene: In Novel after Novel, Writers Grope for Dark Secrets." *Harper's Magazine*, November 1995, 65+.

Susan Nash

SAPPHIRE (Stereotype)

Alongside **Mammy**, the kindly and nurturing servant, and **Jezebel**, the alluring seductress, Sapphire is one of the most widely recognized and rigorously analyzed **stereotypes** associated with U.S. black womanhood. Unlike Mammy, the Sapphire label has no readily associated image. She is, however, readily identifiable by her manner. Just as the Mammy's characteristic contentment and subservience are rooted in her origins in the white antebellum household, so too does the Sapphire stereotype depend on the circumstances through which she was first introduced to the American public.

The Sapphire stereotype takes its name from the highly popular character featured on the groundbreaking television series *Amos 'n' Andy*. The first U.S. television program with an all-black cast, *Amos 'n' Andy* was based on the popular and long-lived radio show of the same name. First broadcast to listeners on March 19, 1928, on WMAQ in Chicago, the program was created by Freeman Gosden and Charles Corell. A pair of white comic actors, Gosden and Corell played the title characters, using an exaggerated and mocking version of southern black dialect. The television version of *Amos 'n' Andy* premiered on CBS in June 1951 and was broadcast weekly for two years. The series was withdrawn from the network in 1953, due to the combined influence of African American advocacy groups who objected to the stereotyped representations of black men and women and white advertisers, many of whom were reluctant to put their support behind a program with an all–African American cast.

The *Amos 'n' Andy* television program features the antics and misadventures of the Uncle Tom–like Amos Jones and the unpredictable Andy Brown, his friend and business partner. Their associates included the unscrupulous Lawyer Brown, the slow-witted janitor Lightnin', the scheming George "Kingfish" Stevens, and Sapphire Stevens, his wife. Played by actress Ernestine Wade, Sapphire entertained viewers with her antagonistic manner and the pointed insults that she directed at her on-screen mate. In her exchanges with Kingfish, she was sharp-tongued and overbearing. Her well-honed wit was most often channeled into put-downs and reprimands directed at her husband and his questionable schemes.

In the years after television's *Amos 'n' Andy* ceased production, Sapphire's name, and its association of her persistent efforts to restrain her husband's behavior, came to symbolize black women's perceived efforts to control or emasculate black men. Today Sapphire is a derogatory label, applied to those African American women whose assertiveness, wit, resistance, or dissent are perceived as infringing on or eroding black male dominance and power.

Works About

Ely, Melvin Patrick. *The Adventures of Amos and Andy: A Social History of an American Phenomenon.* Charlottesville: University of Virginia Press, 2001.

Jewell, K. Sue. *From Mammy to Miss America and Beyond: Cultural Images and the Shaping of U.S. Social Policy.* New York: Routledge, 1992.

Jones, Gerard. *Honey, I'm Home: Sitcoms: Selling the American Dream.* New York: St. Martin's Press, 1993.

Ajuan Maria Mance

SASSAFRASS, CYPRESS & INDIGO

Ntozake Shange wrote *Sassafrass, Cypress & Indigo*, her first novel, in 1982. Her narrative account of three black women artists is interspersed with cooking and **healing** recipes and general observations like the one that opens the book: that the moon can fall from the mouth of a woman who "knows her magic." Shange dedicates the book to all women in struggle, continuing the themes of her "choreopoems"—genre-blurring works of **drama**—into the medium of narrative **fiction**. But while *for colored girls who have considered suicide/when the rainbow is enuf* presents seven different women's voices reading/dancing/singing a dozen poems, *Sassafrass, Cypress & Indigo* (1976) focuses on three sisters, named after natural dyes by their mother, Hilda Effania, a prominent weaver in Charleston, South Carolina. The novel form lends itself well to in-depth portrayals of characters' sensibilities, their relationships, and their struggles, but while Shange uses this form, she also transforms it with her inimitable, innovative style.

Shange has said that when she writes, she is thinking of creating books or performances that can benefit young black girls. She wants to provide them with more artistic rainbows, and she does this with Indigo's seemingly magical talent. It is significant that the youngest of the three sisters, Indigo, is the first perspective to be developed. Uncle John gives her his fiddle when she tells him the sad (to her) news that she has been forbidden to carry her doll and best friend, Miranda, out of the house anymore. When she protests that she does not know how to play the fiddle, Uncle John tells her that she does and that she should play something for her doll, Miranda, to "call her out" with her music since she cannot be reaching for her doll anymore. Indigo teaches herself to play the instrument, refusing the lessons her Mama offered. At first, she produces "noise" so offensive the neighbors complain. Eventually, however, she develops a sound of her own, a potent art that enthralls adolescent boys and heals an old man. As a girl just beginning to menstruate, Indigo marks a key turning point in refocusing childhood imagination into creative expression.

Allusions to the **ancestor** through the repeated phrase "the slaves who are ourselves" ties together the arts of all four women: Hilda's weaving,

774 Sassafrass, Cypress & Indigo

Sassafrass's textile arts, Cypress's dancing, and Indigo's fiddle-playing. The ancestors helped Indigo with her music, we learn, and they are behind the other women as well. As Sassafrass and Cypress leave home, their stories are interspersed with letters from Hilda Effania. Cypress's dancing career resembles Shange's in some ways, as she moves to New York and learns to accept her **body** for the **beauty** it is, the power of her legs and buttocks as a dancer of her own style. Sassafrass finally untangles herself from her musician-lover Mitch, pouring honey down his saxophone and symbolically freeing herself to do her own art. The novels ends with all four women back in South Carolina for the birth of Sassafrass's baby. Indigo, however, has moved out of Charleston and into Aunt Haydee's "tabby hut." She is not just interested in **folklore**, as her mother thinks; she has become "the folks," dancing with ancestral men who came out of the sea. The sisters' stories are like the **blues**, as the many allusions to blues music suggest: open, not closed, incomplete, longing, laughing, and all at the same time.

Arlene Elder states that in *Sassafrass, Cypress & Indigo*, Shange has grounded this tripartite coming-of-age story in African American cultural inheritances, not only in the content but also in the form of the novel. There are overt communal gestures to include the reader, as in the recipe "If Your Beloved Has Eyes for Another."

Orality is also a trait of the narrative, as in Sassafrass's poem about a "rooted" blues with some ripening berries "happenin" inside. There is vivid description of Cypress's dance movements, not only in her rehearsals and performances with her troupe, "The Cushites Returned," but also when she is just moving around her apartment by herself. The richness of imagery is not, however, without historical focus. Elder notes that Shange's novel emphasizes a post–civil rights setting since it is "paradoxically reflective . . . of the illusion of political liberation, the problematic of sexual freedom, and the reality of Black female bonding" (136). However, while acknowledging the disillusionments of the post–civil rights era, the novel does not end with its protagonists in a state of alienation; rather, they are centered in their artistic processes, with no guarantees of security but with no boundaries either. Shange's work breaks new ground even as it draws from old traditions.

Works About

Elder, Arlene. "*Sassafrass, Cypress & Indigo*: Ntozake Shange's Neo-Slave/Blues Narrative." *African American Review* 25.1 (Spring 92): 99–108.

Gofrit, Leslie. "Women Dancing Back: Disruption and the Politics of Pleasure." *Postmodernism, Feminism and Cultural Politics*. Ed. Henry A. Giroux. Albany: State University of New York Press, 1991. 174–195.

Lester, Neal A. "At the Heart of Shange's Feminism: An Interview." *Black American Literature Forum* 24 (1990): 717–730.

Sharon Jessee and Fayme Perry

SCHOMBURG LIBRARY OF NINETEENTH-CENTURY BLACK WOMEN WRITERS

The Schomburg Library of Nineteenth-Century Black Women Writers (1988), a thirty-volume series edited by Henry Louis Gates, Jr., in collaboration with the Schomburg Center for Research in Black Culture and Oxford University Press, demonstrates the talent and scope of forty-five black women writers whose work revealed and defied the racial and gender oppression of their cultural climate. Each work includes an introduction by a prominent literary expert in the field. Feminist in its goals, the series challenges previous beliefs that little had been written by African American women in the nineteenth century. Indeed, black women's writing experienced a particularly prolific period between 1890 and 1910; however, much of that work had become inaccessible to late-twentieth-century readers and literary scholars. Out of print and relegated to shelves in rare book collections, these buried works taken collectively suggest that African American women published more in the last decade of the nineteenth century than African American male writers had in the latter half of the century. In total the series includes seven volumes of **fiction**, three volumes of essays, eleven biographies, and nine books of **poetry**.

In the early 1980s, Henry Louis Gates, Jr., inspired by the discovery of **Harriet E. Wilson**'s novel *Our Nig* (1859), began working with several scholars, research assistants, and librarians to create a bibliography of African American women's writing published before 1910. The decision to locate and reprint many of these works as a "library" became possible through the assistance of the Schomburg Center for Research and Black Culture, which held several of the texts in its own collection. The thirty-volume set contains previously rare texts, such as **Amelia E. Johnson**'s *The Hazeley Family* (1894) and *Clarence and Corinne* (1890), **Emma Dunham Kelley-Hawkins**'s *Four Girls at Cottage City* (1895), **Ann Plato**'s *Essays* (1841), and several obscure women's **slave narratives**. The series also includes recovered works by well-known African American women writers, such as the most complete collection of **Phillis Wheatley**'s poetry and letters, the first complete edition of **Frances E. W. Harper**'s poetry, and three magazine novels by **Pauline Hopkins** that had never been published beyond their appearance in nineteenth-century periodicals. Several seminal works published between 1890 and 1910 are also reprinted here, including **Anna Julia Cooper**'s *A Voice from the South* (1892), Frances Harper's *Iola Leroy* (1892), **Paul Laurence Dunbar**'s short stories, and Pauline Hopkins's *Contending Forces* (1900).

The Schomburg Library of Nineteenth-Century Black Women Writers strengthens both the African American and African American women's literary traditions, interwoven legacies founded by the poet Phillis Wheatley with her 1773 publication of *Poems on Various Subjects, Religious and Moral*. For decades feminist scholars have attempted to trace a fuller tradition between Wheatley's groundbreaking verse and the rich and diverse literary works by African American women of the twentieth century and beyond. The resurrected texts included in the Schomburg Library of Nineteenth-Century Black Women Writers allow us a much broader understanding of both traditions, as well as of black women writers' significant contribution to the study of American **literature**.

Works About

Anderson, Kamili. "Schomburg Library of Nineteenth-Century Black Women Writers, 10 vols." *Belles Lettres: A Review of Books by Women* 7.2 (Winter 1992): 5–8.

Foster, Frances Smith. "The Schomburg Library of Nineteenth-Century Black Women Writers: Supplement, 10 vols." *Tulsa Studies in Women's Literature* 11.2 (Fall 1992): 349–355.

Fraser, C. Gerald. "Tracing 'Lost' Literature of Black Women." *New York Times*, April 21, 1988, C23.

Sundquist, Eric J. "The Schomburg Library of Nineteenth-Century Black Women Writers." *New York Times Book Review*, July 3, 1988, 1.

Elizabeth Armistead Lemon

SENNA, DANZY (1970–)

Danzy Senna has quickly established herself in literary and academic circles for candidly and intelligently tackling contemporary issues of **race** and **identity**. In interviews, Senna calls our attention to the "new **mulatto**," the one who has emerged in America's popular culture as "exotic," "in," "hot," and "improved." But Senna does not embrace this pop idea as easily as the populace; she dismisses stylish notions of racial identity as simplistic and incapable of addressing the complexity that is human, a complexity that Senna reveals through the development of strong female characters. Her novels displace what she calls pseudoscientific "one-drop" notions of race that attempt to define personal identity based on a drop of blood. Her conception of race is instead as much about one's **history**, experience, and consciousness as it is about one's color, an idea she credits to the Black Power movement. Senna creates female characters who face difficult dilemmas about race, rather than gender, and in this way subordinates feminist concerns to concerns about race.

Senna was born in Boston in 1970, the daughter of a black Mexican father, writer Carl Senna, and a white Anglo-Saxon Protestant mother, poet Fanny Howe, both of whom were activists in the **civil rights movement**. Having been born biracial and raised bicultural, Senna brings to her writing personal experiences of growing up in a racially conflicted 1970s urban American society, and this lends a tangible authenticity to her writing. While Senna has always considered herself black, this is not because of the one-drop rule but rather because of her own and her parents' consciousness. She points out that in Boston in 1975 "mixed" was not an option: People were either black or white, there was no in between, and she *chose* black. Senna admits that in her youth her thinking was a product of that dichotomy; she had even gone so far as to think of those who identified themselves as mixed as being irresolute. As a woman who identifies herself as black and yet is frequently mistaken for being white, she has found herself simultaneously inside and outside the boundaries of the racial dichotomy that exists in America. As such she has had the strange experience of being "gray" in a world that thinks only in "black" and "white." Because of this precarious positioning, Senna grew up privy to conversations that are generally limited to exclusively white audiences. In this way she has described herself as feeling like a "spy" and both unfortunate and fortunate to hear talk that usually goes on behind closed doors.

Senna's characters Birdie and Cole, in her first novel, **Caucasia** (1998), are children who also find themselves growing up in a world that seeks to construct their identity for them and limit it to a one-dimensional racial category. The two are sisters, the daughters of a black father and white mother, like Senna, who also happen to be intellectuals and activists for civil rights. The autobiographical elements become clear at different moments, but the story is not a memoir. Senna says she likes to think of her narrators as cousins, that is, **family** but not immediate family, and she likes to present what could have happened in her own "story" but did not. The bond between sisters is in some ways celebrated in Birdie and Cole as they share something of a "twin's" language: Elemeno. But while the girls are presented as so close that they create their own private form of communication, their relationship is not without complication. Birdie appears white to the outside world, whereas Cole appears black, and despite their sisterly bond, this color difference does not make them sisters in the world outside of Elemeno. In this way race supplants gender as their distinguishing characteristic.

Senna published *Caucasia* in 1998 when she was only twenty-eight years old. Her second book, **Symptomatic**, published in 2004, also confronts issues of racial identity through strong female characters, but it is unlike *Caucasia* in many respects. Senna describes the book as coming from her subconscious— she says she went into a sort of dream state while writing it–and more psychological than her first book, which she describes as social. While her debut novel might be called a coming-of-age tale, her second is more of a psychological thriller. Senna said she wanted to write something more hard-edged and minimalist after *Caucasia.* Since her adult character in *Symptomatic* is a woman living in New York who becomes the obsession of another woman, Senna had a greater opportunity to address head-on the difficulty of "**passing**" for white in a way that was not realistic for Birdie in *Caucasia.*

Senna received her B.A. from Stanford University and her M.F.A. in creative writing from the University of California, Irvine. *Caucasia* won the Book-of-the-Month Club's Stephen Crane First Fiction Award, the American Library Association's Alex Award, was listed as a *Los Angeles Times* Best Book of the Year, and one of *School Library Journal*'s best books of the year for young adults. It was nominated for both the Orange Prize and the International IMPAC Dublin Literary Prize. Senna received a 2002 Whiting Writer's Award. She currently holds the Jenks Chair of Contemporary American Letters at the College of the Holy Cross and lives in New York City.

Works By

Caucasia. New York: Riverhead Books, 1998.
"The Color of Love." *The Beacon Best of 2001: Great Writing by Women and Men of All Colors and Cultures.* Ed. Junot Díaz. Boston: Beacon Press, 2001. 49–54.
"The Mulatto Millennium." *Half and Half: Writers on Growing Up Biracial and Bicultural.* Ed. Claudine O'Hearn. New York: Pantheon, 1998. 12–27.
Symptomatic. New York: Riverhead Books, 2004.

Works About

"First Person Singular Danzy Senna." *Essence* 35.3 (July 2004): 126.
Milian Arias, Claudia. "An Interview with Danzy Senna." *Callaloo: A Journal of African-American and African Arts and Letters* 25.2 (Spring 2002): 447–452.
Stuhr, Rebecca. *"Symptomatic." Library Journal* 129.7 (April 15, 2004): 126.
"Symptomatic." Kirkus Reviews 72.5 (March 1, 2004): 200.
Wieder, Tamara. "Saving Race." *Boston Phoenix.Com,* May 14, 2004. www .bostonphoenix.com/boston/news_features/qa/multi_1/documents/03827943 .asp.

Deirdre Fagan

SERAPH ON THE SUWANEE

Seraph on the Suwanee (1948) was the last of **Zora Neale Hurston**'s novels to be accepted for publication. It is distinctive because it is a narrative built primarily around a cast of white characters. It is also a noteworthy text because, except for ***Their Eyes Were Watching God*** (1937), it most obviously addresses the sociopolitical limitations placed on women in early twentieth-century America. The female protagonists—black Janie in *Eyes* and white Arvay in *Seraph*—are poor women who struggle to identify and establish **identity** in a male-dominated world.

Marriage is introduced early in *Seraph on the Suwanee* as one of the few options available to a poor woman. The arrival of Jim Meserve in Arvay's hometown forces the question as he is determined that he will marry Arvay. The situation goes from interesting to disturbing when Jim "**rapes**" Arvay under the cover of her favorite retreat, the huge mulberry tree that up to this point has been symbolic of her youthful innocence. This is where Jim takes that innocence away. It is problematic for many readers that the "rape" is romanticized rather than depicted as the violent act that rape is. Arvay then marries Jim without further protest. The child born nine months later, Earl, was never quite right, perhaps Hurston's way of personifying the destructive act of rape and of a society that allows the Jim Meserves ("serve me"?) of the world to brutalize women.

A number of critics note the constant suggestion of **violence** in Jim's determination to establish his power over Arvay: putting turpentine in her eye to "cure" her of her "fits"; raping her in the one place where she had felt safe; and tormenting her with the rattlesnake, knowing her deathly fear of snakes. The first episode was purely violent; however, the other two acts demonstrate the merging of **sexuality** with violence and suggest the man's attempt to totally subdue the woman.

Jim gives the impression that his primary concern is to show how much he loves and wants to take care of Arvay, but it soon becomes clear that all of his actions are self-serving and are aimed at binding Arvay to him. He tries to convince her that a woman needs a man to take care of her because a woman cannot think on her own. In return, the woman should constantly praise the man for these efforts. Because Arvay does not (cannot?) do so, Jim paints her as a failed wife and mother—the traditional roles of a woman. When Jim's act of bravado with a rattlesnake backfires and Arvay, frozen in her fear, fails to help him get free, Jim leaves her with the pronouncement that two people are not really married until they reach the same point of view—meaning his, of course. Jim goes to the coast to live on his boat, and Arvay is left to consider her options.

The ending of the novel leaves many questions unanswered. When Arvay decides to go to Jim on his boat and resume her position as his wife on his terms, some say that she weighed her options and made a choice, choosing to be subordinate to Jim in the institution of marriage. Others interpret Arvay's action as Hurston's way of showing that a woman entering into marriage has to relinquish herself for the sake of her husband's sense of security, thereby affording her no real options within that institution. The main question one might ask regarding the ending of the novel is, "If a 'seraph' is a protecting angel, who is the seraph in this novel, Jim or Arvay?" If it is Jim, then the oppressive condition of patriarchy is preserved. Ironically, if it is Arvay, then the oppressive condition of patriarchy is still preserved.

Works About

Marsh-Lockett, Carol P. "What Ever Happened to Jochebed? Motherhood as Marginality in Zora Neale Hurston's *Seraph on the Suwanee*." *Southern Mothers: Fact and Fictions in Southern Women's Writing*. Ed. Nagueyalti Warren and Dally Wolff. Baton Rouge: Louisiana State University Press, 1999. 100–110.

St. Clair, Janet. "The Courageous Undertow of Zora Neale Hurston's *Seraph on the Suwanee*." *Modern Language Quarterly: A Journal of Literary History* 50.1 (March 1989): 38–57.

Johnnie M. Stover

SERMON TRADITION

The African American sermon tradition, an eloquent art form, has generated a richly varied and distinct voice in and out of the church. Originating in the infamous years of American **slavery**, the black preacher's sermon has a characteristic **history** of serving as a testament to fundamental faith, social responsibility, and individual accountability.

The ministerial vernacular has produced a sermonic structure marked by rich flexibility within defined standards. Black preachers mount the pulpit as storytellers, singers, actors, and religious and social activists. Despite historical changes in the church in dress, music, and public activism, the gospel message has remained steadfast in its impassioned adherence to biblical text and hyperbolic metaphor. Early-twentieth-century sermons reflect contemporary homilies. There is typically a vision of God who stands at the mountaintop of heaven and who tosses the devil and his sinners into the depths of hell.

The sermon can be readily divided into a series of characteristics, as identified by the folklorist Gerald L. Davis: The preacher clarifies that the day's message is inspired by God and is not the preacher's personal testimony; the sermon is founded on a biblical passage; and the main message often includes anecdotal testimony, homiletical musicality, and a closing statement intended to inspire the congregants toward self-reflection. The sermon, delivered in a jazzlike improvisational mode, relies on rhythmically sophisticated statements enforced with repetitions, long pauses, shifts in tone and pitch, and musical scores. The minister's sermonic narrative is punctuated with moans, chants, singing, and other voice inflections, while the message engages an audience energized by signs of dance, arm waving, and amen shouting. The homily is deemed to be practical and accessible, to incarnate religious abstraction.

The African American sermon tradition originated in the days of slavery, offering a welcomed voice for salvation and social change. Services were communal and held in informal settings when time and opportunity permitted. Richard Allen, a slave for decades before the Civil War, became the founder of the African Methodist Episcopal denomination. As a slave, Allen held a church meeting at the **home** of his master where he preached to other slaves on "Thou are weighed in the balance and found wanting." His master, who attended the service, converted to Methodism and declared slavery to be wrong. Another pioneering nineteenth-century black preacher was the Episcopalian minister Alexander Crummell. After twenty years as a missionary in Liberia, he returned to Washington, D.C., where he preached that the church should act as a foundation for not only worship but social service as well. Crummell's topics emphasized human destruction and restoration by the hand of an almighty God. Crummell served his congregation in both words and deeds; he went on to establish numerous charitable institutes. This same tradition in which Crummell and other early church leaders stressed moral guidance has continued with those like Peter Gomes, who in 1974 became the first black preacher to become the Plummer Professor of Christian Morals at Harvard University.

Women have long served in the evolution of the sermon tradition, influencing the pulpit from the earliest days of slavery in America. These spirited female voices have injected the practice of preaching with an articulation that both followed the prescribed male oration delivery and custom and struggled to gain an acceptance of the female presence and oration at the pulpit. Women have often sermonized on the twin towers of spirit and social responsibility. Two central themes have emerged from this long history of female sermons: that women share the same religious faith and calling to the ministry as professed by their male counterparts and that women enjoy a divine right to ascend to the pulpit to preach about religious and social issues. As noted in *Daughters of Thunder: Black Women Preachers and Their Sermons, 1850–1979*, one fundamental aspect of the female sermon tradition has been the recurrent theme on the authority of the female preacher. Leora Ross and R. H. Harris, both in 1926, were the first women preachers to audio record their sermons for wider audiences and posterity.

From the codified and recognizable form of religious witness from the pulpit, the black preacher has migrated to the streets, assembly halls, rallies, schools, and the public airwaves to create a dialogue for change within the social context. The popular message of preparing congregants for a promised land has at times been transformed into a rhetoric directed at social transformation.

One of the most influential trends in sermon history is the electronic message delivered via radio and television. These ubiquitous media have become major outlets for the gospel message. Television broadcasts abound with Christian soldiers marching into viewers' homes, delivering faith and requesting donations. The preacher turned televangelist has adopted the skills of an actor to broadcast messages to a wide audience of faithful.

The sermon rhetoric has also transcended church walls with an often emotive, even radical, rhetoric targeted toward sociopolitical change. This voice, rising to national debate, explores **race** relations, politics, human rights, and national leadership. Martin Luther King, Jr., **Malcolm X**, and Cornel West, in particular, have taken the pulpit to the streets to influence a world assembly. King's eloquent "I Have a Dream" (1963) and "Letter from Birmingham Jail" (1963) balance his strong Christian religious background and his polished oratory skills to argue eloquently for equal rights for black Americans. Malcolm X, in contrast, was a Muslim who in "The Ballot or the Bullet" (1964) describes his role as a Black Nationalist **freedom** fighter. Cornel West weaves together in the traditional fabric of the church threads of transcendentalism, socialism, and pragmatism and lectures on moral authority from the pulpit, in the classroom, and in such books as *Race Matters* (1993).

The sermon has played an important role in **literature**, often with a realistic tone that reflects actual church sermonizing. Works by **James Baldwin**, **Ralph Ellison**, **Zora Neale Hurston**, **James Weldon Johnson**, and others include an admixture of black religious biblical fervor and anecdotal passages dressed in interactive sounds, shifting tones, and culturally compelling rhythms of the preacher's voice and congregation response. Johnson's acclaimed *God's Trombones* (1927) offers a series of seven sermons in verse form in which he pays homage to the "old-time Negro preacher." Johnson's fictional verse reflects with authenticity the tone and message heard in Sunday sermons. These addresses are highly charged with extended metaphors and abstractions. In Johnson's "Go Down Death—A Funeral Sermon," God, sitting on his throne and surrounded by a band of angels, summons **Death** to the side of a woman lying in mortal pain.

African American sermonic rhetoric has evolved as a dynamic and improvisational oratory form with recognizable differences ranging from **religion**, denomination, sect, parish, and location. From the small Baptist church in the **South** to the Islam mosque in the North, the religious message varies in style and content. But despite variations in outward trappings, it is the preacher, flamboyant and spirited, who stands as a hub of a wheel of celebration and witness.

See also Christianity

Works About

Benston, Kimberly W. *Performing Blackness*. London: Routledge, 2000.
Collier-Thomas, Bettye. *Daughters of Thunder: Women Preachers and Their Sermons, 1850–1979*. San Francisco: Jossey-Bass Publishers, 1998.
Dance, Daryl Cumber, ed. *From My People*. New York: W. W. Norton, 2003.
Hubbard, Dolan. *The Sermon and the African American Literary Imagination*. Columbia: University of Missouri Press, 1994.
Raboteau, Albert J. *A Fire in the Bones: Reflections on African American Religious History*. Boston: Beacon Press, 1995.
Rosenberg, Bruce A. *The Art of the American Folk Preacher*. New York: Oxford University Press, 1970.

Michael D. Sollars

SEXUALITY

The representation of black female sexuality since the nineteenth century has always been constructed as a binary opposite to white women. On the whole, such portrayals of sexuality have been made hypervisible, and also pathologic, within dominant discourses on sexuality. Such discursive portrayals have had effects on the lived experiences of various black communities in the United States. It would not be erroneous to state that to date there has not been a historically specific analysis on black female sexuality in the United States. It is important to inquire as to the reasons behind these silences. Black women's sexuality is often described in metaphors of absence. Hegemonic discourses tend to equate the black female **body** within images of deviant sexuality. The task ahead of black female scholars—social scientists, historians, literary critics—is to examine the reasons behind these silences and to find discursive ways to address these silences.

The nineteenth century saw European colonization of Africa being undertaken on a large scale. The **history** of the representation of black female sexuality in the Western imagination can be traced to this time period, with Europe's contact with people from the African continent. Sander Gilman has examined how, in the iconography of the period, the prostitute was equated with the black female through the image of the Hottentot Venus—a black female from Africa. The Hottentot Venus most represented in Western discourses was Sarah Bartman, who was captured from South Africa. She was crudely exhibited and objectified by the European public and the scientific **community** because of what was regarded as unusual aspects of her physiognomy, her genitilia and buttocks. These were regarded as evidence of her primitive sexual appetites. Thus, the black female body was seen as antithetical to the white body and assigned to the lowest position on the human scale. By the end of the nineteenth century, disciplinary scholarship in the various social and scientific fields—anthropology, public health, biology, and psychology—concluded scientifically that the black female embodied the notion of uncontrolled sexuality. But there were also other sociopolitical events that made it possible for such a scientific conclusion. There was a fear among European elites, at this time, of sexually transmitted diseases; high rates of these diseases among black women were used to equate corrupt and deviant sexuality with the female body. Moreover, Western colonization in the nineteenth century also saw attempts by the Europeans to codify and control nonwhite sexuality, defined as the "other," within a framework of deviancy.

The nineteenth century also saw issues of citizenship rights of nonenslaved blacks being debated in the United States. Racial and sexual differences legitimized why blacks would be denied full franchise to citizenship. Ideologically, it was argued that blacks were disenfranchised due to their unrestrained sexuality, specifically that of black women. To a large extent, in order to maintain white superiority, sexual difference between blacks and whites had to be maintained. **Slavery** was also justified by using a range of images of the sexually deviant black body. **Stereotypes**, also made possible by biological notions of essential difference, allowed justification of the enslavement, **rape**, and sexual abuse of black women by white men and the lynching of black men. Moreover, as African American women were considered property, they were denied social, political, and legal rights. What is surprising to many African American feminist scholars is how black women, under slavery, were able to devise ways of addressing **identity** by asserting a positive attitude toward their sexuality.

At the end of the nineteenth century, the binary opposition between black and white female sexuality was buttressed by the Victorian ideology. White women were cast as chaste, virtuous, and sexless and positioned in opposition to black women, who were considered impure and sexually promiscuous.

The middle-class American public considered the sexuality of blacks in urban centers and the new immigrants as undermining the moral values of the country. The dominant ideology of the Cult of True Womanhood always excluded black women. By the late nineteenth century, despite the fact that slavery had been abolished, black women reformers were engaged in strategizing ways through which they could rework dominant stereotypes regarding their sexuality that had been used to justify rape. It was, after all, not a simple method of reclaiming those characteristics of virtuous female sexuality.

One has to keep in mind that white female sexuality also worked in ways that undermined the black subject, both male and female. One of the important feminists of this period, **Ida B. Wells-Barnett**, drew attention to the connection between sex and politics and the reason behind state-sanctioned lynching and murder of black men. Despite the franchise given by the American state to blacks, they were denied the means to protect that right. Rape was construed as any interaction between white women and black men, and the state sanctioned the lynching and conviction of black men on the grounds that the sexualities of white women had to be protected. The black women's club movement has to be seen as also involved in the antilynching movement. Hazel Carby draws attention to the fact that the representation of black female sexuality was central to how these clubs operated. The clubs also focused on the fact that white women were to be made aware of their complicity in the oppression of black women.

By the early twentieth century, black women reformers changed their approach to how they engaged with dominant discourses on black female sexuality. A public silence regarding black sexuality was promoted. Evelyn Brooks Higginbotham has argued that such a strategy was undertaken in the hope that by doing so it would be possible to promote Victorian notions of morality to describe the sexuality of black women. By portraying a super-moral black woman, it was hoped that these images would enable the inner lives of black women to be protected from the dominant negative public discourses. This would allow black women to gain more respectability and justice and subsequently create opportunities for all black women. But this was not a very successful strategy. It did not end the negative stereotyping of black women. Moreover, middle-class women were involved in policing the behaviors of poor and working-class women on behalf of the race. But most important, what was seen as problematic was in the fact that by refusing to engage in ways to challenge dominant discourses on black sexuality, the politics of silence disempowered black women to articulate and describe their own sexualities.

To a large extent, this silence could be explained by the fact that the early twentieth century in the Western world saw the primitivist movement: a fascination with the exotic primitive. Black women were seen as sexually exotic other. Silence was accompanied by the fact that sexuality was displaced onto another terrain—mostly music, notably the **blues**. The early blues singers, who were from the working classes, were able to reclaim a certain element of sexual subjectivity. Even as the image of the supermoral black woman was being written to counterengage women's sexuality, the blues singers defied and exploited those stereotypes. But neither of these two strategies was effective in dismantling the dominant discourses on black female sexuality. For that matter, black women were unable to successfully gain control of how their sexuality was to be portrayed.

Despite the fact that the socioeconomic conditions of black women have changed, a silence still envelopes their sexuality. Not only do black women not have a space from within which they can articulate their sexuality, but black feminist theorists are also unable to do the same. Black churches and black colleges have contributed in maintaining this silence. Positioned between race and gender, the black female subject is denied a position from which she can articulate herself. To a certain extent, this is the result of how power operates at the institutional and social levels. Undoubtedly, what feminist scholars in the present attempt to do is conceptualize ways of looking at how it is possible to articulate their sexualities; this is only possible if black women participate as social and cultural agents.

Silences of a different nature afflict black feminist scholars, as a result of their racial identity. Even if black women in academia are engaged in reclaiming a space from within which they can speak, a common concern often articulated is that they are not seen beyond their physical bodies and recognized as producers of knowledge, or as speaking subjects. The difficulty involved in breaking the silence is commented upon by scholars like Patricia J. Williams, bell hooks, **Audre Lorde**, and Ann du Cille. Because of the hypervisibility of black women in academia (as there are so few) and the dominant sex-inflected ideological constructions of black femininity, it limits the nature of their scholarship—of what they can and cannot speak. A kind of control operates whereby black women, in positions of power, are seen as "other" by the institution of academia.

What we should be aware of is that, at the present moment, silences imposed on the black female body have a material effect on the lives of black women. A large percentage of black women are affected with acquired immunodeficiency syndrome (AIDS), and the state is unwilling to extend its resources to find ways to cure them. Such an attitude can be explained if we consider the nature of dominant representations of black female sexuality, which is seen as promiscuous. Black women who are infected with AIDS usually tend to be poor, working-class single mothers, and they are frequently represented as drug users and possessing uncontrolled sexuality. This equation that the state makes regarding black women and AIDS reveals the dominant, institutional view of deviant black female sexuality.

We also need to be critical of the fact that black female sexuality is usually defined as heterosexual. Notable exceptions are in the works of **Cheryl Clarke**, **Jewelle Gomez**, Barbara Smith, and Audre Lorde. A heteronormative approach elides the possibility of black female queerness and lesbian sexuality. The usual scholarship on **lesbianism** tends to focus on the differences between black lesbian sexualities and white sexualities, without acknowledging that black lesbians share a history with other black women. Doing so defines black lesbians as outsiders within the black community, which is why many black women are wary of identifying themselves as homosexuals or writing about queer desires. Audre Lorde is an exception. Her writings, with its emphasis on the erotics of lesbian desire, can be seen as one way of reclaiming the sexuality of the black female. This is one way in which the silence can be negated, and black female sexuality can be reclaimed.

See also Autobiography; Black Feminism; Black Feminist Criticism; Baker, Josephine; Combahee River Collection; Holiday, Billie; Jazz

Works About

Carby, Hazel. *Reconstructing Womanhood: The Emergence of the Afro-American Woman Novelist.* New York: Oxford University Press, 1987.

Collins, Patricia Hill. *Black Feminist Thought: Knowledge, Consciousness, and the Politics of Empowerment.* Boston: Unwin Press, 1990.

Fout, John, and Maura Tantillo, eds. *American Sexual Politics: Sex, Gender and Race since the Civil War.* Chicago: University of Chicago Press, 1993.

Gilman, Sander. "Black Bodies, White Bodies: Toward an Iconography of Female Sexuality in Late Nineteenth Century Art, Medicine, and Literature." *Critical Inquiry* 12.1 (1985): 204–242.

Higginbotham, Evelyn Brooks. "African-American Women's History and the Metalanguage of Race." *Signs* 17.2 (1992): 251–274.

hooks, bell. *Black Looks: Race and Representation.* Boston: South End Press, 1992.

Sheftall-Guy, Beverly. *Daughters of Sorrow: Attitudes toward Black Women, 1880–1920. Black Women in United States History.* Vol. 11. Brooklyn, NY: Carlson Publishing, 1990.

Tapati Bharadwaj

SHANGE, NTOZAKE (1948–   )

Ntozake Shange (*en*-toe-zah-kay *shang-ay*) was born on October 18, 1948, in Trenton, New Jersey. Originally named Paulette Williams, Shange is the daughter of Paul and Eloise Williams, a surgeon and psychiatric social worker/ educator, respectively. Shange has a daughter, Savannah. She has earned degrees from Barnard College (B.A. with honors, 1970) and the University of Southern California (M.A., 1973). Shange's career as an artist and activist began in earnest in California while she was attending the University of California at Los Angeles (UCLA), but the groundwork of her thirty-plus years as a writer/artist/performer was laid in her girlhood. Her parents knew W.E.B. Du Bois, and his presence at her parents' **home**, along with frequent visits by other African American intellectuals and **jazz** musicians, influenced Shange's direction as an artist, according to her.

Shange's work has contributed to the shape of African American feminist culture for over thirty years. She has won numerous awards and prizes, such as those given in one year, 1977, for her play *for colored girls who have considered suicide/when the rainbow is enuf*: Obie Award, Outer Critics Circle Award, Audience Development Committee (Audelco) Award, Mademoiselle Award, and Tony, Grammy and Emmy nominations. Recognition of Shange's work has continued; in the 1980s she was awarded the *Los Angeles Times* Prize for Poetry and a Guggenheim Fellowship, and her 1980 adaptation of Brecht's *Mother Courage and Her Children* won an Obie in 1981. A Paul Robeson Achievement Award came to her in 1992, followed by various achievement awards from numerous organizations, including the National Coalition of 100 Black Women, Inc.; the National Black Theatre Festival; and the Pushcart Prize for Poetry.

When she adopted her African name in the early 1970s, she also adopted its etymology as the foundation of her **identity** as a black female artist: "she who comes with her own things" and "who walks like a lion." Frustrated by sexist, patriarchal culture, Shange fought through the gender "barricades," as the sites of resistance to women gaining power were called in that era. Women were fighting to enter the professional workforce and to develop personal relationships with men and women that were based on mutual equality rather than on the patriarchal model. Shange was in the middle of this political climate at UCLA and in San Francisco. In graduate school, Shange was attempting to do **work** as a war correspondent and play jazz music. She began writing poems and choreographing modern dances and performing them along with other women. The venues for these performance pieces were clubs in Los Angeles and San Francisco. What became of them eventually, by the time they reached the stage in New York in 1975, is the groundbreaking dramatic work *for colored girls who have considered suicide/when the rainbow is enuf.*

This "choreopoem," as Shange defines it, was a new art form that synthesized **poetry** with **drama**, dance, and music. *For colored girls* opened up an entirely new genre and an artistic "mooring space," in Karla Holloway's words, which has had a profound influence on African American dance and drama. The improvisational nature of the early forms of the piece when it was performed in San Francisco is retained even into the 1976 published version of the work; the seven women's voices merge and separate from one poem to the next. The ways in which Shange deftly merged dance and oral arts—poetry, music, and drama—in *for colored girls* is furthermore an aesthetic and political argument that carries over into Shange's subsequent works.

Shange's artistry testifies to **womanist** liberations in the post–black liberation age. In the novel *Sassafrass, Cypress & Indigo* (1982) when Sassafrass pours honey into her lover Mitch's horn, she is finally answering with a defiant "no" to his many subtle and not-so-subtle subjugations of her artistic expression. Sassafrass's weaving, like the honey she pours into the saxophone, can render ineffective the patriarchal dominations of black women. Shange's works are rich with images of womanist art and aesthetic expression: **healing** recipes, lunar influences, sexual and erotic affirmations of the female **body**, weaving, dancing, playing music. This playfulness, however, is quite serious. Women's creativity and wisdom are rendered into a radical language and style, creating linguistic spaces of resistance and empowerment for women of color. Recovery of female power and sensibility is not just play; it is a serious undertaking to redefine female subjectivity or identity in a sexist, racist culture.

In her introduction to *for colored girls*, Shange said that women's studies had connected her to other women, past and present, and thus to "an articulated female heritage and imperative." However, she goes on to say that modern dance had become her central medium for expression, because dance "insisted that everything African, everything halfway colloquial, a grimace, a strut, an arched back over a yawn, waz mine." Shange's work, like that of African American women writers such as **Audre Lorde** and **Toni Morrison**, creates discourse on the black female body that defies ideals and **stereotypes** of **beauty** repressing black women's looks and intelligence. Just as Claudia defies doll-beauty culture in *The Bluest Eye* (1970), so does the lady in brown who opens *for colored girls* with the declaration that this is a black female's art form, to teach her to remember her own voice and body because she has been "closed in silence so long" that she has forgotten them. Other choreopoems take up various threads of this project, from "dark phrases" through "latent rapists" and "sechita" to "somebody walked off with alla my stuff" and "a laying on of hands." In *for colored girls*, Shange breaks the silence that was still surrounding sexual abuse, patriarchal relations with black men, black lesbian relationships, and black women's **sexuality**.

Shange's next major dramatic works form a trilogy. First is *A Photograph: Still Life with Shadows/A Photograph: A Study of Cruelty* (1977). The second work is *Spell #7* (1979), which presents the audience with nine characters in a bar in New York discussing racial barriers for black artists and the stereotyped masks that even the successful ones must wear. Last in the trilogy is *Boogie Woogie Landscapes* (1979), one of Shange's most radical experiments in form, blending surrealist and fantastic elements into dramatic portrayals of being black and female in the United States. Shange wants to wake people up with her art; for her, this is the artist's job. Firmly within the context of the African American oral tradition, her works call for visceral responses, asking the readers to enter them, not just passively think about them.

Shange's **fiction** and poetry are radically experimental in form and subject matter as well. In her novel *Sassafrass, Cypress & Indigo*, the form is that of a narrative interspersed with recipes and letters. A very lyrical prose style develops the experiences of the three sisters, who were named after the natural dyes used by their mother, a prominent cloth-weaver in Charleston, South Carolina. Each woman eventually perseveres as an artist, though not without hard work and overcoming difficulties. Sassafrass's weaving poem articulates what each one is experiencing, with images of berries ripening "inside" themselves, and the moon falling out of their mouths. **Liliane: Resurrection of the Daughter**, Shange's 1994 novel, presents fragments of Liliane Lincoln's sessions in psychoanalysis. She is trying to sort out her memories of her mother, who left Liliane and her father when she was a little girl to be with a white man. The overall texture is dense in **memory** and meditation.

Somewhat different than either the novels or choreopoems are several notable collections. One, a 1978 collection of poetry called *Nappy Edges*, demonstrates Shange's dexterity with language. There is an abiding emphasis on the beauty of words, their sounds and images, their movements toward compassion or humor. Syncopations, variations of themes, no full stops: These are a few of the qualities of the poems that perch at the edge of sense and logic. Nonstandard spellings and punctuation make her language dance. Yet these dancing words are also creating a form of resistance to standard English that teaches "colored girls" to hate themselves. Another significant work is *If I Can Cook/You Know God Can*, a 1998 collection of essays, recipes, remembrances, and meditations. These conversational, lyrical fragments are organized around topics. For example, in the section "Better Late Than Never," Shange narrates some of the **history** of the numerous all-black communities of Texas, Oklahoma, and Indian territories in the latter half of the nineteenth century. She narrates the creation of the celebration of "Juneteenth," that day in 1867, two full years after the Civil War, when a proclamation was made by Major General Granger that "all slaves are free," the first time Texas blacks heard about it. But turn the page and you will find a recipe for "Texas Shredded-Beef Barbeque," followed by more history of African American cowboys and the "Cotton-Eyed Joe," a still-popular dance form that resonates with the African ring shout as well as the swing and square dance. After "Daddy's Barbeque Sauce" and a discourse on female hairdos, the section has its finale in "Chicken Fried Steak" and a commentary on the appetites of those hungry migrants who walked to Kansas and Oklahoma from Louisiana and Mississippi in the 1890s, the same historical context that figures prominently in Toni Morrison's novel *Paradise* (1998).

Shange's body of "word-work," to use a phrase from Morrison, emphasizes orality and bodily movement as well as textuality in reframing subjectivity and **community** for "colored girls." Her verbal irony and humor, her sensual descriptions and cadenced voices, and her dances/dancers that people her works all capture a sense of committed passion. Her work is political but not dogmatic. It takes cognizance of difference while it performs communal rituals. Most of all, it is still growing out of Shange's vigilance over what it feels like, and what it means, to grow up black and female in the United States.

See also Betsey Brown; Black Feminism; Folklore; Lesbianism; Love; Rape; Spirituality; Womanism

Works By

Betsey Brown: A Novel. New York: St. Martin's Press, 1985.

Black and White: Two Dimensional Planes. First produced at Sounds in Motion Studio Works, New York City, 1979.

Boogie Woogie Landscapes. First produced at Frank Silvera's Writers' Workshop, New York City; first produced on Broadway at the Symphony Space Theatre, 1978; published 1979.

A Daughter's Geography. New York: St. Martin's Press, 1983.

for colored girls who have considered suicide/when the rainbow is enuf: a choreopoem. First produced at Studio Rivbea, New York City, 1975; produced off-Broadway at the Anspacher Public Theatre, 1976; produced on Broadway at the Booth Theatre, 1976; published by MacMillan, 1977.

From Okra to Greens: Poems. Minneapolis, MN: Coffee House Press, 1984.

If I Can Cook/You Know God Can. Boston: Beacon Press, 1998.

Liliane: Resurrection of the Daughter. New York: St. Martin's Press, 1994.

Nappy Edges: Poems. New York: St. Martin's Press, 1978.

Natural Disasters and Other Festive Occasions. San Francisco: Heirs International, 1997.

A Photograph: Lovers in Motion. First produced Off-Broadway at the Public Theatre, 1977.

Sassafrass, Cypress & Indigo: A Novel. New York: St. Martin's Press, 1982.

Spell #7. First produced off-Broadway at Joseph Papp's New York Shakespeare Festival Public Theatre, 1979.

Three for a Full Moon and *Bocas.* First produced at the Mark Taper Forum, Los Angeles, 1982.

Three Pieces. New York: St. Martin's Press, 1992.

Three Views of Mt. Fuji. First produced at the Lorraine Hansberry Theatre, San Francisco; first produced at the New Dramatists, New York City, 1987.

Whitewash. Illustrated by Michael Sporn. New York: Walker, 1997.

Works About

Betsko, Kathleen, and Rachel Koenig, eds. *Interviews with Contemporary Women Playwrights.* New York: Beech Tree Books, 1987.

Brown-Guillory, Elizabeth, ed. *Their Place on the Stage: Black Women Playwrights in America.* Westport, CT: Praeger, 1990.

Elder, Arlene. "*Sassafrass, Cypress, and Indigo*: Ntozake Shange's Neo Slave/Blues Narrative." *African American Review* 26 (1992): 99–107.

Gofrit, Leslie. "Women Dancing Back: Disruption and the Politics of Pleasure." *Postmodernism, Feminism and Cultural Politics.* Ed. Henry A. Giroux. Albany: State University of New York, 1991. 174–195.

Lester, Neal A. "At the Heart of Shange's Feminism: An Interview." *Black American Literature Forum* 24 (1990): 717–730.

———. *Ntozake Shange: A Critical Study of the Plays.* New York: Garland, 1995.

Lyons, Brenda. "Interview with Ntozake Shange." *Massachusetts Review* 28 (1987): 687–696.

Olaniyan, Tejumola. *Scars of Conquest/Masks of Resistance: The Invention of Cultural Identities in African, African-American, and Caribbean Drama.* New York: Oxford University Press, 1995.

Saradha, Y. S. *Black Women's Writing: Quest for Identity in the Plays of Lorraine Hansberry and Ntozake Shange.* New Delhi, India: Prestige, 1998.

Squier, Susan Merrill. *Women Writers and the City: Essays in Feminist Literary Criticism.* Knoxville: University of Tennessee Press, 1984.

Waxman, Barbara Frey. "Dancing Out of Form, Dancing into Self: Genre and Metaphor in Marshall, Shange, and Walker." *MELUS* 19.3 (1994): 91–106.

Sharon Jessee

SHOCKLEY, ANN ALLEN (1927–)

Ann Allen Shockley began both her life and her writing career in Louisville, Kentucky. She published her first **fiction** in the *Louisville Defender* when she was eighteen before moving to Nashville, Tennessee, to attend Fisk University. After graduating from Fisk, Shockley earned her degree in library science from Case Western, working at several libraries before returning to Fisk in 1969, where she served as head of special collections until her retirement in 1998. Shockley has contributed to African American **literature** as a journalist, a librarian who published books and articles on collecting black texts and materials, an anthologist, and a fiction writer who was one of the first African American women to address the subject of **lesbianism** in her work. The latter two areas are especially pertinent in their relation to feminism.

In 1988, Shockley published a seminal anthology titled *Afro American Women Writers 1746–1933: An Anthology and Critical Guide*, which was the culmination of much of the earlier **work** she had done as an archivist in recovering the work of black women writers. The anthology includes not only well-known writers such as **Phillis Wheatley** but also more obscure writers such as **Victoria Earle Matthews**, a prolific journalist in turn-of-the-century New York, and Zara Wright, a Chicago novelist who offered a melodramatic revision of the tragic **mulatto** story in *Black and White Tangled Threads* (1920). The anthology is valuable both for its inclusion of writers who would otherwise be forgotten and the thorough introductions Shockley provides.

It is for her fiction that Shockley deserves the most recognition. At a time when few black women writers were addressing the subject of lesbianism, Shockley was tackling it in two novels and a collection of short stories. *Loving*

Her (1974) told the story of a black woman disappointed with heterosexual **love** who then turns to a white female lover. While the novel was criticized for its literary weaknesses, it nonetheless remains historically significant for its treatment not only of lesbianism but also of an interracial lesbian relationship. Shockley's short-story collection *The Black and White of It* (1980) is, according to bibliographer Rita B. Dandridge in *Ann Allen Shockley*, "generally considered the first published short story collection about lesbians written by a black woman" (xi). The stories explore a variety of lesbian characters, such as a famed concert singer who remains closeted fearing the prejudiced reaction she will get from her **family** when she and her white partner attend a family reunion. Shockley's most daring work is her novel *Say Jesus and Come to Me* (1982), which recounts the story of Reverend Myrtle Black, a charismatic minister who seduces the women of her congregation; the novel offers a biting critique of homophobia within the black church, which Shockley herself has said she intended. While Shockley's lesbian fiction has not always been highly regarded for its literary quality, she nonetheless deserves her place as a pioneer in the genre, paving the way for such later writers such as **Jewelle Gomez**, April Sinclair, and Shay Youngblood.

Works By

Afro American Women Writers 1746–1933: An Anthology and Critical Guide. Boston: G. K. Hall, 1988.

"Afro-American Women Writers: The New Negro Movement 1924–1933." *Rereading Modernism: New Directions in Feminist Criticism.* Ed. Lisa Rado. New York: Garland, 1994. 123–135.

The Black and White of It. Tallahassee, FL: Naiad Press, 1980.

"The Black Lesbian in American Literature: An Overview." *Home Girls: A Black Feminist Anthology.* Ed. Barbara Smith. 1983. New Brunswick, NJ: Rutgers University Press, 2000. 83–93.

Living Black American Authors: A Biographical Directory. With Sue P. Chandler. New York: R. R. Bowker, 1973.

Loving Her. Indianapolis and New York: Bobbs-Merrill, 1974.

"On Lesbian/Feminist Book Reviewing." *Sojourner: The Women's Forum* 9 (April 1984): 18.

Say Jesus and Come to Me. New York: Avon, 1982.

Works About

Bogus, Diane Adams. *Ann Allen Shockley: An Annotated Primary and Secondary Bibliography.* Westport, CT: Greenwood Press, 1987.

——. "Theme and Portraiture in the Fiction of Ann Allen Shockley." Ph.D. diss., Miami University, 1988.

Christina G. Bucher

SINGING IN THE COMEBACK CHOIR

Bebe Moore Campbell's third work of **fiction** explores the intergenerational relationship between Maxine McCoy, a successful television producer in her mid-thirties, and her aging grandmother Lindy, a former singer with a penchant for men, cigarettes, and alcohol. Central to this work is the notion of **community** and the **family** ties that call a young professional African American woman, Maxine, **home** to her roots. The journey from Los Angeles back to Philadelphia is a symbolic one for Maxine; returning to her past she must consider the life she has carved out for herself as an accomplished African American professional whose success in the hostile world of Hollywood masks the emotional void and frustration she feels in her personal life. In this sense, *Singing in the Comeback Choir* (1998) is indicative of Campbell's earlier fiction in which introspective female protagonists engage in probing self-analysis to reach a point of reconciliation with their personal histories.

Maxine is five when her father dies in the Vietnam War; her mother wastes away shortly afterward, and it is Lindy who raises the young Maxine. Years later, when roles shift and Maxine returns to North Philadelphia to take care of Lindy, she finds a home once filled with laughter and people a silent tomb of bitterness and longing. Not only has the neighborhood, which is now filled with abandoned buildings that are littered with graffiti and drug dealers, changed; Lindy has changed as well. Gone is the woman whose life revolved around song, and in her place is a woman who refuses to participate in the shaping of her own life narrative at the end of her days. But Maxine is no mere rescuer; initially she cannot save Lindy because Lindy refuses to be saved. What granddaughter and grandmother realize is that they must rescue themselves, and doing so involves inserting themselves into a larger dialogue of what opportunities are available to African American women, what it means to find success, and what personal responsibilities they, as women, bear to themselves, to the community, and to others.

In *Singing in the Comeback Choir* **healing** is a central theme. Maxine learns from her grandmother to exercise kindness and forgiveness in her own life, particularly in her intimate relationship with her husband, Satchel. When Maxine suffers a miscarriage, she begins to withdraw from Satchel, who responds to her coldness and their loss by having an ill-conceived affair. His action drives Maxine to a further state of grief and isolation, which leaves her angry and bereft. From Lindy, who slowly comes alive under Maxine's affection and care, Maxine learns the power of forgiveness as a tool to redress the wrongs of the past and to create possibility in the present and future. Neither wants anger and despair, which has turned Lindy's neighborhood and Maxine's former girlhood home into a dim and lifeless world, to root in their own hearts. From this mutual acknowledgment, unspoken at first, they come to learn that faith in themselves and a belief in the possibility of change create an opportunity for redemption and hope. As the title suggests, each is able to make a "comeback" to heal the wounds of the past and to firmly locate themselves in the power of the present. While Campbell addresses the problem of urban blight and the plight of young, single African American mothers and underemployed African American men that now scar Maxine's childhood landscape and Lindy's neighborhood, she suggests that the ability to change lies in the need for both communal and personal responsibility. As in many of Campbell's works, African American women must revisit painful histories, personally and collectively informed, that gave birth to them in order to give life to themselves.

Works About

Richard, Phillip. "Moll Flanders in L.A." A Review of *Singing in the Comeback Choir. Times Literary Supplement*, August 28, 1998, 16.

Seaman, Donna. "Review of *Singing in the Comeback Choir.*" *Booklist*, December 15, 1997, 666.

Jennifer Driscoll

SLAVE NARRATIVE

African American **literacy** allowed black voices to at last authentically frame black experience. The slave narrative became the sword African Americans thrust into the heart of the inhumanity of **slavery** and white atrocities. The slave narrative is considered by most scholars to be the founding form of African American literary traditions, though the earliest form of the autobiographical slave narrative appeared in Great Britain in 1789 with Olaudah Equiano's *The Interesting Narrative of the Life of Olaudah Equiano, or Gustavus Vassa, the African, Written by Himself*, the first African-born slave to write his narrative free of white collaboration. Briton Hammon enjoys the distinction of being recognized as the author of the first published African American narrative, *The Narrative of the Uncommon Sufferings and Surprizing Deliverance of Briton Hammon, a Negro Man* (1760). But it was the more developed form of American slave narratives such as **Frederick Douglass**'s *Narrative of the Life of Frederick Douglass, an American Slave, Written by Himself* (1845), Leonard Black's *The Life and Sufferings of Leonard Black, a Fugitive from Slavery, Written by Himself* (1847), and Henry Watson's *Narrative of Henry Watson, Fugitive Slave, Written by Himself* (1848) that set the standard for publication between 1760 and 1894 of over 200 book-length slave narratives in the United States and England. From the early 1800s to the official end of slavery in 1865, the slave narrative dominated antebellum America; numerous American slave narrative books and pamphlets were published and well circulated before 1865. The slave narrative became the literary mouthpiece of choice for African American hopes, fears, aspirations, and resistance. Slave narratives and their graphic tales of the inhuman treatment by white masters functioned in part as a highly effective tool to fuel antislavery sentiment.

The first slave narratives followed a literary structure that mimicked early white Protestant religious testimonials and the Judeo-Christian redemption mythology tales. The author is first lost in the wilderness of slavery, then achieves awareness of his/her humanity, then the desire for betterment or escape, and finally the journey to **freedom**. The narrative structure appealed to white audiences as it emphasized the black desire for Judeo-Christian ideals; many slave narratives include numerous biblical analogies and metaphors and an unconscious acceptance of white dominance. Yet the structure also allowed for detailed descriptions of the hellish reality of slavery and the barbaric cruelty of white owners within the context of religious references and a hero's journey, so much so that slave narratives became a popular propaganda tool to further support for abolition. Early black authors often had to include introductory testimonials by whites that validated the black author's character and trustworthiness. Slave narratives usually begin with a humble plea for the white reader to sympathize with the trials and sufferings of the author. Slave narratives often examine in detail the mental anguish of what it meant to be a human slave, usually opening with the innocence of childhood and an account of a significant traumatizing event that illuminated to the author his/her condition as a slave. Some early slave narratives include George White, *A Brief Account of the Life, Experience, Travels, and Gospel Labours of George White, an African, Written by Himself* (1810); Nat Turner, *Confessions of Nat Turner* (1831); Moses Roper, *A Narrative of the Adventures and Escape of Moses Roper, from American Slavery* (1838); Solomon Northup, *Twelve Years a Slave. Narrative of Solomon Northup, a Citizen of New-York, Kidnapped in Washington City in 1841* (1853); Lunsford Lane, *Narrative of Lunsford Lane* (1842); Moses Grandy, *Narrative of the Life of Moses Grandy* (1843); George Horton, *Life of George M. Horton. The Colored Bard of North Carolina, from The Poetical Works of George M. Horton, the Colored Bard of North Carolina, to which is Prefixed the Life of the Author, written by Himself* (1845); and **William Wells Brown**, *Narrative of William Wells Brown, an American Slave* (1849).

For men, the slave narrative became a way to expose a nonthreatening **black masculinity** and to exert desire for autonomy while bringing to light the social and ethical complexities inherent in slavery. Men wrote of the horrors of the slave experience, the brutality of white masters, and the barbarous cruelty of white punishment and dehumanization of black men. For black men, the slave narrative became a compelling device in the fight for their right to humanity. But for male slaves, their masculinity, though assaulted through the machinations of slavery, was never in doubt. Rather, white men feared the perceived superior prowess of the black male. Male slave narratives presented a masculinity that met extreme adversity with spirit and manliness intact, though presented in a humble, intelligent, and nonthreatening way. But for female slaves, whites continually questioned their humanity and womanness. Slave women who undertook to write their narratives exhibited both a desire for autonomy and the struggle for affirmation of their very femininity.

The slave narrative became the most popular medium that female slaves adopted to voice their experience at the hands of white male masters. Male slave narrative authors tended to paint a picture of the helpless black woman who was resigned to her lot. But when African American female slaves penned their own stories, the horrific truth they divulged put to rest any previous portrayal of the romanticized weak and helpless female slave. **Harriet Jacobs**'s *Incidents in the Life of a Slave Girl* (1861) was the first published slave narrative written by a black woman. Jacobs's account reveals in disturbing detail the horrendous sexual abuse and oppression that many female slaves endured. Along with the sexual abuse by white owners, female slaves suffered the unconscionable sale of their children as well as numerous physical atrocities.

Whites, acting as ghostwriters, often transcribed some of the early female slave narratives. One of the earliest narratives, the first about a female slave, **Mary Prince**'s *The History of Mary Prince, a West Indian Slave* (1831), was transcribed by a white man, Thomas Pringle. Pringle describes Prince as somewhat disagreeable, temperamental, and easily angered, which is an instance of the white lens shaping reader perception of slavery and Prince's experiences. In her narrative, Prince relates tales of extreme abuse and humiliations against her by her white owners, in response to their perception of improper slave conduct or Mary "giving herself airs." The narrative of **Jarena Lee**, *The Life and Experience of Jarena Lee, A Coloured Lady, Giving an Account of Her Call to Preach the Gospel* (1836), was the first African American woman's spiritual narrative, and though Lee was not a slave (she was born to free parents), her spiritual experiences marked a new form of the women's slave narrative, one that illustrated the evils of slavery alongside the journey to spiritual awakening. The *Memoir of Old Elizabeth, a Coloured Woman* (1863) was unique in that ninety-seven-year-old Elizabeth's ghostwriter was also a black woman. Elizabeth's experiences as a slave mingle with her evangelical faith in a demonstration of how **Christianity** became a source of strength and comfort for female slaves. In her later years, Elizabeth was a minister of the gospel, believing herself divinely ordained, and she braved threats of imprisonment in her steadfast belief in preaching against the sin of slavery. The contradiction between Christian ideology and the practice of slavery became, for slaves like Elizabeth, a source of courage and empowerment in the struggle for an autonomous identity.

Slave narratives functioned as humanizing agents for African Americans in the face of white beastialization of blacks. For women, the struggle was twofold, as African American women were not viewed as *women* but rather as female animals. The acquisition of literacy by blacks allowed female slaves the means to construct for themselves both their humanity and their womanhood. Slave narratives functioned as a testament to the suffering endured by female slaves at the hands of male and female masters. The dramatic cruelty of white women toward black women is one arcane element of slavery that female slave narratives exposed. Female narratives also acted as a celebration of self, a validation of both black **motherhood** and black femininity, keenly captured by **Sojourner Truth**, who asked, "Ar'n't I a woman?" in 1851. Slave mothers were often forcibly separated from their children by slave owners who regularly sold black children, who were viewed as commodity much like horses or cattle. Slave women regularly witnessed the sale of their children, and the unimaginable emotional toll is clearly voiced in their narratives. For African American slave women the exercise of composing or reciting their narrative served as a luminous, yet powerful discourse that afforded them the freedom to claim their right to humanity.

See also Neo-Slave Narrative

Works About

Andrews, William L., ed. *Classic African American Women's Narratives.* New York: Oxford University Press, 2003.

——. *Six Women's Slave Narratives.* New York: Oxford University Press, 1988.

Andrews, William L., and Henry Louis Gates, Jr., eds. *The Civitas Anthology of African American Slave Narratives.* Washington, DC: Civitas/Counterpoint, 1999.

Sharpe, Jenny. *Ghosts of Slavery: A Literary Archaeology of Black Women's Lives.* Minneapolis: University of Minnesota Press, 2003.

Yetman, Norman R., ed. *When I Was a Slave: Memoirs from the Slave Narrative Collection.* Mineola, NY: Dover Publications, 2002.

Debbie Clare Olson

SLAVERY

Slavery has existed at various times and in diverse ways throughout **history**. It was practiced in Greece, Rome, Egypt, China, Japan, Korea, India, Europe, Africa, and other areas. In many cases, human beings were captured either through warfare or outright and forced to become slaves. Slavery was rarely voluntary and was the result of the strong exercising authority and dominion over the weak. The status of the slave in society was low and often involved treatment that was severe, cruel, and demeaning.

Some of the first black people who came to North America were not slaves but explorers. Some Africans, as well as others, came to the continent as indentured laborers and were freed after working for a specified number of years. However, chattel slavery was cheaper and more economically advantageous than other types of labor, and it eventually became institutionalized. From the mid-sixteenth to nineteenth centuries, millions of Africans were forcefully taken from their homes, held in dungeons, packed into ships, and sent off on the **Middle Passage**. Those who survived the arduous trip across the ocean were sold to white masters and were expected to lose their **identity** and past and completely subordinate themselves to their masters' wills.

A slave was viewed as a piece of property that was owned by the master. The slave usually had no rights, was restricted in moving about geographically, and had little input regarding the daily jobs to be performed.

Frequently the slave had no control over the placement of **family** members, including children. Thus, it was not uncommon for families to be split up and for fathers and/or mothers to be separated from their children. The most common type of slave was found in a household or **domestic** setting and usually worked in the **home** or outside in the fields. A slave was often treated like an animal and was completely subject to the master, who could punish and rebuke at will. Furthermore, the slave could not possess anything; technically, everything the slave had belonged to the master.

The master-slave relationship, in which one human being exerts power and authority over another human being, has come to represent a model for other relationships. For example, in a patriarchal society it can be viewed metaphorically as a paradigm for the relationship between men and women. In many civilizations, men have held the position of master of the home, even in relation to their own wives and daughters. For centuries, women in many cultures have been subject to their fathers and husbands. It can be said, therefore, that a female slave experiences double subordination. First, she is a woman who is expected to be subject to a man, and second, she is a slave, who is required to obey her master.

In most African societies, the patriarch was the head of the household, and women as daughters, wives, and mothers were subject to him. In this situation women experienced one level of servitude, yet it was one that included some respect, especially for mothers who brought forth and reared the new generation. However, when 10 to 11 million Africans were involuntarily taken from the home and sold into slavery, the women in particular experienced a second level of subjugation. They were no longer responsible to simply please a father or husband but were now also expected to **work** for a foreign master as well. Some women were born into this situation.

Young black girls on plantations in the **South** usually started to work at an earlier age than their male counterparts. Most frequently, they would begin by working completely or partially inside the house and would eventually be sent out to the fields. Girls were sometimes more industrious than boys and excelled at certain jobs, such as at picking cotton. Most slaves, both male and female, worked outside in the fields during their prime years. Some of the chores included planting, hoeing, and harvesting such crops as corn, peas, potatoes, turnips, wheat, rice, and cotton. Slaves would also prepare the land for planting, clean ditches and drains, work on roads and fences, and perform other miscellaneous jobs. Women who did not work outside were often employed in other capacities inside the home, serving as cooks, housekeepers, laundresses, seamstresses, and nurses. Slaves, despite their particular jobs, worked hard, long hours and were often exhausted after a day's labor. Women frequently returned to their cabins and performed additional tasks for their own families, such as cooking, washing, cleaning, sewing, knitting, **quilting**, and weaving. Their physical and mental health often suffered from overwork, and they frequently lacked the energy to nurture and interact extensively with their families and children.

Sunday, however, was a day of rest for both the slaveholder and the slave, which provided a break from the week's labor. Some masters also allowed slaves a day off for religious holidays, particularly Christmas. Although some slaves spent time catching up on personal chores during days of rest, many enjoyed the leisure time in various ways such as visiting with friends, dancing, singing, and telling stories. Through such interaction, the slave **community** provided strength to its members and helped provide relief from difficult and physically demanding burdens. Visiting with one another provided slaves the chance to articulate feelings, experiences, and challenges and to share in a common quest for emotional and physical survival.

Dancing and singing were a means of outwardly demonstrating inner frustrations. Slave dances were often less formal and controlled than those of the master (such as reels and minuets) and frequently included lustful **body** movements, with rhythmic footwork and somewhat wild motions of the arms and shoulders. Music also offered a sense of community and a means of expressing various experiences. Songs included details of their history, their daily lives, their dreams, and their fantasies. They sang of hard work, oppression, masters, slave patrollers, slave traders, as well as romance, sex, food, and **freedom**.

Slaves also told stories that not only perpetuated oral tradition but also passed on the wisdom of former generations. Although the stories provided rich entertainment, they also contained important messages and themes pertaining to survival and perseverance. There were tales of animal and slave tricksters, stories coded with lessons on life, tales explaining how things came to be, and stories of surviving in the briar patch of life. These stories were originally intended for oral transmission, and the tellers were often dramatic in their performances. A particular rendition often included nonverbal sounds, changes of volume from a whisper to a loud call, asides, and responses from the audience. Sometimes storytellers were competitive and attempted to outdo one another during a particular session. In some cases, a story might be started by one teller and completed by one or more subsequent tellers. Some of these tales were recorded and written. Two stories that deal specifically with women include "Why the Sister in Black Works Hardest" and "Why Women Always Take Advantage of Men."

Regarding male/female slave relationships, according to the slave codes, slaves could not be legally married. It was argued that a slave was a chattel, or thing, and chattels and things did not have the right to be married. Furthermore, the slave had no right to a legal contract and therefore could not be included in a marriage contract. However, in practice, many slaveholders in the United States encouraged marriage and child bearing among slaves and believed that a man who was happy with his wife and children was less likely to cause trouble or run away. Some masters encouraged and promoted sexual morality, while others did not interfere with the sexual habits of their slaves. It was not uncommon for enslaved women to give birth to children fathered by a variety of different men, both black and white. Some male slaves preferred to marry women from other plantations so they would not have to see their spouse beaten, ill-treated, or raped. However, most slaveholders made final decisions regarding the marriages of their slaves and often encouraged unions among slaves on their own plantations. The marriage ceremony was usually simple, and in some cases the couple jumped over a stick to become husband and wife. Other times the pair might simply receive the master's permission to live in the same cabin.

One of the great challenges experienced by many female slaves was being raped and sexually abused by the master, his sons, and/or other men of authority. Many white men considered female slaves to be property that could be used to fulfill their own physical lusts and desires. Although some men offered small gifts in return for their pleasure, slave women were often expected to offer themselves freely and willingly. Refusal to comply could result in a beating or some other type of punishment. Slave fathers and husbands had little control over the sexual mistreatment of their daughters and wives. Furthermore, the mistress of the home was often hurt and angry by her husband's philandering and frequently retaliated by punishing the female slave in subtle or even overt ways.

It was against slave codes to teach a slave to read or write, so most slaves were illiterate. Specific rules varied from state to state in this regard, but there was usually some type of fine imposed on anyone who aided a slave in receiving instruction. For example, in North Carolina, if a free Negro gave a slave a book or pamphlet or taught a slave to read and write, the punishment was thirty-nine lashes or imprisonment. When a white person was guilty of such violations, the fine was $200. Most slaveholders wanted slaves to remain uneducated and feared that increased **literacy** would cause problems and revolts on the plantation. Some masters believed that black slaves were incapable of academic learning. However, a small percentage of slaves received instruction in one way or another. For example, sometimes when a slave girl worked intimately with a slaveholder's daughter in the big house, she was exposed to books and writing. As the master's daughter was instructed in letters, she, in turn, would sometimes teach her favorite slave to read and write. Also, despite the code, some mistresses and daughters felt a responsibility to read the Bible to slaves and to include them in family prayers.

In addition to denying slaves the opportunity of becoming educated, the slave codes also refused them religious rights. The slave was viewed as a thing, not a being, and therefore in theory was not entitled to religious enlightenment. Furthermore, it was reasoned that **religion** was associated with the free agency of human beings, and slaves were not free agents. Basically, slaves were at the mercy of their owners, who could completely decline or allow them access to religious instruction and gatherings. In addition, the slaveholder could force his slaves to be exposed to religious teachings contrary to their own beliefs. In practice, many slaves were introduced to **Christianity** through camp meetings. The slaves in turn held their own services, where white preachers were frequently imitated. The black slave preacher was often intelligent, articulate, imaginative, and charismatic. He understood the plight and misery of the slaves and gave them hope in their times of trial and tribulation. However, since he was observed by whites, he also taught the slaves to be obedient to their masters because failure to do so could result in a whipping.

The struggles, challenges, and agonies experienced by some men and women in slavery gave rise to a powerful and historically significant literary form: the **slave narrative**. Some former slaves with sufficient education wrote about their experiences and trials. **Frederick Douglass**'s **autobiography**, titled *Narrative of the Life of Frederick Douglass, an American Slave* (1845), provides a rich and informative account of his life in slavery and of his successful escape. Another significant narrative is **Harriet Jacobs**'s *Incidents in the Life of a Slave Girl* (1861), which describes her life with a lustful and controlling master and her eventual escape to freedom. Writing a narrative provided former slaves the opportunity to reflect upon their past, to attempt to come to terms with it, to move forward in life, and to document and share their experiences with others.

The slave narrative provides a firsthand account of the challenges the writer faced to survive slavery. Jacobs penned one of the few extant memoirs by a female slave, and her account reflects some of the characteristics of slavery discussed above. For example, she was born a slave and lived in slavery twenty-seven years. Her parents were of light skin, were considered of mixed parentage, and were called **mulattoes**. Her maternal grandmother worked as a cook, wet nurse, and seamstress and performed miscellaneous other duties in the household of her master. Jacobs reiterates in her narrative that a slave is property and therefore cannot hold property. One of her early mistresses taught her to spell, read, and learn some passages from the Bible, which was a rare privilege for a slave. When Jacobs became the property of a new master, Dr. Flint, she was ordered to be obedient in all things, including **sexuality**, and her mistress, rather than helping her, reacted with fury and jealousy. In the narrative, Jacob relates a powerful account of her attempt to escape bondage and her ultimate success in this endeavor.

The theme of bondage and escape continues in some modern and contemporary **literature** today, in a genre called the **neo-slave narrative**. The works are predominantly fictional, often pay homage to oral traditions, and vary in emphasis and form. Some neo-slave narratives imitate the basic slave narrative, such as **Sherley Anne Williams**'s *Dessa Rose* (1986). Some represent a genealogical narrative, in which slavery is documented through the lives of a particular family and its **ancestors**, as can be seen in **J. California Cooper**'s *Family* (1991). There are also narratives that deal with the relationship between contemporary society and slavery and include a connection between the past and present, as in **Octavia Butler**'s *Kindred* (1979). In addition, one can find historical novels that take place during the times of slavery, such as **Barbara Chase-Riboud**'s *Sally Hemings* (1979). One common theme in the neo-slave narrative is the rejection of the obedient, complacent slave often seen in plantation romance works and the promotion of a slave society that was culturally vibrant.

Thus slavery has been the source of a literary tradition that continues in our current times. The oral tradition that was cultivated and enjoyed by slaves represented a means of dealing with the challenges of subjugation and oppression. The telling of colorful and vivid stories of human nature, survival, and freedom provided entertainment, encouragement, and education. Furthermore, the slave narrative became an invaluable record of personal experience and testimony that documents life from a slave's perspective. For many, the theme of slavery has been and continues to be a topic of intense interest, debate, and dialogue. The relationship of the master and slave is an ongoing topic in numerous cultures, contexts, and disciplines and is an integral part of the American literary tradition in general.

See also Folklore; Historical Fiction; Motherhood; Spirituals

Works About

"African-American Women." Online Archival Collections. Special Collections Library, Duke Univeristy. scriptorium.lib.duke.edu/collections/african-american-women.

Blassingame, John W. *The Slave Community: Plantation Life in the Antebellum South*. Rev. ed. New York: Oxford University Press, 1979.

Fleischner, Jennifer. *Mastering Slavery: Memory, Family, and Identity in Women's Slave Narratives*. New York: New York University Press, 1996.

Fox-Genovese, Elizabeth. *Within the Plantation Household: Black and White Women of the Old South*. Chapel Hill: University of North Carolina Press, 1988.

Gaspar, David Barry, and Darlene Clark Hine, eds. *More Than Chattel: Black Women and Slavery in the Americas*. Bloomington: Indiana University Press, 1996.

Goodell, William. *The American Slave Code in Theory and Practice*. 4th ed. New York: American and Foreign Anti-Slavery Society, 1853.

Morton, Patricia, ed. *Discovering the Women in Slavery: Emancipating Perspectives on the American Past*. Athens: University of Georgia Press, 1996.

Rawick, George P. *The American Slave: A Composite Autobiography*. Multiple volumes. Westport, CT: Greenwood Press, 1972. Additional Supplements, 1977, 1979.

Six Women's Slave Narratives. Introduction by William L. Andrews. New York: Oxford University Press, 1988.

Deborah Weagel

SMITH, ANNA DEAVERE (1950–)

Anna Deavere Smith was born in Baltimore, Maryland, in September 1950, the eldest of five children in the middle-class **family** of college-educated parents who worked in business and primary education. She received her B.A. (1971) from Beaver College (now Arcadia University) and her M.F.A. (1977) from the American Conservatory Theatre. Her awards include a MacArthur Foundation "Genius" Award in 1996, and she was nominated for

3

an APEX Award for her performance in *The American President* (1995). Her play *Fires in the Mirror: Crown Heights, Brooklyn, and Other Identities* won Obie and Drama Desk Awards, as did her work *Twilight: Los Angeles*, and she also was nominated for a Pulitzer Prize. In 2002, Smith was included in *Fortune* magazine's list of the fifty most powerful women in business.

Smith has taught at some of America's most prestigious institutions, including Carnegie-Mellon, New York University, University of Southern California, Yale, and Stanford. Her most influential theater experiments are *Fires in the Mirror* and *Twilight: Los Angeles*. In both she undertakes to explore real incidents where **race** has contributed to violent confrontation and retaliation. *Fires in the Mirror* is the result of extensive interviews with participants and observers of Jewish-black clashes in Crown Heights, Brooklyn, in 1991; *Twilight: Los Angeles* attempts the same exploration of the riot that followed in the wake of the infamous Rodney King verdict in 1992.

Performance is Smith's primary avenue of exploration regarding social issues and **identity**. Although she has appeared in a number of **film** and television projects, the stage is at the core of her work, which resists the American model of method acting (which universalizes and naturalizes all human experience) and embraces the Brechtian model of alienation (which demands cultural and historical contextualization). Smith's contribution to the practice of American theater has been through her technique of interview, selection, and performance in which she dramatizes issues and incidents of race, gender, and **class** through such radical and alienating choices as playing, for example, a Jewish man, using his own words, gestures, and inflections, in spite of the fact that she is a black woman. In this way, clearly, the actor does not merge with the character but rather performs a constructed identity external to the actor's own.

Works By

Aye Aye Aye I'm Integrated. American Place Theatre, New York, 1984.
Fires in the Mirror. Joseph Papp Public Theatre, New York, 1992.
From the Inside Looking In. Eureka Theatre, San Francisco, 1990.
House Arrest. Arena Stage, Washington, DC, 1997.
On Black Identity and Black Theatre. Crossroads Theatre, New Brunswick, NJ, 1990.
On the Road: A Search for American Character. Cleare Space, New York, 1983.
Piano. Institute on the Arts and Civic Dialogue, Harvard University, Cambridge, MA, 2000.
Talk to Me: Listening Between the Lines. New York: Random House, 2000.
Twilight: Los Angeles, 1992. Mark Taper Forum, Los Angeles, 1993.

Works About

Lyons, Charles R. "Anna Deavere Smith: Perspectives on Her Performance within the Context of Critical Theory." *Journal of Dramatic Theory and Criticism* 9.1 (Fall 1994): 43–66.

Modleski, Tania. "Doing Justice to the Subjects: Mimetic Art in a Multicultural Society: The Work of Anna Deavere Smith." *Female Subjects in Black and White: Race, Psychoanalysis, Feminism.* Ed. Elizabeth Abel, Barbara Christian, and Helene Moglen. Berkeley: University of California Press, 1997. 57–76.

Reinelt, Janelle. "Performing Race: Anna Deavere Smith's *Fires in the Mirror.*" *Modern Drama* 39.4 (1996): 609–617.

Thompson, Debby. "Is Race a Trope?: Anna Deavere Smith and the Question of Racial Performativity." *African American Review* 37.1 (Spring 2003): 127–138.

A. Mary Murphy

SONG OF SOLOMON

In **Toni Morrison**'s third novel, *Song of Solomon* (1977), she revises many of the themes explored in her first two: **identity**, **love**, marriage, **motherhood**, **sexuality**, traditional morality, **black masculinity**, and the effects of white racism within the black **community**. The story, set in Michigan and spanning the 1930s to the 1960s, follows Milkman Dead as he journeys to find lost gold and finds instead a sense of self, a flying tribe of Africans, and a **history** linking past to present.

Milkman's father, Macon Dead, embodies the novel's critique of both patriarchy and capitalism. In Macon's unforgiving resistance to change, his unwavering belief in the power of property, and his full investment in patriarchal values, he prefigures the character of Steward Morgan in Morrison's seventh novel, ***Paradise*** (1998). Like Steward, and Cholly Breedlove in Morrison's first novel ***The Bluest Eye*** (1970), Macon is also psychologically traumatized by white racism. As a child, he and his sister Pilate (whose mixed-race mother Sing dies in childbirth) witness two whites murder their father for his land. Macon retaliates by accumulating property, including his wife Ruth, daughter of the first black doctor in town. To the extent his marriage increases his financial assets, it also bolsters his self-respect and masculinity. However, after the first few years of marriage, Macon refrains from sexual relations, suspecting Ruth of an incestuous affection for her father. The stern and distant Macon becomes abusive, and when Ruth becomes pregnant with Milkman after she slips Macon an aphrodisiac, Macon forces her into several unsuccessful abortions. As his son grows to adulthood, however, Macon sees him as an extension of himself, encouraging Milkman to learn the **family** business of property ownership and accumulation.

Ruth Foster Dead, whose mother died in Ruth's childhood, has her own plans for her son: to be a doctor, like her father. Ruth copes with her husband's overt scorn, physical abuse, and sexual neglect by focusing on her roles as mother and daughter. In those roles, Ruth commits the novel's unspeakable act that Morrison readers come to expect. However, rather than one overwhelming act—the **rape** of a daughter, the murder of a child—Ruth engages in a string of only potentially horrific acts, thus allowing the novel to explore the line between love and desire. As a teenager, Ruth meets the kisses she demands from her father each night with ecstasy; she kneels in her slip at her father's deathbed to kiss his dead but still-beautiful hands; she nurses her son until his feet can touch the floor; she makes secret night visits to her father's grave. Each of these acts is an attempt to fill an absence Ruth feels in herself, one created by a lack of self-esteem and the overwhelming desire for a father's approval, a desire she displaces onto her son. Because Ruth understands her identity only in relationship to the men in her life—idealized daughter, rejected wife, devoted mother—she fails to achieve any sense of self-knowledge and remains as static as her husband.

Ruth's daughters are scarred by their mother's overt devotion to their brother; however, they are affected even more by their father's stern indifference. College educated and raised to hold themselves above local blacks, the sisters are also isolated from the community. Their lives, like their mother's, are sterile and delimited by a desire for their father's approval. Although Magdalene, called Lena, never escapes her father's house, she does finally stand up to her brother. Referencing an incident when Milkman accidentally urinated on her as a child—symbolic of the relationship between the Dead men and their women—Lena tells Milkman that he has pissed his last in their house. First Corinthians fares better than her sister, managing (in her forties) to attain both independence and a mature sexual relationship. Returning **home** from her **domestic** job—which she represents to her **class**-conscious mother as an amanuensis position—she meets Henry Porter, introduced earlier in the novel in an unsuccessful, drunken attempt at suicide. Armed with a shotgun in an attic window, Porter first demands something to "fuck" and then urinates over the heads of the female spectators below. However, Porter is ultimately revealed as a passionate and compassionate man, and although at first ashamed of him, Corinthians finally escapes her crippling desire for her father's approval and chooses mature love over a classist pride.

Unlike his sisters, Milkman has more access to the world outside their turbulent home. Despite his father's prohibition, he finds refuge in the home of his aunt Pilate. As does Morrison's **Sula** (1973), *Song of Solomon* offers readers an alternative to the patriarchal family. *Sula*'s matriarchal triad of Eva, Hannah, and Sula is revised in Pilate, Reba (short for Rebecca), and Hagar. The six-foot-tall Pilate, whose lack of a navel marks her as something greater than flesh, stands outside the community, refusing to submit to patriarchal authority or traditional morality. Her own moral integrity, however, is clear: She refuses to take the gold of the white man Macon (may have) killed as a teenager and carries what she believes to be his bones as her "inheritance." Pilate's only child, Reba, wins things without trying and gives away anything, including her **body**. Reminiscent of *Sula*'s Hannah, Reba's open celebration of sexuality and human contact exonerates her from a charge of immorality within the text, if not within her community.

Hagar is different from both Reba and Pilate, whom she calls Mama. Wild and spoiled, Hagar likes pretty things, one of which is her seventeen-year-old cousin Milkman. Although she is five years his senior, the two begin a sexual relationship that lasts fourteen years and ultimately consumes Hagar. Filled with a love that has grown into her one driving passion and spurred by the dispassionate "thank you" in his "Dear John" letter, Hagar attempts to kill Milkman. But unlike *Beloved*'s (1987) Sethe, Hagar is unable to kill what she loves and is left temporarily paralyzed, arms upraised in killing stroke. Indicative of his disdain for women, Milkman dismisses her with the suggestion that she drive the knife into her sexual organs. After days in a stupor followed by a frantic, fevered shopping spree to make herself beautiful for Milkman, Hagar dies. Her **death** embodies the dangers of a too-thick love that overwhelms individual female identity.

When Hagar dies, Milkman has already gone to seek his father's mythical abandoned gold. In Shalimar, Virginia, he finds instead comfort and rejuvenation in a woman named Sweet, a prostitute and the only woman in the novel unscarred by men. He then unravels his family's history, connecting past to present, **folklore** to family. The bones in Pilate's green bag are not the white man's but her father's. Milkman's great-grandfather, named alternately Solomon, Shalimar, or Sugarman, leapt off a cliff and flew back to Africa, leaving twenty-one children and a wife named Ryna who, like Hagar, could not live without the man she loved. Milkman's psychological and emotional growth on his somewhat Faulkneresque quest ultimately allows him to feel a compassionate responsibility for Hagar's death.

Pilate returns with Milkman to bury her father's bones on Solomon's Leap. She rises from her father's grave; a loud crack brings her back down. As she dies from a gunshot wound, a bird plucks from the grave the gold box earring that holds her name and flies away. The novel ends with Milkman's leap toward his friend Guitar, who is set on killing him, in a gesture of self-knowledge, surrender, celebration, and defiance. If Milkman spends the majority of his life working for his father, playing the role of the patriarch, he learns something vastly different at novel's end: that you can fly without leaving the ground.

See also Myth, Use of

Works About

Ashe, Bertram D. "'Why Don't He Like My Hair?': Constructing African-American Standards of Beauty in Toni Morrison's *Song of Solomon* and Zora Neale Hurston's *Their Eyes Were Watching God.*" *African American Review* 29.4 (Winter 1995): 579–592.

Buehrer, David. "American History X, Morrison's *Song of Solomon*, and the Psychological Intersections of Race, Class, and Place in Contemporary America." *Journal of Evolutionary Psychology* 25.1–2 (2004): 18–23.

Conner, Marc C. "From the Sublime to the Beautiful: The Aesthetic Progression of Toni Morrison." *The Aesthetics of Toni Morrison: Speaking the Unspeakable.* Ed. Marc C. Conner. Jackson: University Press of Mississippi, 2000. 49–76.

Furman, Jan, ed. *Toni Morrison's "Song of Solomon": A Casebook.* Oxford, England: Oxford University Press, 2003.

Murray, Rolland. "The Long Strut: *Song of Solomon* and the Emancipatory Limits of Black Patriarchy." *Callaloo* 22.1 (Winter 1999): 121–133.

Weems, Renita. " 'Artists without Art Form': A Look at One Black Woman's World of Unrevered Black Women." *Home Girls: A Black Feminist Anthology.* Ed. Barbara Smith. New Brunswick, NJ: Rutgers University Press, 2000.

Julie Cary Nerad

SOUTH, INFLUENCE OF THE

The first slave ship's landing at Jamestown in 1619 began an indelible link between African Americans and the South. Indeed, the legacy of **slavery** often overshadows any other considerations of African American connections to the South, although there are many. Much of the art, music, food, and culture associated with African Americans have roots in the South. Moreover, following the Civil War and Jim Crow period, the Great Migration to the North proved only temporary to many African Americans. Their return to the South as well as the preoccupation among many writers of color with the South as setting necessitate a consideration of its special influence upon African American women writers.

For African Americans the South represents a terrible duality; the worst experiences of African Americans occur in the birthplace of their major contributions to American culture. That duality is coterminous with the southern literary tradition. As southern authors wrote of the confrontation between a feminine landscape and a patriarchal governance, African American writers explored their existence in a region that denied them **identity** and value. As the marginalized Others in the South, African Americans moved to the North to leave behind the place tied to their oppression. In the wake of their return, a reshaping of their cultural **history** began. In effect, debates over issues like **passing** and **class** status became all but moot in the southern landscape—debates that began not in wealth and privilege but in division and poverty.

Inclusions to the modern southern canon include **Zora Neale Hurston**, **Richard Wright**, and **Ralph Ellison**—major literary figures already established within the African American tradition. Hurston's South, however, differs in tone from the one explored and chronicled by the men. Critics of southern **literature** who often dismiss that body of writing as a collection of racist prose oversimplify its themes and miss the importance in connecting the contributions of African Americans to the South. They also miss Hurston's Florida setting of Eatonville in *Their Eyes Were Watching God* (1937) and Joe Starks's transformation of Eatonville from its rural, agrarian inception to preindustrial town. Hurston's major novel as a work of southern literature seemed at first an oddity. However, more and more critics open themselves to consider the import of the novel's influence in southern literature in general and see the value of Hurston's anthropological background as she preserves language, customs, and social history of the South itself. Likewise, in *Seraph on the Suwanee* (1948), Hurston's chronicle of Arvay Henson, a Florida "cracker" devoid of self-**love**, the hierarchical relationship between the races becomes secondary to the experience of Jim Meserve's attempts to provide for his **family** through an industrialized mastery of nature. In contrast to the more popular and critically considered African American southern literature of Wright or Ellison, Hurston's writing falls into a more traditional thematic of encountering a changing landscape and its people's response to it.

Wright's *Uncle Tom's Children* (1938) and Ellison's *Invisible Man* (1952) offer the more popular notion of African Americans in the South and their tales of escape, alive or dead, from white persecution. While Ellison's unnamed narrator reaches his epiphany only after his migration north, he remains aware of his southern birthright and connection. Wright's characters encounter a dark and more violent South where physical **violence** is the accepted result of black and white encounters. The lynching of Bobo, for example, as seen from a distance by Big Boy in "Big Boy Leaves Home," plunges readers into a South that is sharply divided by color and ascribes a much different list of southern traits to the literature. Similarly, Wright's autobiographical essay "The Ethics of Living Jim Crow" (1940) reduces the South to a simplistically racist place. The larger gulf existing between Hurston and Wright in their political outlooks deepens when they are considered in a more broadly southern context. However, both authors are equally important when we consider how African American literature expands the view of southern literature.

Still, beyond Hurston's southern African American characters, few, if any, African American women writers use the South as setting within the literature of the 1940s through the 1960s, for they find little redemption within the landscape. Instead, theirs is an existence categorized by the cultivation of the same determination that slaves demonstrated in their escape plans of the 1800s to leave the South behind. The women novelists of the 1970s forward provide the most deliberate exploration of the South for African Americans. **Alice Walker**, **Toni Cade Bambara**, **Ntozake Shange**, **Paule Marshall**, and especially **Toni Morrison** explore the cultural and psychic landscape that the South remains to African Americans after more than a century of life there. Through their writing, the South becomes the great place of origin for African Americans. Due attention is paid to the cultural contributions made by African Americans to the region, and the resulting literature answers the oft-asked question on the future of southern letters in such a way as to give African American writing a primacy in a southern imagination that often takes Faulkner as synecdoche for its entire tradition. The African American presence in the South, long ignored or dismissed by white southern authors, fills out the region's literature and mandates a reconsideration of earlier texts in addition to a revision of traditional southern themes.

That impetus in African American southern literature to explore thought-fully rather than merely indict historical atrocities helps move both the southern and African American traditions forward. Though vestiges of the Old South continue to exist in areas where **race** hatred proliferates, the **fiction** of African Americans does not shy away from confrontation. Morrison's thought-provoking meditation on the murder of Emmett Till in *Song of Solomon* (1977), for instance, makes clear the geographic line bordering the backward and racist South from the rest of the country. The historicity of the event is indisputable—it remains as it occurs—but the questions of how one responds to such an event resound as Milkman Dead learns from Guitar Bains the responsibility to stand up to injustice. In that example, the South acts as an inclusive and othered body of white racists who collectively murder Emmett Till and strike a blow to the collective African American population. While in part through the trial that acquitted Till's killers did the idea that the South murdered him become known, contemporary women writers see more to the South today than its racist **stereotype**. One cannot forget Morrison's placement within *Beloved* (1987) of Paul D in Alfred, Georgia, and its depiction of slavery as such a warning that the past of the South still reverberates within a changed landscape.

The resulting confrontation of African American writers with white southern history suggests more **work** is needed, but not all of it entails an adversarial placement of African Americans within the South. For Shange's Indigo in *Sassafrass, Cypress & Indigo* (1982), the South is a positive part of her identity. Shange uses the image of **community** to show how despite Indigo's growing awareness of the patriarchal, white South's cultural oppression, she finds within her own culture rich means to progress and thrive. Through acts of **conjuring** and **healing**, Indigo maintains her connection to the people existing in a South, contrary to traditional notions. Likewise, Paule Marshall's Avey Johnson in *Praisesong for the Widow* (1983) recalls her great aunt Cuney's recitation of the triumphant return to Africa by the Ibos that reshapes the historical record of their mass-suicide. The South, for Avey Johnson, becomes the true connecting point for order in her life, due, in part, to the **memory** of Cuney and the associations with the Ibo spirit unifying the landscape. Outside of a racially disparate region, Shange's Indigo and Marshall's Cuney embody the best the South has to offer the African American. Such portrayals suggest that the influence of the South remains a vital part of African American literature due to its reentry into discourse by these female authors. The Old South was never intended by twentieth-century southern writers to be enshrined but rather seen as a tragic landscape; in contemporary African American women's writing it finds a deepened presence as those characters earlier consumed by the tragedy around them take control of that place and bring a sense of ownership to it in order to transform a once racist South into a territory worthy of reconsideration. Certainly, one moving from *The Color Purple*'s (1982) depiction of Celie as lacking wholeness to *The Salt Eater*'s (1980) healing of Velma Henry sees the scope of southern progress in a changed setting.

Today, the South remains a place of change. No longer relegated to a population of poor whites and poorer African Americans, the contemporary South of southern African American literature continues to expand and clarify the African American presence and contribution to the South throughout history. **Tina McElroy Ansa**'s *Baby of the Family* (1989) and **Randall Kenan**'s *A Visitation of Spirits* (1989) both illustrate an ongoing exploration of the spiritual dimensions brought to and cultivated in the South, as well as a reworking of the southern journey motif as inward and psychological over physical. Toni Morrison's *Love* (2003) shows the upper-class side of African Americans in the South through Bill Cosey's Florida hotel frequented by the elite African Americans who summered there; at the same time the novel shows the problematic idea of southern womanhood.

Further, African American women writers also enter into an intertextual dialogue with southern literary figures in order to amend and expand a traditionally white vision of blackness in the South. Morrison has noted William Faulkner's experimentation with race in *Absalom, Absalom!* (1936)—and indeed the question of color permeates much of his work; Dilsey Gibson in *The Sound and the Fury* (1929), Nancy Mannigoe in "That Evening Sun," and Joe Christmas in *Light in August* (1932) offer points of departure to further such consideration. The fugitive poets also find their vision of a patriarchal South corrected on one level of Morrison's *Paradise* (1998) when the novel shows that memory alone cannot govern a culture in the midst of change. Likewise, Alice Walker mentions Flannery O'Connor's work, alongside that of Faulkner, Carson McCullers, and Eudora Welty, as seemingly having a preoccupation with race in the South. Walker ultimately comes to see that O'Connor's work offers something beyond the question of color and finds value in its technique and construction.

Through correctives as well as cultural explorations, African American women writers continue to mine the South and find within it a place of great worth. The pulsing improvisations of **jazz**, the lamentations of **blues**, the healing properties of food and herbs, and the **spirituality** inside and out of southern African American churches all commingle into a flourishing tradition. As the gaze of women writers focuses on the South, memory retains its historical wrongs but approaches them in myriad ways in order to clarify and amplify the positive contributions of a triumphant people who left only to return and reclaim a land as their own.

Works About

Davis, Thadious. "Expanding the Limits: The Intersection of Race and Region." *Southern Literary Journal* 20 (Spring 1988): 3–11.

Harris, Trudier. *The Power of the Porch: The Storyteller's Craft in Zora Neale Hurston, Gloria Naylor, and Randall Kenan.* Athens: University of Georgia Press, 1996.

MacKethan, Lucinda. *Daughters of Time: Creating Woman's Voice in Southern Story.* Athens: University of Georgia Press, 1990.

Towner, Theresa M. *Faulkner on the Color Line: The Later Novels.* Jackson: University Press of Mississippi, 2000.

Yaeger, Patricia. *Dirt and Desire: Reconstructing Southern Women's Writing, 1930–1990.* Chicago: University of Chicago Press, 1999.

F. Gregory Stewart

SPENCER, ANNE (1882–1975)

One of the most remarkable and distinctive poets to emerge from the **Harlem Renaissance** was Anne Spencer. Spencer's complex and compelling blend of biblical, mythological, and botanical themes established her place as an important figure in African American **literature**.

Spencer was born Annie Bethel Bannister (later Scales) on a Virginia tobacco **plantation** on February 6, 1882, to Sarah Louise Scales Bannister and Joel Cephus, who owned a local saloon. She attended the Virginia Seminary and Normal School, graduating valedictorian in 1899 at the age of seventeen. She married her longtime sweetheart, Edward Alexander Spencer, on May 15, 1901. They had a son and two daughters. In 1924 Spencer began working as the librarian at the all-black Dunbar High School, Lynchburg, Virginia, a position she held for twenty years.

During her lifetime, Spencer published selected works in various periodicals and was anthologized frequently. To date, however, no collected volume of Spencer's work exists. Some of her most frequently anthologized poems include "At the Carnival," "White Things," "Before the Feast of Shushan," "Life-Long, Poor Browning," "Translation," "For Jim, Easter Eve," "Letter to my Sister," and "I Have a Friend." Her **poetry** was included in *The Book of American Negro Poetry*, edited by **James Weldon Johnson** (1922); *Caroling Dusk: An Anthology of Verse by Negro Poets*, edited by **Countee Cullen** (1927); *Ebony and Topaz: A Collectanea*, edited by **Charles Johnson** (1927); *The Poetry of the Negro, 1746–1970*, edited by **Langston Hughes** and Arna Bontemps (1949); as well as many other anthologies over the years.

Spencer's poetry reflects her nonconformist nature, and she was criticized at times for her lack of focus on racial issues. Instead, Spencer's poetry often comments on women's issues, particularly women's relationships with men. Spencer advocated women breaking away from patriarchal domination, and her poems frequently espouse a lyrical tartness that impels women to reject their subordination to men. Despite the criticism, however, Spencer was very active in civil rights and, with the help of James Weldon Johnson, was instrumental in founding the Lynchburg, Virginia, chapter of the NAACP (National Association for the Advancement of Colored People). When Spencer did write about racial conflict, she did it with such verve and ambiance that her images keenly capture the raw malevolence of American racism, as in "White Things." Spencer used her beloved garden, Edankraar, as the backdrop for many of her poems in which she frequently compared the resplendent array of nature with the social iniquitousness surrounding her. Spencer's verse reveals her experience and observations of the tumultuous world in which she asks: "is Life itself but many ways of thought?" ("Substitution"). And indeed, Spencer's extraordinary thoughts, offered in poetry, richly capture the authentic complexity of life itself.

Works By

Brown, Sterling, Arthur P. Davis, and Ulysses Lee, eds. *The Negro Caravan: Writings by American Negroes*. Salem, NH: Ayer Co., 1969.

Greene, J. Lee. *Time's Unfading Garden: Anne Spencer's Life and Poetry*. Baton Rouge: Louisiana University Press, 1977.

Stetson, Erlene, ed. *Black Sister: Poetry by Black American Women*. Bloomington: Indiana University Press, 1981.

Works About

Smith, Jessie Carney, ed. *Notable Black American Women*. Detroit: Gale Research, 1992.

Stetson, Erlene. "Anne Spencer." *CLA Journal* 21 (1978): 400–409.

Debbie Clare Olson

SPIRITUALITY

Spirituality is always a contested dimension of human experience, and this applies particularly to the context of African American and feminist studies. Spiritually based studies of faith, self, and **identity** can seem in this context to be counterproductive to notions both of African American cultures and feminism, since "spirituality" and religious topics can be read as necessarily restrictive, overladen with white-privileged notions of ethnicity and identity, archaic traditions, and oppressive reasonings that support a **history** of phallocentric white and culturally dominative patriarchial Judeo-Christian thought. Cultural materialist feminists argue that it is necessarily repressive and discriminatory. Yet "spirituality" may also have a liberatory and self-affirming agenda. Questions of spiritual identity and faith description are embedded deep within the texts of African American **literature**, and from their early beginnings in **slave narrative**, many feminists, female and male writers alike, have explored spiritual identity from an African American feminist perspective.

Maya Angelou, in her autobiographical series that begins with *I Know Why the Caged Bird Sings* (1970) speaks of spirituality and ethical formation in the context of a broadly Christian pathway toward redemption and self-acceptance, but within a context of narrative storytelling that seeks to dismantle the traditional distinction between respectable society and the social-religious outcast. Describing her time in a "whorehouse," she dismantles the socio-economic and moralistic divisions drawn between ideas of social "good," respectability, and those who have seemingly sinned. She also draws attention to the manner in which religious ideologies have sought to label, confine, and constrict black women's **sexuality** in a negative frame. Angelou and her contemporaries present an African American women's spirituality of growth, wholeness, and depth of experience. In this iconography even negative experiences of oppression, **violence**, and suffering can serve as a crucible for the development of better, wiser, stronger African American women, able to stand up on behalf of others and themselves, and capable of deep qualities of interpersonal understanding and compassion. Unlike many traditional religious definitions, African American feminist spirituality of this type sees little or no distinction between the political struggle for **freedom** and self-development, the self-determination of the human **body** (equalling sexual freedom), and the health of the human soul. Contemporary spiritualities of African American feminist identity, while famously diverse and hybrid, tend to share in this common affirmatory and liberatory theme.

Literary consideration of African American feminist spirituality has also led to a reassertion of normative, nonalienation "bedrock" theistic values. **Alice Walker** famously allows her heroine in *The Color Purple* (1982) to journey beyond what she sees as "God" as part of her journey toward feminist and lesbian maturity. The religious values she encounters as a child are dominating and oppressive. Her journey beyond them requires engagement with the wholeness of life and human values. At the same time she reencounters and reenvisages the biblical narratives, exploring the narratives of African and post-African history. This does not lead to atheism, however; instead, Celie moves toward a more holistic vision of world and woman-affirming spirituality at the end of the book. Enthusiastically received, this work has underscored attempts to integrate accounts of spiritual liberation into African American experience.

At the other extreme, **Toni Morrison**'s *Beloved* (1987) creates a transgressive spirituality of ghost-hood that challenges comfortable spiritualities of belonging that attempt to deny social reality or bury the crimes of the past. At the same time Morrison forcibly reminds American culture of an authentic African American spirituality of storytelling that encompasses **folklore**, **myth**, and supernatural belief systems. This inclusive pattern challenges simplistic readings of American spirituality that would base all African American experience around the stories of the Bible. Morrison also challenges comfortable renderings of African American spirituality that would seek to place it too simplistically within the redemptive and patriarchial model of faith tradition favored by the West. By contrast, **Lucille Clifton**'s poetic work intersperses civil rights and political themes with a lyrical mysticism that draws from other faith traditions such as Judaism (the Old Testament) and Hinduism. Texts such as these present spiritual narratives of passionate engagement with society while also representing the walk of the human journey in spiritually inspirational and positivistic terms.

Other faith signifiers have also played a strong role in the development of a distinctively African American feminist spirituality. Magic, retrospective diasporic perspectives, and even Islamic voices have all been part of the pattern as feminist women have sought to define themselves against a white male tradition of sympathetic **fiction** that has nonetheless laid boundaries of domination between African American men and women. The wisdom tradition of spirituality is also represented imaginatively in African American literature, the perspectives and standards of older women repeatedly shedding light on the **domestic** sphere and also on the perspectives of younger generations. Such women appear repeatedly in both adult and children's African American literature. The example of Mama in **Mildred Taylor's** *Roll of Thunder, Hear My Cry* (1976) is an example of **home**-based black feminist leadership, dispensing guidance and instruction on sensitive spiritual themes.

Yet women have always played a crucial social role in the politics of public spirituality, too. Slave narratives such as **Harriet Jacobs**'s *Incidents in the Life of a Slave Girl* (1861) explore spirituality from the paradigm of the oppressed, drawing upon religious and spiritual as well as humanistic values. Examples of African American women preachers such as Old Elizabeth are celebrated by feminist historians today. In the public sphere, black women leaders of faith such as Shakers **Rebecca Cox Jackson** and Rebecca Perot have been cited by writers like Alice Walker as forming part of a historical **womanist** spiritual tradition; they may be productively juxtaposed to male African Americans Martin Luther King and **Malcolm X**, to provide a more inclusive reading of women's spiritual leadership up to the present time.

In recent years many attempts have been made to separate spirituality and **religion**. Founded in 1966, Kwanzaa is an attempt to separate religious faith and spiritual-cultural practice. Rather, it attempts to incarnate an inherent spiritual quality—a respect for the transcendent, the sacred, the good, the right. A spiritual rather than a religious holiday, Kwanzaa is practiced by Muslims, Christians, black Hebrews, Jews, Buddhists, Bahai, and Hindus as well as those who follow the ancient traditions of Maat, Yoruba, Ashanti, Dogon, and others. "Cynth'ya lewis reed" is one of the many female poets who has written on this theme. Kwanzaa affirms a nondogmatic and inclusive African American cultural paradigm of spiritual life.

In recent years more attention has been paid to the boundary between spirituality and psychotherapy. Nancy Boyd-Franklin's *Black Families in Therapy: Understanding the African American Experience* explores issues of psychoanalysis and of spirituality. **Audre Lorde**'s **poetry** and life writing describes the development of a contemporary lesbian African American spirituality. She speaks particularly powerfully of the dangers of silence in colluding with oppression and of the need for an African American spirituality of woman to be clearly articulated and voiced. Jacqueline Amos's work in both art and poetry draws upon the politics of disability and spirituality while making a clearly voiced appeal to consider transcendence and spiritual identity as the birthright of all. With particular force she urges us to consider the need to turn to the spirits of traditional West African and Ghanaian spirituality, as well as the spiritual traditions present in America today.

The work of anthology making has been critical, too; a pattern of **quilting** and mutual collaboration among women of color reflects the postdiasporic experience of diffusion and reemergence and the encompassing of multiple perspectives. Gloria Wade-Gayles's *My Soul Is a Witness: Black American Women's Spirituality* may be considered a work of art in its own terms, so powerfully does it encompass so many African American women's spiritual perspectives.

Recent developments in theology have seen Alice Walker's womanist theory come to dominate African American spirituality studies. Like Angelou, Walker emphasizes how woman is connected to her spirituality not just through religious environment (often artificial and damaging) but through the rhythms of nature and her own body. This creates a strong demand for African American women's spirituality to be taken seriously, not just with regard to the ongoing struggle for women's rights but with regard to the increasingly serious situation with regard to environmental degradation. Cultural theorist Delores Williams argues that there is a symbiosis between disrespect for "people of the earth," such as African American women, and disrespect for the earth itself. Karen Baxter-Fletcher's prose and poetry provide eloquent meditation on this.

Other writers such as Morrison and **Ntozake Shange** have also created strong fictional role models for the development of a people-centered womanist theology. In recent years the development of diaspora studies has created a strand of interest in the African spiritual tradition and its effect upon African American women's themes. Cultural scholars Marsha Foster Boyd and Carolyn Stahl Bohler argue for a new ethic of collaboration between feminist and womanist political-spiritual thought. At the same time, emergent scholars such as Marla Frederick have begun to look at the politics of African American women's religious experience.

In such a vibrant environment there is clear cause for celebration. At one extreme, the spiritualities of women of color are being celebrated, published, and discussed as never before. However, women of color need also to guard and preserve their distinctive identities from too great an identification with dominant norms of contemporary American culture. The clear emergence of an accommodation and welcome reception for African American feminist literary spirituality in mainstream American culture is, however, a fact appropriately symbolized by Toni Morrison's Nobel Prize for Literature in 1993, the staggering popularity of Walker's *The Color Purple* in American universities, and the fact of Maya Angelou's presence at President William Clinton's inauguration ceremony in 1991.

See also Womanism

Works About

Baker, Houston A. *Workings of the Spirit: The Poetics of Afro-American Women's Writings.* Chicago: University of Chicago Press, 1991.

Boyd, Marsha Foster, and Carolyn Stahl Bohler. "Womanist-Feminist Alliances: Meeting on the Bridge." *Feminist and Womanist Pastoral Theology.* Ed. Bonny J. Miller McLemore and Brita L. Gill-Austern. Nashville: Abingdon, 1999.

Boyd-Franklin, Nancy. *Black Families in Therapy: Understanding the African American Experience.* New York: Guilford Press, 2003.

Grant, Jacquelyn, ed. *Perspectives on Womanist Theology.* Atlanta, GA: ITC Press, 1995.

Hull, Akasha Gloria. *Soul Talk: The New Spirituality of African American Women.* New York: Inner Traditions, 2002.

Kendrick, Dolores. *The Women of Plums: Poems in the Voices of Slave Women.* New York: Morrow, 1989.

Wade-Gayles, Gloria. *My Soul Is a Witness: Black American Women's Spirituality.* Boston: Beacon Press, 2002.

Kerry Kidd

SPIRITUALS

The musical heritage of African Americans that grew out of **slavery** is fraught with pain and struggle. African American slaves first created the sacred music known as "spirituals" in rural spaces of **plantation** slave communities. In opposition to slave owners who prohibited slave worship, African American slaves met in "praise houses" or "hush harbors," which might have been a cabin in the slave quarters or even a secluded area under a tree in the woods. These clandestine places became sacred spaces where slaves worshipped stealthily but freely. In *The Souls of Black Folk* (1903) W.E.B. Du Bois called spirituals "sorrow songs" that expressed the soul of African American slaves and were "not simply . . . the sole American music, but . . . the most beautiful expression of human experience born this side the seas" (7). Representing a worldview that sees little distinction between the sacred and the secular, enslaved African Americans sang spirituals to transcend their physical environment while laboring in plantation fields and homes as well as in worship meetings.

Spirituals are a uniquely African American art form in that they are grounded in oral traditions from West and Central African cultures and the American experience of slavery. Although many enslaved Africans adopted the tenets of **Christianity** for moral and spiritual guidance, their religious worship practices and beliefs reflected African rhythms, structures, and worldview. For instance, many spirituals are adaptations of Protestant lined-out hymns. This practice was particularly effective for African American oral culture. However, in the tradition of African American spirituals, the hymns are infused with distinctly African characteristics. These elements include call and response, which demonstrates a relationship between the leader and the group; complex rhythms with syncopation and polyrhythms of hand-clapping, foot-tapping, exclamations, and percussive sounds; often a five-note pentatonic scale that is African based as opposed to the eight-note scale found in much of European music; an existentialist religious outlook concerned with day-to-day lived experience; concreteness of abstractions such as **death** viewed in everyday experience; a lack of distance between God, Jesus, the Holy Spirit, and humans, which, though blasphemous by European standards, is reflective of an African worldview of gods not being "Sunday gods" but involved in day-to-day situations; and a philosophy in which feeling takes priority over meaning, that is, **religion** is not only a philosophical or theological system but an emotional experience.

The significance of the Africanist aspects of spirituals culminates in the yearning for liberation they express. The oral tradition of spirituals is embedded in the slave experience and the desire for **freedom** and deliverance—freedom to own the self, to worship and live autonomously, and deliverance from the dehumanizing practices of forced labor, **rape**, familial separations, and the arbitrary **violence** of slavery. American slave owners institutionalized illiteracy to prevent slaves from challenging their authority, on the premise that illiterates could not participate in legal or public discourses. Yet not only did many slaves gain **literacy**; in developing an active, powerful oral discourse, slaves appealed to a higher authority to challenge the very inhumane practices of and racist ideology supporting the slave institution. Some spirituals contain lyrics explicitly about freedom, like the traditional song "Oh Freedom." Other lyrics were more covert and implicit. Biblical stories of deliverance and freedom often were sung to express faith in ultimate justice. Often the complexity of these allusions rendered powerful speech acts of agency and insurgence. For example, "Mary Don You Weep" combines two seemingly disparate stories, Jesus's resurrection of Lazarus in the New Testament and the Old Testament's story of the Israelites' deliverance from Egyptian slavery—a situation commonly paralleled with African American enslavement—in a celebration of life (freedom) and triumph of justice (defeat of an enemy). The lyrics are consoling, celebratory, and subversive. Certain lines suggest slaves take an active role in the defeat of slavery. Just as Moses was empowered by God to destroy Pharaoh and his army, this spiritual calls enslaved African Americans to be agents in slavery's abolition.

With Emancipation, spirituals took on a more public presence that was less threatening to the American sociopolitical landscape. In 1871 at a fund-raising concert in Oberlin, Ohio, the Fisk Jubilee Singers of Fisk University stunned the audience with their rendition of spirituals. The economic success of the tour convinced Fisk, Hampton College, and other black colleges that concert choirs with a repertoire of spirituals was a lucrative enterprise to fund black higher education. These choirs adopted both the vocal tonalities of European classical choirs and physical deportment of restrained motion with members firmly holding their arms at their sides or clasping their hands. In this more rigid format spirituals—exuding the proper amount of dignity and restraint—became an acceptable musical genre to be performed before mainstream audiences, that is, both black and white middle-**class** Americans of the late Victorian era. Indeed many African Americans gained prominence on the concert stage singing spirituals. Artists such as Roland Hayes, Paul Robeson, and Marion Anderson garnered worldwide attention with spiritual repertoires. The success of black college choruses gave rise to many **community**-based groups called "jubilee quartets" who performed spirituals in the manner adopted by black college chorales.

As opposed to the more formal performance style of spirituals by black college choirs and stage performers, members of traditional black churches in the rural **South** continued to praise and worship in song and service with African aesthetics. These African American denominations were mostly Baptist, Methodist, and Pentecostal (including Holiness, Sanctified, and Church of God in Christ) churches.

The dawn of the new century saw the beginnings of the Great Migration of African Americans from rural southern areas to urban centers; African Americans responded to the constraints and opportunities of migration through sacred music. Unfortunately, the change in geography did not mean change in socioeconomic and political structures. In urban spaces African American migrants struggled with racial subjugation, economic deprivation, and housing discrimination. In spite of and to combat these circumstances, many migrants continued their worship and praise practices that sustained their mental and physical survival in the rural South. The genre of gospel music grew out of this location of sacred music. Concurrent with the development of **blues** and **jazz** in the secular world, the birth of gospel represents the continuum of cultural traditions in the quest for freedom and wholeness in a repressive environment.

Gospel was nurtured in African American folk churches, small storefront churches that functioned as the contemporary counterpart to the praise houses of the past. Founded on a theological philosophy that promoted emotional expressions and physical manifestations of the Holy Spirit as evidence of godliness, these churches permitted congregants to worship freely and praise vocally—in the forms of testimonials, prayers, and invocative interjections—and physically—through hand-clapping, foot-stomping, hand raising, body swaying, and dancing. Anthropologist **Zora Neale Hurston** argued that gospel originated in sanctified churches but migrated to other black church denominations. Primarily the domain of black Pentecostal denominations, gospel music founded on this form of worship is evidenced in black Baptist and Methodist churches as well.

In addition to bodily involvement, gospel songs were accompanied by musical instruments—guitars, pianos, tambourines, drums—played with lively rhythms and driving intensity. Often acknowledged as the "father of gospel music," Thomas A. Dorsey, in the late 1920s, combined the rhythms of blues and jazz with sacred lyrics and coined the term *gospel* to distinguish this music from the other sacred music. Although initially Dorsey, Mahalia Jackson, and other performers of gospel were rejected and often prohibited by some churches because of the blues and jazz influences, gospel became accepted as a more liberating musical form based on performance meant to inspire spiritual transcendence and individual wholeness. The musical representation of the original philosophy of Bishop Charles H. Mason, founder of the Church of God in Christ denomination, gospel embodied the whole of the African American experience in song and became a means of survival. This philosophy called for liberation themes as well as style. The tradition of spirituals as liberation texts that are multivalenced informed the new gospel musical form. For African Americans in the early twentieth century, freedom from slavery did not mean freedom from despair, and so the desire for deliverance from racial, economic, social, and political subjugation is evidenced in gospels for spiritual and communal uplift. Far from being the passive lamentations of a victimized people, gospel music functioned as an active oral discursive method of historiography and sociopolitical analysis. As such, black women gospel singers became arbiters empowered to interpret African American experience and American injustice in a biblical context of sin and redemption.

Across denominations, African American women have pioneered gospel through composing, singing, and performing. In the Church of God in Christ, Arizona Dranes's up-tempo piano-style gospel, mixing ragtime and barrelhouse forms, influenced other gospel and blues artists as varied as Sisters Ernestine Washington and Rosetta Tharpe and Aaron "T-Bone" Walker. Born blind in Dallas, Texas, Dranes was not only the first black woman religious soloist to record exclusively on "**race** records," she composed songs and traveled to churches throughout Texas, Tennessee, Oklahoma, and Missouri. More significant to the development of gospel, Lucie E. Campbell composed over 100 songs that have become standards in the repertoire of black religious institutions. Although Thomas A. Dorsey is often called the "father of gospel music," Campbell introduced Dorsey to the National Baptist Convention, USA, Inc., the world's largest organization of African American Christians with over 6 million members. Elected the music director of the Baptist Training Union Congress in 1916, Campbell commanded great influence on the National Baptist Convention's musical program from 1919 to 1962. Second in popularity only to Dorsey's "Precious Lord," the lyrics of her 1933 composition "He Understands; He'll Say, 'Well Done'" were so powerful that scores of individuals experienced religious conversion after hearing it performed by her protégé J. Robert Bradley. While Campbell preferred to write gospels in the classical choral tradition, later compositions like "Jesus Gave Me Water" (1946), recorded by Sam Cooke and the Soul Stirrers in 1951, and "In the Upper Room" (1947), recorded by Mahalia Jackson in 1952, have assured Campbell's place as, if not mother, at least midwife of gospel music.

Composing aside, African American women have made the greatest impact on gospel in the church through performance. As members of choirs, duet and quartet groups, and soloists, women performers wield authority and power, spiritually moving listeners not just to consider their souls in relation to eternity but—as gospel is born of African American experience—to recognize the assaults on both their bodies and souls caused by racial injustices. Achieving success and fame as no other gospel singer, male or female, has ever done (thirty years after her death, she is still roundly regarded as the greatest gospel singer), Mahalia Jackson epitomized black women gospel singers with the authority to move, if not mountains, then people to spiritual and social action. Gospel performance then allowed women to take center stage, so to speak, as voices inveighed against subjugation and discrimination and for liberation and social justice in America.

Works About

Du Bois, W.E.B. *The Souls of Black Folk*. 1903. New York: Dover, 1994.

Jackson, Joyce Marie. "The Changing Nature of Gospel Music: A Southern Case Study." *African American Review* 29.2 (1995): 185–200.

Peters, Erskine. *Lyrics of the Afro-American Spiritual: A Documentary Collection*. Westport, CT: Greenwood Press, 1993.

Reagon, Bernice Johnson. *We'll Understand It Better By and By: Pioneering African American Gospel Composers*. Washington, DC: Smithsonian Institution Press, 1992.

Shaw, Arnold. *Black Popular Music in America: From the Spirituals, Minstrels, and Ragtime to Soul, Disco, and Hip-hop*. New York: Schirmer Books, 1986.

Young, Alan. *Woke Me Up This Morning: Black Gospel Singers and the Gospel Life*. Jackson: University Press of Mississippi, 1997.

DoVeanna S. Fulton

STEREOTYPES

African American women's writing has been deeply influenced by the individual black women authors' experience of "double consciousness," the phenomenon described by W.E.B. Du Bois as the condition of being ever cognizant of the way that you are perceived by others outside of your specific **identity** category. For black women writers this double consciousness is characterized by an awareness of that set of stereotypes by which, in the popular imagination, African American womanhood is ordered and defined. Aware of those negative images and ideas disseminated about black female identity and the limits that they impose of black women's movement and status within the larger society, African American women writers have historically used their **literature** to respond to these stereotypes. Writing against and in the context of the widespread familiarity of mainstream American readers with negative icons like the **Mammy**, the **Jezebel**, the **Sapphire**, and (more recently) the Welfare Queen, the Matriarch, and the Strong

Black Woman, many African American women have created their fictional narratives, poems, autobiographical writings, and plays with an eye toward both the stereotypes themselves and challenging the second-class treatment of black women that they tacitly endorse.

The capacity of stereotypes to shape the perception and treatment of a given identity group is one of the elements of negative iconography referred to by the use of the term "controlling image." The concept of the controlling image, popularized by Patricia Hill Collins in her landmark study *Black Feminist Thought*, refers to the way that the widespread embrace of negative icons of black womanhood necessitates that black women first engage with and dismantle those stereotypes that define the ways that African American womanhood becomes visible in order to create a space for the depiction of black female subjects whose interests and characteristics contradict the popular understanding of the limits of African American women's identity. The notion of the controlling image also, however, points to some of the important and often detrimental ways that negative stereotypes can shape and define the treatment and status accorded to a given ethnic, racial, **class**, or gender group.

Black women's attention to the dismantling of negative stereotypes is most dramatically illustrated in the literature of the antebellum and post-Reconstruction periods, in which writers like **Harriet Jacobs**, **Harriet E. Wilson**, and **Frances E. W. Harper** created genteel, feminine, pious, often vulnerable African American women protagonists, as a counter to both the image of the Mammy, which depicted the black woman as a neuter or masculine figure, and the Jezebel stereotype, which depicted black women as oversexed seductresses, always already available for and desirous of penetration by any available males.

Stereotypes continue to shape and influence black women's writing even in the contemporary period. African American women's engagement with more recently evolved controlling images like the Matriarch, the Welfare Queen, and the Strong Black Woman are, however, less overt. African American women writers now rely on their representation of diverse black female experiences, none of which truly corresponds with any stereotype of black women's identity, to demonstrate their rejection of even the most deeply ingrained understanding of black female subjectivity. Indirectly destabilizing the foundation on which widely held stereotypes of black womanhood are embraced, while directly addressing the broad spectrum of experiences that comprise African American female subjectivity, works like **Ntozake Shange**'s *for colored girls who have considered suicide/when the rainbow is enuf* (1976), **Toni Morrison**'s *Sula* (1973), and **Lucille Clifton**'s *Blessing the Boats* (2000) exceed the narrow spaces left open in the popular imagination for black female visibility and, in so doing, necessitate a renegotiation and eventually a wholesale abandonment of the limits and expectations for African American women's identity.

See also Aunt Jemima

Works About

Collins, Patricia Hill. *Black Feminist Thought: Knowledge, Consciousness, and the Politics of Empowerment.* New York: Routledge, 1991.

Jewell, K. Sue. *From Mammy to Miss America and Beyond: Cultural Images and the Shaping of U.S. Social Policy.* New York: Routledge, 1993.

Ajuan Maria Mance

STEWART, MARIA (1803–1879)

Born Maria Miller in Hartford, Connecticut, to unknown parents who died before she was five, Maria Stewart spent her youth indentured to a minister's **family**. At age fifteen, she left the family and began a difficult existence as a **domestic** servant. She married black businessman James W. Stewart of Boston on August 10, 1826. Stewart, a veteran of the War of 1812, was several years her senior and quite successful. He introduced his new wife to Boston's lively free black **community**, which included his associate David Walker. When James Stewart died in 1829, though, Stewart was cheated out of her inheritance.

In the months following her husband's **death**, Walker was murdered and Stewart had a conversion experience. She began writing and, in 1831, published the pamphlet *Religion and the Pure Principles of Morality*, one of the earliest texts written by an African American woman. She published other essays soon after—in both pamphlet form and in the pages of William Lloyd Garrison's *Liberator*. In 1832, she gave her first public lecture, arguably the first such speech by a black woman; in 1833, hoping to build on her lectures in Boston, she moved to New York, where she became active in the Female Literary Society. In 1835, she published a collection of her speeches and essays, *Productions of Mrs. Maria W. Stewart*. Her work from this period focused on encouraging antislavery and antiracist activism within an evangelical Christian framework. She specifically emphasized the egalitarianism she saw within Christian thought and considered radical means to achieve that ideal; in this, her work's evocation of Walker's infamous *Appeal* (1829) is marked. But the lectures and essays are also important in both their early attention to women's rights—Stewart has often and rightly been characterized as an early feminist—and for their construction of an audience of northern free blacks.

Though she attended both the 1837 and the 1850 Women's Antislavery Conventions, she essentially left the public lectern for the classroom. For four decades after leaving Boston, she taught in a range of schools—first in and around New York City, then in Baltimore, and finally, in and after the Civil War, in Washington, D.C. Her final years were spent as the Matron of the Freedmen's Hospital in Washington; as she had throughout her life, she also continued to teach Sunday school.

It was while in Washington in 1879 that she finally filed and won a claim for her husband's naval service in the War of 1812; with the funds she received, she published an enlarged version of her collected works under the title *Meditations by Mrs. Maria W. Stewart* (1879).

Works By

Meditations by Mrs. Maria W. Stewart. Washington, DC: Printed for the Author, 1879.

Productions of Mrs. Maria W. Stewart. Boston: Friends of Freedom and Virtue [Garrison and Knapp], 1835.

Religion and the Pure Principles of Morality. Boston: Garrison and Knapp, 1831.

Works About

Moody, Joycelyn. *Sentimental Confessions: Spiritual Narratives of Nineteenth Century African American Women.* Athens: University of Georgia Press, 2003.

Peterson, Carla. *"Doers of the Word": African American Women Speakers and Writers in the North (1830–1880).* New Brunswick, NJ: Rutgers University Press, 1998.

Richardson, Marilyn. Introduction to *Maria W. Stewart, America's First Black Woman Political Writer: Essays and Speeches.* Bloomington: Indiana University Press, 1987.

Eric Gardner

STIGMATA

In her novel *Stigmata* (1998), **Phyllis Alesia Perry** uses fictional characters to document the painful sojourn of the black female in America, beginning with her capture in Africa. Perry provides a somewhat complex genealogy of three black women. However, the genealogical chart at the beginning of the book is helpful. Elizabeth, "Lizzie" DuBose, the principal character in the novel, serves as the presence of black womanhood dating back to the capture in Africa of her great-great-grandmother, Ayo, moving through succeeding generations to Ayo's daughter, Joy, Lizzie's great-grandmother; Joy's daughter Grace, Lizzie's grandmother; Grace's daughter Sarah, Lizzie's mother.

Significantly, Perry uses female **family** members to tell the story of the wounds, both emotional and physical, that were inflicted on the black female culture bearers who nurture and prepare succeeding females to carry on their collective presences. These females recognize no time boundaries or parameters; they suffer no such limitations. They, in this case, the African female who gives life to the African American female, are the "forever" people. Young Elizabeth "Lizzie" DuBose, the only child of the middle-**class**, educated Drs. John and Sarah DuBose, inherits the responsibility of connecting to the past, an incomplete journey started by her grandmother Grace who dies before Lizzie's birth. Grace writes to her sister Mary Nell in a letter dated 1945 instructing her to pass Grace's trunk and its content, which are the keys to the past, on to her granddaughter, the yet unborn Lizzie.

Even as a young person, Lizzie already possesses a strong, pervading sense of the past. At age fourteen, as she awaits the memorial services for Aunt Eva, her last remaining maternal great-aunt, Lizzie recalls, "I feel older than old." Later, as a young adult, she tells Father Tom Jay, a visiting priest who provides her with the true explanation of the cause of her suffering, that she "is an old soul in a young **body**."

Father Tom Jay, who is at once the church and Lizzie's liberator, explains that the wounds she experienced come as a result of her intense identification with the sufferings of her great-great-grandmother, Ayo. He further tells her of the Christians, early as well as recent, who identified so closely with the sufferings of Christ that they experienced body wounds that corresponded with the sites on which the crucified Christ was wounded, for instance, ankles, hands, feet, forehead, shoulders, and back. Similarly, Lizzie experienced Ayo's bleeding wounds caused by the chains that bound her hands and feet during the time she was kidnapped after she had strayed away from her mother in the village. Later on during the **Middle Passage**, the reopened sores on Ayo's wrists bleed profusely, as do Lizzie's wrists. The bloody beating of Ayo's back inflicted by her mistress, Miz Ward, left deep scars. Lizzie also bleeds from her deeply scarred back.

The arts play a major role in Lizzie's search for the past. Early on, the illiterate Ayo demands that her semiilliterate daughter Joy write Ayo's recall of the events, mostly cruel, that shaped her life. Actually, the writing is a memoir, dictated to a close, trusted recorder. One could think, justifiably so, that Joy's recording of her mother's **history** is a forerunner of the **slave narrative**. Just as in the slave narrative, Ayo establishes her **identity**. She dismisses the name Bessie, assigned to her by whites. In doing so she emerges as an African capable of doing what only she, symbolic of millions of Africans can do: tell her own story, establish her own identity, recognize her own history uncluttered and distorted by outside forces. "I am Ayo. I remember."

As Lizzie gets in touch with her past, she finds that the journal Dr. Brun insists that she keeps draws her one step toward the completion of her journey. The art of **quilting** and the quilt itself are of vital importance to Lizzie. Ayo quilts as she dictates her memoir to Joy. Lizzie, at age fourteen, starts the journey to the past, when she engulfs herself in Grace's quilt, pulling it up her chin. Lizzie and Sarah put the closing stitches on a quilt made in **memory** of Sarah's mother, Grace. As mother and daughter recognize that they are Ayo, Joy, Grace, the journey is completed.

Works About

Long, Lisa. "A Relative Pain: The Rape of History in Octavia Butler's *Kindred* and Phyllis Alesia Perry's *Stigmata*." *College English* 64.4 (March 2002): 459–483.

Sievers, Stefanie. "Embodied Memories–Sharable Stories? The Legacies of Slavery as a Problem of Representation in Phyllis Alesia Perry's *Stigmata.*" In *Monuments of the Black Atlantic: Slavery and Memory.* Ed. Joanne M. Braxton and Maria I. Diedrich. Münster, Germany: LIT, 2004.

Shirley Walker Moore

STREET, THE

Ann Petry's first novel, *The Street* (1946), follows the life of Lutie Johnson as she strives to transcend the constraints of **race, class**, and gender and seize a life of happiness for herself and her son. Earning Petry the Houghton Mifflin Literary Award and selling over a million copies–the first novel by a black woman to do so–*The Street* recasts a tradition of African American sociological realism introduced by **Richard Wright**'s *Native Son* (1940) within the context of black female experience. Its focus on the life of a black woman situates *The Street* within a tradition of **black feminism** and black feminist **literature** where African American women adapt established themes, popular tropes, and literary conventions to reflect experiences overwhelmingly informed, and often constrained, by race and gender.

Fair-skinned, hardworking, and well-educated Lutie moves from Long Island to Connecticut to **work** as a maid for the Chandler **family**. While coping with her employers' improprieties, she learns that her husband, who takes care of their son Bud, and to whom she has been sending money, has a mistress. After divorcing her husband, Lutie takes custody of her son and moves to Harlem with the hope that life there will be much improved.

Lutie soon learns that life on 116th Street in Harlem is too harsh to nurture her seeds of hope. The American dream Lutie pursues is made elusive by institutionalized values that she had no hand in fashioning and is powerless against dismantling. Overwhelmed by **violence**, racism, and sexism, Lutie's story, while depressing to many, reads more like a **blues** song than a suicide note. In the tradition of **Harriet Jacobs** who, in *Incidents in the Life of a Slave Girl* (1861), placed **freedom** over marriage, and **Gwendolyn Brooks**'s poetic rendering of the otherwise simple life of Maud Martha, Lutie Johnson lives on to sing her song. Like the blues woman who sings the melody of her "brutal experience," Petry, however sorrowfully, gives voice to Lutie's song of transcendence. Lutie's transcendence comes through her survival, albeit brutal and horrific, not from her "success." Where rugged individualism, financial prosperity, and social success define classic white, male, mainstream versions of the American dream, Petry suggests that for black women who face race, sex, class, and gender oppressions in the same institutions from which they are expected to find prosperity, survival supersedes success. By the end of the novel, although Bud has turned to crime and his mother to murder, Lutie nevertheless departs for Chicago ready to begin again.

Works About

Brody, Jennifer DeVere. "Effaced into Flesh: Black Women's Subjectivity." *Genders* 24 (1996): 184–206.

Hicks, Heather. " 'This Strange Communion': Surveillance and Spectatorship in Ann Petry's *The Street*." *African American Review* 37.1 (Spring 2003): 21–37.

Shanna Greene Benjamin

SULA

Toni Morrison's second novel *Sula* (1973) is set in the "bottom of heaven," the black **community** perched in the hills above Medallion, Ohio, and spans five decades, from 1919 to 1965. The novel follows the divergent paths of two girlhood friends, Sula Peace and Nel Wright, recounting both the difficulties of living outside of community and the dangers of living within it. The novel also explores various representations of **motherhood**, each marked by alienation, dysfunction, and its own form of **love**.

Nel Wright is the daughter of an obsessively respectable woman who has disowned her own mother, a New Orleans Creole prostitute. Journeying to her great-grandmother's funeral, Nel is repulsed by her mother's submission to a white train conductor. The trauma of her excursion into the white-dominated world extinguishes Nel's desire to leave Medallion ever again; however, the nascent separation from her mother provides a sense of individuality that empowers Nel to befriend Sula Peace.

Sula's disorderly **home** life is set in distinct contrast to the sterility and stability of Nel's. While Nel's mother (and eventually Nel herself) embodies the community's traditional morality in her roles as wife and mother, Sula's mother, Hannah, exudes an open **sexuality** that delights the community's men and confounds its women. Sula's grandmother, Eva, who reportedly sacrificed a leg for enough money to support her children, presides over the Peace home, a rambling and anything-but-peaceful maternal space that prefigures *Beloved*'s (1987) 124 Bluestone: It shelters the dispossessed, the newly married, and the un-homed. But as in *Beloved*, the house is an uncertain refuge: After Eva's son Plum returns from the war strung out on heroin, she douses him with kerosene and lights him on fire so that he can die like a man. As in other Morrison novels, an act of **violence** serves in the perpetrator's eyes as a form of love, protection, and a way to regain some lost thing, here her son's **black masculinity**, independence, and selfhood. Later, however, Eva sees judgment upon her when Hannah catches fire while burning leaves. Eva throws herself from a third-story window but cannot save her daughter. Pervaded by a distant sense of satisfaction, Sula mutely witnesses her mother's **death**.

Sula's emotional distance from her mother crystallizes earlier when she overhears Hannah confess that she loves but does not like her. The declaration—heard by the young girl as a denunciation—is followed by Sula's accidental murder of a boy named Chicken Little, a death Nel mutely witnesses. The calm control Nel shows at Chicken's death is matched only by Sula's fierce devotion; she slices off the tip of a finger to show four white bullies the lengths she will go to in order to protect herself and her friend.

On Nel's wedding day, Sula leaves town, returning ten years later in 1937 with a plague of robins, a college degree, and an open sexuality that resembles her mother's. Sula sleeps with any man she wants, but unlike her mother, she subsequently spurns her conquests. The women who could at least accept Hannah's sexual attentions as a compliment to their men feel Sula's scorn as a judgment upon themselves. The birthmark on Sula's eyelid, seen as a rose, a snake, a fish, represents to the community an evil that makes their own lives cleaner, purer, surer. Nel, too, condemns her girlhood friend after Jude, her husband and the father of her two children, becomes one of Sula's men. Nel cannot forgive Sula for the failure of her marriage, and Sula cannot understand Nel's possessiveness. To Sula, sex is disconnected from emotion, a disembodied act of the **body** that allows her to feel a sorrow unattainable through any other means. Not until Sula begins a sexual relationship with Albert Jacks (Ajax), a man ten years her senior, does she begin to understand Nel's possessiveness. But at her first signs of nesting, Ajax leaves, abandoning Sula to a self that now understands a difference between loneliness and being alone.

By 1940, Sula is dying. During Nel's last visit to her childhood friend, she articulates the crux of the community's resentment. Sula cannot just live like a man: independent, free, playing sexual havoc. However, rejecting traditional concepts of gendered and raced morality, Sula suggests that being a colored woman and being a man are no different and that the only difference between her and other women is what they do on the way to dying. In this alternate configuration of morality, Sula suggests that it was she, not Nel, who was the "good" one all along. Sula dies, comforted by the finality and security of Eva's boarded-up bedroom window.

Twenty-five years later, after being confused for Sula by an ailing Eva Peace, Nel finally refigures and understands her own pervasive sense of loss: Jude came between her and Sula. As in Morrison's eighth novel *Love* (2003), the bond between women, forged in preadolescence, ultimately overrides the mature and restrictive sexual relationship between husband and wife. Although *Sula* is about the relationships between women—especially girl-friendships and different ways of mother love—it is as much an exploration of self and other, love and sorrow, independence and interdependence within the black community.

Works About

Bakerman, Jane S. "Failures of Love: Female Initiation in the Novels of Toni Morrison." *American Literature: A Journal of Literary History, Criticism, and Bibliography* 52.4 (January 1981): 541–563.

Bleich, David. "What Literature Is 'Ours'?" In *Reading Sites: Social Difference and Reader Response*. Ed. Patrocinio P. Schweickart and Elizabeth A. Flynn. New York: Modern Language Association of America, 2004. 286–313.

Iyasere, Solomon O., and Marla W. Iyasere, eds. *Understanding Toni Morrison's "Beloved" and "Sula": Selected Essays and Criticisms of the Works by the Nobel Prize-Winning Author*. Troy, NY: Whitston, 2000.

Mayberry, Susan Neal. "Something Other Than a Family Quarrel: The Beautiful Boys in Morrison's *Sula*." *African American Review* 37.4 (Winter 2003): 517–533.

Rand, Lizabeth A. "'We All That's Left': Identity Formation and the Relationship between Eva and Sula Peace." *CLA Journal* 44.3 (March 2001): 341–349.

Weems, Renita. "'Artists without Art Form': A Look at One Black Woman's World of Unrevered Black Women." *Home Girls: A Black Feminist Anthology*. Ed. Barbara Smith. New Brunswick, NJ: Rutgers University Press, 2000. 94–105.

Julie Cary Nerad

SYMPTOMATIC

Danzy Senna is interested in the claustrophobia of **identity** and **race** and in relationships that degenerate from comforting to smothering. In her psychological thriller *Symptomatic* (2004), Senna focuses on two women of mixed race who find themselves in a bizarre, somewhat codependent, and tumultuous friendship based on their feelings of estrangement in a divided black and white world.

Unlike *Caucasia* (1998), the characters are adults, the protagonist (and unnamed first-person narrator) fresh out of college, and the antagonist a middle-aged coworker who, we eventually discover, has multiple identities. We first know her as Greta but later learn that she is also Vera and that her adoption of identities is not limited to these two. Senna describes her nameless narrator as a weak character, someone whom others project onto, and who is as yet unformed. She is such not because of her femaleness but because of her racelessness.

The narrator has moved to New York City to accept a fellowship at a magazine when she meets Andrew on the subway. The two quickly become lovers and are soon cohabitating, not through any real desire on the narrator's part but rather out of her desperation to escape residence at a dilapidated women's boardinghouse. Andrew represents the preparatory school world of wealthy white racists. When the protagonist reluctantly attends a party with Andrew's school friends, a game turns to bigotry for humor, and she retreats to the bathroom where, oddly, she falls asleep.

Enter jaded, bitter, and unstable Greta. Greta aids the narrator in securing a rent-controlled sublet belonging to Vera, whom Greta reports has fled the country, and thus begins their bizarre symbiotic relationship. The narrator leaves Andrew and lives at Vera's, and much of the book develops the odd relationship she shares with Greta. Greta is half full of **love** and half full of hate for her "twin." She swings between glorification and loathing of the narrator, who eventually begins to suffer from the smothering nature of their relationship, while working carefully to escape Greta's grasp.

When given an opportunity to write a piece for the magazine, the narrator is confronted with the black and seemingly bigoted artist Ivers Greene. He does not seem to see her as black enough, as he asks if she is a "quadroon." He then asks whether she pronounces an epithet in "proper" English or in "black" English. The narrator is offended, curbing the interview, and exiting abruptly. Strangely, a romance is born.

The novel takes a dramatic turn when Greta is exposed as Vera, the sublet is revealed as having been her apartment all along, and Greta, the frightening doppelgänger, turns violent.

The book addresses many of the same themes as *Caucasia*: identity, mixed race, "twin" relationships, prejudice, and **violence**. Senna continues to tackle the dark issue of "**passing**" in America and in the process exposes something far darker: how such lack of identity, such namelessness, can lead to compliance or submission rather than resistance and strength.

Works About

"First Person Singular Danzy Senna." *Essence* 35.3 (July 2004): 126.
Milian Arias, Claudia. "An Interview with Danzy Senna." *Callaloo: A Journal of African-American and African Arts and Letters* 25.2 (Spring 2002): 447–452.
Stuhr, Rebecca. *Symptomatic. Library Journal* 129.7 (April 15, 2004): 126.
Symptomatic. Kirkus Reviews 72.5 (March 1, 2004): 200.

Deirdre Fagan

 **T**

TAR BABY

Toni Morrison's fourth novel, *Tar Baby* (1981), is set in the 1970s at the villa L'Arbe de le Croix on the Isle de Chevaliers, a Caribbean island that, according to **folklore**, made slaves go blind when they saw it. The Americanized isle is juxtaposed with the Caribbean town Queen of France, the rural black town of Eloe, Florida, and the urban metropolises of New York and Paris. The island itself is a microcosmic representation—a sociological greenhouse—of the complex interconnectedness of **race**, gender, **class**, nation, and **identity**. *Tar Baby* also explores the deep, delicate, and difficult relationship between blacks and whites and how that culturally articulated racial division affects individual identity.

Throughout the novel, Jadine Childs struggles with what it means to be a black woman in a racist, patriarchal, classist world and which of the three—race, gender, or class—forms the core of her identity. Her emotional paralysis stems from an inability to reconcile her disparate identities: Jade is a successful African American model with an art **history** degree from the Sorbonne; Jadine is an orphaned black girl from a working-class **family**. The novel opens with Jade already anxious that her white suitor, Ryk, loves only her exoticized blackness, but her repressed anxiety over her identity only fully surfaces when, in a Parisian market, Jade encounters a dark-skinned African woman in a bright yellow dress who looks at her and spits. The woman's disdain sends Jadine to L'Arbe de la Croix less for the advice of the aunt and uncle who raised her than for some temporary escape from her own psychological confusion over her racial identity and responsibility.

Jadine's position at L'Arbe de le Croix, the **home** of the white Valerian and Margaret Street, encapsulates her liminality. Jadine is the niece of Sydney and Ondine Childs, who have been the Streets' primary servants for over thirty years. She is also serving as a paid companion to Margaret through the Christmas holidays and is further indebted to the Streets for financing her education. However, rather than sleeping and eating with her family in the servants' quarters, the pampered Jade sleeps upstairs in a guest room and eats with the Streets.

Jade feels safe in her retreat until the unexpected intrusion of the nomadic Son Green, a black man who, after a dishonorable discharge, returned to his hometown of Eloe and killed his wife Cheyenne when he found her having sex with a thirteen-year-old boy. Although Son is initially an intruder in the Street household, he soon becomes a guest, much to the Childs' dismay. Sydney and Ondine represent an older generation of African Americans, linked by profession to **slavery** but by pride to financially stable blacks who perpetuated their own sense of classist superiority. They are self-proclaimed "Philadelphia Negroes," always proper and perfect in their service and unwilling to recognize a shared heritage with Son or the novel's diasporic people. Jade, too, initially treats Son with disdain; however, she is also forcefully attracted to him.

The novel's crisis comes at the Christmas dinner Margaret cooks and their son Michael does not come to, the one dinner where black and white families sit down together to eat. After a dispute between the Streets and the Childs over who controls the hired help, Ondine confesses the secret she has kept for almost three decades: Margaret physically abused her son Michael. Thus Margaret commits the morally reprehensible act that is common in Morrison's fiction. Although direct culpability lies with Margaret (who suffers from guilt-induced mental lapses), the text also exposes the other characters' complicity. Valerian ignored clear signs of abuse to maintain the illusion of himself as loving father, and Ondine failed to expose the abuse for economic security; she feared losing her position.

In the Streets' dysfunctional marriage and the abuse of Michael, the text further exposes the corrosive pressures of a gendered class system on individual relationships: Margaret was a poor, ignorant girl married just out of high school and just off the **beauty**-queen float. Valerian was the Philadelphia candy king. Marking Margaret's lack of education and youth as significant liabilities, the rich women in her husband's set tell her that she should "get to **work** fast" (i.e., become pregnant). **Motherhood** is here understood as the primary way to maintain a higher class status for an uneducated woman. Margaret takes the advice but, unready for motherhood, begins to abuse the son she also idealizes; as Ondine explains, Margaret was hurting Valerian's baby, not her own. Valerian's horror over his wife's behavior and his own blindness to the abuse drives him into a mental feebleness that Margaret and the Childs promptly capitalize on by assuming power over him.

The explosive dinner also facilitates the consummation of Jadine and Son's relationship. Although the Childs disapprove of their niece marrying a white man, they disapprove more of her relationship with Son: Here, class trumps race. The pair flees to New York, where they spend a blissful few months replete with sexual and emotional intimacy. However, when they visit Eloe, the **community**'s strict moral code demands they sleep in separate houses. In the home of Aunt Rosa, who calls her "daughter," Jade is haunted by all the women in her life, specters who surround the bed, their breasts exposed. Her horror at their silent demand is linked to her confusion over her own identity. She recognizes that she and Son are both black but believes they are from disparate worlds, divided by class and defined by gender. Her objectification of the people of Eloe through the lens of her camera, however, merely mimics the objectification of her own black female **body** through the photographer's lens in Europe. The text uses photographs—the magazine image of Jade as the bronze Venus and the black-and-whites of the citizens of Eloe—to illustrate how people frame cultural difference through their own objectifying gazes. After Jade and Son return to New York, their relationship quickly degenerates into one of abuse interspersed with raw **sexuality**. Jade finally leaves Son when she recognizes in their relationship what she foreswore as a child: a pack of dogs copulating with a bitch in heat.

During Jade's stop at the Isle de la Chevalier on route to Paris, the novel's discussion of what it means to be a black woman takes center stage. Ondine tells her niece that she has to learn to be a daughter first before she can be a wife, mother, or any kind of woman. But Jade hears in her aunt's words not only the echo of Aunt Rosa's "daughter" but also a plea for her to "mother" them in their old age, a shackling to a soldier-ant way of life that demands hard labor, sacrifice, and no dreams, as well as an identity limited by race, class, and gender.

The novel ends without clear resolution for either Jadine or Son, who pursues her. Thérèse, the blind, second-sighted woman, rows Son to the Isle de Chevaliers and urges him to choose the blind and naked ghost men who ride the hills and to forget Jade, who has lost her ancient properties. In the novel's closing lines, the reader leaves Son, after language indicative of a symbolic rebirth, running lickety-split toward the trees. Jade returns to Paris, perhaps as divided as she is at novel's beginning, perhaps ready to face all that haunted her: the women in her dreams, the leashed and straining dogs, her own self-doubts. The novel ultimately refrains from articulating a single definition of black womanhood or offering any wax wings to escape the intricate maze of race, gender, class, nation, and identity.

Works About

Duvall, John N. "Descent in the 'House of Chloe': Race, Rape, and Identity in Toni Morrison's *Tar Baby*." *Contemporary Literature* 38.2 (Summer 1997): 325–349.

Fultz, Lucille P. "To Make Herself: Mother-Daughter Conflicts in Toni Morrison's *Sula* and *Tar Baby*." *Women of Color: Mother-Daughter Relationships in 20th Century Literature.* Ed. Elizabeth Brown-Guillory. Austin: University of Texas Press, 1996. 228–243.

Johnson, Cheryl Lynn. "A Womanist Way of Speaking: An Analysis of Language in Alice Walker's *The Color Purple*, Toni Morrison's *Tar Baby*, and Gloria Naylor's *Women of Brewster Place*." *The Critical Response to Gloria Naylor*. Ed. Sharon Felton and Michelle C. Loris. Westport, CT: Greenwood Press, 1997. 23–26.

Mahaffey, Paul. "Rethinking Biracial Female Sexuality in Toni Morrison's *Tar Baby*." *Proteus: A Journal of Ideas* 21.2 (2004): 38–42.

Moffitt, Letitia. "Finding the Door: Vision/Revision and Stereotype in Toni Morrison's *Tar Baby*." *Critique: Studies in Contemporary Fiction* 46.1 (2004): 12–26.

O'Reilly, Andrea. "Maternal Conceptions in Toni Morrison's *The Bluest Eye* and *Tar Baby*: 'A Woman Has to Be a Daughter Before She Can Be Any Kind of Woman.'" *This Giving Birth: Pregnancy and Childbirth in American Women's Writing*. Ed. Julie Tharp and Susan MacCallum-Whitcomb. Bowling Green, OH: Bowling Green University Popular Press, 2000. 83–102.

Otten, Terry. "The Crime of Innocence in Toni Morrison's *Tar Baby*." *Studies in American Fiction* 14.2 (Autumn 1986): 153–164.

Rayson, Ann. "Foreign Exotic or Domestic Drudge? The African-American Woman in *Quicksand* and *Tar Baby*." *Constructions and Confrontations: Changing Representations of Women and Feminisms, East and West: Selected Essays*. Ed. Cristina Bacchilega and Cornelia N. Moore. Honolulu: University of Hawaii Press, 1996. 182–193.

Julie Cary Nerad

TATE, ELEANORA E. (1948–   )

Eleanora Tate was born in Canton, Missouri, where she experienced segregation during her early years. She graduated from Drake University in 1973, worked in journalism and public relations, and in 1981 won a fellowship in children's **literature** for the Bread Loaf Writers Conference. She lives in Morehead City, North Carolina, and speaks frequently about **children's and young adult literature** at schools, public libraries, and universities. Her books for middle-grade children deal with complicated issues including the importance of racial **identity**, understanding and appreciating black **history** and culture, and positive images of black **family** relationships, especially between fathers and daughters. She also discusses the importance of making the best of situations one cannot change. Tate's young heroines and their struggles are engaging and realistic, so the stories avoid the didacticism some of her themes imply.

Her first novel, *Just an Overnight Guest* (1980), set in small-town Missouri, deals with a nine-year-old's resentment when her parents take in an abused child who exhibits abusive behavior. Her loving father helps Margie accept the situation and take responsibility for the girl. A **film** version of the book was aired on *Nickelodeon* and *Wonderworks*. The sequel, *Front Porch Stories at the One-Room School* (1992), concerns the stories Margie's father tells outside the abandoned one-room school about the **community** and its history, which lead the abused girl to tell her own sad story.

Three other novels concern a loving South Carolina family. *The Secret of Gumbo Grove* (1987) is about an eleven-year-old unhappy about her teacher telling the class that blacks had never done anything important in their coastal resort town. An elderly lady challenges Raisin Stackhouse to restore an abandoned church cemetery, and the curious history lover learns that the city's founder, a black man, is buried there and that the reason the community does not talk about its history is its sorrow about the segregated past and the fear stirring up white resentment. Feisty Raisin eventually sees her oral history tapes become a source of pride to her community. *Thank you, Dr. Martin Luther King, Jr.!* (1990) discusses the sensitive issue of skin color as Mary Elouise's white teacher and classmates disparage black history and show black people as victims. Mary Elouise also envies a popular white classmate and prefers her white dolls over her black ones. Through the encouragement of a visiting black storyteller, she learns to have pride in her heritage and produces a school play about black history. *A Blessing in Disguise* (1995) portrays Zambia, a twelve-year-old who lives with her loving and strict aunt and uncle but glamorizes her absent drug-dealing father. When she sees firsthand what drugs and crime do to a community, she joins the battle against them. Zambia also develops a realistic attitude toward her father. In Tate's latest novel, *The Minstrel's Melody* (2001), twelve-year-old Orphelia runs away from **home** in 1904 to join an all-black minstrel show on its way to the St. Louis World's Fair and learns some family secrets.

Works By

African-American Musicians. New York: Wiley, 2002.
A Blessing in Disguise. New York: Delacorte, 1995.
Don't Split the Pole: Tales of Down Home Folk Wisdom. New York: Delacorte, 1997.
Front Porch Stories at the One-Room School. New York: Bantam, 1992.
Just an Overnight Guest. New York: Dial, 1980. Reprint, East Orange, NJ: Just Us Books, 1997.
The Minstrel's Melody. Middleton, WI: Pleasant Co., 2001.
The Secret of Gumbo Grove. New York: Watts, 1987.
Thank you, Dr. Martin Luther King, Jr.! New York: Watts, 1990.

Works About

Kutenplom, Deborah, and Ellen Olmstead. *Young Adult Fiction by African American Writers, 1968–1993: A Critical and Annotated Guide.* New York: Garland, 1996. 265–274.

Murphy, Barbara Thrash. *Black Authors and Illustrators of Books for Children and Young Adults.* 3rd ed. New York: Garland, 1999. 373–374.

Pendergast, Sara, and Tom Pendergast, eds. *St. James Guide to Children's Writers.* 5th ed. Detroit: St. James Press, 1999. 1038–1039.

Susan L. Golden

TAYLOR, MILDRED D. (1943–   )

One of this country's most distinguished and honored authors of **fiction** for children and young adults, Mildred Taylor was born in Mississippi but moved north with her **family** while a baby. She attended Toledo, Ohio's newly integrated schools and was often the only black child in her classes. She always felt intense scrutiny, as though all African Americans were to be judged by her behavior, and also noticed the dissonance between what little she read of black **history** in school textbooks and what she knew of her heritage from the oral history of her family in the South, whom she often visited. After her graduation from the University of Toledo in 1965, Taylor became a Peace Corps volunteer. She completed an M.A. in journalism at the University of Colorado, and she currently lives in Boulder.

In 1973 she won a prize for the manuscript of *Song of the Trees.* Published by Dial in 1975, it introduced the subject of most of her books: the Logan family of Mississippi. Grandfather Logan, a freed slave and skilled carpenter, bought the first 200 acres of the farm the family holds on to so tenaciously over the next century. Set during the Great Depression, Cassie Logan's father is away earning money to pay taxes when white men threaten to cut down trees on their land. Fortunately, Mr. Logan returns in time to stand up to the men. Strong feelings of family unity, racial **identity**, **love** of the land, and standing up to white racism are major themes of this book and the powerful, beautifully written books that followed, all of which are based on stories told and retold in Taylor's family and which follow the Logans up to the early 1950s. Southern history is masterfully interwoven into these novels.

Roll of Thunder, Hear My Cry (1976), the second novel, explores Cassie's first exposure to racism in everyday life. She and her brothers walk to an inferior black school with hand-me-down texts, while the white children are picked up by the school bus, which splatters the Logan children with mud as they trudge along. Mama is fired from her teaching job because she infuses black history into her curriculum. A terrible incident in which several black men are set on fire leads to a store boycott instigated by the Logans of the suspected ringleader and yet more repercussions for the black **community**. The impossibility of friendship between Cassie and a white boy is also highlighted. Although racism is a strong theme, there are several sympathetic white characters, and there are some villainous black characters as well. This Newbery Award book is widely taught in middle schools, as are other novels in the series. Taylor has won numerous other awards, including three Coretta Scott

King Awards. In 2003 she won the first NSK Neustadt Prize for Children's Literature, awarded by the University of Oklahoma, and in 2004 the University of Mississippi's Oxford Conference for the Book celebrated Mildred D. Taylor Day in the state.

See also Children's and Young Adult Literature

Works By

The Friendship. New York: Dial, 1987.
The Gold Cadillac. New York: Dial, 1987.
The Land. New York: Phyllis Fogelman Books, 2001.
Let the Circle Be Unbroken. New York: Dial, 1981.
Mississippi Bridge. New York: Dial, 1990.
The Road to Memphis. New York: Dial, 1990.
Roll of Thunder, Hear My Cry. New York: Dial, 1976.
Song of the Trees. New York: Dial, 1975.
The Well: David's Story. New York: Dial, 1995.

Works About

Crowe, Chris. *Presenting Mildred D. Taylor.* New York: Twayne, 1999.
Kirk, Suzanne P. "Mildred Delois Taylor." *Writers for Young Adults.* Ed. Ted Hipple. New York: Scribner's, 1997. 3:273–282.
Kutenplon, Deborah, and Ellen Olmstead. *Young Adult Fiction by African American Writers, 1968–1998.* New York: Garland, 1996. 273–282.
Moss, Anita. "Mildred D. Taylor." *Writers of Multicultural Fiction for Young Adults: A Bio-Critical Sourcebook.* Ed. Daphne M. Kutzer. Westport, CT: Greenwood Press, 1996. 401–413.
Smith, Karen Patricia. "A Chronicle of Family Honor: Balancing Rage and Triumph in the Novels of Mildred D. Taylor." *African-American Voices in Young Adult Literature: Tradition, Transition, Transformation.* Metuchen, NJ: Scarecrow, 1994. 232–235.
Something about the Author. Vol. 135. Detroit: Thomson Gale, 2003. 205–209.

Susan L. Golden

TAYLOR, SUSIE KING (1848–1912)

While there is no dearth of eyewitness accounts of the Civil War, Susie King Taylor's *Reminiscences of My Life in Camp W the 33rd United States Colored Troops, Late 1st S.C.* (1902) is the only such surviving document by an African American woman. As such, it provides invaluable information about the operations of the nation's first black regiment and importantly chronicles the shifting mood of African Americans during and following the Civil War.

While Taylor's title foregrounds her military service, it is notable that her account opens instead with a chronology of her female **ancestors** and their achievements. Beginning with her great-great-grandmother, Taylor details her matrilineage, finally coming to her parents, Raymond and Hagar Ann Baker. While this emphasis on her matrilineal line in part reflects the realities of **slavery**, Taylor's knowledge of her antecedents is atypical and signals the specificity of her situation. Grest Farm, the Taylors' home, was on the Isle of Wight, Liberty County, Georgia, a **community** founded by Puritans and considered liberal by contemporary standards. Mrs. Grest was fond of Susie, and in 1854 Taylor and two siblings were allowed to move to Savannah to live with their grandmother, Dolly Reed, nominally freed by the Grests.

In Savannah, Taylor's grandmother ensured that the children received an education. **Literacy**—already a rebellious act—enabled the young girl to engage in further rebellions, writing passes and following "Yankee activity" in newspaper accounts. When the war reached Savannah in 1862, many African Americans fled. Taylor found herself on St. Catherine Island under the protection of the Union fleet. Upon learning that she could read and write, Commodore Goldsborough placed her in charge of the school on St. Simon's Island. There she met Sgt. Edward King of the First South Carolina Volunteers (later known as the 33rd Regiment), whom she married within the year. When the regiment was ordered to Camp Saxton in Beaufort, Taylor followed as a laundress. However, other skills were desperately needed, and Taylor was soon a practiced nurse. More is said of smallpox than of her marriage, reflecting the tenor of the war and the seriousness with which she treated her duties and those in her charge.

Taylor's position enabled her to interact with many notable whites, including Clara Barton, founder of the American Red Cross, and Colonel Thomas Wentworth Higginson and Col. C. T. Trowbridge, both of whom wrote letters that preface Taylor's narrative. Yet while her genuine respect for them is apparent, it is the compassion with which she describes individual African American soldiers that most deeply characterizes her account of the war.

After being mustered out February 9, 1866, Taylor and her husband opened a school in Savannah. Unable to make ends meet, King took other **work**, sustaining injuries that resulted in his **death** on September 16, 1866. The arrival of free schools caused the young widow and new mother to give up school teaching for profit. However, her work as a laundress for a **family** that vacationed in New England introduced her to Boston, where she settled circa 1874.

In Boston, Taylor met her second husband, Russell Taylor, whom she married in 1879. There she also continued as an advocate for African American veterans, becoming a founding member of the Corps 67 Women's Relief Corps in 1886 and president in 1893. The death of her son in 1898 was a debilitating blow, not only emotionally but also in the insidious role racism played in hastening his demise. In her reflections on the lack of progress, Taylor muses, "Was the war in vain? Has it brought freedom, in the full sense of the word, or has it not made our condition more hopeless?"

Taylor died on October 6, 1912, at the age of sixty-one, ten years after the publication of her memoirs. She served the Union army for over four years without pay and struggled in the cause of racial uplift. She is buried next to her second husband in an unmarked grave in Mount Hope Cemetery, Roslindale, Massachusetts.

Works About

Mason, Mary G. "Travel as Metaphor and Reality in Afro-American Women's Autobiography, 1850–1972." *Black American Literature Forum* 24.2 (Summer 1990): 337–356.

Nulton, Karen S., and Monika M. Elbert, eds. "The War of Susie King Taylor." *Separate Spheres No More: Gender Convergence in American Literature, 1830–1930.* Tuscaloosa: University of Alabama Press, 2000. 73–91.

Stover, Johnnie M. "African American 'Mother Tongue' Resistance in Nineteenth-Century Postbellum Black Women's Autobiography: Elizabeth Keckley and Susie King Taylor." *A/B: Auto/Biography Studies* 18.1 (Summer 2003): 117–144.

Jennifer Harris

TEMPLE OF MY FAMILIAR, THE

Alice Walker's 1989 novel *The Temple of My Familiar* attempts in **fiction** to relate the **history** of the world through an African and female lens; it is, as the author calls it, a romance of the last 500,000 years. The novel includes a whole host of characters including Shug and a relative of Celie's from *The Color Purple* (1982). Instead of a book determined to create narrative tension, fiction writer Ursula K. Le Guin notes characters seek answers to moral questions and push one another toward self-reflection, knowledge, and truth. Miss Lissie is a reincarnated woman who remembers each life of her past clearly except the first few that she recalls as dreamlike. She tells of her prehistoric lives in Africa, her time as a pygmy, her various returns as slaves, and many others, including her existence as a lion. Suwelo, a professor of American history, is Lissie's audience as he resides in his newly inherited house to escape temporarily from his wife Franny and lover Carlotta. Carlotta is married to musician Arveyda, who takes up with her mother Zedé, a South American exile rescued by a white woman. It is through these characters that readers are swept into a **myth** that inverts the hierarchy of man and woman, Europe and Africa. This myth sets Africa as the true center of all **religion** and civilization and casts man as a deformed female with an elongated clitoris and without breasts and a vagina. After listening to Lissie's past, Suwelo is able to return **home** to his wife, where he quits the academy by the end of the novel. Carlotta and Arveyda remain married but maintain separate residences. Zede marries a shaman in Mexico.

Critics have, on the whole, been negative in their reception of Walker's fourth novel, which followed the Pulitzer Prize–winning *The Color Purple*.

These writers focused on a number of aspects including viewing it as a mythic fantasy, a **love** fable, a feminist manifesto, and a retold history. Some feminist scholars have centered on Walker's retelling of the historically documented goddess-worshiping past that was systematically destroyed by **Christianity** and other religions, though continued to crop up in small pockets through the eons. Other writers centralize their analysis of the novel on the **family** saga in southern **literature**, diaspora writing from a postcolonial perspective, Jungian influences on Walker's works, and the rewriting of history looking bottom up rather than top down.

See also Possessing the Secret of Joy; Womanism

Works About

Gates, Henry Louis, Jr., and K. A. Appiah, eds. *Alice Walker: Critical Perspectives Past and Present.* New York: Amistad, 1993. 22–26.
Lauret, Maria. *Alice Walker.* New York: St. Martin's Press, 2000. 121–158.
White, Evelyn C. *Alice Walker: A Life.* New York: W. W. Norton, 2004. 445–449.
Winchell, Donna Haisty. *Alice Walker.* New York: Twayne Publishers, 1992. 115–131.

Laura Madeline Wiseman

TERRELL, MARY CHURCH (1863–1954)

Mary Church was born the daughter of slaves in Memphis, Tennessee, in 1863, the year of the Emancipation Proclamation. Her father emerged from **slavery** to become a prominent Memphis businessman and the first black millionaire through his real estate investments. She was sent to Ohio for the best education available for a black woman, and she eventually graduated with a bachelor's and a master's degree from Oberlin College. After graduating in 1884, she became a schoolteacher and traveled to Europe before settling in Washington, D.C., and marrying lawyer Robert Terrell. The couple settled in Washington, D.C., and raised daughters, Phyllis (named after black American colonial-era poet **Phillis Wheatley**) and Mary. Although Terrell had given up a prestigious position at Oberlin to marry, after marriage she pursued a variety of social reform and **community** activities. Terrell ultimately emerged as one of the preeminent advocates of social justice of the first half of the twentieth century.

Terrell became the first woman president of the Bethel Literary and Historical Association and served on the board of education for Washington, D.C. Increasingly, Terrell was drawn into the feminist cause and worked tirelessly for the rights of black women in particular. She became the founder in 1892 of the Colored Woman's League, which in 1896 merged with another organization to become the hugely influential National Federation of Colored

Women (NACW), with Terrell as its first president. The NACW sought to bring together black women's voices on a range of issues of concern to their sex and **race**. Terrell was a suffragist, women's rights activist, and peace activist who fought against the segregation of other women's organizations, such as the predominantly white General Federation of Women's Clubs, which had many of the same goals as the NACW. As head of the NACW between 1896 and 1901 Terrell urged white reformers, and especially white suffragists, in the national organizations to join with their black sisters. She herself was involved in almost all of the major women's groups of the era, both nationally and internationally. She was one of the few black members of the Women's International League for Peace and Freedom and served as a delegate to the 1904 International Congress of Women in Berlin.

In addition to her travels and organizational duties, Terrell was also a speaker and a writer who published in periodicals within both the white and black reform communities. Her numerous essays and lectures addressed women's rights and education, the **work** of the women reformers, segregation, antilynching, prison reform, and the accomplishments of individuals in **history**, such as her tribute to "Susan B. Anthony, the Abolitionist" (1906) and "Phillis Wheatley—An African Genius" (1928). Terrell's most substantial written work was her **autobiography**, *A Colored Woman in a White World*, published in 1940 and, as the title indicates, a reflection on the issues of racial segregation and of woman's subordination that had been at the forefront of Terrell's career as a reformer. She lived another fourteen years after her book was published and continued to be active in the feminist movement and the **civil rights movement** until her **death**. She lived long enough to be honored by her alma mater when Oberlin granted her an honorary doctorate in 1948.

Works By

"Club Work of Colored Women." *Southern Workman*, August 8, 1901, 435–438.

A Colored Woman in a White World. New York: Ransdell, 1940.

"Duty of the National Association of Colored Women to the Race." *A.M.E. Church Review* (January 1900): 340–354.

"An Interview with W. T. Stead on the Race Problem." *Voice of the Negro* (July 1907): 327–330.

"I Remember Frederick Douglass." *Ebony* (1953): 73–80.

"Lynching from a Negro's Point of View." *North American Review* 178 (June 1904): 853–868.

"Paul Lawrence Dunbar." *Voice of the Negro* (April 1906): 271–277.

"Peonage in the United States: The Convict Lease System and the Chain Gangs." *Nineteenth Century* 62 (August 1907): 306–322.

"Phillis Wheatley—An African Genius." *Baha'i Magazine: Star of the West* 19.7 (October 1928): 221–223.

"A Plea for the White South by a Coloured Woman." *Nineteenth Century* (July 1906): 70–84.

"Purity and the Negro." *Light* (June 1905): 19–25.

"Society among the Colored People of Washington." *Voice of the Negro* (April 1904): 150–156.

"Susan B. Anthony, the Abolitionist." *Voice of the Negro* (June 1906): 411–416.

"The Washington Conservatory of Music for Colored People." *Voice of the Negro* (November 1904): 525–530.

"What It Means to Be Colored in the Capital of the United States." *Independent*, January 24, 1907, 181–186.

Works About

Fradin, Dennis Brindell, and Judith Bloom Fradin. *"Fight On!: Mary Church Terrell's Battle for Integration.* New York: Clarion Books, 2003.

Jones, Beverly Washington. *Quest for Equality: The Life and Writings of Mary Eliza Church Terrell, 1863–1954.* Brooklyn, NY: Carlson, 1990.

Sterling, Dorothy. *Black Foremothers: Three Lives.* New York: Feminist Press at the City University of New York, 1988.

Tiffany K. Wayne

TERRY, LUCY (c. 1730–1821)

Born in Africa, Terry (who is also listed in some records as "Luce") became the slave of Ebenezer Wells of Deerfield, Massachusetts, in 1735. She was taught to read and write by an area minister and joined his church in 1744. Only two years later she composed the poem she is best known for—and what seems to be the only example of her **work** and the first poem by an African American to survive—"Bars Fight." In ballad form, the poem describes an attack by Native Americans on two white families just outside of Deerfield (at the time, *bars* was a commonly used term for "meadows") on August 25, 1746. Some critics have argued that while it does contain some interesting formal variations, it is otherwise unremarkable. Still, it had notable power over a local audience; though not published until 1855, it seems to have been regularly sung for more than a century after its composition.

Abijah Prince (also known as Obijah or Bijah), a free black man more than two decades her senior, seems to have purchased Terry's **freedom** in 1756, and the two were married on May 17 of that year. Prince had been the slave of Northfield minister Benjamin Doolittle, and Doolittle seems to have both freed him and left him a small parcel of land at his **death**. Prince also acquired land in Guilford and Sunderland, Vermont, and the couple moved to Guilford soon after being married. Between 1757 and 1769, they had six children: Caesar, Duruxa, Drusilla, Festus, Tatnai, and Abijah.

They seem to have moved back and forth between Deerfield and Guilford during the early years of their marriage and between Guilford and Sunderland in the later years. While local histories mark the Princes positively when talking of the area's few blacks (mainly because of Terry's reputation as a storyteller), what seems to have been a **race**-centered dispute with the neighboring white Noyes **family** turned into a series of threats. The Princes appealed successfully for protection to the Vermont Governor's Council in 1785.

While modern historian David R. Proper has raised doubts about their accuracy, later-nineteenth-century sources also argue that Terry made a reputation as an orator through two public performances. When one of her sons was denied admission to Williams College, she supposedly spoke eloquently—but in vain—at a meeting of the trustees. Later, when the white Eli Bronson waged a protracted legal battle to take some of the Princes' land, Terry supposedly made successful arguments before the Vermont Supreme Court.

Abijah died on January 19, 1794, in Guilford, and some sources suggest the family lost some of the Guilford land. Still, they stayed in Guilford for several years before moving to Sunderland. Terry is listed in the 1810 Sunderland census as living with three other free blacks—most likely some of her children. Proper speculates that she spent her final days in Sunderland with her son Caesar.

Work By

"Bars Fight." *The History of Western Massachusetts,* by Josiah Holland. Springfield, MA: Willey and Company, 1855. 2:360.

Works About

Foster, Frances Smith. *Written by Herself: Literary Production by African American Women, 1746–1892.* Bloomington: Indiana University Press, 1993.

Proper, David R. *Lucy Terry Prince: Singer of History.* Deerfield, MA: Pocumtuck Valley Memorial Association, 1997.

Sheldon, George. *A History of Deerfield, Massachusetts.* Somersworth: New Hampshire Publishing Company, 1895–1896.

——. "Negro Slavery in Old Deerfield." *New England Magazine* 7.1 (March 1893): 49–60.

Eric Gardner

THEIR EYES WERE WATCHING GOD

Zora Neale Hurston's *Their Eyes Were Watching God* was published in 1937 and continues to be Hurston's most read and most analyzed novel. On the broadest level, *Their Eyes Were Watching God* represents an African American woman's search for self-**identity**, self-knowledge, and self-understanding. The primary character, Janie Crawford, knows that there are adventures in the world and a life for her beyond the horizon, and she devotes herself to experiencing that life.

Janie is the product of **rape**, as had been her mother. After her mother deserts her, she is raised by her grandmother on property owned by the white **family** for whom "Nanny" works. Janie has been so sheltered by Nanny that she does not even realize she is not white like the children on the property until she sees herself in a group picture. Nanny is convinced that black women are destined to be the "mules of the world," destined to be objectified and used by men. One day, as Janie is reaching young womanhood, Nanny sees her kissing a young local boy and decides that the only way to guarantee Janie's future is to marry her off to a settled, financially secure man. Janie, believing her grandmother, equates **love** with marriage and agrees to the union. Thus begins her search and the first of the journeys that are to determine her sense of self.

Janie's growth and development are tied to her relationships with men, beginning with her first husband, Logan Killicks. Logan is a middle-aged, unattractive man who is obsessed with Janie's **beauty** and sees her as a possession he has been lucky enough to have acquired. When Janie realizes that the blossoming passions of love she had felt when kissing Johnny Taylor do not exist in her marriage, she learns her first lesson—that love and marriage are not synonymous. She begins to resent the trap that her marriage has become; the more obvious she is in voicing her discontent, the more Logan tries to control her, to break her. He becomes verbally abusive and finally decides to stop treating Janie like a prize and to put her to **work** in the fields. While Logan is away, purchasing a mule that Janie can use for plowing, Joe Starks, the man who is to become Janie's second husband, comes along. Joe (Jody) is a big talker and seems to share Janie's ideas of adventure and passion, awakening the sense of blossoming in Janie that Logan "Killicks" had killed. So Janie leaves Logan, marries Jody, and heads off with him toward the horizon and the dream of a little, all-black **community** that Jody had heard about—Eatonville, Florida.

Jody is ambitious and is soon accepted by the residents as the leader of their community. Janie, however, finds that Jody is not prepared to share that leadership with her. While his "big voice" frees him, it silences Janie; Jody goes out of his way to depict Janie as someone without anything to say, and she "made her face laugh." Again, Janie becomes an object, trapped in a relationship where she is merely one of the beautiful things that this man, "Mr. Mayor," owns, just like he owns the store he has built and the big white house he has constructed on top of a hill. Jody even forces Janie to tie up her long, thick hair when she works in the store to further mark her as his possession and one not to be coveted by the eyes of other men. Janie remains married to Jody for seventeen years, until **death** takes him. They are years of silence and oppression for Janie, seventeen years in which she is reduced to being no more than "Mrs. Mayor." Although outwardly Janie accepts her role, inwardly she resents this repressive condition. She knows that she has a voice, too, and that she could take part in community activities and tell stories on the front porch, just like the men. However, as Hurston shows in her ethnography **Mules and Men** (1935), leadership and the telling of "lies" were the provinces of the men of the community.

A few years into their marriage, when Janie makes a comment to Jody while they are at **home** that threatens Jody's control over her, he slaps her. At that point, something in Janie closes against him, and it never opens up again. It seems that both Logan and Jody react abusively when they feel that they are losing power over Janie—verbal abuse from Logan and physical abuse from Jody. Both acts seem to awaken Janie from her sleepwalk through life. While Janie continues to play her role in public as Mrs. Mayor, her heart is now closed to Jody. She also begins to use her voice, subtly and covertly criticizing some of the men in their beliefs about women—for instance, that a woman is so weak and helpless that a man has to do her thinking for her, the same as he does for "chillun and chickens and cows." Janie wonders—out loud—how strong a man really is if all he has to strain against is "women and chickens." Like she does with the character of Lucy Potts in **Jonah's Gourd Vine** (1934), Hurston notes the talent that Janie has with wordplay when given the opportunity.

Janie gets the opportunity to demonstrate her prowess with word games and signifyin' when Jody becomes frustrated that he is showing his age while Janie continues to appear young and beautiful. He seizes upon an opportunity in his store one day to ridicule her in front of the other men of the community. The insult is so intimate and reductive in its attack on the female that it receives only embarrassed laughter from these listeners. Janie, however, has come into full voice and signifies right back, referring to Jody's sagging manhood. While the men appreciate the quick wit and cleverness of Janie's response, Jody feels emasculated and never recovers from this embarrassment. He dies soon afterward, and Mrs. Mayor takes over the store. It is not until Vergible "Tea Cake" Woods walks into the store and into her life that Janie experiences the full blossoming of love and mutual respect in a marriage.

With Tea Cake, Janie is not only encouraged to express herself—to play and to explore—she is expected to do those things. Tea Cake is important, not because he gives Janie **freedom** but because he does not claim possession of her, thereby making it possible for her to explore her own horizons and limitations. Unlike Logan and Jody, Tea Cake encourages and enjoys Janie's verbal wit, and when they move to the muck with its atmosphere of passion and blooming, Janie is just as much a part of the lying sessions and wordplay as he is. The drawback, however, is that, isolated as it is, the muck and those living there still experience and respond to the gender-based influences of the larger community. Tea Cake's one act of cruelty toward Janie results from his need to show the other men that he is the boss—the man—of his house. He beats Janie in order to establish his male superiority. Although Janie forgives him, Hurston has established a pattern in this novel. Tea Cake's **violence** toward Janie, even after he has been a major factor in her discovery of self, cannot go unpunished. Tea Cake has to die because, in the end, as long as the male-female relationship exists within a system that is defined by the man's domination—that is, marriage—the woman cannot achieve selfhood. As in many of Hurston's other novels, especially in ***Seraph on the Suwanee*** (1948), the institution of marriage is problematic.

Janie returns to Eatonville as a woman who has gone on an adventure, a coming-of-age activity usually reserved for men. She does not return home furtively; she walks down the middle of the street, head held high, wearing men's overalls. She has grown as a person and a woman, having refused the limiting restrictions of Nanny, Logan, Jody, and even her true love Tea Cake, and her only advice to her friend Pheoby is that everyone must do two things for themselves: Go to God and "find out about livin'."

Works About

Clarke, Deborah. "'The Porch Couldn't Talk for Looking': Voice and Vision in *Their Eyes Were Watching God.*" *African American Review* 35.4 (Winter 2001): 599–613.

DuPlessis, Rachel Blau. "Power, Judgment, and Narrative in a Work of Zora Neale Hurston: Feminist Cultural Studies." *New Essays on "Their Eyes Were Watching God."* Ed. Michael Awkward. Cambridge: Cambridge University Press, 1990. 95–123.

Haurykiewicz, Julie A. "From Mules to Muliebrity: Speech and Silence in *Their Eyes Were Watching God.*" *Southern Literary Journal* 29.2 (Spring 1997): 45–60.

Newman, Judie. "'Dis Ain't Gimme, Florida': Zora Neale Hurston's *Their Eyes Were Watching God.*" *Modern Language Review* 98.4 (October 2003): 817–826.

Johnnie M. Stover

THERE IS CONFUSION

The first novel by **Jessie Redmon Fauset**, published by Boni and Liveright in 1924, has been both criticized and praised for its scale and ambition. *There Is Confusion* is a historical novel, set in the early twentieth century; it also contains elements of the bildungsroman and romance genres. Although there are many fully developed characters, two New York females dominate: Joanna is a light-skinned (**mulatta**) daughter of middle-**class** black man Joel Marshall; Maggie Ellersley is a black girl from an impoverished **family**. The novel traces the girls' journeys into adulthood, describing their troubled routes to maturity. Maturity occurs when characters rise to succeed and to challenge white society's discrimination against African Americans. The "confusion" of the title is the malaise of fecklessness that blacks can succumb to, because of their limited scope for betterment.

Maggie is the less brattish girl. Her first passion for Joanna's brother, Philip, is thwarted by Joanna, who writes a callous latter to Maggie, pointing out that Philip could do better than to marry a girl of "lowly aims." Maggie then endures trials, including a marriage to an abusive conman, before finding her calling when nursing maimed soldiers in war-torn France. Here she has a surprising meeting with Philip, whom she marries despite his possibly fatal wounds. Joanna, too, has a tough journey to maturity. A talented dancer and singer, Joanna is driven to succeed: "I want fame. I've got to have it." Joanna places her ambitions above all else and is exasperated by her sweetheart Peter Bye's lack of ambition. Provoked by a bitter family **history**, Peter has a "mad" on white men, hating them all. Fighting in France changes him; he realizes that racist whites want blacks to become disillusioned, embittered, and directionless. Instead of perpetuating rueful idleness, he resolves to become a skilled surgeon, earning, eventually, the approval and heart of Joanna.

The ambitions of Joanna are influenced by her reading of accounts of exemplary black women, but her ambitions involve pleasing white people, not bettering the status of her own **community**. Despite numerous career disappointments caused by color-based prejudice against her, she maintains that her color will not hinder her. It is only after a media backlash for the disgrace of her representing "America" in a vulgar stage show that Joanna finally comprehends the scale of discrimination against African Americans. A meeting with an old friend who passes for white—who tells her about the wicked things that whites say about blacks—also convinces her of the necessity of fighting racism, not ignoring it.

After the Great War, Joanna marries Peter, abandons all thoughts of stardom, and determines to **work** hard to establish a family that will serve as an exemplary, hardworking, selfless unit for other African Americans to emulate. The trajectory of Joanna's and Maggie's lives, and the Bye family's convoluted history, is told by an intrusive, frequently comic, ironic, and even self-reflexive omniscient narrator. *There Is Confusion* is multitextured, complicated, sometimes grueling, and bitter about the lowly status of blacks and especially black women. But the main characters' eventual acquisitions of inspired insight and personal maturity mean that Fauset's first novel is ultimately rousing and upbeat.

See also Chinaberry Tree, The; Comedy: American Style; Plum Bun

Works About

Davis, Thadious M. Foreword to *There Is Confusion*, by Jessie Redmon Fauset. Boston: Northeastern University Press, 1989. v–xxvi.

Kuenz, Jane. "The Face of America: Performing Race and Nation in Jessie Fauset's *There Is Confusion*." *Yale Journal of Criticism* 12.1 (1999): 89–111.

Levinson, Susan. "Performance and the 'Strange Place' of Jessie Redmon Fauset's *There Is Confusion*." *Meddelanden Fran Strindbergssallskapet* 46.4 (2000): 825–848.

McCoy, Beth A. " 'Is This Really What You Wanted Me to Be?': The Daughter's Disintegration in Jessie Redmon Fauset's *There Is Confusion*." *Meddelanden Fran Strindbergssallskapet* 40.1 (1994): 101–117.

Miller, Nina. "Femininity, Publicity, and the Class Division of Cultural Labor: Jessie Redmon Fauset's *There Is Confusion.*" *African American Review* 30.2 (1996): 205–220.

Sylvander, Carolyn Wedin. *Jessie Redmon Fauset: Black American Writer.* Troy, NY: Whitston Publishing, 1981. 141–192.

Kevin De Ornellas

THIRD LIFE OF GRANGE COPELAND, THE

Alice Walker's first novel, *The Third Life of Grange Copeland*, was published in 1970 while she was living in Jackson, Mississippi, and working in the **civil rights movement**. At the time she was married to Mel Levanthal; their daughter Rebecca had been born only one year prior to the novel's publication.

The Third Life of Grange Copeland follows the three intertwined stories of Grange, Brownfield, and Ruth Copeland, African Americans living in Baker County, Georgia, during the first half of the twentieth century. The novel begins with Brownfield, shifts back to his father, Grange, and then focuses on Ruth, Brownfield's daughter and Grange's granddaughter. The narrative time shifts and interdependent plotlines cohere in Walker's omniscient narrator, illustrating how specific incidents influence all three main characters' lives.

In Grange Copeland's "first life," he is a sharecropper, like Walker's own father, and is rendered desperate by his poverty, hopelessness, and lack of control over his life. After his wife, Margaret, gives birth to a child who is clearly the progeny of their white landowner, Mr. Shipley, Grange abandons Margaret, Brownfield, and the baby, living for a time with the prostitute Josie and in New York City. Grange's "second life," one characterized by racial hatred, reaches an apex when he watches a pregnant white woman drown in a Central Park pond; his resentment of whites then leads him to believe that the only way he can survive is to live separately from whites. His return to Baker County is marked by his marriage to Josie and his use of her money to fund his farm, separated both literally and figuratively from the white **community**. But Grange's "third life" revolves around his **love** for his granddaughter Ruth, whom he raises after Brownfield kills his wife Mem. In caring for Ruth, Grange breaks from his previous abusiveness—both that exacted on him in the form of sharecropping and racial prejudice and that he exacts in his beating of Margaret, abandonment of Brownfield, and manipulation of Josie.

Brownfield's story parodies that of Grange; he too escapes the subjugation of sharecropping to go north and stays with Josie for a time. After marrying Josie's niece Mem, Brownfield returns to Baker County, where his descent into poverty and jealousy of white landowners like Mr. J. L. fills him with bitterness. His abusiveness, like Grange's, is visited upon his wife and children. The nadir of Brownfield's bitterness is when he shoots Mem in the face with a shotgun; Grange's degradation leads him to abandon his **family**, but Brownfield actively destroys his own.

When Brownfield is sent to prison for Mem's murder, his youngest daughter Ruth moves in with Grange. For both Grange and the reader, Ruth represents what Grange and Brownfield might have been, had they escaped their oppressive poverty and racial subjugation. Grange teaches Ruth self-respect and self-reliance through trickster **folklore**, dance, and the story of Moses. At the end of the text, when Ruth is a teenager interested in joining the civil rights movement, Grange sacrifices himself to save her from Brownfield, redeeming at least partially his previous two lives.

Redemption is at the heart of *The Third Life of Grange Copeland*. The endless abuse visited upon all of the female characters represents an interesting take on **black masculinity**—that black men, so degraded by racial oppression, must hurt black women in order to assert their own humanity. Most feminist critics focus on that abusiveness, as well as on Ruth's status as Walker's first **womanist** character. But Grange's transformation in his "third life" redeems not only himself but also Ruth, whose spiritual survival he esteems more than his own life.

See also Womanism

Works About

Butler, Robert. "Alice Walker's Vision of the South in *The Third Life of Grange Copeland*." *African American Review* 27.2 (1993): 195–204.
——. "Making a Way Out of No Way: The Open Journey in Alice Walker's *The Third Life of Grange Copeland*." *Black American Literature Forum* 22.1 (1988): 65–79.
Cochran, Kate. " 'When the Lessons Hurt': *The Third Life of Grange Copeland* as Joban Allegory." *Southern Literary Journal* 34.1 (2001): 79–100.
Ensslen, Klaus. "Collective Experience and Individual Responsibility: Alice Walker's *The Third Life of Grange Copeland*." *The Afro-American Novel since 1960*. Ed. Peter Bruck and Wolfgang Karrer. Amsterdam: B. R. Gruner Publishing, 1982. 189–218.
Harris, Trudier. "Violence in *The Third Life of Grange Copeland*." *CLA Journal* 19 (1975): 238–247.
Hellenbrand, Harold. "Speech, after Silence: Alice Walker's *The Third Life of Grange Copeland*." *Black American Literature Forum* 20.1–2 (1986): 113–128.
Mason, Theodore O., Jr. "Alice Walker's *The Third Life of Grange Copeland*: The Dynamics of Enclosure." *Callaloo* 12.2 (1989): 297–309.

Kate Cochran

THOMAS, JOYCE CAROL (1938–)

Joyce Carol Thomas is the author of adolescent novels, books of **poetry**, and plays. She was born on May 25, 1938, in Ponca City, Oklahoma. Her father, Floyd David, was a bricklayer, and her mother, Leona, was a hair stylist. The **family** lived in Oklahoma until Thomas turned ten, when she moved to Tracy,

California. Thomas grew up in a large family, as she was the fifth of nine children. They all worked hard picking cotton, grapes, and tomatoes alongside migrant workers, even missing the first few months of school during the harvest time. To alleviate the hard **work**, they told stories to each other. Working as a telephone operator, Thomas put herself through college while raising four children. She began her career teaching public high school and then went on to teach at several universities, including California State University, Purdue University, and the University of Tennessee at Knoxville.

Thomas' body of work includes both adolescent and adult **literature**. She began her writing career primarily as a playwright in the San Francisco Bay area during the 1970s. At that time, she also had several collections of poetry published. Her first novel, *Marked by Fire*, was published in 1981 and earned her critical recognition that elevated her status as a professional writer. A sequel, *Bright Shadow*, was published in 1983 and has since been followed by many other novels, as well as several new plays and collections of poetry.

The hard work, large family, multicultural experience, and rural upbringing can all be noted as influences that found their way into the themes of Thomas's writing. Food is always a focus in her novels, due to her mother's ability to feed so many on a limited budget. Rural images, such as insects, are common in Thomas's novels as well. Thomas incorporates a childhood experience of finding a nest of black widows under her bed into the novel *Journey* (1990). The power of nature is also a recurring theme in her writing, particularly the power of storms. In *Marked by Fire*, Abby is born in a field while a tornado rages; in *Water Girl* (1986), earthquakes haunt Amber; and in *When the Nightingale Sings* (1986), Marigold experiences a hurricane.

Feminist themes are prominent in Thomas's work. In her novels, the main character is often female and is usually portrayed with strength, courage, and tenacity. *Marked by Fire*, *Bright Shadow*, and *House of Light* (2001) all trace the life of Abyssinia, who is raped at the age of ten but goes on to complete college and become a physician. *Water Girl* tells the story of Abyssinia's teenage daughter, Amber, who was given up for adoption. *When the Nightingale Sings* is a Cinderella-inspired story about a young woman named Marigold. Thomas's poetry contains feminist themes, as well. Poems like "Ambrosia," which is dedicated to black women, exemplify her concern with women's experiences. *A Mother's Heart, a Daughter's Love* (2001) honors the mother-daughter bond. Writing mostly about young women's experiences and the struggle for **identity**, Thomas also emphasizes the role of **community** and the role older women play in the lives of the younger women. For her work she has received the National Book Award, three Coretta Scott King awards, and three American Library Association awards, among others. Thomas currently resides in Berkeley, California.

Works By

Bright Shadow. New York: Avon Books, 1983.
Brown Honey in Broomwheat Tea. New York: Spoken Arts, 1993.

Cherish Me! New York: HarperCollins, 1998.

A Gathering of Flowers: Stories About Being Young in America. New York: Harper and Row, 1990.

The Gospel Cinderella. New York: Amistad, 2004.

House of Light: A Novel. New York: Hyperion, 2001.

Hush Songs: African American Lullabies. New York: Jump at the Sun/Hyperion Books for Children, 2000.

I Have Heard of a Land. New York: HarperCollins, 1998.

Linda Brown, You Are Not Alone: The Brown v. Board of Education Decision. New York: Hyperion Books for Children, 2003.

Marked by Fire. New York: William Morrow, 1981.

A Mother's Heart, a Daughter's Love: Poems for Us to Share. New York: J. Cotler Books, 2001.

The Six Fools. Collected by Zora Neale Hurston and adapted by Joyce Carol Thomas. New York: HarperCollins, 2006.

The Skunk Talks Back and Other Haunting Tales. New York: HarperCollins, 2004.

Water Girl. New York: Avon Books, 1986.

When the Nightingale Sings. New York: HarperTrophy, 1986.

Kyla Heflin

THOMAS AND BEULAH

Known by many as **Rita Dove**'s definitive collection of **poetry**, the publication of *Thomas and Beulah* by Carnegie-Mellon University Press in 1986 earned Rita Dove the 1987 Pulitzer Prize for Poetry. She became the second African American poet besides **Gwendolyn Brooks** to win the Pulitzer Prize. The poems are organized in sequence and chart the lives of Dove's maternal grandparents in the context of larger **history** that encompassed the migration of blacks from the **South** to the North, several wars, and the **civil rights movement**, among other social events that would affect blacks. Though *Thomas and Beulah* is not about a specific place, Dove asserts that the grandmother and grandfather function as one unit that is "defined" and "confined" to a particular place, Akron, Ohio. The theme of **home** and personal understanding and growth recur in many of her works. For Dove, the poems took charge of themselves, and each fell into place within the collection.

When Dove was in Germany in 1981, she wrote five or six poems about her grandfather's youth and thought that these would work well by themselves. While she was a writer-in-residence at Tuskegee Institute in Alabama for the summer, she wrote several more poems about her grandfather. Later on, as a creative writing professor at Arizona State University, she revised these and sent them to the *Ohio Review*, where they were published as the chapbook "Mandolin." The poems about her grandfather would expand, especially after Dove was awarded a Guggenheim Fellowship for the 1983–1984 academic year, allowing her the **freedom** to focus on her writing. One night, while Dove looked over a poem from *Museum* (1983) titled "Dusting," she recognized that the solarium in the poem was her grandmother's, and the woman who was trying to remember her lover's name was, in fact, her grandmother. Dove felt that her grandmother spoke to her through the poem, asking to have her story told. At that moment, the poetry collection *Thomas and Beulah* was born.

The creation of *Thomas and Beulah* would span many years, and the idea of the collection was generated from some of Dove's earlier experiences. Many of Dove's poems derive from single words. In this sense, for Dove building poetry is similar to constructing a house. She met someone with the name "Maurice," and thought the name would be interesting to use for a future poem. Later, while in Berlin, she heard a story about a goldfish that became frozen in its fishbowl because its owners left the window open in winter while they were away. When they returned, the fish was frozen, so they warmed it up slowly on the stove, and it came back to life. Dove wrote this story down as well. She also remembered the name "Beulah" and looked up its biblical connotations. The name means "desert in peace." During that time, she was reading Gaston Bachelard's *Poetics of Space* (1964), and he notes that when people dust, the dusting is an act of restoring or excavating something. Dove decided to write a poem about Beulah dusting and include the fish story as well as her first **love**, Maurice. The poem is about restoring **memory**. Beulah's act would become "Dusting," the first of many poems that would later become *Thomas and Beulah.*

Works About

Gabbon, Joanne V., ed. *The Furious Flowering of African American Poetry.* Charlottesville: University Press of Virginia, 1999.

Ingersoll, Earl, ed. *Conversations with Rita Dove.* Jackson: University Press of Mississippi, 2003.

Pereira, Malin. *Rita Dove's Cosmopolitanism.* Urbana: University of Illinois Press, 2003.

Reddy, Maureen T., Martha Roth, and Amy Sheldon, eds. *Mother Journeys: Feminists Write about Mothering.* Minneapolis: Spinsters Ink, 1994.

Earl F. Yarington

TILLMAN, KATHERINE DAVIS CHAPMAN (1870–?)

Katherine Chapman was born in 1870 into a poor **family** in Mound City, Illinois. She had no formal education until the family moved to South Dakota, and she first enrolled in school at the age of twelve. She graduated from high school and soon began publishing her poems, essays, and short stories in papers such as the *Christian Recorder* and the *Indianapolis Freeman.* Her first poem, titled "Memory," was published in 1888. She attended college at the

State University of Louisville in Kentucky and at Wilberforce University in Ohio. Sometime before 1893, Chapman met and married George M. Tillman, a minister with the African Methodist Episcopal (AME) church.

Tillman led an active life as the wife of a minister. She engaged in a variety of activities that especially reflected her talents and interests as a woman and as a writer. She served as editor of the *Women's Missionary Recorder* and held official roles in women's missionary societies. Tillman continued to write after her marriage and published many pieces in various publications of the AME church. Her longest works were two novellas serialized in the *AME Church Review: Beryl Weston's Ambition: The Story of an Afro-American Girl's Life* (1893) and *Clancy Street* (1898–1899). Her two other major pieces of **fiction** were the short stories "Miles the Conqueror" (1894) and "The Preacher at Hill Station" (1903). In addition to these works, Tillman is perhaps best known as a dramatist. Her play *Fifty Years of Freedom, or From Cabin to Congress* (1910) is a celebration of the fifty-year anniversary of the Emancipation Proclamation.

The *AME Church Review* was also the forum for many of Tillman's most important essays. A theme she particularly engaged was the subject of racial uplift and opportunities for African American women and, specifically, the role of the African American writer, in articles such as "Some Girls That I Know" (1893), "Afro-American Women and Their Work" (1895), "Afro-American Poets and Their Verse" (1898), "The Negro among Angle-Saxon Poets" (1898), and "Paying Professions for Colored Girls" (1907). As a middle-**class** black woman writer, Tillman must be considered as part of the larger social reform movements for racial progress that characterized the late nineteenth and early twentieth century. She participated in the women's club movement and was a member of some of the most significant **race** reform organizations of the era, such as the National Colored Women's League, the National Federation of Afro-American Women, and the National Association of Colored Women's Clubs (NACWC). She served as an officer of the NACWC at one time.

As a writer and reformer, Tillman worked to secure and prove the abilities of African Americans, and women in particular, in a post–Reconstruction era characterized by racial politics and the **violence** of white supremacy.

Works By

"Afro-American Poets and Their Verse." *AME Church Review* 14 (April 1898): 421–428.

"Afro-American Women and Their Work." *AME Church Review* 11 (April 1895): 477–499.

"Alexander Dumas, Père." *AME Church Review* 24 (January 1907): 257–263.

"Alexander Sergeivich Pushkin." *AME Church Review* 25 (July 1909): 27–32.

Aunt Betsy's Thanksgiving. Philadephia: AME Book Concern, n.d.

Beryl Weston's Ambition: The Story of an Afro-American Girl's Life. AME Church Review 10 (July 1893): 173–191; (October 1893): 308–322.

Clancy Street. AME Church Review 15 (October 1898): 643–650; (January 1899): 748–753; (July 1899): 152–159; (October 1899): 241–251.

Fifty Years of Freedom, or From Cabin to Congress: A Drama in Five Acts. Philadelphia: AME Book Concern, 1910.

Heirs of Slavery: A Little Drama of To-day. AME Church Review 17 (January 1901): 199–203.

"The Negro among Anglo-Saxon Poets." *AME Church Review* 14 (July 1898): 106–112.

"Paying Professions for Colored Girls." *Voice of the Negro.* (January–February 1907): 54–56.

Quotations from Negro Authors. Fort Scott, KS: N.p., 1921.

Recitations. Philadelphia: AME Book Concern, 1902.

"Some Girls That I Know." *AME Church Review* 9 (January 1893): 288–292.

The Spirit of Allen: A Pageant of African Methodism. N.p., 1922.

Thirty Years of Freedom: A Drama in Four Acts. Philadelphia: AME Book Concern, 1902.

Works About

Tate, Claudia. *Domestic Allegories of Political Desire: The Black Heroine's Text at the Turn of the Century.* New York: Oxford University Press, 1992.

——. Introduction to *The Works of Katherine Davis Chapman Tillman.* New York: Oxford University Press, 1991. 3–62.

Tiffany K. Wayne

TOOMER, JEAN (1894–1967)

Jean Toomer is best known as the author of *Cane* (1923), a collage of short **fiction**, **poetry**, and **drama** credited with being the first **work** of the **Harlem Renaissance** as well as a landmark of literary **modernism**. But Toomer was not to repeat this literary success. He was a spiritual seeker, and the pursuit of insight and truth mattered more to him than literary achievement. Although he wrote prolifically throughout the 1920s and 1930s, publishers repeatedly rejected his book-length manuscripts, and only a few of his poems and essays, and one of his plays, found their way into print. It is the verbal portraits of rural southern women in *Cane* that have earned Toomer a place in a feminist encyclopedia of African American **literature**. **Alice Walker** has called them "essential" to her own development as a writer. Toomer was among the first writers to choose rural southern African American women as complex subjects for fiction, exploring sympathetically their consciousness as well as their symbolic value.

Born in December 1894 to Nina Pinchback and Nathan Toomer, Nathan Eugene Toomer grew up in the household of his maternal grandparents in Washington, D.C. After his father deserted him and his mother when Eugene was only a few months old, his maternal grandfather P.B.S. Pinchback insisted that his grandson be called Eugene Pinchback and forbid the mention of Nathan Toomer in his presence. P.B.S. Pinchback, famous as the African American lieutenant governor of Louisiana during Reconstruction, was a highly successful light-skinned man who could have passed for white but chose instead to identify with his African American heritage. After leaving New Orleans for Washington, D.C., in the early 1890s, he built a new house in an almost all-white section of the city. It was in this house and neighborhood that Eugene spent his first decade of life. When his mother remarried a white man, Eugene moved with them to mostly white neighborhoods in Brooklyn and New Rochelle, New York, but returned to his grandparents' home in Washington after his mother's **death** in 1909. His grandparents, meanwhile, had moved to a black section of the city where Toomer attended M Street High School, a public secondary school for Negroes, his first experience living and studying in an African American environment. During his high school years Eugene rejected his grandfather's surname and shortened his given name Eugene to Jean, thus renaming himself Jean Toomer. Both Toomer and his grandfather could have passed for white. While his grandfather P.B.S. Pinchback had chosen to identify with African Americans, Toomer—with the crisscrossing of black and white contexts in his own life— called himself "American" by the end of his high school years and spent much of his adult life attempting to articulate the concept of a new American who was not racially defined.

Toomer entered college at the University of Wisconsin to study agriculture but quickly realized he had little talent or interest in the field and left before the year was finished. He repeated this pattern at five other educational institutions without ever taking a degree. In 1919 he moved to Greenwich Village, where he came into contact with modernist writers such as Waldo Frank and Lola Ridge and embarked on an intensive study of American and European literature. In 1920 he encountered idealist philosophy and devoted the better part of a year to reading Eastern classics. When he returned to writing after this immersion, he was attracted to imagist and symbolist aesthetics. He completed his first poem, "The First American," in 1921 but was not satisfied with his literary voice, although this poem articulated a theme that would become a primary one in his later writings.

In the fall of 1921, Toomer traveled to Sparta, Georgia, accepting the position of substitute head teacher in a small rural school. This was Toomer's first trip to the **South**, and it proved a memorable one. His first personal contact with the lives of African Americans in rural Georgia, and the opportunity to hear their stories, folksongs, and **spirituals**, inspired him to begin writing *Cane* on the train ride back to New York. Toomer called *Cane* a "swansong," meaning that it was a tribute to what he perceived as disappearing cultural riches—the songs, stories, and lives of rural black southerners. Even as he captured the pathos and spiritual **beauty** of this cultural heritage in *Cane*'s portraits of women, and his own ambivalence toward his southern cultural heritage in the character of Kabnis, he also meant to say "good-bye" to notions of racial **identity** and heritage in this volume in order to begin the project of articulating his concept of the new American who transcended **race**.

From his adolescent immersion in tales of chivalry to an absorbed study of the French symbolists and of Eastern religious texts in his young adulthood, Toomer was an avid and prodigious reader. *Cane* reflects not only Toomer's experiences and observations in rural Georgia but also his reading of Baudelaire's *Petits poems en prose* and the imagist theories of Ezra Pound, his **love** of Robert Frost's New England poems, and his admiration for Sherwood Anderson's *Winesburg, Ohio*. Thus *Cane* merges both American regionalism and a modernist aesthetic with African American subject matter. Many of Toomer's acquaintances at the time of the publication of *Cane* were also leading American modernists: Hart Crane, Waldo Frank, Georgia O'Keeffe, Alfred Stieglitz, Allen Tate. Leading African American literary figures also encouraged and praised Toomer's efforts. **Jessie Redmon Fauset**, editor of the *Crisis*, wrote frequently to encourage him during the composition of *Cane*. W.E.B. Du Bois, Jessie Fauset, Alain Locke, **Countee Cullen**, and **Claude McKay** wrote to congratulate Toomer upon its publication, which was lauded as the first sign of a new artistic era in African American letters. According to critic Robert B. Jones, *Cane* deserves a place as one of the great African American literary achievements of the twentieth century, alongside **Richard Wright**'s *Native Son* (1940) and **Ralph Ellison**'s *Invisible Man* (1952). However, Toomer resisted efforts on the part of his publisher to market him as a New Negro writer.

Cane is composed of three sections. The first, set in rural Georgia, consists of six sketches interspersed with ten poems. The sketches and stories of this section focus on female characters and, with the exception of the final story, "Blood-Burning Moon," are titled after the central female character: Karintha, Becky, Carma, Fern, and Esther. The second section, set in Washington, D.C., provides an urban contrast to the rural setting and lyricism of the first. The second section consists of seven sketches and stories interspersed with five poems. The third and final section of the book is a single work, "Kabnis," titled after its central male character, modeled on Toomer himself. "Kabnis" combines the rural and urban settings of parts one and two in an uneasy dialectic through the central character, an urban northerner who returns to the South. His story, written in the style of a play, with stage directions and dialogue tags, incorporates fragments of five Negro spirituals. It dramatizes the spiritual nadir of the cycle of *Cane*, balancing the spiritual zenith in the mytical dimensions of the first section. It has been suggested that, in fact, Kabnis is a Cain figure, punning on the volume's title, *Cane*, named for the crop whose growing, processing, and marketing drives the economic lives of so many of the book's characters.

The first and third sections of *Cane* were written in response to Toomer's visit to Georgia, but the second section was actually written earlier and added to make the manuscript large enough for a book. This middle section reflects the struggle for identity and wholeness of characters whose lives are marked by city life. Many of the episodes are based on Toomer's experiences from his fragmented college years.

Cane's first section will be of greatest interest to students of feminist approaches to African American literature. The female characters are portrayed as human beings on a journey of self-realization, struggling with the economic, social, and gender restrictions of their societies. Each of the women constitutes a different part of the racial/cultural spectrum. Karintha is a young black woman whose essence attracts the desires of men young and old; her inevitable pregnancy results in infanticide. Toomer sympathetically portrays the effects of the projections of men onto Karintha—they stunt her identity. Becky is a white woman who was two black sons; she is a pariah in the **community**, an unredeemed Hester Prynne. Carma is as strong as a man and her powers of attraction compared to those of a goddess. Fern's sensual attractions are accompanied by the imagery of a Jewish cantor. Esther is a pasty white girl attracted to the blackness of an itinerant man named Barlo. Toomer portrays their spiritual and sexual longings, refusing to impose conventions. Instead he explores how these women find themselves trapped by desire—their own and others'—as well as by larger cultural expectations. Furthermore, he examines the ways in which the characters' identities are shaped by these expectations. In portraying such diversity among the women of *Cane*, Toomer also challenges essentialist notions of race by showing complexity in the lives and complexions of his characters. He moves beyond personal psychology to the social construction of reality by symbolizing the ways in which what Charles Scruggs and Lee Vandemarr call the "terrors of American **history**" impinge on the lives of his fictional subjects. Louisa of "Blood-Burning Moon" is trapped between her love of a black man and a white man's desire for her; the love triangle results in a lynching. Scruggs and Vandemarr point out how Toomer's "Blood-Burning Moon" was a response to Waldo Frank's *Holiday*, written at about the same time. Both works end in a lynching and the madness of the black woman who is bereaved of her love. But Frank's work essentializes race, reinforcing binary notions of black and white, while Toomer's work complicates it.

By the time *Cane* was published, Toomer was already pursuing another interest, the work of Georges I. Gurdjieff, which also attracted his friend Waldo Frank and such literary types as Katherine Mansfield. Toomer trained at Gurdjieff's "Institute for the Harmonious Development of Man" near Fontainbleau, France, then returned to the United States to become an advocate and teacher for Gurdjieff's ideas, leading several Gurdjieff groups in Harlem and Chicago. In Portage, Wisconsin, at a six-month experimental living community inspired by Gurdjieff's Institute for the Harmonious Development of Man, he met Marjery Latimer, a writer, and married her in 1932. The couple had a daughter, also named Marjery, but unfortunately Marjery Latimer died from complications of childbirth. In 1934 Toomer married again, this time to Marjorie Content, daughter of a wealthy New York Stock Exchange broker. The couple settled in Doylestown, Pennsylvania, on a farm given to them by Content's wealthy father, where they spent the rest of their lives. Both of Toomer's marriages were highly publicized because they were considered interracial. Once again Toomer was caught in the trap of racialized American thinking.

Although Toomer split with Gurdjieff during the mid-1930s, he continued to espouse the Gurdjieff philosophy. Between 1936 and 1939, the Toomers attempted to run another experimental living community, modeled after the Portage, Wisconsin, attempt, on their farm. And in 1939 the Toomer **family** spent nine months in India. After their return Toomer began suffering from health problems that forced him to dissolve the community living experiment. Toomer's search for spiritual growth and fulfillment included explorations of the teachings of Edgar Cayce, Jungian psychoanalysis, and scientology. He continued to write prolifically throughout his life, publishing very little. He joined the Society of Friends and became a spokesman for Quakerism in the 1940s and 1950s. His last published work was a series of essays on Quaker **spirituality**.

In 1967, the year of Toomer's death, *Cane* was reissued by New York University Press, a few years after Toomer's wife, Marjorie Latimer, had given his manuscripts to the Fisk University Library, where Arna Bontemps was curator. (Toomer's papers and manuscripts are now housed at the Beinecke Rare Book and Manuscript Library, Yale University.) A paperback edition of *Cane*, with an introduction by Bontemps, was published in 1970. The republication of *Cane* was greeted with the same enthusiasm that followed its original publication, and scholars discovered the cache of unpublished work by Toomer. Subsequently, several volumes of Toomer's unpublished work have appeared in print. Darwin T. Turner's *The Wayward and the Seeking* made accessible to the reading public for the first time many of Toomer's experimental plays, stories, and writings about race; however, some of Toomer's African American critics chastised him for "abandoning the race" by denying his African American identity when they read his work that sought to articulate a theory of the fully realized human being that transcends race. More recent work on Toomer, however, acknowledges the greater complexity of his vision as one that challenged the binary, essentialist understanding of race in America. Toomer identified seven strands of ethnicity in his own bloodlines—French, Dutch, Welsh, Negro, German, Jewish, and Indian—and sought to "fuse" them imaginatively and spiritually in his thinking about race at a time when America saw race in only black or white.

Although it is generally agreed that Toomer's unpublished manuscripts are didactic and dogmatic and lack the literary qualities of *Cane*, his spiritual journey is more resonant at the turn of the twenty-first century than it was with literary critics and publishers at the heart of modernism. His spiritual and philosophical journey became the subject of several studies in the 1990s, and he has been named as a literary mentor by contemporary African American writers such as **Charles Johnson** and Alice Walker, who also embrace a spiritual view of life. Evidence of his influence is also present in the work of **Ernest Gaines**, Michael S. Harper, and **Gloria Naylor**. Clearly Toomer was at his strongest as an artist when his artistic eye was responding to the material manifestations of African American culture rooted in place and lived experience, and his ear was attuned to the "lower frequencies" that his intellect did not always fully comprehend.

Works By

Cane. Boni and Liveright, 1923. New York: New York University Press, 1967.

The Collected Poems of Jean Toomer. Ed. Robert B. Jones et al. Chapel Hill: University of North Carolina Press, 1988.

Essentials. 1931.

A Jean Toomer Reader: Selected Unpublished Writings. Ed. Frederick L. Rusch. New York: Oxford University Press, 1993.

Jean Toomer: Selected Essays and Literary Criticism. Ed. Robert B. Jones. Chattanooga: University of Tennessee Press, 1996.

The Wayward and the Seeking: A Collection of Writings by Jean Toomer. Ed. Darwin T. Turner. Washington, DC: Howard University Press, 1980.

Works About

Jones, Robert B. *Jean Toomer and the Prison-House of Thought: A Phenomenology of the Spirit.* Amherst: University of Massachusetts Press, 1993.

Kerman, Cynthia Earl and Richard Eldridge. *The Lives of Jean Toomer: A Hunger for Wholeness.* Baton Rouge: Louisiana State University Press, 1989.

Larson, Charles R. *Invisible Darkness: Jean Toomer and Nella Larsen.* Iowa City: University of Iowa Press, 1993.

McKay, Nellie Y. *Jean Toomer, Artist: A Study of His Literary Life and Work, 1894–1936.* Chapel Hill: University of North Carolina Press, 1984.

Scruggs, Charles, and Lee Vandemarr. *Jean Toomer and the Terrors of American History.* Philadelphia: University of Pennsylvania Press, 1998.

Turner, Darwin T. *In a Minor Chord: Three African American Writers and Their Search for Identity.* Carbondale: Southern Illinois University Press, 1971.

Ann Hostetler

TOPDOG/UNDERDOG

In *Topdog/Underdog* (2001), on the surface it appears as if **Suzan-Lori Parks** creates a typical sibling rivalry in this work of **drama**, but as the brothers confront their abandonment by their parents and their feelings toward each other, it becomes clear that the playwright has embedded a deeper meaning. No longer making a living by street hustling, Lincoln works in whiteface in an arcade, clothed in a false beard, stovepipe hat, and frock coat; for paying patrons he reenacts Abraham Lincoln's assassination. After a day's **work**, Lincoln comes **home** to eat and drink and think about his childhood. Booth, the younger brother, makes his living off of his brother's pay and by stealing whatever else is necessary to make ends meet. He is determined to make his future by learning the three-card monte, a con that his brother made legendary. However, his brother will not teach it to him. Booth is not successful at convincing Lincoln, who vowed not to return to the streets after the murder of his partner, to reenter a life of hustling.

The play ends when an enraged Booth kills his brother after losing the **family** legacy, $500 rolled in a stocking left to each son when their parents abandoned them. Although Lincoln's **death** is foreshadowed by his job and by the historical significance of both of their names, where Parks recreates **history** so that the Emancipator and murderer are black, there is a deeper layer to Parks's play: The play is her exploration of the paradox between inevitability and the chance for change. Each brother has an opportunity to change the historical narrative of his fate. Lincoln considers his new line of work honest, but in fact he is only staged as the Emancipator; he has no real power. Booth remains the perennial underdog and resorts to **violence** instead of creating a different meaning or ending for himself. What remains is Parks's implicit question: What would happen if black men refuse to step into the role of "underdog," hustler, killer, masquerader behind the whiteface that symbolizes what is expected?

Works About

Chaudhuri, Una. "*Topdog/Underdog* by Suzan-Lori Parks." *Theatre Journal* 54.2 (2002): 289–291.
"For the First Time, the Drama Pulitzer Goes to a Black Woman." *Journal of Blacks in Higher Education*, no. 36 (Summer 2002): 60.

Brandon L. A. Hutchinson

TRUTH, SOJOURNER (c. 1797–1883)

Originally born Isabella Baumfree, Sojourner Truth was the child of James and Elizabeth Baumfree, slaves in Ulster County, New York. Truth was shuffled among several owners—most notably John Dumont—during the first three decades of her life. She married another of Dumont's slaves, Thomas, around 1815, and the couple had five children: Diana (c. 1815), an unknown second child (perhaps named Jane), Peter (1821), Elizabeth (1825), and Sophia (1826). We know little of Truth's **family** life, though in 1826–1827, as New York's emancipation grew closer, she left her husband and all of her children, save Sophia, with Dumont. (Her later interactions with her children varied throughout the rest of her life. In 1828, she would sue for custody of Peter, though he had left her life by 1841. Her daughters lived with or near her intermittently after 1840.)

Feeling she had heard the voice of God, she immersed herself in evangelical Methodism and moved to New York City. Her experiences with Methodist Perfectionists there eventually led her to the commune headed by

Robert Matthews (known as the Prophet Matthias), where she lived from 1833 to 1835. In 1835, when the commune was disbanded in the midst of a spectacular scandal (involving murder, **violence**, and sex), Truth returned to **domestic work** but did not set aside the combination of evangelical **Christianity** and millennialism that shaped much of her early life. On June 1, 1843, she changed her name to Sojourner Truth and began preaching throughout the New York City/Connecticut area. Eventually, Truth settled at the utopian Northampton Association in Massachusetts, where antislavery and nascent feminism, as well as spiritualism, became linked to her faith.

The Association folded in 1846, the year Truth began dictating her **autobiography** to Olive Gilbert (a white member of the Association; Truth was illiterate) and one year after her first major antislavery speech. By 1850, when *The Narrative of Sojourner Truth* was published, Truth had already gained fame in the movement, in part for answering **Frederick Douglass**'s 1847 call for slave insurrection by calling out from the audience, "Frederick, is God dead?" The weaving together of abolition and Christianity that marked her comment also mark the book, which, while certainly a narrative of **slavery**, is also, in many ways, a spiritual autobiography. She lectured extensively after 1850, and in May 1851, she gave the speech that critics later dubbed (making her Afro-Dutch sound much more southern) "Ain't I a Woman?" and that led twentieth-century feminists to mark her as an important **ancestor**.

Her 1856 move to Michigan (she settled in Battle Creek, though she spent time at the utopian community of Harmonia) did nothing to stop her activism. When the Civil War came, she met with Abraham Lincoln, composed a battle song (to the tune of "John Brown's Body") for the First Michigan Colored Infantry, was immortalized by Harriet Beecher Stowe in an article for the *Atlantic Monthly* that christened her "the Libyan Sibyl," and worked to aid newly freed slaves. It was her work in this last role that shaped her sense that the West might hold the greatest hope for freed slaves and her later support for the Exodusters who migrated to Kansas in 1879.

In 1875, with the aid of friend Frances Titus, she prepared a new, enlarged version of her *Narrative*, including a scrapbook-style update titled the "Book of Life." Truth's last years were spent in Michigan, where she was cared for by three of her daughters.

Works By

The Narrative of Sojourner Truth. With Olive Gilbert. Boston: For the author, 1850.

The Narrative of Sojourner Truth. With Frances Titus. Boston: For the author, 1875.

Works About

Mabee, Carlton. *Sojourner Truth.* New York: New York University Press, 1993.

Painter, Nell Irvin. *Sojourner Truth: A Life, a Symbol.* New York: W. W. Norton, 1996.

Peterson, Carla. *"Doers of the Word": African American Women Speakers and Writers in the North (1830–1880).* New Brunswick, NJ: Rutgers University Press, 1998.

Yellin, Jean Fagan. *Women and Sisters: The Antislavery Feminists in American Culture.* New Haven, CT: Yale University Press, 1989.

Eric Gardner

 **U**

UGLY WAYS

Tina McElroy Ansa's second novel, *Ugly Ways* (1993), focuses on the Lovejoy women, the recently deceased Esther and her three daughters, Betty, Emily, and Annie Ruth. The story, set in Ansa's fictional Mulberry, Georgia, covers several days following the **death** of Esther, called "Mudear" by her daughters. The Lovejoy sisters are all successful career women, but they share an essential unhappiness caused by their resentment toward Mudear and their feeling that they have not been properly nurtured. By allowing each sister to tell her own story as well as allowing us to hear from the father, Ernest, and from the deceased Esther, Ansa gives us all sides in this story of **family** expectations, misunderstandings, and **love**.

The family expectations are seen in the early years of Esther and Ernest Lovejoy's marriage when Esther waited on Ernest and gave all her time to him and her three small daughters. When her obedience begets the expectation on Ernest's part that he can boss her around and abuse her, Esther goes through what her family calls The Change and retreats to her bedroom. The Lovejoy sisters had expected her to be a nurturing mother, and when she refuses to even prepare food for them, they have to turn to one another for nurturing. Even though Mudear has abandoned her traditional roles, the family still expects her to perform them, leading to all the family misunderstandings. The sisters gather to bury Mudear, but in reality they are trying to come to terms with her living **memory** in their lives and with their current realities.

Sections told by Mudear's spirit as she watches the girls prepare for her funeral balance the sisters' condemnation of their mother. Mudear asserts that she has taught them how to survive in a hostile world, and in a way she has. She condemns what she calls the girls' ugly ways of disrespecting her, but we see that by abandoning her maternal role, she has also exhibited some ugly ways. By novel's end, the girls are reconciled to what Mudear was and are united in their support for one another, especially for the pregnant Annie Ruth.

By turns grim and comic, the story is, on the whole, hopeful. The catharsis comes near the novel's end. In a wildly comic scene set at Parkinson's funeral home, the sisters manage to tip Mudear's coffin and wind up on the floor with Mudear across their laps, thus literally uniting the Lovejoy women. Mudear has the novel's last word as she declares that she will continue watching the girls, especially Annie Ruth and her future granddaughter, since she now has nothing else to do.

In *Ugly Ways*, Ansa explores sisters' relationships with one another and with their absent mother. Ansa's belief in the spirit world comes through in Mudear's vibrant voice from the dead that allows us to hear Mudear's side of the story. Ansa reaffirms her themes of the primacy of love and forgiveness in this story of the struggles and reconciliations of the Lovejoy women.

See also Motherhood

Works About

Grooms, Anthony. Review of *Ugly Ways*. *Callaloo* 17.2 (Spring 1994): 653–656.

Peterson, V. R. Review of *Ugly Ways*. *Essence* 24.8 (December 1993): 54.

Review of *Ugly Ways*. *Belles Lettres: A Review of Books by Women* 10.2 (Spring 1995): 93.

Seaman, Donna. Review of *Ugly Ways*. *Booklist* 89.21 (July 1993): 1942.

Warren, Nagueyalti. "Resistant Mothers in Alice Walker's *Meridian* and Tina McElroy Ansa's *Ugly Ways*." *Southern Mothers: Fact and Fictions in Southern Women's Writing*. Ed. Nagueyalti Warren and Sally Wolff. Baton Rouge: Louisiana State University Press, 1999. 182–203.

Zingman, Barbara. Review of *Ugly Ways*. *New York Times Book Review*, October 10, 1993, 20.

Harriette C. Buchanan

UNDERGROUND RAILROAD

The Underground Railroad is defined as an occasionally organized, frequently serendipitous, network of assistance that enabled individuals to escape from **slavery**, most often traveling from the American **South** to the North. Though there have long been mythologized interpretations of the

Underground Railroad as an example of benevolent white people helping the downtrodden enslaved blacks, recent research has revealed that, more often than not, it was a situation of African Americans helping each other and helping themselves to escape from the hell of slavery. Certainly, some white abolitionists, such as Levi Coffin and John Rankin, did participate vigorously, but it was more commonly the unsung free and enslaved African Americans who put their lives on the line to help others. Often, the fugitives simply traveled alone and with no systematic assistance.

Due to the tremendous risks inherent to working with the Underground Railroad, most dangerously after 1850 with the enactment of the Fugitive Slave Law, scant records remain. Nevertheless, a few brave souls managed to write of their experiences escaping themselves and assisting others, resulting in what now is considered Underground Railroad **literature**. Consisting of **slave narratives**, historical documents, and works of **fiction**, this body of writing reveals the profound dangers undertaken by such remarkable nineteenth-century authors as Harriet Tubman, **Frederick Douglass**, John Parker, **William Wells Brown**, **Ellen and William Craft**, **Hannah Crafts**, Harriet Beecher Stowe, and **Harriet Jacobs**. A significant early source, William Still's 1872 volume *The Underground Railroad* provides a wealth of historical material about the many refugees from slavery Still and others helped to escape. Later writers—including **Toni Morrison**, **Sherley Anne Williams**, and **Octavia Butler**—sought to capture this powerful time in **history** through fictional accounts, often in the unique genre of **neo-slave narrative**.

No matter the category of writing, several themes pervade Underground Railroad works, with particular attention to matters of feminism. In describing the circumstances of escape, these works regularly refer to slavery's forces of oppression and mistreatment that cause enslaved people to flee. Though the works depict men who seek **freedom** for a variety of reasons, enslaved women experience uniquely gender-specific humiliation. This oppression, often of a sexual nature, results in enslaved women subject to unbearable abuse from white men. For these women, the systematic degradation of slavery often prevents them from keeping a **family** together, assaults their **identity** as women, denies them the agency of **motherhood**, and results in their often innovative attempts at resistance.

One of the earliest Underground Railroad texts is Frederick Douglass's 1845 *Narrative of the Life of Frederick Douglass, an American Slave, Written by Himself*. In this slave narrative, Douglass explores issues of identity through his trials in learning to read and in his rebellion with the slave breaker Edward Covey, as well as his later failed and then successful attempts at escape. Douglass reveals his feminist concerns in several ways in this text. Early on, he recounts a horrific experience watching his Aunt Hester being severely beaten by an overseer, and he alludes to the probable sexual exploitation she undergoes at the hands of this man. In addition, when Douglass writes about Sophia Auld, the white Baltimore mistress who initially begins teaching him to read, he shows that slavery corrupts her nature too, causing it to devolve from relatively kind to thoroughly evil. Following the time of the narrative, throughout Douglass's long life, he worked for equality for all, remaining committed to women's suffrage long after slavery ended.

Hannah Crafts's autobiographical novel *The Bondwoman's Narrative* was written in the 1850s, though not published until 2002 in an edition edited by Henry Louis Gates, Jr. Now considered to be the earliest novel written by an African American woman, and the only novel written by an enslaved black woman, this text relates the ordeals that its protagonist undergoes in slavery as well as her eventual escape. Interestingly, in its feminist perspective, the novel also reveals the shared plight of sexual abuse between enslaved woman and slave mistress, particularly considering the fluid definitions of **race**. And in describing Hannah's escape from North Carolina to New Jersey, the novel fits well into the Underground Railroad tradition.

In 1861, Harriet Jacobs published *Incidents in the Life of a Slave Girl* under the pseudonym Linda Brent. One of the earliest slave narratives published by a woman, *Incidents* breaks many taboos through its representation of the sexual exploitation of enslaved women. Jacobs is particularly revolutionary in using her own **sexuality** as resistance, when she becomes pregnant by an unmarried white man of her own choosing, in order to fend off the unwanted advances of her married white master. Through her descriptions of the excruciating circumstances and confused identity of at once being an enslaved woman and a mother, Jacobs reveals the depths of this unique torment. Although she eventually flees northward in a classic Underground Railroad escape, this is preceded by her unprecedented experience hiding for seven years in her grandmother's attic, managing to watch over her two children, however distantly.

In the second half of the twentieth century, the Underground Railroad influenced many works of fiction, ranging from **Margaret Walker**'s *Jubilee* (1966) to **Ishmael Reed**'s *Flight to Canada* (1976) to Toni Morrison's *Beloved* (1987). While many of these works employ the approach of the neo-slave narrative, others, such as Reed's *Flight* and Octavia Butler's *Kindred* (1979), defy genre, at once incorporating the slave narrative, along with speculative fiction, fantasy, and science fiction.

In *Kindred*, Butler weaves an intricate story of life in 1970s California, time travel, and slavery in the early nineteenth century in Maryland. The experiences of the novel's protagonist, Dana, redefine the Underground Railroad to include a journey of time as well as space. Suddenly ripped from her 1976 home, Dana finds herself forced to interact with, and compelled to protect, a sometimes repellant white slave owner, Rufus Weylin, who will eventually become her great-grandfather. In part because of Dana's biracial contemporary marriage, complex relationships abound in *Kindred*, with poignant revelations about both contemporary and antebellum issues of racial and gender interaction. Butler's novel is especially noteworthy for its commentary on the inadequacies of twentieth-century teaching on slavery, particularly regarding the plight of enslaved women.

Sherley Anne Williams's 1986 neo-slave narrative *Dessa Rose* delivers an important message about the complexities of gender dynamics in ante- and postbellum American society. Though centered on the perspectives of an enslaved African American woman, the eponymous Dessa, the novel also emphasizes the growing sense of female solidarity possible for white and black women suffering gender and race oppression. Through her interaction with the mostly sympathetic white character Ruth ("Rufel"), Dessa learns that there is a diversity of white viewpoints on the humanity of African Americans. By novel's end, Ruth, Dessa, Nathan, Harker, and the other refugees from slavery **work** together in a scheme to thwart the slaveholding system. With Ruth pretending to sell the African Americans, the group raises enough money for the blacks to take a less typical Underground Railroad journey: They strike out for the American West.

Perhaps the most acclaimed Underground Railroad text of the twentieth century, Toni Morrison's *Beloved* won the 1988 Pulitzer Prize for fiction and was certainly a key ingredient in the decision to award Morrison the Nobel Prize for Literature in 1993. A neo-slave narrative inspired, like *Dessa Rose*, by historical events, *Beloved* focuses intensely on the protagonist Sethe's efforts to be a mother. Morrison has said in many interviews that when she learned of the historical Margaret Garner's decision in 1856 to kill her child rather than allowing her to be reenslaved, she was struck with what it must have taken to make such a decision. Daring to decide what would happen to her children, Garner took a revolutionary stand to assert her right to do so. As the fictionalized Sethe makes the same harsh choice, Morrison reveals the poignancy and repercussions of such a decision. Parallel to Douglass fighting back with Covey and Jacobs choosing to have an affair with a man not her master, Sethe chooses an innovative approach to resisting slavery, here through infanticide. Yet before this development, Sethe and others from Sweet Home also plan to escape northward, from northern Kentucky to Cincinnati, participating in an organized plan of Underground Railroad intent.

Morrison is not the only African American woman author inspired by Margaret Garner's radical action. In 1857, **Frances E. W. Harper** published her powerful poem "The Slave Mother: A Tale of the Ohio" that also recounts this mother's painful decision. Revealing the fact that a "slave mother" is, by definition, an oxymoron, Harper's poem evokes the emotional torment attendant on Garner's decision, while simultaneously imploring that her readers take action to end slavery. While she laments that Ohio can no longer provide a refuge for an enslaved woman fleeing hell, Harper sympathizes with the desperation Garner faced and reveals the ripple effect of this mother's decision, far beyond her own time and place. Once her cousin's house in Cincinnati was surrounded, there was no Underground Railroad refuge possible for Margaret Garner and her family.

Throughout African American literature, the Underground Railroad is a powerful vehicle for revealing much about slavery, particularly what might cause an enslaved woman to believe she could strike out for freedom and take the terrible risks inherent in an escape attempt.

See also Historical Fiction; Quilting

Works About

National Underground Railroad Freedom Center. www.freedomcenter.org.

Still, William. *The Underground Railroad.* 1872. Salem, NH: Ayer, 1992.

Kristine Yohe

 **V**

VENUS

Suzan-Lori Parks's 1996 play *Venus* is loosely based on the story of a South African woman, Saartjie Baartman, who was taken to London in the early nineteenth century, encaged, and exhibited in a traveling sideshow due to her unconventional physiognomy. Parks combines retelling with reimagining as she brings to the forefront how Baartman was an image of both fascination and revulsion for the white audience who came to see her nude public display in London and Paris in the early nineteenth century. The popularity of the exhibit sparked a debate as to whether the "Hottentot Venus" display constituted **slavery**; ultimately, a court heard a case to determine whether the exhibitioner should be sentenced under England's antislavery laws.

Parks uses Baartman's **history** as the backdrop of the play but does not focus solely on the familiar objectification of the black woman's **body** but instead reaches back to reconfigure and make tangible the woman, not just the image of desire who became known for her sexual organs and posterior. In fact, after her death, Baartman's body was dissected and her sexual organs and buttocks were preserved and housed in the Musee de l'Homme in Paris until the late twentieth century. Parks, however, places her focus on imagining Baartman as a sexual woman, not one who was just "sexualized." While we see her through a typical lens—being labeled by whites as lascivious—underneath she surfaces as a woman who uses her body to her advantage. It is true that one could argue that Venus does come to perpetuate her own exploitation, but it is also possible that she is aware of how she could change her situation somewhat, even on a miniscule level. She is aware that the scientist is fascinated by her, and may even **love** her, and therefore has a willing sexual relationship with him that wins her towering wigs, perfume, and being taken care of, to some degree.

Although she is eventually abandoned and dissected by the scientist who both loves and loathes her simultaneously, Parks reconfigures her as more than the sideshow freak—as a woman, who like other black women characters in her writing, uses her situation as an opportunity to move, as best as possible, from a position of victimhood. In her retelling of Baartman's story, Parks not only interrogates the enslaved woman's coping mechanisms, but she also exposes one of the world's most abhorrent stories of racism, objectification, envy, and oppression.

Works About

Basting, Anne Davis. "Performance Review: *Venus* by Suzan-Lori Parks." *Theatre Journal* 49.2 (May 1997): 223–225.

Elam, Harry. "Body Parts: Between Story and Spectacle in *Venus* by Suzan-Lori Parks." In Jeanne Colleran and Jenny S. Spencer eds., *Staging Resistance: Essays on Political Theater*. Ann Arbor: University of Michigan Press, 1998. 265–286.

Lyman, Elizabeth Dyrud. "The Page Refigured: The Verbal and Visual Language of Suzan-Lori Parks's *Venus*." *Performance Research* 7.1 (March 2002): 90–100.

Miller, Greg. "The Bottom of Desire in Suzan-Lori Parks's *Venus*." *Modern Drama* 45.1 (Spring 2002): 125.

Wright, Laura. " 'Macerations' French for 'Lunch': Reading the Vampire in Suzan-Lori Parks's *Venus*." *Journal of Dramatic Theory and Criticism* 17.1 (Fall 2002): 69–86.

Young, Jean. "The Re-Objectification and Re-Commodification of Saartjie Baartman in Suzan Lori-Parks' *Venus*." *African American Review* 31.4 (Winter 1997): 699–708.

Brandon L. A. Hutchinson

VIOLENCE

"Violence" exceeds the boundaries of a single narrative, character, voice, historical viewpoint, cultural context, place, or event because its effects often cannot be separated from its causes. For those who experience violence and its effects, it is also a traumatic reality that overwhelms and exceeds the affected individual's cognitive comprehension, ordinary **memory**, and speech capacity. Because violence is both a painful or traumatic historical reality and a symptom of ideological oppression such as racism, the African American women writers who seek to interrogate and represent the effects of violence voice their struggle with the discursive or linguistic constraints that simultaneously expose and conceal these effects.

Toni Morrison, in her afterword to *The Bluest Eye* (1970), discusses her choice to use the image of marigold seeds that do not, and indeed cannot, grow in the ground because of the land's hostile conditions. It is, however, the case that flowers of evil have grown in the land, that incest, **rape**, **family** violence, emotional abuse, physical and spiritual scarification, which are the direct effects of racism, provide a toxic "ground" for growing victims, which the **community** at large will later say "had no right to live" (206). By foregrounding the infertility of the land and of the marigold seeds planted that tragic autumn by Pecola's two friends, Frieda and Claudia, Morrison feels that she was best able to access the background of "illicit, traumatic, incomprehensible sex coming to its dreaded fruition" (213). Reflecting on her authorial ability to capture the horrors of self-hatred and misrecognition caused by endemic racism, Morrison expresses her satisfaction at how, in the novel's opening, she was able to capture the insidious dynamics of community secrecy and intergenerational trauma. But she also laments her own inability to adequately represent the silence. That Pecola wants blue eyes and will go to any length to get them, even if they are blue marbles implanted by a colored, xenophobic, male pedophile who disavows his own African heritage, means that the "bluest eye" will come to symbolize a number of things in the novel in relation to different scenes and types of violence. For instance, the "bluest eye" symbolizes the violence inherent in the complicity of various members of the society with respect to rape, incest, and **domestic** violence. It also symbolizes the violence that is inherent in internalized racism and self-hatred; and as such, it becomes coextensive with externalized racism, sexism, and social abjection. Also symbolizing forms of ideological "blindness" that manifest themselves symptomatically in and through intergenerational trauma, human **sexuality**, **myths**, and perceptions of childhood or, especially in this case, girlhood, "the bluest eye" indexes invisible as well as visible forms of social insanity. As important and very poignantly, Pecola's blue eyes represent the gender-specific insanity women can experience as a result of sexual violence, social abjection, emotional abuse, and psychological trauma.

There are many more things that the black girl's blue eyes may symbolize in this novel. However, as Morrison has observed, there are limits to what a literary symbol or figure can achieve with respect to probing the depths of suffering experienced by rape survivors or victims of violence, or with respect to representing the complex dynamics of individual, community, and audience witnessing. Morrison adamantly refuses to accept that rape and domestic abuse associated with racial violence constitute a social enigma, nor is she willing to accept the fact that African American writers, such as herself, cannot find new or better ways of addressing and representing the nature of the victims' or community's silence on the matter of women's sexual torture and emotional torment. In her afterword to *The Bluest Eye*, Morrison finds, in retrospect, that the "silence" and "void" corresponding to Pecola's traumatic experiences "should have had a shape–like the emptiness left by a boom or a cry. It required a sophistication unavailable to me, and some deft manipulation of the voices around her [Pecola]" (215). Though she confesses her perceived failure to capture this void, by having Pecola's incestuous rape experience with her father turn into an unwanted, teenage pregnancy, and by having her girlfriends indirectly testify to their limited knowledge of the circumstances surrounding Pecola's sexual abuse, Morrison delves into the matter of what is known by whom, at what time, under what circumstances, and at whose expense.

In taking this approach, this author crucially considers what the violated, black female **body** bears witness to, consciously or not. The body's silent affects or corporeal markers of emotional, physical, psychic, and spiritual distress can bear witness to the loss of voice and ability to articulate, let alone conceive of, the wrongs that were suffered as a result of various assaults or violences to being; it can bear witness to the loss of memory, sanity, sense of self, belonging, or being through various means, tears and crying being only two of the more obvious physical signs. Pecola develops unsightly twitches and erratic body movements; however, in other African American women's writings on the subject of rape and violence, the body may be screened by language, only partially imaginable as that which bears witness to specific or generalized violence against African American individuals, or utterly detached and dissociated from other aspects of being, such as psychic or spiritual integrity. For example, **Maya Angelou**'s narrator, in "The Detached," enunciates self-**death** as being "internal." Some biographical **slave narratives**, such as the one written by **Octavia V. Rogers Albert** in *The House of Bondage or Charlotte Brooks and Other Slaves* (1890), document accounts of the emotional and physical torments of slave mothers. In Albert's interview with Charlotte Brooks later in the text, Brooks attributes the deaths of all her children, one of whom was her first master's son, to a lack of motherly attention. Using the interview style as a more direct form of testimony and witnessing, Albert illustrates how **slavery**'s destruction of emotional and physical bonds between a mother and her children constitutes a form of violence that produces "milk tears" in addition to lacrimal tears, that produces children's death as a result of imposed, maternal neglect.

What the different literary approaches, styles, and forms adopted by these African American women writers testify to is the importance of witnessing in survivors' and victims' lives. While such witnessing may be a way of acting out or working through the various obstacles to comprehension, memory, desire, mourning, and **love**, or as a means of negotiating new ways of overcoming traumatic memories and stress disorders (being thought of by the present generation of trauma scholars as a pathology of **history** rather than self), it can also expose the ways in which violence manifests itself in various love relationships. **Literature** thus plays a vital role with respect to witnessing traumatic events and mediating forms of violence, since, as Holocaust historian Dominick LaCapra argues, "violence in unmediated form may be more likely when there are no accepted or legitimated modes of symbolizing difference and conflict in an effective manner that enables them to be addressed and to some extent dealt with" (60). The question that African American women writers struggle with when representing violence and its effects is the question of how to re-present violence without perpetuating its traumatic effects and sustaining its pathological, historical legacy. LaCapra's larger point about the mediation of violence through socially or politically legitimated avenues of resistance and recovery is that anyone can suffer from "structural trauma," which he defines as the speaking subject's alienated relation to language, to nature, to "species-being," and to "transhistorical absence" (77). Not everyone, however, suffers from "historical trauma," which entails a subject position that is incommensurable with the subjective, witnessing positions occupied by perpetrators and other witnesses.

In *Fires in the Mirror*, **Anna Deavere Smith** experiments with voice in ways that place the female body—her own body—at the center of performance consisting of a series of witness interviews about a traumatic car accident involving two black children and the ensuing racial violence that erupted between blacks and Hasidic Jews in the Crown Heights section of Brooklyn, New York, on August 19, 1991. Smith's theory about ways of presenting as well as negotiating racial and ethnic difference involves experimenting with the "travel" from other to the self, which is a departure from acting techniques based on "psychological realism." Desiring an acting technique that did not rely on experience based on a performer's "real life," Smith set to prove her hypothesis, namely, that "[i]f we were to inhabit the speech pattern of another, and walk in the speech of another, we could find the individuality of the other and experience that individuality viscerally" (xxvii). In other words, she was proposing that performing the other could be a useful way of learning about the other, that instead of using the self as a frame of reference as in conventional acting methods, the feat of enacting difference would require that "the frame of reference for the other would *be* the other" (xxvii). What Smith believed was that if we are resistant to acting like another human being, we also may have strong inhibitions about hearing, seeing, and empathizing with the other. These inhibitions further would prevent us from comprehending the violent actions or histories of other persons considered to be unlike ourselves. In the course of her vocal and bodily performance of various witnesses or characters associated in some way with the Crown Heights eruption of violence, Smith enacts or takes on the otherness of the Reverend Al Sharpton (a well-known New York activist and minister), Rivkah Siegal (a Lubavitcher woman), Norman Rosenbaum (the brother of the man who was mobbed and killed after the accident), Michael S. Miller (executive director at the Jewish Community Relations Council), Monique "Big Mo" Matthews (a Los Angeles rapper), and various other Crown Heights residents of different gender, **race**, religious affiliation, educational level, and **class**. Smith's female body undergoes startling and surprising transformations during the course of her performance, and even without the benefit of seeing this performance live, it is possible for readers of her text to bear witness to the other's uncanny presence that is given to be seen in her still photographs and the written script. What Smith wishes to impress upon her audiences is that "[t]he mirrors of society do not mirror society" (xxviii). This recognition affords the reader or spectator (or indeed, tertiary witness) an opportunity to examine the ways in which literary devices, such as the symbol, figure of speech, or image, operate as partial mirrors that do not mirror society but rather imperfectly mirror a given society's dominant belief systems or worldview.

When African American women writers such as Smith, Angelou, Albert, and Morrison deploy literary devices or adopt narrative strategies so as to expose the blind spots within the oppressive ideologies and representational systems they wish to contest, different issues will emerge in their writings as to how to represent the invisible, the ineffable, the unknown, or the unspeakable dimensions of violence and its wide-ranging effects. Traumatic, corporeal affects such as numbing, partial paralysis, irregular breathing or menstrual bleeding, and other "silent" markers of violence's indelible effects, are sometimes represented in African American women's writing through the use of sensory cues such as smells, sounds, colors, rhythms, sensations, or emotions. An author's strategic use of such sensory cues effectively may index different forms of sensory conversion or synaesthesia, different registers of emotional shock or psychic disturbance, different levels of consciousness or perception, and different orders of traumatic representation and visceral response. For example, by using color to signify volatile and mutable emotional states that correspond indirectly with the experience of violence, women writers find novel ways to express the psychic, emotional, corporeal, and spiritual changes in a human being that result from violence.

The blue color of indigo-stained hands, in Julie Dash's *Daughters of the Dust* (1991), for instance, symbolizes slavery and rape as well as spiritual legacy and continuity. Despite having historically accurate information about the impermanence of the poisonous indigo dye used in the indigo processing plants on Florida's Sea Islands from Dr. Margaret Washington Creel, an expert on the Gullah, Dash decides to deploy the image of Nana Peazant's blue-stained hands in an anachronistic manner to "create a new kind of icon [and symbol] around slavery rather than the traditional showing of the whip marks or the chains" (Dash 31). This is one of the ways that African American women writers, playwrights, and filmmakers readjust the "mirrors of society" to interrogate the intergenerational legacy of violence and to discover new ways of averting the effects of a potentially violent gaze or demeaning approach. That is to say, Dash employs an entire spectrum of adjectival meanings for the word *violent* instead of adopting the obselete verb form, "to violence," or the noun form, "violence," as a means of achieving her vision of the Ibo tribe's American acculturation and assimilation. To artistically play with the adjectival senses of the word *violent*, as many of these writers do, is to expand the lexicon for what qualifies as violence in modern society, while simultaneously pointing out the deficiences of these English terms and meanings for African Americans who are the descendants and heirs of racial, ethnic, class, gender, and religious violence.

In her interview with Julie Dash, feminist critic bell hooks applauds this filmmaker's use of creative anachronism, avowing that it is crucial for black female writers and filmmakers to depart from dominant culture's dependence on "reality," "accuracy," "authenticity" by taking flight into the imaginative realms of utopia, fantasy, folly, and even nonsense. It is precisely because, in the process of documenting, representing, and rearticulating violent histories, truth claims cannot be verified as a result of the often fragmented, incomplete, and inaccurate accounts of primary eyewitnesses, victims, and bystanders, it can be liberating and **healing** for artists such as Dash to avert the cinematic "white gaze" by resituating the audience's vision and perceptions of African American slavery. Dash does this by taking aesthetic liberties with historical accounts of slavery and sexual violence, thereby transforming such forms of violence into a cinematic experience that is sensual but not pornographic in its display of beautiful black women. By directing the cinematic gaze to the black female body but refusing to eroticize the suffering and **beauty** of that body, this black feminist filmmaker intervenes in historical debates about pornography and visual culture.

Carolyn J. Dean proposes that the numbness many trauma scholars and others exposed to violence, or images and thoughts of violence on a regular basis, experience can result in "empathy" or "compassion" fatigue. The pervasive perception of a "numb" public, held by humanitarian organizations such as Amnesty International and the French Doctors without Borders, informs our daily consumption of violent images in the media, to the point where "pornography allegorizes the causes and effects of our numbness and thereby of threats to empathic identification in a wide variety of Holocaust discussions" (93). Some black historians calculate that the lives lost to the black slave trade far outnumber those lost to the Holocaust by hundreds of millions, and a number of African American women writers (such as Angelou and Smith) judiciously use the word *holocaust* to describe black suffering; however, the point is not that these two things are comparable or in any way coextensive with one another in terms of their historical specificity but that the insights gained from these and other historical traumas can, and do, affect twentieth-century black female authors' and playwrights' representations of women's suffering. What Dash, **Toni Cade Bambara**, and bell hooks think is important, in terms of how black female sexuality is portrayed in literature, **film**, the theater, and academic criticism, is an ethics and aesthetics that allow numbed or traumatized audiences, whatever their particular histories might be, to revisualize how black women have lived their legacies of violence as mothers, lovers, prostitutes, lesbians, daughters, and unwitting matriarchs. Dash, Bambara, and hooks believe that it can be an affirmative artistic exercise not to mirror and thus not to replicate the violence(s) experienced by members of a given society. The production of fantastic or utopian images of black societies, such as the kind witnessed in Dash's *Daughters of the Dust* or **Zora Neale Hurston**'s ***Their Eyes Were Watching God*** (1937), may be a valuable way of shortcircuiting violence as an overt or subliminal means of communication, such that an ethics of responsibility can emerge as a supplement to, or in place of, nonetheless prevalent, artistic spectacles of pain, trauma, and suffering.

One of Dash's solutions to the issue of pornographic representation and sexual violence is the figure of The Unborn Child, who represents ancestral spirits and continuity in the form of a wise, prepubescent girl. Wearing an indigo-colored ribbon in her hair to symbolize her **ancestors**' slavery, The Unborn Child narrates the Peazant family's history on Ibo island. Her spiritual roots in Africa and her future place on the U.S. mainland allow this figure to symbolize aspects of intergenerational **spirituality**, violence, and memory. In Dash's *Daughters of the Dust*, the audience becomes aware of how powerful the use of color can be as a means of evoking different emotional, sensory, mnemonic, and corporeal registers and multifarious dimensions of cultural and historical meaning. By acknowledging that violence, whether as a historical event and traumatic cause or as an experienced symptom, can function in multifarious ways to blur the conceptual boundaries between the human and nonhuman, community and personhood, victim and perpetrator, good and evil, voice and silence, slavery and **freedom**, right and wrong, childhood and adulthood, the present and the past (or future), this African American filmmaker and writer seeks to address the corporeal, spiritual, psychic, as well as abstract, dimensions of violence but does so through the use of visual tropes that index metaphysical, abstract, ephemeral, and otherwise invisible links between family members and their individual histories. In the course of the film, the color blue comes to represent different kinds of metamorphoses or conversions; that is, it concretizes the conversion of one sensory affect (i.e., joy or pain) into another (i.e., sadness or anger), marks the transformation of one sensory experience or bodily memory for another (Nana's for The Unborn Child), and helps to chart the evolution of women's experiences of rape or abuse into childbirth, nonheterosexual sexuality, and corporeal memory.

Thus when Morrison and other African American women writers, such as Angelou, Dash, Smith, and Hurston, address the relation between voice and silence so as to interrogate the shape of violence and its effects upon African American communities and the individuals that comprise them, these writers act as cartographers that map out both the known and unknown dimensions of racial, ethnic, sexual, class, and religious violence. For these and other women writers, such cartography is as much a question of how not to make history repeat itself as a question of how to differentiate between different witnessing positions and modes of traumatic representation and how to make these things matter differently in the lives of those (still) affected by violence.

Works About

Dash, Julie. *Daughters of the Dust: The Making of an African American Woman's Film*. New York: New York Press, 1992.

Dean, Carolyn. "Empathy, Pornography, and Suffering." *differences* 14.1 (Spring 2003): 88–124.

hooks, bell. "Dialogue between bell hooks and Julie Dash, April 26, 1992." *Daughters of the Dust: The Making of an African American Woman's Film.* New York: New York Press, 1992. 27–67.

LaCapra, Dominick. *Writing History, Writing Trauma.* Baltimore, MD: Johns Hopkins University Press, 2001.

Lorelee Kippen

VOICE FROM THE SOUTH, A

Anna Julia Cooper's first published—and most celebrated—work, *A Voice from the South* (1892) represents one of the first African American feminist texts. Boldly attacking the problems afflicting African Americans, particularly black women, in the wake of Emancipation and Reconstruction, she compellingly reveals the racial, gender, and **class** prejudices responsible for their ongoing oppression. Yet throughout this collection of speeches and essays, Cooper consistently elevates the invaluable yet unacknowledged contributions black women make to **family**, **community**, and American society.

Structurally, the text is divided into two parts: "Soprano Obligato," signifying the individual voice of one black woman from the **South**, and "Tutti ad Libitum," suggesting the collective **identity** of the larger African American community. Whereas the four essays in the second half more broadly consider questions impacting all African Americans such as widespread national racism or theories of racial uplift, part one, also composed of four essays, examines the special case of the African American woman, opening with an arresting metaphor of her hitherto muted, silenced voice.

In her short prologue "Our Raison d'Être," Cooper first introduces her peerless narrator, the Black Woman from the South. Here she also delineates the need for such a text, for this Black Woman, embodying a formerly voiceless constituency of American society, must speak and be heard. Charged with communicating her own experiences as well as those of "her people," she adopts a peculiarly grand, authoritative tone, which has led a number of critics to analyze the seeming irreconcilability of the competing voices within *A Voice from the South.* Certainly those moments where Cooper endeavors to speak for a black female majority that remained largely uneducated reveal her own vexed position. (As a highly educated African American woman, she was uniquely accomplished; her engagement with ancient and contemporary writers throughout these essays demonstrates her intelligence and proficiency as an academic.) And periodically, Cooper invokes rather traditional constructions of womanhood, appearing torn between lingering **domestic** ideals and an evolving feminist consciousness.

Despite such tensions, *A Voice from the South* emerges as unequivocally feminist and humanist in its outlook and agenda. Promoting black women's status through education, Cooper extends her argument to other people of color in "Woman versus the Indian," her direct response to white suffragist

Anna Shaw's address at the 1891 National Woman's Council. In the midst of her universalism, she condemns white feminists' exclusionary practices—their overt racism. Thus at the peculiar juncture of racial and sexual politics (the woman's movement), Cooper remains uncompromising in her frankness. She appears equally prepared to criticize black men's sexism through biting sarcasm and the use of personal anecdotes. In place of these flawed visions, she champions the black woman, whose unique voice and moral vision renew hope for the nation's future. Such is the abiding hope—glimpsed through her intellectual alacrity, relentless drive, and passionate appeals on behalf of all African American women—Cooper herself so clearly exemplified.

Works About

Alexander, Elizabeth. "'We Must Be about Our Father's Business': Anna Julia Cooper and the In-Corporation of the Nineteenth Century African-American Woman Intellectual." *Signs: Journal of Women in Culture and Society* 20.2 (Winter 1995): 336–356.

Carby, Hazel. "'On the Threshold of the Woman's Era': Lynching, Empire, and Sexuality in Black Feminist Theory." *Critical Inquiry* 12.1 (Autumn 1985): 262–277.

May, Vivian M. "Thinking from the Margins, Acting at the Intersections: Anna J. Cooper's *A Voice from the South*." *Hypatia: A Journal of Feminist Philosophy* 19.2 (Spring 2004): 74–91.

McCaskill, Barbara. "Anna Julia Cooper, Pauline Elizabeth Hopkins, and the African American Feminization of Du Bois's Discourse." *The Souls of Black Folk One Hundred Years Later*. Ed. Dolan Hubbard. Columbia: University of Missouri Press, 2003. 70–84.

Wallinger, Hanna. "The Five Million Women of My Race: Negotiations of Gender in W.E.B. Du Bois and Anna Julia Cooper." *Soft Canons: American Women Writers and Masculine Tradition*. Ed. Karen L. Kilcup. Iowa City: University of Iowa Press, 1999. 262–280.

Washington, Mary Helen. "Anna Julia Cooper: The Black Feminist Voice of the 1890s." *Legacy: A Journal of Women Writers* 4.2 (1987): 3–15.

Mary Alice Kirkpatrick

VROMAN, MARY ELIZABETH (192?–1967)

Born in Buffalo, New York, in the 1920s and raised in the West Indies, short **fiction** writer, novelist, and screenwriter Mary Elizabeth Vroman was the first African American woman invited to join the Screen Actors Guild. A graduate of the Alabama State Teacher's college, Vroman's **literature** demonstrates her commitment to the realistic yet optimistic portrayal of black life in the segregated **South** as well as her interest in preserving the legacy of early black women's organizations.

Best known for the short story "See How They Run," Vroman's other published works include *Esther* (1963), a novel about a black woman's quest to become a nurse; *Shaped to Its Purpose* (1965), a **history** of Delta Sigma Theta Sorority, Incorporated (of which Vroman was a member); and *Harlem Summer* (1967), a story about an Alabama boy's summer trip to Harlem. "See How They Run" chronicles the experiences of Miss Richards, a black teacher who presides over forty-three students in a one-room, segregated school. This story exposes how basic needs—housing, sustenance, and health care—precede learning. Vroman's tale anticipates **Alice Walker**'s *Meridian* (1976) in its discussion of the humanist prerequisites for activism.

The story focuses on the recalcitrant C. T., an unlikely achiever who, through Miss Richard's care and encouragement, comes to realize his full potential as a student and a person. Like **Toni Cade Bambara**'s "The Lesson," "See How They Run" demonstrates the commitment of black women to **community** uplift. First published in *Ladies' Home Journal*, "See How They Run" was adapted into the **film** *Bright Road* (1953) and featured Dorothy Dandridge and Harry Belafonte in starring roles.

Of Vroman's other works, *Shaped to Its Purpose* stands alone in its importance to black women's feminist history. Written to record the history of Delta Sigma Theta, the second black Greek-lettered organization founded by college-educated women, this text documents an important outgrowth of the nineteenth century's black women's club movement. Founded in January 1913 at Howard University, Delta Sigma Theta made service and activism a priority, participating in the Women's Suffrage March in Washington, D.C., in March of that same year. *Shaped to Its Purpose* paved the way for Paula Giddings's *In Search of Sisterhood: Delta Sigma Theta and the Challenge of the Black Sorority Movement* (1994) and documents the importance of black sororities in the ever-expanding feminist movement. Vroman died in April 1967 of surgical complications.

Works By

Esther. New York: Bantam, 1963.
Harlem Summer. New York: Putnam's, 1967.
Shaped to Its Purpose: Delta Sigma Theta, the First Fifty Years. New York: Random House, 1965.

Works About

Bachner, Saul. "Writing School Marm: Alabama Teacher Finds Literary Movie Success with First Short Story." *Ebony* (July 1952): 23–28.
Blicksilver, Edith. "See How They Run." *The Ethnic American Woman: Problems, Protests, Lifestyle*. Dubuque, IA: Kendall/Hunt, 1978. 125–143.

Shanna Greene Benjamin

WAITING TO EXHALE

Criticized by some black scholars for its poor representation of black male and female relationships coupled with the "in search of a good black man" motif, *Waiting to Exhale* (1992), a *New York Times* bestseller, is **Terry McMillan**'s third novel about the challenges of coming of age as a black female. The four protagonists, Savannah, Gloria, Robin, and Bernadette, take a journey toward self-**love** and self-acceptance. It can be argued that each woman individually quests for a resolution to the one aspect of her life that she feels could solve all of her problems. However, when viewed collectively, these women make up a composite of a self-assured, self-loving black woman.

The Rapunzel-like Bernadette's quest focuses on redefining her **identity** into a more self-constructed sense of herself. Gloria, on the other hand, quests for self-acceptance. An overweight single mother of a teenager, Gloria goes on one diet after another in order to possess a quality, thinness, that she feels will bring her the things that she thinks she lacks in life: a loving husband, more respect from her son, and physical **beauty**. Robin, along with Gloria, suffers from self-devaluation. Ironically, however, her extreme dedication to her appearance and the belief that she can get any man she wants do not replace the fact that she values herself so little that she ends up being used and abandoned by the very men she gets. The fourth woman in the novel is the single and childless Savannah. Although beautiful, smart, and professionally successful, thirty-six year-old Savannah sees her life as empty because it lacks emotional attachments that she believes can only be gotten from an intimate relationship with a man. Thus, Savannah gets involved in an affair with a married man and ends up spending most of her time alone.

Through close examination, readers can recognize McMillan's purpose for writing this third novel. The characters in the novel represent the bad decisions that many women unknowingly make that stifle their personal growth. The testimony of each character helps readers challenge socially constructed notions of romantic narratives. Moreover, although *Exhale* has universal appeal, McMillan, at times, through the use of call-and-response narrative, speaks directly to black women readers not only about the challenges of fighting the master narrative of romance but also about the implications of **race**, **class**, and gender. Through these characters, readers learn about the downfalls that come with buying into the Eurocentric construct of love relationships.

Thus, McMillan returns to her discussion about self-empowerment through personal reflection and reaffirms female identity in general and black female identity in particular. *Waiting to Exhale* was made into a film in 1995.

Works About

Harris, Tina M. "Interrogating the Representation of African American Female Identity in the Films *Waiting to Exhale* and *Set It Off.*" *Popular Culture Review* 10.2 (1999): 43.

——. "'Waiting to Exhale' or 'Breath(ing) Again': A Search for Identity, Empowerment, and Love in the 1990's." *Women and Language* 21.2 (1998).

Holland, Sharon P. "On *Waiting to Exhale*; or What to Do When You're Feeling Black and Blue: A Review of Recent Black Feminist Criticism." *Feminist Studies* 26.1 (2000): 101.

Jackson, Edward M. "Images of Black Males in Terry McMillan's *Waiting to Exhale.*" *MAWA Review* 8.1 (1993): 20.

Catherine Ross-Stroud

WALKER, ALICE (1944–   )

Alice Walker is the author of numerous novels, collections of **fiction**, **poetry**, essays, and children's books. There have been several collections of academic essays published about her and her **work**, countless reviews of her writing, and most recently, a biography in 2004, Evelyn White's *Alice Walker: A Life*. Though highly published in several genres before writing the acclaimed Book Award–, Townsend Prize–, and Pulitzer Prize–winning novel ***The Color Purple***, this 1982 text brought her to the forefront of the literary world. Central to her works is her idea of **womanism**, which she defines in the beginning of her collection of nonfiction ***In Search of Our Mothers' Gardens*** (1983). Other important themes she fully develops in her work are the relationships between black men and women, **family** members, and their **community**, southern culture, **folklore**, and the **civil rights movement**.

Walker was born on February 9, 1944, the eighth and final child to Willie Lee and Minnie Tallulah Grant Walker, sharecroppers in the small and poor town of Eatonton, Georgia. The Walkers made between $200 and $300 a year in the cotton fields to support and raise their children. In 1952, when Alice was eight, she was disfigured and partially blinded when she was accidentally shot in the eye by pellets from her brother's BB gun. Until the scar tissue was removed six years later in Boston, Walker fantasized about suicide because she considered herself ugly and disfigured. However, this incident allowed her to observe more closely the relationships between people. After the minor operation she became class valedictorian and high school prom queen, graduating from Butler-Baker High School in 1961.

This injury made her eligible for a scholarship to Spelman College, a black women's school in Atlanta. Her mother gave her three parting gifts: a suitcase for independence, a typewriter for creativity, and a sewing machine for self-sufficiency. At Spelman faculty members such as Howard Zinn and Staughton Lynn influenced her as well as the civil rights activities in Atlanta in which she was involved. However, Spelman's training for proper young women did not bode well with Walker.

She accepted a scholarship to Sarah Lawrence College in 1964, a predominantly white women's school in Bronxville, New York, where she began her writing career. In her education she discovered nineteenth-century Russian writers, Ovid, Chopin, the Brontës, Doris Lessing, and Simone de Beauvoir. She was lucky enough to travel to Africa in 1965. However, during the winter of her senior year she found herself pregnant in a world where reproductive health care was hard to come by and abortion was illegal, particularly inaccessible to people of color and those of low income. She felt her only choices were to kill herself or get an abortion but almost was unable to secure one until a friend gave her a phone number and her life back. After, she wrote poems incessantly and gave them to Muriel Ruykeyser, a teacher and well-known poet on campus. The professor helped the collection reach the publisher Harcourt Brace and Jovanovich. Walker graduated from Sarah Lawrence in 1966 with a B.A.

After graduation, she worked in the welfare department in New York City. She received a writing fellowship from Spelman to collect biographies and autobiographies of black women and spent the summer working in civil rights programs in Mississippi. There she met Melvyn Rosenman Leventhal, a white civil rights lawyer. They lived together in New York for a year, where she published a short story "To Hell with Dying," and an essay, "The Civil Rights Movement: What Good Was It?" which won a $300 prize from the American Scholar. On March 17, 1967, Walker and Leventhal married, becoming the first legally married interracial couple in Mississippi where previously an interracial couple could not live together, legally married or not. During those seven years in Mississippi, Walker worked with Head Start programs and served as writer-in-residence at Jackson State University and Tougaloo College.

Harcourt Brace and Jovanovich published her first book of poems, titled *Once*, in 1968. The poems focus on Africa, the **South**, **love**, and suicide and are almost in haiku form. The African poems describe the realities of African people and nature. The pieces on the South discuss the civil rights movement and are ironical even as they express sympathy. The verses on love examine complications, desire, loneliness, uncertainties, and forgiveness. This collection received little attention from critics, but the notice it did receive was positive.

During 1968 and 1969, the couple tried desperately to get pregnant and endured one miscarriage to avoid the draft. On November 17, 1969, Rebecca Grant, Walker's daughter, was born. In several essays Walker describes her fears that **motherhood** might disallow her career as a writer. At the time there were no models of successful black women who were mothers and writers. Fortunately, she was able to overcome her anxiety and continued to publish extensively over the years. Walker explains that much of her earlier writing was her method to maintain health, to avoid crises, and to survive.

In 1970 Walker was awarded the Radcliffe Institute Fellowship, and Harcourt Brace and Jovanovich published her first novel, *The Third Life of Grange Copeland*. This story examines three generations of a black share-cropping family whose experiences lead to abandonment, promiscuity, self-hatred, abuse, and murder via a southern landscape of harsh working conditions, racism, economic oppression, frustration, and little hope for the characters. Hope is given through African American folk culture and the civil rights movement. The novel's central character Grange Copeland and then Brownfield believe that sharecropping will cultivate success; however, this shortsightedness leads to frustration, rage, self-hatred, **domestic** abuse, and infidelity. The novel utilizes the themes of moral responsibility, hope through love, secular redemption, and black characters finding a way out on their own. Though the novel showcases the relationships of fathers and sons, how they treat black women becomes a theme that Walker continued to explore in her future works.

In 1972 Walker accepted temporary teaching positions while her husband remained in Mississippi. She taught at the University of Massachusetts, Boston, and Wellesley College, where she instructed one of the first classes in the nation on gender focusing on African American women's **literature**. In her classes at Wellesley she taught black women writers like **Phillis Wheatley** alongside Virginia Woolf.

She published *Revolutionary Petunias*, a book of poems in 1973, and *Langston Hughes: American Poet*, a children's biography of the famous poet in 1974. *Revolutionary Petunias* further develops some of her earlier themes: valuing the past, the difficulties of the present, and the hope for the future. Her book of short stories *In Love & Trouble* (1973) won the Rosenthal Award of the National Institute of Arts and Letters. "Everyday Use" and "The Revenge of Hannah Kemhufff" of that collection were published in *Best American Short Stories*. The former story first gave her access to anthropologist and writer **Zora Neale Hurston**. Though some of the stories were published previously in periodicals, many of them were new and told narratives of black women experiencing **violence**, injustice, oppression, false ideals, **death**, and dignity.

In 1974 the family of three moved to New York. In the following year Walker became a contributing editor to the feminist magazine *Ms.* In 1976 Walker and Leventhal divorced on good terms, and she returned to her maiden name, reclaiming the **history** of her **ancestors** walking to escape **slavery**. She later changed her name to Alice Tallulah-Kate Walker. That same year, her second novel, ***Meridan***, was published. *Meridian*, in one sense, is a continuation of the story of Grange Copeland. In this novel womanhood is depicted as problematic via tales of women who come to violent ends through their actions. Meridian Hill marries her high school friend, who never matures or understands her. She loves and wants to kill her own child. Through the civil rights movement, Meridan feels possibility for liberation and purpose in her life. This book has been described as a study of women and the inner dynamics of the civil rights movement. It addresses the morality of racism and asks in the novel: Would you kill for the revolution?

In 1977 Walker became associate professor at Yale University. She reunited with Robert Allen, editor of *Black Scholar*, whom she had known at Spelman. In 1978 she received the Guggenheim Fellowship. The following year brought two publications, an anthology of writings by Zora Neale Hurston, *I Love Myself When I'm Laughing . . . and Then Again When I'm Mean and Impressive*, and her third book of poems, *Good Night, Willie Lee, I'll See You in the Morning*. The collection of **poetry** deals with themes of her earlier works of poetry but diverges more fully into feminist ideals. The book is divided into five sections that examine love, history, disappointments in relationships, life as an artist, strong men like Martin Luther King, Jr., and **Malcolm X**, and women's connection to male power. Walker left New York for San Francisco to give her time to fully develop her next novel. In 1981 her second collection of stories, ***You Can't Keep a Good Woman Down***, was published by Harcourt.

The Color Purple, published in 1982, remained on the *New York Times* bestseller list for more than a year and was made into a movie directed by Steven Spielberg and starring Whoopi Goldberg, Danny Glover, and Oprah Winfrey in 1985. The **film** was nominated for several Academy Awards, though it did not win any. In 1983 she was awarded the Pulitzer Prize for the book and was the first African American woman ever to win the Pulitzer Prize for fiction. *The Color Purple* is an epistolary novel of ninety letters telling the story of Celie, an abused woman living in the Deep South. It covers some of the themes of her earlier work including women's relationship to men, domestic abuse, **rape**, and desire. It is told entirely in black folk English or vernacular. This book, similar to her story of Copeland Grange, exposed a particular type of black male behavior toward women and initiated a dialogue on what this abuse means for black women. Some critics felt her depictions revealed too much and called the characterization of Mr. — harsh, but this particular reading fails to see, as Walker points out, the necessity of this discussion as well as the evolution of the male characters as they begin to find their place in the world. In 2000 this novel went into its forty-second printing, and in 2004 it became a Broadway musical production premiering in Atlanta. She later published a collection of essays, unseen letters, and screenplay excerpts, *The Same River Twice: Honoring the Difficult: A Meditation of Life, Spirit, Art, and the Making of the Film*, The Color Purple, *Ten Years Later* (1996).

In 1983 she published her first nonfiction collection of essays on herself, the civil rights movement, literature, and black women, *In Search of Our Mothers' Gardens*. The title essay suggests looking low to reclaim our foremothers' art because creativity is in many types of work, including gardening, storytelling, and **quilting**. She believes that all writers are important and necessary, contributing to the full picture of humanity. This collection of thirty-six pieces also explores her **womanist** perspective, antinuclear activism, the need for black women literary models, Zora Neale Hurston, the women's movement, **Langston Hughes**, Cuba, and other topics. In the following year, she started her own publishing company with Robert Allen, Wild Tree Press, which closed in 1988. Soon after, Walker and Robert Allen ended their relationship, and she eventually announced her bisexuality.

During her involvement with the film *The Color Purple*, Walker became interested in female genital mutilation, an initiation rite that removes various parts of the female genitalia and is performed on an estimated 100 million girls and women in the Middle East, the Far East, and Africa. On this topic, she coproduced the Pratibha Parmar film *Warrior Marks* (1993) and wrote her fifth novel ***Possessing the Secret of Joy*** (1992). In this novel several characters from *The Color Purple* tell their story.

Walker continues to write in a variety of venues. Her nonfiction collections include *Living by the Word* (1988) and *Anything We Love Can Be Saved: A Writer's Activism* (1997). Her poetry includes *Horses Make the Landscape Look More Beautiful* (1984), *Her Blue Body Everything We Know: Earthling Poems, 1965–1990* (1991), *Sent by Earth: A Message from the Grandmother Spirit After the Bombing of the World Trade Center and the Pentagon* (2001), *Absolute Trust in the Goodness of the Earth: New Poems* (2003), and *A Poem Traveled Down My Arm* (2003). Her fiction includes ***The Temple of My Familiar*** (1989), ***By the Light of My Father's Smile*** (1998), *The Way Forward Is with a Broken Heart* (2000), and *Now Is the Time to Open Your Heart* (2004). Her children's books include *To Hell with Dying* (1988) and *Finding the Green Stone* (1991). Walker currently lives in northern California.

Works By

Alice Walker Banned. San Francisco: Aunt Lute Books, 1996.

The Color Purple: A Novel. New York: Harcourt Brace Jovanovich, 1982.

Everyday Use. New Brunswick, NJ: Rutgers University Press, 1994.

Good Night, Willie Lee, I'll See You in the Morning: Poems. New York: Dial, 1979.

I Love Myself When I'm Laughing . . . and Then Again When I'm Mean and Impressive: A Zora Neale Hurston Reader. Old Westbury, NY: Feminist Press, 1979.

In Love & Trouble: Stories of Black Women. New York: Harcourt Brace Jovanovich, 1973.

In Search of Our Mothers' Gardens: Womanist Prose. San Diego: Harcourt Brace Jovanovich, 1983.

Langston Hughes: American Poet. New York: Crowell, 1974 and 2002.

Meridian. New York: Harcourt Brace Jovanovich, 1976.

Once: Poems. New York: Harcourt Brace Jovanovich, 1968.

Possessing the Secret of Joy. New York: Harcourt Brace Jovanovich, 1992.

Revolutionary Petunias, and Other Poems. New York: Harcourt Brace Jovanovich, 1973.

The Temple of My Familiar. San Diego: Harcourt Brace Jovanovich, 1989.

The Third Life of Grange Copeland. New York: Harcourt Brace Jovanovich, 1970.

Warrior Marks: Female Genital Mutilation and the Sexual Blinding of Women. With Pratibha Parmar. New York: Harcourt, Brace, 1993.

You Can't Keep a Good Woman Down: Stories. New York: Harcourt Brace Jovanovich, 1981.

Works About

Banks, Erma Davis, and Keith Byerman. *Alice Walker: An Annotated Bibliography 1968–1986.* New York: Garland, 1989.

Gates, Henry Louis, Jr., and K. A. Appiah, eds. *Alice Walker: Critical Perspectives Past and Present.* New York: Amistad, 1993.

Lauret, Maria. *Alice Walker.* New York: St. Martin's Press, 2000.

White, Evelyn C. *Alice Walker: A Life.* New York: W. W. Norton, 2004.

Winchell, Donna Haisty. *Alice Walker.* New York: Twayne Publishers, 1992.

Wiseman, Laura Madeline. "Alice Walker." *Empowerment4Women* (January–February 2005). www.empowerment4women.org/respect.

Laura Madeline Wiseman

WALKER, MARGARET (1915–1998)

Margaret Abigail Walker Alexander was born in Birmingham, Alabama, on July 7, 1915. Encouraged at an early age by her parents Reverend Sigismund and Marion Dozier Walker to read, she immersed her life in **poetry** and philosophy. Though Walker read widely, the Holy Bible and the Bhagavad-Gita were chief among the texts that influenced her thinking and subsequent development as a writer.

A graduate of Northwestern University in 1935, she received her Bachelor of Arts degree and in 1936 began to **work** for the Federal Writers' Project. She met and worked with such writers as **Gwendolyn Brooks**, Frank Yerby, and **Richard Wright**. The two collaborated on Wright's endeavors; Walker provided significant research and seminal ideas on Wright's *Black Boy* (1945).

No single day in Walker's young life was ordinary, as she became an astute observer of life and **history**. Her **love** for languages, words, and ideas helped to determine and shape her literary activism. Her father's strong and proactive oratories against racial repression and oppression of American blacks in the **South** and across the nation as well influenced her perspective and outlook.

From the journey across the South with her parents and sister to relocate to New Orleans, Louisiana, and the harrowing experience she remembered it to be, Walker never forgot what the threats to personal safety felt like to her and to her **family**. As they traveled that distance on American highways without being able to use public facilities, this was only one remarkable impression of history upon her life.

Subsequently, she used her writing, and acquaintance with the power of words, the highest treasure of her life, and helped repeal the social, spiritual, and economic devastation of **race** hatred. As a writer, as a person, as a woman, she saw in herself an important and reasonable agent of social change to which she prolifically responded.

Her very first literary missive was the award-winning collection of poetry she titled *For My People* (1942). And that is how Walker saw the struggle for equal liberty in America—as beyond herself, beyond her interests, even beyond the borders of the South—and for the people of her color, deep into the total African diaspora of the Western Hemisphere.

Despite her formal training and education, and as part of the elite social structure of higher education in Mississippi, Walker retained a close cultural connection to the life and ethos of the struggle of black people, to be epitomized throughout her life in *For My People*. She utilized every aspect of black folk culture to contest social alienation that ranged from **drama** to ballad folk poetry to "badman" songs that told stories originating from African Americans in the South.

Also the author of the historical novel *Jubilee* (1966), Walker died on November 30, 1998, at the age of eighty-three.

Works By

The Ballad of the Free. Detroit: Broadside Press, 1970.

For My People. New Haven, CT: Yale University Press, 1942.

How I Wrote Jubilee and Other Essays on Life and Literature. Ed. Maryemma Graham. New York: Feminist Press at the City University of New York, 1990.

Jubilee. Boston: Houghton Mifflin, 1966.

October Journey. Detroit: Broadside Press, 1970.

On Being Female, Black, and Free: Essays by Margaret Walker, 1932–1992. Knoxville: University of Tennessee Press, 1997.

A Poetic Equation: Conversations between Nikki Giovanni and Margaret Walker. Washington, DC: Howard University, 1974.

Prophets for a New Day. Detroit: Broadside Press, 1966.

Richard Wright, Daemonic Genius: A Portrait of the Man, a Critical Look at His Work. New York: Warner Books, 1988.

Works About

Barksdale, Richard. "Margaret Walker: Folk Orature and Historical Prophecy." *Black American Poets between Worlds, 1940–1960*. Ed. R. Baxter Miller. Knoxville: University of Tennessee Press, 1986.

Bonetti, Kay. "An Interview with Margaret Walker Alexander." *Missouri Review* 15.1 (1992): 112–131.

Caton, Bill. "Margaret Walker Alexander." *Fighting Words: Words on Writing from 21 of the Heart of Dixie's Best Contemporary Authors.* Ed. Bill Caton and Bert Hitchcock. Montgomery, AL: Black Belt, 1995.

Collier, Eugenia. "Fields Watered with Blood: Myth and Ritual in the Poetry of Margaret Walker." *Black Women Writers (1950–1980): A Critical Evaluation.* Ed. Mari Evans. Garden City, NY: Anchor Press/Doubleday, 1984. 499–510.

Graham, Maryemma. "The Fusion of Ideas–An Interview with Margaret Walker Alexander." *African American Review* 27.2 (Summer 1993): 279–286.

Elisabeth S. James

WALTER, MILDRED PITTS (1922–   )

Experience has been the inspiration for Mildred Pitts Walter's writing. Born in Sweetville, Louisiana, the seventh of seven children to Paul, a log cutter, and Mary, a midwife and beautician, Walter had a childhood that was characterized by the challenges of poverty and the joys of **community**. Her **family** lived in two small houses owned by a lumber company, and the yard between the houses served as a community meeting place. Neighbors would congregate there on Saturday nights for food, dancing, and storytelling. These experiences had a powerful influence on Walter's later writing.

Walter's long, varied career has also had an impact on her books. At times a shipwright helper, dye salesperson, teacher, and lecturer, Mildred Walter—with her husband, Earl Walter—was also an activist for the Congress of Racial Equality (CORE) during the **civil rights movement**. Her activism was the embodiment of her beliefs that differences between people are not wrong and that all people are entitled to the same rights from the moment of birth. These core beliefs surely influenced her writing career. Walter was inspired to write when, as a teacher in southern California, she noticed a lack of African American characters in **children's and young adult literature**. She decided to write, and Lillie, the birthday girl character of her first book, was born.

Lillie of Watts: A Birthday Discovery (1969) is about a girl facing hardship on her eleventh birthday who is sustained by the strength of her family's **love**. Lillie returns in Walter's second book, *Lillie of Watts Takes a Giant Step* (1971), in which Lillie joins a campaign to celebrate the birthday of **Malcolm X** at her school.

Walter's award-winning writing celebrates the positive aspects of African American life. Families are important in her writing, as are friends and community members. In her writing, Walter often addresses themes of poverty, prejudice, courage, community, change, and strength. Heritage is also important, as her African American characters often develop and recognize their **identity**.

Walter has received many awards for her work. In 1984, *Because We Are* was named a Coretta Scott King honorable mention book; two years later, *Trouble's Child* received the same honor. In 1987, *Justin and the Best Biscuits in the World* was a Coretta Scott King winner. Walter missed the award ceremony. Ever an activist with a cause, Walter was marching in the Soviet Union for world peace.

Works By

Because We Are. New York: Lothrop, Lee and Shepard, 1983.

Brother to the Wind. New York: Lothrop, Lee and Shepard, 1985.

Darkness. New York: Simon and Schuster, 1995.

The Girl on the Outside. New York: Lothrop, Lee and Shepard, 1982.

Have a Happy... New York: Lothrop, Lee and Shepard, 1989.

Justin and the Best Biscuits in the World. New York: Lothrop, Lee and Shepard, 1986.

Kwanzaa: A Family Affair. New York: Lothrop, Lee and Shepard, 1995.

Lillie of Watts: A Birthday Discovery. Los Angeles: Ritchie, 1969.

Lillie of Watts Takes a Giant Step. New York: Doubleday, 1971.

The Liquid Trap. New York: Scholastic, 1975.

Mariah Keeps Cool. New York: Bradbury, 1990.

Mariah Loves Rock. New York: Bradbury, 1988.

The Mississippi Challenge. New York: Bradbury, 1992.

My Mamma Needs Me. New York: Lothrop, Lee and Shepard, 1983.

Second Daughter: The Story of a Slave Girl. New York: Scholastic, 1996.

Suitcase. New York: Lothrop, Lee and Shepard, 1999.

Tiger Ride. New York: Bradbury, 1993.

Trouble's Child. New York: Lothrop, Lee and Shepard, 1985.

Two and Too Much. New York: Bradbury, 1990.

Ty's One-Man Band. New York: Four Winds, 1980.

Work About

Henderson, Darwin L., and Consuelo W. Harris. "Profile: Choice, Courage, and Change Yield Character: An Interview with Mildred Pitts Walter." *Language Arts* (November 1992).

Heidi Hauser Green

WEDDING, THE

The Wedding (1995) by **Harlem Renaissance** author **Dorothy West** first began life as the manuscript "Where the Wild Grapes Grow." While publishers Houghton Mifflin felt that it was well written, they were equally concerned that a novel about middle-class blacks would not sell. West abandoned the project and in the 1960s incorporated the background into *The*

Wedding. She received a Mary Roberts Rinehart grant for the novel and a contract from Harper and Row. Yet this time it was West who would lay it aside, convinced that the era was not right for a novel about the concerns of light-skinned upper-class African Americans. West's concerns had less to do with salability and more to do with politics and reception; she feared that the prevalent mood of black militancy would generate hostile reviews from black and white reviewers alike. Over twenty years later, Jacqueline Kennedy Onassis, fellow Martha's Vineyard vacationer, convinced West that the time was right to resume **work** on the novel. Their literary partnership is memorialized in *The Wedding*'s dedication.

The Wedding is set on Oak Bluffs, Martha's Vineyard, at the end of the 1950s. Its characters are light-skinned black professionals who populate "The Oval," a carefully guarded geographic and social circle. The penetration of that circle by the darker-skinned, socially inferior Lute forms the primary conflict of the novel. Shelby Coles, engaged daughter of one of the prominent families, must decide between marriage to a white man whose profession as a **jazz** musician invites her **family**'s disdain and her attraction to the intruder who tries to convince her that she is fleeing her racial heritage by marrying white. Lute's argument holds sway temporarily as Shelby is forced to evaluate her family's social snobbery and articulated preference for those who can pass for white.

West maps the origins of the Coleses' preferences through flashbacks to earlier generations, demonstrating that the family has a long-standing anxiety about **race**, **class**, skin color, and sexual desire. In order to maintain the border around their world, they struggle against their ever-erupting attractions to those who do not meet their standards. Yet the very fact that this border requires such policing suggests its fraught and tenuous nature. West presents the threats to their world throughout, embodied in a cast of characters whose longings draw attention to the limitations of a world that defines itself in differing degrees as both "not black" and "not white," while simultaneously expressing longings for elements of what they attribute to each.

West's novel was well received by critics; Susan Kenney noted its "range of scope of language and imagery as well as the [novel's] broadness of vision," comparing her favorably to William Faulkner. In 1998, a less-successful television version appeared, produced by Oprah Winfrey, which replaced *The Wedding*'s light-skinned subjects with visibly black actors, suggesting that, once again, some were not yet ready for West's story.

See also Passing

Works About

Dalsgard, Katrine. "Alive and Well and Living on the Island of Martha's Vineyard: An Interview with Dorothy West, October 29, 1988." *Langston Hughes Review* (Fall 1993): 28–44.

Kenney, Susan. "Shades of Difference." *New York Times Book Review*, February 12, 1995, 11–12.

McDowell, Deborah E. "Conversations with Dorothy West." *The Harlem Renaissance Re-examined.* Ed. Victor A. Kramer. New York: AMS, 1987. 265–282.

Roses, Lorraine Elena. "Interviews with Black Women Writers: Dorothy West at Oak Bluffs, Massachusetts." *Sage* (Spring 1985): 47–49.

Steinberg, Sybil. "Dorothy West: Her Own Renaissance." *Publishers Weekly*, July 3, 1995, 34–35.

Jennifer Harris

WELLS-BARNETT, IDA B. (1862–1931)

Like **Frances E. W. Harper** and **Anna Julia Cooper**, Ida B. Wells-Barnett devoted much of her energy in the decades between Reconstruction and the turn into the twentieth century to causes of vital importance to the women of her **race**. Accounts of Wells's extended campaign against lynching often stress the tendency of white opponents (and even some African Americans) of her own day to view her as a radical political figure who regularly violated norms for ladylike behavior. However, such characterizations can obscure more gendered aspects of her activist social agenda, such as her lifelong involvement with women's groups (especially African American clubwomen) and her sustained commitment to nurturing children (particularly after her 1895 marriage to Chicago attorney Ferdinand Barnett).

Among the many allies who supported Wells's antilynching campaign, African American and British women played a particularly crucial role. In the early 1890s, Wells came to the attention of women leaders such as Josephine St. Pierre Ruffin and **Gertrude Bostell Mossell** through writing published in the *New York Age*. Wells had earlier established herself as a journalist in Memphis, Tennessee. She had originally moved there from her Mississippi birthplace to seek improved pay for the schoolteaching she had been doing since the **death** of both parents made her the major breadwinner for herself and her younger siblings. Biographers understandably tend to emphasize one event from her 1880s time in Memphis as pivotal in forging her dedication to racial justice: the unsuccessful lawsuit Wells brought against the Chesapeake and Ohio and Southwestern Railroad for removing her from a coach reserved for whites. But Wells's own **autobiography** also highlights another important dimension of this period, one that shows her clear understanding of writing as an avenue to support racial uplift. In that vein, she first published articles in the *Evening Star*, a local paper linked to a lyceum she had joined, and then for a column in the *Living Way*, a religious weekly that was soon syndicating the essays she signed as "Iola." By the early 1890s, Wells had gone on to become editor, co-owner, and major writer for a Memphis newspaper, the *Free Speech*. When several local Memphis men whom Wells knew to be of good character were lynched because their People's Grocery Store was undermining one run by local whites, Wells published an account in the *Free Speech* that raised such ire among whites that she had to abandon Memphis and the newspaper for her own safety. But a *New York*

Age feature story she wrote about her enforced exile prompted **Victoria Earle Matthews** and other prominent clubwomen to organize a gala dinner raising funds to support Wells's **work** against lynching. Wells's autobiography credits this occasion with promoting the founding of the Boston Woman's Era Club, whose *Woman's Era* publication regularly printed writings by leaders such as **Mary Church Terrell** and Josephine St. Pierre Ruffin. Wells also linked this event with the start of her public speaking career, which in turn led to an invitation from women activists in the British Isles to visit and share her anti-lynching message.

Wells would remain proactively connected with the clubwomen's movement, even after her marriage to Ferdinand Barnett, when she repeatedly took on leadership roles through local club work in Chicago. As her autobiography emphasizes, Wells-Barnett reveled in **motherhood**, while seeking at the same time to balance those responsibilities with public duties associated with her membership in an influential social **class** and her reputation as a well-known figure supporting causes such as recognition of African American achievements at the 1893 Columbian Exposition, continued integration of Chicago schools, and collaborations between black women and local white activists like Jane Addams, Celia Parker Wooley, and Mrs. George Plummer.

Works By

Crusade for Justice: The Autobiography of Ida B. Wells. Ed. Alfreda M. Duster. Chicago: University of Chicago Press, 1970.

"Lynch Law." 1893. *The Reason Why the Colored American Is Not in the World's Columbian,* by Ida B. Wells, Frederick Douglass, Irvine Garland Penn, and Ferdinand L. Barnett. *Exposition.* Ed. Robert W. Rydell. Urbana: University of Illinois Press, 1999. 29–43.

Lynch Law in Georgia. Chicago: Pamphlet circulated by Chicago colored citizens, 1899.

On Lynchings: Southern Horrors, a Red Record, Mob Rule in New Orleans. New York: Arno Press, 1969.

Works About

DeCosta-Willis, Miriam, ed. *Ida B. Wells: The Memphis Diaries.* Boston: Beacon Press, 1994.

Royster, Jacqueline Jones, ed. *Southern Horrors and Other Writings: The Anti-Lynching Campaign of Ida B. Wells, 1892–1900.* Boston: Bedford Books, 1997.

———. " 'To Call a Thing by Its True Name': The Rhetoric of Ida B. Wells." *Reclaiming Rhetorica.* Ed. Andrea Lunsford. Pittsburgh: University of Pittsburgh Press, 1995. 167–184.

Schechter, Patricia Ann. *Ida B. Wells-Barnett and American Reform, 1880–1930.* Chapel Hill: University of North Carolina Press, 2001.

Sarah R. Robbins

WEST, DOROTHY (1907–1998)

It is appropriate that Dorothy West's novels concern familial relations: While West was the only child of transplanted southerners Rachel Benson and Isaac West, she was raised in a household populated by maternal aunts and their children. With the exception of West's mother, all were in **domestic** service, the two others who had children leaving them behind to be educated by a governess. It is therefore not surprising that by her teen years the money West earned through writing helped support the **family**.

In 1926 West entered *Opportunity*'s literary contest, tying with **Zora Neale Hurston** in the short-story category. She and **Helene Johnson**, a cousin whose **poetry** had received honorable mention, traveled to New York for the ceremony. Hurston was one of many luminaries of the **Harlem Renaissance** who welcomed the cousins, establishing a long-lasting friendship with them. West was less influenced by the movement's other female writers, **Nella Larsen** and **Jessie Redmon Fauset**, though she knew the latter. Instead, she was a favorite of the male writers; Wallace Thurman represented West kindly in his satirical novel *Infants of the Spring* (1932), while **Claude McKay** mentored her as a writer. Indeed, McKay, **Countee Cullen**, and **Langston Hughes**–among others–proposed marriage. That West received multiple marriage proposals from gay men is interesting; her reservation appeared to provoke a protective impulse in others, including A'Lelia Walker, who chastised Carl Van Vechten for his advances to West. Certainly, friends of West's mother cared for her in New York, making sure she was fed and employed. One even helped her to secure a part in the original production of DuBose Heyward's *Porgy*, which traveled to London. Three years later West was again overseas, this time as part of a group of twenty-two African Americans who journeyed to Russia–including Hughes, Henry Lee Moon, Ted Poston, and Louise Thompson–to make a never-completed **film** about American racism.

Returning to America upon the **death** of her father, West continued to live in New York, working for the Public Welfare Department and, in 1934, launching the magazine *Challenge*, an attempt to counter the impact of the depression upon black artists. Her supporters included Cullen, Hughes, Hurston, McKay, Van Vechten, and others, while her detractors claimed that the magazine did not reflect the socialism with which many artists were then enamored. *Challenge* was revised accordingly, becoming *New Challenge* in 1937, with West as editor and Marian Minus and **Richard Wright** as associate editors. But West's opposition to communism and status as proprietor and primary backer meant that the magazine did not survive.

West continued to write throughout these years; her employment with the Works Progress Administration produced some of her most powerful writings of the period. In 1940 she secured an arrangement to provide the *New York Daily News* with two stories a month, initiating a relationship with the paper that lasted almost twenty years. However, within six years the author would permanently retire from New York, to Oak Bluffs, Martha's Vineyard.

It was there her grandfather had bought a **home** after following his daughters North, it was there that the family had summered, and it was there that she finished her first novel, *The Living Is Easy* (1948). While its proposed serialization by the *Ladies' Home Journal* was canceled when editors feared a backlash from southern subscribers, the story of a selfish matron and her family was reviewed favorably in the North.

The novel was loosely based on West's own family and domineering mother and included a thinly veiled portrait of Monroe Trotter, West having been a pupil of his sister Bessie and a goddaughter of his sister Maude. Some relatives were outraged by what they saw as West's betrayal of family and friends. From there she became a columnist for the *Vineyard Gazette*. By 1968 she was regularly reporting on the activities of vacationing elite African Americans; by 1973 her scope extended to all residents of the Island, regardless of color.

It was not until 1995 that West published her second novel, *The Wedding*, begun in the 1960s, an era West felt was unsympathetic to the lives of those light-skinned upper-class blacks who were its subjects. Another local vacationer and editor for Doubleday, Jacqueline Kennedy Onassis, had convinced West to resume work on the novel, and the two formed a meaningful literary partnership. The publication was timely; the renewed interest in West, as the last surviving writer of the Harlem Renaissance, meant that her final literary production was received as she wished, by those who were attuned to the nuances of **race**, gender, **class**, and their impact upon families. The last remaining years of West's life were busy; in 1997 the residents of Martha's Vineyard threw her a birthday party attended by Hilary Clinton, Henry Louis Gates, Jr., Anita Hill, and Jessye Norman and renamed a street in her honor. The event was televised by Cable News Network; a year later a film version of *The Wedding* also aired, produced by Oprah Winfrey and starring Halle Berry. While West lived her middle years in obscurity, she died in 1998 better known than she had ever anticipated.

Works By

The Dorothy West Martha's Vineyard: Stories, Essays, and Reminiscences by Dorothy West Writing in the Vineyard Gazette. Jefferson, NC: McFarland, 2001.
The Living Is Easy. 1948. New York: Feminist Press, 1982.
A Renaissance in Harlem: Lost Voices of an American Community. Ed. Lionel C. Bascom. New York: Avon, 1999.
The Richer, the Poorer: Stories, Sketches, and Reminiscences. New York: Doubleday, 1995.
The Wedding. New York: Doubleday, 1995.

Works About

Cromwell, Adelaide M. Afterword to *The Living Is Easy*, by Dorothy West. New York: Feminist Press, 1982. 349–364.

Dalsgard, Katrine. "Alive and Well and Living on the Island of Martha's Vineyard: An Interview with Dorothy West, October 29, 1988." *Langston Hughes Review* (Fall 1993): 28–44.

McDowell, Deborah E. "Conversations with Dorothy West." *The Harlem Renaissance Re-examined.* Ed. Victor A. Kramer. New York: AMS Press, 1987. 265–282.

McGrath, Abigail. "Afterward: A Daughter Reminisces." *This Waiting for Love: Helene Johnson, Poet of the Harlem Renaissance.* Ed. Verner D. Mitchell. Amherst: University of Massachusetts Press, 2000.

Mitchell, Verner D., ed. *This Waiting for Love: Helene Johnson, Poet of the Harlem Renaissance.* Amherst: University of Massachusetts Press, 2000.

Newson, Adele S. "An Interview with Dorothy West." *Zora Neale Huston Forum* 2 (1987): 19–24.

Roses, Lorraine Elena. "Interviews with Black Women Writers: Dorothy West at Oak Bluffs, Massachusetts." *Sage* (Spring 1985): 47–49.

Saunders, James Robert, and Renae Nadine Shackelford. Introduction to *The Dorothy West Martha's Vineyard*, by Dorothy West. Jefferson, NC: McFarland, 2001. 1–11.

Steinberg, Sybil. "Dorothy West: Her Own Renaissance." *Publishers Weekly*, July 3, 1995, 34–35.

Thurman, Wallace. *Infants of the Spring.* 1932. New York: AMS Press, 1975.

Jennifer Harris

WHAT YOU OWE ME

Bebe Moore Campbell's most recent work *What You Owe Me* (2001), winner of *Los Angeles Times* Best Book of the New Year, tells the story of friendship, betrayal, and recognition that occurs between two women, Hosanna Dark, who is African American, and Gilda Rosenstein, a Jewish immigrant. The two women meet while working as maids in Los Angeles' oldest white-owned hotel, the Braddock, and quickly and quietly form a fast friendship. In post–World War II California, each recognizes within the other the narrative not only of a survivor but an unfolding story of ambition and the desire to succeed—to **work** for themselves rather than labor for others.

Gilda's father, prewar, was a cosmetic factory owner, and Hosanna and Gilda borrow on and perfect his recipe for making lotion, which they then market to women of color, to launch their careers in the **beauty** industry. Until discovered and subsequently fired, they use the hotel's tubs as a laboratory to mix and bottle cosmetics. What the women learn from each other is the power of innovation and collaboration—the ability of like-minded women, regardless of **race**, to form a partnership forged in an entrepreneurial spirit.

It is men who betray this partnership and the sting of racism that poisons female friendship. Shortly after their firing from the Braddock, Hosanna and Gilda lose contact with one another. Gilda's husband, an older, domineering, and racist man of Jewish descent, learns of his young wife's business partnership with an African American woman and abruptly puts an end to it by having Gilda turn all bank accounts over to him. Because as a black woman Hosanna's name was never on the company's account, when she attempts to withdraw her share of their savings, she cannot. Unknown to Gilda, whose husband has secretly closed the account, he has her write a bad check to Hosanna for funds that are rightfully hers. Hosanna must start anew, and she does so by marketing her own line of cosmetics to African American women. However, she carries her anger and bitterness at Gilda with her to the grave. It is up to Hosanna's daughter, Matriece, to right a mother's assumed betrayal by a woman she once called not just business partner but friend.

Reconciliation is at the heart of *What You Owe Me*. Gilda has amassed a fortune, and Matriece, who works for another cosmetic company, becomes the head of Gilda's cosmetics division, which caters to women of color. Initially, Matriece keeps the secret that she is Hosanna's daughter from Gilda. Expecting to loathe Gilda, when Matriece meets her she begins to understand the narrowness of Hosanna's narrative and the gulf of Gilda's grief, which is borne out of an inability to explain circumstance to the friend she was never able to locate after their rift occurred. Once Matriece's **identity** is revealed and her mother's past made known, Gilda acknowledges the debt she owes Hosanna and secedes the part of her business that caters to cosmetics for African American women to Matriece. In this act, amends are made.

What the women in this narrative realize is that human beings are essentially flawed and that they must recognize the flaws in one another not so much to seek retribution but to reconcile themselves with past and current hurt. Gilda has survived the Holocaust, and Hosanna, regardless of her bitterness, survived a hostile world that indicated to her that an African American woman must always be someone else's maid. Hosanna is a minor success in her own right, and her legacy lives on in a daughter who has corrected the wrongs of the past through the diligence, hard work, and courage that she inherits from her mother. Forgiveness and reconciliation are central to a novel that celebrates women's tenacity to survive with dignity and integrity despite the burden of racism, xenophobia, and men's suspicion of strong women.

Work About

Gamble, Althia. "Fiction Reviews." A Review of *What You Owe Me*. *Black Issues Book Review* 3.4 (July–August 2001): 27.

Jennifer Driscoll

WHEATLEY, PHILLIS (1752–1784)

Phillis Wheatley was probably born in the Senegal/Gambia area in Africa. Because she was enslaved at a young age, Wheatley had few memories of her life in Africa. In a letter to her close friend, Obour Tanner, she recalled seeing her mother pouring libations to the sun and then prostrating herself on the ground. Whether her mother was engaged in sun worship or praying to Mecca is difficult to determine; what is clear, however, is the importance that **religion** would continue to play in Wheatley's life and **work**.

At the age of seven, Wheatley was captured and taken to the United States to be sold as a slave. She was purchased in Boston in 1761 by John Wheatley as a servant for his wife Susannah. The Wheatleys decided to name her Phillis, after the slave ship that brought her from Africa. As a relatively well off **family** and because primary educational opportunities had been extended to middle-class young women, the Wheatley daughters were well educated. The daughters of the Wheatley family used the skills they had learned to teach Phillis English. Within four years, Wheatley accumulated a swift and sure command of the language. An unusually quick and apt pupil, Phillis would go on to study Latin and **literature**.

She began writing poems soon after she began studying literature. Her first piece of published writing, a poem about the miraculous survival of two men during a hurricane off Cape Cod, "On Messrs. Hussey and Coffin," appeared in 1767 in the *Newport Mercury*. Although she would continue to occasionally publish, most of her published poems were frequently preceded by mention of her **race** and sex.

She would go on to publish others, including the immensely popular "On the Death of the Rev. Mr. George Whitefield" (1770). By 1772 she had written enough poems to fill a volume. For a variety of reasons including racism and the stagnation of the American economy at the run-up to the Revolutionary War, which hit Boston pretty hard, Wheatley was unable to get enough subscribers to warrant publication in Boston. Whitefield had been the valued chaplain to the countess of Huntington, Selina Hastings. Phillis sent her a copy of the poems along with her letter of condolence. The countess was impressed and invited Wheatley to London, in order to facilitate publication of the volume.

In 1773, she went to London with Nathaniel Wheatley. While there she met Lady Huntington, who helped bring her book of **poetry**, *Poems on Various Subjects, Religious and Moral*, into publication. Wheatley spent six weeks in London and met many British intellectuals and writers including Granville Sharpe, Benjamin Franklin, and Thomas Gibbon. Her book was extremely popular. She tried to get the book published in the United States when she returned. It was only published after she had proved to a group of white men in a tribunal that she had actually written the poems.

She continued writing poetry. In 1773, Mrs. Wheatley died, and Wheatley was manumitted a year later. She continued to live with the Wheatleys and to write poetry. She also wrote many letters, including one to George Washington in 1775. Washington was so impressed with the poem that he invited Wheatley to his Cambridge, Massachusetts, headquarters.

In 1778, much to the chagrin of Obour Tanner and other friends, Wheatley married a black freeman, John Peters. She still continued to write poetry but would frequently use her married name, Phillis Peters. She was unable to be published again, but this did not stop her from continuing to try to earn a living from her writing.

Most of her poetry is concerned with religious and moral themes. As a result, she is often castigated for not appearing feminist enough. She does not talk about feminist or female-centered topics. However, if we consider that at the time she was writing, religious writing was deemed particularly suited to women, it is difficult to find fault with her.

Wheatley did address issues of **slavery** in several of her poems and letters, most famously in "On Being Brought from Africa to America" (1773). Although Wheatley does seem to accept much of the prevailing ideology about blacks and Africa as uncivilized, she frequently asserts that blacks are just as worthy of **Christianity** as whites. Indeed in her poem "To the University of Cambridge in New England" (1773), Wheatley, a black enslaved woman, appropriates the power of the muses and uses it to offer advice to the young white male collegians.

Recent criticism has caused scholars to look anew at Wheatley and consider her feminism in a new light. The mere fact that she, as a **domestic** female servant, felt comfortable adding her voice to popular discussion on a variety of political and religious topics should not be underestimated. She also wrote many praise poems and commentaries on topics of the day. It was quite unusual for a woman of her time to publicly comment on issues other than religion and private domestic matters. As a result, one can interpret the assertion of her voice into the public venue as an expression of a type of feminism. Additionally, one can also catch a glimpse of what might be considered latent feminism in her poetry through hidden messages within her texts. Because she could not write explicitly about her experience as a black woman, it is possible that Wheatley felt compelled to encode it in her poems.

Work By

Poems on Various Subjects, Religious and Moral. London: Printed for Archibald Bell and Sold in Boston by Cox and Berry, 1773.

Works About

Balkun, Mary McAleer. "Phillis Wheatley's Construction of Otherness and the Rhetoric of Performed Identity." *African American Review* 36.1 (Spring 2002): 121–135.

Flanzbaum, Hilene. "Unprecedented Liberties: Re-reading Phillis Wheatley." *MELUS* 18.3 (Fall 1993): 71.

Gates, Henry Louis, Jr. *The Trials of Phillis Wheatley: America's First Black Poet and Her Encounters with the Founding Fathers.* New York: Basic Civitas, 2003.

Robinson, William H. *Critical Essays on Phillis Wheatley.* Boston: G. K. Hall, 1982.

Nicole N. Aljoe

WHITE, PAULETTE CHILDRESS (1948–   )

Paulette Childress White, writer of **poetry** and prose, was born in Detroit, Michigan, on December 1, 1948. White's **fiction** is often set in Detroit, where she grew up. Initially, White longed to be an artist, but a number of circumstances, including financial problems, prevented her from being able to realize her dream. After years of marriage to an artist and giving birth to several children, White began writing poetry. In 1972 her first published poem was included in *Deep Rivers*. With the help of her mentor, Naomi Long Madgett, she published *Love Poem to a Black Junkie* in 1975. Two years later her first published short story, "Alice," appeared in *Essence* magazine. In "Alice," White poetically describes the necessity of female friendships. In 1978, "The Bird Cage" was published in *Redbook*. "The Bird Cage" and "Alice" were included in Mary Helen Washington's *Black-Eyed Susans/Midnight Birds: Stories by and about Black Women*, published in 1990.

"The Bird Cage," in addition to repeating the caged bird motif that can be found in the works of **Paul Laurence Dunbar**, **Maya Angelou**, and others, explores the thwarted artist motif. This motif seems to run through White's oeuvre and is somewhat autobiographical, as she, a mother of five children, has written about the strain the roles wife and mother have on her as a budding artist. White also discontinued her art education when she became pregnant with her first child. White says she writes about personal experiences in an attempt to reflect upon her life. The protagonist in "The Bird Cage" is unable to finish her **work**. She is a housewife who can only find a few moments to write late at night after her four sons are asleep. She says, "Even as [my children] sleep, I sense the cling of their eyes, hear their voices circling round me, 'Momma, Momma!' I am theirs." To make matters worse, while the housewife-artist tries to "distill a line or two of poetry," a crowd in front of the Bird Cage, a nightclub, distracts her. Thus, her roles—wife and mother—restrict her internally, while externally her creativity is hampered by the noise coming from the Bird Cage.

Artistic expression, sisterhood, marriage, domesticity, **community**, **motherhood**, **identity**, and self-actualization are recurring ideas explored in her poetry and short stories. Other work by White includes two short stories, "Paper Man," published in 1986 in the *Michigan Quarterly Review*, and "Dear Akua," also published in 1986 in *Harbor Review*, and a narrative poem titled *The Watermelon Dress: Portrait of a Woman: Poems and Illustrations*, published in 1984. Her work has also appeared in books—*Consonance and Continuity in Poetry: Detroit Black Writers* (1988); *Sturdy Black Bridges* (1979); *Growing Up Female: Stories by Women Writers from the American Mosaic* (1993); *Rites of Passage* (1994); *Mending the World: Stories of Family by Contemporary Black Writers* (2003)—and a number of periodicals including *Essence*, *Redbook*, and *Callaloo*.

Works By

Lost Your Momma. Detroit: Lotus Press, 1977.
Love Poem to a Black Junkie. Detroit: Lotus Press, 1975.

The Watermelon Dress: Portrait of a Woman: Poems and Illustrations. Detroit: Lotus Press, 1984.

Works About

Barrax, Gerald. "Six Poets: From Poetry to Verse." Review of *The Watermelon Dress: Portrait of a Woman. Callaloo* 26 (Winter 1986): 248–269.
Brown, Beth. "Four From Lotus Press." Review of *The Watermelon Dress: Portrait of a Woman. CLA Journal* 29.2 (December 1985): 250–252.

KaaVonia Hinton-Johnson

WHITENESS

In the past decade, the study of whiteness has become a focus of mainstream scholarship and the popular press. The central emphasis of recent scholarship is making visible the signs of white **identity**: the constructions and operations of a category that has tended to be marked as "natural" in the United States. From this perspective, the alleged universalism of the term *American* is revealed as an *un*marked sign of whiteness. **James Baldwin**'s essays of the 1980s, such as "On Being 'White'...And Other Lies" and others collected in *The Price of the Ticket* (1985), and **Toni Morrison**'s *Playing in the Dark: Whiteness and the Literary Imagination* (1992) have suggested some of the parameters of recent studies seeking to emphasize whiteness as a historical, political, and moral problem. Baldwin argues that whites are "impaled" on the lies of their **history**, a situation that "hideously menaces this country" (Roediger, *Black on White* 321). Morrison describes, through analyses of American literary texts, the "parasitical nature of white freedom" (57). Subsequent studies, such as Ruth Frankenberg's *White Women, Race Matters: The Social Construction of Race* (1994) and David R. Roediger's *Colored White: Transcending the Racial Past* (2002) have continued to specify how white identity is inextricably related to the exercise of power and the maintenance of privilege.

However, this new scholarship on whiteness has had the effect of suggesting that whiteness is just one more "ethnic" identity to be added to multicultural studies, as the title of a popular press article, "Getting Credit for Being White" (Talbot), illustrates. The popularization of what whites say about their racial identities can dilute issues of racism in social practices and obscure the serious parameters of the study of whiteness as it has been historically practiced. Moreover, to characterize whiteness studies as a project of white scholars is to perpetuate the tendency to place whites at the front and center of the discourse. The inability to imagine or acknowledge that black people can see—and have seen—them (i.e., identify their "whiteness") constitutes a powerful illusion that is connected to the exigencies of racial dominance.

African Americans' expertise in identifying the various operations of whiteness have frequently been unacknowledged or misinterpreted in mainstream scholarship. W.E.B. Du Bois's famous articulation "the problem of the color line" has largely been characterized as a statement about African Americans and their problems due to racism rather than as the broader problem of a "color-line" drawn by whiteness. White identities and behaviors have been observed and analyzed by African Americans for several centuries, not only academically but practically as well. From before David Walker's "Whites as Heathens and Christians" (1830) to beyond bell hooks's "Representations of Whiteness in the Black Imagination" (1992) stretches a substantial and un-surpassed discourse on whiteness by African Americans. In the fifty-one texts collected in Roediger's *Black on White: Black Writers on What It Means to Be White* (1998), writers delineate whiteness variously: as a form of property, a site of **violence** and terror, a corrupting and corrosive ideology of privilege, a psychological bulwark, and a coercive delusion. The title of an article published in 1860 by "Ethiop" (William J. Wilson)—"What Shall We Do With the White People?"—is a question that still reverberates in current letters.

Feminist approaches to the study of whiteness have also developed in the past decades. Women of color have been calling on white women to acknowledge and critique their own participation in maintaining racism and dominance. Recent work on **literature** by white women is attempting to identify frameworks of whiteness in their writing, frameworks about which the writers themselves reveal little understanding or awareness. One such work is Renee Curry's *White Women Writing White* (2000), a study of poets H. D., Elizabeth Bishop, and Sylvia Plath. Furthermore, the whiteness of much feminist scholarship has been identified as another area in need of rigorous and honest re-vision.

Hopefully, whiteness studies will continue to underscore the racist implications of ignoring the insidious power of, in the words of **Malcolm X**, "white-ism."

Works About

Allen, Theodore W. *The Invention of the White Race*. New York: Verso, 1994.

Baldwin, James. *The Price of the Ticket*. New York: St. Martin's Press, 1985.

Basso, Keith H. *Portraits of "The Whiteman": Linguistic Play and Cultural Symbols among the Western Apache*. Cambridge: Cambridge University Press, 1978.

Bay, Mia. *The White Image in the Black Mind*. New York: Oxford University Press, 2000.

Brodkin, Karen. *How Jews Became White Folks*. New Brunswick, NJ: Rutgers University Press, 1998.

Curry, Renee R. *White Women Writing White: H. D., Elizabeth Bishop, Sylvia Plath, and Whiteness*. Westport, CT: Greenwood Press, 2000.

Davis, Jane. *The White Image in the Black Mind: A Study in African American Literature*. Westport, CT: Greenwood Press, 2000.

Dyer, Richard. *White*. London and New York: Routledge, 1997.

Frankenberg, Ruth. *White Women, Race Matters: The Social Construction of Race*. Minneapolis: University of Minnesota Press, 1994.

Harris, Cheryl. "Whiteness as Property." *Harvard Law Review* 106 (June 1993): 1710–1791.

hooks, bell. "Representations of Whiteness in the Black Imagination." *Black Looks: Race and Representation*. Boston: South End Press, 1992. 165–178.

Ignatiev, Noel. *How the Irish Became White*. New York and London: Routledge, 1995.

Morrison, Toni. *Playing in the Dark: Whiteness and the Literary Imagination*. Cambridge, MA: Harvard University Press, 1992.

Roediger, David R., ed. *Black on White: Black Writers on What It Means to Be White*. New York: Schocken Books, 1998.

——. *Colored White: Transcending the Racial Past*. Berkeley: University of California Press, 2002.

Talbot, Margaret. "Getting Credit for Being White." *New York Times,* November 30, 1997, 116–118.

Sharon Jessee

WIDEMAN, JOHN EDGAR (1941–)

John Edgar Wideman was born on June 14, 1941, in Washington, D.C. Wideman was a Rhodes Scholar and in 1966 married Judith Ann Goldman and fathered two children, Daniel Jerome and Jacob Edgar. Wideman founded the University of Pennsylvania's African American Studies program and became the first writer to win the PEN/Faulkner Award twice: first, for *Sent for You Yesterday* in 1984 and again in 1991 for *Philadelphia Fire*. A former basketball player, Wideman's seeming disassociation of inner-city life through his own existence is discarded in his **fiction**, where he has long been recognized for his understanding of the inner-city African American experience.

Wideman's primary works include *A Glance Away* (1967); *Hurry Home* (1970); *The Lynchers* (1973); *Damballah* (1981); *Hiding Place* (1981); *Sent for You Yesterday* (1983); *Brothers and Keepers* (1984); *Reuben* (1987); *Fever* (1989); *Philadelphia Fire* (1990); *All Stories Are True* (1993); *Fatheralong: A Meditation on Fathers and Sons, Race and Society* (1994); *The Cattle Killing* (1996); *Two Cities* (1998); and *The Stories of John Edgar Wideman* (1992).

The world of Wideman's fiction functions through its critique and association with contemporary black existence. Since his brother's arrest and conviction for murder in 1976 and his son's arrest in 1986, Wideman's fiction has focused on dealing with the turmoil that these two incidents created in his **family**. Wideman's work draws on the experiences of his individual familial **history** and also the cultural life of African Americans. His fragmented, postmodern prose delves into the contradictions and hopelessness often associated with the modern black inner-city experience—oftentimes not offering any solution or help in the end. He especially understands how different that experience is for women. The female characters in Wideman's fiction occupy a peculiar role within the complex world of the inner city, becoming the keepers of cultural, familial, and societal **memory**. His fiction draws on cultural experiences as the backdrop, and characters, male and female, in his multilayered, multinarrated works, search for a place of hope and existence in the turmoil of modern life.

In his earlier fiction, Wideman uses female characters to save or teach his often distraught male characters something about their past. Bess in *Hiding Place* (1981) and Freeda from *Sent for You Yesterday* (1983) both act as keepers of memory. They help their male counterparts emotionally and physically recover from the trauma of urban black life. These earlier characters give way to two characters in Wideman's later fiction that serve the same roles. Margaret Jones in *Philadelphia Fire* (1990) and Kassima in *Two Cities* (1998) are both the full realization of Wideman's characterization of women as keepers of memory. Wideman has long struggled with the role women in the inner city play. He has noted that women are witness to the horrors of the inner-city life and are left to clean up the mess after the **violence** created by men is over. This role of viewer provides them with a powerful understanding, and their role as keeper of memory is one that is the hope for the future.

Philadelphia Fire (1990) is a novel that recounts ex-Philadelphia native Cudjoe's return to the city in search of the lone survivor from the MOVE bombing. In *Philadelphia Fire* readers see Wideman's ties to realism within his multiple narrator form, and Cudjoe, one of three narrators in the text, is the cohesive force among all three. The novel's treatment of women is interestingly personal. The narrators provide insight into Wideman's thoughts on interracial marriage, memory, and trauma.

The first narrator, Cudjoe, is widely considered to embody the voice of Wideman. His return to Philadelphia after a ten-year sabbatical away from the city begins the action of the novel. He has come to research the MOVE bombing, and his motivations for doing so are transparent. Cudjoe is haunted by the loss of his wife and children, the loss of his boyhood friends, and the loss of the city of his past. The loss of his wife and children is interesting because the reader is not given her voice in the text. She occupies a space that is only objectified through Cudjoe's eyes. Cudjoe, like Wideman, married a white woman and fathered half-white children. The wife is the haunting memory of what Cudjoe became once he left the city. For Cudjoe she comes to represent his point of departure from the city of his youth. She becomes for him the link between his present state and the past, but he has failed her and his children and cannot reclaim what he once attained. Wideman's voice here explicitly comes through, and readers are left to contemplate what the white wife is thinking.

The interracial marriage has many cultural implications. Cudjoe is aware of those implications, and part of the issue is that he has not given the white wife a voice. She is left out of the narrative other than third-person mention because she is never named or given an **identity**. Nameless and depthless, she is nothing more than an idea—a cultural marker left out of the discussion.

Another narrative voice in *Philadelphia Fire* is Margaret Jones, a former member of MOVE. She is the keeper of memory, and her retelling of the events surrounding the MOVE bombing help Cudjoe recover an understanding of the past. When Cudjoe first meets Jones, he is nervous that she knows he has been gone and she does. She shares with Cudjoe the loss and trauma of a past. Jones has lost two families—the family she left to join the MOVE and the family of MOVE—and mourns not only the loss of them but also the loss of Philadelphia. She is the voice of the cultural memory. She is the voice through which Wideman tells the story of the MOVE bombing, and her retelling accomplishes two things. First, the reader gains an understanding of the events that led to and followed the bombing in Philadelphia; furthermore, she details the demise of the city. The wreckage left behind after the bombing becomes the metaphor for what Philadelphia has become. Jones cannot reconcile the fact that the city of her past is lost.

Jones awakens in Cudjoe the memories of his past—the way things used to be, especially the park where he used to play basketball. Through their interaction Wideman can critique the causes of and show his concerns for what Philadelphia has become. Through her story Wideman can show the remorse that many have over the dilapidation of Philadelphia. If, in fact, Cudjoe is Wideman, then Wideman is releasing into the text the pivotal role that women play in the inner city. Margaret is the witness to the bombing and the relayer of cultural information. Her roles as cultural and familial memory keeper are a voice of pain and trauma for the specific historical and personal memory, but it also becomes a metaphor for the loss of the past and an inability to reclaim it.

Margaret Jones shares characteristics with other female characters in Wideman's fiction. He often casts a woman in the role of storyteller, either as the narrator within his multilayered texts or as a speaker within someone else's sections. In either case, Jones is given a voice in this section, and she exhibits the power of memory and voice through her narration of the story for which Cudjoe is looking.

In *Two Cities* (1998) the initial narrator shares many characteristics with Margaret Jones and other female characters that Wideman has portrayed. Wideman again enlists a woman to portray and relate memory to the reader and other characters. Through her relationships with the men in her life, Kassima is the embodiment of all inner-city women that Wideman characterizes in his fiction. Her loss, **love**, and care taking are coupled with and troubled by her memories of the past trauma.

Wideman creates a narrator in Kassima that thrusts into the foreground the horrors of the inner city. Wideman even says that she and other women are forced into the role of observers of violence. Kassima lost her two sons and her husband in ten months; one son died playing Russian roulette and the other in a botched drug deal, and their father is in jail with AIDS (acquired immunodeficiency syndrome). As a mother and a wife, Kassima must reconstruct her life following the tragedies of her past and relearn how to live. Prior to her losses, Kassima had devoted her life to the three men, and now, upon their absence, she must learn how to live life for herself. She knows that there is no way to forget the past, and so she balances the memories of trauma and the hope for the future.

At the novel's opening, the reader sees Kassima taking control of her loneliness. She is on her way out of the house for the first time since the tragedies and finds her eventual love interest, Robert. Kassima explicitly wants sex and is not interested in a relationship but ends up in a relationship with Robert. In this section of the text, Kassima becomes both healer and healed. Her relationship with Robert helps her put the past memories of trauma behind and participate in loving again, but she specifically notes that she does not want to give herself up like she did before. And when Robert is nearly killed on the basketball courts by a young gang member, she ends the relationship because she is unable to endure more traumatic experience in her life. She has known tragedy, and the relationship cannot release her from the memories of the loss of her son and her husband. The rain that follows the near **death** of Robert does not purify or cleanse her; it serves as a metaphor for her entrapped life.

Kassima's voice disappears from the narrative after the breakup with Robert but reappears suddenly after the death of Mr. Mallory. Her relationship with Mallory helps to assert that she can get beyond the memories of the deaths of her sons and husband. She realizes that she cannot occupy the ghostlike state she has since their deaths because of the silent stepping of Mr. Mallory. He has walked through life with his camera without participating, and she is not willing to do that anymore. His pictures show her the existence of hope in the inner city, and upon Mallory's death, she calls Robert to come help her. She has taken a step toward recapturing love in her life, but it is not until Mallory's funeral that she is able to fully recognize the need for getting beyond the traumatic memories of her past.

Like Margaret Jones, Kassima is witness to trauma and comes to serve as a metaphor for the female inner-city African American experience. Kassima has hope for the future but is still wary of the past. Mr. Mallory's funeral, the last scene of the novel, provides a cathartic release for Kassima. Mallory's **body** is caught between rival gangs and is mistakenly taken to the street and desecrated. Before Mallory's death, Kassima promised to burn his photos, but in the end she cannot destroy them. With Mallory's casket in the street and broken, she grabs the box of pictures and dumps them on the ground. They float like snow, and the violence breaks for a moment. Kassima is healed to continue loving, and she makes the violent city pause and take notice of the present suffering.

Although Wideman's narratives take a fragmented approach to storytelling, often he recruits women as central storytellers and providers of memory that provide cohesion in the text. His female characters sometimes embody the stereotypical trapped female, but when Wideman is at his best, the women in his fiction are not objectified or subjugated because of their womanhood. They are in fact given central power in the texts by exercising their ability to transfer cultural memory and trauma. They are the hope of the inner city of Wideman's fiction.

Works By

All Stories Are True. New York: Vintage, 1993.
Brothers and Keepers. New York: Holt, 1984.

The Cattle Killing. Boston: Houghton Mifflin, 1996.
Damballah. New York: Avon, 1981.
Fatheralong: A Meditation on Fathers and Sons, Race and Society. New York: Pantheon, 1994.
Fever. New York: Holt, 1989.
A Glance Away. New York: Harcourt, 1967.
Hiding Place. New York: Vintage, 1981.
Hoop Roots. Boston: Houghton Mifflin, 2001.
Hurry Home. New York: Harcourt, 1970.
The Lynchers. New York: Harcourt, 1973.
Philadelphia Fire. New York: Holt, 1990.
Reuben. New York: Holt, 1987.
Sent for You Yesterday. New York: Avon, 1983.
The Stories of John Edgar Wideman. New York: Pantheon, 1992.
Two Cities. Boston: Houghton Mifflin, 1998.

Works About

Abu-Jamal, Mumia. "The Fictive Realism of John Edgar Wideman." *Black Scholar* 28.1 (Spring 1998): 75–79.
Baker, Lisa. "Storytelling and Democracy (in the Radical Sense)." *African American Review* 34.2 (Summer 2000): 263–273.
Coleman, James W. *Blackness and Modernism: The Literary Development of John Edgar Wideman.* Jackson: University of Mississippi Press, 1989.
Dewilde, Door Marceau. "This City of Brotherly Love: Race, Community and the Transition from Modernism to Postmodernism in the Works of John Edgar Wideman." www.zaan.be/jwthesis.
Dubey, Madhu. "Literature and Urban Crisis: John Edgar Wideman's *Philadelphia Fire.*" *African American Review* 32.4 (Winter 1998): 579–595.
Howell, Charles H. "John Edgar Wideman: An Interview and Selected Works." *Callaloo* 13.1 (Winter 1990): 47–61.
Janifer, Raymond E. "Two Cities: A Postmodern Love Story." www.ship.edu/~rejani/twocities.html.

John D. Miles

WILKINSON, BRENDA (1946–)

Brenda Wilkinson's childhood as an African American girl in Georgia provided her with ample material when she turned her attention to writing for children and young adults. The daughter of construction worker Malcolm and nurse Ethel, Brenda gained an understanding of rural black life during her childhood in Moultrie.

Wilkinson's first book, *Ludell* (1975), begins a trilogy about a poor African American girl growing up in Waycross, Georgia, during the 1905s and 1960s.

Other books in the series are *Ludell and Willie* (1976) and *Ludell's New York Time* (1980). Over the course of the series, Ludell, a talented young girl at the beginning, matures. She moves from Georgia to Harlem, New York, and faces decisions about school, **love**, marriage, and career. Some critics have suggested that the trilogy is an extension of the **Harlem Renaissance** stories that characterized African Americans migrating from the South to the North and the challenges they faced in the process. *Ludell* was nominated for the National Book Award (1976); *Ludell and Willie* was recognized as an outstanding children's book of the year by the *New York Times* and as a best book for young adults by the American Library Association (1977).

Brenda Wilkinson's fictional writing is characterized by a controversial use of dialect. While some critics praise her use of dialect, jive talk, and rap, others find it objectionable, feeling that it is inconsistent and makes her books more difficult to read. Wilkinson's writing is sensitive and compassionate. She focuses on the comforting importance of **family** and **community** while addressing weighty issues of integration and social justice.

Brenda Wilkinson also has a keen interest in **history**, particularly African American history, and this reveals itself in her writing. Critics have suggested that her stories have a universal quality and that Wilkinson is able to write about past events from a contemporary perspective. She integrates history into her fictional writing, and recently has focused here attention on a series of nonfiction books about African Americans in American history, including *Black Stars of Colonial and Revolutionary Times* (2002), *Black Stars of the Harlem Renaissance* (2003), and *Black Stars of the Civil Rights Movement* (2003).

After twenty-seven years, Wilkinson retired from her position as staff writer with the United Methodist Church's Board of Global Ministries in 2003. Separated from her husband, Wilkinson has two daughters, Lori and Kim, and lives in New York City.

Works By

African American Women Writers. New York: Wiley, 2000.
Black Stars of Colonial and Revolutionary Times. New York: Wiley, 2002.
Black Stars of the Civil Rights Movement. New York: Wiley, 2003.
Black Stars of the Harlem Renaissance. New York: Wiley, 2003.
Definitely Cool. New York: Scholastic, 1993.
Jesse Jackson: Still Fighting for the Dream. Morristown, NJ: Silver Burdett, 1990.
Ludell. New York: Harper, 1975.
Ludell and Willie. New York: Harper, 1976.
Ludell's New York Time. New York: Harper, 1980.
Not Separate, Not Equal. New York: Harper, 1987.

Works About

Commire, Ann. "Brenda Wilkinson." *Something about the Author.* Vol. 14. Detroit: Gale Group, 1978.

Kornfeld, Matilda R. "Ludell (Book Review)." *School Library Journal* 22.4 (December 1975): 62.

Pollack, Pamela D. "Ludell's New York Time (Book Review)." *School Library Journal* 26.6 (February 1980): 73.

Senick, Gerard J., and Sharon R. Gunton. "Brenda Wilkinson." *Children's Literature Review*. Vol. 20. Detroit: Gale Group, 1990.

Silver, Linda. "Ludell and Willie (Book Review)." *School Library Journal* 24.2 (October 1977): 128.

Heidi Hauser Green

WILLIAMS, PAULETTE. See Shange, Ntozake

WILLIAMS, SHERLEY ANNE (1944–1999)

Poet, novelist, short-story writer, dramatist, and critic, Sherley Anne Williams's artistic project is rooted in the African American **blues** tradition. Her work seeks to establish a continuity between the expression of the collective historical experience found in successive generations of blues music and the representation of black life in **literature**. Williams sees in the blues the missing links from a disrupted and distorted historical record. She recognizes that the patterns of blues music are a highly effective means of representing the black self to the black self and in turn incorporates this ritualized means of expression and passing on of **history** into her writing. In her work, Williams features black vernacular and folk culture along with Western literary conventions in order to rework African American literary tradition.

Williams was born on August 25, 1944, in Bakersfield, California, to Lena-Leila Marie Siler and Jessee Winson Williams. The third of four daughters, Williams grew up in a Fresno housing project and spent her youth picking fruit and cotton alongside her parents and sisters in the San Joaquin Valley. This experience was one that she would revisit in her literary work. Williams lost both her parents early in life. Her father died when she seven and her mother when she was sixteen. After her mother's **death** Williams was reared by her older sister, whom Williams would later cite as an inspirational figure in her life.

While an academic and literary career was by no means a foregone conclusion, Williams, nevertheless, entered Fresno State College (now California State University, Fresno) and was awarded her B.A. in 1966. A period of graduate study followed at Howard University before she completed her M.A. at Brown University in 1972. In the following year she became the first African American literature professor at the University of California at San Diego (UCSD), La Jolla, and began a distinguished teaching career. During this period Williams's career advanced considerably with the publication of her first book, *Give Birth to Brightness: A Thematic Study in Neo-Black Literature* (1972), an examination of the heroic tradition in contemporary African American literature, focusing on **Amiri Baraka**'s *Dutchman* (1964) and *The Slave* (1964), **James Baldwin**'s *Blues for Mr. Charlie* (1964), and **Ernest Gaines**'s *Of Love and Dust* (1967). In this work Williams traces the history of the black hero from the rebel leaders who revolted against **slavery**, to the contemporary revolutionaries who oppose hegemonic society, to the tricksters and game runners who draw their inspiration from black **folklore**.

Williams chaired the UCSD Department of Literature from 1977 to 1980. Subsequently she was invited to teach at several universities, and in 1984, under the aegis of a Fulbright scholarship, she traveled to Africa, where she taught at the University of Ghana. She was also an advisory editor of *Callaloo* and *Langston Hughes Review*. At the time of her death in 1999 she was head of the writing section of the UCSD Department of Literature.

Both as a writer and an academic, Williams received several awards and nominations. In 1976, her first book of **poetry**, *The Peacock Poems* (1975), was nominated for a Pulitzer Prize and a National Book Award. Williams's performance of poems from her second book of poetry, *Some One Sweet Angel Chile* (1982), won an Emmy Award for television in 1982. This book also received a National Book Award nomination. In 1987 Williams was named Distinguished Professor of the Year by the UCSD Alumni Association. *Working Cotton*, Williams's first children's book, published in 1992, won an American Library Association Caldecott Award and a Coretta Scott King Book Award. A considerable honor was bestowed upon Williams in 1998 when the city of San Diego declared May 15 "Sherley Anne Williams' Day." In the same year Williams won the Stephen Henderson Award for Outstanding Achievement in Literature and Poetry granted by the AALCS.

Williams published her first short story, "Tell Martha Not to Moan," in the *Massachusetts Review* in 1967. The themes and the narrative patterns of this composition, such as a low-income black woman's perspective on male/female relationships and **motherhood**, and Williams's keen sense of black vernacular are features of her later works. In this short story, Williams uses a first-person narrative as a medium through which to represent the voice of the silenced female. While the domain of the utterance belongs to the characters that attempt to assert their control over the protagonist's life and **identity** (her lover, mother, and roommate), the expression of her thoughts, unfiltered by the intrusion of a third-person narrator, allows Martha to reclaim control over her narrative and her life.

In *The Peacock Poems*, Williams continues to use the first-person female perspective. Significantly here, the blues provides the idiom through which the personal narrative finds meaning and echoes in the shared African American experience. In this compilation, the blues functions both as a ritualized means of expression and as a channel of self-discovery. In the first of the three primary sections of *The Peacock Poems*, the journey to the self, marked by blues rhythms and rhymes, parallels the physical journey from west to east; from the dry heat of California and the comfort of the familiar to the blistering cold of Rhode Island and the facing of the unknown. In this section, the form reflects the feelings of uncertainty of the poetic persona. The more conventional poetic forms alternate with autobiographical sketches and dictionary entries, emphasizing the improvisational and experimental mode of this section and denoting the speaker's struggle to make order out of chaos. This effort of coming to terms with past experiences and working through contradictory feelings unveils a journey of self-awareness that is circular rather than linear. This circularity is mirrored in the patterns of repetition and variation within the text. Titles of poems are repeated, or presented with small variations. The first line of one composition, for example, becomes the title of another, introducing a notion of time that is ruled by imagination and emotion rather than chronology. This circular structure is also indicative of the tradition of call-and-response that informs the text. The poet's points of departure vary from blues songs to an anonymous poem found between the pages of a library book, or memories of conversations held with her **family** and lover, or a dedication of the writer Michael S. Harper to Williams, illustrating a continuous dialogue between artist and **community**.

Exploring history, motherhood, family, intimate relationships between women and men, individual and community, particularly the communities formed by women in support of each other, *The Peacock Poems* map out the themes and concerns of Williams's subsequent work. In this collection, the blues language forms a creative synthesis where misunderstanding, hurt, and **love** are expressed and reveal a self that like the peacock is burdened with heavy feathers but is able to keep its tail from dragging.

In *Some One Sweet Angel Chile*, the poetic personae are also female. In this collection, the woman's voice establishes a line of continuity between African American women of different historical periods. In "Letters from a New England Negro," the epistolary form of the poems, presented with dates and arranged in chronological order, serves to illustrate the speaker's evolving historical and cultural awareness, while she establishes her identity. In her letters to her northern friends, Hannah, a young African American working as a teacher in the **South** during the Reconstruction period, contrasts her experience as a freeborn northerner with that of the newly emancipated women and men, cautioning the reader against the homogeneity of black life in antebellum America. In this section, Williams considers W.E.B. Du Bois's concept of double consciousness, describing the tensions between Hannah's formative years in the North, her exposure to black southern life, and the pressures imposed upon her by white society. The white southern females lift her skirts as she passes, the white northern women attempt to control her identity by keeping her away from the Quarters with its music, tales, prayers, and shared memories, while the ex-slaves, in an effort to reclaim her, rename her. Negotiating racial and social-cultural boundaries, Hannah resists the fixed identities that others try to enforce upon her. In "Letters from a New England Negro," which was later adapted into a one-woman **drama**, Williams presents the autobiographical chronicle as the unwritten collective history of African Americans.

In the second section of this compilation titled "Regular Reefer," the usage of blues language and forms further develops the notion that the artist's personal testimony mirrors the communal experience of her audience. These poems alternate between the biographical and the autobiographical, between the reimagined songs of the blues singer Bessie Smith and the voices of the women whose lives she touched. In this dialogue based on call-and-response patterns, the stories of physical abuse, lost love, betrayal, and abandonment, or in other words, the silenced female narrative, become utterance in the singer's throat. In choosing Bessie Smith to sing the song of the shared African American experience, an artist whose work reflects the hostility and hurdles of the black urban experience in the early twentieth century, Williams moves away from middle-**class** concerns. The emphasis on underprivileged African Americans suggests that Williams's work is more indebted to **Zora Neale Hurston** than to **Nella Larsen**.

In "The Songs of the Grown," the third and final part of *Some One Sweet Angel Chile*, Williams goes back to her own past. In this section the writer uses her childhood recollections but does not construct a linear narrative. Instead she recreates her past through a series of images, those seemingly disconnected visual and sound imprints from which the thread of the life story is interlaced. The poems evoke the rhythms of the housing project with the voices of the adults mingled with the music of Ray Charles or Thelonious Monk—the oral and musical traditions that constitute the fabric of Williams's work. In addition, the landscape of the San Joaquin Valley, where the cultivated fields are bisected by the freeway and the engine of a solitary car is echoed by a crying coyote, is also featured. However, there is no sense of sentimentality in the poet's treatment of the natural environment. The bus route, which links the projects to the cotton fields and the vineyards, ends in the line of the County Hospital or the County Welfare. The fertility of the land contrasts with the deprivation of the people who **work** it. In this section, the speaker, like the blues singer, assumes the voice of her community, singing both her song and that of her parents' generation, recreating her mother's accent and reimagining her father's lost tale.

Working Cotton, Williams's first children's book, also evokes the life of the migrant fieldworkers. This text, based on an earlier composition from her first volume of poetry, "The Peacock Poems:1," signals not only the writer's return to her childhood but also her continuous effort to establish a literary account of the life of low-income African Americans. The "Author's Note," drawing attention to a society where minimum wages and education translate into a near absence of opportunity for children, shows Williams's commitment to a literature infused with social responsibility. In this book, significantly dedicated to her grandchildren and the children of the Valley, the writer bears witness to her familiar past to pass it on to future generations as representative of their history. The untold narrative of the cotton pickers is emphasized by the anonymity of their faces, which are covered by the darkness of dawn and dusk. In this text, consistent with Williams's previous work, the voice of the silenced is validated through a first-person narrative as Shelan describes an ordinary day in the life of her family. The harshness of the work under the burning sun is interrupted by work songs, the children's laughter, and a late cotton flower, a sign of luck. In this text, the rhythms of the black vernacular evoke the endurance of the human spirit, celebrating the roughness and the poetry of life.

In her second picture book, *Girls Together* (1999), Williams recreates a Saturday morning in the Fresno projects. The girls get up early in order to avoid house chores and errands. If in *Working Cotton* Williams evokes a child's perspective on family life, here she creates a children's world, where the adults are near but astutely excluded. In the streets of the project, stories are acted out, new dances tried, and lyrics of songs are reinvented. However, the girls are not indifferent to the desolation of the urban landscape around the projects with its vacant lots and derelict buildings. Walking away from their neighborhood, the four friends see the detached houses with their green lawns and trees. They are attracted to a magnolia tree, a symbol of the rural American South. Climbing the branches of the tree and picking flowers to adorn their hair, the girls do not forget their absent friend, Lois, who was not allowed out to play. The small present of a white creamy flower attests to and celebrates childhood friendships.

In 1986 Williams published her novel **Dessa Rose**. Many critics identify the short story "Meditations on History" (1980) as the genesis of this work. In fact, in the poem "I Sing This Song for Our Mothers" (1975), the writer already traces the story line that she will later develop in her novel. In the "Author's Note" to *Dessa Rose*, Williams explains that her story is based on two historical episodes. From **Angela Davis**'s article published in the *Black Scholar* in 1971, "Reflections on the Black Woman's Role in the Community of Slaves," Williams learned about an 1829 uprising on a coffle in Kentucky led by a pregnant woman. Reading Herbert Aptheker's *American Negro Revolts* (1947), she came across the second incident: In North Carolina in 1830, a white woman living in a remote area offered refuge to runaway slaves. In reality these two women never met, but their encounter in Williams's imaginative world provides a space where they are forced to confront their preconceived notions of **race** and gender by questioning the validity of socially assigned roles.

In *Dessa Rose*, the writer exposes the cultural constructs involved in the production of the historical record and the distortion of the history of the voiceless. Nevertheless, in Williams's work, the slave's silence becomes an act of resistance. In keeping with Williams's overall artistic project, the black vernacular and call-and-response patterns of the slaves' songs provide the necessary means not only to escape slavery but also to liberate the self. In the final of the three main sections of the novel, Dessa assumes control over her narrative, and the third-person narrator fades away. In her account Dessa remains a speaker, a storyteller, validating African American oral tradition as both a literary and historical record.

By the time of her death Williams was working on a sequel to *Dessa Rose* and had begun a work set in the Central Valley of California in the late 1960s.

See also Historical Fiction; Neo-Slave Narrative

Works By

"Anonymous in America." *Boundary 2: A Journal of Postmodern Literature* 6 (1978): 435–442.

"The Blues Roots of Contemporary Afro-American Poetry." *Chant of Saints: A Gathering of Afro-American Literature, Art, and Scholarship.* Cfhicago: University of Illinois Press, 1979. 123–135.

Dessa Rose. New York: William Morrow, 1986.

Girls Together. San Diego: Harcourt Brace, 1999.

Give Birth to Brightness: A Thematic Study in Neo-Black Literature. New York: Dial Press, 1972.

"The Lion's History: The Ghetto Writes Back." *Soundings: An Interdisciplinary Journal* 76.2–3 (Summer–Fall 1993): 245–259.

"Papa Dick and Sister-Woman: Reflections on Women in the Fiction of Richard Wright." *American Novelists Revisited: Essays in Feminist Criticism.* Ed. Fritz Fleischmann. Boston: G. K. Hall, 1982.

The Peacock Poems. Hanover: Wesleyan University Press, 1975.

"Remembering Prof. Sterling Brown, 1901–1989." *Black American Literature Forum* 23.1 (1989): 106–108.

"Returning to the Blues: Esther Philips and Contemporary Blues Culture." *Callaloo* 14.4 (1991): 816–828.

"Some Implications of Feminist Theory." *Griot* 6.2 (1987): 40–45.

Some One Sweet Angel Chile. New York: William Morrow, 1982.

"Telling the Teller: Memoir and Story." *The Seductions of Biography.* Ed. Mary Rhiel and David Suchoff. New York: Routledge, 1996. 179–184.

Working Cotton. San Diego: Harcourt Brace, 1992.

Works About

Henderson, Mae Gwendolyn. "In Memory of Sherley Anne Williams: 'Some One Sweet Angel Chile.'" *Callaloo* 22.4 (1999): 763–767.

McDowell, Deborah E. "Conversation: Sherley Anne Williams and Deborah McDowell." *The Furious Flowering of African American Poetry.* Ed. Joanne V. Gabbin. Charlottesville: University of Virginia Press, 1999. 194–205.

Ana Nunes

WILSON, AUGUST (1945–2005)

Playwright August Wilson is renowned as one of America's most important dramatists, having achieved both popular and critical acclaim for his cycle of plays focusing on African American life in each decade of the twentieth century. Not only have his plays been commercial hits on Broadway, but he has won the New York Drama Critics Circle Awards, Drama Desk Awards, Tony Awards, and two Pulitzer Prizes for his **drama**.

Born in Pittsburgh, Pennsylvania, to an African American mother and a German immigrant father, Wilson's original name was Frederick August Kittel. Later, he changed his name to Wilson to honor his mother, Daisy Wilson, and reject his father, who abandoned the **family** when August was a baby. Wilson dropped out of school in the tenth grade, ending his formal schooling at age fifteen. He studied widely on his own, however, using the public library and the streets of Pittsburgh as his school. Although many critics have compared Wilson to canonical playwrights such as Arthur Miller and Eugene O'Neill, Wilson claims unfamiliarity with their work. The Black Nationalist movement of the 1960s has been integral to his philosophy, however. Wilson also cites painter Romare Bearden, poet and activist **Amiri Baraka**, Argentine writer Jorge Luis Borges, and most important, the **blues** tradition in music as the major influences on his work. Wilson's earliest creative forays were in **poetry**, but eventually he switched to writing plays, where he found his voice by capturing the poetry of everyday black speech.

Wilson's plays seek to chronicle the realities faced by African Americans throughout the twentieth century. His dramas fuse social realism with supernatural elements rooted in African **spirituality** and oral traditions. His Afrocentric perspective reminds his audience of the unique culture that people of African heritage have forged in this country. A cultural contribution of particular importance to Wilson is the blues aesthetic, which permeates all of his works. The blues philosophy, he believes, captures the essence of African American culture—both its tragedy and its strength.

The struggle African Americans face forging a strong **identity** as both individuals and as part of a tradition provides a common thread throughout Wilson's oeuvre. Many of his characters are lost because they have denied, or been denied, their African roots. Wilson's work suggests that only when African Americans find their authentic identity firmly rooted in their own traditions—what he metaphorically terms their "song"—are they able to lead rich, satisfying lives.

Wilson's body of work unquestionably focuses on African American men, not on women. However, his cycle of twentieth-century plays does include a significant number of female characters. Although some of Wilson's women function mainly as appendages to the more interesting male characters, he has created several complex women characters whose words and actions provide a sharp critique of gender inequities within African American culture. While it is beyond the scope here to discuss all of Wilson's female characters, it is nonetheless possible to categorize these females into three types who recur throughout his oeuvre: the nurturers/sustainers, the artists, and the rebels.

Bertha Holly of *Joe Turner's Come and Gone* (1988) and Rose Maxson of *Fences* (1987) exemplify the female sustainers in Wilson's work. These women provide warmth, support, and nourishment not only for their own families but often for other members of the **community** as well. In *Joe Turner*, for example, Seth and Bertha Holly's boardinghouse serves as a **home** for the many displaced blacks who have come up north from the **South**. Bertha's generous spirit helps to make the boardinghouse seem like a home. In particular, Bertha feeds people as a way of building community and nourishing both **body** and soul; most of the stage directions depict Bertha cooking, serving food, or cleaning up after meals. In addition to feeding people, Bertha also defends and comforts them. Overall, she is a warmhearted, level-headed woman whose spirit helps to heal these troubled souls.

However, Bertha Holly, like most other female characters in Wilson's oeuvre, is not the major focus of the work. She is only a supporting player, not only in the play but also in her own life. Indeed, some feminist scholars have criticized Wilson for his tendency to relegate his female characters to the margins rather than the center of his plays. Such a critique is justified; Wilson's major characters are almost all male. However, to Wilson's credit, he has created a number of plays that highlight specifically female struggles.

With Rose Maxson of *Fences*, for example, we see the drawbacks of being a female sustainer. Rose is a responsible, nurturing woman who sacrifices her own desires in order to keep peace in the family. Married to domineering Troy Maxson, Rose has cared for Troy and their son Cory for seventeen years, putting up with Troy's flaws with little complaint. Like Bertha, Rose also spends much of her time on stage serving food and trying to create peace between squabbling characters.

Unlike Bertha, however, Rose questions her decision to devote herself entirely to her family after discovering that Troy has been having an affair and that his mistress is about to give birth to their child. Troy is not only unapologetic about his affair, but he even asks Rose to raise the illegitimate child when its mother dies in childbirth. When Rose reflects upon her marriage, she realizes that she went overboard in her desire to nurture Troy. In the end she is left with neither a full identity nor a husband. *Fences* emphasizes that devoting oneself to family at the expense of the self is not a good choice for women because they may well be left with nothing in the end.

Not all of Wilson's female characters can be classified as nurturers, however. Wilson has also created characters such as Ma Rainey of *Ma Rainey's Black Bottom* (1985) and Berniece of *The Piano Lesson* (1990). These women are artist figures who need to do more than nurture others; they need to play music in order to be whole. *Ma Rainey* is loosely based on the historical figure of Ma Rainey, known as "the Mother of the Blues." This play, which is set in the 1920s, explores the historical exploitation of black musicians by white producers. Even though Ma Rainey is a successful artist, she knows that the white publishers control and manipulate her career for their own benefit. In fact, she compares the relationship of black musician–white publisher to that of a prostitute and pimp.

But though the publishers may have the ultimate power, Wilson's Ma Rainey is no submissive doormat. On the contrary, Wilson portrays her as a confident artist who knows her own worth. She is also brash, independent, sexually adventurous, and domineering. Although Ma is a flawed character whose bossiness is so extreme it is almost comical, she is one of the few Wilson female characters whose identity does not come from her relationship to the male characters of the play. Her identity, rather, comes from her integrity as a blues artist. She is a woman who has already found her song. Because her identity is so firmly rooted in African American traditions, she is one of Wilson's strongest and most vibrant characters.

Like Ma Rainey, piano player Berniece of Wilson's *The Piano Lesson* exemplifies another of Wilson's female artists. Unlike Ma, however, Berniece's artistic impulses are frustrated. The major conflict of this play revolves around a piano that Berniece and her brother Boy Willie inherited from their parents. The piano is much more than a musical instrument to Berniece; it is a precious family legacy gained through her **ancestors**' long struggles with the slaveholding Sutter family. Berniece cherishes the piano as a way to honor the **memory** of her ancestors and the horrors they experienced because of **slavery** and its aftermath. In a sense, this piano represents her soul, one thing that cannot be bought or sold. So when her brother Boy Willie wants to sell the piano in order to buy a farm, Berniece categorically refuses. She is so adamant in her refusal that she is willing to shoot her brother if he tries to take it by force.

Wilson is sympathetic to Berniece's desire to retain her family legacy. However, the play reveals that honoring one's past involves more than holding on to a piece of furniture, no matter how precious it is. Berniece is missing part of the picture, however; although she keeps the piano, she never plays it because she does not want to wake the spirits of her family's ghosts. Not only does Berniece refuse to play the piano; she also refuses to "play" the game of life. Still mourning the **death** of her husband three years earlier, Berniece has stopped living fully; she goes out very little and pushes away any attempts at intimacy.

By holding on to the piano without playing it, Berniece demonstrates that she is afraid of the family ghosts, afraid of the past. This fear paralyzes her for the present and the future, keeping her frozen and unable to live fully. In order to both honor the past and live in the present, Wilson suggests, she must play the piano, to keep the song of the family alive. Berniece finally recognizes this truth at the end of the play. When Berniece sits down to the piano to play and sing, asking her ancestors to help her, the ghost of Sutter finally disappears, and there is peace in the home. Berniece has finally reclaimed her song by conquering her fear and facing her legacy head-on. In so doing, the play suggests that she is on the road to living a fuller life as an artist.

In addition to sustainers and artists, Wilson also portrays another recurring type of female: the rebel. Characters such as Molly Cunningham of *Joe Turner's Come and Gone* and Risa of *Two Trains Running* (1993) rebel against culturally imposed standards of proper femininity. Like most Wilson characters, these women have emotional scars and are in need of **love** and **healing**. However, unlike submissive characters such as Mattie Campbell who roams the countryside looking for the husband who abandoned her, Molly and Risa choose to fight their demons in ways that defy proper female codes of behavior.

Molly is a beautiful woman to whom many men are attracted. She has learned through observation and experience, however, that sexual relationships can be a trap to women, and she consciously tries not to fall into that trap. She refuses to perform conventional female behavior such as ironing other people's clothes, having children, or even searching for a committed relationship because she sees how other women have been hurt or worn out before their time by looking after men and children. Although Molly enjoys male company, she makes sure to maintain her independence within a sexual relationship by being the one to set the rules.

Like Molly, Risa of *Two Trains Running* is also a woman who attracts a great deal of male attention. Risa, however, tries to keep male advances at bay through an unusual technique, deliberately scarring her legs in order to make herself unattractive. As the stage directions note, Risa has done this in order to carve out an identity that does not depend on her sexual organs. She wants men to consider her personality, not just her body. By scarring herself, she forces men to think about her in ways that they otherwise would not have.

To be sure, Wilson is not suggesting that either Molly's or Risa's fear of intimacy is something to be emulated. Both of these characters are wounded and, the plays suggest, in need of love. However, Wilson does demonstrate through his creation of these characters an implicit critique of gender relations—specifically the emotional dangers women confront when they are treated like sexual game by men.

In conclusion, while Wilson's work focuses more deeply on African American men's issues than on female issues, he has succeeded in creating a number of complex portraits of women who challenge the prevailing norms of proper female behavior.

See also Black Nationalism

Works By

Fences. New York: New American Library [Plume], 1987.
Gem of the Ocean. Unpublished.
The Janitor. Literature and Its Writers: An Introduction, by Ann Charters and Samuel Charters. Boston: Bedford, 1997. 1901–1902.
Jitney. New York: Overlook Press, 2003.
Joe Turner's Come and Gone. New York: New American Library [Plume], 1988.
King Hedley II. Unpublished.
Ma Rainey's Black Bottom. New York: New American Library [Plume], 1985.
The Piano Lesson. New York: Plume, 1990.
Seven Guitars. New York: Dutton, 1996.
Testimonies. Antaeus 66 (Spring 1991): 474–479.
Three Plays. Pittsburgh: University of Pittsburgh Press, 1991. (Includes *Ma Rainey's Black Bottom*, *Fences*, and *Joe Turner's Come and Gone*.)
Two Trains Running. New York: Plume, 1993.

Works About

Bogumil, Mary L. *Understanding August Wilson*. Columbia: University of South Carolina Press, 1999.

Elkins, Marilyn, ed. *August Wilson: A Casebook*. New York: Garland, 1994.

Nadel, Alan, ed. *May All Your Fences Have Gates: Essays on the Drama of August Wilson*. Iowa City: University of Iowa Press, 1994.

Pereira, Kim. *August Wilson and the African-American Odyssey*. Urbana: University of Illinois Press, 1995.

Shannon, Sandra G. *The Dramatic Vision of August Wilson*. Washington, DC: Howard University Press, 1995.

Wolfe, Peter. *August Wilson*. Twayne's United States Author Series. New York: Twayne, 1999.

Debra Beilke

WILSON, HARRIET E. (1828?–1863?)

Since the 1983 republication of ***Our Nig; or, Sketches from the Life of a Free Black, In a Two Story White House, North, Showing That Slavery's Shadows Fall Even There***, Harriet E. Wilson has been considered the first black person known to have published a novel in the United States. Despite her historical significance, Wilson's text and her life story lingered on the brink of obscurity until fairly recently. Scholars' attempts to locate biographical information about Wilson and to map her text's literary legacy reveal the specific challenges of researching nineteenth-century African American women writers. Every biographical or critical writing published about Wilson laments the paucity of detail about her life, and this entry is no different.

Wilson is known to us through her only literary work, *Our Nig*, which was published for the author in 1859 in Boston by George C. Rand and Avery. Wilson was all but ignored for most of the years following the publication of *Our Nig*. Moreover, for much of the twentieth century, critics and rare booksellers believed H. Wilson to be male and, quite likely, a white male. It was not until the 1983 reprinting of *Our Nig* (edited by Henry Louis Gates Jr.) that Wilson's gender and **race** were confirmed through careful scrutiny of federal and state census data, birth and **death** records, city directories, newspapers, and a range of other documents by Gates and David A. Curtis. More recently, Barbara A. White builds on the work of Gates and Curtis and locates Wilson in the (June 1) 1840 census for Milford, New Hampshire. From this information, White ascertains that Wilson lived with the Nehemiah Hayward **family**, not the Samuel Boyleses, as originally believed. In this census, Wilson is listed as being a free colored person between ten and twenty-four years of age. Gates's first record of Wilson is the 1850 federal census of New Hampshire, which lists Harriet Adams living in Milford, New Hampshire. Her age is stated as twenty-two and her race as black. Gates contends that if this information is accurate, Wilson was a free black, born as Harriet Adams in 1827 or 1828. In the 1860 Boston federal census, a Mrs. Harriet E. Wilson is listed with a birthdate of 1807 or 1808 and a birthplace of Fredericksburg, Virginia. These absences and inconsistencies highlight several of the obstacles facing scholars investigating the lives of nineteenth-century African American women. Inconsistencies or errors within early censuses are not unusual, nor is the absence of records about African American women. As Barbara A. White observes, it is not surprising that the birth of a poor black female went unrecorded. White further notes that the absence of records regarding Wilson stands in sharp contrast to the plentiful property records of white men in the **community**.

Our Nig, which makes claims at being an **autobiography**, has also helped to provide leads and context for many of these archival findings. White's research into the Hayward family verifies that many of the stories in *Our Nig* are true, including the ill treatment she received at the hands of Rebecca Hayward, who was, in all likelihood, the inspiration for the "she-devil" Mrs. Bellmont. White's important research also confirms the social and economic difficulties Wilson confronted. In the 1850 "Report of the Overseers of the Poor for the Town of Milford, for the Year ending February 15, 1850," Wilson is listed as "Poor not on the farm"; White suggests at this time Wilson avoided the town pauper farm and was living with a family who was reimbursed by the town for keeping her. Reports for 1851–1854 are missing, so little evidence exists about this period of Wilson's life. Records at the Milford Town Clerk's office reveal that Harriet Adams married Thomas Wilson on October 6, 1851. Their only child, George Mason Wilson, was born approximately nine months later. In a document appended to the text, "Allida" alludes to Wilson's husband leaving her, returning once, and then disappearing for good; ill health and single **motherhood** would have compounded the economic hardships facing a free African American woman at this time.

White found documentation to confirm Wilson's struggles with poverty and failing health. Wilson appears to have worked as a straw sewer and to have sold hair dye or tonic but was plagued by ill health. Records of the Hillsborough County farm show that Wilson's son, age three, was admitted to this farm for four weeks. White's research into this county farm reveals horrific conditions. There is little doubt that Wilson would have worried about her son's emotional and physical well-being at such a place. Records also suggest that Wilson left George with a foster family while she went to Boston to find **work**. Gates located a widow named Harriet Wilson living in Boston between 1856 and 1863 in the Boston city directories. This Boston connection is important since *Our Nig* was printed in Boston and was registered with the Clerk's office of the District Court of the District of Massachusetts in 1859. It is uncertain when Wilson left Massachusetts; however, White asserts that Wilson was back in New Hampshire in 1863. All traces of Harriet E. Wilson end there.

Despite her aspirations, *Our Nig* seems to have offered Wilson little, if any, critical notice or remunerative success. To date, scholars have not been able to find published notices or reviews of the novel upon its publication nor references to Wilson as an author. Six months after the novel's publication, Wilson's son died of fever. In a sad twist of fate, the discovery of George's death certificate was what unequivocally established Wilson's race and gender and what finally brought Wilson the readership she desired, albeit 125 years later.

Although the details of her life remain, in Gates's words, "frustratingly sparse," Wilson is, unfortunately, not an isolated case. Many African American women's significant achievements have also hovered on the brink of obscurity or have been lost over the years. There is hope that scholars may yet, as did Barbara A. White, discover missing pieces of Wilson's life to help flesh out her role in the vibrant narrative of African American women's **history**.

Work By

Our Nig; or, Sketches from the Life of a Free Black. 2nd ed. New York: Vintage, 1983.

Works About

Carby, Hazel. *Reconstructing Womanhood: The Emergence of the Afro-American Woman Novelist.* New York: Oxford University Press, 1987.

Gates, Henry Louis, Jr. Introduction to *Our Nig; or, Sketches from the Life of a Free Black,* by Harriet. E. Wilson. 2nd ed. New York: Vintage, 1983.

Holloway, Karla F. C. "Economies of Space: Markets and Marketability in *Our Nig* and *Iola Leroy.*" *The (Other) American Traditions: Nineteenth-Century American Women Writers.* Ed. Joyce Warren. New Brunswick, NJ: Rutgers University Press, 1992. 126–140.

White, Barbara A. "'Our Nig' and the She-Devil: New Information about Harriet Wilson and the 'Bellmont' Family." *American Literature* 65.1 (March 1993): 19–52.

Heidi L. M. Jacobs

WOFFORD, CHLOE ANTHONY. See Morrison, Toni

WOMANISM

Womanism is a concept that defines the desire for wholeness of self, a celebration of black women's **identity**, and an appreciation and **love** for all things woman, including the roles of mother and wife. Womanism separates itself from white feminism in that white female feminist ideology espouses significant differences from the issues affecting black women.

White feminists focus on issues related to power disparities within gender relationships and are most concerned with attaining social equality with white males. White feminism concentrates on achieving a socially valid individual selfhood outside the dominant socially constructed patriarchal expectations of subordination by white men. White feminists believe the oppression of white males and social patriarchal structure to be the biggest threat to women's lives, an idea rooted in the white woman's past subjugation as property owned by white males. White women's feminism encourages the struggle to achieve self-empowerment through feminist dialogue and an emphasis on female inclusion in areas formally the sole realm of white males, most particularly in employment and political structures and opportunities. White female feminist ideology also attempts to decommodify women's bodies, particularly within male-dominated visual media. White feminists support reproductive rights and equal educational opportunities as a way to combat what they see as the tyranny of white males. For white female feminists, women's struggle for equality is reduced to a simple dualism: All males are the oppressor. White females also promote their feminist ideology on a global scale, often without a clear understanding of the very significant cultural differences within non-Western countries. White feminism approaches what most consider important women's issues through the lens of Western privilege, rather than from a broader scope that encompasses issues more vital to the majority of the world's women.

In contrast, womanism encompasses issues that are important to African American women beyond those that concern white feminism. Black women's issues differ significantly from white feminist ideology in part because the core ideals of womanism are significantly different from the egotistically based power struggle that undergirds white feminism.

The term *womanism* was coined by **Alice Walker** in her book ***In Search of Our Mothers' Gardens*** (1983). Womanism referred to black women whose focus is black women's culture, the **family**, and combating racism together with men. An important distinction between white feminism and womanism is the attitude toward men. White feminists view all males as the enemy, the oppressive force of patriarchy that must be overcome. Womanists do not view black men as oppressors but rather as partners in the fight against white racism and domination. Womanists celebrate women's issues but embrace black men within the context of their common cultural traditions. In traditional African culture, black women and men are equal; there is no passive female role in African society, which is reflected in African American culture. Black women do not feel the patriarchal oppression from black men but rather from white society as a whole: both men *and* woman. For the womanist, the fight against white racism is the core from which womanism springs. White feminists are centered on the self and establishing an individual female autonomy separate from their male oppressors. Black women already hold a position of autonomy within black gender relationships, so the womanist struggle against men is transformed to a struggle against the oppression of whites against all genders of African Americans and people of color.

Womanists privilege the family and **work** to advocate the family and family empowerment. While the majority of white feminists view the role of mother and wife as subordinate and unfulfilling, a patriarchal suppression of the woman's ability to become a whole person (a wholeness most often defined by the economic value of her labor), womanists believe that **motherhood** should be embraced as an integral part of a woman's wholeness. For womanists, motherhood is not reduced to its economic profitability but is viewed as a key element in the health and well-being of future African Americans. Womanism promotes communal issues of **race**, gender, and identity and the unity that comes from furthering pluralistic social ideologies, rather than individual self-realization. Womanists espouse social justice issues as a means to improve the economic and social disparities that affect people of color all over the world. Womanism is a unique ideal that unites African Americans by their common **history** of suffering under **slavery** and as a connection to and preservation of traditional African heritage.

See also Black Feminism; Black Feminist Criticism; Womanist Conjure

Works About

Allan, Tuzyline J. *Womanist and Feminist Aesthetics: A Comparative Review.* Athens: Ohio University Press, 1995.

Gates, Henry Louis, Jr. *Reading Black, Reading Feminist: A Critical Anthology.* New York: Meridian Books, 1990.

hooks, bell. *Feminist Theory: From Margin to Center.* Boston: South End Press, 1984.

Hudson-Weems, Clenora. *Africana Womanism: Reclaiming Ourselves.* New York: Bedford, 1993.

——. *Africana Womanist Literary Theory.* Trenton, NJ: Africa World Press, 2004.

McCaskill, Barbara, and Layli Phillips. "We Are All 'Good Woman': A Womanist Critique of the Current Feminist Conflict." *Bad Girls/Good Girls: Women, Sex, and Power in the Nineties.* Ed. Nan Bauer Maglin and Donna Perry. New Brunswick, NJ: Rutgers University Press, 1996. 106–122.

Ogunyemi, Chikwenye. "Womanism: The Dynamics of the Contemporary Black Female Novel in English." *Signs* 11 (1985): 63–80.

Walker, Alice. *In Search of Our Mothers' Gardens: Womanist Prose.* New York: Harcourt/Brace, 1983.

Williams, Sherley Anne. "Some Implications of Womanist Theory." *Callaloo* 9.2 (Spring 1986): 303–308.

Debbie Clare Olson

WOMANIST CONJURE

Womanist conjure is a black aesthetic grounded in the religious symbols, rituals, **myth**, and **folklore** of voodoo and hoodoo. Black women writers who use as their creative models the mythologies of African **religion** to articulate issues related to black female life and appropriate the character of the conjure woman as a strong symbol of black female creative and spiritual agency are engaging in the literary act of womanist conjure.

The texts of womanist conjure carry as their essence the idea of wholeness and **healing**. Books such as ***Beloved*** (1987) by **Toni Morrison**, ***Mama Day*** by **Gloria Naylor** (1988), and ***The Salt Eaters*** (1980) by **Toni Cade Bambara** explore various journeys of healing for black people, but they also place black women who act as healers at the center of that journey.

In its traditional context, *conjure* is both verb and noun; therefore, *conjure* refers to the creative process of black women and the product of that creativity. Within this framework, themes of mother-daughter creativity and cultural inheritance are evident. Examples include Mayse Conde's *I, Tituba, Black Witch of Salem* (1992) and Jewel Parker Rhodes's *Voodoo Dreams: A Novel of Marie Leveau* (1993), both works that attempt to reclaim the lives of legendary conjure woman as creative foremothers. These novels affirm the lives of real-life conjurers to tell the stories of women whose voices have been historically silenced.

The role and influence of the conjure woman in black communities worldwide are vast. The conjure woman may be a priestess or spiritual guide in the religion of voodoo or Santería, a midwife, and/or healer. Black women who represent these variations of the conjure woman in their art are engaging in womanist conjure.

In the African American literary tradition, conjure and conjurers both male and female can be traced back to the **slave narratives** of **Frederick Douglass** and **Harriet Jacobs**, but it is not until **Charles Waddell Chesnutt**'s *The Conjure Woman and Other Conjure Tales* (1899) that conjure comes into its own as a literary device. Although Chesnutt utilizes the conjure woman as a powerful woman who uses magic or conjure as a way to empower her **community**, his conjure woman, Aunt Peggy, is not a layered, complex character, as she becomes in womanist conjure narratives.

Zora Neale Hurston's work is the first to truly employ womanist conjure. In ***Mules and Men*** (1935), Hurston goes in search of conjure and studies under a descendant of Marie Leveau, the famous nineteenth-century voodoo queen of New Orleans. Hurston, a voodoo priestess in her own right, frequently employed the imagery and mythology of voodoo and conjure in ***Their Eyes Were Watching God*** (1937), and ***Jonah's Gourd Vine*** (1934). In her own **autobiography** ***Dust Tracks on a Road*** (1942) she makes reference to herself as a "seer," which in the world of conjure is another term for a two-headed doctor or conjurer. Womanist conjure preserves the ethnic and cultural elements of the conjure woman in black communities while reaffirming black female agency.

See also Ancestor, Use of; *Baby of the Family*; Conjuring; *Hand I Fan With, The*; *In Love & Trouble: Stories of Black Women*; *In Search of Our Mothers' Gardens: Womanist Prose*; *Meridian*; *Sassafrass, Cypress & Indigo*; *Song of Solomon*; Womanism

Works About

Baker, Houston A. *Workings of the Spirit: The Poetics of Afro-American Women's Writings.* Chicago: University of Chicago Press, 1991.

Bell, Bernard. *The Afro-American Novel and Its Foundation.* Amherst: University of Massachusetts Press, 1994.

Lee, Valerie. *Granny Midwives and Black Women Writers: Double-Dutched Readings.* New York: Routledge, 1996.

Pryse, Majorie, and Hortense J. Spillers, eds. *Conjuring: Black Women, Fiction, and Literary Tradition.* Bloomington: Indiana University Press, 1985.

Tucker, Lindsey. "Recovering the Conjure Woman: Texts and Contexts in Gloria Naylor's *Mama Day.*" *African American Review* 28.2 (1994): 173–188.

Kelly Norman Ellis

WOMEN OF BREWSTER PLACE, THE

A hint of *The Women of Brewster Place* (1982) first appeared in *Essence Magazine* in 1979 as "A Life on Beekman Place." The *Essence* story expanded into the collection of seven stories that became **Gloria Naylor**'s first novel. The novel tackles the various stories that lead black women to a bleak place like Brewster Place. The stories and issues that entangle them are many and diverse.

The most pronounced character in the novel is Mattie Michael. She emerges from Tennessee after her relationship with her father, once an inseparable bond, becomes intractable. Mattie is not sent away to live with relatives when her parents learn of her out-of-wedlock pregnancy, as was a common custom of the rural **South** of the past. Her father accepts the pregnancy but cannot bear his daughter's refusal to divulge the name of the baby's father. His rage immediately manifests as physical brutality. Only the blast from Mrs. Michael's shotgun interrupts the beating and pulls Mr. Michael from his trance. From this house in Tennessee to Brewster Place is still a long distance and many years in between, but his story is just one of several that reveals the vicissitudes of life that lead the characters of the novel to the dead-end street of Brewster Place.

Brewster Place is separated from the rest of the city by a brick wall. It has been the residence of other people of color before blacks, mostly black women, settle on Brewster Place. The reader is introduced to the street in Mattie Michael's story. Her son has skipped bail after she puts up her house to ensure that he will appear at his court date just two weeks from the bail posting. On Brewster Place, Mattie becomes the mother figure. Her nurturing spirit is even a place of solace for her childhood friend Etta Mae Johnson.

Etta Mae has rejected the strictures placed on a black woman of her time. She fled her native Rock Vale, Tennessee, after an undisclosed matter with a white man. The reader is left to fill in the blanks that Etta Mae had refused the sexual advances of a white man, a rejection felt so deeply and widely among the whites of Rock Vale that her father's barn was burned down. Etta Mae has never felt the need to apologize for her **race** or her gender, but this stalwart confidence leads her on a search for herself that loops throughout the United States—St. Louis, Chicago, San Francisco, Harlem, Florida, and to the primary setting of Naylor's first novel. Finding no place to blossom as an individual, she resolves that her only success will come from ties with a man. However, she is left emotionally wounded from her one-night tryst with Rev. Moreland T. Woods. When she saw him, she had dreamed of a respectable life as his wife.

Kiswana Browne is an idealist from black upper-**class** Linden Hills who rejects her bourgeois background, what she deems a sell-out lifestyle. She, with her college classmates, fought for political and social revolution. Her first declaration of revolution might have been changing her name from Melanie to Kiswana. She dropped out of college to fight authentically among the people, not as her classmates had done by graduating and taking traditional jobs with corporations and law firms. She lives on Brewster Place to fight the revolution that she views as continuing.

She begins her fight against the slumlord who owns the buildings on Brewster Place by organizing a tenant association. In this process she meets Cora Lee, a woman with seven children, and immediately Cora becomes a situation to revolutionize. Kiswana invites Cora Lee and her children to an all-black production of Shakespeare's *A Midsummer Night's Dream*. While the production exposes Cora Lee to an expanded worldview, it cannot be and is not enough to magically transform her into an attentive mother. And despite Mattie Michael's admonishment for her to stop having children, she continues. By the novel's end, she is pregnant with her eighth.

Part of Naylor's message in *The Women of Brewster Place* is that stories exist beneath the assumptions that are made about people who live on a street like Brewster Place. For instance, Cora Lee is a mother of seven on welfare, but her current state has developed from a childhood fascination with dolls that was ignored even when she mutilated the dolls that were not baby dolls. Her father's alarm was always quieted by her mother.

Whereas Mattie places her son before all else, including any interest in a romantic relationship, Luciela (Ciel) Louise Turner invests herself in a man to the detriment of her children. Only after she aborts her child to preserve her romantic relationship and just as her daughter Serena is being electrocuted does she realize that her **love** for Eugene is not worth holding. She is finally ready to let him go when she hears Serena's screams of **death**. Ciel spirals into a pit of despondence and despair that Mattie pulls her from by nurturing her back to reality.

Toward the end of the novel, Naylor broaches the subject of homosexuality in the black **community** with the chapter "The Two." Lorraine and Theresa have been skirted to Brewster Place because of Lorraine's discomfort with the questioning eyes of neighbors. They began in Linden Hills, and Brewster Place is the end of the line for them. Lorraine, the more friendly of the two, has noticed that the greetings of neighbors have waned. She suspects that the neighbors know that they are lesbians. Although she claims that she fears rumors reaching the principal on the other side of town where she teaches, she is actually dealing with her need to be an accepted member of her community. Theresa is so self-contained that she feels she does not need her community to survive. Lorraine finds in Ben, the perpetually intoxicated handyman, a surrogate father, but she bludgeons him to death after she confuses him for one of the gang of men who raped her in the alley.

The action of the novel ebbs as Mattie dreams of the women of Brewster Place banding together to tear down the brick wall, an act of solidarity that pulls Theresa, Cora Lee, Etta Mae, and the other women from the fringes to express their rebellion against the kind of life that is lived on a dead-end street. While this is Mattie's dream, it probably portends what is to come.

See also Lesbianism; *Men of Brewster Place, The*

Works About

Christian, Barbara. "No More Buried Lives: The Theme of Lesbianism in Audre Lorde's *Zami*, Gloria Naylor's *The Women of Brewster Place*, Ntozake Shange's *Sassafras, Cypress, and Indigo*, and Alice Walker's *The Color Purple*." *Black Feminist Criticism: Perspectives on Black Women Writers*. New York: Pergamon Press, 1985. 187–204.

Fraser, Celeste. "Stealing B(l)ack Voices: The Myth of the Black Matriarchy and *The Women of Brewster Place*." *Critical Matrix* 5 (Fall–Winter 1989).

Stanford, Ann Folwell. "Mechanism of Disease: African-American Women Writers, Social Pathologies, and the Limits of Medicine." *NWSA Journal* 6.1 (Spring 1994): 28–47.

Wells, Linda, Sandra E. Bowen (reply), and Suzanne Stutman (reply). " 'What Shall I Give My Children?' ": The Role of Mentor in Gloria Naylor's *The Women of Brewster Place* and Paule Marshall's *Praisesong for the Widow*." *Explorations in Ethnic Studies* 13.2 (1990): 41–60.

Sharese Terrell Willis

WOODSON, JACQUELINE (1964–)

Jacqueline Woodson was born on February 12, 1964, in Columbus, Ohio, though she grew up in Greenville, South Carolina, and Brooklyn, New York. She received a B.A. degree in English at Adelphi University in 1985 and studied creative writing at the New School for Social Research. In addition to being a writer, Woodson is also a teacher and editor. She has contributed to a number of short-story collections (e.g., *Queer 13: Lesbian and Gay Writers Recall Seventh Grade*) and journals (e.g., *Essence* and *Horn Book*).

She writes for multiple audiences, but she has received critical acclaim for her picture books and **children's and young adult literature**. With over fifteen books to her credit, she began publishing for young people in the early 1990s.

Her first publication, *Last Summer with Maizon* (1990) (first book in a trilogy), introduces the friendship that exists between the title character Maizon and her neighbor Margaret. Within the story, the girls' bond is strengthened as they help each other cope with serious issues such as **death** and loneliness. Woodson's works are consistent in that they focus on realistic and oftentimes controversial issues such as **sexuality**, **lesbianism**, teen pregnancy, molestation, and imprisonment. The majority of her young adult books feature female characters that face issues pertinent to female adolescent **identity** development. The characters often confront racism, discrimination, and abandonment, among other contemporary social issues. Serious social issues are not confined to her books for teenagers; they appear in her books for younger readers as well.

In one of her recent picture books, *Our Gracie Aunt* (2002), siblings, Beebee and Johnson, are in need of an "othermother" because their own mother, who is accustomed to leaving them **home** alone, has left and may not return. When their mother's sister, Aunt Gracie, agrees to take care of them, the children have to grow to trust and **love** her, though they fear she will also abandon them. Another picture book, *Visiting Day* (2002), is about a girl who, along with her grandmother, prepares to visit her father in prison. When asked about the topics she chooses to address in her work, Woodson said,

I write about what's important to me.... It's interesting to me when people say I write about "tough" issues or that the issues are "edgy" because, for me, they are things we talk about in my community everyday. It's the things that are important to us that pretty much change the course of our lives. The issue of the high number of Black men in prison is a big issue and not only because the numbers are so imbalanced in terms of how many people of color are incarcerated, but also because in families it doesn't get talked about. So there is a lot of shame around that, and I think the issue of shame is a big issue for me because I don't think anyone should feel it for any reason." (Hinton 27)

Womanist concerns around **community**, women friends, and love of self are prevalent throughout her work.

Works By

Between Madison and Palmetto. 1993. New York: Putnam, 2002.
"Common Ground." *Essence* (May 1999): 148–150.
The Dear One. New York: Delacorte Press, 1991.
From the Notebooks of Melanin Sun. New York: Scholastic, 1995.
I Hadn't Meant to Tell You This. New York: Bantam Doubleday, 1994.
Locomotion. New York: G. P. Putnam's Sons, 2003.
"A Sign of Having Been Here." *Horn Book Magazine* (November–December 1995): 711–715.
A Way Out of No Way: Writings about Growing Up Black in America. Ed. Jacqueline Woodson. New York: Holt, 1996.

Works About

Bush, Catherine. "A World without Childhood." *New York Times Book Review* 26 (February 1995): 14.

Cart, Michael. "Woodson, Jacqueline." *St. James Guide to Young Adult Writers.* Detroit: St. James Press, 1999. 911–913.

Hinton, KaaVonia. "Jacqueline Woodson: Keeping It Real about Social Issues." *Journal of Children's Literature* 30.1 (2004): 26–30.

Stover, Lois Thomas. *Jacqueline Woodson: The Real Thing.* Lantham, MD: Rowman and Littlefield, 2004.

KaaVonia Hinton-Johnson

WORK

From the earliest origins of the United States, African American women workers have faced challenges based on their marginalization in the realms of **race**, **class**, and gender status. During **slavery**, they were treated as property, taken away from their children and families, and forced into backbreaking work. They were sexually objectified, abused, and mistreated, all the while working long, hard hours in devastatingly harsh working conditions. Dating back to the days of slavery, African American women held the majority of work positions within the **domestic** sphere. In their stations as domestics, African American women workers would often have to suppress their own needs and those of their loved ones in order to care for the families of their owners. Whether working in the **home** or in the fields, it appears that work was a constant reminder for female slaves of their race, class, and gender status. Works such as **Frances E. W. Harper**'s "The Slave Mother" (1854), **Harriet E. Wilson**'s *Our Nig* (1859), and **Harriet Jacobs**'s *Incidents in the Life of a Slave Girl* (1861) make clear how difficult the lives of slave women were. These texts tell of the pain and suffering many women slaves had to endure because their lives were not their own. Whether told in the form of autobiographical narrative, poem, or **fiction**, these women make clear that the conditions in which they had to work were physically and emotionally devastating.

However, at the same time, these works are rich in their representation of the empowerment African American women could gain through the written word and in the way these narratives demonstrate how many of these workers eventually found means of escape. Though these women often had to write in between work and **family** obligations, they still found ways to make known their lived experience. Furthermore, in works such as *Incidents in the Life of a Slave Girl,* Jacobs describes her own struggles with physical and sexual abuse at the hands of her owner and her eventual retreat from his abuse. Jacobs's **slave narrative** is merely one example of the empowerment many of these women gained through their writing and the strength they possessed to finally escape from such harsh conditions.

Aside from these narratives and poems, there were other, more universally known works at the time that greatly affected the lives of women slaves. While writing their memoirs and poems offered at least a temporary escape from the reality of their lives, so too did work songs and **spirituals** offer these women opportunities to concentrate on issues other than their work. The spirituals, particularly, demonstrate the religiosity and faith present in so many African American workers before and during the Civil War, and many of these songs, such as "Swing Low, Sweet Chariot" and "Go Down, Moses," have made their way into our cultural **memory** and psyche throughout **history**. The work songs also served many of the same purposes, offering slaves opportunities to unite as a community and express themselves creatively while working in the fields or as domestics. Many of these songs offer rich examples of the promise of **freedom** and the hope for a better future.

The period of Reconstruction also presented specific challenges to African American workers, and most particularly women. In a period that was known for vast changes in historical, political, and socioeconomic realms, former slaves had to work hard to determine their roles in an ever-changing economic atmosphere. Though now officially "freed," African American workers often found themselves in the same jobs they had held as slaves, simply because it was difficult to find the economic means to make major life changes. Despite governmental initiatives like the Freedman's Bureau, which was established by Congress in 1866 to help in educating and finding jobs for former slaves, many African American workers found it difficult, if not impossible, to make changes in their socioeconomic positions. Furthermore, their freed status was often ignored by society, especially former owners. As such, the period after the Civil War brought little change for many African American workers.

Yet, at the same time, writings by such women as **Sojourner Truth** and **Maria Stewart** demonstrate that the period during and after the Civil War brought about a body of **literature** that was no longer focused only on chronicling the lived experience of slaves. Now, there was also a sense that writers had the opportunities to write of moral, religious, political, and gender issues. Truth's speech to the 1851 Women's Rights Convention—"Ain't I a Woman?"—demonstrates how African American women now focused their attentions on changing society for the better in the realms of both race and gender. Furthermore, the nineteenth century was a particularly influential time in the development of African American women's writing and history. As **literacy** rates increased among former slaves in the United States, African American women from all walks of life began to write about their experiences in memoirs, letters, diaries, and **autobiography**, and creative, imaginative literature also began to take shape in new and meaningful ways. However, while these women were writing, little was being done with their literary accomplishments. It was not until much later, during the 1960s, that publishers and scholars began to take interest in these women's writings.

Yet despite their new status as "freed" and their increasing literacy rates, African American women have had to contend with many of the same issues of race, class, and gender marginalization within various work environments throughout history. It is true that African American women began to gain greater opportunities in some realms, particularly in terms of garnering positions outside of the domestic sphere. However, as Fannie Barrier Williams pointed out in her 1893 speech, "The Intellectual Progress of the Colored Women of the United States since the Emancipation Proclamation," black women were still struggling to find work outside of teaching in African American schools and the domestic sphere. It seems these women were isolated to jobs in traditionally "pink-collar" realms—as domestic workers, teachers, and caregivers. Yet even within these spheres, African American women themselves were marginalized not just due to their class and gender status but also due to their race. As a result, they were given the most menial jobs available.

As the twentieth century dawned, it seemed black women had more far-reaching job opportunities, though these possibilities often depended on geographic location. For instance, during the **Harlem Renaissance**, African American women had creative and artistic opportunities that had before been virtually absent. Living in such a rich and empowering **community** as Harlem allowed many women occasions to collaborate, create, and commune with fellow writers, artists, musicians, and intellectuals. It is not surprising, therefore, that the Harlem Renaissance offers a view of the "Golden Age" of African American creative expression and, most particularly, numerous examples of women authors, such as **Nella Larsen**, **Zora Neale Hurston**, **Jessie Redmon Fauset**, and **Marita Bonner** seeking to make known their intellectual and artistic passions. What is perhaps complicated about the Harlem Renaissance, however, is that many argue that this period represents only particular segments of African American society: those of the middle and upper classes. It is true that many of these women had to struggle to make ends meet so that they could provide themselves with the time and opportunity to write; yet these women, for the most part, are decidedly middle and upper class. Through works such as Marita Bonner's "On Being Young—a Woman—and Colored" (1925), Nella Larsen's *Passing* (1929), and Jessie Redmon Fauset's *Plum Bun* (1929), we learn what a difficult position it was to be young, African American, female, and intellectual during this period. At the same time, these works represent concerns very different than those of working-class women.

However, Zora Neale Hurston, both a writer of the Harlem Renaissance and an outspoken opponent of the era's elitism, made attempts, along with other writers, to make heard the voices of African American working-class women. Through her participation in the Federal Writers' Project (FWP), for instance, Hurston chronicled the lives of women domestics, laundry workers, dancing girls, and others who were not members of the Harlem intelligentsia. Instead, Hurston and her FWP colleagues sought to tell the stories of working-class women of color in an attempt to show the multivariant and diverse aspects of African American, particularly Harlem, life. Hurston also writes of black working-class experience in her fictional works. In texts such as *Mules and Men* (1935) and *Their Eyes Were Watching God* (1937), Hurston chronicles the lives of the African American working class, and many of the stories in these texts draw from her experiences in the FWP.

Throughout the World War II era, as well, many African American women workers had greater opportunities as women from all walks of life moved into the factories to replace male workers sent overseas. However, even working in the factories that so needed workers did not come without struggle. It seems that many defense industry factories tolerated both implicit and explicit racial discrimination, and it was not until President Franklin D. Roosevelt's Executive Order 8802 was passed, which forbade racial discrimination in the defense industry, that African American women were given equal opportunities. In the military, too, black women served important roles in nursing, the Women's Army Corps, and even as pilots in the air force. What is challenging, however, is finding stories of these African American women from the World War II era. It seems that most of the writings and narratives that reflect the work and struggles that African American women faced during the World War II era are present mainly in periodicals of the times such as *Negro Digest* and *Crisis*. These popular magazines are important in giving readers a sense of the work and lives of black women during this period.

During the 1950s and 1960s, when African American women were making their voices heard in the **civil rights movement** and the feminist movement, women workers still struggled to contend with oppression both in the workplace and in society. In the famous bus boycotts of the 1950s and 1960s, African American women, particularly domestic workers, sought alternative means of transportation to their jobs as a form of protest against racial discrimination. Though standing up for their rights and making a stand on principle, this move made it even more difficult for many women to find and maintain employment. It was during the 1950s and 1960s that many African American writers were telling of working-class experience through their works, while also pointing out the great disparities in American social class status. **Lorraine Hansberry**'s famous *A Raisin in the Sun* (1959), for instance, deals with issues of upward mobility and social class struggle among an African American family during the post–World War II era.

Despite all these struggles, it is important not to generalize the type of jobs African American women workers pursued throughout history. While it is true that many were subjugated to low-paying, menial work on their basis of their race, class, and gender, this is not the whole story. On the contrary, there is also a rich and powerful history of black professional women in the United States. Even during the Jim Crow era, African American women worked in positions as teachers, librarians, social workers, and nurses. Furthermore, many African American women, particularly in more recent history, have made names for themselves in white-collar professions such as medicine, law, and the sciences. And while African American women were making strides in a variety of professions, there was also renewed interest in their legacy. It was during the 1960s, with the Black Power and feminist movements specifically, that scholars began to take notice of the writings of past African American women. While most of the works published during this time period were of African American male writers, authors like **Phillis Wheatley**, **Ann Plato**, and Harriet Wilson also began to garner interest. In many ways, these women, who often wrote of the everyday lives of black women, made clear to more contemporary scholars the rich and diverse legacy of African American women's literature.

The 1970s made evident the multitude of African American feminist writers acutely interested in class issues. It seems there was a renaissance of sorts during this period with such important works as **Alice Walker**'s *The Third Life of Grange Copeland* (1970) and **Toni Morrison**'s *The Bluest Eye* (1970). Walker and Morrison have continued to look at the intersections of race, class, and gender in their more contemporary writings and theoretical works as well. Other women writers, too, have found opportunities to discuss class and work implications for African American women, particularly in theory and scholarly works. **June Jordan**, bell hooks, and Rebecca Walker are just a few of the contemporary African American women writers and scholars who have also found outlets through which to chronicle their class histories. In works such as hooks's *Where We Stand: Class Matters* (2000), one gains perspective on the working lives of black women and theoretical constructs by which to better understand their lives.

Work is an all-encompassing entity in the lives of many African American women, and many of the struggles and complexities of such a relationship with work are represented in a variety of social, historical, and literary documents. African American women workers have had to contend with a multitude of oppressions stemming from their status as workers marginalized in many realms. Whether working as slaves, domestic workers, or professionals or in "pink-collar" jobs, African American women workers' lives represent the complicated intersections of race, class, and gender. Work, therefore, becomes a part of African American feminine and feminist existence that makes clear the numerous sites of marginalization in which these women must struggle.

Works About

Bascom, Lionel C., ed. *A Renaissance in Harlem: Lost Essays of the WPA, by Ralph Ellison, Dorothy West, and Other Voices of a Generation.* New York: Amistad, 1999.

Honey, Maureen, ed. *Bitter Fruit: African American Women in World War II.* Columbia: University of Missouri Press, 1999.

Shaw, Stephanie J. *What a Woman Ought to Be and to Do: Black Professional Women Workers during the Jim Crow Era.* Chicago: University of Chicago Press, 1995.

Lisa A. Kirby

WRIGHT, RICHARD (1908–1960)

Richard Wright is one of the most well known and highly acclaimed black American writers. He produced various genres of writings: novels, poems, short stories, **drama**, essays, autobiographies, and haikus. His most acknowledged works are *Native Son* (1940), a novel, and his **autobiography**, *Black Boy: A Record of Childhood and Youth* (1945). Although some traditional critics dismiss these works as simple social statements, many critics highly regard them as masterpieces of American **literature**. His works present the complexities and problems of dehumanizing society through the vivid portrayal of the brutality of racism. He was influenced by a wide range of political and literary theories including communism, naturalism, realism, existentialism, and Pan-Africanism.

Wright had a harsh life as a child. He was born to Nathaniel and Ella on September 4, 1908. When he was born, his **family** lived on a plantation near Natchez, Mississippi, where his father Nathaniel worked as a sharecropper. His mother was a well-educated woman who had been a schoolteacher. His father was illiterate and an alcoholic. His family was extremely poor and lived often without food. When Richard was six years old, to get out of their extreme poverty, his family moved to Memphis. However, soon after they moved, his father abandoned the family to live with another woman, and his mother had to support the family with low-paying menial jobs. Richard and his brother Leon suffered from the economic hardship early on. They were always hungry and psychologically insecure. Richard even had to stay in an orphanage once. Before he turned ten years old, he experienced extreme racial hatred. When he was staying with his uncle, white men murdered his uncle so that they could take his property. His family ran away to Arkansas to save their lives but came back to Tennessee later on.

Wright first received his formal education in 1916, but after his mother fell ill, he dropped out of school to take care of her. His family moved to his maternal grandmother's **home** in Jackson, Mississippi. Because his grandmother was a fervent Seventh-Day Adventist, she sent Wright to the Seventh-Day Adventist school in Huntsville and forced him to go to her fundamental Christian church. He grew to loathe **religion** and developed a critical view of the function of the black church in the black **community** in the Deep **South**. Wright explains in his autobiography that he was bright and sensible but misunderstood as mischievous by adults during his adolescence. He constantly revolted against his grandmother and his aunt who lived with them.

From 1921 to 1925, he attended Jim Hill Public School and Smith-Robinson Public School, which was the longest formal education he ever received. Since his family was too poor and unstable, his schooling was often interrupted. However, he enjoyed reading. Reading provided him an escape from hardship and racial **violence** in the South. In 1924, his short story "The Voodoo of Hell's Half Acre" was published in *Southern Register*, a local black newspaper. After he graduated and moved to Memphis in 1925, he became self-educated by reading. He avidly read books by H. L. Mencken, Theodore Dreiser, Fedor Dostoevski, Sinclair Lewis, and Sherwood Anderson while he was working menial jobs in Memphis and Chicago. He lived in Chicago after 1927 for a decade, where he had various odd jobs and learned about the urban life of black people. For example, one of his jobs was at an insurance company that took advantage of black clients, and he became quickly disillusioned by the urban life. These experiences appeared in many of his stories. Working during the nightshift at the post office, a job he lost during the Great Depression, he could spend his daytime reading and writing. In 1931, he published a short story "Superstition," his second publication, in *Abbott's Monthly Magazine*.

During the Great Depression, Wright started to get involved with the Communist Party. He became a member of the Works Progress Administration (WPA) Writers' Project and participated at the John Reed Club, a communist literary organization. The John Reed Club inspired and encouraged him to be a writer and supported his writing. The club also influenced his mode of writing greatly as well as stimulating his racial and **class** consciousness. He found a sympathetic white readership among communists. He published stories and poems in *Daily Worker*, *New Masses*, and *International Literature*, which are communist journals. He also worked as an editor for communist-affiliated journals in New York for a while. In 1944, after several years of serious commitment to communism, he left the Communist Party. He felt that his fellow communists were too narrow-minded to understand more progressive ideas, and he felt their views were suffocating to creative writers like him. Wright also had relationships with two white women, Dhimah Rose Meadman and Ellen Poplar, in 1938. The next year, he married Dhimah, a dancer, but divorced shortly thereafter. He married Ellen, a Communist Party member, in 1941 and had two daughters with her.

In 1938, Wright's *Uncle Tom's Children: Four Novellas* (1938), a collection of four long stories, won a contest offered by *Story* magazine. Another story was added in the second edition. Stories in this collection were inspired by a black communist in Chicago, and each story describes the racism and violence black people experience in the South. Some critics criticized Wright, claiming that these stories were sentimental and ideological, but this collection was largely accepted as successful. Many white readers, especially Marxist critics, gave positive reviews. On the other hand, **Zora Neale Hurston**, who valued the black folk tradition, disagreed often with Wright and gave negative criticism on this collection. Even Wright felt troubled by his readership's upbeat response to this book. He thought that these stories were received as adorable touchy stories to mass readers. What he wanted to achieve was to reveal the cruel reality of society, which would make people feel uncomfortable and question society. Therefore, in his next book, he aimed to create characters without empathy and avoided sentimentalism.

Wright received the Guggenheim fellowship in 1939, which helped him finish *Native Son*. *Native Son* is regarded as one of the best black novels. This novel narrates the story of Bigger Thomas, a common, ignorant young black man from a ghetto. He describes the character without emotional involvement to reveal the dehumanization and alienation of the social system. The character of the communist lawyer eloquently gives a long speech, in the later part of the novel, on how society creates a murderer and how the murderer is also a victim of society. The story of Bigger Thomas presents straight-forwardly the horrors of urban black life. Wright tries diverse stylistic experiments in *Native Son*. It incorporates a **detective** story quality as well as elements from the gothic romance tradition of horror and mystery in order to uncover the **race** issue more fully. It is also a naturalistic novel influenced by Theodore Dreiser's *An American Tragedy* (1925). Many white critics praised it for exposing the ruthless reality of racism in America. Some black reviewers, although they highly acclaimed his book, were concerned about the **stereotypes** of black people in it. **James Baldwin** criticized Wright, charging that he failed to present blacks' sense of collective reality. Baldwin points out that because Bigger Thomas does not have the psychological depth to go beyond the stereotypical level, black people do not relate to the character or to his experiences. Despite such criticism, *Native Son* quickly became a bestseller. For the general readership as well as the academy, *Native Son* is the most powerful and well received book Wright authored.

Wright published the censored version of his autobiography *Black Boy* in 1943. *Black Boy* is a story of himself as a willful, bright, and sensitive black boy growing up in the Deep South. The young black protagonist overcomes many obstacles and finally achieves **freedom** and individual success. Wright avows in this book that he is a self-made man and writing is the means of self-realization for him. Like *Native Son*, this novel was a bestseller and was well reviewed. In spite of its commercial success, the autobiography was controversial. Some black readers were unhappy at being reminded about the truth of many blacks' condition in the Deep South, while other critics were uneasy with his narrative style. *Black Boy* is claimed to be an autobiography; however, it is, in fact, more than a faithful record of facts. As an imaginative and sensitive man, Wright created a fictionalized version of his life story in this book. In addition to these critics' concerns, communist critics, who had been supportive of him since he started his career as a writer, turned against him after he left the Communist Party and negatively reviewed *Black Boy*.

After World War II, Wright visited France with an invitation from the French government. While there, he was hailed as a great American author and became friends with leading French intellectuals, including Simone de Beauvoir, Jean-Paul Sartre, and Albert Camus. He found a new intellectual world of existentialism and worried about the racism his daughters would experience in America; he moved his family residence to Paris in 1946. Some critics argue that Wright lost touch with black people's reality when he moved to France. He seemed unable to produce such powerful works like he had before. His second novel, *The Outsider* (1953), is one of the first American existentialist novels, but many did not see *The Outsider* as a successful work. His next novels, *Savage Holiday* (1954) and *The Long Dream* (1958), did not receive good reviews from critics or readers. Many critics evaluate Wright's later novels as inferior to *Native Son* and *Black Boy*.

The most important **fiction** Wright produced in the 1950s is "The Man Who Lived Underground," which is a selection from *Eight Men* (1961), a collection of short stories published posthumously. The story is similar to Dostoveski's *Notes from the Underground* (1864) and **Ralph Ellison**'s later publication, *Invisible Man* (1952). There are two other posthumously published books, *Lawd Today!* (1963) and *American Hunger* (1977). *Lawd Today!* was not very well received, but *American Hunger* drew attention to Wright again. *American Hunger* is his memoir that notes his relationship with communism and his development as a writer.

In addition to Wright's stylistic achievement and prominent vision on the issues of black people, the presentation of masculinity and femininity in his works has been a central topic among critics. Many readers argue that women characters in Wright's works are stereotypical. **Black feminist** critics point out the hate and fear against women in his works. They argue that in his novels mothers are threatening and oppressive to young protagonist men, and young women are hysterical, whorish lovers. Many of his female characters are presented as senseless and suffocating, and the male characters take women as obstacles holding them back from achieving their **black masculinity** and their freedom. Feminist critics claim that women characters in his major works are either asexual, oppressive mothers or loveless sex objects. The presentation of women and masculinity in Wright's works remains a volatile issue in black literary criticism.

In addition to novels and autobiographies, Wright tried writing in various genres and created diverse works. After his works were translated into many languages, and he gained international fame in the 1950s, he traveled throughout many countries in Europe, Asia, and Africa. Based on his experience during these trips, he produced many nonfictional works such as *Black Power* (1954), *Pagan Spain* (1957), and *The Color Curtain: A Report on the Bandung Conference* (1956). In these books, he observed and discussed race and **class** issues in Ghana, Spain, and Asia, extending his concerns about race internationally. Besides nonfiction, he also produced radio plays, a drama and a **film** script for *Native Son*, and haikus. He wrote a total of 4,000 haikus, but most of them were unpublished until recently.

Wright died from a heart attack on November 29, 1960, in France. He suffered from illness and financial difficulties in his last years. He was a seminal figure for the next generation of black writers, such as James Baldwin, who was his protégé, and Ralph Ellison. He influenced Baldwin and Ellison greatly, and they wrote several brilliant criticisms on Wright's works in their attempt to move beyond him. In black literary history, Wright remains one of the most acknowledged black writers. His works, especially *Native Son* and *Black Boy*, were highly acclaimed by most critics and well read for years. Wright's writing technique, philosophy, and insight on society make his works an important contribution to American literary history.

Works By

Black Boy: A Record of Childhood and Youth. New York: Harper, 1945.
Black Power: A Record of Reactions in a Land of Pathos. New York: Harper, 1954.

The Color Curtain: A Report on the Bandung Conference. Cleveland and New York: World, 1956.

Eight Men. Cleveland and New York: World, 1961.

Haiku: This Other World. Ed. Yoshinobu Hakatuni and Robert L. Tener. New York: Arcade, 1998.

How "Bigger" Was Born: The Story of Native Son. New York: Harper, 1940.

Lawd Today! New York: Walker, 1963.

The Long Dream. Garden City, NY: Doubleday, 1958.

Native Son. New York: Harper, 1940.

The Outsider. New York: Harper, 1953.

Pagan Spain. New York: Harper, 1957.

Savage Holiday. New York: Avon, 1954.

"Superstition." *Abbott's Monthly Magazine* 2 (April 1931): 45+.

12 Million Black Voices: A Folk History of the Negro in the United States. New York: Viking, 1941.

Uncle Tom's Children: Five Long Stories. New York: Harper, 1938.

Uncle Tom's Children: Four Novellas. New York: Harper, 1938.

White Man, Listen! Garden City, NY: Doubleday, 1957.

Works About

Baldwin, James. "Everybody's Protest Novel." *Notes of a Native Son.* Boston: Beacon, 1955. 85–114.

Bloom, Harold, ed. *Bigger Thomas.* New York: Chelsea House, 1990.

———. *Richard Wright.* New York: Chelsea House, 1987.

Du Bois, W. E. Burghardt. "Richard Wright Looks Back." *New York Herald Tribune Weekly Book Review,* March 4, 1945, 2.

Ellison, Ralph. "Richard Wright's Blues." *Shadow and Act.* New York: Random House, 1964. 77–94.

Fabre, Michel. *The Unfinished Quest of Richard Wright.* Trans. Isabel Barzun. 2nd ed. Urbana: University of Illinois Press, 1993.

Felgar, Robert. *Richard Wright.* Boston: Twayne, 1980.

———. *Student Companion to Richard Wright.* Westport, CT: Greenwood Press, 2000.

Gates, Henry Louis, and K. A. Appiah, eds. *Richard Wright: Critical Perspectives Past and Present.* New York: Amistad, 1993.

Gayle, Addison. *Richard Wright: Ordeal of a Native Son.* Garden City, NY: Anchor Press/Doubleday, 1980.

Hakutani, Yoshinobu, ed. *Critical Essays on Richard Wright.* Boston: G. K. Hall, 1982.

Hurston, Zora Neale. "Stories of Conflict." *Saturday Review of Literature* 17 (April 2, 1938): 32.

Miller, Eugene E. *Voice of a Native Son: The Poetics of Richard Wright.* Jackson: University Press of Mississippi, 1990.

Reilly, John M. *Richard Wright: The Critical Reception.* New York: Franklin, 1978.

Smethurst, James Edward. *The New Red Negro: The Literary Left and African American Poetry, 1930–1946.* New York: Oxford University Press, 1999.

Walker, Margaret. *Richard Wright: Demonic Genius.* New York: Warren Books, 1988.

Webb, Constance. *Richard Wright: A Biography.* New York: G. P. Putnam's Sons, 1968.

Williams, John A. *The Most Native of Sons.* Garden City, NY: Doubleday, 1970.

Youngsook Jeong

WRIGHT, SARAH ELIZABETH (1928–)

Born and reared in Wetipquin, on the Eastern Shore of Maryland on December 9, 1928, Wright knows how politics, **history**, and culture govern gender issues. As a novelist, poet, essayist, and activist, she also is aware of the treatment of women of color, in particular, and "anti-woman" laws nationally. With the support of her public school teachers in Wetipquin, Wright attended Howard University from 1945 to 1949 and received further training at such schools as Cheney State College (now University), the University of Pennsylvania (where she attended writers' workshops), New York State University, and Regents College in Albany, New York, where she received her B.A. degree in 1979. Wright's education, which she has used to **work** as a **poetry** therapist and **fiction** writing instructor, matches her multilayered literary output. Her first work was a collection of poems, *Give Me a Child* (1955), coauthored with Lucy Smith. She is a contributor to such poetry collections as *Poetry of the Negro* (1970) and *Poetry of Black America* (1973). She has published a children's biography, *A. Philip Randolph: Integration in the Workplace* (1990), and has provided the forward for Rashidah Ismaili's collection of poems *Missing in Action and Presumed Dead* (1992).

It is no accident that the Feminist Press rekindled Wright's novel *This Child's Gonna Live* (1969) in 1986, for it celebrates and critiques the range of a black woman's experiences as she struggles in a world created by whites and supported by black men and their older black women enablers. Although the title of the novel suggests a singular theme of a mother's determination to leave and, thereby, save her children from the physical, economic, and racial degradation of "the Neck" (Tangierneck, a small, fictional **community** on Maryland's Eastern Shore) during the depression, Wright blends slave history, black folk culture, the unique world of black Eastern Shore oyster pickers, and migration and miscegenation with the depiction of Mariah Upshur, a vital, central character through whom the reader sees the virtues and pitfalls of black women's communal relationships; the oppression and power of black women in marriage; **sexuality** and sexual transgression; the resilience of a black woman's self-image against economic, racial, communal, and familial belittlement; and the resolve to live, even in relentless, abject poverty, for familial survival.

The details of Eastern Shore poverty may overwhelm the reader, but they enhance Wright's portrait of Mariah's spiritual resilience. Because work in oyster fishing was sporadic, Mariah helps to support her husband Jacob and three children by digging potatoes, trying to raise crops in poor soil and collecting ferns for wreaths to send to Baltimore. There is little food, and the weight of **domestic** work falls on the pregnant Mariah's shoulders. With an occasional stewed muskrat for meat, Mariah and her **family** are perpetually ill with bronchiallike colds. It is Mariah's spiritual vitality against great odds that offers the reader a reverse ending from that in Kate Chopin's *The Awakening* (1899). This is not a male-bashing novel. One is left with the implication that black men have scars—but so do black women.

Wright has managed to meld her activism with a **love** of writing. While in Philadelphia in the 1950s, she helped found a writer's workshop. She was a member and officer in the Harlem Writer's Guild from 1957 to 1972 and helped plan and initiate two black writers' conferences. In her introductory speech to the 1965 conference panel, "The Negro Woman in American Literature," Wright advocates a strong belief in the writer's responsibility to depict multiple and complex images of black women characters.

Works By

A. Philip Randolph: Integration in the Workplace. Englewood Cliffs, NJ: Silver Burdett Press, 1990.
"Black Writers' Views of America." *Freedomways* 19.3 (1979): 161–162.
Give Me a Child. With Lucy Smith. Philadelphia: Kraft Publishing, 1955.
Missing in Action and Presumed Dead, by Rashidah Ismaili. Foreword by Sarah E. Wright. Trenton, NJ: Africa World Press, 1992. vii–x.
This Child's Gonna Live. 1969. New York: Feminist Press, 1986.

Works About

Campbell, Jennifer. " 'It Is a Time in the Land' : Gendering Black Power and Sarah E. Wright's Place in the Tradition of Black Women's Writing." *African American Review* 31.2 (Summer 1997): 211–223.
Harris, Trudier. "Three Black Women Writers and Humanism: A Folk Perspective." *Black American Literature and Humanism.* Ed. R. Baxter Miller. Lexington: University Press of Kentucky, 1981. 51–73.
Mickelson, Anne Z. "Winging Upward: Black Women: Sarah E. Wright, Toni Morrison, Alice Walker." *Reaching Out: Sensitivity and Order in Recent American Fiction by Women.* Ed. Anne Z. Mickelson. Metuchen, NJ: Scarecrow Press, 1979. 113–174.

Australia Tarver

 **X**

XENOGENESIS TRILOGY

Octavia Butler's Xenogenesis trilogy consists of *Dawn* (1987), *Adulthood Rites* (1988), and *Imago* (1989). In some ways this trilogy is traditional science fiction, with aliens, a postapocalyptic setting, and a first contact plot. However, Butler's use of these motifs is original and provocative, infused with a feminist perspective and grounded in a theory about the human race as troubling as it is convincing. In 1989 the trilogy was republished as a single volume titled *Lilith's Brood.*

Butler's protagonist is Lilith, an allusion, of course, to Adam's first mate. In legend, Lilith was created Adam's equal, but Adam wanted a subordinate— some say especially in his sexual life. Finally God banished Lilith and created Eve, Adam's new mate, using one of Adam's ribs to make clear woman's intended subservience to man. Here, Butler's Lilith helps rid the Earth of its hierarchical **history**.

Lilith awakens in a spaceship where she has been kept in stasis by aliens who have rescued survivors of a nuclear war that made Earth uninhabitable. During her 250-year sleep the Oankali have healed Earth; now Lilith is given a chance to return, but only if she agrees to mate with an Oankali. From now on, she hears, no all-human child shall be born. The Oankalis' survival depends on dramatically transforming their genetic structure every few generations; they plan to effect this through interbreeding with human beings.

The Oankali are benevolent beings who have healed the human survivors of cancers and made their bodies able to live much longer lives. But they are adamant that the human race must cease to exist except as a genetic component of a new Oankali-human hybrid species. Lilith is repulsed by the offer. Not only are the Oankali a three-sexed alien species, but they are only vaguely humanoid, with bodies covered in tentacles that make them look, she thinks, like sea-slugs.

The Oankalis refuse to let all-human children be conceived because two dominant but incompatible genetic traits are wired into human consciousness: Human beings are by nature both intelligent and hierarchical. Intelligence, though, is a much newer trait and thus is subservient to the more entrenched impulse for hierarchy. Human history, therefore, will always be conflict ridden; over time, these conflicts will inevitably escalate to self-destruction. Mixing Oankali DNA with human genes, however, should mitigate the urge for hierarchy, so genetic sharing could save not just one but both species. The Oankali ask Lilith to lead the way, an example for her fellow survivors.

The trilogy examines the deep psychological hold that prejudice against those unlike us has on the human psyche. Despite the loving natures of the Oankali, many human beings choose sterility over having a child with mixed genetic "blood," even at the cost of seeing the human race last only one more generation. To the Oankali this decision defies logic, but even human beings who feel drawn to the Oankalis find it psychologically difficult to think of bearing offspring only partly human. Readers are likely to feel ambivalent over which is the admirable route–to overcome repulsion and genetically merge with the gentle Oankali or to let the human race die out rather than participate in forced genetic sharing. The dilemma invites readers to think about the power of prejudice, resistance to interracial or same-sex marriages, and historic attempts to achieve genetic "purity." To have an African American author write such a story is a powerful statement. To have Lilith be the novel's focal character places woman at the center of social history instead of on its periphery.

Adulthood Rites focuses on Lilith's toddler Akin, the first male allowed to be born to a female human. All Earth children are now genetic constructs, products of families made up of a male and female human, a male and female Oankali, and an ooloi, the third-sexed Oankali. Before Akin, all males had Oankali birth mothers for fear that human-born males would carry the innate compulsion for hierarchy. Now, however, the Oankali feel confident of their ability to genetically engineer a human-born male child who will not endanger others; Lilith's Akin will be the test of their success.

Akin's superior sensory perceptions and his rapid intellectual growth reflect his Oankali genes, but he looks surprisingly human (as long as he hides his Oankali sensory probe tongue and until he reaches metamorphosis age, when he will grow an array of sensory tentacles). The young Akin is kidnapped and sold to a **community** of sterile human "resistors" who refuse to mate with aliens; he is the closest they have seen to a human-looking baby in years. The story follows Akin's attempts to stay safe among these people and his quest to understand their emotional needs and psychological drives. Readers already know the Oankali grasp of human psychology is weak. Their attempts to acculturate humans into a new social order have suffered from misreadings and faulty assumptions, sometimes resulting in murders, suicides, or accidental deaths. Much as they would like to, the Oankali cannot understand needs basic for human contentment. Now Akin has a chance to learn more about human psychology than any Oankali has ever known. Then he will have to decide what to do with his knowledge.

The third book, *Imago*, follows a later child of Lilith, Jadahs. Although all had assumed this child would become male, once metamorphosis begins, they realize Jadahs is ooloi, the powerful third-sexed healers and genetic engineers of the Oankali. Jadahs is an accident: No child born to a human female has been allowed the genetic construction to become ooloi, for no one knows the ramifications of this most risky of birth possibilities. Like the books preceding it, *Imago* is about experiencing frightening difference and the isolation attendant to breaking new cultural ground. In Butler's world, being different is a lonely place to be, but it is also an opportunity to make a real contribution in life.

Butler's first book in this trilogy will most interest feminist readers because it features Lilith, one of Butler's strong female protagonists. Her central role in *Dawn* suggests that women have the capacity to effect significant change on the course of civilization. If this should happen, Butler speculates, our social history might take a new—and more tolerant—turn.

See also Bloodchild and Other Stories; *Kindred*; Parable Series; Patternist Series

Works About

Boulter, Amanda. "Polymorphous Futures: Octavia E. Butler's Xenogenesis Trilogy." *American Bodies: Cultural Histories of the Physique.* Ed. Tim Armstrong. New York: New York University Press, 1996. 170–185.

Holden, Rebecca J. "The High Cost of Cyborg Survival: Octavia Butler's Xenogenesis Trilogy." *Foundation* 72 (1998): 49–56.

Michaels, Michael Benn. "Political Science Fiction." *New Literary History* 31.4 (2000): 649–664.

Osherow, Michele. "The Dawn of a New Lilith: Revisionary Mythmaking in Women's Science Fiction." *NWSA Journal* 12.1 (2000): 68–83.

Grace McEntee

 **Y**

YARBROUGH, CAMILLE (1935–)

She might have made a living as a dancer or actress, but Camille Yarbrough uses her cultural talent and imagination to forge an independent life. The author of the widely touted and inspirational children's book *Cornrows* (1979) and novel *The Shimmershine Queens* (1989), never sought the easy road to success. She follows her passion for a commitment she made early in her twenties to foster African American pride and dignity. So the dancer, actress, singer, poet, and self-dubbed griot or storyteller creates art to meet what she sees as a dire need for hope and self-**love** in black youth culture. Yarbrough said she wants to help young people gain a sense of self and heal broken spirits. Her writings counter the cash-obsessed mantra in U.S. society that preaches a person is nothing without money as the kind of thought that fosters black self-hatred and alienation. Today, through her New York City–based organization, the African American Traditions Workshop, Yarbrough performs songs and stories at schools and on campuses to inspire cultural pride, hope, and unity.

The author's strength and direction come from cultural **ancestors**, particularly her father, who always urged, "Do better." Others role models include the late international dancer and civil rights advocate **Josephine Baker**, whom she met in 1958; the late playwright and children's author **Alice Childress**; playwright and friend **Lorraine Hansberry**; and the late **blues** singer Nina Simone, to whose voice and style music critics compared Yarbrough's acclaimed 1975 spoken-word album *The Iron Pot Cooker*, reissued in 2000 by Vanguard Records.

At 6214 Champlain Avenue on Chicago's south end, Camille grew up as the seventh of eight children born to Anna May and Ernest Yarbrough, a precinct captain for more than thirty years. Dance became her fascination long before she graduated from Englewood High School in 1953. After a couple of false starts as a dancer in Montreal and New York, she returned to Chicago. In 1955, Yarbrough auditioned and was accepted into the Hollywood-based troupe of her idol Katherine Dunham. Until the company broke up in 1961, Yarbrough was steeped in an exploration of black diaspora culture through dances inspired by Dunham's research on African, Caribbean, and Latin American forms. In the early 1970s Yarbrough's reputation as a performer and poet landed her a spot in New York City's Jazz Mobile, a **drama** and **poetry** program in the city schools.

Yarbrough was outraged by the unruliness of many black students and the way they ripped each other apart psychologically with slurs and putdowns about their hair, skin color, and facial features. She responded with "Cornrows," a poem about the heritage and **beauty** of African Americans' braided hair. Through an introduction to a publisher arranged by Hansberry's husband, Robert Nemiroff, the sentiments were transformed into a 1979 children's book, illustrated by Carol Bayard, which won the prestigious American Library Association Coretta Scott King Award (1980). Yarbrough's tales, as staples in **children's and young adult literature**, highlight the wisdom of elders, women's dignity and beauty, self-love, and the importance of **community**, heritage, and education.

The Shimmershine Queens (1989) tells of Angie, who learns from Cousin Seatta, an elder, to value herself, her classmates, and the chance for schooling. Like Yarbrough's later works, *Tamika and the Wisdom Rings* (1994) and *The Little Tree Growing in the Shade* (1996), the novel encourages youths to shun fighting and name calling as acts of racism. *Watch Hour*, aimed at four- to eight-year-olds, was published in 2005.

Works By

Cornrows. New York: Coward-McCann, 1979.
The Little Tree Growing in the Shade. New York: Putnam, 1996.
The Shimmershine Queens. New York: Putnam, 1989.
Tamika and the Wisdom Rings. New York: Demco, 1994.
Watch Hour. New York: Putnam, 2005.

Works About

Abner, Allison. *The Black Parenting Book.* New York: Broadway, 1998.
Afua, Queen. *Sacred Women: A Guide to Healing the Body, Mind and Spirit.* New York: One World/Ballantine, 2000.

Frazier, DuEwa M. "Taking Her Praise: Profile of Camille Yarbrough, a Renaissance Woman." African American Literature Book Club. aalbc.com/authors/article.htm.

Senich, Gerald. "Camille Yarbrough." *Children's Literature Review* 29 (1993): 262–275.

Sims, Rudine. *Shadow and Substance: Afro-American Experience in Contemporary Children's Literature.* Urbana, IL: National Council of Teachers of English, 1982.

Vincent F. A. Golphin

YOU CAN'T KEEP A GOOD WOMAN DOWN

You Can't Keep a Good Woman Down is the second published collection of short stories by **Alice Walker**. Published in 1981, the collection consists of fourteen stories, some of which were previously published in a variety of magazines including *Ms.*, *Mother Jones*, and *Essence*.

As with her previous collection of stories, *In Love & Trouble* (1973), Walker's second collection is also centered on the lives of black women. Walker not only gives voice to a seldom-heard group, but she also takes a critical look at the oppressive society that makes being heard so difficult. She engages major issues such as **rape** and pornography, perhaps influenced by the Second Wave feminist movement of the 1970s.

The book is dedicated in part to the women **blues** singers who have influenced her work: Ma Rainey, Bessie Smith, and Mamie Smith. The blues is significant to this collection in a number of ways. The title plays off of the blues songs "You Can't Keep a Good Man Down," recorded by Mamie Smith in 1920, and "You Just Can't Keep a Good Woman Down," recorded by Lillian Miller in 1928. Walker thanks this generation of singers for defining themselves and finding value in what they did, a tradition that Walker sees herself carrying on.

In addition to sharing a title with these songs, Walker incorporates the blues woman as a character in the opening story, "Nineteen Fifty-Five." The story is based on Elvis Presley's rise to stardom and the borrowing of music from black singers who received little or no compensation for their songs. Gracie Mae Still is the blues singer who sells her song to a young white singer named Traynor, who then goes on to become the Emperor of Rock and Roll.

The collection also shares a common blues theme of being resilient in times of trouble. Walker's stories show black women who resist **stereotypes** and conventions, refuse to sacrifice their dignity, and like the blues women mentioned in the dedication, define themselves as valuable human beings. Despite the prevalence of racist and sexist stereotypes that attempt to circumscribe their role in society, these women define fulfillment for themselves and, significantly, act in accordance with their definitions.

The capacity for self-fulfillment shows a development in Walker's characters. Earlier works featured women who were able to define fulfillment for themselves but were not always able to act accordingly because they felt limited by societal conventions. In this collection Walker celebrates the strength and resilience of black women who stay true to themselves and attempt self-fulfillment regardless of the limited choices they face.

However, critics have found fault with some of the stories, claiming that characters were now empowered to an extent that they were not credible. In general, a major critique of *You Can't Keep a Good Woman Down* was that it lacked the cohesiveness of Walker's first collection of stories. Some stories, particularly "Porn," "Coming Apart," and "Advancing Luna—and Ida B. Wells," were criticized for being dogmatic and obvious in making a point at the expense of the development of characters and narrative.

See also In Search of Our Mothers' Gardens: Womanist Prose; Womanism

Works About

Christian, Barbara. *Black Feminist Criticism: Perspectives on Black Women Writers.* New York: Pergamon Press, 1985.

Johnson, Maria V. "You Just Can't Keep a Good Woman Down: Alice Walker Sings the Blues." *African American Review* 30.2 (1996): 221–236.

Petry, Alice Hall. "Alice Walker: The Achievement of the Short Fiction." *Modern Language Studies* 19.1 (1989): 12–27.

Pollitt, Katha. "Stretching the Short Story." *New York Times*, May 24, 1981, sec. 7, 6.

Winchell, Donna Haisty. *Alice Walker.* New York: Twayne Publishers, 1992.

Raquel Rodriguez

YOU KNOW BETTER

Tina McElroy Ansa's fourth novel is *You Know Better* (2002), a ghost story in which three generations of women in the Pines **family** are visited by three spirits on one momentous day in their lives. The Pines women are on a downward spiral, with the youngest, LaShawndra, about to run away from **home** to escape her mistakes and to seek a career as a dancer in music videos. With help from the spirit world, each woman faces her shortcomings and accepts her and her family members' failures as learning experiences from which they can move to mutual support and **love**.

You Know Better, like Ansa's other novels, is set in Mulberry, Georgia. The novel opens at midnight as Lily Paine Pines sets out to drive around Mulberry, looking for her granddaughter LaShawndra. She picks up a passenger, Miss Grace Moses, who mostly listens as Lily talks through her worries about LaShawndra, LaShawndra's mother, her daughter Sandra, and her ex-husband Charles. At 6:00 AM the scene shifts to Sandra, who arrives at her real estate office to drive Nurse Joanna Bloom around Mulberry to look at property. At noon, we shift again to LaShawndra, who is hitchhiking out of Mulberry to attend Freaknik in Atlanta. LaShawndra is picked up by Miss Liza Jane Dryer, who tells LaShawndra that she lives with Miss Moses and Nurse Bloom. We realize that all three of the women with whom the Pines women drive around are spirits whose purpose is to listen to the Pines women and, by asking questions or making comments, to lead the Pines women from self-absorption to genuine attention to one another's needs.

Lily has been overly focused on her career as a teacher and school administrator and on her reputation in the **community**. Sandra has been overly hurt by rejection from LaShawndra's father and his family and has buried herself in her real estate career. LaShawndra has been overly concerned with her "coochie" girl image and her dreams of a music video career and has taken advantage of her grandmother, her mother, and her friend and housemate Crystal. During their conversations with the spirit guides, each of the Pines women comes to the recognition that being absorbed by her own desires and demons has led her to neglect truly loving and meaningful relationships with the others. The novel's epilogue, told by LaShawndra one year after their momentous rides, shows the three women in Lily's kitchen coming to terms with one another. Lily has reconciled with Charles, and Sandra is trying to be openly affectionate with LaShawndra. LaShawndra ends the novel by remembering Miss Liza Jane's admonition that people can change, and the Pines women have each changed for the better by reaching out to one another in love and forgiveness.

In *You Know Better* Ansa depicts how LaShawndra's generation has gotten lost and holds out hope for their and their parents' and grandparents' redemption through love, understanding, and forgiveness.

See also Baby of the Family; Motherhood; Spirituality

Works About

Jones, Lynda. Review of *You Know Better* by Tina McElroy Ansa. *Black Issues Book Review* 4.2 (March–April 2002): 32.

Lewis, Lillian. Review of *You Know Better* by Tina McElroy Ansa. *Booklist* 98.13 (March 1, 2002): 1086.

Zaleski, Jeff. Review of *You Know Better* by Tina McElroy Ansa. *Publishers Weekly* 249.10 (March 11, 2002): 52–54.

Harriette C. Buchanan

Z

ZAMI: A NEW SPELLING OF MY NAME

Audre Lorde's *Zami: A New Spelling of My Name* (1982) is an experimental text of feminist life writing. Although she relates many events of her depression-era girlhood and her young womanhood in the 1950s, Lorde describes the book not as **autobiography** or memoir but as "biomythography." Interviewed by Karen Nölle-Fischer for Germany's *Virginia* magazine, she explained that *Zami* encompasses many genres, including **history**, **myth**, and psychology. Nölle-Fischer translated the book into German for Orlanda in Berlin, a leading feminist press whose editor, Dagmar Schultz, was instrumental in introducing Lorde to many European women's communities. Lorde told Nölle-Fischer that *Zami* explores the crucial role of women's **love** in her life, from her mother's love during Lorde's rebellious childhood to the lesbian love scenes that underscore an erotic life force. Lorde's 1978 essay "Uses of the Erotic: The Erotic as Power," reprinted in her *Sister Outsider: Essays and Speeches* (1984), develops the concept of eroticism as a female, spiritual source of energy and creativity that threatens patriarchy and rejects the pornographic.

The word *Zami*, as Lorde defines it in the epilogue, is a Carriacou term for Caribbean women bound by ties of love and friendship as they plant, tend goats, build, harvest, and raise children together during their men's long absences at sea. Such love, she adds, lasts after the return of the seafarers. Because her parents, Linda Belmar Lorde and Frederic Byron Lorde, were immigrants who always hoped to go back to the Caribbean, Lorde grew up in Harlem with a sense of dislocation from her true **home**. In titling her bio-mythography *Zami*, she views intense female relationships as a crucial inheritance, both from the islands and from the even more distant Africa, home of the great mother MawuLisa and her trickster daughter Afrekete.

A female bildungsroman, *Zami* traces Lorde's growth and development from a silent little girl to an articulate woman. One important early influence was Augusta Baker, a children's librarian who inspired the pre-school-aged Audre not only to read but also to speak up. Until she was four, Lorde explains, she rarely said a word, but soon she was communicating with her **family** by reciting **poetry**. Later, at the all-girls' Hunter High School, she was part of an outsider group that called themselves The Branded and "raised the ghosts of Byron and Keats." She also developed an early political consciousness, envying Jewish classmates who planned to **work** on a kibbutz in post–World War II Israel.

As a teenager, Lorde's closest friends were girls, especially the dance student Gennie, the first person she was "conscious of loving." After Gennie's suicide and an affair with a white boy that resulted in a "homemade abortion," Lorde found that writing poetry about "death, destruction, and deep despair" was the only activity that made her feel alive. Bored at Hunter College, she worked at blue-collar jobs in Stamford, Connecticut, and as a clinic clerk in New York to earn the money to travel to Cuernavaca, Mexico, where she had her first lesbian affair. Back in New York, she became part of the 1950s "gay girl" scene.

Lesbians, she says, were probably the only African American and white women in the city at that time who made "any real attempt to communicate with one another," predating by several years the coalitions she would join during the 1960s **civil rights movement**. Female connection was "our power," adds Lorde, who credits each black woman she met in Greenwich Village with "some part in my survival" in a hostile world. Cassie Premo Steele emphasizes that the sensuous lover Afrekete in the final chapter of *Zami* is a "sexual/spiritual mother" who links the author to the African motherland. Thus, says Steele, Lorde "fits her narrative into the traditions of American women's writing, black women's autobiography, and lesbian narratives" (120).

See also Black Feminism; *Cancer Journals, The*; Lesbianism

Works About

Alexander, Elizabeth. " 'Coming Out Blackened and Whole': Fragmentation and Reintegration in Audre Lorde's *Zami* and *The Cancer Journals*." *American Literary History* 6.4 (Winter 1994): 695–715.

De Hernandez, Jennifer Browdy. "Mothering the Self: Writing the Lesbian Sublime in Audre Lorde's *Zami* and Gloria Anzaldúa's *Borderlands/La Frontera*." *Other Sisterhoods: Literary Theory and U.S. Women of Color*. Ed. Sandra Kumamoto Stanley. Urbana: University of Illinois Press, 1998. 244–262.

DiBernard, Barbara. "*Zami*: A Portrait of an Artist as a Black Lesbian." *Kenyon Review* 13.4 (Fall 1991): 195–213.

Kader, Cheryl. "'The Very House of Difference': *Zami*, Audre Lorde's Lesbian-Centered Text." *Critical Essays: Gay and Lesbian Writers of Color*. Ed. Emmanuel S. Nelson. New York: Haworth, 1993. 181–194.

Nölle-Fischer, Karen. "Poetry and Day-by-Day Experience: Excerpts from a Conversation on 12 June 1986 in Berlin." Trans. Francis J. Devlin. *Conversations with Audre Lorde*. Ed. Joan Wylie Hall. Jackson: University Press of Mississippi, 2004. 154–157.

Steele, Cassie Premo. *We Heal from Memory: Sexton, Lorde, Anzaldúa, and the Poetry of Witness*. New York: Palgrave, 2000.

Joan Wylie Hall

✼ Timeline

Boldfaced items are "firsts" for an African American.

1746   **Lucy Terry writes "Bars Fight" (published 1855). First known poem by an African American.**

1773   **Phillis Wheatley,** *Poems on Various Subjects, Religious and Moral* **in London. First book published by an African American; second book published by an American woman.**

1841   **Ann Plato,** *Essays.* **First African American to publish a book of essays.**

1848   Frederick Douglass addresses the first Women's Rights Convention, Seneca Falls, New York.

1849   Harriet Tubman escapes from slavery and begins working on the Underground Railroad.

1851   Sojourner Truth delivers her "Ar'n't I a Woman?" address at the Women's Rights Convention, Akron, Ohio.

1854   Frances E. W. Harper, *Poems on Miscellaneous Subjects.*

1859   **Harriet E. Wilson,** *Our Nig.* **First African American to publish a novel in America.**

1861   Harriet Jacobs, *Incidents in the Life of a Slave Girl.*
        Frances E. W. Harper, "The Two Offers." First short story published by an African American woman.

1865   **Julia C. Collins, *The Curse of Caste*. First serialized novel by an African American woman.**

1892   Anna Julia Cooper, *A Voice from the South*.
       Frances E. W. Harper, *Iola Leroy*.

1900   Pauline Hopkins, *Contending Forces*.

1916   **Angelina Grimké, *Rachel*. First successful full-length play written, produced, and performed by African Americans.**

1928   Nella Larsen, *Quicksand*.

1929   Nella Larsen, *Passing*.
       Jessie Redmon Fauset, *Plum Bun*.

1937   Zora Neale Hurston, *Their Eyes Were Watching God*.

1942   Margaret Walker, *For My People*.

1946   Ann Petry, *The Street*.

1949   Gwendolyn Brooks, *Annie Allen*.

1950   **Gwendolyn Brooks wins the Pulitzer Prize in Poetry for *Annie Allen*. First African American to win a Pulitzer in any category.**

1953   Gwendolyn Brooks, *Maud Martha*.

1959   **Lorraine Hansberry, *A Raisin in the Sun*. First Broadway play by an African American.**

1968   Alice Walker, *Once*.

1970   Maya Angelou, *I Know Why the Caged Bird Sings*.
       Toni Morrison, *The Bluest Eye*.
       Toni Cade, *The Black Woman* (editor).

1974   Mary Helen Washington, "Black Women Image Makers."

1975   Ntozake Shange, *for colored girls who have considered suicide/when the rainbow is enuf*.
       Gayl Jones, *Corregidora*.

1977   Barbara Smith, "Towards a Black Feminist Criticism."

1980   Toni Cade Bambara, *The Salt Eaters*.
       Barbara Christian, *Black Women Writers: The Development of a Tradition. 1892–1976*.

1981   bell hooks, *Ain't I a Woman? Black Women and Feminism*.

1982   Gloria Naylor, *The Women of Brewster Place*.
       Alice Walker, *The Color Purple*.
       Gloria Hull et al., *All the Women Are White, All the Blacks Are Men, But Some of Us Are Brave: Black Women's Studies*.

1983   **Alice Walker wins the Pulitzer Prize in fiction for *The Color Purple*.**
       Alice Walker, *In Search of Our Mothers' Gardens: Womanist Prose*.

1985   Film version of *The Color Purple*.

1986   Sherley Anne Williams, *Dessa Rose*.
       Rita Dove, *Thomas and Beulah*.

1987   **Rita Dove wins the Pulitzer Prize in Poetry for *Thomas and Beulah*.**
Toni Morrison, *Beloved*.

1988   **Toni Morrison wins the Pulitzer Prize in fiction for *Beloved*.**
Gloria Naylor, *Mama Day*.

1989   Barbara Christian, "But What Do We Think We're Doing Anyway: The State of Black Feminist Criticism(s) or My Version of a Little Bit of History."

1992   Terry McMillan, *Waiting to Exhale*.

1993   **Toni Morrison is the first African American to win the Nobel Prize for Literature.**
Maya Angelou, "On the Pulse of Morning," read at the inauguration of President William Clinton.

1994   Rita Dove named U.S. Poet Laureate.

1995   Film version of *Waiting to Exhale*.

2001   Henry Louis Gates, Jr., purchases and authenticates the manuscript *The Bondwoman's Narrative* by Hannah Crafts, believed to have been written in the mid- to late 1850s. Published in 2003. **This work is now considered the first novel by an African American woman.**

2002   **Suzan-Lori Parks wins the Pulitzer Prize in Drama for *Topdog/Underdog*.**

❀ Selected Bibliography

Abel, Elizabeth, Barbara Christian, and Helene Moglen, eds. *Female Subjects in Black and White: Race, Psychoanalysis, Feminism*. Berkeley: University of California Press, 1997.

Andrews, William L., Frances Smith Foster, and Trudier Harris, eds. *The Oxford Companion to African American Literature*. New York: Oxford University Press, 1997.

Awkward, Michael. *Inspiriting Influences: Tradition, Revision, and Afro-American Women's Novels*. New York: Columbia University Press, 1989.

Baker, Houston A. *Workings of the Spirit: The Poetics of Afro-American Women's Writing*. Chicago: University of Chicago Press, 1991.

Bassard, Katherine Clay. *Spiritual Interrogations: Culture, Gender, and Community in Early African American Women's Writing*. Princeton, NJ: Princeton University Press, 1999.

Beaulieu, Elizabeth Ann. *Black Women Writers and the American Neo-Slave Narrative: Femininity Unfettered*. Westport, CT: Greenwood Press, 1999.

Bell, Roseann P., Bettye J. Parker, and Beverly Guy-Sheftall, eds. *Sturdy Black Bridges: Visions of Black Women in Literature*. Garden City, NY: Anchor Press/Doubleday, 1979.

Bloom, Harold, ed. *Black American Women Fiction Writers*. New York: Chelsea House Publishers, 1994.

———. *Black American Women Poets and Dramatists*. New York: Chelsea House Publishers, 1996.

Braxton, Joanne M. *Black Women Writing Autobiography: A Tradition within a Tradition*. Philadelphia: Temple University Press, 1989.

Braxton, Joanne M., and Andrée Nicola McLaughlin, eds. *Wild Women in the Whirlwind: Afra-American Culture and the Contemporary Literary Renaissance*. New Brunswick, NJ: Rutgers University Press, 1990.

Brown-Guillory, Elizabeth, ed. *Their Place on the Stage: Black Women Playwrights in America*. Westport, CT: Greenwood Press, 1988.

Cade, Toni, ed. *The Black Woman*. New York: New American Library, 1970.

Carby, Hazel. *Reconstructing Womanhood: The Emergence of the Afro-American Woman Novelist*. New York: Oxford University Press, 1987.

Carroll, Rebecca, ed. *I Know What the Red Clay Looks Like: The Voice and Vision of Black Women Writers.* New York: Crown Trade Paperbacks, 1994.

Chapman, Dorothy Hilton, comp. *Index to Poetry by Black American Women.* Westport, CT: Greenwood Press, 1986.

Christian, Barbara. *Black Feminist Criticism: Perspectives on Black Women Writers.* New York: Pergamon Press, 1985.

———. *Black Women Novelists: The Development of a Tradition, 1892–1976.* Westport, CT: Greenwood Press, 1980.

Collins, Patricia Hill. *Black Feminist Thought: Knowledge, Consciousness, and the Politics of Empowerment.* New York: Routledge, 1991.

Connor, Kimberly Rae. *Conversions and Visions in the Writings of African-American Women.* Knoxville: University of Tennessee Press, 1994.

Danquah, Meri Nana-Ama. *Shaking the Tree: A Collection of New Fiction and Memoir by Black Women.* New York: W. W. Norton, 2003.

Davies, Carole Boyce. *Black Women, Writing and Identity: Migrations of the Subject.* New York: Routledge, 1994.

Davis, Angela Y. *Women, Race, & Class.* New York: Random House, 1981.

duCille, Ann. *The Coupling Convention: Sex, Text, and Tradition in Black Women's Fiction.* New York: Oxford University Press, 1993.

Evans, Mari, ed. *Black Women Writers (1950–1980): A Critical Evaluation.* Garden City, NY: Anchor Press/Doubleday, 1984.

Fleischner, Jennifer. *Mastering Slavery: Memory, Family, and Identity in Women's Slave Narratives.* New York: New York University Press, 1996.

Foster, Frances Smith. *Written by Herself: Literary Production by African American Women, 1746–1892.* Bloomington: Indiana University Press, 1993.

Fox-Genovese, Elizabeth. *Within the Plantation Household: Black and White Women of the Old South.* Chapel Hill: University of North Carolina Press, 1988.

Gates, Henry Louis, Jr., ed. *Reading Black, Reading Feminist: A Critical Anthology.* New York: Meridian Books, 1990.

Gavin, Christy, ed. *African American Women Playwrights: A Research Guide.* New York: Garland, 1999.

Giddings, Paula. *When and Where I Enter: The Impact of Black Women on Race and Sex in America.* New York: William Morrow, 1984.

Gwin, Minrose. *Black and White Women of the Old South: The Peculiar Sisterhood in American Literature.* Knoxville: University of Tennessee Press, 1985.

Harley, Sharon, and Rosalyn Terborg-Penn, eds. *The Afro-American Woman: Struggles and Images.* Port Washington, NY: National University Publications, 1978.

Harris, Trudier. *From Mammies to Militants: Domestics in Black American Literature.* Philadelphia: Temple University Press, 1982.

———. *Saints, Sinners, Saviors: Strong Black Women in African American Literature.* New York: Palgrave, 2001.

Hernton, Calvin C. *The Sexual Mountain and Black Women Writers: Adventures in Sex, Literature, and Real Life.* New York: Anchor Press, 1987.

Holloway, Karla. *Moorings and Metaphors: Figures of Culture and Gender in Black Women's Literature.* New Brunswick, NJ: Rutgers University Press, 1992.

Honey, Maureen, ed. *Shadowed Dreams: Women's Poetry of the Harlem Renaissance.* New Brunswick, NJ: Rutgers University Press, 1989.

hooks, bell. *Ain't I a Woman: Black Women and Feminism.* Boston: South End Press, 1981.

———. *Feminist Theory from Margin to Center.* Boston: South End Press, 1984.

———. *Talking Back: Thinking Feminist, Thinking Black.* Boston: South End Press, 1989.

———. *Yearning: Race, Gender, and Cultural Politics.* Boston: South End Press, 1990.

Hull, Gloria T., Patricia Bell Scott, and Barbara Smith, eds. *All the Women Are White, All the Blacks Are Men, but Some of Us Are Brave: Black Women's Studies.* Old Westbury, NY: Feminist Press, 1982.

Jones, Jacqueline. *Labor of Love, Labor of Sorrow: Black Women, Work, and the Family from Slavery to the Present.* New York: Basic Books, 1985.

Jordan, Casper LeRoy. *A Bibliographical Guide to African-American Women Writers.* Westport, CT: Greenwood Press, 1993.

Kafka, Phillipa. *The Great White Way: African American Women Writers and American Success Mythologies.* New York: Garland, 1993.

Kubitschek, Missy Dehn. *Claiming the Heritage: African-American Women Novelists and History.* Jackson: University Press of Mississippi, 1991.

Kutenplon, Deborah, and Ellen Olmstead. *Young Adult Fiction by African American Writers, 1968– 1993: A Critical and Annotated Guide.* New York: Garland, 1996.

Ladner, Joyce A. *Tomorrow's Tomorrow: The Black Woman.* Garden City, NY: Doubleday, 1971.

Lerner, Gerda. *Black Women in White America: A Documentary History.* New York: Pantheon Books, 1972.

Levin, Amy K. *Africanism and Authenticity in African-American Women's Novels.* Gainesville: University Press of Florida, 2003.

McDowell, Deborah E. *"The Changing Same": Black Women's Literature, Criticism, and Theory.* Bloomington: Indiana University Press, 1995.

Mitchell, Angelyn. *The Freedom to Remember: Narrative, Slavery, and Gender in Contemporary Black Women's Fiction.* New Brunswick, NJ: Rutgers University Press, 2002.

Moraga, Cherríe, and Gloria Anzaldúa, eds. *This Bridge Called My Back: Writings by Radical Women of Color.* Watertown, MA: Persephone Press, 1981.

Newby, James Edward. *Black Authors: A Selected Annotated Bibliography.* New York: Garland, 1991.

Noble, Jeanne L. *Beautiful, Also, Are the Souls of My Black Sisters: A History of the Black Woman in America.* Englewood Cliffs, NJ: Prentice-Hall, 1978.

Peterson, Bernard L. *Contemporary Black American Playwrights and Their Plays: A Biographical Dictionary and Dramatic Index.* New York: Greenwood Press, 1988.

Pryse, Marjorie, and Hortense J. Spillers, eds. *Conjuring: Black Women, Fiction, and Literary Tradition.* Bloomington: Indiana University Press, 1985.

Roses, Lorraine Elena, and Ruth Elizabeth Randolph, eds. *Harlem's Glory: Black Women Writing, 1900–1950.* Cambridge, MA: Harvard University Press, 1996.

Russell, Sandi. *Render Me My Song: African-American Women Writers from Slavery to the Present.* New York: St. Martin's Press, 1990.

Shockley, Ann Allen, ed. *Afro-American Women Writers, 1746–1933: An Anthology and Critical Guide.* Boston: G. K. Hall, 1988.

Staples, Robert. *The Black Woman in America: Sex, Marriage, and the Family.* Chicago: Nelson-Hall Publishers, 1973.

Stover, Johnnie M. *Rhetoric and Resistance in Black Women's Autobiography.* Gainesville: University Press of Florida, 2003.

Tate, Claudia, ed. *Black Women Writers at Work.* New York: Continuum, 1983.

——. *Domestic Allegories of Political Desire: The Black Heroine's Text at the Turn of the Century.* New York: Oxford University Press, 1992.

Terborg-Penn, Rosalyn. *The Afro-American Woman: Struggles and Images.* Port Washington, NY: National University Publications, 1978.

Wade-Gayles, Gloria Jean. *No Crystal Stair: Visions of Race and Gender in Black Women's Fiction.* Cleveland, OH: Pilgrim Press, 1997.

Wall, Cheryl A., ed. *Changing Our Own Words: Essays on Criticism, Theory, and Writing by Black Women.* New Brunswick, NJ: Rutgers University Press, 1989.

Wallace, Michele. *Black Macho and the Myth of the Superwoman.* New York: Verso, 1990.

Washington, Mary Helen, ed. *Invented Lives: Narratives of Black Women, 1860–1960.* Garden City, NY: Anchor Press, 1987.

White, Deborah Gray. *Ar'n't I a Woman?: Female Slaves in the Plantation South.* New York: Norton, 1985.

Williams, Dana A. *Contemporary African American Female Playwrights: An Annotated Bibliography.* Westport, CT: Greenwood Press, 1998.

Willis, Susan. *Specifying: Black Women Writing the American Experience.* Madison: University of Wisconsin Press, 1987.

Zackodnik, Teresa C. *The Mulatta and the Politics of Race.* Jackson: University Press of Mississippi, 2004.

Index

Encyclopedia entry numbers are boldfaced.

611; pseudonyms of, 609; on women, 716

McKissack, Patricia, **612–14**

McMillan, Terry, **614–17**: and *A Day Late and a Dollar Short*, 250–51; and *Disappearing Acts*, 270–71; early life of, 613–15; and *How Stella Got Her Groove Back*, 431–32; and *The Interruption of Everything*, 453–54; literary influences of, 613; and *Mama*, 594–95; teaching career of, 615; and *Waiting to Exhale*, 881–82; writing career of, 615–16

Meditations on the Rainbow, 769–70

Memoirs of Mrs. Zilpha Elaw, 299–300

Memories of Childhood's Slavery Days, 136–37

Memory, in literature, 243, 413–14, **617–19**, 904–7

Memphis Blues, 252

Men of Brewster Place, The, **619–21**

Meridian, **621–23**, 743, 885

Meriwether, Louise, **623–25**

Micklebury, Penny, 264

Middle Passage, 414–15, 481–82

Middle Passage, 414–15, 481–82, **625–26**, 725–27

Midnight Birds, 580

Milk in my Coffee, 269

Miller, May, **626–28**

Millican, Arthenia J. Bates, **628–29**

Mind of My Mind, 703–4

Minstrel's Melody, The, 835

Miscegenation, and black identity, 441–42

Modernism, African Americans and, **629–32**

Moms, 169

Montgomery bus boycott, 694–96

Moody, Anne, 180, **633–34**

Moore, Opal, **634–35**

Moraga, Cherrie, 525–26

Morris, Tracie, 720

Morrison, Toni, **636–41**: awards won by, 637–38; and *Beloved*, 54–58; and *Bluest Eye, The*, 97–99; on death, 253; early life of, 636–37; on history, 417;

influence of the South on, 809; and *Jazz*, 471–74; and *Love*, 581–83; and Nobel Prize, 326; and *Paradise*, 689–92; and *Song of Solomon*, 804–7; on spirituality, 813; and *Sula*, 826–28; and *Tar Baby*, 831–34; and use of ancestor, 9; on violence, 871–72; work as teacher and editor, 637

Moses, Man of the Mountain, **641–42**

Moss, Thylias, **642–44**

Mossell, Gertrude, **644–45**

Mostly Womenfolk and a Man or Two, 10

Mother-daughter relationships: in autobiographical fiction, 520–21; in fiction, 18–19, 30–32, 115–16, 233, 318, 596, 948–49

"Mother, The," 718

Mothers, motherhood, **645–49**: Clarence Majors on, 587–88; in drama, 750–51; effects of slavery on, 647–48; in feminist literature, 648–49; in fiction, 54–58, 151, 260, 389, 472–73, 584–85, 601, 620, 832; grandmothers' roles, 646–47; James Baldwin on, 41; Maya Angelou on, 446; in poetry, 718–19, 910–11; as redemptive feature, 102; rejection of, 558–59; relationships to children, 646; stereotypes of, 647; Terry McMillan on, 594–95; and violence, 872

"Mother's Tale, The," 718–19

Moynihan Report, The, 209, 315

Mr. Potter, 521

Mulatto, 100

Mulatto/a, **649–52**, 735–36

Mules and Men, **652–54**, 744

Mullen, Harryette, **654–55**

Mumbo Jumbo, 755–56

Murphy, Beatrice M., **655–56**

Murray, Pauli, **657–58**

Muse-Echo Blues, 152

Museum, 280

Music, gospel, 818–19

Music, jazz, 469–71

Muslims, in slavery, 757

My Blood in Your Veins, 37

My Brother, 521

My Garden (Book), 521–22

Myth, use of, **659–62**: African creation, 233; Biblical, in literature, 659–71; of black families, 271; of black women, 474–75; in literature, 409, 659–62, 839

Name changes, by African Americans: of Aishah Rahman, 746; of Amiri Baraka, 47–48; of Audre Lorde, 572; in fiction, 636–37; of Frederick Douglass, 275; of Johari Amini, 8; of Maya Angelou, 13–14; of Ntozake Shange, 787; reasons for, 63; of Sapphire, 769; of Sojourner Truth, 861; of Toni Bambara, 42; of Toni Morrison, 636

Nappy Edges, 789

Nappy Hair, 52, 408–9

Narrative of Sojourner Truth, 659

Narrative of the Life of Frederick Douglass, 275, 865–66

Narratives, 184

Narrows, The, 579, **663–64**, 708

Nash, Diane, 180

Nathaniel Talking, 376

Nation of Islam, 592–93, 757, 766

National Black Feminist Organization, 68–69

National Council of Negro Women (NCNW), 562–63

National Federation of Colored Women (NCAW), 840–41

Native Son, 100, 935–36

Natural Birth, 258, 719

Naylor, Gloria, **664–68**: and *Bailey's Café*, 34–36; on death, 254; early life of, 664–65; feminist heritage of, 664–65; and *Linden Hills*, 547–49; and *Mama Day*, 595–97; and *The Men of Brewster Place*, 619–21; ministerial work of, 665; novels of, 666–68; professional career of, 666; and *The Women of Brewster Place*, 925–27

Neely, Barbara, 87–92, 263–64, **668–71**

Nelson, Marilyn, **671–73**

Racial identity, Josephine Baker and, 36–37

Racism: art, in fight against, 489; and black feminists, 68–69, 892; in fiction, 148, 152–53, 207–8, 214–15, 222–23, 292, 450–51, 663–64, 708, 714–15, 836–37, 846–48; internalized, revealed, 417; and literacy, 551; marginalization of black people, 563; and plantation tradition, 709–12; in poetry, 765; and tar baby symbol, 338; in the theater, 167; women activists and, 742–43. *See also* Color hierarchy, among African Americans

Rahman, Aishah, **746–48**

Rainbow Jordan, 168

Rainbow Remnants in Rock Bottom, 643

Rainbow Roun Mah Shoulder, 126–27, **748–49**

Raisin in the Sun, A, **749–52**: analysis of, 391, 749–52; and the Civil Rights Movement, 563–64; ancestor figure in, 9; effect on audiences, 287; patriarchism in, 662; role of education in, 743

Rape, **752–55**: in autobiography, 445; definitions of, 752; and feminist movements, 753–54; in literature, 100, 482, 670, 752–55, 754, 770, 778–79, 885; and myth of black rapist, 753; of slave women, 730, 752–53

Rattlebone, 183

Reading Race, 630

Reed, Ishmael, **755–56**

Religion, 453, 510, **757–58**. *See also* Christianity; Preachers, black female; Sermon tradition; Spirituality

Religious Experience and Journal of Mrs. Jarena Lee, 542

Reminiscences of My Life in Camp W, 837–39

Rice, 333–34

Rodgers, Carolyn, 177, 565, **758–60**

Roll of Thunder, Hear My Cry, 836–37

Roosevelt, Eleanor, 561

Roots, 25, 384

"Roselily," 450

Running a Thousand Miles for Freedom, 226–29

Sally Hemings, 155, 651, **761–62**

Salt Eaters, The, 44, 103, 407, **762–64**

Sambo, stereotype of, 710, 711

Sanchez, Sonia, **764–68**: collegiate career of, 764, 766; on death, 254; early life of, 764–65; and the FBI, 766; on individuality, 662; in Nation of Islam, 766; poetry of, 765–66; theatrical career of, 287–88; and theme of love, 579

Sanders, Dori, **768–69**

Sapphire (author), **769–72**

Sapphire, (stereotype), 475, **772–73**

Sarah Phillips, 541

Sassafrass, Cypress & Indigo, **773–74**, 787, 788–89, 809

Savage, Augusta Fells, 399

Say Jesus and Come to Me, 792

Scar imagery, 102

Schomburg Library of Nineteenth-Century Black Women Writers, 419, **775–76**

Science fiction, 92–94, 139–42, 523–25, 687–89, 941–43

Scripture, as basis for novel, 34–36

Secret of Gumbo Grove, The, 835

"See How They Run," 879

Seeds beneath the Snow, 629

Segregation, 744

Senna, Danzy, 152–53, **776–78**, 828–29

Seraph on the Suwanee, **778–79**

Sermon tradition, **780–82**

Seven for Luck, 283

Sexism: in the 1990s, 568–69; of Amiri Baraka, 48–49; and black feminist criticism, 71, 73; and black feminists, 68–69; in fiction, 450–51, 559, 641–42, 689–92, 751; internalized, revealed, 417; in protest tradition, 733

Sexual abuse: in autobiography, 727–28; in fiction, 91–92, 97, 113–14, 205, 222–23, 581–83, 588–89, 638, 689–92, 804–6, 885; of men, 754; during

Middle Passage, 625; in poetry, 223–25, 529; in slavery, 67, 83, 465, 474, 651, 800. *See also* Rape

Sexuality, **782–86**: black female, 69, 142, 782–86; in fiction, 638–39, 826–27; and HIV, 405; invisibility of, for bisexuals, 404; and stereotypes, 474–75

Shaker community, black women in, 463–65

Shange, Ntozake, **786–91**: awards won by, 787; and *Betsey Brown,* 60; and choreopoem, 288, 342–45, 787; and *for colored girls,* 288, 342–45, 787; influence of the South on, 809; life and career of, 786–87; and *Liliane,* 546–47; and *Sassafrass, Cypress & Indigo,* 773–74; writings of, 787–89

Shimmershine Queens, The, 946

Shockley, Ann Allen, **791–92**

Short Walk, A, 168

Sign in Sidney Brustein's Window, The, 391

Simple (Jesse B. Semple), 436

Singing in the Comeback Choir, **793–94**

"Sis Cat," 653

Sketches of Southern Life, 402

"Sky Is Gray, The," 358

Slave Girl's Story, A, 289–90

"Slave Mother, The," 867

Slave narratives, **794–97**: of Annie Louise Burton, 136–37; in antebellum period, 794–95; effects on slavery, 794; of Elizabeth Keckley, 53–54; of Ellen and William Craft, 226–29; in fiction, 824; folklore in, 337–38; of Frederick Douglass, 275, 276; of Harriet Jacobs, 447–50, 466–68, 801; of Mary Prince, 727–28; and the Middle Passage, 625; mother-child breakups in, 648; as testimonials to freedom, 349–50; themes of, 577–78; Underground Railroad in, 865–67; use of conjuring in, 212–13; by women, 555, 795–96. *See also* Neo-slave narratives; Slavery

About the Editor and Contributors

ELIZABETH ANN BEAULIEU is the author of *Black Women Writers and the American Neo-Slave Narrative: Femininity Unfettered* (1999) and the editor of *The Toni Morrison Encyclopedia* (2003). She is an assistant professor in the Department of Interdisciplinary Studies at Appalachian State University, where she works in the areas of women's studies, food studies, and learning communities, sometimes simultaneously.

WANDA G. ADDISON is pursuing her Ph.D. in the Department of English at the University of Louisiana at Lafayette. Her concentration is in folklore studies, but she also works in the areas of women's studies, American literature, and nineteenth-century British literature. She was awarded the 2003 American Folklore Society's Zora Neale Hurston Prize for Outstanding Essay on African American Folklore.

JENNIFER DAWES ADKISON is an assistant professor of English at Idaho State University, where she teaches American literature. Her areas of scholarship include nineteenth-century women writers, Western literature, and ecocriticism. Her article on Susan Fenimore Cooper was published in *Susan Fenimore Cooper: New Essays on Rural Hours and Other Works* (2001). She is currently working on a new edition of Sarah Royce's Gold Rush narrative.

NICOLE N. ALJOE is an assistant professor of English at the University of Utah. She earned her Ph.D. from Tufts University in 2005.

WILLIAM L. ANDREWS is E. Maynard Adams Professor of English and senior associate dean for the Fine Arts and Humanities in the College of Arts and Sciences at the University of North Carolina at Chapel Hill. He is the author of *The Literary Career of Charles W. Chesnutt* (1980) and *To Tell a Free Story: The First Century of Afro-American Autobiography, 1760–1865* (1986). He is coeditor of *The Norton Anthology of African American Literature* (1997, 2003), *The Oxford*

Companion to African American Literature (1997), and *The Curse of Caste and Other Writings by Julia C. Collins* (2006).

MONIFA A. LOVE ASANTE is the author of *Provisions* (1989), *My Magic Pours Secret Libations* (1996), *Freedom in the Dismal* (1998), and *Dreaming Underground* (2004). She is an associate professor at Morgan State University, where she coordinates the creative writing program. She lives in Maryland with her family.

ANN BEEBE is an assistant professor of English at the University of Texas at Tyler. She is currently working on a short article about Langston Hughes as well as an essay on counterfeiting in the works of Charles Brockden Brown and James Fenimore Cooper.

DEBRA BEILKE is a professor of English at Concordia University–St. Paul, where she teaches courses in American literature, writing, and world literature. She has published articles and presented numerous papers on southern literature, African American literature, and women's writing.

SHANNA GREENE BENJAMIN is a Ford Foundation Postdoctoral Fellow working on a project entitled *The Ananse Aesthetic: Transformations of the Trickster Spider in African American Folklore, Fiction, and Fine Art* which examines the presence of the Ghanaian trickster Kwaku Ananse in black oral traditions, the novels of select black women writers, and the art of John Biggers. In addition to publishing on Toni Cade Bambara, Toni Morrison, and Victor Sejour, she has authored the essays "Weaving the Web of Reintegration: Tracing Threads of A(unt) Nancy in Paule Marshall's *Praisesong for the Widow*" and "Race, Faces, and False Fronts: Shakespearean Signifying in the Colored American Magazine."

TAPATI BHARADWAJ is a doctoral candidate in the English Department at Loyola University, Chicago. Her dissertation looks at the emergence of print culture in the colonial South Asian context. Her academic interests are in nineteenth-century literatures and feminist and postcolonial theories.

KIMBERLY BLACK-PARKER is an assistant professor of library and information science at the University of Kentucky. She earned her doctorate from Florida State University and has worked as an academic librarian and researcher.

ELLESIA ANN BLAQUE is the author of " 'I Am More Than a Victim': The Slave Woman Stereotype in Antebellum Narratives by Black Men" and "Black Nationalism" in *Blackberries and Redbones: Critical Articulations of Black Hair/Body Politics in Africana Communities*. A doctoral candidate at Wayne State University, she also teaches in the Department of English at Queensborough Community College–City University of New York, where she focuses her research in the areas of African American literature and history, 1760–1919, black feminist studies, and slave narratives specifically.

RITA BODE is assistant professor in the Department of English Literature at Trent University, Ontario, Canada, where she teaches a wide range of courses including drama and the literature of social justice. She has published articles on both British and American writers, and among her research interests are literary representations of the maternal.

J. BROOKS BOUSON is a professor of English at Loyola University in Chicago. She has published essays and book chapters on a variety of authors, and she is the author of four books: *The Empathic Reader: A Study of the Narcissistic Character and the Drama of the Self* (1989); *Brutal Choreographies: Oppositional Strategies and Narrative Design in the Novels of Margaret Atwood*

(1993); *Quiet as It's Kept: Shame, Trauma and Race in the Novels of Toni Morrison* (2000); and *Jamaica Kincaid: Writing Memory, Writing Back to the Mother* (2005). Her areas of specialization are modern British literature and twentieth-century women's literature. Her other areas of interest include psychoanalysis and literature, feminist theory, especially the history of feminist theory, emotions and literature, shame in literature, and trauma and narrative.

LINDA JOYCE BROWN is an assistant professor of writing and literature at Mitchell College. Her research has focused on American women writers, immigration, visual culture, and critical race and ethnicity studies. She is the author of *The Literature of Immigration and Racial Formation: Becoming White, Becoming Other, Becoming American* (2004).

JOSIE BROWN-ROSE is assistant professor of English and director of the minor in African American studies at Western New England College. She received her Ph.D. from Stony Brook University, focusing on African American, Caribbean, and black British literatures.

DIANE TODD BUCCI is assistant professor of communications skills and coordinator of the Communications Skills Program at Robert Morris University. In addition to teaching communications skills, she teaches literature classes at the university.

HARRIETTE C. BUCHANAN is a professor of interdisciplinary studies at Appalachian State University, Boone, North Carolina. She has published numerous articles on women writers, especially such Appalachian writers as Lisa Alther and Lee Smith. Other research interests include contemporary southern writers and women mystery writers.

CHRISTINA G. BUCHER is an associate professor of English, rhetoric, and writing at Berry College in Rome, Georgia, where she teaches nineteenth-century American, African American, and women's literatures. She has published articles in the *Mississippi Quarterly* and the *North Carolina Literary Review*.

ZISCA ISABEL BURTON has been teaching freshman composition at the University of Miami since 2002, where she codirects the University Writing Center. She earned her B.A. in English and M.A in African American studies from the University of Wisconsin, Madison.

KEELY A. BYARS-NICHOLS is currently pursuing her Ph.D. in American literature from the University of Georgia. Her areas of interest are multicultural American literatures and specifically how Native American and African American studies can be balanced with a broader understanding of multicultural theory, pedagogy, and American identity.

LICIA MORROW CALLOWAY is author of *Black Family (Dys)Function in Novels by Jessie Fauset, Nella Larsen, and Fannie Hurst* (2003). She is an assistant professor of English at The Citadel, specializing in the study of race, class, and gender in twentieth-century American literature.

BENJAMIN D. CARSON is an assistant professor of ethnic American literature at Bridgewater State College, Bridgewater, Massachusetts.

KAREN ARNETT CHACHERE is an assistant professor in the Departments of English and Interdisciplinary Studies at Aurora University, where she teaches courses in American, African American, and multicultural literature.

MICHELLE CHILCOAT is associate professor of French and Francophone studies at Union College, Schenectady, New York, where she is also affiliated with the Women's and Gender

Studies program. Her research focuses on how race, gender, and class inflect constructions of citizenship in colonial and postcolonial France.

KATE COCHRAN is an assistant professor in the Department of Literature and Language at Northern Kentucky University, where she teaches courses in southern literature, English education, women's studies, and American literature. She previously published an article on Alice Walker's *The Third Life of Grange Copeland* in the *Southern Literary Journal* and has delivered papers and talks on Walker's life and work.

JANELLE COLLINS is an associate professor in the Department of English and Philosophy at Arkansas State University, where she specializes in African American women writers and civil rights movement literature. Her articles have appeared in *Genders*, *MELUS*, the *College Language Association Journal*, and *Midwest Quarterly*.

CALEB A. CORKERY is assistant professor of English at Millersville University of Pennsylvania.

ANGELA COTTEN is visiting professor of ethnic and gender studies at California State University, Stanislaus. Her areas of research and teaching are women and political economy and philosophy, aesthetics, and women's cultural production. She has edited two anthologies, *Cultural Sites of Critical Insight* and *(Un)making Race, Re-Making Soul: Transformative Aesthetics and the Practice of Freedom*. Currently, she is completing a book on womanism as critical tradition in the writings of Alice Walker titled *Womanist Thought Reconsidered: Its Origins and Travels in the Works of Alice Walker*.

KARLYN CROWLEY is assistant professor of English at St. Norbert College in De Pere, Wisconsin, where she focuses on issues of gender, race, and ethnicity. Her current project, "When Spirits Take Over: Gender and American New Age Culture," investigates how a decline in certain public feminisms in the United States has led to a rise in very popular and yet more private "female-centered" spirituality.

KEVIN DE ORNELLAS has lectured at Queen's University, Belfast, and the University of Wales, Bangor, and is presently at the University of Ulster. He has two books scheduled for publication in 2007: *The Horse in Early Modern English Culture* and *Horse*. He has published widely on English Renaissance drama and on twentieth-century American, British, Canadian, and Irish drama and prose.

KWAKIUTL L. DREHER is assistant professor of English and African American studies at the University of Nebraska, Lincoln. Her research interests include film and visual culture, twentieth-century American literature (1970–present), African American literature, and black autobiography. She is currently at work on her book titled *Dancing on the White Page: The Black Entertainer 1940–1970*.

JENNIFER DRISCOLL's scholarly work focuses on discourses of the emotions, particularly outrage, in nineteenth- and twentieth-century women's writing. She is a lecturer at Yeshiva College, where she teaches rhetoric and composition. She is currently working on a project that considers medical rhetoric and the framing of female illness from the 1950s to the present.

KELLY NORMAN ELLIS is the author of *Tougaloo Blues*. Her poems and essays have appeared in *The Toni Morrison Encyclopedia*, *Maud Martha: Critical Essays*, and *Caylx*. She is an associate professor of English and creative writing at Chicago State University and associate director of the M.F.A. program in creative writing.

SHERRY ENGLE is the author of *Portraits and Plays: New Women Dramatists in America, 1890–1920*. She is an assistant professor in the Department of Speech, Communications and Theatre Arts at Borough of Manhattan Community College, as well as a produced playwright.

DEIRDRE FAGAN is the author of *Critical Companion to Robert Frost* (forthcoming). She currently teaches composition and American literature at the University of Miami. Her primary fields of interest are twentieth-century American poetry and the contemporary memoir.

KATRIN FISCHER has published articles on American literature and on teaching English as a foreign language. Her dissertation on the representation of Native Americans in contemporary crime fiction, *Time to Tear Down Barriers: Raum, Kultur und 'indianische' Identität im Kriminalroman*, was published in 2003. Currently a research associate at Harvard University, she is writing a book on captivity narratives by and about Germans.

JOHANNA FRANK is assistant professor of English at the University of Windsor, where she teaches courses in modern and contemporary drama. Former Mellon Fellow at Cornell University, she is a cofounder of SteinSemble Performance Group, a collection of actors and scholars dedicated to performing avant-garde, modernist, and other generally unstaged texts of the twentieth century.

VALERIE FRAZIER is an assistant professor at the College of Charleston, where she teaches courses in African American literature, women's literature, and multicultural literature. She has published articles in *African American Review* and the *Zora Neale Hurston Forum* and is currently working on a book on the critical reception of Gwendolyn Brooks.

DOVEANNA S. FULTON is the author of *Speaking Power: Black Feminist Orality in Women's Slave Narratives* (2005). She is an associate professor in the English Department at Arizona State University, where she teaches courses in African American literature and culture, American literature, and women's literature. She has published and lectured in the United States, France, England, and Ethiopia on African American literature and manifestations of oral traditions by black women. Her current research is on African American activism in the temperance movement for which she has received a grant from the National Endowment for the Humanities.

ERIC GARDNER is the editor of *Major Voices: The Drama of Slavery* (2005) and author of articles on Chloe Russel, Harriet Wilson, Frank Webb, and Mary Webb. He is an associate professor of English at Saginaw Valley State University.

SHENNETTE GARRETT is a graduate student in the History Department of the University of Texas at Austin. She works in the areas of gender, culture, and late-nineteenth- to early-twentieth-century black entreprenuership in America.

ROXANE GAY is pursuing a doctoral degree in rhetoric and technical communication at Michigan Technological University. Her essays and short fiction have been widely anthologized in books ranging from the *Mammoth Book of Tales from the Road* to *Father-Daughter Travel Adventures*.

MONIKA GIACOPPE, assistant professor of comparative/world literature at Ramapo College of New Jersey, publishes on women's writing, translation studies, and inter-American literature. Her co-translation of fiction by S. Corinna Bille, *The Transparent Girl and Other Stories*, is due out in 2006.

ARACELIS GIRMAY is the writer and collagist of *changing, changing* (2005). She has received writing grants from the Watson Foundation and the Toor Cummings Center. She earned undergraduate and graduate degrees from Connecticut College and New York University, respectively.

SUSAN L. GOLDEN is a professor and collection development librarian at Appalachian State University, where her field of expertise is children's literature. She is currently working on a monograph for the American Library Association on evaluating and selecting children's and young adult literature for academic librarians without a background in the field.

VINCENT F. A. GOLPHIN is an award-winning journalist and author who teaches writing, African American studies, literature and religion, and literary and cultural studies at the Rochester Institute of Technology in Rochester, New York. His latest works include *African-American Children's Stories* and *Grandma Loves You: A Child's First Primer*.

HEIDI HAUSER GREEN is a book reviewer for *Children's Literature* and *KLIATT*. She also edits newsletters and materials for *Breastfeeding Outlook*. She has earned graduate degrees in English from Illinois State University and library and information science from the University of Pittsburgh. Her interests include women's studies, children's literature, young adult literature, and social sciences.

STACY GROOTERS is a doctoral candidate at the University of Washington, Seattle. Her dissertation examines liberal and liberatory narratives of education in nineteenth-century British and twentieth-century Jamaican literature.

JOAN WYLIE HALL is the author of *Shirley Jackson: A Study of the Short Fiction* (1993) and the editor of *Conversations with Audre Lorde* (2004). A book reviewer for several journals, she teaches in the English Department at the University of Mississippi and has published essays on Willa Cather, Eudora Welty, Lee Smith, Ruth McEnery Stuart, Ann Patchett, and other American women writers.

WILLIAM S. HAMPL is the author of articles and reviews that have appeared in *Studies in the Novel* and *Modern Fiction Studies*. He works for the Department of Defense as an instructor of English in the BOOST/STA-21 Program in Newport, Rhode Island.

ROXANNE HARDE is an assistant professor in the Department of English at the University of Alberta, Augustana Faculty. Her research focuses on early American women's writing, including writing for children, and feminist theology. She has recently published articles on abolition literature in *Mosaic*, on Emily Dickinson in *Christianity and Literature*, and on Anne Bradstreet in *Studies in Puritan American Spirituality*.

JENNIFER HARRIS is assistant professor of English at Mount Allison University, Canada. Her essays have appeared in *English Language Notes*, *Canadian Review of American Studies*, and elsewhere.

KYLA HEFLIN is the director of Extended Studies for the College of Education at the University of Colorado at Colorado Springs. She is a Ph.D. candidate in literature at Indiana University of Pennsylvania.

KATHLEEN M. HELAL has taught courses on women's writing and English literature for several years. She has published articles on Virginia Woolf and Dorothy Parker and is writing a book on women's writing and celebrity culture.

KAAVONIA HINTON-JOHNSON is an assistant professor in the Department of Educational Curriculum & Instruction at Old Dominion University in Norfolk, Virginia. Her specialization is English education, and her research surrounds the teaching of multicultural literature, particularly African American literature. She is currently completing a book about young adult author Angela Johnson.

ELVIN HOLT is a professor of English at Texas State University at San Marcos, specializing in African American literature and cultural studies, autobiography, American literature, and African literature. Holt's essays and reviews have appeared in *Zora Neale Hurston Forum*, *Griot*, *Xavier Review*, *Studies in American Humor*, *Texas Books in Review*, *Southwestern American Literature*, and elsewhere.

ANN HOSTETLER is associate professor of English at Goshen College in Goshen, Indiana, where she teaches American literature and creative writing. She is the author of *Empty Room with Light* (2002) and the editor of *A Cappella: Mennonite Voices in Poetry* (2003). Her work has appeared in *PMLA* and *American Scholar*.

BRANDON L. A. HUTCHINSON is an assistant professor of English at Southern Connecticut State University. She teaches courses in the area of African American literature, with a special focus on black women writers.

HEIDI L. M. JACOBS coedited *American Women Prose Writers, 1870–1920* and has published numerous essays and articles on nineteenth-century American women writers.

ELISABETH S. JAMES is an independent scholar living in West Palm Beach, Florida.

YOUNGSOOK JEONG is the author of the "Nellie Wong" entry for *The Dictionary of Literary Biography: Asian American Writers* (2005). She is an instructor at Rider University and Burlington County College. Her area of interest is second-generation Asian American women's literature and Asian American diasporic literature.

SHARON JESSEE has published several essays on Ishmael Reed and Toni Morrison and is currently finishing a book manuscript on *Beloved*, *Jazz*, and *Paradise* as a Polyrhythmic trilogy. She is an associate professor at the University of Wisconsin at La Crosse, where she teaches American literatures.

NANCY KANG is a doctoral candidate at the University of Toronto Department of English. She is a Social Sciences and Humanities Research Council of Canada (SSHRCC) Doctoral Fellow, a Chancellor Jackman Graduate Fellow in the Humanities, and a Governor General of Canada's Academic Medalist. She works in race and ethnicity studies.

PRATIBHA KELAPURE is an independent scholar. Her literary interests include African American literature and Indian poetry.

KERRY KIDD did her first degree at Trinity College, Oxford, in English. She then spent a year working in community health theater development projects, followed by a Ph.D. in modern theater and cultural studies at Sheffield University. She is a postdoctoral Wellcome Research Fellow at the University of Nottingham, England.

LORELEE KIPPEN has published articles on Holocaust testimony, the South African Truth and Reconciliation Commission, Japanese and American AIDS testimonial, twentieth-century neuroscientific research, South African women's writing, medieval women's writing, and

Corpus Christi pageantry. She is a doctoral candidate at the University of Alberta, where she works in the areas of American literature, performance studies, medical history, and trauma studies.

LISA A. KIRBY is an assistant professor of English at North Carolina Wesleyan College in Rocky Mount, North Carolina. She specializes in American literature, working-class studies, and women's literature. Her work has appeared in *Left History*, *Working USA: The Journal of Labor and Society*, *Indiana English*, and *Oregon English Journal*.

MARY ALICE KIRKPATRICK is a contributing editor for *The North Carolina Roots of African American Literature* (2006). A Ph.D. candidate and teaching fellow at the University of North Carolina, Chapel Hill, she works in the areas of African American women's fiction, postcolonial literature, and theory.

AMY SPARKS KOLKER is chairperson of the Liberal Arts and Science Department at Black Hawk College, East Campus, as well as an assistant professor of English. Her interests are in American women writers, especially poets, and in serving the needs of students at a rural community college. She earned her Ph.D. in English from the University of Kansas.

JESSICA LABBÉ holds a Ph.D. in American literature and women's studies from the University of South Carolina, Columbia. She melds these interests in her work on women writers, feminist theory, and cultural criticism and in her pedagogical approaches to American literature, women in culture and society, as well as women and witchcraft/mythology. She is the author of several book reviews and scholarly publications.

SUZANNE LANE is assistant professor of English at California State University, San Bernardino, where she teaches American and African American literature. Her primary research focuses on the intersections of contemporary African American literature and folk traditions.

JENNIFER LARSON is a Ph.D. candidate and teaching fellow in the English Department at the University of North Carolina at Chapel Hill. Her research areas include nineteenth-century African American literature and nationalism.

ELIZABETH ARMISTEAD LEMON is a contributing editor of *The North Carolina Roots of African American Literature* (2006). She is a Ph.D. candidate at the University of North Carolina at Chapel Hill, where she works in the areas of twentieth-century American literature and African American literature.

CATHERINE E. LEWIS received her Ph.D. from the University of South Carolina. She teaches African American literature and composition at Louisiana State University. Her current research and teaching interests examine the connections between the nonfiction of African American writers and their fiction.

BETH L. LUECK is the author of *American Writers and the Picturesque Tour: The Search for National Identity, 1790–1860* (1997). She is an associate professor in the Department of Languages and Literatures at the University of Wisconsin, Whitewater, where she teaches nineteenth-century American literature, particularly women writers.

REI MAGOSAKI is a Ph.D. candidate in English at the University of Virginia, working on her dissertation on postwar women's fiction, titled "Sexing the City: Postwar U.S. Women's Fiction and the Postindustrial Metropolis." Her field of research finds itself at the intersection of twentieth-century American fiction, issues of gender, recent theories of modernity, and global studies.

DEVONA MALLORY is a Ph.D. candidate in English studies at Illinois State University in Normal, Illinois. Her research areas are magical realism literature, women's literature, and comparative literature.

AJUAN MARIA MANCE is the author of *Inventing Black Women: African American Women Poets and Self-Representation*, forthcoming from the University of Tennessee Press. She is an associate professor in the English Department at Mills College in Oakland, California.

ANNE MANGUM is professor of English and chair of the Humanities Division at Bennett College for Women in Greensboro, North Carolina. Her areas of specialty are seventeenth-century and Renaissance literature, and she works in Africana women's studies, early-twentieth-century poetry, and southern gothic fiction as well.

YOLANDA M. MANORA is an assistant professor in the Department of English at the University of Alabama, where she specializes in twentieth-century American literature with concentrations in African American women's literature, African American studies, and women's studies.

BARBARA McCASKILL is coeditor of *Post-Bellum–Pre-Harlem: African American Literature and Culture, 1877–1919* (2006), with Caroline Gebhard, and cofounder of *Womanist Theory & Research*. She is an associate professor of English and General Sandy Beaver Teaching Professor (2005–2008) at the University of Georgia. She is writing a book on fugitive slaves William and Ellen Craft.

GRACE McENTEE is a professor in the English Department at Appalachian State University, where she teaches nineteenth-century American literature and African American literature. Her publications and presentations in African American literature focus on the emergence of African American writers into mass-market genres.

LAURIE McMILLAN is an assistant professor of English at Marywood University. Her dissertation is titled "Practice, Practice, Practice: Innovative Feminist Literary Criticism," and she has published journal articles on feminism in contemporary literature.

REBECCA MEACHAM is the author of the award-winning story collection *Let's Do* (2004). She is an assistant professor of English and women's studies at the University of Wisconsin, Green Bay, where she teaches courses on ethnic American writers.

JOHN D. MILES is a doctoral candidate at the University of New Mexico. He is assistant director of the Rhetoric and Writing Program, and his research interests include feminist rhetorical strategies, Native American literature, and composition theory.

VERNER D. MITCHELL is the editor of *This Waiting for Love: Helene Johnson, Poet of the Harlem Renaissance* (2000) and the coeditor of *Dorothy West: Where the Wild Grape Grows, Selected Writings 1930–1950* (2005), both published by the University of Massachusetts Press. He is an associate professor of English at the University of Memphis.

KARA L. MOLLIS is a Ph.D. candidate in the Department of English at Duquesne University, where she has taught composition and literature courses. She is currently completing her doctoral dissertation, which examines the political and aesthetic relationships between the nineteenth-century sentimental novelistic tradition and contemporary American fiction by women.

SHIRLEY WALKER MOORE is chairperson of the Department of English and Foreign Languages at Texas Southern University in Houston, Texas.

LISA MUIR teaches composition and American literature at Wilkes Community College. Her research and writing deals with varyingly autobiographical American and ethnic American literature, and her most recent works can be found in *Western American Memoir and Autobiography*, *Teaching with Technology in the College Classroom*, and *College Literature*.

JUDITH MULCAHY is the author of several articles on African American and American literature and history. She teaches literature at Hunter College and John Jay College. Currently she is a doctoral candidate at the Graduate Center of the City University of New York. Her current scholarship addresses U.S. literature, religion, and doctrines of nationalism in the nineteenth century.

A. MARY MURPHY writes both as a scholar and as a poet. Her primary area of academic expertise is life writing, and she contributes entries to numerous encyclopedia projects. She currently teaches at St. Mary's University College in Calgary, Canada.

SUSAN NASH is a professor of English at Capital University in Columbus, Ohio, where she teaches a variety of traditional (Romantic, Victorian, and British literature) and thematic (black women writers, Paris in the 1920s and 1930s) classes and a general education humanities course. Her scholarly work also crosses disciplinary boundaries, focusing most recently on eighteenth-century travelers and caricatures.

JULIE CARY NERAD is assistant professor of American literature at Morgan State University. Her articles have appeared in *American Literature*, *African American Review*, and *ESQ*. She is currently completing a book on racial passing from 1850 to 1920 and editing a collection of essays on women in U.S. race riots in the nineteenth and twentieth centuries.

TERRY D. NOVAK is an associate professor of English at Johnson & Wales University in Providence, Rhode Island, where she teaches a variety of writing and literature courses, including interdisciplinary and learning community-centered courses. She has published several articles on African American women writers and works particularly in the areas of nineteenth- and early-twentieth-century American women and African American authors.

ANA NUNES took English and Portuguese coursework at the University of Coimbra, Portugal. A period of graduate study followed at University College Dublin, Ireland, before she completed her master's in American studies at the University of Coimbra in 2000. She is currently finalizing her doctorate at University College Dublin. Her research focuses on African American historical fiction. Recent publications include articles on the neo-slave narrative and on authors such as Paule Marshall and Gayl Jones. Nunes is a senior tutor in the School of English at University College Dublin, where she also teaches a seminar on African American fiction.

MENDI LEWIS OBADIKE is the author of *Armor and Flesh* (poems) and the librettist of the Internet opera *The Sour Thunder*. She has received commissions from the Whitney Museum, Yale University, the New York African Film Festival, and Electronic Arts Intermix. She received a Rockefeller Fellowship for her opera *TaRonda, Who Wore White Gloves*. She will launch *Four Electric Ghosts* at Toni Morrison's Atelier at Princeton. Mendi earned a Ph.D. in literature from Duke

University and currently teaches English at Montclair State University. She works with her husband, composer and conceptual artist Keith Obadike. They are based in the New York metropolitan area.

DEBBIE CLARE OLSON is an instructor of English and film/media studies at Central Washington University. She has published numerous book reviews for *Material Culture: Journal of the Pioneer America Society*, the *Journal of Contemporary Thought*, and others. She is pursuing her doctorate at Oklahoma State University in film, African film, and critical theory.

JAMES N. ORTEGO II has written entries for other reference works on writers such as William Shakespeare, Thomas Hardy, and Bernard McClaverty. He is an assistant professor at Troy University in Dothan, Alabama, where he teaches various courses on medieval and Renaissance literature.

JULUETTE BARTLETT PACK is the author of "The Plight of Poor Women in Modernity and Tradition in Tess Onwueme's *Tell It to Women*," in *Urbanization and African Cultures*; "Sweetness: A Trap or Freedom in Zulu Sofola's *The Sweet Trap*," in *Yoruba Creativity*; and "Modernity and Tradition in Tess Onwueme's Plays," in *Nigeria in the Twentieth Century*. She is an assistant professor at DeVry University and the University of Phoenix, where she teaches courses in composition, communications, and literature.

CHRYSAVGI PAPAGIANNI has contributed to *The Encyclopedia of Multiethnic American Literature*. She has taught film, literature, and writing classes in the English Department at the State University of New York, Buffalo, where she is a Ph.D. candidate. She is currently completing her dissertation on twentieth-century American women writers and directors.

FAYME PERRY has been a research and writing assistant for contributor Sharon Jessee for this encyclopedia; she has also completed an Undergraduate Research Award at the University of Wisconsin, La Crosse. She has a B.A. from La Crosse and plans to attend graduate school in Oregon.

AIMEE L. POZORSKI is an assistant professor in the Department of English at Central Connecticut State University, where she teaches contemporary literature and American fiction. She has recently published articles on Philip Roth, Ernest Hemingway, and Mina Loy as well as reviews of new poetry by Maxine Kumin, Eavan Boland, and Kathryn Kirkpatrick.

LISA HAMMOND RASHLEY is an associate professor of English and women's studies at the University of South Carolina, Lancaster. She has published on gender issues and technology in *Kairos* and the *National Women's Studies Association Journal*. She is also a poet.

ANTHONY J. RATCLIFF is ABD (all but dissertation) in Afro-American studies at the University of Massachusetts, Amherst, where he teaches American cultural diversity studies. His scholarly interests include Afro-American (diaspora) cultural and literary history; Pan-African cultural politics; and Afro-diasporic social movements, specifically interaction between African American and Afro-Latina*b*s. Anthony has written articles for publication on the National Association for the Advancement of Colored People and Black Arts Movement performers Sarah Webster Fabio and Camille Yarbrough in the *Encyclopedia of American History* and *An Encyclopedia of African American Literature*, respectively.

SARAH R. ROBBINS is the author of *Managing Literacy, Mothering America: Women's Narratives on Reading and Writing in the Nineteenth Century* (2004) and the coeditor of *Writing America: Classroom Literacy and Public Engagement* (2004) and *Writing Our Communities: Local Learning and*

Public Culture (2005). She is professor of English and English education at Kennesaw State University, where she teaches courses in American literature, American studies, literacy studies, women's studies, and teacher education. She is the director of the Keeping and Creating American Communities program, funded by the National Endowment for the Humanities, and of the Kennesaw Mountain Writing Project, a site of the National Writing Project serving northwest Georgia.

STÉPHANE ROBOLIN is a visiting instructor at Rutgers University, New Brunswick, where he teaches postcolonial African and African diasporic literature and culture and is at work on a manuscript titled *Constructive Engagements*. He has published and essays on African literature and the literary connections between South African and African American cultures.

KATHARINE RODIER is coeditor of *American Women Prose Writers, 1820–1870* (2001) and *Reinventing the Peabody Sisters* (forthcoming). She is professor of English at Marshall University, where she directs her department's graduate program.

RAQUEL RODRIGUEZ is the librarian for the African American Collection in Hillman Library at the University of Pittsburgh.

CATHERINE ROSS-STROUD is an assistant professor of teacher education at Cleveland State University, where she teaches courses in literacy studies, language arts, and adolescent literature.

JENNIFER DENISE RYAN has published articles on blues singer Bessie Smith and feminist approaches to service learning. She is an assistant professor of English at Buffalo State College, where she teaches courses in American poetry, women's literature, and African American literature.

CATHERINE E. SAUNDERS is an assistant professor in the Department of English at George Mason University. Her 2002 dissertation, *Houses Divided: Sentimentality and the Function of Biracial Characters in American Abolitionist Fiction*, examines the history of the term "tragic mulatto" and the use of biracial characters in abolitionist literature. Her other writing/research interests include local (Virginia) history and environmental issues.

J. SHANTZ teaches cultural studies at York University in Toronto, Canada. His writings have appeared in such journals as *Feminist Review, Feminism and Psychology*, and *Feminist Media Studies* as well as in numerous anthologies.

LAURA BAKER SHEARER is an adjunct professor and freelance writer in Dallas, Texas. She holds a Ph.D. in nineteenth-century American literature and specializes in working-class literary theory and women's studies.

EVIE SHOCKLEY is an assistant professor in the English Department at Rutgers University. The author of a poetry chapbook, *The Gorgon Goddess* (2001), Shockley is completing a scholarly book on the gothic in African American literature, tentatively titled *Gothic Homelessness: Domestic Ideology, Identity, and Social Terror in African American Literature*, and has begun a project on race and innovation in African American poetry.

TONI E. SMITH is an English instructor at Black Hawk College, East Campus, a community college located in Illinois.

RASHELL R. SMITH-SPEARS is an English doctoral candidate at the University of Missouri, Columbia. Her research interests include nineteenth-century literature and African American literature, particularly the discourse of black family life as it relates to questions of national identity at the turn of the century.

MICHAEL D. SOLLARS is the editor of *The Compendium of World Novelists and Novels*. His essays have appeared in many journals such as *LISA* and *Journal for the Interdisciplinary Study of the Arts*. He is an associate professor in the Department of English and Foreign Languages at Texas Southern University, where he teaches modern literature and literary criticism.

F. GREGORY STEWART lectures in the School of Arts and Humanities at the University of Texas at Dallas, where he works in the areas of southern and African American literature and culture. He is revising his dissertation on Toni Morrison's place within southern letters and most recently published work in the *Southern Quarterly* and *The Toni Morrison Encyclopedia*.

JOHNNIE M. STOVER is the author of *Rhetoric and Resistance in Black Women's Autobiography* (2003). She is an associate professor in the Department of English at Florida Atlantic University with specialization in American literatures of the nineteenth and twentieth centuries. Her current research involves female multicultural tricksterism.

AUSTRALIA TARVER is associate professor of English at Texas Christian University, where she teaches American, African American, and multiethnic literatures. She has contributed entries to the *Oxford Companion to African American Literature*; *Black Women in America*; and *The Dictionary of Literary Biography*; and articles to *Contemporary Literature in the African Diaspora*; *Winds of Change: The Transforming Voices of Caribbean Women Writers and Scholars*; and *Arms Akimbo: Africana Women in Contemporary Literature*. With Paula Barnes, she has edited a forthcoming volume of essays, *New Voices in the Harlem Renaissance*, and is completing a study, "Black Southern Novelists' Views of the South."

DEBORAH THOMPSON is an associate professor in the Department of English at Colorado State University, where she teaches classes in modern drama, literary theory, cultural studies, and multicultural literature. She is currently completing a book titled *Casting Suspicions: The Post-Identity Politics of Race in American Theater*, which explores the ways contemporary performances and theater practices both participate in and interrogate U.S. American racial constructions in an era of postidentity politics.

ELIZABETH ELY TOLMAN is the author of *¡A su salud!: Spanish for Health Professionals*, a set of multimedia and text materials based on an original medical soap opera designed to teach intermediate Spanish to health-care workers. A visiting professor in the School of Public Health at the University of North Carolina at Chapel Hill, her other interests include Latin American and American twentieth-century literature.

BETTIE JACKSON VARNER previously worked as a technical writer in the space and oil industries before moving into the field of education. She is a short-story writer and has taught both high school and college. She is also a member of the Houston Reading Commission and the National Council of Teachers of English.

NAGUEYALTI WARREN is associate dean in the Office for Undergraduate Education at Emory University. She coedited *Southern Mothers: Fact and Fictions Essays on Southern Women's Writing* (1999), authored a collection of poetry, *Lodestar and Other Night Lights* (1992), and edited the forthcoming poetry anthology *Temba Tupu (Walking Naked): Africana Women's Poetic Self Portrait*.

TIFFANY K. WAYNE is the author of *Woman Thinking: Feminism and Transcendentalism in Nineteenth-Century America* (2005) and *The Facts on File Encyclopedia of Transcendentalism* (2005). She recently completed a term as Affiliated Scholar with the Institute for Research on Women and Gender at Stanford University and is an independent scholar working in the fields of literary studies, intellectual history, and women's history. She is currently writing a history of American women in the nineteenth century.

DEBORAH WEAGEL is the author of *Interconnections: Essays on Music, Art, Literature, and Gender* as well as articles on contemporary literature, feminism/gender studies, and postcolonial literature. She is a doctoral student at the University of New Mexico.

LORNA J. RAVEN WHEELER is a retired chef who returned to the academy later in life. She is finishing up her Ph.D. at the University of Colorado at Boulder. Her project involves queering the Harlem Renaissance. Publications include "Straight Up Sex in The L Word," to be published in *Representing Lesbians*, and a couple of biographical contributions to *The Encyclopedia of Ethnic American Literature*. Wheeler's teaching interests include queer theory/rhetoric/literature, African American literature, and food studies/foodways.

QIANA J. WHITTED is an assistant professor in the Department of English at the University of South Carolina. Her essays on African American literature, religion, and culture have appeared in *African American Review* and *Southern Literary Journal*.

NICOLE LYNNE WILLEY has published articles and presented papers on the topics of the American slave narrative, African feminism, and nineteenth-century American sentimental novels. She is an assistant professor of English at Kent State University, Tuscarawas, where she teaches African American literature and composition and works in the areas of nineteenth-century literature and gender, class, and race studies.

LAMARA WILLIAMS-HACKETT is currently a news researcher with the *News and Observer (N&O)* in Raleigh, North Carolina. Before coming to the *N&O* she was a reference/instruction librarian at Louisiana State University in Baton Rouge, Louisiana. In addition to her teaching, she was very active on the Library Outreach Committee as well as being a selector in the arts and humanities.

SHARESE TERRELL WILLIS has also published in *The Encyclopedia of African American Literature*. Her literary interests include African American women's literature and Gloria Naylor's work in particular. She is pursuing a doctorate in professional writing at the University of Memphis, where she is concentrating in medical writing. She holds a master's degree from Clark Atlanta University.

LAURA MADELINE WISEMAN is an award-winning writer teaching at the University of Arizona and The Learning Curve. Her works have appeared in *13th Moon, Comstock Review, Fiction International, Poetry Motel, Driftwood, apostrophe, Moondance, Familiar, Spire Magazine, Colere, Clare, Flyway Literature Review, Nebula,* and other publications. She is the literary editor for *IntheFray* and a regular contributor to *Empowerment4Women*.

LORETTA G. WOODARD is associate professor of English at Marygrove College and the president of the African American Literature and Culture Society. Her scholarly work has appeared in *Contemporary African American Novelists* (1999), *African American Authors, 1745–1945* (2000), *African American Autobiographers* (2002), *Women in Literature* (2003), *African American Dramatists* (2004), *Obsidian III, Journal of African American History,* and *African American Review*.

EARL F. YARINGTON is an English faculty member at Burlington County College in New Jersey. He has recently published entries on Thomas Paine, Mary Austin, and Elizabeth Stoddard for the Greenwood *Encyclopedia of American Poetry*.

KRISTINE YOHE is an associate professor in the Department of Literature and Language at Northern Kentucky University, where she has taught since 1997. Her teaching and scholarship focus on African American literature, especially Toni Morrison, and particularly *Beloved* and *Paradise*. Other research and teaching interests center on Underground Railroad literature, as well as other African American and Afro-Caribbean writers, including Edwidge Danticat and Jean-Robert Cadet.